THE PENGUIN DICTIONARY OF

M U S I C

FIFTH EDITION

Arthur Jacobs

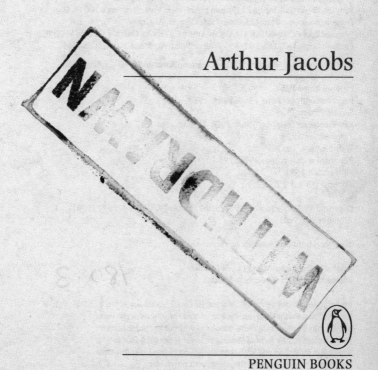

PENGUIN BOOKS

0140 511 598 1320

PENGUIN BOOKS

Published by the Penguin Group
Penguin Books Ltd, 27 Wrights Lane, London W8 5TZ, England
Penguin Books USA Inc., 375 Hudson Street, New York, New York 10014, USA
Penguin Books Australia Ltd, Ringwood, Victoria, Australia
Penguin Books Canada Ltd, 10 Alcorn Avenue, Toronto, Ontario, Canada M4V 3B2
Penguin Books (NZ) Ltd, 182–190 Wairau Road, Auckland 10, New Zealand

Penguin Books Ltd, Registered Offices: Harmondsworth, Middlesex, England

First published 1958
Reprinted with revisions 1960, 1961, 1963
Second edition 1967
Reprinted with revisions, 1968, 1970
Third edition 1973
Fourth edition 1977
Reprinted with revisions 1978, 1982
Fifth edition 1991
10 9 8 7 6 5 4 3 2 1

Printed in England by Clays Ltd, St Ives plc
Filmset in 8½/10 pt Monophoto Photina

480·3

Introduction

More than thirty years after its first edition (1958), this dictionary is offered by its compiler in a revised form, taking account of recent happenings in the world of music: new works, newly emergent composers, newly appointed conductors of major orchestras, and so forth. To keep abreast not only of modern composition but of the ever-growing cultivation of early music, new technical terms have been added (including *early music* itself) and others improved.

In general, the principles on which the book was founded have been maintained. In a single alphabetical list will be found composers, living and dead; titles of musical works; names and brief descriptions of instruments and voice-types; musical institutions (for instance, Glyndebourne, the Boston Symphony Orchestra); technical terms both English and foreign; and authors on whose writings important musical works have been based. As before, space compels some restriction on the inclusion of conductors, instrumentalists and singers: persons listed are those whose achievement may be ranked as historic. Entries for many more performers, with greater detail of information, may be found in my *Penguin Dictionary of Musical Performers*.

Due attention has been paid to differences between British and North American usage (for an example, see **bar**). For note-lengths, the more logical North American nomenclature of *half-note*, *quarter-note*, etc., has been followed; entries for the British equivalents (*minim*, *crotchet*) carry a cross-reference. In the spelling of Russian names and others of original non-roman script, the example of *The New Grove Dictionary of Music and Musicians* has generally been followed – as in 'Rakhmaninov', 'Skryabin', 'Tchaikovsky'.

For a further explanation of forms of names and their alphabetical order, see the section which follows, 'How to Use this Book'.

In personal entries, State honours are sparingly indicated. It may be useful, especially for readers outside the United Kingdom, to clarify the relevant British terminology. Next in rank to a *peer*, marked by the title 'Lord' or 'Lady', is a *baronet* (male only), a title now almost obsolete. Next in rank is the *knight* (male) or *dame* (female), with the title 'Sir' or 'Dame'; then come the awards of CBE (Commander of the British Empire) and OBE (Order of the British Empire). All these are 'political' honours, government-controlled; royal patronage more directly governs the award of OM (Order of Merit) and CH (Companion of

Honour), limited respectively to twenty-four and sixty-five at any one time, both recognizing special intellectual distinction.

The debt of this dictionary to such larger works as *The New Grove Dictionary of Music and Musicians* (1980, edited by Stanley Sadie) is gratefully acknowledged. The American *Baker's Biographical Dictionary of Musicians* (seventh edition, 1984) and *Music Since 1900* (fourth edition, 1971, with supplement, 1986) – both edited by Nicolas Slonimsky – were much consulted. David Cummings, editor of the sixth edition (1988) of *Everyman's Dictionary of Music*, was generous in personally drawing attention to entries requiring updating or alteration, and a significant element of valuable updating arose from observations by Hugh Davies. Other useful suggestions came from Kate Parker of the copy-editorial department of Viking/Penguin and from various friends, correspondents and reviewers. For future revisions of the book, any new suggestions or comments will be welcome and should be sent to me care of Penguin Books, 27 Wrights Lane, London W8 5TZ.

Arthur Jacobs
October 1990

How to Use This Book

All entries, whether people, things or terms, are given in a single alphabetical list. 'A' and 'The' and their foreign-language equivalents are disregarded in alphabetization. Musical works known in a numerical form are spelt out as commonly spoken – e.g. '1812' as 'Eighteen-Twelve'.

Entries are listed alphabetically by letter, ignoring the gaps between words. Thus:

> in
> Incredible Flutist, The
> indeterminacy
> Indian Queen, The
> in modo di
> In Nature's Realm
> In nomine
> In the South
> In the Steppes of Central Asia

and not:

> in
> in modo di
> In Nature's Realm
> In nomine
> In the South
> In the Steppes of Central Asia
> Incredible Flutist, The
> indeterminacy
> Indian Queen, The

Where an abbreviation is the entry-word itself, it normally falls in its due alphabetical place ('sop.' comes before 'soprano'). Similarly, abbreviations beginning with a detached initial letter ('B.Mus.') or consisting of several initials ('BBC') are to be found listed alphabetically by letter, hence 'BBC' follows 'Bazzoni'. Names beginning with the prefix 'Mc' are all listed as if spelt 'Mac'. Likewise, entries beginning 'St' are listed as if spelt 'Saint'.

Where possible, full names of composers and performers – and not only their commonly used professional names – are given. But where a part or parts of the holder's full name are not in general use, then such parts are enclosed in [square brackets]. Such bracketed names are disregarded for the purpose of alphabetical listing.

Most of the abbreviations, symbols and conventions are self-explanatory, or familiar from general reference books. Names of languages are abbreviated as convenient: Cz(ech), Dan(ish), Du(tch), Eng(lish), Fr(ench), Gael(ic), Ger(man), G(ree)k, Heb(rew), Hung(arian), It(alian), Jap(anese), Lat(in), Nor(wegian), Rus(sian), Sp(anish), Swe(dish).

Where SMALL CAPITALS are used in the course of entry, a cross-reference is indicated: i.e. 'Look up this term for further information'.

Where a date is marked c. (circa, i.e. approximately), this refers only to the figure immediately following. Thus 'c. 1555–1602' means 'born about 1555, known definitely to have died in 1602'.

A

A, note of the scale (commonly used for tuning instruments). So A FLAT (Ab), DOUBLE-FLAT (Abb), NATURAL (A♮), SHARP (A♯), DOUBLE-SHARP (A𝄪); *A major, A minor,* etc. – see MAJOR. So also *in A*, either (1) in the key of A (major, understood), or (2) indication of a TRANSPOSING INSTRUMENT on which the note written C sounds as A (and correspondingly with other notes): e.g. *clarinet in A*, or, colloquially, *A clarinet*.

A, abbr. for Associate (in musical diplomas – e.g. ARCM, Associate of the Royal College of Music).

A, term used in analysis to symbolize the first section of a piece. So e.g. ABA represents a piece containing one section followed by a different section followed by a repeat of the first.

a, à (It., Fr.), to, at, with, etc. So *a 2, a 3,* etc., indication either that a piece is written in so many PARTS, or that a single line of music is to be played by so many instruments in unison; so also *a* CAPPELLA, *a* PIACERE, *a* TEMPO, etc. (in all such cases see under next word).

ab (Ger.), off, away. So *Dampfer ab,* take mute(s) off.

ABA (and similar combinations of letters in musical analysis), see A (third entry).

Abbado, Claudio (b. 1933), Italian conductor; musical director, La Scala (opera), Milan, from 1972; principal conductor, London Symphony Orchestra, 1979–87; in 1989 he succeeded Karajan as conductor of the Berlin Philharmonic Orchestra.

'Abegg' Variations, Schumann's opus 1 for piano (1830), dedicated by him to a 'Countess Abegg' and consisting of variations on a theme made up of the notes A–Bb–E–G–G (German B = English Bb). Meta von Abegg was a friend of his, but the rank of Countess was imaginary.

Abel, Carl Friedrich (1723–87), German player of the bass viol (also of the harpsichord) and composer of chamber music, symphonies, etc. Trained in boyhood under J. S. Bach; settled in London (where he died) and gave concerts there with J. C. Bach.

Absil, Jean (1893–1974), Belgian composer of four symphonies; Divertimento for four saxophones and chamber orchestra; three piano concertos; ballets; etc.

absolute music, music without direct reference to anything outside itself, i.e. not having words and not being ILLUSTRATIVE MUSIC depicting story, scene, etc.

1

absolute pitch, see PITCH.

abstract music, same as ABSOLUTE MUSIC.

Abt, Franz (1819–85), German composer, especially of songs and part-songs in the German style of his period; also conductor in Germany and Switzerland.

Abu Hassan, one-act comic opera by Weber, produced in Munich, 1811. Libretto by F. C. Hiemer, after an *Arabian Nights* adventure of escaping debtors.

Academic Festival Overture (Ger., *Akademische Fest-Ouvertüre*), concert-overture by Brahms, first performed in 1881, composed in acknowledgement of a doctorate from Breslau University, 1879. Made up of favourite German student songs.

Academy, (1) a teaching institution, e.g. Royal Academy of Music; (2, actually the earlier meaning) a society for the promotion of science or art, hence a performing organization. The *Academy of St Martin-in-the-Fields* is a London chamber orchestra, named after a London church, founded (1959) and directed by Neville Marriner, with a speciality in string music of the Bach–Vivaldi period; the *Academy of Ancient Music*, founded in 1973 by Christopher Hogwood (and taking its title from an 18th-century organization) is a London group of expandable forces, using period instruments to perform mainly 18th-century music. See also SING-AKADEMIE.

Accardo, Salvatore (b. 1941), Italian violinist particularly associated with Paganini; he was the first to record all six of Paganini's concertos.

accelerando (It.), quickening the pace.

acciaccatura (It., a crushing), an 'extra' note struck just before (or simultaneously with) the main note, but immediately released. Notated with the stem of the note crossed through (♪).

accidental, a sharp, flat, double-sharp, double-flat, or natural sign occurring temporarily in the course of a piece, and not forming part of the key-signature. It conventionally refers only to the bar where it occurs – not to any succeeding bars, unless repeated there.

accompanied recitative (or, It., *recitativo accompagnato*), see RECITATIVE.

accompany, to perform with another performer, but in a subordinate capacity; so *accompanist, accompaniment* – a piano being commonly understood as the instrument unless another is specified. (So *unaccompanied song, sonata for unaccompanied violin*, etc., indicating absence of piano or other keyboard instrument.) When the performers are thought of as equal partners, e.g. in a violin and piano sonata, then *accompany* and its derivatives are to be avoided.

accordion, portable, box-shaped instrument having metal reeds which are made to vibrate by the access of air from bellows, actuated by the player's hands pushing and pulling. The notes are selected through the action of the player's fingers on studs or (*piano-accordion*) on studs for the left hand and a piano-like keyboard for the right. An instrument using only studs is sometimes called a *button-accordion*. On the standard piano-accordion some of the left-hand studs actuate individual bass-notes while others actuate pre-set chords; the *free-bass accordion* is one where all left-hand studs actuate individual notes. Much used in informal music-making, the instrument makes rare appearances in the concert-hall: see HARRIS (R.).

achtel (Ger., eighth part), EIGHTH-NOTE, quaver.

Acis and Galatea, dramatic cantata by Handel with text probably by John Gay, variously called a 'mask' (i.e. MASQUE), 'serenata' and 'pastoral'; first performed privately near London, 1718. It had then no connection with Handel's earlier Italian cantata on the same story (of two pastoral lovers and a villainous giant); but when reviving the English work in 1732, Handel incorporated part of the Italian one.

acoustic, term sometimes used to distinguish a 'normal' (non-electric) instrument from its electric counterpart – e.g. *acoustic guitar* (see GUITAR). See also the following.

acoustic bass, a type of organ pedal stop which makes use of an acoustic phenomenon, the RESULTANT TONE, to produce notes an octave lower than the pipes seemingly permit. When the note ordinarily representing 16-FOOT C is depressed, this stop brings into action that note together with the G above it; this then appears to sound the C an octave below, i.e. 32-foot C. Similarly for other notes. This stop is thus said to simulate 32-foot tone.

acoustics, (1) the science of sound; (2) the sound-properties of a building, etc.

action, the operation of mechanical or other devices used in construction of musical instruments – e.g. *tracker action,* a direct mechanical link between an organ key and the sounding

of the pipe, as alternative to *pneumatic* or *electric action.*

act tune, piece played between the scenes of an English 17th-century theatrical work; cp. ENTR'ACTE, INTERMEZZO.

adagietto (It., a little adagio), not quite so slow as ADAGIO; used as title of the fourth movement (out of five) of Mahler's Symphony no. 5, often played separately, being scored only for harp and strings.

adagio (It.), slow, a slow movement – slower than ANDANTE, faster than LARGO. *Adagio for Strings,* title of an orchestral work (in elegiac vein) by Barber, first performed in 1938 – originally the slow movement of a string quartet. See also ALBINONI.

Adam, Adolphe [Charles] (1803–56), French composer of operas including *If I were King*; ballets including GISELLE; choral and church music; etc. Also a critic.

Adam, Theo (b. 1926), German bass-baritone eminent in Wagner; member of (East) Berlin State Opera; sang at Bayreuth Festival from 1952.

Adamis, Michael [George] (b. 1929), Greek composer and conductor who studied in USA. Works (many with Greek titles) include *Apocalypse* (*The Sixth Seal*) for chorus, narrator, piano and tape; *Genesis* for three choruses, reciter, tape, painter and dance.

Adams, John [Coolidge] (b. 1947), American composer of opera NIXON IN CHINA, also of *Grand Pianola Music* for two sopranos, two pianos and small orchestra; chamber music, etc. Composer-in-residence to San Francisco Symphony Orchestra, 1982–5.

Adaskin, Murray (b. 1906), Canadian composer and university teacher. Works include opera *Grant, Warden of the Plains*; *Qalala and Nilaula of the North* for woodwind, strings and percussion, based on Inuit tunes; Trio for flute, cello, piano.

added sixth, the major sixth added to the major or minor triad –

e.g. ♩♩♩ or ♩♩♩ , A being the added note, the result being called an *added-sixth chord*. Used e.g. by Mahler and Delius and in jazz and later popular music.

Addinsell, Richard [Stewart] (1904–77), British composer of music particularly for films and plays – including *Warsaw Concerto* (fragment for piano and orchestra) in film *Dangerous Moonlight* (1941).

'Adélaïde' Concerto, a violin concerto alleged to have been written by Mozart, aged 10, and dedicated to a French princess, Adélaïde. The work is now known to be spurious.

Adieux, Les (in full *Les Adieux, l'absence et le retour*), title given by Beethoven to his Piano Sonata in E♭, op. 81a (1809); the 'farewell, absence and return' are depicted successively in three movements.

Adler, Larry (originally Lawrence Cecil Adler) (b. 1914), American player of the harmonica (mouth-organ) – an instrument which he elevated to concert rank, works having been specially written for him by Milhaud, Vaughan Williams, M. Arnold, etc. Resident in England since 1949.

ad lib. (Lat., *ad libitum*), at discretion, to be performed as the performer wishes – especially meaning that strict time need not be observed, or that the inclusion of a particular voice or instrument in the ensemble is optional.

Adrienne Lecouvreur (It., *Adriana . . .*), opera by Cilèa, produced in Milan, 1902. Libretto by A. Colautti, about an (historical) actress of the Comédie Française, 1730.

aeolian harp, primitive instrument with strings of different thicknesses, but all tuned to the same note, across which the wind is allowed to blow: various HARMONICS result. Named from Aeolus, legendary keeper of the winds. For a modern electronic simulation, using vibrating metal bands instead of strings, see DAVIES (Hugh).

Aeolian mode, the MODE which may be represented by the white keys of the piano from A to A.

aerophone, term used scientifically to classify an instrument in which a vibrating column of air produces the musical sound – including pipe-organ, accordion, etc., as well as conventional mouth-blown woodwind and brass instruments.

affettuoso (It.), with feeling.

affrettando (It.), becoming faster or more agitated.

African, The (Fr., *L'Africaine*), opera by Meyerbeer, produced in Paris, 1865, with libretto by Scribe. The (female) 'African', who loves the explorer Vasco da Gama, would appear to be a geographical aberration as her community is Hindu.

Afternoon of a Faun, The (Fr., *L'Après-midi d'un faune*), orchestral piece by

Debussy, 1892–4, composed as a musical illustration of Mallarmé's poem. Strictly called 'Prelude to "The Afternoon of a Faun"': Debussy originally intended two other pieces to follow it.

Age of Anxiety, The, title (from W. H. Auden's poem) of Bernstein's Symphony no. 2, for piano and orchestra, first performed in 1949 and used for ballet in 1950.

agitato (It.), agitated, restless.

Agnus Dei (Lat., [O] Lamb of God), see MASS.

Agon (Gk., contest), ballet with music by Stravinsky, produced in New York, 1957.

agrément (Fr.) = ORNAMENT.

Agricola, Alexander (1446–1506), Flemish composer of church and secular music, possibly pupil of Ockeghem; died while employed in Spain.

Ahronovitch, Yuri (b. 1932), Russian-born Israeli conductor; since 1982, conductor of the Stockholm Philharmonic Orchestra.

ai (It.), at the, to the (pl.).

Aichinger, Gregor (1564–1628), German composer who visited Rome and Venice, and became cathedral choirmaster in Augsburg. Wrote Latin church music.

Aida, opera by Verdi, produced in Cairo, 1871. Libretto by A. Ghislanzoni, set in ancient Egypt and named after the Ethiopian princess who is its heroine. (The spelling 'Aïda', with diaeresis, is incorrect in Italian.)

air, a simple tune for voice or instrument. (The old English spelling AYRE, and the Italian equivalent ARIA, have

acquired more specialized meanings.) *Air on the G String* is a name given to an arrangement by Wilhelmj (1871) of the second movement of Bach's Suite no. 3 in D for orchestra; in this arrangement, for violin and piano, the piece is transposed from D to C and the violinist plays on the lowest (G) string.

Akhnaten, opera by Glass, produced in Stuttgart, 1984. Libretto by the composer and others, about the Pharaoh Akhnaten (otherwise 'Akhnaton' or 'Ikhnaton') of *c.*1350 BC.

Akiyama, Kuniharu (b. 1929), Japanese composer, pupil of Cage and Xenakis. Works include *Music for Bells* (stone instruments and glass bottles on four-channel tape) and *Music for Farting* (for clarinet, trumpet, trombone and tuba).

al (It.), to the. (For phrases beginning thus, see under the word following.)

Alabiev, Alexander Alexandrovitch, see ALYABIEV.

Alain, Jehan (1911–40), French organist and composer mainly of organ and choral music. See the following.

Alain, Marie-Claire (b. 1926), French organist who has recorded music by her brother (preceding) and other composers.

Alban Berg Quartet, Austrian string quartet, named after the composer; founded 1971, it includes all Berg's and Webern's quartets in its repertory.

Albee, Edward (b. 1928), American dramatist. See FLANAGAN.

Albéniz, Isaac (1860–1909), Spanish composer of music in Spanish 'national' style. Child prodigy as composer and pianist; pupil of Liszt in Weimar; spent much of later life in London and Paris. Works include operas (two in English), songs and many piano pieces, e.g. the cyle IBERIA.

Albéniz, Mateo [Antonio Perez de] (c.1755–1831), Spanish organist, composer and author of a musical treatise.

Albert, Eugène [Francis Charles] **d'** (1864–1932), Scottish-born composer-pianist, French-English by descent and German by adoption (therefore known also as Eugen d'Albert). Pupil of Liszt; teacher in Berlin; died in Riga. Composed *Lowland* (Ger., *Tiefland*) and 20 other operas, etc.

Albert Herring, comic opera by Britten, produced at Glyndebourne, 1947; libretto by E. Crozier, after a story by Maupassant about a male 'May Queen'.

Alberti bass, the spreading-out of a left-hand keyboard chord in a rhythmical pattern – e.g.

from ♪ Named after Domenico Alberti (1710–40), Italian composer, who used it extensively.

Albinoni, Tomaso (1671–1750), Italian violinist and composer of works of CONCERTO GROSSO type; also of more than 40 operas, etc. Bach studied, and adapted from, his music. An ADAGIO ascribed to him is principally the work of his biographer, Remo Giazotto (b. 1910).

alborada (Sp.), morning song (cp. AUBADE); *Alborada del gracioso* (. . . of

the Jester), piano piece by Ravel in the set *Mirrors* (1905).

Albrechtsberger, Johann Georg (1736–1809), Austrian composer and theorist under whom Beethoven studied counterpoint.

Alceste, Alcestis, see ALKESTIS.

Alcina, opera by Handel, produced in London, 1735. Libretto (after Ariosto's narrative poem of chivalry, *Orlando Furioso*) about an enchantress.

alcuna licenza, see LICENZA.

Aldrich, Henry (1648–1710), English composer of church music, the round 'Great Tom is Cast', etc.; also theologian and architect.

aleatoric, malformed word (presumably from Ger. *Aleatorik*, noun not adjective) ignorantly used in place of the standard English term: see next entry.

aleatory, dependent on chance or on the throw of the dice (Lat., *alea*). This is rather loosely applied to a tendency (since the 1950s) of some composers to leave elements in their compositions in an indeterminate state. But it might be more strictly confined to compositions in which random chance genuinely plays a part in performance (see CAGE), not to those in which a decision of the performer replaces a decision of the composer. See INDETERMINACY.

Alexander Nevsky, cantata (drawn from film score) by Prokofiev, first performed in 1939, celebrating the victories of the 13th-century Russian prince.

Alexander's Feast, cantata by Handel, first performed in 1736; words mainly from Dryden's poem, referring to Alexander the Great and celebrating the power of music.

Alexeev (more correctly Alexeyev), **Dmitry** (b. 1947), Russian pianist who won the Moscow (International Tchaikovsky) and Leeds competitions and has pursued concert and recording careers both in the USSR and in the West.

Alfano, Franco (1875–1954), Italian composer of operas including *Cyrano de Bergerac* (after Rostand); also symphonies, string quartets, etc. Completed Puccini's TURANDOT from sketches left by the composer.

Alfonso and Estrella, Schubert's only all-sung opera (D732), produced posthumously in Weimar, 1854. Libretto by F. von Schober, about two lovers, children of a deposed king and a usurping one.

Alfred, masque by T. A. Arne, produced at Cliveden, Bucks, 1740. Words by J. Thomson and D. Mallet, celebrating King Alfred. It contains 'Rule, Britannia!' (of which the version often sung today is corrupt – but see SARGENT).

Alfvén, Hugo (1872–1960), Swedish composer of five symphonies and three orchestral *Swedish Rhapsodies* (no. 1, *Midsummer Vigil*, is the one sometimes called simply *Swedish Rhapsody*); also of cantatas, a violin sonata, etc.

Aliabiev, Alexander Alexandrovitch, see ALYABIEV.

Alison, Richard (16th–17th century), English composer of songs, lute solos, etc.

Alkan, (original surname Morhange), **Charles-Valentin** (1813–88), French pianist and composer of works for the normal piano and the PEDAL-PIANO; his music has some 'advanced' chromatic harmonies.

Alkestis, name given to operas by many composers, after Euripides' tragedy: as *Alceste,* (1) by Lully (libretto, P. Quinault) produced in Paris, 1674; (2) by Gluck (Italian libretto by R. Calzabigi), Vienna, 1767.

alla (It.), to the, at the; in the manner of (like Fr. *à la*). See also the following.

alla breve, a tempo-direction (chiefly 18th-century) indicating that, in a bar nominally of four beats, the pace is to be so fast that it is heard as having two beats only (on the original first and third beats).

allargando (It.), broadening, becoming slower.

Alldis, John (b. 1929), British chorus-master and conductor; chorus-master, London Philharmonic Choir 1969–82; director, Groupe Vocal de France, 1978–83.

allegretto (It., a little allegro), not quite so lively as ALLEGRO.

Allegri, Gregorio (1582–1652), Italian composer, and singer in the Papal chapel. His *Miserere* was written down by Mozart, aged 14, after one hearing (and checked after a second hearing).

allegro (It.), lively, i.e. rather fast (but not as fast as PRESTO).

Alleluia (Mozart), see EXSULTATE, JUBILATE.

allemande, dance-movement often opening the baroque SUITE, in moderate 4-4 time; it was divided into two sections and usually began with a short note just before the bar-line. The term is French for 'German', but this is not the same as a GERMAN DANCE.

Allen, Thomas [Boaz] (b. 1944), British baritone, noted in opera; at Covent Garden from 1972, Metropolitan Opera from 1981.

Allende(-Saron), [Pedró] **Humberto** (1885–1959), Chilean composer (also violinist, teacher and folk-music researcher). Works include 12 *Tonadas*, of popular Chilean character, for piano (some also orchestrated); *The Voice of the Street* for orchestra; songs.

almain, almand, almond, old English equivalents of ALLEMANDE.

alphorn, wind instrument having a straight wooden tube sometimes as much as 12 ft long. It sounds one HARMONIC SERIES only (like a bugle) with very powerful tone, and is used in Switzerland for attracting cattle (and tourists). The German name is *Alpenhorn*. Extremely rare in the concert-hall: see SCHWERTSIK.

Alpine Symphony, An (Ger., *Eine Alpensinfonie*), the last of R. Strauss's descriptive orchestral works, first performed in 1915.

Alsina, Carlos Roqué (b. 1941), Argentinian composer, also pianist and conductor (in Germany 1964–6). Works include piano solos, chamber music (his *Rendezvous* uses an alphorn) and *Layers* (Ger., *Schichten*) for orchestra.

Also sprach Zarathustra, see THUS SPAKE ZARATHUSTRA.

alt, term signifying 'high' in special vocal sense – *in alt*, in the octave written immediately above the treble clef, beginning with G; *in altissimo*, in the octave above that.

altissimo (It., very high), see preceding entry.

alto (It., high), (1) an unusually high type of adult male voice, employing falsetto – see also COUNTER-TENOR; (2) the lower type of female voice – so designated in choirs, elsewhere usually CONTRALTO (see also next entry); also, sometimes, the corresponding child's voice; (3), in a 'family' of instruments, having range approximately that of an alto voice – e.g. *alto* FLUTE, *alto* SAXOPHONE; (4, *alto clef*) type of clef, written 𝄡 ; it is the normal clef for viola but is otherwise little used; (5, Fr.) = viola.

Alto Rhapsody, usual English title for Brahms's Rhapsody for contralto solo, male chorus and orchestra, first performed in 1870; it has a philosophical text by Goethe.

Alva, Luigi (originally Luis) (b. 1927), Peruvian tenor who studied in Milan and made an international operatic career with speciality in Mozart and Rossini (Covent Garden from 1960).

Alwyn, William (1905–85), British composer, pupil of McEwen. Formerly flautist. Works include four symphonies; concerto *Lyra Angelica* for harp and strings; two string quartets; also much film music.

Alyabiev, Alexander Alexandrovich (1787–1851), Russian composer of song 'The Nightingale' (formerly often interpolated into the Lesson Scene of Rossini's *Barber of Seville*); also of operas, etc. (The name is wrongly transliterated as 'Alabiev' in most English references.)

Amadeus Quartet, British string quartet (three of its members Austrian-Jewish refugees from the Nazis) which took Mozart's middle name; made its

London début in 1948 and continued with unbroken membership. It disbanded on the death of its viola-player, Peter Schidlof, in 1987.

Amahl and the Night Visitors, opera for television by Menotti, produced in New York, 1951; later on stage. Libretto by composer, on the legend of the Magi.

Amati, family of violin-makers of Cremona, active from mid 16th to early 18th century.

Ambrosian chant, type of PLAINSONG associated with Bishop (St) Ambrose of Milan (340–97), differing from GREGORIAN chant.

Amelia Goes to the Ball, Menotti's first opera, produced in Philadelphia, 1937. Libretto by composer, originally in Italian (*Amelia al ballo*), mocking woman's outlook on social priorities.

Ameling, Elly (really Elisabeth Sara) (b. 1934), Dutch soprano well known in German and French song, Bach's church music, etc., with a few appearances in opera.

American in Paris, An, descriptive piece for orchestra (including four taxi-horns) by Gershwin, first performed in 1928.

American organ, type of REED-ORGAN in which air is sucked in through bellows. (US term: cabinet-organ.)

'American' Quartet, nickname for Dvořák's String Quartet in F, op. 96 (1893), composed in USA and partly prompted by Negro melodies; hence also called 'Negro' Quartet and (in former usage) 'Nigger' Quartet.

Amfiparnaso, L', see AMPHIPAR-NASSUS.

Amid Nature (Cz., *V přírodě*), overture by Dvořák, 1891; see also CARNIVAL.

Amor brujo, see LOVE, THE SORCERER.

amore, d'; amour, d' (It., Fr.), term applied to some old instruments, indicating an ingratiating tone (literally, 'of love'); see main name of instrument, e.g. VIOLA D'AMORE.

amoroso (It., lovingly), tenderly.

Amphiparnassus, The (It., *L'Amfiparnaso*), name given by Vecchi to a sequence of madrigals in the form of a dramatic comedy; published 1597, but not intended to be staged, therefore not a forerunner of opera. Title means 'The lower slopes of Parnassus' (mountain sacred to the Muses).

Amsterdam Baroque Orchestra, see KOOPMAN.

Amy, Gilbert (b. 1936), French composer, conductor and writer on music; director of Lyons Conservatory; pupil of Boulez. Works include *Trajectories* for violin and orchestra, *Play* (*Jeu*) for 1–4 oboes, *Cycle* for six percussionists.

anacrusis (term borrowed from the analysis of verse), an initial upbeat, which may be one note or more – i.e. whatever is heard before the first strong accent (downbeat). A phrase beginning *on* the downbeat has no anacrusis.

Anchieta, Juan de (1462–1523), Spanish composer in service to Spanish royal family (also priest); wrote Latin church music and secular songs with Spanish words.

ancora (It., cp. Fr. ENCORE), still, yet; *ancora più presto,* still more quickly.

Anda, Geza (1921–76), Hungarian

pianist, pupil of E. Dohnányi; resident in Switzerland from 1942, taking Swiss nationality.

andante (It., going), at a walking pace, at moderate speed (between ALLEGRETTO and ADAGIO).

andantino (It., a little ANDANTE), term apparently indicating either a little slower than andante, or (now more usually) not quite so slow as andante.

Andersen, Hans Christian (1805–75), Danish writer. See HARTMANN (J. P. E.), HENRIQUES, HØFFDING.

Anderson, June (b. 1950), American soprano who made her opera début with New York City Opera, 1978, and developed a speciality in coloratura roles, e.g. title-role of Rossini's *Semiramide*.

Anderson, Marian (b. 1902), American contralto; overcame various disabilities imposed on her race; in 1955 became the first black singer to perform in the Metropolitan Opera, New York.

André Chénier (It., *Andrea* . . .), opera by Giordano, produced in Milan, 1896. Libretto by L. Illica, about the historical French Revolutionary poet.

André, Maurice (b. 1933), French trumpeter, noted soloist in baroque and modern music; Blacher and other composers have written works for him.

Andriessen, Hendrik [Franciscus] (1892–1981), Dutch composer of much Roman Catholic church music, including Masses making use of Gregorian chant; also of opera, four symphonies, etc. Father of the two following composers.

Andriessen, Juriaan (b. 1925), Dutch composer, pupil of his father (preceding), also pianist and conductor. Works include Sinfonietta Concertante for four trumpets and orchestra; *Homage to Milhaud* for 11 instruments.

Andriessen, Louis (b. 1939), Dutch composer, pupil of his father (Hendrik, above), and of Berio. Works include *Sweet* for recorder; two orchestral compositions called *Anachronie*; *Contra tempus* (Lat., Against Time) for 23 musicians. See SCHAT.

Anerio, Felice (1560–1614), Italian composer, mainly of church music; Palestrina's successor as composer to the Papal Chapel. Brother of the following.

Anerio, Giovanni (*c*.1577–1630), Italian composer (also priest), brother of the preceding. Worked as choirmaster in Italy; also visited Poland and died in Austria on a journey from Poland to Italy. Wrote Masses, motets, madrigals, etc.

Anfossi, Pasquale (1727–97), Italian composer, especially of operas – including *La Finta Giardiniera* (The Mock Girl-gardener) to a libretto later used by Mozart; also church musician in Rome.

Angel of Fire, The, see FIERY ANGEL.

Anglican chant, type of harmonized melody used for psalm-singing in the Church of England. The melody is four-square in itself, but made metrically irregular by having to accommodate a varying number of syllables.

animato (It.), animated, lively.

Anna Bolena, see ANNE BOLEYN.

Anne Boleyn (It., *Anna Bolena*), opera by Donizetti, produced in Milan, 1830. Libretto, by F. Romani, culminates in Anne's execution.

Années de pèlerinage, see YEARS OF PILGRIMAGE.

Ansermet, Ernest (1883–1969), Swiss conductor – worked with Diaghilev, then (1918) founder-conductor of the Geneva orchestra (Orchestre de la Suisse Romande); gave many first performances of important modern works, especially of Stravinsky. Also writer on music.

answer, a musical phrase appearing to respond to another – particularly in a FUGUE, where the first entry of the main theme is called the subject and the second (at the interval of a fifth upwards from the subject) is called the answer, and so on alternately. If the answer exactly reproduces the subject (apart from the displacement of a fifth), it is called a *real answer* and the fugue a 'real fugue'; if the internal intervals of the subject are (as usually) slightly modified in the answer, so as to keep the music within the key, then the answer is a *tonal answer* and the fugue a 'tonal fugue'.

Antheil, George (1900–1959), American composer and pianist; also author of fiction and an autobiography. Wrote *Ballet Mécanique* (for aeroplane propellers, bells, motor-horns, etc.), 1927, and also six symphonies, opera *Volpone* (after Jonson) and many film scores.

anthem, short solemn vocal composition (hence *national anthem*, authorized for expression of patriotic sentiment); specifically, a short choral work, to a text not necessarily forming part of the liturgy, included in Church of England services – sometimes with organ accompaniment, and either with or without solo parts. Cp. MOTET.

anticipation, the sounding of a note before the chord of which it forms part, so that at first it is heard as a discord with the preceding chord.

Antigone, title (after Sophocles' play) of operas by various composers, including one by Honegger, produced in Brussels, 1927 (libretto by Cocteau); another by Orff (with unorthodox, mainly percussive orchestra), directly setting Hölderlin's German version of Sophocles, produced in Salzburg, 1949.

antiphon (from Gk. for 'sounding across'), part of Roman Catholic and Greek Orthodox church services sung as responses between single and many voices or between two groups of singers; hence *antiphonal*, descriptive term for musical effects drawn from the use of groups of performers stationed apart.

antique cymbal, see CROTALE.

Antony and Cleopatra, opera by Barber, produced in New York, 1966, with libretto after Shakespeare by Franco Zeffirelli (libretto later revised by Menotti).

anvil, orchestra bar-and-striker instrument imitating real anvil; first used by Auber, 1825. Wagner's *The Rhinegold* demands 18.

Apollinaire, Guillaume (1880–1918), French poet. See BREASTS OF TIRESIAS.

Apollo Musagetes (Gk., Apollo, Leader of the Muses), ballet with music by Stravinsky, produced in Washington, 1928. The French version of the title, *Apollon Musagète*, has no claim to usage in English.

Apostel, Hans Erich (1901–72), German-born Austrian composer, pupil of Schoenberg and Berg. Works include two string quartets (no. 1, variations on a theme from WOZZECK for Berg's birthday), a Requiem, piano solos.

Apostles, The, oratorio by Elgar (text from the Bible), first performed in 1903. The first part of Elgar's intended trilogy of oratorios; no. 2 is *The Kingdom*, no. 3 was never completed.

Appalachian Spring, ballet with music by Copland, produced in 1944. (Title chosen by Martha Graham, for whose company the work was composed; the setting is a 'primitive' American rural community.)

appoggiatura (It., a leaning), (1) musical ornament (chiefly 18th-century, now obsolete) consisting of unharmonized auxiliary note falling (or, less frequently, rising) to an adjacent note which is harmonized or implied to be so. Appoggiatura can be either 'written' using an auxiliary note in smaller type – e.g. played or 'unwritten', i.e. to be inserted by performer according to conventions of the period – e.g. a recitative in Handel or Mozart ending was intended to be sung as ; (2, derived from above) term used in modern harmonic analysis for accenting non-harmonized note like the D in the first example (whether or not notated in the above obsolete way) adjacent to following harmonized note less accented than itself.

Apprenti sorcier, L', see SORCERER'S APPRENTICE.

Arabella, opera by R. Strauss, produced in Dresden, 1933. Libretto by H. von Hofmannsthal, based on a widower's courtship of a new bride.

arabesque (Fr., Eng.; also *Arabeske*, Ger.), title borrowed from visual art and sometimes given to short piece with decorative qualities – e.g. by Schumann and Debussy, for piano.

Aragall, Giacomo (originally, in Spanish, Jaime) (b. 1939), Spanish tenor who made an international reputation, particularly in Italian opera, from the 1960s.

Arányi, Jelly [Eva] **d'** (1893–1966), Hungarian-born British violinist, great-niece of Joachim; works by Bartók, Ravel and Vaughan Williams were dedicated to her.

Araujo or Arauxo, Francisco Correa de, see CORREA DE ARAUJO.

Arbós, Enrique Fernandez (1863–1939), Spanish violinist, conductor and arranger; orchestrated part of IBERIA by Albéniz.

Arcadelt, Jacob (*c.*1505–68), Flemish composer of Masses, motets, madrigals, etc. (one of the earliest practitioners of the madrigal), working in Rome as Papal musician.

'Archduke' Trio, nickname of Beethoven's Piano Trio in B♭ (1811), op. 97, dedicated to Archduke Rudolph of Austria.

Archer, Violet [Balestreri] (b. 1913), Canadian composer (also university teacher) who studied with Hindemith and Bartók. Works include a piano concerto, violin concerto and *Cantata Sacra* (to her own text) for solo singers and chamber orchestra.

archlute, generic name for a long-necked LUTE with extra bass strings; see CHITARRONE, THEORBO.

arco (It.), bow (of a stringed instrument); (instruction to) play with the bow (cancelling the instruction PIZZICATO).

Arden Must Die, opera by Goehr, with libretto (originally in German, as *Arden muss sterben,* by Erich Fried), produced in Hamburg, 1967; the plot of violent intrigue is based on the (anonymous) Elizabethan play *Arden of Faversham.*

Arditi, Luigi (1822–1903), Italian composer of waltz-song 'Il Bacio' (The Kiss), etc., and conductor; settled in England, 1858, and died there.

Arditti Quartet, British string quartet, founded 1974 and led by Irving Arditti; its high reputation rests on its devotion to modern works.

Arensky, Anton Stepanovich (1861–1906), Russian composer, pupil of Rimsky-Korsakov but not sharing his teacher's pronounced 'nationalism' in music; works include three operas, two symphonies, and (now chiefly heard) piano pieces, chamber music and songs.

Argento, Dominick [Joseph] (b. 1927), American composer of 10 operas, including *Postcard from Morocco* and *The Aspern Papers* (after Henry James); *Letters from Composers* for tenor and guitar; incidental music for plays; etc. His teachers included Dallapiccola.

Argerich, Martha (b. 1941), Argentinan pianist, pupil of Gulda, Michelangeli and others; prizewinner in Geneva at 16, then internationally prominent.

aria (It.), air, song, especially one of some complexity in opera or oratorio; '*da capo*' *aria* (as used, e.g., by Handel), one in which the first section is finally repeated after a contrasting section.

Ariadne on Naxos (Ger., *Ariadne auf Naxos*), opera by Richard Strauss with libretto by H. von Hofmannsthal – original version, 1912, designed to be performed after Molière's play *Le Bourgeois Gentilhomme* (with Strauss's incidental music); longer self-contained version, 1916. (Naxos is the island on which Ariadne, at first deserted, later finds consolation with Bacchus.)

arietta (It.), a little or a light ARIA.

ariette (Fr.), literally a 'little air', but historically (e.g. in Rameau) a term indicating an operatic song of considerable dimensions and great vocal display.

arioso (It.), aria-like, i.e. 'normally' sung (as distinct from RECITATIVE) though not necessarily constructed according to the formal balance usually accorded to an ARIA. The term is occasionally used as a title: for Henze's *Ariosi,* see SEEFRIED.

Ariosto, Ludovico (1474–1533), Italian poet. See ALCINA, ORLANDO, PETRASSI.

Arkhipova, Irina (b. 1925), Russian mezzo-soprano, prominent in opera in USSR and (since appearing in Milan, 1967) in the West.

Arlésienne, L'

Arlésienne, L', see WOMAN OF ARLES.

Armida (or, Fr., *Armide*), name of operas by several composers, based on Tasso's poem of the Crusades, *Jerusalem Delivered*; e.g. (1) by Lully, produced in Paris, 1686 (libretto by P. Quinault); (2) by Gluck, Paris, 1777 (libretto by P. Quinault); (3) by Haydn, Eszterháza, 1784 (Hob. XXVIII: 12; libretto, in Italian, by J. Durandi); (4) by Rossini, Naples, 1817 (libretto by G. Schmidt); (5) by Dvořák, Prague, 1904 (libretto by J. Vrchlitzky). See also RINALDO – he and Armida being Tasso's principal male and female characters.

armonica, Italian name for the GLASS HARMONICA.

Armstrong, Karan (b. 1941), American soprano well known in opera, notably in title-role of Berg's *Lulu*.

Arne, Michael (b. 1740 or 1741; d. 1786). British singer and, from childhood, a composer. Works include song 'The Lass with the Delicate Air', and much music for the stage. Illegitimate son of Thomas Arne (below).

Arne, Thomas Augustine (1710–78), British composer mainly of operas (one in Italian), other stage works, and songs; also of oratorio JUDITH. Wrote masques ALFRED (in which 'Rule, Britannia!' occurs) and COMUS. See also LOVE IN A VILLAGE. Composed much music for the London pleasure gardens, Drury Lane Theatre, etc. D. Mus., Oxford, 1759. Was generally known as Dr Arne. Michael Arne was his illegitimate son.

Arnell, Richard [Anthony Sayer] (b. 1917), British composer of seven symphonies, a *Symphonic Portrait: Lord Byron*, chamber music, etc.; also

conductor and pianist. Lived in USA, 1939–47 and later. Authority on film music.

Arnold, Malcolm (b. 1921), British composer, pupil of Jacob; formerly orchestral trumpeter. Works include symphonies and a TOY SYMPHONY; various concertos (one for harmonica, one for piano duet and orchestra); a number of instrumental sonatas; many film scores. Created CBE, 1970.

Arnold, Matthew (1822–88), British poet. See BARBER.

Arnold, Samuel (1740–1802), British composer of many operas and plays with music, church music, harpsichord pieces, etc. Was also organist and editor of first collected edition of Handel.

arpa (It.), harp.

arpeggio (It., from preceding), chord (on piano, etc.) which is performed 'spread out' – i.e. the notes sounded not simultaneously but in succession (nearly always starting at the bottom) as normally on the harp.

arpeggione, a six-stringed instrument invented in 1824, fretted and tuned like a guitar but bowed like a cello. The sonata that Schubert wrote for it (with piano) in that year (D821) is now commonly taken over by cellists and identified as the 'Arpeggione' Sonata.

arr., abbr. for *arranger, arranged*. See following.

arrange, to set out for one performing medium a composition written for another. (Normally this indicates stricter fidelity to the composer's notes, and less artistic licence, than does TRANSCRIBE.)

Arrau, Claudio (b. 1903), Chilean pianist who gave first recital at age five, and studied in Berlin under Krause (pupil of Liszt); appeared in USA, 1924, and then began world tours. Continued to perform into his 80s; returned in 1974 to Chile after a 17-year absence. His authority in the classics is considered unsurpassed.

Arriaga [y Balzola], **Juan Crisostomo Antonio** (1806–26), Spanish composer who studied in Paris and, before early death, wrote opera, symphony and three string quartets.

Arrigo, Girolamo (b. 1930), Italian composer resident in Paris. Has written many vocal works (texts in French, Italian, Spanish); *Infra-red* for 16 instruments; *From the Mist to the Mist* for 16 cellos and six double-basses; etc.

Arroyo, Martina (b. 1936), American soprano whose Aida at the Metropolitan Opera, New York, 1965, began her celebrity in heavier Italian operatic roles. She also performs modern works.

ars antiqua (Lat., old art), term for the style of Western European medieval music (based on PLAINSONG and OR-GANUM) practised, e.g., by Pérotin and preceding the ARS NOVA.

ars nova (Lat., new art), term for the musical style current in 14th-century France and Italy, free from the restrictions of ARS ANTIQUA, introducing duple (instead of only triple) time and having much independence of part-writing; practised, e.g., by LANDINI, MACHAUT.

Artaxerxes, opera by Arne, produced in London, 1762; libretto by composer, translated from Metastasio, about the ancient Persian king Artaxerxes I (5th century BC).

Art of the Fugue, The (Ger., *Die Kunst der Fuge*), work by Bach, a series of fugues and canons all on the same theme – showing prodigious resource in contrapuntal technique. No instrument is indicated, but the work was demonstrably intended for keyboard (harpsichord or organ) – though versions with other instrumentation have been made by several 20th-century musicians. Begun in 1748; the final fugue was left incomplete on Bach's death in 1750 (see TOVEY).

Arts Florissants, Les, see CHRISTIE.

art-song, term sometimes used in contradiction to FOLK-SONG or popular song to indicate a 'serious' composition intended for formal concert performance.

Arutiunian, Alexander Grigorievich (b. 1920), Soviet-Armenian composer of a piano concerto, trumpet concerto, horn concerto, opera *Savat-Nova*, etc.; also writer on music.

Asafiev, Boris (1884–1949), Russian composer (*The Fountain of Bakhchisarai* and other ballets; also operas, five symphonies, etc.); and, under the name Igor Glebov, music critic and writer.

ASCAP, (name formed from the initials of) American Society of Composers, Authors and Publishers, a performing-rights agency, created in 1914.

Ashkenazy, Vladimir [Davidovich] (b. 1937), Russian pianist, naturalized Icelandic, 1972; joint winner, with John Ogdon, of the International Tchaikovsky Contest in Moscow, 1962. Emigrated to the West in 1963, won acclaim as pianist-conductor, later as conductor alone; music director, Royal Philharmonic Orchestra, 1987.

Ashley, Robert (b. 1930), American composer with special interest in film, multimedia, electronics, etc. Works include *The Wolfman Motorcity Revue* and other 'electronic music theatre' pieces; also *Quartet for any Number of Instruments*, etc.

assai (It.), very; *allegro assai*, very quick.

Assassinio nella Cattedrale, see MURDER IN THE CATHEDRAL.

Aston, Hugh (*c*.1485–1522), English composer of a HORNPIPE – the earliest known piece for virginals – Masses and other vocal works.

Atherton, David (b. 1944), British conductor, principal conductor of the Royal Liverpool Philharmonic Orchestra, 1980–83; especially noted in modern music, including opera.

atonal, not in any key; hence *atonality, atonalism*. (The term *pantonal*, indicating the synthesis of all keys rather than the absence of any, was preferred by Schoenberg but never won general acceptance.) TWELVE-NOTE music developed as a systematization of atonal music.

attacca (It.), attack (verb), i.e. go on to the next section without a break; so also *attacca subito* (immediately).

Atterberg, Kurt [Magnus] (1887–1974), Swedish composer, conductor and critic. Wrote nine symphonies, five operas, etc., sometimes making direct use of Swedish folk-music.

Attwood, Thomas (1765–1838), British organist (at St Paul's Cathedral, London, from 1796), and composer of church and other music, including notable songs. Pupil of Mozart in Vienna.

au, aux (Fr.), at the, to the, etc.

aubade (Fr.), morning song (cp. SERENADE). See also ALBORADA.

Auber, Daniel François Esprit (1782–1871), French composer of more than 40 operas including *The Dumb Girl of Portici* (*La Muette de Portici* – see MASANIELLO), MANON LESCAUT and FRA DIAVOLO; also of a violin concerto, etc. Director of the Paris Conservatory.

Auden, Wystan Hugh (1907–73), British-born US poet. See AGE OF ANXIETY, BASSARIDS, BRITTEN, ELEGY FOR YOUNG LOVERS, HYMN TO ST CECILIA, PAUL BUNYAN, RAKE'S PROGRESS.

Audran, Edmond (1840–1901), French composer chiefly of operettas including *The Mascot* (*La Mascotte*).

Auer, Leopold (1845–1930), Hungarian violinist who settled in St Petersburg and became a performer and teacher of worldwide renown; moved to USA, 1918.

Aufführungspraxis, see PERFORMANCE PRACTICE.

Aufstieg und Fall der Stadt Mahagonny, see RISE AND FALL OF THE CITY OF MAHAGONNY.

aug., abbr. for AUGMENTED as applied to intervals.

augment, (1) to supplement the numbers of a performing group; so *augmented choir*, etc.; (2) to 'increase' certain intervals – see AUGMENTED; (3) to subject a melody to AUGMENTATION.

augmentation, the treatment of a melody in such a way as to lengthen (usually doubling) the time-values of its notes. The device is used, e.g., in some fugues.

augmented, term applied to a type of interval regarded as an 'increased' version of a certain other interval. So *augmented first* (e.g. C up to C♯); *augmented second* (C up to D♯); *augmented fourth* (C up to F♯); *augmented fifth* (C up to G♯); *augmented sixth* (C up to A♯ – see FRENCH, GERMAN, ITALIAN SIXTHS); *augmented eighth* or *augmented octave* (C up to next C♯ but one). Note that the *augmented fifth* carries the harmonic implication of the major third too; e.g. the *augmented-fifth chord* on C is C-E-G♯, which chord is referred to in popular music, etc., as *C augmented* (abbr. *C aug.*).

Auletta, Pietro (1698–1771), Italian composer, one of whose operas was attributed to Pergolesi when published in Paris (with accretions) in 1753. See MUSIC MASTER.

aulos, ancient Greek oboe-like wind instrument always played in pairs, the player holding two reed-pipes in V-formation, one hand fingering each.

Auric, Georges (1899–1983), French composer, youngest member of THE SIX. Wrote much for ballet (e.g. *Phèdre*, after Racine's play) and for films; also a piano concerto, piano sonata, etc. Administrator of the two Paris opera-houses, 1962–8.

Aurora's Wedding, see SLEEPING BEAUTY.

Austin, Frederic (1872–1952), British baritone and composer; arranged the music of THE BEGGAR'S OPERA for its exceptionally successful London revival, 1920. Made a similar arrangement of POLLY.

Austin, Larry [Don] (b. 1930), American composer (pupil of Milhaud) with special interest in electronics and multimedia, also in co-ordinated improvisation. Works include *Plastic Surgery* for piano, percussion, tape and film; *A Broken Consort* for seven instruments. Also writer on music and university teacher.

authentic, authenticity, terms broadly referring to correctness in performance achieved by observing the conventions that apply to the composer's period – e.g. 'They played it with authentic trills.' Specifically, from the 1970s, *authenticity* refers to the use of the instruments (and the instrumental and vocal techniques) of a bygone period for performing music of the same era. In this sense no differentiation is made between still surviving old instruments and modern replicas.

authentic modes, see MODE.

autograph, term used by literary and musical scholars to denominate a manuscript (not just a signature) written in an author's or composer's own hand, with the implication that it carries authority over a mere copy. Hence, 'No autograph exists of Mozart's Clarinet Quintet.' The term 'holograph' is sometimes used to indicate a manuscript text completely, not partially, written in its orginator's hand.

auxiliary note, in harmony, a note which forms a discord with the chord with which it is heard, but is 'justified' because it lies adjacent (higher or lower) to a note of the chord which is heard immediately before and after –

e.g. the D in the following example:

Ave Maria (Lat., Hail, Mary), Roman Catholic prayer of partly biblical source. It has been variously set to music. The setting usually described as 'Bach-Gounod' consists of the first prelude of Bach's THE WELL-TEMPERED CLAVIER plus a melody which Gounod wrote over this (with the title 'Meditation'); to this melody the words of the 'Ave Maria' were fitted by someone else.

Avison, Charles (1709–70), British composer and organist who worked in Newcastle-on-Tyne, and probably studied with Geminiani in London. Works include concertos for string orchestra; also edited Marcello's psalm-settings with English texts. See also GIARDINI.

Avni, Zvi [Jacob] (b. 1927), German-born Israeli composer, pupil of Copland, Foss and Ben-Haim. Works include *Summer Strings* for string quartet; *Collage* for voice, flute, percussion and electric guitar; *Meditations on a Drama* for orchestra.

Avodath hakodesh, see SACRED SERVICE.

Avshalomov, Aaron (1894–1965), Russian-born composer-conductor, active in Shanghai, 1928–46; died in New York. Wrote a piano concerto on Chinese themes and other works attempting an integration of Chinese and Western music. Father of the following.

Avshalomov, Jacob (b. 1919), American composer and conductor; born in China of a Russian father (preceding). Works include Sinfonietta; *Slow Dance* for orchestra; *Inscriptions at the City of Brass* for narrator, chorus and orchestra without strings.

ayre, old spelling of 'air', retained in modern English for a type of English song composed (e.g. by J. Dowland) about 1600; usually STROPHIC, its main melodic interest is focused in the top vocal line, with accompaniment for lute (or other voices).

B

B, note of the scale. So *B* FLAT (B♭),
DOUBLE-FLAT (B♭♭), NATURAL (B♮),
SHARP (B♯), DOUBLE-SHARP (B𝄪); *B
major*, *B minor*, etc. – see MAJOR. So
also *in B♭*, either (1) in the key of B♭
(major, understood); or (2) indication
of a TRANSPOSING INSTRUMENT on
which the note C sounds as B♭ (and
correspondingly with other notes); e.g.
clarinet in B♭, or, colloquially, *B♭ clarinet*. In German the note represented
in English by B is represented by H,
the Germans using B to mean what is
in English B♭. Hence clarinets in
German scores may be marked *in B*,
etc.

B., abbr. for (1) Bachelor (in university
degrees, e.g. B.MUS. or Mus.B., Bachelor of Music); (2) British (cp. BBC);
(3) Bach, as in BWV – see BACH, J. S.

Baal Shem, suite for violin and piano
by Bloch, subtitled 'Three Pictures of
Chassidic Life'; named after Baal Shem
Tov (Master of the Good Name), 17th-
century founder of the Jewish pietist
sect of Chassidism.

Baaren, Kees van (1906–70), Dutch
composer who studied in Germany.
Works include Variations for orchestra, a piano concerto, wind quartet.

Baba Yaga, a 'fairy-tale for orchestra'
by Lyadov, 1904, describing the flight
of the witch named in the title.

Babbitt, Milton (b. 1916), American
composer (also influential theorist and
teacher), pupil of Sessions. Works include string quartets; piano pieces; *Phi-
lomel* for soprano, recorded soprano
and synthesized accompaniment on
tape.

Babi Yar, nickname for Shostakovich's
Symphony no. 13 for bass voice, male
chorus and orchestra, with words by
Yevtushenko, first performed in 1962.
'Babi Yar' is actually the title of the
first movement, referring to the place
in the Ukraine where thousands of
Jews were killed by the Nazis in 1941.

baby grand, a grand piano of the
smallest size.

Baccaloni, Salvatore (1900–1969),
Italian bass whose long operatic
career from 1922 was distinguished
by his performances in Italian comic
roles.

bacchetta (It., pl. *-ette*, stick), drumstick.

Bacchus and Ariadne (Fr., *Bacchus et
Ariane*), ballet with music by Roussel,
produced in Paris, 1931. (Based on
the same legend as R. Strauss's
ARIADNE ON NAXOS.) Two orchestral
suites are drawn from it.

Bacewicz, Grażyna (1909–69), Polish composer of symphonies, cello concerto, seven violin concertos, seven string quartets, etc.; she was also a violinist.

Bach, German family of musicians, some of whom are listed below; *Bach* without prefaced name or initials indicates Johann Sebastian Bach. For *Bach bow*, see BOW; for *Bach trumpet*, see TRUMPET. The letters B-A-C-H happen to represent, in German nomenclature, the notes B♭-A-C-B♮; J. S. Bach himself conceived the idea of using these notes as a theme of the unfinished final fugue of THE ART OF FUGUE, and the same combination has been used by many subsequent composers (e.g. Schumann, Liszt, Busoni), generally in tribute to Bach.

Bach, Anna Magdalena (1701–60), second wife of J. S. Bach, who compiled two books of music (by himself and others) for her musical instruction, 1722 and 1725.

Bach, Carl Philipp Emanuel (1714–88), German composer, fifth child of J. S. Bach, pupil of his father. Domestic musician to Frederick the Great of Prussia, until assuming a church post at Hamburg in 1767. Noted keyboard-player, adapting his music progressively to suit trend from harpsichord to piano; wrote treatise on keyboard-playing. Works, showing departure from J. S. Bach's style towards that of Haydn and Mozart, include keyboard concertos and sonatas, symphonies, chamber music; also oratorio and church music. His work is indexed by 'Wq' numbers, referring to the thematic catalogue made by Alfred Wotquenne in 1905.

Bach, Johann Christian (1735–82), German composer, 18th child of J. S. Bach; studied under his father and under his brother C. P. E. Bach. Went in 1756 to Italy, in 1762 to London where he remained, eventually dying there. He was known as 'the English Bach'; influenced Mozart on his visit (aged eight) to London. Works include Italian operas, English songs, about 40 piano concertos and other orchestral works, church music in Latin and English.

Bach, Johann Christoph (1642–1703), German composer, cousin of J. S. Bach's father. Wrote organ music, cantatas, motets including *Ich lasse dich nicht* (literally 'I leave thee not', but in English usually known as *I wrestle and pray*), formerly ascribed in error to J. S. Bach.

Bach, Johann Sebastian (1685–1750), German composer, the best-known of a distinguished musical family (see other BACH entries). Of high repute in his time as organist, but achieved major standing as composer only with posthumous (19th-century) revival. Born at Eisenach; studied under his brother Johann Christoph (not the preceding) and, as boy chorister at Lüneburg, was apparently influenced by Georg Böhm. Held organist's or other posts at Weimar, 1703; Arnstadt, later in 1703; Mühlhausen, 1707; Weimar, 1708; Köthen, 1717; then in 1723 in Leipzig as Cantor (director of music) at St Thomas's church, in which post he died shortly after becoming blind. Twice married, father of 20 children. Works, mostly written as official duty or with some other definite performance in view, include over 200 church cantatas (Lutheran), with orchestral accompaniment; ST JOHN and ST MATTHEW PASSIONS, both using his harmonizations of Lutheran chorales; CHRISTMAS and EASTER ORATORIOS; the so-called 'Mass in B minor' (see MASS); COFFEE CANTATA, PHOEBUS AND PAN and some other secular vocal works; preludes, fugues and other works for organ; CHROMATIC FANTASIA AND FUGUE, GOLDBERG VARIATIONS, ITALIAN CONCERTO, THE WELL-TEMPERED CLAVIER and other works for harpsichord and/or clavichord including ENGLISH SUITES, FRENCH SUITES; concertos for one, two, three and (arranged from Vivaldi) four harpsichords, also for one and two violins; six BRANDENBURG CONCERTOS (orchestral); THE MUSICAL OFFERING and THE ART OF FUGUE, both demonstrating prodigious contrapuntal skill. See also BOW and CHACONNE. Bach's works are indexed by BWV numbers (*Bach Werke-Verzeichnis* – i.e. Index to Bach's Works), according to the thematic catalogue made by Wolfgang Schmieder.

Bach, K. P. E. or **K. Ph. E.**, the customary German way (modernizing Carl to Karl) of referring to the composer known as C. P. E. Bach in general non-German usage.

Bach, Wilhelm Friedemann (1710–84), German composer; eldest son and second child of J. S. Bach, who wrote some music specially for his instruction. Became church organist, died in poverty; wrote church cantatas, nine symphonies, organ and harpsichord music, etc.

Bachauer, Gina (1913–76), Greek-born pianist (of Greek, Italian, Russian and Austrian descent); first appeared in Britain, 1946, later in USA.

Bachianas Brasileiras, title given by Villa-Lobos to a set of nine works (for various instrumental groups with or without voice) intended to combine the spirit of J. S. Bach's music and that of the traditional music of Villa-Lobos's native Brazil.

Bäck, Sven-Erik (b. 1919), Swedish composer, pupil of Petrassi in Rome. Works include Symphony for strings; *Sinfonia sacra* for choir and orchestra; Sonata for solo flute; opera *Crane Feathers*.

Backhaus, Wilhelm (1884–1969), German pianist (latterly became Swiss citizen), renowned for playing Beethoven; taught in Manchester, 1905–9; performed up to a few days before his death.

Bacquier, Gabriel (b. 1924), French baritone, internationally celebrated in opera (Covent Garden from 1962).

badinerie (Fr., a jest), title of certain 2/4 movements in the 18th century, e.g. in Bach's Suite in B minor for flute and strings.

Badings, Henk (1907–87), Dutch composer, born in Java; largely self-taught at first, then pupil of Pijper. Works, showing some affinity with Hindemith's style, include 14 symphonies, four violin concertos; Sonata for carillon, electronic music.

Badura-Skoda, Paul (b. 1927), Austrian pianist; has toured widely. Also writer on music, an authority on Mozart and composer of cadenzas for his concertos.

bagatelle (Fr., trifle), short, light piece, often for piano – Beethoven wrote 26.

bagpipe(s), reed-pipe instrument for which wind is stored in a bag, either (e.g. Scottish Highland pipes) mouth-filled, or (e.g. Northumbrian pipes and

Irish 'Uillean' or 'Union' pipes) filled by bellows under player's arm; the former type is the louder. Similar types are found in other countries; most have one or more drone pipes (giving unaltered bass-notes) as well as a pipe for the melody (chanter). The Scottish Highland pipe, though its scale does not correspond exactly to the normal one of the concert-hall, is used with orchestra in P. M. Davies's *Orkney Wedding with Sunrise*, 1985. See also MUSETTE.

baguette (Fr.), (1) drumstick; (2) a conductor's baton (the French do not use their word *bâton* in this sense).

Bailey, Norman [Stanley] (b. 1933), British baritone celebrated for Wagner roles sung in English and German.

Baillot, Pierre [Marie François de Sales] (1771–1842), French violinist, composer of violin music and writer of an instructional textbook on his instrument.

Bainbridge, Simon (b. 1952), British composer. Works include a viola concerto, wind quintet, *Landscape and Woods* for soprano and instrumental ensemble.

Bainton, Edgar L[eslie] (1880–1956), British composer and educationist; went to Sydney, 1934, as director of the Conservatorium, and died there.

Baird, Tadeusz (1928–81), Polish composer of *Erotics* (six songs for soprano and orchestra), *Variations without a theme* and other orchestral works, a piano concerto, theatre and film music, etc.

Bairstow, Edward Cuthbert (1874–1946), British organist (at York Minster from 1913), composer chiefly of

church music, conductor, and professor at Durham University; knighted, 1932.

Baker, Janet [Abbott] (b. 1933), British mezzo-soprano, formerly styling herself contralto; noted in concerts (Edinburgh Festival, 1960; first New York recital, 1966) and in operas, especially Handel's and Britten's. Created Dame, 1976.

Balakirev, Mily Alexeyevich (1837–1910), Russian composer, leader of the 'nationalist' group of composers called THE MIGHTY HANDFUL; also conductor and musical organizer. After nervous breakdown, retired from music, 1871–6, becoming railway official; 1883, director of music to the Russian court. Works include two symphonies; symphonic poem *Tamara*; much piano music, e.g. ISLAMEY and a sonata; songs and folk-song arrangements.

balalaika, type of Russian plucked instrument usually with three strings and triangular body; made in various sizes, and used singly and in bands for folk-music, etc. Cp. DOMRA.

Balassa, Sándor (b. 1935), Hungarian composer of *Iris* for orchestra; *Requiem for Lajos Kassák*; Trio for violin, viola and harp; etc. On staff of Hungarian Radio.

Balfe, Michael William (1808–70), Irish composer, also baritone singer; came to London as a boy and later studied in Italy. Composed operas in French, Italian and English, these last including THE BOHEMIAN GIRL (internationally successful, combining a cosmopolitan operatic style with provision for the Victorian English taste for 'ballads'), *The Maid of Artois* (see MANON), *The Rose of Castile*; also songs, cantatas, etc.

ballabile (It.), to be danced; in a dancing manner. Cp. CANTABILE.

ballad (derived as 'ball', i.e. from dancing), (1) old song (often a FOLK-SONG) telling a story, the music being repeated for each verse; hence – (2) a self-contained song of a narrative nature, e.g. Goethe's 'Erl King' as set by Schubert and Loewe; (3) song of narrative, explanatory type characteristically found in French opera and also, e.g., in Wagner's *The Flying Dutchman* ('Senta's Ballad'); so Stravinsky called his narrative cantata on Abraham and Isaac a 'sacred ballad'; (4) sentimental English song of 19th-century 'drawing-room' type (also found in English operas of the period); so *ballad concert*, mainly devoted to such songs; (5) see BALLADE. See also BALLAD OPERA.

ballade, (1) instrumental piece, suggesting narrative, e.g. four written for piano by Chopin, said to be inspired by (but certainly not being literal interpretations of) Polish poems by Mickiewicz. (The word is the French version of BALLAD; its use in English may be justified by the convenience of differentiating the instrumental from the vocal term.) (2) a form of French medieval poetry and music; certain polyphonic works, e.g. by Machaut, are so described.

Ballad of Baby Doe, The, opera by Douglas Moore, produced in Central City, Colorado, 1956, with libretto by John Latouche; the 19-century story revolves round Elizabeth 'Baby' Doe who marries a Colorado goldmine-owner.

ballad opera, opera having spoken dia-

logue and using popular tunes of the day adapted to new words, the prototype being THE BEGGAR'S OPERA, 1728. (The term is also used in various looser senses; Vaughan Williams's HUGH THE DROVER, described as 'a romantic ballad opera', has no spoken dialogue, and is not made up of traditional tunes, but it is written in an idiom deliberately evoking such tunes.) Cp. BALLAD (1).

ballata (It.), a form of 14th-century Italian poetry and music, found, e.g., in Landini's works. (Not the same form as Ballade, 2.)

ballet, (1) form of dancing of Italian origin, established at French court in the 16th century and evolving into a recognized art-form with its own traditional technique and conventions; it normally uses orchestral music (specially composed or otherwise) and appropriately full resources of stage decoration. The term was long employed in Britain for almost any piece of stage dancing having an artistic purpose and substantial length; but now, as in the USA, it is commonly withheld from works not based on the 'classical' technique of dancing – e.g. the so-called 'modern dance'. (See also DIVERTISSEMENT.) Hence *opera-ballet* and *ballet-pantomime*, 18th-century French terms differentiating ballet with and without sung words; the term *opera-ballet* is also applied to certain modern ballets with singing, e.g. Prokofiev's CINDERELLA. (But note that the simple classification *ballet* does not exclude the use of voices – as in Ravel's DAPHNIS AND CHLOE – and that Falla's LOVE, THE SORCERER, is styled *ballet-pantomime*, although it has vocal solos.) (2) an alternative spelling of BALLETT, and so pronounced.

ballett, type of concerted vocal composition prominent in England and Italy (*balletto*) about 1600 and similar to the madrigal, but having a dance-like lilt (as the name suggests) and a 'fa-la' refrain.

ballo (It.), a dance; *Overtura di ballo*, idiosyncratic title of a concert-overture by Sullivan, 1870, using dance rhythms.

Ballo in maschera, Un, see MASKED BALL.

Baltsa, Agnes (b. 1944), Greek mezzo-soprano who established an operatic career in Germany, then internationally (Covent Garden from 1976).

bamboo pipe, simple wood instrument of RECORDER type, used mainly educationally, players often making their own instruments; sometimes just called *pipe*, as in Vaughan Williams's *Suite for Pipes* (four of different sizes), published in 1947.

Banchieri, Adriano (1568–1634), Italian composer, also organist, musical theorist and priest. Works include Masses, instrumental works and 'madrigal comedies' (see MADRIGAL).

band, a numerous body of players, especially of wind or percussion instruments – BRASS, MILITARY, DANCE, PERCUSSION *bands*, etc. The use of the term for a full or string orchestra is obsolete or colloquial, and the supposed prestige of the term 'orchestra' was borrowed by dance bands from the 1930s onwards. The term *big band* now refers to the type of dance band of 20 or more musicians

which became a theatrical attraction in the 1930s; it has undergone a post-1960 revival.

bandora, see PANDORA.

bandurría (Sp.), Spanish plucked instrument, usually with six pairs of strings, each pair tuned to a unison.

Banfield, Raffaello de, see DE BANFIELD.

Banister, John (*c.*1625–79), English violinist, composer, and organizer of the first concerts in London to be open to the public on payment of an admission fee, 1672.

banjo, fretted instrument of five or more strings, plucked with fingers or plectrum; taken over from US Negro slaves by black-faced minstrel shows, and also used in early jazz – otherwise not much played in public, except to provide local 'atmosphere', e.g. in the orchestration of Gershwin's PORGY AND BESS and Delius's KOANGA.

Banks, Don[ald Oscar] (1923–80), Australian composer, resident in England from 1950 until appointed to university post in Canberra, 1971; pupil of Seiber in London and of Dallapiccola in Florence. Works include a horn concerto and a setting of Psalm 70 for soprano and chamber orchestra.

Bantock, Granville (1868–1946), British composer of *Fifine at the Fair* and other symphonic poems; also of *Hebridean Symphony*, song-cycles, unaccompanied choral works including a setting of Swinburne's *Atlanta in Calydon*, etc. Professor at Birmingham University, 1908; knighted, 1930. See CHORAL SYMPHONY.

bar, (1) a metrical division of music, marked on paper as the distance between two vertical lines; so 'two beats in the bar', etc.; (2) such a vertical line itself. (In general the first of these uses is English, the second American – Eng. *bar* equals US 'measure'; US *bar* equals Eng. *bar-line*. But two vertical lines close together, indicating the end of a piece or section, are called even in English *double bar*, not *double bar-line*.) (3, a meaning unconnected with previous two), a medieval German unit of song-construction, two similar sections being followed by one in contrast.

bar., abbr. of BARITONE (voice).

Barber, Samuel (1910–81), American composer, also singer (e.g. in his own setting, for voice and string quartet, of Matthew Arnold's 'Dover Beach'). Studied in Italy and USA. Works include operas *Vanessa*, *A Hand of Bridge*, *Antony and Cleopatra*; two symphonies; two *Essays for Orchestra*; *Adagio for Strings* (see ADAGIO); overture to Sheridan's *The School for Scandal*; a cello concerto; *Capricorn Concerto* (flute, oboe, trumpet and strings); a piano sonata; ballet *Medea* (also known as *Cave of the Heart*); cantata *Prayers of Kierkegaard*.

Barber of Baghdad, The (Ger., *Der Barbier von Bagdad*), comic opera by Cornelius, produced in Weimar, 1858. Libretto by the composer, a tale of intrigue (after the *Arabian Nights' Entertainment*).

Barber of Seville, The (It., *Il barbiere di Siviglia*), name of operas by (1) Rossini, produced in Rome, 1816, with libretto by C. Sterbini; (2) Paisiello, produced in St Petersburg, 1782, with libretto by G. Petrosellini – this version achieving international success but being superseded by Rossini's. The plot is that of Beaumarchais's French play, the cunning barber-factotum of the title being Figaro: the plot of Mozart's THE MARRIAGE OF FIGARO is a sequel. See ALYABIEV.

barber-shop singing (US), the singing of home-made arrangements of sentimental songs by amateur male quartets; a 'Society for the Preservation and Encouragement of Barber-shop Singing in America' was founded in 1938.

Barbiere di Siviglia, Il, see BARBER OF SEVILLE.

Barbieri, Francisco [Asenjo] (1823–94), Spanish composer, also singer, instrumentalist and writer on music; composed Spanish comic operas of ZARZUELA type, including *The Little Barber of Lavapies*.

Barbier von Bagdad, Der, see BARBER OF BAGHDAD.

Barbirolli, John (really Giovanni Battista ...) (1899–1970), British conductor of Italian and French parentage, previously cellist. Conductor of the New York Philharmonic-Symphony Orchestra, 1936–42, of the Hallé Orchestra (Manchester), 1943–70, and of the Houston (Texas) Symphony Orchestra, 1961–7. Knighted, 1949; created CH, 1969. Married Evelyn Rothwell (b. 1911), oboist.

barcarolle (Fr., from It.), boating-song, especially of the kind associated with Venetian gondoliers; song or instrumental piece suggestive of this, in swaying 6/8 time (e.g. the famous one in Offenbach's THE TALES OF HOFFMANN).

Barenboim, Daniel (b. 1942), Israeli pianist and conductor, born in

Argentina; studied in Salzburg, Paris, Rome; boy prodigy as pianist (London, 1955; New York, 1957). He conducted internationally (especially as conductor-pianist) from mid-1960s; conductor, Orchestre de Paris, 1975–90; appointed conductor of Chicago Symphony Orchestra from 1991. Married Jacqueline du Pré, 1967.

baritone, (1) man's voice of a range intermediate between tenor and bass; (2, of 'families' of instruments) indication of a range below the 'tenor' type, e.g. *baritone* SAXHORN, *baritone* SAXOPHONE; (3) name used in brass bands as abbreviation for *baritone saxhorn*. See also BARYTON.

Barnby, Joseph (1838–96), British conductor and composer (of part-song 'Sweet and Low', etc.). Principal of Guildhall School of Music, London; knighted, 1892.

Barnett (original surname Beer), **John** (1802–90), British composer (a relative of Meyerbeer), whose works include opera *The Mountain Sylph*, operettas, symphony.

barocco, Barock (It., Ger.) = BAROQUE.

baroque, term borrowed from architecture (where it has connotations of a 'twisting, elaborate, heavy, involved construction') and used to describe characteristics of musical style roughly corresponding to this, *c.* 1600–1750. Applied, e.g., to Monteverdi, Purcell and J. S. Bach, though the liberality of such application makes precise definition awkward. (Cp. ROCOCO.) The term *baroque organ* is applied to the type of this period, more brilliant in tone and less heavy than 19th-century type, with lighter wind-pressure and greater reliance on MUTA-TION STOPS. (This is a 20th-century use of the word *baroque*. In the 18th century the word meant 'uncouth, odd, rough and antiquated in taste'.) Baroque music generally involves CONTINUO.

barrage (Fr.), the use of chords played BARRÉ on the guitar.

Barraine, Elsa (b. 1910), French composer, pupil of Dukas; works include two symphonies, theatre and film music.

Barraqué, Jean (1928–73), French composer, pupil of Messiaen. Works include a piano sonata; Concerto for clarinet, vibraphone and six instrumental ensembles; *Song after Song* for six percussionists, voice and piano.

Barraud, Henry (b. 1900), French composer of orchestral works, *Lavinia* and other operas, three symphonies, a piano concerto, etc.; also critic.

barré (Fr.), (chord on guitar, etc.) played with one finger laid like a rigid bar across all strings, raising the pitch of all these equally.

barrel-organ, automatic organ in which projections on a hand-rotated barrel bring into action the notes required – i.e. a genuine pipe-organ though limited to a number of pre-set tunes, like a musical box; formerly used in some English churches. The HURDY-GURDY is different.

Barrie, [Sir] James (1860–1937), British novelist and dramatist. See O'NEILL (N.).

Barry, Gerald [Anthony] (b. 1952), Irish composer of opera *The Intelligence Park, A Piano Concerto, Sweet Punishment* for brass quintet, etc.

Barshai, Rudolf (b. 1924), Russian viola-player and conductor who founded the Moscow Chamber Orchestra; conductor of the Bournemouth Symphony Orchestra, 1982–8; naturalized British, 1983.

Barstow, Josephine [Clare] (b. 1940), British soprano celebrated in opera, including works by Tippett and Henze. CBE, 1985.

Bartered Bride, The (Cz., *Prodaná nevěsta*), comic opera by Smetana, produced in Prague, 1866. Libretto by K. Sabina, about a village intrigue. The Czech title actually means 'The Sold Fiancée'.

Bartók, Béla (1881–1945), Hungarian composer, settled in USA, 1940, dying there a poor man. From youth, a virtuoso pianist. Cultivated and developed Hungarian national musical style; partly in association with Kodály, collected and edited Hungarian folk-songs, showing them to be different from the gipsy music borrowed by Liszt, Brahms, etc. Active in investigating other folk-music too. His own works – often atonal and cultivating extreme dissonance, especially in his middle life – include opera BLUEBEARD'S CASTLE; mime-plays *The Wooden Prince* and the MIRACULOUS MANDARIN; much piano music, such as MIKROKOSMOS, *Out of Doors* and works for children; orchestral *Dance Suite*; Concerto for Orchestra (see CONCERTO); *Music for Strings, Percussion and Celesta*; three piano concertos, two violin concertos; a viola concerto (posthumous, edited by T. Serly); six string quartets (see PIZZICATO); trio CONTRASTS; songs and folk-song arrangements. See also CANTATA.

Bartók Quartet, Hungarian string quartet founded in 1957, led by Péter Komlós; recipient of a UNESCO prize in 1981.

Bartolozzi, Bruno (1911–80), Italian composer, also violinist and author of important book on new woodwind techniques. Works include Concerto for Orchestra; *The Hollow Man* for any woodwind instrument; *Images* for women's voices and 17 instruments.

Bartós, Jan Zdeněk (1908–81), Czechoslovak composer, also violinist. Works include a horn concerto; an accordion concerto; *From Petrarch's Sonnets to Laura* for tenor, bass, violin, cello and harpsichord.

baryton, obsolete stringed instrument resembling bass viol but having sympathetic strings like the viola d'amore. Haydn wrote extensively for it, because his patron, Prince Nicholas Esterházy, played it; disused thereafter until a modest post-1950 revival.

Bashmet, Yuri (b. 1953), Russian viola-player for whom Schnittke and others have written works specially; internationally prominent soloist, and founder of the ensemble 'Moscow Soloists'.

basic set, term used in TWELVE-NOTE technique for the note-row or series (comprising all 12 notes within the octave) in its original chosen order – i.e. not in an order arrived at by using the row backwards, or upside-down, or both (see INVERSION, RETROGRADE).

bass, (1) the lowest male voice; (2) the lowest note or part in a chord, a composition, etc.; (3) the lower regions of musical pitch generally – especially in antithesis to TREBLE; (4, of a 'family' of instruments) having low range, e.g. *bass* CLARINET, *bass* SAXOPHONE; *bass flute*, usually a misnomer for 'alto flute' – but see FLUTE; (5) colloquial abbreviation for DOUBLE-BASS, or (in military and brass bands) for the TUBA (either size); (6, *bass clef*) clef written 𝄢 and indicating F below middle C as the top line but one of the staff (and so sometimes also called *F clef*); it is normally used for bass voice, for most lower-pitched instruments, for the left-hand part of piano music, etc. See also following entries.

Bassarids, The, opera by Henze, produced in Salzburg, 1966. Libretto by W. H. Auden and Chester Kallman, founded on Euripides' *The Bacchae*. Title means 'the [male or female] followers of Bacchus'.

bass drum (or 'long drum'), large, shallow drum of low but indefinite pitch; used in symphony orchestras, military bands (where it may be carried), dance bands (the drum-stick usually worked by pedal), etc.

basse (Fr.), bass; *basse chantante* = BASSO *cantante*.

basset-clarinet, the modern name for a clarinet of standard size equipped with a downward extension, such as was used by Mozart's soloist Anton Stadler for the former's Clarinet Concerto and Clarinet Quintet.

basset-horn, instrument of same type as clarinet but lower in pitch (down to the F at the bottom of the bass staff). Used, e.g., by Mozart in THE CLEMENCY OF TITUS; also by R. Strauss (*Symphonies for Wind*, 1943–5) but otherwise very rare since Mozart's day. It is a TRANSPOSING INSTRUMENT in F.

bass fiddle, colloquial term for DOUBLE-BASS. (For an eccentric use, see GRAINGER.)

basso (It.), bass. So *basso cantante* ('singing'), a bass voice suitable for lyrical rather than dramatic parts in opera; *basso continuo*, see CONTINUO; *basso ostinato* = GROUND BASS; *basso profondo* (not *profundo*), a bass voice of unusually low range.

bassoon, bass woodwind instrument found in the orchestra and military band, occasionally also as soloist and in chamber music; having a double reed, thus related to the oboe. Compass from the B♭ below the bass stave upwards for about three and a half octaves. The *double-bassoon*, rarely encountered before the 19th century, has a compass an octave lower; it is often called contra-bassoon, but this is an illegitimate, offspring of 'bassoon', and (It.) *contrafagotto* – in modern Italian, *controfagotto*. (The obsolete *Russian bassoon* was not a bassoon at all but a kind of straightened-out SERPENT.)

Bastien and Bastienne, German opera (K50) by Mozart (aged 12), produced in Vienna, 1768. Libretto by F. W. Weiskern and A. Schachter (after a French original), about a pair of pastoral lovers separated and reunited.

Bateson, Thomas (*c.*1570–1630), English composer of madrigals, also organist (latterly in Dublin, where he died).

baton (from the French *bâton*, though in French usage the conductor's stick is a *baguette*), stick used by conductor to indicate time and expression.

battery, an obsolete collective term for percussion instruments.

Battistini, Mattia (1856–1928), Italian baritone, among the most prominent operatic performers of his day; won acclaim in Britain and (every season from 1888 to 1914) in Russia.

Battle, Kathleen (b. 1948), American soprano, prominent in opera (Glyndebourne from 1979) and the concert repertory.

Battle of Vitoria, Battle Symphony, see WELLINGTON'S VICTORY.

battuta (It.), (1) beat; (2) bar; *ritmo di tre battute*, literally 'rhythm of three bars', i.e. with the main accent falling at the beginning of every three bars.

Bauld, Alison (b. 1944), Australian composer, resident in Britain. Various theatrical works include *Exiles* for four actors, mezzo-soprano, tenor, chorus and instruments; has also written *Mad Moll* for soprano alone; *My Own Island* for clarinet and piano; *Van Diemen's Land* for unaccompanied chorus; etc.

Baumann, Hermann [Rudolf Konrad] (b. 1934), German horn-player who occasionally performs on the old valveless horn and has revived long-forgotten works.

Bax, Arnold [Edward Trevor] (1883–1953), British composer – not Irish, but influenced by Irish literature and lore. Also visited Russia, 1910. Knighted, 1937; Master of the King's (later Queen's) Music, 1941. Works, tending to an expansive post-romantic idiom, include seven symphonies; *Tintagel* and other symphonic poems; *Overture to a Picaresque Comedy*; and many piano solos (see COHEN).

bayan (Rus.), a Russian type of button-ACCORDION.

Bayle, François (b. 1932), French composer, born in Madagascar; pupil of Stockhausen and others. Much of his music is electronic and includes *The Acoustic Experience*, designed to last about 10 hours.

Bayreuth, a Bavarian town where a festival theatre was built to Wagner's designs. It opened in 1876 with THE RING and has remained devoted to his music.

Bazelon, Irwin (b. 1922), American composer of *De-Tonations* for brass quintet and orchestra; *Triple Play* for two trombones and solo percussion; a piano concerto, etc.

Bazzini, Antonio (1818–97), Italian violinist and composer of *The Dance of the Goblins* (Fr., *La Ronde des lutins*) for violin and piano; also opera, six string quartets, etc.

BB♭ bass, see TUBA.

BBC, British Broadcasting Corporation; *BBC Symphony Orchestra*, its chief orchestra, is maintained in London – founded in 1930, first conducted by Boult; from 1983, Andrew Davis. Outside London it maintains, among others, the *BBC Philharmonic Orchestra* (Manchester), till 1983 called the *BBC Northern Symphony Orchestra* (principal conductor, 1973–80, Raymond Leppard, then Edward Downes); *BBC Scottish Symphony Orchestra* (Glasgow; principal conductor since 1983, Jerzy Maksymiuk); *BBC Welsh Symphony Orchestra* (Cardiff; principal conductor since 1987, Tadaaki Otaka).

Beach, Mrs H. H. A., style of name used as a composer by Amy Marcy Beach (born Cheney; 1867–1944), whose works include *Gaelic Symphony*, a piano concerto, Mass, etc. – the first American woman to achieve a reputation as composer of such music.

Bear, The, nickname of Haydn's Symphony no. 82 in C, 1786 (Hob. I: 82), one of the PARIS Symphonies; its last movement suggests a captive bear dancing to a bagpipe.

Bear, The, one-act opera by Walton (libretto by Paul Dehn) based on a Chekhov play; produced in Aldeburgh, 1967.

beat, (1) rhythmic pulse ('the waltz has three beats to the bar'), or the physical action corresponding to this ('watch the conductor's beat') – see UP-BEAT, DOWN-BEAT; (2, acoustics) appreciable regular increase and decrease of loudness caused by discrepancy in vibrations of adjacent notes sounded together (a phenomenon utilized, e.g., in piano-tuning); (3) (obsolete word for) APPOGGIATURA; (4) ornament found in old music, probably meaning something similar to MORDENT.

Beatrice and Benedick (Fr., *Béatrice et Bénédict*), opera by Berlioz, produced in Baden-Baden, 1862. Libretto by composer, after Shakespeare's *Much Ado About Nothing*. (There is no reason why Shakespeare's spelling of his hero's name should not be retained in English references to Berlioz's work.)

Beaumarchais, Pierre Augustin Caron de (1732–99), French dramatist. See BARBER OF SEVILLE, MARRIAGE OF FIGARO, MOZART, PAISIELLO, ROSSINI.

Beaux Arts Trio, American piano trio founded in 1955, keeping the same membership (Menahem Pressler, piano; Isidore Cohen, violin; Bernard Greenhouse, cello) until 1987.

be-bop, type of jazz (of agitated character) cultivated in 1940s, mainly by small groups; Charlie Parker (alto saxophone) and Dizzy Gillespie (trumpet) were exponents.

Bebung, see CLAVICHORD.

bécarre (Fr.) = NATURAL, the sign ♮.

Becken (Ger.), cymbals.

Becker, John Joseph (1886–1961), American composer of seven symphonies (no. 7 unfinished); eight *Soundpieces* for various small instrumental groups; *A Marriage with Space* for solo and mass recitation, solo dancer, dance group and orchestra, etc.

Beckett, Samuel (1906–89), Anglo-Irish dramatist and novelist. See HAUBENSTOCK-RAMATI, MIHALOVICI, WILKINSON.

Beckwith, John (b. 1927), Canadian composer, pupil of N. Boulanger in Paris; also writer and university teacher. Works include *Canada Dash, Canada Dot,* words-and-music collage for singers, speakers and orchestra; *Circle with Tangents* for harpsichord and 13 strings.

Bedford, David [Vickerman] (b. 1937), British composer, pupil of Berkeley and Nono. Works include *Star Clusters, Nebulae and Places in Devon* for chorus and brass; *Star's End* for two (rock) guitarists and orchestra; etc. His brother is the conductor Steuart Bedford (b. 1939); they are grandsons of the following.

Bedford, Herbert (1867–1945), British composer (also author, painter); married the singer and composer Liza Lehmann. Works include unaccompanied songs and music for military band.

Beecham, Thomas (1879–1961), British conductor; knighted in 1916 and later that year became baronet in succession to his father, Sir Joseph Beecham (manufacturing chemist and patron of music and ballet). First London orchestral season, 1905–6; important opera seasons, 1910, 1911 (first English performances of R. Strauss's ELEKTRA and SALOME, etc.); founder-conductor in 1932 of London Philharmonic Orchestra, which parted company with him in 1940; founder-conductor of Royal Philharmonic Orchestra, 1946. Champion and biographer of Delius.

Beecroft, Norma [Marian] (b. 1934), Canadian composer (pupil of Copland and Maderna), also organizer of new music concerts, etc. Compositions include *Contrasts* for oboe, viola, harp, marimba, vibraphone, other percussion; choral work *The Living Flame of Love* (words from St John of the Cross).

Beerbohm, [Sir] **Max** (1872–1956), British writer. See GHEDINI.

Beeson, Jack [Hamilton] (b. 1921), American composer of *Lizzie Borden, My Heart's in the Highlands* and other operas, etc.; had some informal tuition from Bartók. Also university teacher.

Bees' Wedding, The, see SONGS WITHOUT WORDS.

Beethoven, Ludwig van (1770–1827), German composer, born in Bonn; son and grandson of musicians. Published a piano piece at the age of 12; worked shortly afterwards as pianist, organist, viola-player. Went to Vienna, 1792 (to study with Haydn, but did not stay with him), and remained and died there. Many love-affairs, but never married. Brought up as a Roman Catholic but came to hold unorthodox deistical views. From 1801, developed deafness, becoming total by about 1824 – after composition of Symphony no. 9 (CHORAL) but before the last five quartets. Vastly extended the form and scope of the symphony (he wrote nine, not including WELLINGTON'S VICTORY; no. 3 is the EROICA), and also of the piano concerto (he wrote five, no. 5 being the so-called EMPEROR), the string quartet (16 and GREAT FUGUE), the piano sonata (32). Other works include opera FIDELIO (see also LEONORA); ballet *The Creatures of Prometheus* (see PROMETHEUS); Mass (*Missa solemnis*) in D and a smaller Mass in C; oratorio *Christ on the Mount of Olives*; a violin concerto and a triple concerto (piano, violin, cello); CHORAL FANTASIA; theatre music – see EGMONT, CORIOLANUS, KING STEPHEN, CONSECRATION OF THE HOUSE; NAME-DAY overture; EQUALI for trombones; 10 violin sonatas (no. 9, KREUTZER); ARCHDUKE and GHOST piano trios; songs; piano pieces including DIABELLI and PROMETHEUS Variations. The so-called JENA Symphony is not by him. His works are indexed by Kinsky. See also PASTORAL SYMPHONY, RAZUMOVSKY QUARTETS, SPRING SONATA.

Beggar's Opera, The, work of BALLAD OPERA type, with words by John Gay, set to tunes then current, produced in London, 1728. Musical arrangements by Pepusch. Later musical arrangements include those of F. Austin (1920, record London run of 1,463 performances) and Britten (Cambridge, 1948, libretto adapted by Tyrone Guthrie). See also POLLY, THREEPENNY OPERA.

Begleitung (Ger.), accompaniment.

Beinum, Eduard [Alexander] **van** (1901–59), Dutch conductor, associated with the London Philharmonic Orchestra and principal conductor of the Concertgebouw Orchestra of Amsterdam from 1945 until his death.

bel canto (It., beautiful singing), term used – often vaguely – by teachers, 'authorities' on singing, etc., with reference to the finely cultivated voice, particularly implying suitability to the agile yet smooth voice-production demanded in the operas of Bellini, Donizetti, etc.

bell, (1) heavy resonating vessel in hollow cup-shape found in churches, etc., and rung either directly by hand-ropes (see CHANGE-RINGING) or by CARILLON; (2) orchestral instrument usually in the form of a free-hanging tube (*tubular bell*) struck by hand with small hammer – a set of such bells sometimes spanning as much as an octave (see also GLOCKENSPIEL); (3) the open end of a wind instrument, at the opposite extremity to the mouth-piece. See also following entries.

Bell Anthem, nickname for Purcell's *Rejoice in the Lord Alway* (Z49, composed *c*.1684–5), alluding to bell-like descending scales in the introduction (for strings).

Belle Hélène, La (Fr., The Beautiful Helen), operetta by Offenbach, produced in Paris, 1864. Libretto by Meilhac and L. Halévy, mocking the classical story of Helen of Troy.

Bellini, Vincenzo (1801–35), Italian composer of opera, pupil of Zingarelli. Visited London and Paris, 1833; wrote his last completed opera, THE PURI-TANS, for performance in Paris, and died near there. The other operas he composed in his short life – making great demand on agility and refinement of voice – include *The Capulets and the Montagues* (not directly based on *Romeo and Juliet*), *The Sleep-walker* (see SONNAMBULA) and NORMA.

Bell Rondo (It., *Rondo alla campanella*), the finale of Paganini's Violin concerto in B minor (*c*.1824), with bell-like effect. Liszt's *La campanella* for piano (1838, revised in 1851) is based on it.

Bells, The (Rus., *Kolokola*), cantata by Rakhmaninov, first performed in St Petersburg, 1915; text, translated from Poe, concerns the 'voices' of bells.

belly, the upper surface (i.e. that lying directly under the strings) of a stringed instrument.

Belshazzar's Feast, (1) suite by Sibelius drawn from his incidental music to a play by H. Procope (1906); (2) work for baritone, chorus and orchestra by Walton (words arranged by Osbert Sitwell, chiefly from the Bible), first performed in Leeds, 1931.

bémol (Fr.) = FLAT, the sign ♭.

ben, bene (It.), well, very.

Benda, Jiří Antonín (1722–95), Bohemian oboist, keyboard-player and composer, one of a family of many musicians. Worked in Germany (known there as Georg Benda) and died there. Notable for his melodramas (in the technical sense; see MELODRAMA); also wrote symphonies, operas, church music, etc.

Benedetti Michelangeli, see MICHELANGELI.

Benedicite (Lat., Bless ye . . .), a name in Anglican Church use for the canticle taken from the 'Song of the Three Holy Children' found in the Apocrypha. This text is combined with a poem by J. Austin (1613–69) in Vaughan William's cantata *Benedicite* (first performed, 1930). See also GESANG.

Benedict, Julius (1804–85), German-born composer (also conductor), pupil of Weber, who settled in England 1835, becoming naturalized; knighted, 1871. Works include two symphonies, two piano concertos, and operas in Italian and English including THE LILY OF KILLARNEY, formerly a favourite of the British public.

Benedictus, (1) part of the Mass (starting *'Benedictus qui venit'*, 'Blessed is he that cometh'); (2) canticle sung during Anglican morning service and based on Luke i. 68ff.

Benguerel, Xavier (b. 1931), Spanish composer, mainly self-taught. Works include a violin concerto, an organ concerto, *Successions* for wind quintet.

Ben-Haim, Paul (1897–1984), Israeli composer, German-born, changed his surname from Frankenburger after emigrating to Palestine, 1933. Works include two symphonies, a piano concerto, chamber music, setting of biblical Hebrew texts.

Benjamin, Arthur (1893–1960), Australian composer and pianist resident in London and for a time in Vancouver. Wrote comic operas *The Devil Take Her* and *Prima Donna*, a piano concerto, film music, and many smaller pieces including JAMAICAN RUMBA.

Benjamin, George (b. 1960; no relation to the preceding), British composer, also pianist; precociously gifted, he had an orchestral work performed at the Proms before he was 21 – *Ringed by the Flat Horizon*. Has also written a piano sonata; *Flight* for unaccompanied flute; etc.

Bennet, John (*c*.1575–?), English composer of madrigals (contributor to THE TRIUMPHS OF ORIANA) and church music, etc.

Bennett, Richard Rodney (b. 1936), British composer of operas *The Ledge*, THE MINES OF SULPHUR, *A Penny for a Song*, *Victory*; various concertos; chamber works – some called *commedia* (It., comedy); film music. Studied with H. Ferguson and (in Paris) Boulez. Also pianist who plays his own transcriptions of Cole Porter, etc. CBE, 1977.

Bennett, Robert Russell (1894–1981), American composer (symphonies, film music, etc.) and arranger of 'symphonic pictures' drawn from the scores of musicals by Gershwin, Kern, etc. Pupil of N. Boulanger in Paris.

Bennett, William Sterndale (1816–75), British composer and pianist, pupil of Mendelssohn at Leipzig; friend of Schumann, who dedicated his *Symphonic Studies* (for piano) to him. Professor at Cambridge; knighted, 1871. Works include cantata *The May Queen*, five piano concertos, overture *The Naiads*, piano pieces and songs.

Bentoiu, Pascal (b. 1927), Romanian composer of opera *Hamlet*, Symphony for three saxophones and orchestra, two piano concertos; is also folk-music researcher.

Bentzon, Jørgen (1897–1951), Danish composer, pupil of C. Nielsen and Karg-Elert; has written mainly chamber music, including *Racconti* (one-movement works using 3–5 instruments suggesting narrative, hence this Italian title). Other works include *A Dickens Symphony*. Cousin of the following.

Bentzon, Niels Viggo (b. 1919), Danish composer and pianist (also writer on music), cousin of preceding. Works include ballet *The Courtesan*; Symphonic Variations for orchestra; nine string quartets; 11 piano sonatas (some named, e.g. 'Napoleon' Sonata) and many other piano works.

Benvenuto Cellini, opera by Berlioz, produced in Paris, 1838. Libretto by L. de Wailly and A. Barbier, after Cellini's autobiography (*c.*1560). See also ROMAN CARNIVAL.

bequadro (It.) = NATURAL, the sign ♮.

Berberian, Cathy (1925–83), American mezzo-soprano, mainly devoted to modern music, e.g. by Cage, Bussotti, Pousseur and especially Berio (to whom she was married, 1950–65) and of whose music she gave many first performances. Also composer of *Stripsody* (for unaccompanied voice, based on comic-strip sounds), 1966.

Berceuse (Fr.), cradle-song, lullaby; instrumental piece suggestive of this.

Berenice, opera by Handel, produced in London, 1737. Libretto by A. Salvi; Berenice is the wife of an ancient Egyptian king. The well-known minuet occurs in the overture.

Berezovsky (also spelt Berezowsky), **Nikolai** (1900–1953), Russian-born composer who settled in USA, 1922; also conductor, violinist, viola-player (soloist in first performance of his Viola Concerto, 1941). Other works include four symphonies, oratorio *Gil-*

gamesh (text from Babylonian poem of 1750 BC); children's opera *Babar the Elephant* (1953).

Berg, Alban (1885–1935), Austrian composer; born, worked and died in Vienna; pupil of Schoenberg, whose methods he developed. Used a free-atonal idiom combined with very closely worked structures (passacaglia, variations, etc.) in opera WOZZECK, completed in 1922; shortly afterwards turned to strict TWELVE-NOTE technique, e.g. in his Chamber Concerto (piano, violin, wind), completed in 1925. Other works include 12-note opera, LULU; a string quartet and (also for string quartet) *Lyric Suite*; songs with orchestra and with piano; a violin concerto 'in memory of an angel' (i.e. Manon Gropius, 18-year-old daughter of Mahler's widow by her second marriage), written shortly before his own death and not performed till after it (1936).

bergamasca (It.; also Fr., *bergamasque*, and Eng., *bergomask*), (1) tune and chord-sequence apparently from Bergamo, Italy, widely used in 16th and 17th centuries, e.g. as ground bass; (2) folk-dance from Bergamo; (3) now a term used by composers with only the vaguest picturesque significance – e.g. by Debussy in *Suite Bergamasque* for piano (composed at intervals between 1890 and 1905), which includes 'Clair de lune'.

Berganza, Teresa (b. 1935), Spanish mezzo-soprano noted in florid roles of Italian opera; at La Scala, Milan, from 1957, Glyndebourne from 1958, etc.

Berger, Arthur [Victor] (b. 1912), American composer, pupil of Piston, N. Boulanger (in Paris) and others; works include a chamber concerto, woodwind quintet, string quartet, songs. Also writer and university teacher.

Berger, Jean (b. 1909), German-born composer resident in France and then (from 1941) in USA – naturalized, 1943. Also writer. Works include *Brazilian Psalm* and other pieces for choir; cantata *The Blood of Others*; *Caribbean Concerto* for harmonica and orchestra; etc.

Berger, Theodor (b. 1905), Austrian composer, pupil of F. Schmidt. He has written *The Elements* (cycle of symphonic poems); two string quartets; *Manual Concerto* for two pianos, percussion and strings.

bergerette (Fr.), light French song cultivating a pastoral style that is highly idealized (like Dresden-china shepherdesses). From Fr., *berger*, shepherd.

Berglund, Paavo [Engelbert] (b. 1929), Finnish conductor; principal conductor of Bournemouth Symphony Orchestra, 1972–9, and of Helsinki Philharmonic Orchestra, 1974–9.

Bergonzi, Carlo (b. 1924), Italian tenor (originally sang as baritone); noted in Italian opera, especially Verdi – heard in London from 1953, New York (Metropolitan Opera) from 1956.

Bergsma, William (b. 1921), American composer, pupil of Hanson. He has composed a symphony and *The Fortunate Island* for orchestra (after visit to West Indies); *Tangents* and other works for piano; opera *The Wife of Martin Guerre*; etc.

Berio, Luciano (b. 1925), Italian composer, pupil of Dallapiccola. He has employed spatial effects, e.g. in *Circles* (text by E. E. Cummings) for voice, harp and two percussion instruments; has also written electronic music and works allowing free choice by performers (see INDETERMINACY). His operas include *A King Listening* (*Un Re in ascolto*). A series of pieces each called *Sequence* (It., *Sequenza*) is for different solo instruments – no. 5 for trombone, no. 6 for viola. His Sinfonia (orchestra, organ, piano, harpsichord, chorus, reciters) incorporates a section of Mahler's Symphony no. 2.

Bériot, Charles [Auguste] **de** (1802–70), Belgian violinist and composer, chiefly for his instrument. Toured much; first visited London in 1826.

Berkeley, Lennox [Randal Francis] (1903–89), British composer, pupil of N. Boulanger in Paris. Collaborated with Britten in *Mont Juic*, orchestral suite of Catalan dances. Wrote operas including *Nelson* and A DINNER ENGAGEMENT; four symphonies; two concertos for piano, one for two pianos; many piano solos; *Four Poems of St Teresa* for contralto and orchestra, and a few other works to texts with Roman Catholic associations; film music. Knighted, 1974.

Berkoff, Steven (b. 1937), British playwright. See GREEK.

Berlin, Irving (originally Israel Baline) (1888–1989), Russian-born composer, resident in USA from 1893. Composer of popular songs markedly successful from 'Alexander's Ragtime Band' (1911) and including the now perennial 'I'm Dreaming of a White Christmas' (from film *Holiday Inn*, 1942); see also OCARINA.

Berlin Philharmonic Orchestra, orchestra founded in 1882; conductor 1955–89, Herbert von Karajan (succeeding Furtwängler); Abbado was appointed his successor.

Berlioz, [Louis] **Hector** (1803–69), French composer; learnt guitar and had general musical training at Paris Conservatory, but became proficient neither on piano nor on any orchestral instrument – yet a great master and innovator in orchestration (on which he wrote a book), also noted as conductor and music critic. Nearly all his works have some literary or other extra-musical allusion (typical ROMANTIC trait; cp. SCHUMANN). His love for the English Shakespearian actress Harriet Smithson is expressed in his FANTASTIC SYMPHONY, 1830; he married her in 1833 and separated from her in 1842. Other works include operas BENVENUTO CELLINI, BEATRICE AND BENEDICK, THE TROJANS; choral works including THE DAMNATION OF FAUST (in which occurs his arrangement of the RÁKÓCZI MARCH), THE CHILDHOOD OF CHRIST and GRANDE MESSE DES MORTS (see also REQUIEM); symphony ROMEO AND JULIET; HAROLD IN ITALY for viola and orchestra; *Lélio* (intended sequel to the *Fantastic Symphony*) for reciter, singers and orchestra; ROMAN CARNIVAL, THE CORSAIR, KING LEAR and other overtures; songs with orchestra and with piano.

Berman, Lazar [Naumovich] (b. 1930), Russian pianist, pupil of Richter, who played in London in 1958 but did not develop his major international career until after 1970.

Bernac (real surname Bertin), **Pierre** (1899–1979), French baritone, par-

ticularly distinguished in recitals of French songs; Poulenc was often his accompanist.

Bernanos, Georges (1888–1948), French novelist. See DIALOGUES OF THE CARMELITES.

Berners, Lord [Gerald Hugh Tyrwhitt-Wilson] (1883–1950), British composer (also painter, author, diplomat). Works include ballets *The Wedding Bouquet* (words by Gertrude Stein, stage-settings of Berners's own design) and *The Triumph of Neptune*; *Valses bourgeoises* for piano duet; and songs.

Bernstein, Leonard (1918–90), American composer, also conductor, pianist and celebrated television commenter on music. Pupil of Piston and others; conductor of the New York Philharmonic Orchestra, 1958; 'laureate conductor', 1969. Works include 'Jeremiah' Symphony; Symphony no. 2 with piano (THE AGE OF ANXIETY, after Auden); Symphony no. 3 (KADDISH); opera *Trouble in Tahiti*; operetta *Candide* (after Voltaire); musicals *On the Town* (based on his ballet *Fancy Free*) and *West Side Story*; songs; chamber music; *Chichester Psalms* (in Hebrew) for Chichester Cathedral (choir and orchestra). See also MASS (second entry) and RIFF. His style was influenced by jazz.

Béroff, Michel (b. 1950), French pianist, chiefly noted in Messiaen's works and other modern music.

Berwald, Franz Adolf (1796–1868), Swedish composer and violinist who studied in Germany; little appreciated in his lifetime, only no. 1 (*Sérieuse*) of his four symphonies receiving performance. Also wrote opera *Estrella di Soria*, a violin concerto, chamber music, etc. in an individual ROMANTIC style.

Bésard, Jean-Baptiste (b. 1567; d. after 1617), French lutenist and composer whose publications include music for lute by himself and others.

Bethlehem, 'choral drama' by Broughton, produced in Glastonbury, 1916. Libretto from the medieval Coventry play.

Betrothal in a Monastery, The, see DUENNA.

Betterton, Thomas (1635–1710), English actor and playwright. See DIOCLESIAN.

Bibalo, Antonio (b. 1922), Italian composer (also pianist), resident in Norway; has written opera *The Smile at the Foot of the Ladder* (after Henry Miller), orchestral and piano works, etc.

Biber, Heinrich Johann Franz von (1644–1704), Austrian violinist, musical director of the Archbishop of Salzburg's court, and composer of violin sonatas and chamber music; also wrote opera and church music. An early user of SCORDATURA.

big band, see BAND.

Biggs, E. [Edward George] **Power** (1906–77), British-born concert organist who settled in USA and had international career; also editor of organ music.

Billings, William (1746–1800), one of the earliest American-born composers, but a tanner by trade; wrote 'fuguing tunes' (with primitive IMITATION), words and music of hymns, music to American patriotic songs, etc. Also concert promoter. See COWELL, SCHUMAN.

Billy Budd, (1) opera by Britten, produced in London, 1951; libretto by E. M. Forster and E. Crozier, after Melville's novel of the British navy at the time of the mutiny of the Nore (1797); (2) opera by Ghedini, produced in Venice, 1949; libretto by Quasimodo, after the same source.

Billy the Kid, ballet (about an outlaw) with music by Copland, 1938; a well-known orchestral suite is drawn from the score.

binary, in two sections; *binary form,* classification used of a simple movement (e.g. in an early 18th-century keyboard suite) which is in two sections, the first modulating to another key and the second returning to the original key. (Cp. TERNARY.) The above form developed historically into SONATA-FORM, an alternative name for which is, accordingly, *compound binary form.*

Binchois, Gilles [Egidius] (*c.* 1400–1460), Netherlands composer of chansons, motets, etc., who worked at the court of Burgundy.

Binkerd, Gordon [Ware] (b. 1916), American composer of three symphonies, choral works, songs, etc.

Birds, The (It., *Gli uccelli*), orchestral suite by Respighi, first performed in 1927, based on 17th- and 18th-century pieces.

Birmingham Symphony Orchestra, see CITY OF BIRMINGHAM SYMPHONY ORCHESTRA.

Birtwistle, Harrison (b. 1934), British composer, pupil of R. Hall. Works include *The Triumph of Time* for orchestra; *Refrains and Choruses* for wind quintet; *Music for Sleep* for child

37

singers and instrumentalists; *Tragoedia* for 10 players (the wind instrumentalists also playing claves); operas PUNCH AND JUDY and *The Mask of Orpheus* (see ORPHEUS). Is actively associated with the National Theatre (London). Knighted, 1987.

bis (Fr., twice), word actually used in French where the English use 'encore'; *bisser*, to encore. Also instruction that a section of music is to be performed twice.

bisbigliando (It., whispering), repeating the notes softly and quickly, as a special effect in playing the harp.

biscroma (It.), THIRTY-SECOND-NOTE, demisemiquaver.

Bishop, Henry [Rowley] (1786–1855), British composer, chiefly of operas; also adapted Mozart's and other operas. Prominent as conductor; knighted in 1842, the first musician to receive knighthood at the hands of a British sovereign. His opera *Clari*, or *The Maid of Milan* (1823) includes his 'Home, Sweet Home' used in a recurrent way anticipating the REMINISCENCE-MOTIVE.

Bishop-Kovacevich, Stephen (b. 1940), American pianist of Yugoslav parentage. Came to London in 1959 to study with Myra Hess and remained there. Noted in Beethoven; he is also associated with Richard Rodney Bennett's music. (Known until 1975 as Stephen Bishop.)

bitonality, the use of two keys (see TONALITY) simultaneously; e.g. by Stravinsky (a famous early use in PETRUSHKA, 1911), Holst, Milhaud.

biwa, a Japanese form of lute, normally with four silk strings.

Bizet, Georges (first names really Alexandre César Léopold) (1838–75), French composer, born in Paris, pupil of Halévy, whose daughter he married after Halévy's death. At 19 won prize for an operetta, *Doctor Miracle*; later composed operas including THE PEARL-FISHERS, THE FAIR MAID OF PERTH, IVAN THE TERRIBLE (not performed till 1946) and CARMEN – at first only a moderate success; Bizet died three months after its first performance. His work, marked by its clarity and melodic gifts, was later championed (e.g. by Nietzsche) as a counterblast to Wagner. It also includes incidental music to Daudet's play THE WOMAN OF ARLES (*L'Arlésienne*); a symphony (written at age 17 but not performed till 1935); suite CHILDREN'S GAMES (originally for piano duet).

Björling, Jussi (1911–60), Swedish tenor, eminent in Italian opera at Metropolitan Opera House (New York) and elsewhere.

Bjørnson, Bjørnstjerne (1832–1910), Norwegian writer. See GRIEG, HOMAGE MARCH.

Blacher, Boris (1903–75), German composer born of Russian parents in China; from 1953 director of the (West) Berlin High School of Music. Works include *Romeo and Juliet*, *Prussian Fairy-tale* and other operas; oratorio *The Grand Inquisitor* (after Dostoyevsky's *Crime and Punishment*); two piano concertos; orchestral *Variations on a Theme of Paganini* (see PAGANINI).

Blades, James (b. 1901), British percussionist, pioneer in new effects (working with Britten); author of historical textbook on percussion.

Blake, David [Leonard] (b. 1936), British composer (and York University teacher), pupil of Eisler in East Berlin. Works include Variations for piano, Chamber Symphony, unaccompanied choral music, opera *Toussaint*.

Blake, Howard (b. 1938), British composer of works appealing to young audiences, e.g. *The Snowman* for narrator, boy soprano and orchestra; also of a clarinet concerto, piano quartet, etc.

Blake, William (1757–1827), British poet and artist. See GOEHR, JOB, WEBER (B.).

Blaník, see MY COUNTRY.

blasen (Ger.), to blow; *Bläser*, wind instruments, wind-players; *Blasinstrument(e)*, wind instrument(s); *Blasmusik*, music for wind.

Blavet, Michel (1700–1768), French flautist and composer of flute music, operas, etc.

Blech (Ger.), brass (section of an orchestra); *Blechmusik*, brass band, music for brass.

Blech, Harry (b. 1910), British conductor, formerly violinist; founder-conductor of London Mozart Players (chamber orchestra), 1949–84. OBE, 1962.

Blessed Damozel, The, cantata by Debussy, 1887–8, on a French translation ('La Damoiselle élue') of Rossetti's poem.

Bliss, Arthur (1891–1975), composer, pupil of C. Wood, Stanford, Vaughan Williams and Holst. BBC director of music, 1941–5; knighted, 1950; Master of the Queen's Music, 1953. Works include ballet CHECKMATE; opera *The Olympians* (libretto by J. B. Priestley); symphony *Morning Heroes* (with speaker and chorus); orchestral *Meditations on a Theme by John Blow*; a piano concerto and a violin concerto; *Music for Strings*; A COLOUR SYMPHONY; a piano sonata; a clarinet quintet and other chamber music; *Seven American Poems* and other songs. Wrote one of the first important film scores, *The Shape of Things to Come* (1935).

Blitheman, John (1525–91), English organist (at the Chapel Royal, London), and composer of church music and keyboard pieces; teacher of J. Bull.

Blitzstein, Marc (1905–64), American composer (pupil of N. Boulanger and Schoenberg) and pianist. Composed music expressing militantly democratic and pro-labour ideas – e.g. operas *The Cradle Will Rock* and *No for an Answer*, symphonic poem *Freedom Morning*.

Bloch, Ernest (1888–1959), Swiss-born American-naturalized composer, pupil of Knorr in Frankfurt. Went to USA, 1916, but returned to Switzerland, 1930–38. Much of his work has specific Jewish associations – e.g. SHELOMO (Solomon) for cello and orchestra; SACRED SERVICE (*Avodath hakodesh*); BAAL SHEM for violin and piano; *Israel Symphony*. Other works include opera MACBETH; rhapsody *America*; a piano quintet (1923, introducing quarter-tones); five string quartets; *Concerto symphonique* for piano and orchestra.

block (percussion instrument), see TEMPLE BLOCK, WOOD BLOCK.

Blockflöte (Ger.), RECORDER.

Blockx, Jan (1851–1912), Belgian

composer of music mainly with Flemish nationalist associations – operas and cantatas with Flemish words, overture *Rubens*, etc.

Blomdahl, Karl-Birger (1916–68), Swedish composer (also conductor), pupil of Rosenberg. Works include three symphonies (no. 3 called *Facets*); cantata *In the Hall of Mirrors*; chamber music; piano pieces; operas *Aniara* (set on a space-ship) and *Herr von Hancken*.

Blomstedt, Herbert (b. 1927), American-born Swedish conductor; active in Europe, then from 1985 principal conductor of the San Francisco Symphony Orchestra.

Blondel [de Nesle], 12th-century French TROUVÈRE (minstrel) of whom some songs survive; according to legend he discovered (by singing and being answered) the place where Richard Cœur de Lion was held captive.

Blow, John (1649–1708), English composer, pupil of H. Cooke and others; teacher of Purcell; organist of Westminster Abbey, 1668–79 (Purcell succeeding him) and again, 1695–1708. Works include English and Latin anthems, services, odes on the death of Purcell and on other occasions (10 for New Year's Day); keyboard pieces and songs; masque VENUS AND ADONIS. See BLISS.

Bluebeard (Fr., *Barbe-bleue*), operetta by Offenbach, produced in Paris, 1866. Libretto by H. Meilhac and L. Halévy, based on the legend of the ogre who murdered his successive wives.

Bluebeard's Castle (Hung., *A Kékszakállú Herceg Vára*, 'Duke Bluebeard's Castle'), opera by Bartók, produced in Budapest, 1918. Libretto by Balázs, giving a modern psychological interpretation of the old legend (see preceding).

Blue Danube, The (Ger., *An der schönen blauen Donau*, 'By the beautiful blue Danube'), waltz by Johann Strauss the younger, composed 1867; originally with chorus.

blue note, a note of the scale (especially the third and seventh) characteristically flattened in JAZZ and in light and serious music indebted to jazz idiom. See also BLUES.

blues, type of slow, sad American-Negro song, becoming widely known about 1911; strictly (*12-bar blues*) in three lines of four bars each, the second line exactly or nearly repeating the first, and the whole following a set chord-sequence. (Term also used loosely, e.g. by Copland, as indication of mood only.) See also BLUE NOTE.

Blumine (an invented German word of the early 19th century, representing the goddess Flora), title of the original second movement of Mahler's Symphony no. 1 (1889); discarded by the composer, it has none the less been reinstated in some modern performances.

B.Mus., abbr. of Bachelor of Music.

Boccherini, Luigi (1743–1805), Italian composer and cellist. By invitation, of the Spanish ambassador in Paris, visited Spain in 1768–9; and was there again from 1797 until dying there in poverty and lacking a patron. Works include 11 cello concertos; 30 symphonies; 125 string quintets (from one of which – op. 13, no. 5, in E – comes 'the' Boccherini minuet); 91 string quartets and much other chamber music; Spanish opera *Clementina*; church music.

Boehm, see also BÖHM (alternative spelling).

Boehm, Theobald (1794–1881), German flautist, composer for his instrument, and inventor. His key-mechanism (replacing finger-holes) spread from the flute to oboe, clarinet and bassoon.

Boehm system, woodwind key-mechanism; see preceding entry.

Boëllmann, Léon (1862–97), French organist (latterly at church of St Vincent de Paul, Paris) and composer, principally for organ; also wrote a symphony, Symphonic Variations for cello and orchestra, etc.

Bogusławski, Eduard (b. 1940), Polish composer, pupil of Haubenstock-Ramati in Vienna. Works include *Apocalypse* for narrator, chorus and orchestra; *Intonations* for orchestra.

Bohème, La (Fr., 'Bohemian Life', in artistic sense), name of Italian operas based on Murger's French novel *Scènes de la vie de Bohème* – (1) by Puccini, produced in Turin, 1896; libretto by G. Giacosa and L. Illica; (2) by Leoncavallo, produced in Venice, 1897; libretto by composer. The two were composed contemporaneously, but the latter missed Puccini's success.

Bohemian Girl, The, opera by Balfe, produced in London, 1843. Libretto by A. Bunn; the high-born heroine is abducted as a child by gipsies ('Bohemians') and finally restored.

Böhm, Georg (1661–1733), German organist and composer of a 'St John' Passion, organ music, keyboard suites, etc.; from 1698 at Lüneburg, where

J. S. Bach, as a boy chorister at another church, apparently came to know his music.

Böhm, Karl (1894–1981), Austrian conductor, director of Vienna State Opera, 1943–5 and 1954–6. Noted in Mozart, R. Strauss, etc.

Böhm, Theobald, see BOEHM.

Boïeldieu, François Adrien (1775–1834), French composer, pupil of Cherubini and others. Wrote a piano concerto, chamber music and especially operas – including *The White Lady* (Fr., *La Dame blanche*), after two novels of Scott, which contains some Scottish tunes, and THE CALIPH OF BAGHDAD. Also conductor, e.g. at St Petersburg.

Boismortier, Joseph Bodin de (1689–1755), French composer of operas (including *Don Quixote at the Duchess's*), cantatas, instrumental suits, etc.

Boito, Arrigo (1842–1918), Italian composer (opera MEPHISTOPHELES, etc.) and librettist, e.g. for Verdi's *Otello* and *Falstaff*.

Bolcom, William [Elden] (b. 1938), American composer, pupil of Milhaud (in California and in Paris); works include *Dynamite Tonite* (a 'pop opera' for actors and 11 instruments), nine string quartets, *Dark Music* for kettle-drums and cello.

bolero, Spanish dance, usually with a triplet on the second half of the first beat of bar; accompaniment includes dancers' voices and castanets. Ravel's purely orchestral *Bolero*, 1928, is for ballet, not for dancing a real bolero. Chopin's *Bolero* is for piano, published in 1834.

Bolet, Jorge (1914–1990), Cuban-American pianist, pupil of Godowsky, of commanding ability in large-scale Romantic works; his reputation did not peak until the mid-1970s.

Bolshoi Theatre, Moscow's principal opera and ballet theatre; the present building opened in 1856. (*Bolshoi* means 'large', 'great'.)

bombard, name given to the larger instruments of the obsolete SHAWM family. ('Pommer' is an alternative form.)

bombarde, a 16-FOOT reed stop on the organ.

bombardon, (1) name formerly given in brass and military bands to the two types of bass TUBA used in those bands; (2) organ stop similar to BOMBARDE.

Bond, Carrie Jacobs (1862–1946), American composer of 'The End of a Perfect Day' (which sold over five million copies) and similar popular sentimental songs.

Bond, Edward (b. 1934), British playwright. See WE COME TO THE RIVER.

bones, percussion instrument used in black-faced minstrel shows, etc.; a pair of small bones held between the fingers and clicked together.

bongo, single-headed small drum (tunable or non-tunable) struck with the finger; familiar in Latin-American dance bands and occasionally used elsewhere. Usually in sets of two or three (plural *bongos*).

Bononcini (or Buononcini), **Giovanni** (1670–1747), Italian composer and cellist, one of a family of musicians; worked in Rome, Vienna, Berlin and (1720–32) London, where he rivalled Handel for a time, leaving eventually when plagiarism was proved against him. Works include operas, Masses, funeral anthem for the Duke of Marlborough. Died in poverty in Vienna.

Bonynge, Richard [Alan] (b. 1930), Australian conductor who coached and advised the young Joan Sutherland, married her in 1954 and has been conductor of almost all her performances; also revived unfamiliar ballet scores. CBE, 1977; created Officer of the Order of Australia, 1983.

boogie-woogie, style of fast jazz pianoplaying characterized by OSTINATO bass in BROKEN octaves; popularized in USA from about 1938. Also abbreviated to *boogie*.

Borg, Kim (b. 1919), Finnish bass of multilingual international career, also composer of a trombone concerto and other works.

Boris Godunov, opera by Musorgsky, produced (in revised and cut version) in St Petersburg, 1874; libretto by composer, after Pushkin's drama of the historic tsar (d. 1605). The opera was afterwards edited and altered by Rimsky-Korsakov, in which form it became known also outside Russia, sometimes with the additional 'St Basil scene' revised and altered by Ippolitov-Ivanov. The complete authentic work was produced in Leningrad, 1928. A version has also been made by Shostakovich which (unlike Rimsky-Korsakov's) respects the composer's harmonies but provides new orchestration.

Borodin, Alexander [Porphyrevich] (1833–87), Russian composer – also professor of chemistry, so could spare little time for music. Illegitimate son of a prince; pupil of Balakirev; one of the 'nationalist' group of composers known as THE MIGHTY HANDFUL. Works include opera PRINCE IGOR (unfinished; completed by Rimsky-Korsakov and Glazunov), which includes the 'Polovtsian Dances'; three symphonies (no. 3 unfinished, but two movements of it advanced enough to be completed by Glazunov); symphonic poem IN THE STEPPES OF CENTRAL ASIA; two string quartets; songs.

Borodin Quartet, Moscow-based string quartet founded in 1946, retaining its international distinction (with some changes of membership) for more than 40 years.

Bortnyansky, Dmitri Stepanovich (1751–1825), Russian composer who studied in Italy, returned to Russia and became director of the court church choir, which he reformed. Composed chiefly church music, but also Italian operas.

Boscovich, Alexander Uriah (1907–64), Romanian-born Israeli composer who emigrated to Palestine, 1937. Works include a violin concerto, an oboe concerto, *Semitic Suite* for orchestra or piano, songs.

Boskovsky, Willi (b. 1909), Austrian violinist who specialized in the music of the Strauss family and conducted the Vienna Philharmonic's New Year's Day concerts from 1954 to 1979.

Bossi, [Marco] Enrico (1861–1925), Italian composer and concert organist; works include an organ concerto and many organ solos, also operas, oratorios, etc.

Boston Pops Orchestra, an offshoot of the Boston Symphony Orchestra; founded 1885, it has an annual season presenting the lighter repertory.

Boston Symphony Orchestra, an orchestra founded in Boston, Mass., 1881. Koussevitzky's conductorship (1924–49) made it especially famous. Conductor since 1973, Seiji Ozawa.

Bottesini, Giovanni (1821–89), Italian double-bass virtuoso who appeared as soloist in London and elsewhere; also composer and conductor.

bouche fermée (Fr.), with the mouth closed, i.e. (as instruction to singers) humming.

Boucourechliev, André (b. 1925), Bulgarian composer, naturalized French in 1956; also critic. Has written several chamber works, each called *Archipelago* (Fr., *Archipel*), which are performable in more than one version; also a piano sonata and *Night Music* for clarinet, harp and piano.

bouffe, see OPERA.

Boughton, Rutland (1878–1960), British composer (also conductor and writer on music). In emulation of Wagner and Bayreuth, organized a festival operatic centre (not only for his own works) at Glastonbury, 1914–25; it opened with his THE IMMORTAL HOUR which later ran for 216 successive performances in London. None of his later stage works – including BETHLEHEM – achieved such success.

Boulanger, Lili (properly Marie-Juliette) (1893–1918), French composer, pupil of her sister Nadia and others; first woman to win the 'Rome Prize', principal French award to young composers. Works include cantata *Faust and Helen* (after Goethe), psalms with orchestra.

43

Boulanger, Nadia (1887–1979), French composer (orchestral works, songs, etc.), conductor, and teacher of distinguished musicians from many countries, especially USA (e.g. Copland, Piston). Sister of preceding.

Boulez, Pierre (b. 1925), French composer, pupil of Messiaen; extended the methods of TWELVE-NOTE technique to the 'organizing' (in mathematical relationships) of rhythms, volume, etc., and has also employed spatial effects. Works include piano pieces (often of great complexity, with some choice of order left to performer); LE MARTEAU SANS MAÎTRE (The Hammer without a Master) for contralto and chamber orchestra; two works for soprano and instrumental ensemble called *Improvisation sur Mallarmé* (see IMPROVISE). Also conductor, e.g. at Bayreuth Wagner Festival; principal conductor of BBC Symphony Orchestra, 1971–5, of New York Philharmonic Orchestra, 1971–7; director of musical-acoustical research centre in Paris (see IRCAM).

Boult, Adrian [Cedric] (1889–1983), British conductor who studied in Germany. Musical director of BBC, 1930–42; formed and conducted BBC Symphony Orchestra, 1931–50, then chief conductor of London Philharmonic Orchestra till 1957. Knighted, 1937.

bourdon, a 16-FOOT organ stop of stopped DIAPASON type.

Bourgeois, Louis (*c.*1510–*c.*1561), French musician who contributed harmonizations (including that of the 'Old Hundredth') to Calvin's Genevan Psalter, 1551.

Bourgeois Gentilhomme, Le (Fr., The Tradesman as Gentleman), (1) play by Molière (1670) with incidental music by Lully; (2) incidental music by R. Strauss to a shortened version of Molière's play, intended to precede the original version of Strauss's ARIADNE ON NAXOS.

Bourguignon, Francis de (1890–1961), Belgian composer (also pianist, formerly accompanist to Melba) and critic; works, some using polytonality, include piano concertos, songs, chamber music.

Bournemouth Municipal Orchestra, see BOURNEMOUTH SYMPHONY ORCHESTRA.

Bournemouth Sinfonietta, a chamber orchestra founded 1968 under the same management as the Bournemouth Symphony Orchestra; principal conductor from 1989, Tamás Vásáry.

Bournemouth Symphony Orchestra, the successor in 1954 to the former Bournemouth Municipal Orchestra, founded in 1893 under Sir Dan Godfrey's conductorship. Conductor from 1988, Andrew Litton.

bourrée (Fr.), dance-movement (found, e.g., in the baroque SUITE) in quick duple time beginning with an up-beat.

bouzouki (Gk.), a modern Greek type of mandolin.

bow, stick with horsehair stretched across it, used to set in vibration the strings of the violin and related instruments, also the viols; *Tourte bow*, name for the ordinary modern kind of bow (after François Tourte, inventor, 1747–1835), with stick curved inward to the hair. The earlier type, with an outward-curving stick, has been revived for 'old' music (but the idea that it could play simultaneous four-string chords as written by Bach is false). The term *Bach bow* sometimes alludes to a 20th-century invention associated with the violinist Emil Telmányi (b. 1892), supposedly suitable for Bach's music. So also *to bow*, i.e. to play with the bow or to mark an instrumental part for up-bow and down-bow.

Bowen, [Edwin] **York** (1884–1961), British pianist and composer (also played violin and horn); composer, generally in conservative ROMANTIC style, of three piano concertos, many piano solos, etc.

Bowles, Paul [Frederic] (b. 1910), American composer, pupil of N. Boulanger, Sessions and others; studied folk-music in Spain and Latin America. Works include orchestral *Danza Mexicana*, operas, chamber music, theatre and film scores. Also novelist.

Bowman, James [Thomas] (b. 1941), British counter-tenor, formerly boy chorister; London concert début, 1967, followed by operatic appearances in works of Handel, Britten, etc.

Boyce, William (1711–79), British composer and organist; D.Mus., Oxford. Boy chorister at St Paul's Cathedral, London, later a pupil of Greene and (1755) Master of the King's Band; organist of the Chapel Royal, 1758. Works include church and stage music, eight symphonies, songs including 'Heart of Oak'; editor of a notable collection of English cathedral music.

Bozay, Attila (b. 1939), Hungarian composer of *Outcries* for tenor and chamber ensemble; Variations for piano; *Symphonic Piece* for orchestra, etc.

Br., abbr. of Ger., BRATSCHE(N), i.e. viola(s).

Brade, William (1560–1630), English viol-player and musical director who worked mainly in Germany and died in Hamburg. Composed dance-music for instrumental ensemble, etc.

Braga, Gaetano (1829–1907), Italian cellist, composer of popular vocal 'Serenade', also of operas, etc.

Braham (real surname Abraham), **John** (1774–1856), British tenor, the original male lead in Weber's OBERON; sang also on the Continent; composer of songs including the once very popular 'The Death of Nelson'.

Brahms, Johannes (1833–97), German composer, also pianist; born in Hamburg, where as a youngster he played in sailors' taverns; pupil of Marxsen. In 1853 met Joachim, Liszt, Schumann and others who became interested in him; visited Vienna, 1862, settled there, 1863 (also died there). Never married. Entirely devoted to composition from 1864, but did not write the first of his four symphonies till 1875. Composed no opera, and did not follow widely prevalent Lisztian ideal of PROGRAMME MUSIC, but developed the forms of Beethoven's period and showed notable rhythmic originality. Works include two piano concertos, a violin concerto; Double Concerto for violin and cello; ACADEMIC FESTIVAL and TRAGIC overtures; *Variations on the St Anthony Chorale* (see ST ANTHONY CHORALE) – formerly known as *Variations on a Theme of Haydn* – for orchestra or two pianos; variations on themes by Handel and by PAGANINI for piano, and many other piano works; chamber music; songs (including FOUR

SERIOUS SONGS) and part-songs (see LOVE-SONG WALTZES) choral works including A GERMAN REQUIEM and ALTO RHAPSODY.

Brain, Dennis (1921–57), British horn-player, son of an equally eminent horn-player, Aubrey Brain (1893–1955). He made his début in 1938; works by Britten (*Serenade for Tenor, Horn and Strings*), Hindemith, and others were written for him. Died in a car crash.

Brand, Max (1896–1980), Polish-born Austrian composer of opera *Machinist Hopkins* (1929, later banned by the Nazis) and other works. Lived in USA, 1940–75.

Brandenburg Concertos, six works by J. S. Bach, 1721 (BWV 1046–51), for varying instrumental combinations, no two alike; dedicated to the Margrave of Brandenburg. Often classified as CONCERTO GROSSO, they are not really typical, having a wide variety of styles and forms.

branle, bransle, French dance-movement in 2/2 time, something like the gavotte; it is called *brawl* in Shakespeare.

Brant, Henry [Dreyfus] (b. 1913), Canadian composer resident in USA. Works include *Antiphony I* for five separated orchestral groups and five conductors; *The Grand Universal Circus*, spatial theatre piece for eight singing and speaking voices, 32 choristers, 16 instruments; Concerto for trumpet and nine instruments.

brass, collective term for musical instruments made of brass or other metals and blown directly though a cup-shaped or funnel-shaped mouthpiece. (This excludes, e.g., saxophone, because the air is actuated through a reed and not directly; it excludes flute, even if made of metal, because it has no such mouthpiece. See WOODWIND.) Basic brass requirements of the symphony orchestra are four horns, two or three trumpets, two tenor and one bass trombone, and one tuba; *heavy brass*, inexact and unhelpful term for trombones and tuba. See also the following entry.

brass band, combination of BRASS instruments only (MILITARY BAND has woodwind too) with or without percussion; in Britain made up of a fairly rigid combination of cornets, flugelhorn, tenor and baritone saxhorns, euphoniums, trombones, tubas and percussion.

Bratsche (Ger., pl. *-en*), viola.

bravo (It., brave, fine), interjection used to express approval – invariable in English-speaking countries, but *brava, bravi, brave* in Italian for a female performer, male performers, female performers, respectively.

bravura (It.), courage, swagger; *bravura passage*, one calling for a bold and striking display of an executant's technique.

brawl, see BRANLE.

break, (1) a change in tone-quality encountered in some voices and wind instruments in passing between different REGISTERS; (2) a short solo passage, usually improvised, in a concerted jazz piece – i.e. a CADENZA; (3, verb) of the voice, to undergo that change in quality and compass which comes to a young male's voice in puberty (better spoken of as 'to change', as *break* suggests that something has been destroyed and lost).

Bream, Julian [Alexander] (b. 1933), British guitarist who made début at age 12; also lutenist, as soloist and formerly as recital partner of Peter Pears. Britten and others wrote works for him. CBE, 1985.

Breasts of Tiresias, The (Fr., *Les Mamelles de Tirésias*), opera by Poulenc, produced in Paris, 1947; libretto by Apollinaire, a light-hearted modernization of the Greek myth of transsexuality.

Brecht, Bertolt (1898–1956), German dramatist and poet. See DESSAU, EISLER, RISE AND FALL OF THE CITY OF MAHAGONNY, THREEPENNY OPERA.

breit (Ger.), broadly, grandly – an indication of manner of performance, not (except incidentally) of speed.

Brendel, Alfred (b. 1931), Czech-born pianist, resident in Austria, then (since 1972) in Britain. Noted in Mozart; has also recorded Prokofiev, Schoenberg, etc.; is also occasional writer on music. Created honorary KBE, 1989.

breve (note-value), see DOUBLE-WHOLE-NOTE. See also ALLA BREVE (time-direction): there is apparently no connection between the two.

brevis (Lat.), short; *missa brevis*, see MISSA.

Brian, Havergal (1876–1972), British composer of 32 symphonies (some using voices; no. 1, *Gothic*), operas, songs, etc.; also writer on music. Mainly self-taught. (His music was little performed until his last years.)

bridge, (1) on a violin, viol, guitar, etc., the supporting piece of wood which holds the strings up from the belly of the instrument, and transmits their vibrations to the body of the instrument; (2) in a composition, a section (usually *bridge passage*) the main function of which is to link together (sometimes partly by a change of key) two passages more important than itself.

Bridge, Frank (1879–1941), British composer (pupil of Stanford, teacher of Britten), chiefly of chamber music – at first on traditional harmonic lines, later determinedly 'modern' – and songs; also wrote suite *The Sea*, and other orchestral music.

Bridge, [John] Frederick (1844–1924), British organist (Westminster Abbey), choral conductor, composer of church music, author of textbooks; knighted, 1897.

Brigg Fair, 'English rhapsody' by Delius (being variations on a Lincolnshire folk-song) for orchestra; first performed in 1908. It is dedicated to Grainger, who acquainted Delius with the song.

brillant, brillante (Fr., It.), brilliant (as a direction for performance, particularly in solo music).

brindisi (It.), a toast, drinking-song (e.g. in Verdi's LA TRAVIATA).

Brindle, Reginald Smith (b. 1917), British composer and professor (University of Surrey, 1970); pupil of Pizzetti and Dallapiccola. Works include *Cantata da Requiem*; *Homage to H. G. Wells* for orchestra; Quintet for clarinet, piano and strings.

brio (It.), spirit, dash; *con brio*, spiritedly.

Britten, [Edward] Benjamin (1913–76), British composer; also pianist (often in duo-recital with his permanent companion, Peter PEARS) and conductor, chief creator of Aldeburgh Festival and English Opera Group. Pupil of Frank Bridge (from age 12) and later of Ireland; much influenced (e.g. in vocal setting) by Purcell, and had stylistic links also with Mahler and Stravinsky. In USA and Canada, 1939–42 (see PAUL BUNYAN). Unusually successful opera PETER GRIMES, 1945, was followed by THE RAPE OF LUCRETIA and ALBERT HERRING (operas with small cast, chamber orchestra, no chorus), BILLY BUDD (all-male), GLORIANA and (again small-scale) THE TURN OF THE SCREW; LET'S MAKE AN OPERA! for children; NOYE'S FLUDDE, CURLEW RIVER, *The Burning Fiery Furnace* and *The Prodigal Son* (all for church performance); A MIDSUMMER NIGHT'S DREAM, *Owen Wingrave* (for television), DEATH IN VENICE; ballet THE PRINCE OF THE PAGODAS. He edited THE BEGGAR'S OPERA (with the tunes very freely treated). Concert works include SIMPLE SYMPHONY, SINFONIA DA REQUIEM, Cello Symphony (cello and orchestra), choral WAR REQUIEM and SPRING SYMPHONY, CANTATA ACADEMICA (see CANTATA); five CANTICLES; song-settings of Auden, Rimbaud (LES ILLUMINATIONS), Michelangelo, Donne, Pushkin, etc. (see SERENADE and NOCTURNE); three string quartets; folk-song arrangements. See also YOUNG PERSON'S GUIDE and IMPROMPTU. OM, 1965; life peer (Lord Britten), 1976. See also BREAM, FERRIER, LUXON.

Brixi, František Xaver (1732–71), Bohemian organist and composer of much church music, also of instrumental works.

broken chord, a chord of which the notes are not all played simultaneously, but one after the other (or a few followed by another few). Similarly *broken octaves*, a passage of alternate notes an octave apart – especially in piano-writing.

broken consort, see CONSORT.

Brontë, Emily (1818–48), British novelist and poet. See FLOYD, HERRMANN.

Brott, Boris (b. 1944), Canadian conductor; formerly associate conductor, Toronto Symphony Orchestra; conductor of the Hamilton (Ontario) Philharmonic Orchestra from 1969, and (concurrently) of BBC Welsh Orchestra, 1972–9.

Brouwer, Leo (b. 1939), Cuban composer (also guitarist and conductor) who trained in New York and has held official musical posts in Cuba. Has written many film scores; *Songs of the New Era* for actors, children's chorus, piano, harp and two percussion instruments; a guitar concerto.

Brown, Earle (b. 1926), American composer, a pioneer of time-notation (see GRAPHIC) and OPEN forms. Works include *25 Pages* for 1–25 pianos; *Available Forms II* for 98 specified instruments divided between two conductors; a string quartet.

browning, a type of English variation-form current about 1600, based on a tune 'The leaves be green, the nuts be brown'.

Browning, Elizabeth Barrett (1806–61), British poet. See NAYLOR.

Browning, Robert (1812–89), British poet. See GALUPPI, VOGLER.

Bruch, Max (1838–1920), German

composer; also conductor – of Liverpool Philharmonic Society, 1880–83. Works include three violin concertos (no. 1 is well known); KOL NIDREI for cello and orchestra; also three symphonies, operas, choral works.

Bruckner, Anton (1824–96), Austrian composer; also organist – played at Royal Albert Hall, London, 1871. At first church choirboy; went to Vienna and studied with Sechter (with whom Schubert had intended to study) and from 1868 settled in Vienna, becoming professor at the Conservatory there. Heard Wagner's TRISTAN AND ISOLDE, 1865, and became his fervent disciple; wrote, however, no operas but nine symphonies (no. 3 nicknamed his 'Wagner' Symphony; no. 4, ROMANTIC), not including two unnumbered early works later rejected by him. Symphony no. 9 (only three out of four movements finished) is dedicated 'to God' – Bruckner always retaining devout Roman Catholicism and certain unsophisticated 'country' ways. Symphonies nos. 7, 8, 9 use WAGNER TUBAS. There are important differences between the shortened published versions of his symphonies and the 'authentic' texts published after his death. Other works include five Masses, a Te Deum, string quintet.

Brüggen, Frans (b. 1934), Dutch player of the recorder (also of flute); prominent as soloist and in ensembles reviving 17th- and 18th-century music.

Bruhns, Nikolaus (1665–97), German organist and composer of church music, etc.; pupil of Buxtehude.

Brüll, Ignaz (1846–1907), Austrian pianist and composer of 10 operas, two piano concertos, etc.

Brumel, Antoine (c.1460–c.1515), Flemish composer of church music, etc.; choirmaster of Notre Dame, in Paris, 1498–1500, afterwards going to Italy.

Bruneau, [Louis Charles Bonaventure] Alfred (1857–1934), French composer of operas (two with librettos by Zola, whose political and social ideas he shared), three choral symphonies, etc.; also writer on music.

Brunswick, Mark (1902–71), American composer who died in London. Works include choral symphony *Eros and Death*; Quartet for violin, viola, cello and double-bass; opera *The Master Builder* (after Ibsen).

Brusilovsky, Yevgeni [Grigoryevich] (1905–81), Russian composer, dismissed from Moscow Conservatory as academically poor, but studied in Leningrad under M. Steinberg. Researched into folk-music of Kazakhstan, and wrote five operas, six symphonies, etc., with some use of Kazakh themes.

Bruson, Renato (b. 1936), Italian baritone, internationally celebrated in Verdi operas; Covent Garden début, 1976.

Brustwerk (Ger.), CHOIR-ORGAN.

Brymer, Jack (b. 1915), English clarinettist who developed a noted solo career and directed his own ensemble; latterly a successful radio speaker.

Btb., Ger. abbr. of bass TUBA, i.e. the normal orchestral tuba.

Bucchi, Valentino (1916–76), Italian composer and conservatory director, pupil of Dallapiccola. Works include opera *The Double-bass* (after Chekhov); *Concerto lirico* for violin and string orchestra; film scores.

Büchner, Georg (1813–37), German dramatist. See LOPATNIKOFF, WOZZECK.

Buck, Dudley (1839–1909), American composer and organist who studied in Germany; wrote opera *Deseret*, choral works, chamber music, etc.

Budapest Quartet, string quartet founded in 1917, originally Hungarian; but during its celebrated period (from 1936 until it disbanded in 1967) its members were Russian-Jewish, led by Josef Roisman.

buffo, buffa (It.), comic; *basso buffo*, *tenore buffo*, comic bass, comic tenor (in opera). (So also *buffo* by itself is sometimes found, e.g. in the list of singers required for an Italian opera, and then indicates a comic bass.) So also *opera buffa* – literally 'comic opera', but see OPERA.

bugle, brass instrument without valves and so producing only one HARMONIC SERIES (normally in B♭), used by armies, etc., both as a band instrument and to signal movements, etc. *Key bugle, keyed bugle, Kent bugle* – see OPHICLEIDE.

Bühnenweihfestspiel, see PARSIFAL.

Bulgakov, Mikhail Afanasyevich (1891–1940), Russian novelist and playwright. See HÖLLER (Y.).

Bull, John (1562/3–1628), English composer and organist – at Chapel Royal, London; first professor of music at Gresham College, London, 1596. Left England, 1613; in 1617 became cathedral organist at Antwerp, where he died. Wrote notable pieces for keyboard (one of them the probable source of 'God Save the Queen'; and

see PARTHENIA), also music for viols, and church music.

Bull, Ole (1810–80), Norwegian violinist, composer (two violin concertos, etc.), and enthusiast for Norwegian folk-music; gave Grieg early encouragement.

bull-roarer, primitive musical instrument found in Australian aboriginal and other cultures; a sound is produced by the whirling of an object at the end of a rope, the other end being held in the hand.

Bülow, Hans [Guido] **von** (1830–94), German pianist, music-editor and conductor – reckoned the first 'virtuoso' conductor; disciple of Liszt and Wagner, but enthusiast also for Brahms. Married Liszt's daughter, who afterwards left him for Wagner. Died in Cairo.

Bulwer-Lytton, Edward George Earle Lytton [Lord Lytton] (1803–73), British novelist and dramatist. See RIENZI.

Bumbry, Grace [Ann Melzia] (b. 1937), American mezzo-soprano, prominent in opera (first black singer to appear at Bayreuth Festival, 1961), latterly has taken some soprano roles.

Bunyan, John (1628–88), English writer. See PILGRIM'S PROGRESS.

Buononcini, Giovanni, see BONONCINI.

burden, (1) the refrain of a song; (2) in 14th- and 15th-century English music, the lowest strand in a polyphonic complex.

Bürger, Gottfried August (1747–94), German poet. See ACCURSED HUNTSMAN.

Burgmüller, [Johann] Friedrich [Franz]

(1806–74), German composer who settled in Paris and wrote two supplementary numbers for the ballet *Giselle* (mainly by Adam) as well as his own ballet *The Peri*. Also composed many piano pieces.

Burgon, Geoffrey (b. 1941), British composer of a Requiem, orchestral and chamber music, and of television theme music for *Brideshead Revisited*, etc.

Burian, Emil František (1904–59), Czech composer (also singer, author, playright, producer); inventor of 'voice band', an ensemble of voices using vowels as concords, consonants as discords (demonstrated, 1928). Works include operas, ballets, chamber music.

Burkhard, Willy (1900–1955), Swiss composer (also pianist and conductor); pupil of Karg-Elert and somewhat influenced by Hindemith. Works include *The Vision of Isaiah*, and other Protestant oratorios; three symphonies; Toccata for four wind instruments with percussion and strings; Mass; opera *The Black Spider*.

Burleigh, Henry Thacker (1866–1914), American baritone, composer and arranger of Negro spirituals; pupil of Dvořák.

burlesque (Fr., Eng.), **burlesca** (It.), **Burleske** (Ger.), terms indicating a humorous, playful vein (It., *burla*, joke), applied variously in musical titles, usually without an implication of parody. R. Strauss's *Burleske* is for piano and orchestra (1886).

burletta (It.), term used in Britain around 1800 for a light Italian comic opera, or a work in that style.

Burnand, [Sir] **Francis** (1836–1917), British writer. See COX AND BOX, SAVOY OPERAS.

Burney, Charles (1726–1814), British author of a famous history of music and other books; also organist and composer.

Burns, Robert (1759–96), British poet. See SVIRIDOV.

Burrows, Stuart (b. 1933), British tenor, noted in opera, especially Mozart; from Welsh National Opera went to Covent Garden (1967), the Metropolitan, New York (1971), etc.

Burt, Francis (b. 1926), British composer, pupil of Ferguson and (in Berlin) of Blacher; resident in Vienna. Works include *Iambics* for orchestra; two string quartets; opera *Volpone* (after Ben Jonson).

Busch, Adolf [Georg Wilhelm] (1891–1952); German-born violinist who, as anti-Nazi, took Swiss nationality; died in New York. Well known as soloist, leader of the Busch String Quartet and partner of Rudolf SERKIN (who became his son-in-law). Also composer. Brother of Fritz Busch.

Busch, Fritz (1890–51), German-born conductor who, as anti-Nazi, settled in Denmark; noted also as opera conductor at Glyndebourne. Died in London. Brother of Adolf Busch.

Bush, Alan [Dudley] (b. 1900), British composer (also pianist, conductor, writer on music and teacher); studied under John Ireland, and also in Berlin. Communist sympathies give clues to many of his works including operas WAT TYLER and *Men of Blackmoor* (both produced in East Germany), a piano concerto (with male chorus declaiming leftist text in finale),

DIALECTIC for string quartet. See also INTERLUDE.

Bush, Geoffrey (b. 1920), British composer (also writer and university teacher), formerly Salisbury Cathedral choirboy. Works include *Lord Arthur Savile's Crime* (after Wilde) and other operas, two symphonies, an oboe concerto, songs (some with orchestra).

Busnois, the name by which Antoine de Busne (*c.*1430–1492) was known; he was a Flemish (Netherlandish) composer in service to the dukes of Burgundy. Wrote Masses and other church music, also secular CHANSONS.

Busoni, Ferruccio [Benvenuto] (1866–1924), Italian pianist and composer; travelled widely; from 1894 lived mainly in Berlin (was himself of a German mother) and died there. Made wider appeal as a pianist, piano-teacher and arranger (e.g. editions for piano of J. S. Bach's organ works) than as composer. Works, showing an anti-ROMANTIC tendency (he detested Wagner) and an eclectic idiom, include operas *Arlecchino*, DOCTOR FAUST, and TURANDOT; a piano concerto (using male choir); a violin concerto; many piano solos; *Fantasia Contrappuntistica* (It., Contrapuntal Fantasia) for two pianos, based on J. S. Bach's THE ART OF FUGUE.

Büsser, Paul Henri (1872–1973 – the longest-lived composer in this dictionary!), French composer, pupil of Gounod and others, also conductor. Works include seven operas, church and organ music, and orchestrations of piano pieces by Debussy.

Bussotti, Sylvano (b. 1931), Italian composer of *The Passion According to Sade* (a 'staged concert' for voice, instruments, narrator); piano pieces (of an advanced sort); *The Rara Requiem* (for voices and chamber orchestra), etc. Employs highly individualized GRAPHIC NOTATION.

Butt, Clara [Ellen] (1872–1936), British contralto for whom Elgar wrote his *Sea Pictures*; chiefly famous for ballad singing, and the first musician to be created Dame (1920).

Butterfly, Butterfly's Wing(s), unauthorized nicknames for Chopin's Study in G flat for piano, op. 25, no. 9.

Butterley, Nigel [Henry] (b. 1935), Australian composer, pupil of Rainier in London. Works include a violin concerto; *Meditations of Thomas Traherne* for children's recorder group and orchestra; *Explorations* for piano and orchestra; three string quartets.

Butterworth, George [Sainton Kaye] (1885–1916), British composer; collected English folk-songs and shows their influence in, e.g., *A Shropshire Lad* for orchestra. Killed in action as a soldier.

Buxtehude, Diderik (*c.*1637–1707), Danish organist and composer; from 1668 organist at Lübeck, Germany, and therefore better known by the German form of his name as Dietrich Buxtehude. Wrote organ and harpsichord pieces, also church cantatas, etc. Much esteemed in his own day; visited by Bach and Handel as young men, influencing them both.

BWV, the accepted system of numbering Bach's works: see BACH (J. S.).

Bychkov, Semyon (b. 1952), Russian-born conductor, naturalized American, 1983. Left USSR in 1975. Appointed conductor of the Orchestre de Paris from 1990.

Byrd, William (1543–1623), English composer; organist of Lincoln Cathedral, 1563, of the Chapel Royal (jointly with Tallis), 1572. Jointly with Tallis, held from Queen Elizabeth a monopoly of music printing. Roman Catholic; composed for both his own and the Anglican Church. Works, mainly in serious vein and mainly church music, include Masses for three, four and five voices; more than 200 Latin motets (17 in CANTIONES SACRAE, 1575); five Anglican services (one incomplete); also madrigals, rounds and other secular vocal music, many pieces for keyboard (some contributed to PARTHENIA), and FANCIES, etc., for viols.

Byron, George Gordon [Lord] (1788–1824), British poet. See ARNELL, CORSAIR, DE BANFIELD, HAROLD IN ITALY, HOLBROOKE, MANFRED, MAZEPPA, NATHAN, ODE TO NAPOLEON, THOMSON (V.).

Byzantine music, the music of the liturgical chant of the Eastern Orthodox Churches.

C

C, note of the scale. So C FLAT (C♭),
DOUBLE-FLAT (C♭♭), NATURAL (C♮),
SHARP (C♯), DOUBLE-SHARP (C𝄪); C
major, C *minor*, etc. – see MAJOR. So
also *in C*, either (1) in the key of C
(major, understood), or (2) indication
of a non-transposing instrument in
cases where otherwise a TRANSPOS-
ING INSTRUMENT might seem to be
indicated: thus e.g., *trumpets in C* (to
differentiate from trumpets in B♭, in
A, etc.). So also *middle C*, the C situated
about the middle of the piano, and
notated on the line below the treble
staff; *cello C*, the C below the bass staff
(tuning of the cello's lowest note); C
clef, any one of the clefs which indicate
the position of the middle C – e.g. the
ALTO and TENOR clefs, and the obsolete SOPRANO clef. For C *melody saxophone*, see SAXOPHONE.

cabaletta (It.), in 19th-century Italian
opera (and, by analogy, in other operatic contexts), the final, quicker section
of an aria or duet made up of several
(usually two) sections. See CAVATINA.

Caballé, Montserrat (b. 1933), Spanish
soprano, prominent in Italian opera;
at La Scala, Milan, from 1960, Covent
Garden from 1972.

Cabezón, Antonio de (1510–66), Spanish organist, harpsichordist and composer of keyboard music, musician at
the Spanish court; he was blind, apparently from birth. Wrote keyboard variations, etc.

cabinet organ, see AMERICAN ORGAN.

caccia (It., hunt), an Italian poetic and
musical form of the 14th and early
15th centuries, usually for two voices
and dealing with real-life scenes such
as the hunt. For *oboe da caccia*, see
OBOE; for *corno da caccia*, see HORN.

Caccini, Giulio (c.1545–1618), Italian
composer (and lutenist) whose opera
Eurydice (1600) is one of the earliest
operas; as a pioneer of a newly expressive type of music (cp. MONTE-
VERDI), he called his collection of madrigals and canzonets (1601) *Le nuove
musiche*. His daughters, Francesca
(c.1587–1640) and Settimia (c.1591–
1638), were celebrated singers as well
as composers, an opera by the former
being performed in Florence in 1625.

cachucha, a lively Spanish dance
(from Andalusia) in triple time,
borrowed by Sullivan in *The Gondoliers*.

cadence, a progression of chords
(usually two) giving an effect of clos-
ing a 'sentence' in music. Thus *perfect
cadence*, progression of dominant
chord to tonic chord; *plagal cadence*,
subdominant to tonic; *imperfect*

cadence, tonic (or other chord) to dominant; *interrupted cadence*, dominant to submediant (or to some other chord suggesting a substitution for the expected tonic chord); *Phrygian cadence*, progression (deriving from the Phrygian MODE) which, in the key of C major, leads to the chord of E major (and correspondingly with other keys). Note that (1) some of these definitions are open to differences between authorities; (2) the *feminine cadence* is not a specific kind of harmonic progression, as the above, but any cadence in which the final chord comes on a weaker beat than its predecessor (instead of, as normally, the other way round). See also the following.

cadenza (It., cadence; but pronounced as English and used in different sense), solo vocal or instrumental passage, either of an improvised nature or in some other way suggesting an interpolation in the flow of the music – particularly, today, in concertos for solo instrument and orchestra. In these, however, genuine improvisation has for 150 years been very rare, cadenzas being written out in full instead by either the composer, the actual performer, or a third person.

Cadman, Charles Wakefield (1881–1946), American composer of *Pennsylvania Symphony* (orchestration includes banging on iron plate); opera *Shanewis* based on an American-Indian story; songs (including 'At Dawning'); etc.

Cage, John (b. 1912), American composer (also pianist and writer), pupil of Schoenberg. Has written for normal instruments and for his invention the PREPARED PIANO; is especially noted for 'music' which seems to involve the abdication of the composer, e.g. his *Imaginary Landscape No. 4* for 12 radio sets, first performed in 1951, requiring 24 performers (two to each set) and conductor – dynamics, and the ratio of sound to silence, are stipulated but the result obviously depends on chance. See ALEATORY. Other works include *Roaratorio* (1979), after Joyce's *Finnegans Wake*.

caisse (Fr.), drum; *grosse caisse*, bass drum; *caisse claire*, side-drum; *caisse roulante* or *caisse sourde*, tenor drum.

cakewalk, US dance originating in Negro-slave plantations with musical elements foreshadowing RAGTIME; became generally known from late 19th century. For Debussy's version, see CHILDREN'S CORNER.

calando (It.), getting weaker and slower.

Caldara, Antonio (*c.*1670–1736), Italian composer who settled in Vienna, 1716, where he died; works include more than 80 operas, also oratorios, chamber music, church music.

Calderón, Pedro (1600–1681), Spanish dramatist. See WIMBERGER.

Calife de Baghdad, Le, see CALIPH OF BAGHDAD.

Calinda, La, orchestral piece by Delius (excerpt from his opera KOANGA); a dance taking its name from Negro dance imported by African slaves to the American continent.

Caliph of Baghdad, The (Fr., *Le Calife de Baghdad*), opera by Boïeldieu, produced in Paris in 1800. Libretto by C. H. d'A. de Saint-Just; the Caliph assumes a disguise to learn people's real feelings about him.

Calisto, see CALLISTO.

Callas, Maria (form of name used by Maria Anna Kalogeropoulos) (1923–77), American-born soprano of Greek parentage, at first with career based mainly in Italy, then achieving highest international reputation, especially in Rossini, Verdi, etc. Rare operas, e.g. Cherubini's *Medea*, were revived for her. Gave concerts sporadically after last stage appearance in 1965.

Callisto, opera by Cavalli, produced in Venice, 1651; libretto by Faustini, about the nymph of Roman legend who is metamorphosed into a constellation. ('Callisto' is correct Latin spelling; 'Calisto' is the Italian form).

Calvé, Emma (originally Rose-Noémie Calvet de Roquer), (1858–1942), French soprano, celebrated in the (normally mezzo-soprano) role of Carmen. Sang at Covent Garden from 1892.

Cambert, Robert (*c*.1628–77), French composer who lived in London from 1673, and died there. His *Pomona* (1671) is one of the earliest French operas.

cambiata, see NOTA CAMBIATA.

camera, da (It.), for the room – either (1) as distinct from *da chiesa*, for the church, or (2) as implying music for a small gathering, exactly as 'chamber music' does. For *sonata da camera* see SONATA.

camerata, (1, It.) a historical name for a club or society, in musical history usually referring to that which centred on Count Giovanni Bardi in Florence shortly before 1600, the composers Caccini and Peri being members. In this group but also in

others at Florence the new concepts of MONODY and OPERA were shaped. (2) Modern name sometimes used (in various countries) for a chamber orchestra.

Camidge, Matthew (1758–1844), British organist, composer of piano sonatas, editor of a collection of cathedral music.

Camilleri, Charles [Mario] (b. 1931), Maltese composer who worked in Canada, 1960–65. Has used Maltese, African and other musical sources. Works include opera *Melita*; *Abongo* for wind quintet; *Missa Mundi* (Lat., Mass of the World) for organ.

campana, campane (It.), bell, bells.

Campanella, La, see BELL RONDO.

campanology, the study of bells. See BELL; see also CHANGE-RINGING.

Campian, see CAMPION.

Campion (or Campian), **Thomas** (1567–1620), English composer of more than 100 songs to lute accompaniment; also of masques, etc. Wrote poems set to music by himself and others, and was also lawyer and physician.

Campra, André (1660–1744), French composer of operas including TANCRED, opera-ballets, church music, etc.; in charge of music at the church of Notre Dame, Paris.

canarie, canaries, canary, an old dance in triple time (a type of JIG), having a prominent dotted rhythm.

can-can, Parisian dance, sometimes supposedly salacious, in quick 2/4 time; used by Offenbach in ORPHEUS IN THE UNDERWORLD.

cancion (Sp.), song, so *cancionero*, song-book.

cancrizans (made-up Lat.), crab-wise. The term is used (apparently through defective observation of crabs, which move sideways) to indicate a back-to-front order of notes (i.e. RETROGRADE motion); *canon cancrizans*, a canon in which the imitating voice gives out the theme not as the first voice gave it but with the notes in reverse order.

Cannabich, Johann Christian (1731–98), German composer of symphonies (adherent of the so-called MANNHEIM SCHOOL) and of operas, ballets, chamber music, etc.; also violinist and conductor.

Cannon, Philip (b. 1929), British composer of partly French descent, pupil of Imogen Holst. Works include *Songs to Delight* for women's choir; Concertino for piano and strings.

canon, contrapuntal composition, or section of a composition, in which a melody announced by one voice (or instrument) is repeated by one or more other voices (or instruments), each entering before the previous voice has finished so that overlapping results. A *canon at the unison* is when the 'imitating' (i.e. following) voice enters at the same pitch as the first voice; a *canon at the fifth* is when the imitating voice enters a fifth higher than the original. A *canon four in one* indicates four voices entering successively on the same melody; a *canon four in two* (or *double canon*) has two different simultaneous canons for two voices each. So also *accompanied canon*, when there are simultaneous other voices or instruments performing but not taking part in the canon; *perpetual canon*, when each voice as it comes to

the end begins again (see ROUND); *canon* by AUGMENTATION, DIMINUTION, INVERSION, etc., one in which the theme is treated in the imitating voice in one of those ways; *riddle* (or *enigma* or *puzzle*) *canon*, one in which only the opening voice is written out, leaving the notation of the other entries to be deduced.

cantabile (It.), in a 'singing' fashion; flowingly and clearly.

cantata (It., a sung piece), an extended choral work with or without solo voices, and usually with orchestral accompaniment. This is the later meaning of the term, but in Italian baroque usage it denotes solo voice(s) and CONTINUO, and Bach's cantatas have solo voice(s) with accompanying instruments, with or without chorus. The term is much more rarely used as an actual title than its counterpart, SONATA – but Stravinsky composed a *Cantata* (two solo singers, female chorus, five instrumentalists) to old English texts, 1952, and Bartók a *Cantata profana* (subtitle 'The Enchanted Stags', on a legend symbolizing a plea for political freedom) for two soloists, chorus and orchestra, 1930. Britten's *Cantata academica* (in Latin) was written for the 500th anniversary of Basle University, 1960.

cantatrice (It.), woman singer.

cante flamenco, cante hondo (or *jondo*), see FLAMENCO, HONDO.

Cantelli, Guido (1920–56), Italian conductor. He appeared at the 1950 Edinburgh Festival and was chosen as music director of La Scala, Milan, shortly before being killed in an air crash; his gifts were considered outstanding.

Canteloube [de Malaret], **Marie-Joseph** (1879–1957), French pianist, composer and folk-song collector; his *Songs of the Auvergne* (region of France) have accompaniment for piano or orchestra.

canticle, (1) a hymn with biblical words, other than from the Psalms, used in Christian liturgy (distinct from ANTHEM, not on a liturgically obligatory text); so, analogously, (2) a concert work with a religious or quasi-religious text – term used, e.g., as title of five works by Britten.

cantilena (It.), a smooth song-like melodic line.

cantillation, unaccompanied chanting in free rhythm – term used particularly of Jewish liturgical chanting.

Cantiones Sacrae (Lat., Sacred Songs), title sometimes formerly applied to collections of Latin motets (e.g. one composed by Tallis and Byrd, 1575).

canto (It.), song; melody; *marcato il canto*, bring out the melody; *col canto*, let the tempo of the accompaniment be accommodated to that of the soloist's tune; *canto fermo*, same as CANTUS FIRMUS.

cantor (Lat., singer), (1) director of music in a German Lutheran church (in modern German, *Kantor*) – e.g. J. S. Bach's position at St Thomas's, Leipzig; (2) the leader of the chanting in a synagogue.

cantoris (Lat., of the singer, i.e. of the precentor), that section of the choir in a cathedral, etc., which is stationed on the north (i.e. precentor's) side of the chancel; opposite of DECANI.

cantus (Lat.), (1) song, melody; *cantus firmus* (pl. *cantus firmi*), fixed song, i.e.

the 'given' melody borrowed from religious or secular sources which 14th–17th-century composers used as a basis of works by setting other melodies in counterpoint against it – similarly, a melody given to a student, even today, to set a counterpoint against; (2) in, e.g., the 16th century, the upper voice-line of a choir.

canzona, canzone (It.), (1) any song; e.g. 'Canzone del salce', the 'Willow Song' from Verdi's OTELLO; (2) specifically, a type of medieval Italian poem, and hence a musical setting of this; (3) type of short instrumental piece, especially of the 16th to early 18th centuries, often less strongly polyphonic than the RICERCAR – developed from the contemporary French CHANSON.

canzonet (Anglicized from It. *canzonetta*), term used *c.*1600 for a light song for one or more voices, and later (e.g. Haydn's English canzonets) for an English solo song not from an opera.

canzonetta (It.), little song, light song. See CANZONA.

Caoine, see KEEN.

Čapek, Karel (1890–1938), Czech novelist and dramatist. See MAKROPOULOS AFFAIR.

capella, incorrect spelling for CAPPELLA.

Caplet, André (1878–1925), French composer of unaccompanied Mass, song-cycles, etc.; also conductor – at Boston, USA, 1910–14; friend of Debussy, some of whose work he arranged for orchestra.

capo (It., head), (1) see DA CAPO; (2) a device used on the fingerboard of a guitar to shorten the strings equally in order to facilitate playing in various keys – i.e. a form of movable nut (see NUT, 1).

cappella (It.), chapel; in 17th-century usage, a near-synonym for RIPIENO, i.e. full performing forces; later use, *a cappella, alla cappella*, 'in the chapel style', i.e. unaccompanied (of choral music).

Cappuccilli, Piero (b. 1929), Italian baritone, distinguished in Verdi; sang at La Scala, Milan, from 1964.

Capriccio, opera by R. Strauss, produced in Munich, 1942. Styled 'a conversation piece in one act' (2 hours). Libretto by Clemens Krauss, in which a poet and a musician are rival suitors to a young widowed countess; set in the 18th century.

capriccio, caprice (It., Fr,. Eng.), term applied to various types of lively, light piece; and specifically to a 17th-century keyboard work in lively fugal style. See also following.

Capriccio espagnol (It. + Fr.), see SPANISH CAPRICE.

Capriccio italien (It. + Fr.), see ITALIAN CAPRICE.

Capriol, suite for strings by Warlock, 1926, also arranged for full orchestra; in six movements based on old French dances from Thoinot Arbeau's *Orchésographie*, a book on dancing, 1589. ('Capriol' is an imaginary character in the book.)

Carafa (full surname Carafa di Colobrano), **Michele Enrico** (1787–1872). Italian opera-composer who settled in France. See MASANIELLO.

Cardew, Cornelius (1936–81), British composer, pupil of Howard Ferguson, later associated with Stockhausen; works include *Octet 1961* with diagrammatic notation and free choice for performers: 'free use may be made of notes apart from those provided'. (See INDETERMINACY.) Also composed more conventional music for piano, string trio, etc., and some later works with 'popular' simplification in pursuance of Maoist political ideas.

Cardillac, opera by Hindemith, produced at Dresden, 1926. Libretto by F. Lion; it was later revised – the text extensively, the music rather less. Title is the name of the hero, a 17th-century French goldsmith.

Carey, Henry (*c*.1689–1743), English composer (also poet and playwright); wrote words and music of *Chrononhotonthlogos* (burlesque of pompous tragedy) and other stage pieces including *True Blue*; also composed cantatas and songs. Wrote words and a tune (not the best-known one) of 'Sally in our Alley'.

carillon (originally Fr.), (1) set of bells, e.g. in a tower, on which tunes are played either by heavy manual and pedal keyboards or mechanically; (2) bell-like organ stop; (3) title of work by Elgar (1914) for reciter with orchestra, based on a bell-like short theme.

Carissimi, Giacomo (1605–74), Italian composer and church musician who wrote early examples of oratorio (e.g. JEPHTHA); also cantatas, Masses, vocal duets, etc.

Carmelites, The, See DIALOGUES OF THE CARMELITES.

carmen (Lat.), song; the plural is *carmina* – see CARMINA BURANA.

Carmen, Bizet's most successful opera, produced in Paris, 1875. Libretto by H. Meilhac and L. Halévy. Title from the name of the heroine, a gipsy working in a cigarette factory. The opera's well-known HABANERA is taken from a song by YRADIER. See also CONSTANT, SHCHEDRIN.

Carmina Burana, cantata by Orff, intended for mimed action; first performed in Frankfurt, 1937. Title and words from a collection of medieval Latin verse (with old French and old German interpolations) on love and liquor. Title is the Latin for 'Songs from Beuron', where the text was found in a monastery. (*Carmina* is accented on the first syllable.)

Carnaval (Fr.), see CARNIVAL (and similarly for other titles beginning with this word, except *Le Carnaval romain* – see ROMAN CARNIVAL).

Carneval (Ger.), see CARNIVAL.

Carnival, (1) concert-overture (Cz., *Karneval*) by Dvořák, 1891, second of the cycle of three overtures, originally given the collective title *Nature, Life and Love* (no. 1 being AMID NATURE and no. 3 OTHELLO); (2) set of 21 piano pieces by Schumann, 1834–5, subtitled 'dainty scenes on four notes' (Fr., *Carnaval: scènes mignonnes sur quatre notes*), these notes representing the four letters A, S (i.e. 'Es', the German symbol for E♭), C and H (German name for the note B); the word ASCH makes up the home-town of the girl Schumann was then in love with, and also uses the only 'musical' letters in his own name (see also PAPILLONS); (3) orchestral version of the preceding, arranged by Glazunov and others, and used for ballet, 1910; (4) concert-overture by Glazunov, 1894.

Carnival Jest from Vienna (Ger., *Faschingsschwank aus Wien*), piano work in five sections by Schumann, 1839, described by him as a 'grand Romantic sonata'.

Carnival of Animals, The (Fr. *Le Carnaval des animaux*), 'grand zoological fantasy' for two pianos and orchestra by Saint-Saëns, 1886 (the composer permitted no public performances in his lifetime); 14 movements, of which no. 11 is 'Pianists' and no. 13 'The Swan'.

Carnival of Venice, variations for violin and piano by Paganini (1829 or before) on a popular Venetian tune, 'O mamma mia'; the theme was also used for variations by later composers, and an opera with this title (Fr., *Le Carnaval de Venise*) by A. Thomas was produced in 1857.

carol, an English traditional song of joyful character (apparently, in its medieval origins, a danced song). The *Christmas carol* (most current examples dating from the 19th–20th centuries) is only one type.

Carpenter, John Alden (1876–1951), American composer of orchestral suite *Adventures in a Perambulator*, two symphonies (no. 2 incorporating Algerian tunes), ballet *Krazy Kat*, etc.; he combined music with a business career.

Carreras, José [Maria] (b. 1946), Spanish tenor prominent in Italian opera; at Covent Garden since 1974, at La Scala, Milan from 1975. His career was temporarily interrupted by leukaemia, 1987.

Carrillo, Julián (1875–1965), Mexican composer of three operas, Masses symphonies, etc., of 'normal' musical structure; also deviser of harps and other instruments producing intervals of quarter-, eighth- and 16th-tones, and composer of more than 50 works for them.

Carroll, Lewis [C. L. Dodgson] (1832–98), British writer. See DEL TREDICI, RAXACH, TAYLOR (D.).

Carter, Elliott [Cook] (b. 1908), American composer, pupil of Piston and (in Paris) of N. Boulanger; former music director of a ballet company. Works include ballet *The Minotaur*; four string quartets; Double Concerto (harpsichord, piano, two chamber orchestras); a piano and a violin concerto. Is also writer on music.

Carulli, Fernando (1770–1841), Italian guitarist, composer of nearly 400 pieces for his instrument; settled in Paris, taught and died there.

Caruso, Enrico (1873–1921), Italian tenor who made his first public appearance in 1894 in Naples (where he was born and died); appeared in Britain from 1902, USA from 1903. One of the first artists whose enormous success owed much to recording.

Cary, Tristram [Ogilvie] (b. 1925), British composer of electronic music on tape (e.g. *Birth is Life is Power is Death is God is*), and also film and television scores, etc. Holds university post in Adelaide.

Casadesus, Robert [Marcel] (1899–1972), French pianist, noted as soloist and also forming two-piano team with his wife, Gaby (Milhaud wrote for them *The Ball at Martinique*); also composer of piano concertos, symphonies, etc.

Casals, Pablo (he also used the Catalan form of his first name: Pau) (1876–1973), Spanish cellist (also pianist, conductor and composer, e.g. of oratorio *The Manger*) who made his first London appearance in 1898. Won unsurpassed reputation, particularly in J. S. Bach's unaccompanied cello works, and received high state honours from many countries. From 1940 lived outside Spain in protest against Franco's government (latterly in Puerto Rico). Founder-conductor of annual festival at Prades in the French Pyrenees (from 1950).

Casanova, André (b. 1919), French composer, also pianist; trained as lawyer. Works include *The Silver Key* (Fr., *La Clé d'argent*) for soprano, tenor, baritone and orchestra; *Three Poems by Rilke* for chorus; *Strophes* for xylophone, kettledrums and strings; violin concerto.

Casella, Alfredo (1883–1947), Italian composer and pianist; pupil of Fauré in Paris. Works include operas, symphonies, *Puppets* (*Pupazzetti*) for piano duet, many piano solos; chamber music including Concerto for string quartet. Also wrote oratorio *The Desert Challenged* (idealizing Mussolini's conquest of Ethiopia) and other works with topical links.

Casken, John (b. 1949), British composer and university lecturer. Works include string quartet, opera *Golem*.

cassa (It.), drum; *gran cassa*, bass drum; *cassa rullante*, tenor drum.

cassation (derivation uncertain), 18th-century type of composition (e.g. by Mozart) in several movements and in DIVERTIMENTO style for an orchestra or small group of instruments.

Casse-noisette, see NUTCRACKER.

castanets, percussion instruments made of two hollowed-out wooden surfaces rhythmically clicked together by the fingers of Spanish dancers; in the orchestra the clicking pieces of wood are often mounted for convenience at the end of a small stick, which is shaken.

Castelnuovo-Tedesco, Mario (1895–1968), Italian composer, pupil of Pizzetti; settled in USA, 1939, when banned as a Jew from Italian cultural life. Works include operas, oratorio *The Book of Jonah*, three violin concertos, a guitar concerto, song-settings of Shakespeare, music for the synagogue.

Castiglioni, Niccolò (b. 1932), Italian composer and pianist who has worked at US universities. Works include *Granulation* for two flutes, two clarinets; Symphony in C with choral text by Jonson, Dante, Shakespeare and Keats.

castrato (It., castrated), male singer who was castrated at puberty to allow development of a powerful voice in soprano or contralto range. Such singers were employed in Italian churches in the 17th and 18th centuries and became prominent in Italian operas – Handel's for instance being written for their participation.

Castro, Juan José (1895–1968), Argentinian composer and conductor, pupil of d'Indy in Paris. Works include opera *Proserpina and the Stranger* (in Spanish), a piano concerto, etc.

Catalani, Alfredo (1854–93), Italian composer who studied in Paris and composed WALLY and other successful operas; also Mass, symphonic poem *Hero and Leander*, etc.

catch, type of ROUND with tricky, amusing (sometimes bawdy) words, cultivated by Purcell and other English composers from 17th to 19th century.

Cat's Fugue, nickname of one of D. Scarlatti's so-called 'sonatas' for harpsichord (no. 30 in Kirkpatrick's catalogue; published in 1738). Its theme of oddly rising intervals is thought to have been suggested by the steps of a cat on the keyboard; Edward J. Dent, having failed to induce a cat to confirm this hypothesis, suggested another possible origin in the cat's nocturnal cry.

Catullus, Caius Valerius (*c*.84–54 BC), Roman poet. See DENISOV, ORFF.

Causton, Thomas (?–1569), English composer of church music, etc.

Cavalieri, Emilio de' (*c*.1550–1602), Italian composer, mainly at the Medici court at Florence; as well as incidental music for court festivities, he composed THE REPRESENTATION OF SOUL AND BODY – type of 'morality play' set to music, now reckoned the first oratorio (but using costumes and action).

Cavalleria Rusticana (It., The Rustic Code of Honour), opera by Mascagni, produced in Rome, 1890. Libretto by G. Menasci and G. Targioni-Tozzetti: a tale of revenge in a Sicilian village. It is performed without an interval, the well-known Intermezzo being played with the curtain up at a point in the middle when the stage is empty of characters.

Cavalli, Pietro Francesco (1602–76), Italian composer of more than 40 operas, including ORMINDO, CALLISTO, *Eritrea* and *Erismena*, also of church music; worked in Venice as singer (at first under Monteverdi) and organist.

cavatina (It.), (1) operatic song in slow tempo, either complete in itself or (e.g. in Bellini and Verdi) followed by faster, more resolute section – see CABALETTA; hence (2) a rather slow, song-like instrumental movement – title, e.g., of a movement in Beethoven's String Quartet in B flat, op. 130 (1826); of a once-famous piece (originally for violin and piano) by Raff; and of the slow movement of Rubbra's String Quartet no. 2.

Cavazzoni, Girolamo (*c*.1525–after 1577), Italian composer of keyboard works, including some in the forms of RICERCAR and CANZONA. Son of the following.

Cavazzoni, Marco Antonio (*c*.1490–1560), Italian composer, singer and organist, in service to Pope Leo X; works include a collection of keyboard pieces. Father of the preceding.

Cavendish, Michael (*c*.1565–1628), English composer of psalms, madrigals (one in THE TRIUMPHS OF ORIANA), ayres, etc.

cebell, dance of the gavotte type, found in old English music.

Ceccato, Aldo (b. 1934), Italian conductor, formerly pianist. Conducted New York Philharmonic, 1970; also internationally prominent in opera.

Cecilia, Christian saint (now no longer recognized by Roman Catholic Church), supposedly executed in Sicily under the Romans in the second or third century AD. Later called the patron saint of music (commemorated annually on 22 November), though her connection with music is purely legendary and dates only from the 16th century, apparently through the misreading of a Latin text. See HYMN TO ST CECILIA; ODE FOR ST CECILIA'S DAY. See also WALOND.

cédez (Fr., yield), hold the tempo back (usually implying that a return to the previous tempo will shortly follow).

celesta (pronounced as English word; it is not Italian), instrument looking like small upright piano but having hammers striking metal bars giving bell-like sound; used, a few years after its invention in Paris, by Tchaikovsky in the 'Dance of the Sugar-Plum Fairy' (in THE NUTCRACKER) and afterwards by various composers, usually for 'picturesque' effects in the orchestra. Its compass is from middle C upwards for four octaves.

Celibidache, Sergiu (b. 1912), Romanian conductor, trained in Germany; was attached to Berlin Philharmonic Orchestra, 1945–52; sporadic but much-acclaimed appearances since.

Cellier, Alfred (1844–91), British composer, especially of operettas – including *Dorothy* (1886), with a record London run; also organist and conductor.

cello (It.; see end of entry), bowed four-stringed instrument, one of the family (of which the principal member is the violin) that superseded the viols in the 17th and 18th centuries; has compass from C two octaves below middle C, upwards for more than three octaves. The five-stringed cello sometimes demanded, e.g. by Bach, is now obsolete. (The word *cello* is abbr. from *violoncello*, meaning a small violone, this being a large viol; hence it is frequently given the apostrophe, as *'cello*. But it may be accepted, without the apostrophe, as now having become a standard English word on its own, like 'piano', since no 'really English' alternative for it had been recognized. But see GRAINGER.)

Celtic harp, see HARP.

cembalo (It.), literally a dulcimer (cp. CIMBALOM) but used as abbr. for *clavicembalo*, i.e. keyed dulcimer, i.e. HARPSICHORD. (Used also in German; its use in English is affected.)

Cendrillon, see CINDERELLA.

Cenerentola, La, see CINDERELLA.

Cerha, Friedrich [Paul] (b. 1926), Austrian composer, also violinist, conductor and writer. See LULU. Works include *Mirrors* (Ger., *Spiegel*) nos. 1–8 for orchestra.

Certon, Pierre (1510–72), French composer, choirmaster in Paris; works include Masses, psalm-settings, chansons.

Cervantes [Saavedra], **Miguel de** (1547–1616), Spanish writer. See BOISMORTIER, DON QUIXOTE, MASTER PETER'S PUPPET SHOW, MINKUS, PETRASSI.

Cesti, Marc'Antonio (1623–69), Italian composer and Franciscan monk holding church and court musical posts; pupil of Carissimi. Works include operas, solo cantatas, motets.

Ch-, Russian names beginning with this sound are listed (by convention rather than consistency) under TCH-. See, e.g., TCHAIKOVSKY, TCHEREPNIN.

ch., abbr. for choir (as a manual on the organ); *chm.*, abbr. for choirmaster (in some musical diplomas).

Chabrier, [Alexis] **Emmanuel** (1841–94), French composer, also pianist and conductor; originally civil servant. He visited Spain, 1882, and afterwards wrote orchestral rhapsody ESPAÑA. Wrote also *Joyous March* for orchestra; piano and two-piano works; opera *King Despite Himself* (Fr. *Le Roi malgré lui*); etc. In late life suffered melancholic near-madness.

chaconne (Fr., from Sp. *chacona*), type of dance-piece in slow three-beat time, originating in the late 16th century. Using this form, composers often chose to repeat a given theme over and over again in the bass (i.e. a ground bass). In such works as the Chaconne which forms the final movement of Bach's Partita no. 2 in D minor for violin alone (*c.*1720), the theme is harmonically implied even at those points when it is not actually present. The term is applied by modern historians also to vocal numbers (e.g. 'When I am laid in earth' in Purcell's DIDO AND AENEAS) with a similar pattern of repetition. See also PASSACAGLIA.

chacony, term formerly used in England, e.g. by Purcell, for CHACONNE.

Chadwick, George Whitefield (1854–1931), American composer of three symphonies, five string quartets, etc.; reckoned a pioneer establishing a distinctively American type of symphonic composition; pupil of Rheinberger in Germany.

Chailly, Luciano (b. 1920), Italian composer of *The Proposal* (after Chekhov), *Trial by Tea-Party* (*Procedura penale*) and other operas, chamber works, etc.; pupil of Hindemith. Artistic director of La Scala opera house, Milan, 1968–71. Father of the following.

Chailly, Riccardo (b. 1953), Italian conductor, son of Luciano Chailly. Assistant conductor at La Scala, Milan, from age 19; after rapid international rise, became conductor of Concertgebouw Orchestra (Amsterdam) in 1988.

Chaliapin(e), see SHALYAPIN.

chalumeau (Fr.), (1) an obsolete instrument, forerunner of the clarinet; (2) the lowest register of the clarinet, with a distinctively 'dark' tone-colour.

chamber music, music intended for a room (in fact, called by Grainger 'room music', very sensibly), as distinct from a large hall, theatre, church, bandstand, ballroom, etc.; hence, particularly, music calling for 'intimate' presentation, having only a few performers, and treating all these as soloists on equal terms. Conventionally, works for one or two performers only are excluded. (The term is not a precisely defined one; see also following entries. There is every reason for including in it the appropriate kind of vocal music, e.g. madrigal-singing with one to two voices to each part.) Note that Hindemith gave the actual title *Chamber Music* (Ger. *Kammermusik*) to each of a set of seven compositions for various instrumental combinations, 1922–30.

chamber opera, term sometimes used for an opera with few singers and a small orchestra (e.g. THE RAPE OF LUCRETIA and some others by Britten); an inaccurate term, because it falsely suggests (by analogy with CHAMBER MUSIC) that such work should be capable of being performed in an ordinary room, not a theatre.

chamber orchestra, an orchestra small in size, and therefore capable of playing in a room (or anyway a small hall), but not merely a string orchestra. See CHAMBER MUSIC.

chamber sonata, see SONATA.

Chamber Symphony, title of two works by Schoenberg which use only a few players and treat them as soloists (cp. CHAMBER MUSIC). No. 1 (1906) he scored also (1935) for normal orchestra; no. 2, begun 1906, was put aside, completed in USA and first performed in 1940. There are also works of this title by Schreker, Milner and others.

Chaminade, Cécile (1857–1944), French composer (pupil of Godard) and pianist, performing much in England; mainly known for her light piano pieces but also wrote opera, ballet, orchestral suites, etc.

Chamisso, Adalbert von (1781–1838), German poet. See WOMAN'S LOVE AND LIFE.

Champagne, Claude (1891–1965), Canadian composer of *Altitude* for chorus, martenot and orchestra; Concerto for piano with chamber orchestra; French-Canadian folk-song arrangements; etc.

Chandos Anthems, 12 anthems (with orchestra) composed by Handel for his patron James Brydges (later Duke of Chandos), 1717–18.

change-ringing, the British practice of ringing church bells by teams, of which each member pulls the rope controlling one bell; thus with three bells the number of available *changes* (i.e. variations of the order of pulling) is six ($= 3 \times 2 \times 1$), with four bells it is 24 ($= 4 \times 3 \times 2 \times 1$), etc.

changing-note, see NOTA CAMBIATA.

Chanler, Theodore [Ward] (1902–61), American composer of a violin sonata, songs to texts by Walter de la Mare, etc.

chanson (Fr.), song, in particular a type of polyphonic song, sometimes with instruments, current in France from 14th to 16th century – during the latter part of which period Italy and England had the corresponding but different form of the MADRIGAL. The *chanson de geste*, however, was a type of heroic verse chronicle set to music, current in the 11th and 12th centuries. The name is also used in 20th-century titles, e.g. Ravel's *Chansons madécasses* (= of Madagascar), 1926.

chant, (1, Eng.) see ANGLICAN CHANT, PLAINCHANT; (2, Fr.) song, singing.

chanty, see SHANTY.

chapel-master, the director of music in a church – made-up English equivalent for *maître de chapelle, Kapellmeister, maestro di cappella* (Fr., Ger., It.). But the German sense is much wider: see KAPELLE, KAPELLMEISTER.

Chapel Royal, the English court chapel (i.e. a corporate body, not a building) with records going back to 1135; many leading English musicians have been associated with it as choirboys, choir-men or organists.

Chapí [y Lorente], Ruperto (1851–1909), Spanish composer who for a time lived in Rome; wrote ZARZUELAS, also a symphony and other orchestral works, piano pieces, etc.

characteristic piece, Charakterstück (Eng., Ger.), a musical representation of a mood, a place, etc.

Charpentier, Gustave (1860–1956), French composer, pupil of Massenet; wrote notably successful opera LOUISE and unsuccessful sequel *Julien*. Expressed his sympathy for the socially underprivileged both in these works and in founding a music school for working-class girls. Wrote also orchestral *Impressions of Italy*, songs, etc.

Charpentier, Marc-Antoine (*c*.1645–1704), French composer, pupil of Carissimi in Rome; held church posts in France and wrote Masses and other church music, as well as operas, ballets, incidental music to plays by Molière (with whom he collaborated) and Racine, etc.

chasse (Fr.), hunt; *La Chasse* (nickname of a Haydn symphony), see HUNT; *cor de chasse* (hunting-horn), see HORN.

Chaucer, Geoffrey (1340–1400), English poet. See FINNEY, LAY, TROILUS AND CRESSIDA, WOOD (T.).

Chausson, Ernest (1855–99), French composer, pupil of Massenet and then of Franck, stylistically bridging the gap between that generation and Debussy's. Works include POEM for violin and orchestra; a piano quartet; Concerto for violin and piano with string quartet; *Poème de l'amour et de la mer* (Poem of Love and the Sea) for voice and orchestra; and many songs.

Chávez, Carlos (1899–1976), Mexican composer (also conductor, musical organizer and folk-song researcher) who studied in Europe and New York. Used Mexican native instruments, writing for an ensemble of them, e.g. in *Xochipilli-Macuilxochitl* (name of the Aztec god of music). Other works include seven symphonies; *HP* (i.e. Horsepower) and other ballets; piano pieces. Cultivated a Mexican national idiom.

Checkmate, ballet with music by Bliss, produced in Paris, 1937. (A game of chess between Love and Death.)

chef d'attaque (Fr., leader of the attack), an orchestra's first violinist (Eng., leader; US, concertmaster).

chef d'orchestre (Fr.), conductor.

Chekhov, Anton (1806–1904), Russian writer. See BEAR, BUCCHI, CHAILLY (L.).

Cheminée du Roi René, La, see KING RENÉ'S CHIMNEY.

Cherevichki, see LITTLE SLIPPERS.

Cherkassky, Shura, professional name of Alexander (for which Shura is a diminutive) Isakovich Cherkassky (b. 1911), Russian-born pianist who studied in USA and took US nationality; celebrated as virtuoso from the 1930s to the 1980s.

Cherubini, [Maria] Luigi [Carlo Zenobio Salvatore] (1760–1842), Italian-born composer, permanently in Paris from 1788 and head of the Paris Conservatory from 1822; met Beethoven, who admired his music and whose FIDELIO was a 'rescue opera' influenced by Cherubini's *Faniska*. Wrote various other operas in French and Italian including IPHIGENIA IN AULIS, MEDEA, *Lodoiska* and *The Water-Carrier* (French title, *Les Deux Journées*, i.e. The Two Days); also symphony, chamber music, two Requiems and other church music.

chest (of viols), a set of various sizes – usually six instruments in all and so

called because in the 16th century, they were often stored together in a chest or cupboard – for which composers often wrote as an ensemble.

chest voice, that 'register' of the voice which gives the feeling to the singer of coming from the chest – i.e. the lower register, contrasted with HEAD VOICE.

Chevreuille, Raymond (1901–76), Belgian composer of ballet *Cinderella*; eight symphonies; various concertos; *Prayer for Those Condemned to Death* for narrator and orchestra; six string quartets; *Lilliputian Music* for four flutes; etc.

Chicago Symphony Orchestra, American orchestra founded in 1891. From 1991 Barenboim becomes conductor, succeeding Solti.

chiesa, da (It.), for the church (as opposed, e.g., to *da camera*, for the room); for *sonata da chiesa*, see SONATA.

Chilcot, Thomas (?–1766), English organist and composer of harpsichord concertos, songs, etc.

Child, William (1606–97), English composer, particularly of church music, including about 25 services; court musician to Charles II.

Child and the Spells, The (Fr., *L'Enfant et les sortilèges*), opera by Ravel, produced in Monte Carlo, 1925. Libretto by Colette: fantasy in which objects of furniture, etc., come to life. See SWANEE WHISTLE.

Childhood of Christ, The (Fr., *L'Enfance du Christ*), oratorio by Berlioz, first performed in 1854. Words by the composer.

Child of our Time, A, oratorio by Tippett, first performed in 1944. Text (by the composer) forms a modern plea for the oppressed, with special reference to the Nazi persecutions, and the music incorporates Negro spirituals to parallel the traditional chorales in Bach's PASSIONS.

Children's Corner, suite of six piano pieces by Debussy, 1906–8, dedicated to his daughter. No. 1 is 'Doctor GRADUS AD PARNASSUM'; titles of the other pieces, as of the whole suite, are in English (as Debussy conceived it), no. 2 being 'Jimbo's [i.e. Jumbo's] Lullaby' and no. 6 'The Golliwogg's [sic] Cakewalk'.

Children's Games (Fr., *Jeux d'enfants*), suite of 12 pieces by Bizet for piano duet, 1871; he afterwards made an orchestra suite of five, and five more were later orchestrated by Karg-Elert.

Chilingirian Quartet, British string quartet led by Levon Chilingirian; founded 1971.

Chimney of King René, The, see KING RENÉ'S CHIMNEY.

Chinese block, see WOOD BLOCK.

Chinese pavilion, see JINGLING JOHNNY.

Chisholm, Erik (1904–65), British composer – also pianist, conductor and professor at the University of Cape Town. Works include two piano concertos, no. 2 subtitled 'The Indian' (indebted to Indian music); trilogy of short operas *Murder in Three Keys*; also symphonies, chamber music, etc.

chitarra (It.), guitar.

chitarrone (It., big guitar), largest ARCHLUTE with greatly extended neck, cultivated in 16th and 17th centuries; used for CONTINUO, e.g. in opera.

chiuso (It.), closed; (of horn notes) 'stopped' by the placing of the hand in the bell.

Chocolate Soldier, The (Ger., *Der tapfere Soldat*, The Valiant Soldier), operetta by O. Straus, produced in Vienna, 1908. Libretto by L. Jacobson and R. Bernauer, based on Shaw's *Arms and the Man*.

choir, (1) a body of singers, especially in a place of worship ('chorus' or 'choral society' being more used in other contexts); (2) part of a church where singers are seated; (3) usual abbreviation for CHOIR-ORGAN.

choir-organ (or simply *choir*), division of an organ (a manual and the equipment controlled by it) having predominantly soft stops. (Originally 'chair-organ', the pipes being placed behind the organist's chair or stool.)

choke cymbals, see CYMBAL.

Chopin, Frédéric François (French form of Polish 'Fryderyk Franciszek') (1810–49), Polish composer and pianist of partly French descent. Born at Zelazowa Wola, near Warsaw; studied in Warsaw; settled in Paris, touring from there (e.g. to England and Scotland). Never revisited Poland (under Russian occupation) but was keen patriot and student of Polish literature. Never married; met 'George Sand' (real name Aurore Dudevant) in 1838, and lived with her till 1847; suffered from consumption, gave his last public concert in 1848, and died in Paris. Works – nearly all for piano, and equally remarkable for harmonic imagination and for use of piano technique – include three sonatas (no. 2, in B♭ minor, including a funeral march), four scherzos, 25 preludes, 27 studies, 19 nocturnes, 19 waltzes, 10 polonaises, at least 55 mazurkas (these and some other works influenced by Polish folk-music), four ballades; also two piano concertos, Sonata for cello and piano, songs, etc. Contributor to the HEXAMERON. See also SYLPHIDES.

Chopsticks, anonymous short quick-waltz tune for piano, playable with two outstretched forefingers, or with the little fingers if the hand is held vertically like a chopper. Variations have been written on it by, e.g., Borodin, Rimsky-Korsakov and Liszt. The French and German names for it mean 'cutlets' – thus the reference is to chopping (not to chopsticks in the Chinese sense).

choragus, musical office-holder at Oxford University, subordinate to professor – office revived in 1926, after lapsing.

choral, (1, Eng.) relating to a choir or chorus; see CHORAL FANTASIA; CHORAL SYMPHONY; (2, Ger.) = CHOR-ALE (in the sense of a traditional congregational hymn-tune).

chorale, (1) Ger., *Choral,* i.e. type of traditional German metrical hymn-tune for congregational use, e.g. 'A Stronghold Sure' (*Ein' feste Burg*), perhaps composed by Martin Luther; this tune, like many others, was made use of by Bach. So *chorale prelude,* instrumental piece (usually for organ) based on a chorale. (The English word *chorale* is mock-foreign and synthetic, but useful in avoiding 'choral prelude', suggesting a choral work.) For *Passion chorale,* see PASSION. (2) a choir or choral society – French word, also used in the title of some US (and, more rarely, British) choirs.

Choral Fantasia, the name generally given to Beethoven's Fantasy, op. 80, for piano, chorus and orchestra (the words, by C. Kuffner, in praise of music) – first performed in 1808. It appears to have been used as a kind of study for Beethoven's Ninth Symphony (see next entry).

choral symphony, either (1) a symphony in the normal sense but using a chorus as well, or (2) a work of symphonic dimensions but written for voices alone, e.g. Bantock's *Atlanta in Calydon* (after Swinburne), first performed in 1912. The first of these two senses is much the commoner. 'The Choral Symphony', in common usage, is Beethoven's Symphony no. 9 in D minor, first performed in 1824, having three purely orchestral movements followed by a setting of Schiller's 'Ode to Joy' for four solo singers, chorus and orchestra; among other examples (in the first sense) are Mahler's SYMPHONY OF A THOUSAND and Vaughan Williams's SEA SYMPHONY.

chord, any simultaneous combination of notes – but sometimes defined as any simultaneous combination of not less than three notes. (Whether the notes form a CONCORD or discord is irrelevant: the term *chord* is not related to these.) See also following entries.

chording, (1) (satisfactory or unsatisfactory) intonation of a chord by several performers, e.g. a choir; (2) in composition, the spacing of the intervals in a chord; (3, US) the provision of chords, e.g. on a guitar, to accompany a melody.

chordophone, term scientifically used to classify an instrument in which a vibrating string produces the musical sound; e.g. harp, violin, piano.

chord-symbol, type of simple harmonic notation used, e.g., by guitarist in playing pop music: e.g. C7 means a chord of the minor seventh on C (i.e. C-E-G-B♭), but no stipulation is made as to which note should form the bass. Cp. FIGURED BASS.

choreographic poem, a composition for the use of ballet (presumably on the analogy of SYMPHONIC POEM) – description used by Ravel of his LA VALSE.

chôro (Port.), an ensemble of serenaders in late 19th-century Brazil. The title was applied also to characteristic pieces; see VILLA-LOBOS for a particular use.

chorus, (1) a substantial body of singers not all singing separate parts; (2) colloquial term for the REFRAIN of a song, in which a chorus (in the first sense) often joins; (3) term figuratively used for a group of instruments, or organ stops, used in the manner of a chorus (i.e. not for solo effect, but as contributing a mass of sound).

Chou, Wen-Chung (b. 1923), Chinese composer who settled in USA, 1946; works include *Landscapes* for orchestra, *In the Mode of Shang* for chamber orchestra.

Chout, see BUFFOON.

Christie, William (b. 1944), American harpsichordist and conductor. Settled in Paris and founded Les Arts Florissants (1979), an ensemble devoted to baroque music.

Christmas Carol, A, opera by Musgrave, produced in Norfolk, Virginia, 1979, with libretto (after Dickens) by the composer.

Christmas Concerto, name given to Corelli's Concerto Grosso in G minor, op. 6, no. 8, for strings and continuo, 1712 – intended for church use, inscribed 'made for Christmas night', and having a 'Pastorale' at the end. (The name also applies to Torelli's Concerto Grosso in G minor, op. 8 no. 6, of 1708 and other works.)

Christmas Eve (Rus., *Noch pered rozhdestvom*, The Night Before Christmas), opera by Rimsky-Korsakov, produced in St Petersburg, 1895, with libretto (after Gogol's comic village episode) by the composer. See also LITTLE SLIPPERS (Tchaikovsky's opera based on same plot).

Christmas Oratorio, (1) work for soloists, chorus, and orchestra by Bach (Ger., *Weihnachts-Oratorium*), 1734 (BWV 248), in the form of six cantatas – the first for performance on Christmas Day and the others to follow on particular days up to Epiphany. Text, the biblical Christmas story, with commentary; (2) short English title often used for the work by Schütz, literally entitled (in German) 'History of the joyful and merciful birth of God's and Mary's Son, Jesus Christ', 1664.

Christmas Symphony (Haydn), see LAMENTATION SYMPHONY.

Christoff, Boris (b. 1914), Bulgarian bass-baritone who trained in Rome and won international eminence in opera (La Scala, Milan, 1947), e.g. in title-role of BORIS GODUNOV (which he twice recorded).

Christopher Columbus (Fr., *Christophe Colomb*), opera by Milhaud, produced (in German) in Berlin, 1930. Libretto (in French) by Paul Claudel. The opera uses a cinema screen – e.g. to show images of exotic landscapes when Columbus reads Marco Polo's *Travels*.

chromatic, pertaining to intervals outside the diatonic (major or minor) scale; *chromatic scale*, ascending or descending by semitones; *chromatic compass*, see COMPASS. So also *chromatic progression*, a chord-progression which involves departure from the prevailing diatonic scale; *chromaticism*, tendency of a piece or a composer towards the use of intervals outside the prevailing diatonic scale, and thus often towards a plentiful use of modulation (but the term is not used to cover ATONAL music, etc.). So also *chromatic* HARMONICA, *chromatic* HARP. And see following entry.

Chromatic Fantasia and Fugue, by Bach for harpsichord, completed in 1730 (BWV 903), the fantasia being notable for CHROMATIC progressions.

Chung, Kyung-Wha (b. 1948), Korean violinist; she won the Leventritt competition (jointly with Zukerman) in New York in 1967 and appeared in London with the London Symphony Orchestra, 1970. The pianist-conductor Myung-Whun Chung (see next entry) is her brother; the cellist Myung-Wha Chung is her sister.

Chung, Myung-Whun (b. 1953), Korean pianist and conductor, brother of the foregoing. In 1989 he became music director of the new Paris Opera at the Bastille.

church cantata, cantata written for actual performance during church service, though not forming part of the liturgy – e.g. those by Bach.

church modes, see MODE; the term is a misleading one since, though the

modes persisted in church use and are to be heard, e.g., in plainsong and in 16th-century church music, they were by no means specially ecclesiastical and are found equally in the secular music (whether folk-music or works by known composers) of the period.

ciaccona (It., in older spelling *ciacona*) = CHACONNE.

Ciconia, Johannes (*c*.1335–1412), Flemish composer of church music and author of a musical treatise; also priest. Worked for some time in Italy.

Cikker, Jan (b. 1911), Czechoslovak composer of *Resurrection* (after Tolstoy), *Mr Scrooge* (after Dickens) and other operas; also orchestral, chamber and piano works.

Cilèa, Francesco (1866–1950), Italian composer chiefly of operas (including ADRIENNE LECOUVREUR); also of Sonata for cello and piano, piano solos, etc.

Cimarosa, Domenico (1749–1801), Italian composer, chiefly of operas (more than 60); pupil of Sacchini and Piccinni. Held court posts in St Petersburg and then Vienna, where THE SECRET MARRIAGE was produced, 1792; this won wide fame for its combination of dramatic and musical values, in a style near Mozart's. Said to have been condemned to death in Naples for pro-French-Revolutionary sentiment, but reprieved and banished; died in Venice on way back to Russia. Other works include THE MUSICAL DIRECTOR (comic vocal piece) and church music.

cimbalom (Hung.), large concert DULCIMER (having horizontal strings struck with hammers and a damping mechanism) used in Hungarian popular music and in certain works indebted to this – e.g. Kodály's opera HÁRY JÁNOS (and the suite drawn from it).

cimbasso, the term used by Verdi for the lowest brass instrument in most of his opera scores; it apparently means a valved trombone of bass or double-bass range, though most modern performances employ a tuba.

Cinderella, title of various stage works based on Perrault's fairy-tale, e.g.: (1) opera by Isouard, produced in Paris, 1810 (*Cendrillon,* libretto by C. J. Etienne); (2) opera by Rossini, produced in Rome, 1817 (*La Cenerentola,* libretto by J. Ferretti); (3) opera by Massenet, produced in Paris, 1899 (*Cendrillon,* libretto by H. Cain); (4) opera by Wolf-Ferrari, produced in Venice, 1900 (*Cenerentola,* libretto by M. Pezzè-Pescolato); (5) ballet with songs, by Prokofiev, produced in Moscow, 1945 (*Zolushka,* i.e. the Ash-Girl).

cinema organ, see THEATRE ORGAN.

cipher(ing), the continuous sounding, through a mechanical mishap, of a note on the organ.

Cis (Ger.), C sharp; *Cisis,* C double-sharp.

citole, see CITTERN.

cittern (also *cither, cithern*), plucked, wire-strung instrument (used for popular music, *c.*1550–1700) with strings set in pairs tuned to the same note (like lute) but built with flat back (like guitar). An earlier name is 'citole' despite D. G. Rossetti's poem 'The Blessed Damozel', which implies that the two are different; a 'gittern', however, is not a cittern but an old English name for a certain type of guitar.

City of Birmingham Symphony Orchestra, orchestra founded in 1920, becoming full-time, 1944; musical director since 1980, Simon Rattle.

Clair de lune (Fr., Moonlight), piano piece by Debussy (later subjected to multifarious arrangements); see BERGAMASCA.

clarabella, see CLARIBEL.

Clari (opera), see BISHOP (H.).

claribel, claribel flute (or *clarabella*), an organ stop of flute-like tone.

clarinet, woodwind instrument with single reed and normally a wooden (exceptionally, a metal) body, in use since mid-18th century; constituent of symphony orchestra, military band, dance band, etc. Also favoured as solo instrument and in chamber music – *clarinet trio, clarinet quartet,* trio or quartet incorporating clarinet; *clarinet quintet,* string quartet plus clarinet. Standard orchestral sizes of clarinet are those in B♭ (lowest note, D below middle C) and in A, a semitone lower, both being TRANSPOSING INSTRUMENTS with an upward range of more than three octaves. Other instruments found are the *bass clarinet* in B♭, an octave below the standard B♭ (and *bass clarinet* in A; very rare); *high clarinet* in E♭, a fourth above the standard B♭ (and *high clarinet* in D; rare); clarinet in C (not a TRANSPOSING INSTRUMENT) used, e.g., by Beethoven, rarely later; *alto clarinet* (rare; similar to BASSET-HORN); *double-bass clarinet* (also called *pedal clarinet* and very rare) an octave below bass clarinet. See also BASSET-CLARINET.

clarino (It.), name used for high, florid 17th–18th-century trumpet parts or, in usage up to the 18th century, for the (valveless) trumpet itself.

clarionet, obsolete spelling of CLARINET.

Clarke, Jeremiah (*c.*1670–1707), English composer, pupil of Blow; organist, e.g. at St Paul's Cathedral, London. Disappointed in love, he shot himself. Composed church and stage music, choral setting of *Alexander's Feast* (after Dryden), etc., and also harpsichord pieces including *The Prince of Denmark's March* – see TRUMPET VOLUNTARY, under which title (sometimes with a misattribution to Purcell) it is widely known.

Clarke, Rebecca (1886–1979), British viola-player and composer; wrote orchestral and choral music as well as works featuring the viola. Settled in USA, died in New York.

clàrsach (Gael.), ancient small Celtic harp, revived in the 20th century for folk-song accompaniment.

classic(al), classicism, terms commonly used very vaguely, but with three main areas of meaning; (1, as distinct from, e.g., 'popular' or 'folk'), serious, learned, belonging to a sophisticated and written tradition; (2, as opposed to ROMANTIC), aesthetically dependent supposedly more on formal appeal than on emotional stimulation; (3, = *Viennese classic*), belonging to the period and predominant musical style of Haydn, Mozart and Beethoven, *c.*1770–1830. So also, the *classical concerto* (Mozart's); so too (as abstraction), *classicism*. See also NEO-CLASSIC and the following entry.

Classical Symphony, title of Symphony no. 1 by Prokofiev, first performed 1918; its Haydn-sized orchestra and modernized Haydnesque idiom (but with a gavotte instead of the customary minuet of Haydn's period) allude to the first sense given in the preceding entry.

Claudel, Paul (1868–1955), French dramatist and poet. See CHRISTOPHER COLUMBUS, JOAN OF ARC AT THE STAKE, MILHAUD.

clavecin (Fr.), harpsichord; *claveciniste*, harpsichord-player (term also used for a French composer for the harpsichord in the days of that instrument's pre-eminence, e.g. Couperin).

claves (Sp.), a pair of wooden sticks beaten together to mark the rhythm in Latin-American dance music, etc.; see BIRTWISTLE.

clavicembalo (It.), harpsichord. The term literally means 'keyed dulcimer' and is normally abbreviated to *cembalo*.

clavichord, soft-toned keyboard instrument with strings hit by metal 'tangents'; much used from 16th to 18th centuries as a solo instrument (not loud enough, e.g., for concertos for which a harpsichord was used), and revived in the 20th century for old music. (Since the tangents remain in contact with the string while it is vibrating – unlike the hammers of a piano or the quills of a harpsichord – it is possible by 'shaking' the individual notes of a keyboard to produce a kind of vibrato effect; in Ger., *Bebung*.)

clavicytherium, rare 15th–18th century instrument of harpsichord type with perpendicular strings as in the upright piano.

clavier, term originally French and meaning keyboard, or manual (of an organ); taken into German, where the modern spelling is *Klavier*, and there having its meaning extended to include a piano or any keyboard instrument; used in English for contexts in which a definite choice between different keyboard instruments is not implied – e.g. 'Bach's clavier concertos' (intended for harpsichord, but now equally often played on piano); THE WELL-TEMPERED CLAVIER (intended by Bach as suitable for harpsichord or clavichord). See also following entry.

Clavierübung (Ger., Clavier Exercise), title of a work by Bach (who borrowed the title from Kuhnau) in three sections (1731, 1735, 1739), consisting of works for harpsichord (including the ITALIAN CONCERTO) and organ. The GOLDBERG VARIATIONS, 1742, were also headed *Clavierübung* and may be regarded as the fourth section of the work.

Clay, Frederic (1838–89), British composer of 'I'll sing thee songs of Araby' and other favourite Victorian ballads; also of stage music and cantatas.

clef, sign which fixes the location of a particular note on the staff – and hence the location of all other notes; placed normally at the beginning of each line of music and at any point where a new clef cancels the old. The TREBLE clef fixes the note G above middle C; the ALTO and TENOR fix middle C; the BASS fixes the F below middle C. Other clefs are obsolete, but the SOPRANO lingered well into the 19th century.

Clemency of Titus, The (It., *La clemenza di Tito*), opera by Mozart (K621), produced in Prague, 1791; libretto by C. Mazzolà, after Metastasio – extolling imperial magnanimity, and so suiting an opera composed for the coronation of the Austrian Emperor as King of Bohemia. (Previous operas on this plot were composed by Gluck and by Hasse – Mozart heard the latter in 1770.)

Clemens non Papa, nickname given to Jacob Clement (*c.*1510-*c.*1558), Flemish composer of Latin church music, psalms in Flemish, songs, etc. (The nickname, formerly thought to mean 'Clement not the Pope' [i.e. Clement VIII], was probably designed to avoid confusion with a Flemish poet, Clemens Papa, of the composer's home town of Ypres.)

Clementi, Aldo (b. 1925), Italian composer of a series of chamber music pieces called *Ideograms* and another called *Informels*; also Concerto for two pianos and wind orchestra, etc.

Clementi, Muzio (1752–1832), Italian composer and pianist who, showing great gifts as a child, was taken to England by Peter Beckford, MP, and thereafter lived mainly there; died at Evesham. Composed mainly for piano, pioneering a new (non-harpsichord) technique. Works include more than 60 sonatas (some with illustrative intent, e.g. one called *Didone abbandonata*, 'The Forsaken Dido') and a famous collection of studies, GRADUS AD PARNASSUM; in addition to symphonies, chamber music, etc. Also entered the piano-manufacturing trade.

Clemenza di Tito, La, see CLEMENCY OF TITUS.

Clérambault, Louis Nicolas (1676–1749), French composer of cantatas, harpsichord and organ pieces, etc.; church organist in Paris.

Cleveland Orchestra, American orchestra founded in 1918. Its conductor since 1984 has been Christoph von Dohnányi.

Cliburn, Van (real forenames Harvey Lavan) (b. 1934), American pianist, winner of International Tchaikovsky Prize in Moscow, 1958. Endowed a piano competition in Texas, 1962. After some years' absence from concerts, he resumed performances in 1989.

Cloak, The (It., *Il tabarro*), one-act opera by Puccini, produced in New York, 1918, with the other two one-act operas (SISTER ANGELICA and GIANNI SCHICCHI) that follow it to form what Puccini called his Triptych (*Trittico*). It is under a cloak that a husband reveals to his wife the body of her lover whom he has killed.

Clock, The, nickname of Haydn's Symphony no. 101 in D (Hob. I:101) – from the clock-like ticking at the opening of the slow movement.

close, a cadence; *full close,* perfect cadence; *half-close,* imperfect cadence. (See CADENCE.)

close harmony, harmony in which the notes of a chord lie near together – this sometimes implying, e.g. in popular *close-harmony trios,* etc., that the supporting harmonizing notes keep as near to the melody as possible without any particular logic of harmonic PROGRESSION.

cluster, a group of adjacent notes on the piano keyboard played together, e.g. with the flat of the forearm – demonstrated in public by Cowell (aged 15) in 1912; Ives was independently using the device at the same time (see CONCORD SONATA). The usual US term is *tone-cluster,* for which the English would be *note-cluster* (see TONE, 5).

Clutsam, George Howard (1866–1951), Australian-born composer (especially of stage works), pianist and critic who settled in England, 1889; 'edited' (i.e. mauled) Schubert's music for the musical play *Lilac Time.*

Coates, Albert (1882–1953), British composer (operas *Samuel Pepys* and *Pickwick,* etc.), and conductor, born in Russia of English parents; conducted in Russia both before and after the 1917 Revolution, but lived from 1919 mainly in London until going as conductor in 1946 to South Africa, where he died.

Coates, Eric (1886–1957), British composer of light songs (e.g. 'Bird Songs at Eventide'), light orchestral pieces (e.g. *The Three Bears, The Three Elizabeths*), etc.; previously viola-player.

Cockaigne, concert-overture by Elgar, first performed in 1901. Subtitled 'In London Town' and punning on 'Cockaigne' (imaginary land of idle luxury) and 'cockney'.

Cocteau, Jean (1889–1963), French writer. See ANTIGONE, MILHAUD, OEDIPUS REX.

coda (It., tail), in musical analysis, a section of a movement considered to be added at the end as a rounding-off rather than as a structural necessity. Thus in SONATA-FORM, the coda (if there is one) occurs only after both principal subjects have been recapitulated in the tonic key. (As with all such terms of analysis, the meaning here given is of value only as an approximation: Beethoven's codas, for instance, have great importance in his musical design and do not strike the listener as 'stuck on' at the end.) See also CODETTA (diminutive form).

codetta (It., little tail), in musical analysis, a rounding-off passage which does for a section of a movement what a CODA does for a whole movement.

Coffee Cantata, nickname for a humorous cantata by Bach (BWV 211), composed about 1732 (now sometimes given as comic opera), alluding to the contemporary craze for coffee. Known also by its opening words, 'Schweigt stille, plaudert nicht' (Ger., Be silent, do not chatter).

cogli, see CON.

Cohen, Harriet (1895–1967), British pianist for whom a number of British composers wrote music expressly – particularly Bax. CBE, 1938.

Coleman, Edward (c.1605–1669), English viol-player and composer of stage music, songs, etc.; wrote part of the music to THE SIEGE OF RHODES, to which his son, Edward (?–1699), also contributed.

Coleridge, Samuel Taylor (1772–1834), British poet. See GRIFFES.

Coleridge-Taylor, Samuel (1875–1912), British composer, born in Croydon of a British mother and West African father; no relation of the poet Samuel Taylor Coleridge. Pupil of Stanford. Wrote works inclining to exotic and picturesque associations (cantatas HIAWATHA and A Tale of Old Japan; Symphonic Variations on an African Air; etc.), as well as a violin concerto, a string quartet and other chamber music, many piano solos, etc.

Colette [Sidonie Gabrielle Claudine Colette] (1873–1954), French writer. See CHILD AND THE SPELLS.

Colgrass, Michael [Charles] (b. 1932), American composer, also percus-

sionist. He has written several works for percussion; As Quiet As for orchestra; Virgil's Dream for four actor-singers and four mime-musicians; etc.

coll', colla, colle, see CON.

collegium (Lat.), a learned society; collegium musicum, term used in the 18th century for a musical ensemble, and revived in the 20th century mainly by groups at universities, etc., whose members apply historical knowledge to the performance of baroque and older music.

Collingwood, Lawrance [Arthur] (1887–1982), British composer (of operas including Macbeth, etc.) and conductor, especially of opera; CBE, 1948.

coloratura (It.), term applied to an agile, florid style of vocal music or to its performance; coloratura soprano, soprano with voice suited to this.

colour (of musical tone), see TONE-COLOUR. See also following entries.

colour-organ, term used in English for the light-projecting instrument specified in Skryabin's PROMETHEUS, 1911.

Colour Symphony, A, symphony by Bliss, 1922 – its four movements being interpretations of purple, red, blue and green, in the light of their heraldic associations.

come (It.), as, like; come prima, as at first, as at the opening, etc.; come sopra, as above.

comédie-ballet, a type of French theatrical entertainment combining a stage play, songs and dancing, as exemplified by Molière's LE BOURGEOIS GENTILHOMME, with music by Lully.

commedia dell'arte (It., comedy of the profession, i.e. not amateur), type of Italian entertainment originating in the 16th century, using masks, improvisation, and stock types, such as the gullible doctor or boastful soldier, in a parody of social behaviour; of significant influence on Italian comic opera.

commodo, mis-spelling for COMODO.

common chord, see TRIAD.

common metre (in hymns), the metre of a four-line stanza having eight, six, eight and six syllables per line.

common time, four QUARTER-NOTES (crotchets) to the bar, written 4/4 or **c**. (The latter sign is not a 'C' for common time, but derives from an obsolete way of indicating time-values.)

community-singing, singing by the public at a meeting, a sporting event, etc. So *community songs*, those suitable for such occasions.

comodo (It., easy), easily flowing, leisurely.

compass, the range of a voice or instrument from the highest to the lowest note obtainable; *chromatic compass*, the range in which a complete CHROMATIC scale is playable (said of instruments which for part of their compass are not chromatic, e.g. trombone, which has gaps at the lower end of its range).

Compère, Loyset (*c*.1445–1518), Flemish composer who worked in Milan, then served Charles VIII of France. Works include Masses, motets, chansons.

composition, (1) the art of creating original works of music; (2) a piece of music regarded as the result of a deliberate individual creative act – term therefore not usually applied (a) to a folk-tune, which may have reached its present shape through oral tradition and untutored adaptation, and (b) to a musical work not thoroughly original but ARRANGED from some other work. Neither of these senses has any connection with the use of the word in the following entry.

composition pedal, composition piston, foot-operated or hand-operated lever on the organ bringing into action a preselected group of stops simultaneously.

compound time, any musical metre not classifiable as SIMPLE TIME, in which the beat-unit divides into two. Thus 12/8 is a compound time, because the unit of beat is ♩. (the bar having four of these) and this divides not into two but into three sub-units (♪♪♪). (The term is, however, now more academic than practical: it is of no use in analysing, say, a score by Stravinsky, or in classifying a RUMBA in which the beat is of non-uniform length.)

comprimario (It., from *con*, 'with', and *primo*, 'first'), a (male) singer of supporting roles in Italian opera, particularly one who has an aria to himself. The feminine form, *comprimaria*, is also encountered.

computer-composed music, type of music in which some post-1950 composers have used a computer program to determine the succession of notes, a succession which may be (as in some works by Xenakis) random at any one point but conforming to an overall statistical pattern. A *computer organ*, however, is simply an electronic organ in which a digital computer process is used to produce the range of sounds: see ORGAN (3).

Comte Ory, Le, see COUNT ORY.

Comus, (1) masque with words by Milton, originally produced in 1634 with music by H. Lawes; (2) work in which Milton's words were adapted, and new music was provided by T. Arne, 1738; (3) ballet with music arranged by Lambert from Purcell, some of Milton's words being spoken; produced in 1942.

con (It.), with; *cogli, coi, col, coll', colla, colle,* with the. (In general, see next word of phrase.) *Con brio,* with spirit; *colla parte,* the tempo and expression of the accompaniment to be accommodated to that of the soloist; *clarinetti coi flauti,* the clarinets to play the same notes as the flutes.

Concentus Musicus Wien, Vienna-based ensemble founded in 1953 by Harnoncourt; its hundreds of recordings on period instruments set a standard in historical treatment of Bach and other baroque composers.

concert, a substantial performance of music before an audience (other than in conjunction with a stage performance, or as part of a religious service or similar ceremony, etc.); a performance given by one or two, however, is not called a concert but a RECITAL. An older use denotes a body of performers (= CONSORT); for a modern revival, see PINNOCK. See also following entries.

concertant (Fr.), in a concerted form, with interplay between instruments – term used, e.g., by Stravinsky, *Duo concertant* (1932) for violin and piano, avoiding terms 'sonata' or 'suite'; so also (feminine form) *concertante,* as in F. Martin's *Petite symphonie concertante* for harp, harpsichord, piano and two

string orchestras (1945). See also following entry.

concertante, (1, Fr.) see preceding entry; (2, It.) in a concerted form; *sinfonia concertante,* term used for a work for solo instrument(s) and orchestra, with the implication that the form followed is nearer that of the symphony than of the concerto. Similarly *concerto.*

concertato, concertata (It.), concerted (masc., fem. forms). The term *concertato style* is used by some historians for the new style of ensemble writing (vocal or instrumental) of the early 17th century founded on the practice of CONTINUO.

concert band, American type of band of woodwind, brass and percussion instruments (similar to, but not identical with, British MILITARY BAND) for which works have been expressly written by Hindemith, Schoenberg and various American composers.

concerted, pertaining to a performance by several people on more or less equal terms; so a *concerted number* (more usually called 'ensemble') in an opera.

Concertgebouw (Du., concert-building), name of an Amsterdam concert-hall, opened in 1888, and of its resident orchestra (now called the Royal Concertgebouw Orchestra). Conductor, 1961–88, Bernard Haitink (at first jointly with Eugen Jochum); from 1988, Riccardo Chailly.

concertina, hexagonal-bodied instrument with bellows, similar to ACCORDION in principle but having only studs (never a piano-like keyboard) for the fingers. Popular for informal occasions (and even sometimes penetrating the concert-hall) in the last century, it has now been almost entirely superseded by the accordion.

concertino, (1) a little (and usually rather light) CONCERTO, in the first sense given below; (2) in older usage, the smaller group of instruments in a CONCERTO GROSSO.

concertize (US, chiefly promoters' jargon), to give concerts.

concertmaster (US), the first violinist of an orchestra (following German term *Konzertmeister*) – in British usage, 'leader'.

concerto (It., a concert, a concerted performance), (1, in general modern usage) a work making contrasted use of solo instrument(s) and orchestra – generally in three movements, and generally keeping to certain structural principles of which Mozart is regarded as the classic exponent; (2, earlier use) an orchestral work in several movements, with or without solo instruments (see CONCERTO GROSSO and BRANDENBURG CONCERTOS); (3) term used apart from this by composers for exceptional reasons of their own – e.g. Bach's ITALIAN CONCERTO, which, though for a single player, employs an effect of instrumental contrast between the two manuals of a harpsichord; Bartók's Concerto for Orchestra (1944), so called because of the solo functions performed by individual orchestral instruments.

concerto grosso (It., great concerto), (1) type of orchestral work prevalent in 17th and 18th centuries, usually (but not always) having an interplay between the larger body of instruments ('concerto' or 'ripieno') and a smaller group ('concertino') each with its own CONTINUO – as distinct from the modern concerto, in which only one soloist (rarely more, and anyway not a group) provides the contrast with the orchestra; (2) title used for certain 20th-century works based broadly on 17th- and 18th-century models – though Bloch's Concerto Grosso no. 1, for example, has only piano soloist instead of a concertino. (See NEO-CLASSIC.)

concert-overture, see OVERTURE.

concitato (It.), excited; *stile concitato* (= an agitated style), a compositional device defined and used by Monteverdi to represent emotional excitement.

concord, a chord which seems harmonically at rest; its opposite, *discord*, seems unsettled, thus requiring a RESOLUTION to another chord. What constitutes a concord is not something fixed: throughout history composers have tended to admit more and different chords as concords, and in, e.g., much TWELVE-NOTE music, the ideas of concord and discord need not have any structural relevance for the composer.

Concord Sonata, Piano Sonata no. 2 by Ives (inscribed 'Concord, Mass., 1840–60'), completed in 1915, first performed in 1939. The movements are I, Emerson; II, Hawthorne; III, The Alcotts; IV, Thoreau; and the music, in Ives's characteristically experimental vein, uses such devices as CLUSTERS of notes by laying a strip of wood on the keyboard.

concrete music (Fr., *musique concrète*), type of quasi-musical organization of real, 'concrete' sounds (from nature or man-made environment) recorded and arranged on tape – a technique developed chiefly by Pierre Schaeffer at the Paris radio station in 1948–9. The process was soon absorbed in ELECTRONIC MUSIC.

conduct, to direct a performance with the motions of a baton or the hands (but formerly, e.g. in early 19th-century England before the advent of the baton, *to conduct* was simply to be in charge of the performance, usually while also playing the piano or organ). So *conductor*, etc.

conductus, in medieval music, a type of secular vocal composition having one 'given' part (CANTUS FIRMUS) to which other parts were set in close harmony – the 'given' part being either specially composed or taken from some other secular work, not from plainsong. See MOTET.

conga, a modern Afro-Cuban dance with a pronounced syncopation; *conga drum* (or simply *conga*), a long, finger-played drum, taken from Latin-American bands into post-1950 concert percussion. Such drums usually come in sets of two or more pitches.

conjunct motion, see MOTION.

Connolly, Justin [Riveagh] (b. 1933), British composer, pupil of Fricker; also studied law. Teacher at RCM. Compositions include *Anima* for viola and orchestra, and several works called *Triad* (each for some kind of three-some).

Consecration of the House, The (Ger., *Die Weihe des Hauses*), title of a German play to which Beethoven wrote an overture and incidental music, 1822. The play, by C. Meisl, was adapted from an earlier play, Kotzebue's *The Ruins of Athens*, to which Beethoven had also written an overture and incidental music.

consecutive, term applied to harmonic intervals of like kind succeeding one another. E.g. C struck with the E above, and then F struck with the A above (each of these pairs forming the interval of a THIRD) would give *consecutive thirds*. The sounding of *consecutive fifths* (see FIFTH) was avoided for about five centuries before 1890 as a musically poor effect – with certain very rare and deliberate exceptions; consecutive fifths are therefore still banned in academic exercises based on formerly current idiom. *Consecutive octaves* come under a similar ban in strict PART-writing, since two voices singing consecutive octaves would not be singing real parts at all, but just the same tune at an octave's distance. But in writing for an orchestra or piano, for instance, consecutive octaves are recognized as valid. 'Hidden fifths' are consecutive fifths not actually present but thought to be implied, and therefore equally liable to academic disapproval.

conservatoire, -torium, -tory, school of musical training – originally in Italian, *conservatorio*, meaning an orphanage where children were 'conserved' and given musical and other training. (*Conservatoire* should be regarded as French; *conservatory* is unexceptionable English; *conservatorium* is the German form and is used also in Australia.)

console, the part of an organ actually at the player's command – manuals, pedals, stops, pistons, etc.

consonance = CONCORD.

consort, old English word (16th–17th century) for a group of instrumentalists, e.g. *consort of viols*; term revived as name for post-1950 ensembles devoted to such music, e.g. the (British) *Consort of Musicke*: see ROOLEY. The historical meaning of the (rare) terms *broken consort* and *whole consort* is uncertain, but the view that they respectively represent mixed instruments and instruments of one family is now discredited. See also following entry.

consort song, modern term for the type of old English song (dating from the late 16th and early 17th centuries) in which a consort, generally of viols, accompanies a solo voice or voices.

Constant, Marius (b. 1925), composer and conductor born in Romania who settled in France after World War II. Works include small-scale opera *Pygmalion* (not based on Shaw's play); a violin concerto; *Three Complexes* for piano and double-bass; ballet *Paradise Lost*. He compiled the version of *Carmen* (called *The Tragedy of Carmen*) used for Peter Brook's touring production, 1981.

Consul, The, opera by Menotti, produced in Philadelphia, 1950. Libretto by the composer: the action takes place in a modern totalitarian state, from which escape to a 'free' country is made impossible by red tape at that country's consulate. (The consul himself never appears.)

Contes d'Hoffmann, Les, see TALES OF HOFFMANN.

continental fingering, see FINGERING.

continuo (It., abbr. of *basso continuo*), a type of accompaniment (current particularly *c*.1600–1750) played from a bass-line, most commonly on a keyboard instrument. From the bass-notes, the player worked out the correct harmonies, sometimes aided by numerical shorthand indications provided by the composer (see FIGURED BASS). To *play the continuo*, therefore, is not to play a particular kind of instrument; it is to play on a keyboard instrument (or lute, etc.) a harmonized accompaniment from this type of bass – or to reinforce (e.g. on cello and double-bass) this bass-line without the chords. Hence *continuo group* of such instruments, e.g. in a Monteverdi opera orchestra. The historic English equivalent for *continuo* is 'thorough-bass', i.e. 'through-bass'; but *continuo* has now acquired standard usage in English.

contra-, contre-, Kontra-, Italian, French and German prefixes signifying (of an instrument) 'lower in pitch', usually about an octave lower. So, e.g., *contrebasse, Kontrabass,* French and German terms for DOUBLE-BASS; *contre-basson, Kontrafagott,* French and German terms for double-bassoon (see BASSOON). The Italian terms for these instruments are usually found in non-Italian musical contexts as *contrabasso* and *contrafagotto*: correct modern Italian, however, gives *contrabbasso* and *controfagotto*. The practice of introducing *contra-* as an element of made-up English words (*contrabass, contra-bassoon*) is illogical: the true linguistic counterpart of this prefix is 'counter-' (as in COUNTER-TENOR), and the appropriate usage here is 'double-', e.g. double-bassoon.

contrabasso, contrabbasso, contrafagotto, see preceding entry.

contralto, lower type of female voice. See also ALTO.

contrapunctus (made-up Lat.), a counterpoint; used by Bach instead of 'fugue' as a heading for movements in his THE ART OF FUGUE.

contrapuntal, pertaining to COUNTER-POINT.

Contrasts, trio by Bartók, 1938, for clarinet, violin and piano – the violinist using two instruments, one of normal tuning (G, D, A, E) and the other tuned G♯, D, A, E♭. See also MARTIRANO.

contre-, see CONTRA.

contredanse, see COUNTRY DANCE.

controfagotto (It.), double-BASSOON.

Converse, Frederick Shepherd (1871–1940), American composer, pupil of Rheinberger in Munich. Works include four operas, six symphonies and *Flivver 10,000,000* for orchestra (celebrating the manufacture of the 10 millionth Ford car).

Cooke, Arnold [Atkinson] (b. 1906), British composer, pupil of Hindemith. Works include opera *Mary Barton* (after Mrs Gaskell), six symphonies, much chamber and piano music.

Cooke, Benjamin (1734–93), British composer (pupil of Pepusch) and organist; wrote church music, glees and other vocal pieces, organ works, etc.

Cooke, Deryck [Victor] (1919–76), British musicologist who worked extensively for the BBC and who made a completion of Mahler's Symphony no. 10.

Cooke, Henry (*c.*1615–72), English bass singer and composer of church music, songs, part of the music to THE SIEGE OF RHODES, etc.

Cooper, James Fenimore (1789–1851), American novelist. See CORSAIR.

Cooper, John (*c.*1575–1626), English

composer, player of the viol and other instruments; changed name to Giovanni Coperario (or Coprario) while studying in Italy and retained this on returning. Composed music for masques, anthems, songs, fantasies and suites for viols and violins, etc.; author of *Rules how to Compose*. Teacher of the brothers Lawes.

Coperario, see preceding entry.

coperto (It.), covered, e.g. of drums muffled with a cloth to give a muted effect.

Copland, Aaron (1900–90), American composer, pupil of R. Goldmark and (in Paris) N. Boulanger; also pianist, lecturer and writer, prominent in general championing of American music. Born in Brooklyn. His work variously shows an indebtedness to jazz (*Music for the Theatre*, 1925), to cowboy songs and similar indigenous American tunes (ballets BILLY THE KID, RODEO and APPALACHIAN SPRING), and to Latin-American music (EL SALÓN MÉXICO, clarinet concerto); but elsewhere it is sometimes completely abstract, fiercely dissonant, and devoid of 'popular' influences – e.g. piano variations, a piano sonata. Other works include opera *The Tender Land*, three symphonies; QUIET CITY (orchestral suite); A LINCOLN PORTRAIT (with narrator); a piano quartet and other chamber music; film scores.

Coppélia, ballet with music by Delibes, produced in Paris, 1870. (Subtitled 'or, The Girl with Enamel Eyes' – a girl deceiving a toy-maker into thinking her a doll come to life.)

Coprario, see COOPER, JOHN.

Coq d'or, Le, French title of Rimsky-Korsakov's THE GOLDEN COCKEREL;

since this is a Russian work, there is no point in English-speaking countries in using the French title.

cor (Fr.), HORN; *cor anglais*, see ENGLISH HORN; *cor de chasse* (hunting-horn), see HORN; *tenor cor*, see MELLOPHONE.

corda (It.; pl. *corde*), a string. So, in piano-playing, *una corda* (one string) – instruction to play with soft pedal, this pedal achieving its effect (on grand pianos) by causing the hammers to hit only one instead of three strings to each note. The terms *tre corde* or *tutte le corde* (three strings, all the strings) cancel this, indicating that the soft pedal is not to be used.

Corelli, Arcangelo (1653–1713), Italian violinist, composer chiefly for his instrument, of which he was a celebrated exponent. In service as musician to a cardinal at Rome. More than anyone else, established the form of the CONCERTO GROSSO; among his examples in this form is the so-called CHRISTMAS CONCERTO. See also FOLÍA.

Corelli, Franco (b. 1921), Italian operatic tenor; first appearance at La Scala, Milan, 1954, and Metropolitan Opera, New York, 1960.

Corigliano, John [Paul] (b. 1938), American composer who has worked in television and radio music departments; works include a violin sonata, concertos for piano, for oboe and for clarinet.

Coriolanus (Ger., *Coriolan*), overture by Beethoven, 1807, to a play (not related to Shakespeare's) by H. von Collin.

Cornelius, Peter (1824–74), German composer (also critic), pupil of Liszt and admirer of Wagner; wrote THE BARBER OF BAGHDAD and other operas, some notable songs and part-songs, etc.

cornemuse (Fr.) = BAGPIPE.

cornet, (1) brass wind instrument with three valves, resembling trumpet but squatter in appearance, of wider bore and easier to play; a TRANSPOSING INSTRUMENT in B♭, with compass from E below middle C upwards for about two and a half octaves – can be switched to become an instrument in A, half a tone lower. It 'arrived' in 1820s, i.e. before valved trumpet, so found a ready role in being the only brass instrument of its pitch capable of fully chromatic use; but it has now been generally driven out of the symphony orchestra by the valved trumpet (except when called for specially – e.g. by Stravinsky in PETRUSHKA, whose score makes use of trumpets as well). It has also been driven out of dance-music, but was used in early jazz. It is still a basic instrument in the brass band (where a smaller, higher *soprano cornet* in E♭ is also used) and most military bands. (2) = CORNETT.

Cornet, Pierre (16th–17th century), Netherlands organist and composer of organ music; held court post in Brussels.

cornet-à-pistons (Fr.) = CORNET (1).

cornett, old wooden or ivory wind instrument having a cup-shaped mouthpiece (like modern brass) but finger-holes (like modern woodwind); used, e.g., in 17th-century ensemble music, and to reinforce choral soprano parts, as trombones would reinforce the lower vocal parts. The OPHICLEIDE and SERPENT are of the same family. (In modern spelling the word would be 'cornet', but the old spelling is kept to distinguish it from CORNET above.) Its use has been revived in the 20th century.

Cornish, see CORNYSHE.

corno (It.), HORN; corno inglese = ENGLISH HORN; corno di bassetto = BASSET-HORN. ('Corno di Bassetto' was Bernard Shaw's pseudonym as a music critic.)

cornopean, (1) an early form of cornet (brass instrument); (2) organ stop of soft but trumpet-like tone.

Cornyshe, William (also Cornish and other spellings) (c.1468–1523), English composer of songs (including a setting of Skelton), church music, etc.; in service as musician, actor and master to Henry VII and to Henry VIII, whom he accompanied to the Field of the Cloth of Gold, 1520 (cp. FAYRFAX, SERMISY).

Coronation Concerto, nickname for Mozart's Piano Concerto in D, K537, performed by him at coronation festivities for the Emperor Leopold II at Frankfurt, 1790 (composed 1788).

Coronation Mass, (1) nickname for Mozart's Mass in C, K317 (1779), apparently through some association with the annual crowning of a statue of the Virgin; (2) nickname sometimes formerly used for Haydn's Mass in D minor (Hob. XXII: 11), more often called NELSON MASS.

Coronation of Poppaea, The (It., L'incoronazione di Poppea), opera by Monteverdi, produced in Venice, 1642; libretto by G. F. Bussenello, on

Nero's expulsion of his wife in favour of his mistress, Poppaea.

Correa de Araujo (or Arauxo), Francisco (c.1575–1654) Spanish organist and composer of organ works (in the forms of ricercar, variations, etc.), also of psalms, etc.

Corrette, Michel (1709–95), French organist and composer of songs for the theatre, keyboard works and church music; author of an instructional method for violin.

Corsair, The, concert-overture by Berlioz (Fr., Le Corsaire), 1831. Not after Byron's poem, but after Fenimore Cooper's novel The Red Rover – title of overture was originally Le Corsaire rouge.

Cortot, Alfred [Denis] (1877–1962), Swiss-born pianist resident in France – noted as soloist and as chamber-music partner of THIBAUD and Casals, and was also conductor, musical editor and writer.

Così fan tutte, opera by Mozart, produced in Vienna, 1790. Libretto by L. da Ponte, mocking women's vows of fidelity. Title literally means 'So do all women'; subtitle is 'or, The School for Lovers' (La scuola degli amanti).

Costa, Michael [Andrew Agnellus] (1808–84). Italian-born composer-conductor who settled in London, 1829, and achieved leading position as conductor. Knighted, 1869. Composed operas, oratorios, symphonies, etc.

Costeley, Guillaume (c.1531–1606), French organist and composer, in service to French court; works include chansons, motets, organ pieces.

Cotrubas, Ileana (b. 1939), Romanian soprano who appeared at Glyndebourne from 1969, Covent Garden from 1971. She retired from opera in 1989.

counterpoint, the simultaneous combination of two or more melodies to make musical sense, one melody then being spoken of as *the counterpoint of* or *in counterpoint to* another. So *double counterpoint,* when two melodies, one above the other, can exchange position; similarly *triple,* *quadruple counterpoint* (etc.), where three, four (etc.) melodies can take up any positions relative to each other – all these being kinds of *invertible counterpoint,* as practised in FUGUE. A certain academic discipline abstracted from 16th-century practice is called *strict counterpoint*; *free counterpoint* denotes counterpoint not bound by this.

counter-subject, see FUGUE.

counter-tenor, a rare male voice higher than tenor, current in England in Purcell's and Handel's time and revived in the 20th century in concerts and opera; called male ALTO in, e.g., Anglican cathedral usage. See FALSETTO.

Count Ory (Fr., *Le Comte Ory*), opera by Rossini, produced in Paris, 1828. Libretto by E. Scribe and C. G. Delestre-Poirson: the Count is a medieval suitor whose amorous pursuit leads him to disguise himself as a hermit and then as a female pilgrim.

country dance, kind of social dance originating in England (e.g. the 'Sir Roger de Coverley') and cultivated, e.g., by Mozart and Beethoven, who called it *Kontretanz* – based on French *contredanse* (counter-dance), derived by false etymology from the English word.

coup d'archet (Fr.), stroke of the bow, the attack with the bow.

coup de glotte (Fr.), stroke of the glottis; a method of vocal 'attack' counselled by some teachers of singing.

Couperin, French family of musicians (see below). The surname alone is taken to refer to François Couperin.

Couperin, Charles (1638–1679). French organist (in Paris) and composer; father of François Couperin.

Couperin, François (1668–1733), called 'Couperin le grand' (the great), French composer, also harpsichordist and organist; pupil of his father (see preceding entry). Held official post under Louis XIV. Composed over 200 harpsichord pieces, some with picturesque titles; chamber music, organ pieces, church and other vocal music. Wrote famous book on harpsichord-playing. Nephew of Louis Couperin.

Couperin, Louis (*c.*1626–61), French organist (in Paris) and composer. Brother of Charles Couperin and uncle of François Couperin (see preceding entries).

couple (verb), on the organ, to contrive that the stops normally controlled by one manual are available also on another manual (or on pedals); or that the striking of one note should also cause the sounding of the same note an octave higher or lower. Hence *coupler,* mechanism for this, also sometimes available on a harpsichord and on some electronic keyboard instruments. (See ELECTRIC.)

coupler, see preceding entry.

couplet (Fr., not the same meaning as in English), (1) stanza of a poem, the music being repeated for each successive stanza – so an operatic song may take the form of *couplets*; (2) forerunner, e.g. in Couperin's works, of what in RONDO form is called the 'episode'.

courante (Fr.), dance in triple time occurring in the baroque SUITE.

course, term used to distinguish one string from a pair (or more) of strings which are both tuned to the same note (in unison or, rarely, an octave apart). Thus the common form of mandolin has eight strings in four double courses (a pair tuned to each note); on different forms of lute there may be some courses which are double (two strings tuned to each note), others single (one string to a note).

Covent Garden, the usual name for the London theatre whose official title has been the 'Royal Opera House, Covent Garden' since 1892 (previously the 'Royal Italian Opera House'). It has had its own resident opera and ballet companies since 1946, named Royal Opera and Royal Ballet since 1969 and 1957 respectively. The Opera's musical directors have included Solti (1961), Colin Davis (1971), Haitink (1987).

Coward, Noël (1899–1973), British playwright who wrote the music of many songs in his own plays, e.g. 'Bitter Sweet', 'Conversation Piece' – and other songs. Knighted, 1970.

cow-bells, as percussion instrument, specified, e.g., in R. Strauss's ALPINE SYMPHONY with picturesque intent.

Cowell, Henry [Dixon] (1897–1965), American composer and pianist, given to musical experiment; developed the idea of CLUSTERS of adjacent notes played, e.g., with forearm on the piano, and extended this to orchestral technique also; co-inventor of the 'Rhythmicon', electrical instrument reproducing predetermined rhythms. Prolific composer for orchestra, band and various instrumental groups; works (some with synthesized titles like *Synchrony, Tocanta*) include 21 symphonies, *Hymns and Fuguing Tunes* (after BILLINGS), opera, works for piano; also teacher and writer.

Cowen, Frederic [Hymen] (1852–1935), British composer and conductor, born in Jamaica; works include operas, six symphonies (no. 3, *Scandinavian*) and about 300 songs. Knighted, 1911.

cow-horn, brass instrument (roughly of HORN type, but valveless) made to imitate the sound of a rustic horn and used in Britten's SPRING SYMPHONY.

Cox and Box, operetta by Sullivan, produced in London, 1866. Libretto by F. C. Burnand. Cox and Box are alternate tenants (day and night) of the same lodgings.

Crabbe, George (1754–1832), English poet. See PETER GRIMES.

Craft, Robert [Lawson] (b. 1923), American conductor and writer, particularly associated with Stravinsky.

Crawford Seeger, Ruth [Porter] (also known by her maiden name as Ruth (Porter) Crawford) (1901–53), American composer. Works include a string quartet; three songs with piano, oboe, percussion; *Rissolty Rossolty* for 10 wind instruments, drums and strings. Was also collector and arranger of US folk-songs.

Creation, The (Ger., *Die Schöpfung*), oratorio by Haydn (Hob. XXI: 2), first performed in Vienna, 1798. Composed to an unidentified German translation of an English text indebted to Genesis and Milton's *Paradise Lost*. See also CREATION MASS.

Création du monde, La, see CREATION OF THE WORLD.

Creation Mass, nickname (because of a quotation in it from THE CREATION) for Haydn's Mass in B♭, 1801.

Creation of the World, The (Fr., *La Création du monde*), ballet (a long way after Genesis) with music by Milhaud, using jazz idiom; produced in Paris, 1923.

Creatures of Prometheus, The, see PROMETHEUS.

Credo, see MASS.

crescendo (It., growing), increasing in loudness.

Crespin, Régine (b. 1927), French soprano, internationally noted as Tosca (Puccini), Salome (R. Strauss), etc., and in recital.

Creston, Paul (originally Joseph Guttoveggio) (1906–85), American composer, also organist. Works include six symphonies (no. 3 on the Gregorian chant); a saxophone concerto; Concertino for marimba; Fantasia for trombone and orchestra.

Croce, Giovanni (*c.*1557–1609), Italian composer (and priest), pupil of Zarlino; in charge of music at St Mark's, Venice. Wrote motets, psalms, madrigals, etc.

croche (Fr.), EIGHTH-NOTE, quaver. ('Monsieur Croche' was a pseudonym used by Debussy in writing music criticism.)

Croft, William (1678–1727), English organist (at Westminster Abbey,

1708) and composer of songs, harpsichord pieces, stage music, etc., and much church music including hymntune 'St Anne' ('O God our Help in Ages Past').

crook, detachable section of the tube of horns, trumpets, etc., made in various sizes so as to give a different basic key to the instrument when fitted. (A player in Mozart's time, seeing 'horn in D' specified, would fit a *D crook*, giving a HARMONIC SERIES with D as the fundamental.) The use of VALVES, general from about 1850, has almost eliminated the necessity for changing crooks, but on, e.g., an ordinary trumpet in B♭ there is a mechanism which in effect can change the instrument to one having an *A crook*.

croon (particular usage, especially in 1930s), to sing softly and sentimentally into a microphone, as in dance bands.

Cross, Beverley (b. 1931), British playwright. See MINES OF SULPHUR.

Cross, Joan (b. 1900), British operatic soprano (also teacher and operatic stage director); created some of Britten's leading opera roles. CBE, 1951.

Crosse, Gordon (b. 1937), British composer, pupil of Wellesz and (in Italy) Petrassi. Works include *Meet my folks!*, and others involving child singers and instrumentalists; two violin concertos; *Wildboy* for clarinet with cimbalom and seven other instruments; vocal settings of poems by Ted Hughes; operas *Purgatory* and *The Story of Vasco*.

cross-fingering, fingering the ascending or descending scale (on woodwind instruments) in a way that goes against the normal order of lifting up and putting down successive fingers.

cross-relation(s), the relation set up when, for instance, the notes A♮ and A♭ occur simultaneously or in immediate succession in different PARTS – that is, a special effect of harmony in which the parts are not unanimous in whether they treat a particular note as sharp, natural, or flat. (*Cross-relation*, the standard American term, is clearer than 'false relation', more usual in Britain.)

crotal, type of small bell such as a sleigh-bell; for the French form of the term, with a different meaning, see the following.

crotale (Fr.), the normal modern term for the orchestral percussion instrument formerly known as the ancient cymbal or antique cymbal, used e.g. in Debussy's AFTERNOON OF A FAUN; such cymbals differ from the larger standard cymbal in being tuned to a definite pitch and in their more delicate tone.

Crotch, William (1775–1847), British composer; child prodigy as organist and composer whose later works (oratorio *Palestine*, church and organ music, etc.) did not fulfil his exceptional early promise. Professor at Oxford, 1797, and first principal of the Royal Academy of Music, 1822.

crotchet, see QUARTER-NOTE.

crowd (string instrument) = CRWTH.

Crown Imperial, march by Walton for coronation of George VI, 1937 (title from William Dunbar's poem 'In Honour of the City', earlier set as cantata by Walton).

Crucifixion, The, oratorio by Stainer (text written, and selected from the Bible, by J. S. Simpson), first performed in 1887.

Crumb, George [Henry] (b. 1929), American composer, pupil of Blacher (in USA and in Berlin). Works include *Echoes of Time and the River* for orchestra; *Ancient Voices of Children*, song-cycle with instrumental ensemble; *Black Angels* for electric string quartet.

crumhorn (Ger., *krumm*, crooked), type of curved, cylindrically bored, double-reed wind instrument current in Europe in 16th–17th centuries; made in at least six sizes of different pitch (a four-part consort was standard); revived in mid 20th century for old music.

Crusell, Bernhard Henrik (1775–1838), Finnish clarinettist and composer who worked mainly in Stockholm. Wrote clarinet concertos, quartets for clarinet or oboe with strings, opera, songs.

crwth (Welsh; equivalent to obsolete English word 'crowd' as musical instrument), medieval and later British stringed instrument shaped like a lyre but played with a bow, surviving longest in Wales; an ancestor of the violin family. (Sometimes misleadingly called a 'bowed harp'.)

csárdás (Hung.), Hungarian dance in sections, *lassú* (slow) and *friss* (quick). *Die Csárdás-Fürstin*, see GIPSY PRINCESS.

cuckoo, toy instrument, used e.g. in the TOY SYMPHONY formerly ascribed to Haydn.

Cuenod, Hugues (b. 1902), Swiss tenor of unusually high range; noted in recitals (including medieval music) and in opera. He gave an 86th-birthday recital in London.

Cui, César [Antonovich] (1835–

1918), Russian composer of French descent; Russian army general; critic, propagandist for 'national' Russian music, and member of the group of composers called THE MIGHTY HANDFUL. Works include 10 operas, many piano pieces and songs. Completed Dargomizhsky's THE STONE GUEST.

cuivre, cuivré (Fr.), brass, brassy (the latter term used, e.g., in horn-playing to signify a 'forced', ringing tone); *cuivres*, brass instruments.

Cummings, E. E. (1894–1962), American poet. See BERIO.

Cunning Little Vixen, The (Cz. *Příhody lišky Bystroušky*), opera by Janáček, produced in Brno, 1924; libretto by R. Těsnohlídek, using both human and animal characters.

Cupid and Death, masque with words written by J. Shirley, 1653, with music conjecturally by C. Gibbons; revived, 1659, with music (certainly) by C. Gibbons and M. Locke.

Curlew, The, song-cycle by Warlock, 1923, to four linked poems by Yeats; accompaniment for flute, English horn and string quartet.

Curlew River, dramatic work ('parable for church performance') by Britten, first performed at Orford (Suffolk), 1964. Libretto by William Plomer, based on medieval Japanese Noh play.

curtal(l), old English name for obsolete family of wind instruments, the bass member surviving longest, transformed in the 18th century into the BASSOON.

Curtin, Phyllis (b. 1922), American soprano prominent in opera, creating leading roles in works by Carlisle Floyd; latterly dean of arts, Boston University.

Curzon, Clifford [Michael] (1907–82), British pianist, pupil of Schnabel, Landowska and N. Boulanger; London début at age 16; various overseas appearances. Knighted, 1977.

cut time (US usage), the metre expressed as 'C', equivalent to 2/2 – two beats to the bar.

Cutting, Francis (active *c.*1583–*c.*1603), English lutenist and composer of music for his instrument (including an arrangement of 'Greensleeves') and for instrumental consort.

cycle, (1) name given to a set of works, especially songs, intended to be performed as a group and often linked musically or by other means; (2) name given to certain post-1950 pieces where the performer begins at a point of his own choosing, goes through the written score and concludes at the same point – e.g. Stockhausen's *Cycle* (Ger., *Zyklus*) for percussionist, 1959; (3) term used in the expression *cycle of fifths*, the 'chain' by which (given 'equal TEMPERAMENT') a succession of perfect fifths upwards or downwards will lead back to the original note again (at a higher or lower octave) after passing through all the other 11 notes of the chromatic scale. See also CYCLIC FORM.

cyclic form, (1) form of a work in which a theme does duty (often in new guise) in more than one movement – e.g. Franck, Symphony in D minor; Elgar, Symphony no. 1; (2, obsolete; see CYCLE, 1) form of any work with more than one movement.

cymbal, percussion instrument consisting of a plate of metal which is usually either struck with drumstick (single stroke or roll) or clashed against another cymbal. For the so-called *ancient cymbals* or *antique cymbals*, tuned to definite pitch, see CROTALE. Ordinary cymbals are of no definite pitch – but nevertheless one of them may sound higher than another, and three so differing are used, e.g., by Nono, *Epitaph for Lorca*. *Choke cymbals* are two ordinary cymbals mounted face to face on a rod (e.g. in dance bands) and struck with side-drum stick.

cythern, see CITTERN.

czardas, incorrect spelling of CSÁRDÁS.

Czech Philharmonic Orchestra, Prague-based orchestra becoming independent of its operatic origins in 1901. Jiři Belohlavek has been conductor since 1990.

Czerny, Carl (1791–1857), Austrian pianist and composer of an enormous number of piano studies; also of many other piano works (e.g. fantasies on popular operatic and other tunes of the day) and of church music, etc. Contributor to the HEXAMERON. Pupil of Beethoven and himself a famous teacher – e.g. of Liszt.

D

D, note of the scale. So *D* FLAT (D♭), DOUBLE-FLAT (D♭♭), NATURAL (D♮), SHARP (D♯), DOUBLE-SHARP (D𝄪); *D major, D minor,* etc. – see MAJOR. So also *in D,* either (1) in the key of D (major, understood), or (2) indication of a TRANSPOSING INSTRUMENT on which the note written C sounds as D (and correspondingly with other notes) – e.g. *trumpet in D,* or (colloquially) a *D trumpet,* as used by Purcell, Handel, etc.

D, abbr. for (1) *da,* as in *DC, da capo* (see DA); (2) abbreviation for 'Deutsch' in numbering the works of SCHUBERT; (3) Doctor, as in D.Mus. or Mus.D., Doctor of Music.

d, symbol in TONIC SOL-FA notation for the first degree (tonic) of the scale, pronounced *doh.*

d' (Fr., It), of (before a vowel); see under second word of phrase (except for the proper name D'ANNUNZIO: see below).

da (It.), from; *da capo* (abbr. DC), repeat from the beginning. So also *da capo al fine, da capo al segno* (repeat) up to the occurrence of the word 'fine' (end), or up to the sign indicating this (e.g. ⌢ – see PAUSE). Similarly *dal segno,* (repeat) from a specified sign, instead of repeating right from the beginning. (For *da capo* aria, see ARIA.)

da camera, see CAMERA, DA.

da chiesa, see CHIESA, DA.

da Gagliano, Marco, see GAGLIANO.

Dahl, Ingolf (1912–70), American (German-born) composer, also conductor, writer and teacher. Works include Concerto for alto saxophone and wind orchestra; *A Cycle of Sonnets* for voice and piano; *Quodlibet on American Folk-tunes* for two pianos, eight hands (later orchestrated).

dal, see DA.

Dalayrac (also spelt d'Alayrac), **Nicolas** (1753–1809), French composer of songs, string quartets and especially operas – over 50 of them, including *All for Love* (*Tout pour l'amour*), based on *Romeo and Juliet.*

Dalby, Martin (b. 1942), Scottish composer (also viola-player); head of BBC Music in Scotland since 1972. Works include a symphony, viola concerto, string quintet, song-cycle *The Fiddler* (voice and violin).

Dalcroze, Émile Jaques-, see JAQUES-DALCROZE.

Dale, Benjamin James (1885–1943), British composer and teacher; won attention with a piano sonata at 17, and later wrote cantata *Before the Paling of the Stars,* music for one or more violas, etc.

Dallapiccola, Luigi (1904–75), Italian composer (born in Pisino – then part of Austria–Hungary, now of Yugoslavia). Was also pianist and noted teacher, e.g. in USA. Works include operas *Night Flight*, THE PRISONER, JOB, ULYSSES; cantata *Songs of Liberation*; a piano concerto; songs (some in German) with orchestral, piano and other accompaniments.

Dam, José van (originally Joseph Van Damme) (b. 1940), Belgian bass-baritone, internationally prominent in opera (Paris Opera from 1961).

Damase, Jean-Michel (b. 1928), French pianist and composer of ballet scores, e.g. *The Diamond-Cruncher*, and several works for harp, including two concertos – his mother being a harpist.

Damnation of Faust, The (Fr., *La Damnation de Faust*), cantata by Berlioz, 1846; since 1893 also occasionally staged as opera. Words by composer and A. Gandonnière, after Goethe.

Damoiselle élue, La, see BLESSED DAMOZEL.

Dämpfer (Ger.), MUTE.

damping pedal, soft pedal (of piano).

Damrosch, Walter (1862–1950), German-born conductor who went with his father (Leopold Damrosch, 1832–85, also a conductor) to settle in USA in boyhood; championed Wagner, and gave many 'first American performances'. Was himself composer of operas including *Cyrano* (after Rostand's *Cyrano de Bergerac*), and *The Man Without a Country*; also of choral works, etc.

dance band (in modern sense), a band that plays for social dancing; in Europe and North America from the 1920s it generally divided into three – saxophones (some players doubling clarinets), brass (trumpets and trombones) and 'rhythm' (piano, drums, guitar and double-bass usually playing pizzicato). From the 1950s such bands were displaced in popular appeal by 'pop groups' based on electrically amplified guitars of differing types, with percussion and later with synthesizers.

Dance of the Hours, ballet music from Act III of Ponchielli's opera LA GIOCONDA.

dance-poem, description sometimes given by composers (see DUKAS) to a substantial orchestral work intended for ballet and having narrative interest (cp. CHOREOGRAPHIC POEM, SYMPHONIC POEM).

Dances of Galánta, orchestral suite by Kodály, 1933, based on tunes in a collection of gipsy music from Galánta (a small Hungarian market town).

Dandrieu, Jean-François (*c*.1682–1738), French organist, composer of works for harpsichord and for organ, etc.

Dankworth, John [Philip William] (b. 1927), British jazz clarinettist, composer, conductor and festival organizer. Works include film scores and (jointly with Seiber) *Improvisations* for jazz band and orchestra.

D'Annunzio, Gabriele (1863–1938), Italian poet and dramatist. See GIOCONDA, MARTYRDOM OF ST SEBASTIAN, ZANDONAI.

danse (Fr.), dance; *Danse macabre*, orchestral work by Saint-Saëns, 1874 – inspired by the medieval idea of a skeletons' dance, it quotes the DIES IRAE plainsong tune.

Dante Alighieri (1265–1321), Italian poet. See CASTIGLIONI, DANTE SONATA, DANTE SYMPHONY, FRANCESCA DA RIMINI, GIANNI SCHICCHI, LISZT, PACINI.

Dante Sonata, usual short name for Liszt's piano work, 'After a reading of Dante' (Fr., *Après une lecture du Dante*), labelled by him as a 'Fantasia, quasi sonata' and included in the *Années de pèlerinage* (see YEARS OF PILGRIMAGE). Played by Liszt in 1839; revised and given its present form in 1849. Arranged by Lambert for piano and orchestra and used for ballet, *Dante Sonata*, 1940.

Dante Symphony, orchestral work by Liszt (first performed, 1857) – in two movements, 'Inferno' and 'Purgatorio', ending with the MAGNIFICAT sung by a women's chorus. (Liszt wrote two alternative versions of this ending.) See also PACINI.

danza (It., Sp.), dance.

Danzi, Franz (1763–1826), German composer (son of an Italian), also cellist and conductor. Works include wind quintets and much other chamber music, also operas, oratorio, church music.

Daphnis and Chloe, ballet with music by Ravel (using a chorus), produced in Paris, 1912. (The two orchestral suites drawn from it do not comprise the whole.) Based on an ancient Greek story of pastoral love.

da Ponte, Lorenzo (1749–1838), Italian writer. See COSÌ FAN TUTTE, DON GIOVANNI, MARRIAGE OF FIGARO.

Daquin (also spelt d'Acquin), **Louis Claude** (1694–1772), French composer of harpsichord pieces (including

The Cuckoo), church music, etc.; organist from boyhood, holding post at French Chapel Royal from 1739.

d'Arányi, Jelly, see ARANYI.

Dargason, English COUNTRY DANCE, tune incorporated into Holst's ST PAUL'S SUITE.

Dargomizhsky, Alexander Sergeyevich (1813–69), Russian composer, 'nationalist' in musical ideas and associated with the group known as THE MIGHTY HANDFUL, though not a member. Composed THE RUSALKA, THE STONE GUEST and other operas; orchestral works; nearly 100 songs, many satirical.

Dart, [Robert] **Thurston** (1921–71), British harpsichordist, organist, conductor and musicologist; professor of music at Cambridge, then (1964) at London University.

Daudet, Alphonse (1840–97), French writer. See BIZET, WOMAN OF ARLES.

Daughter of the Regiment, The (Fr., *La Fille du régiment*), opera by Donizetti, produced in Paris, 1840. Libretto by J. H. V. de Saint-Georges and J. F. A. Bayard; the heroine, brought up as a regimental 'mascot', turns out to be of noble (if illegitimate) parentage.

da Viadana, Lodovico Grosso (c.1560–1627). Italian composer who took the name Viadana from his birthplace (cp. PALESTRINA); was also monk. Held church musical posts, and wrote madrigals, canzonas, etc., as well as church music – which includes *One Hundred Church Concertos*, giving an early example of CONTINUO-writing, though without figured bass.

David, Félicien [César] (1810–76), French composer (also theatre conductor); travelled in Near East, arranged oriental melodies for piano, and won noted success with descriptive orchestral work *The Desert*. Also composed operas, 25 string quintets, etc.

David, Ferdinand (1810–73), German violinist and composer – mainly for violin, including five concertos.

David, Jonathan Nepomuk (1895–1977), Austrian composer, also conservatory director and editor of old music. Works include eight symphonies, sonatas for solo violin and for solo flute, many church compositions and organ pieces, etc.

Davidovsky, Mario (b. 1934), composer, born in Argentina, naturalized American; has written seven *Synchronisms* for various instrumental or vocal ensembles combined with taped sound, also two string quartets, a cantata with Hebrew biblical text, etc.

Davidsbündler (Ger.), members of Schumann's (imaginary) League of David, opponents of a Philistine attitude to art; hence Schumann's *Davidsbündler-Tänze* (-Dances) for piano, 1837, revised in 1850.

Davie, Cedric Thorpe (1913–83), Scottish composer (pupil of Vaughan Williams and Kodály), also organist, professor at St Andrews University and writer on music. Composed music for Edinburgh Festival revival (1949) of old Scottish play, *The Three Estates*.

Davies, Hugh [Seymour] (b. 1943), British composer, performer and instrument inventor; assistant to Stockhausen, 1964–6. Besides works for traditional instruments, he has composed others for his own new

electro-acoustic instruments, and 'sound sculptures', e.g. *Strata* for quadraphonic aeolian harp plus tape. Also composes for stage presentations with dance and slide-projections.

Davies, Peter Maxwell (b. 1934), British composer. Directed his own ensemble, 'The Fires of London', and often conducts his own (and latterly others') works. Has written operas TAVERNER, THE MARTYRDOM OF ST MAGNUS, THE LIGHTHOUSE and the semi-staged EIGHT SONGS FOR A MAD KING; also three symphonies and *Orkney Wedding with Sunrise* (cp. BAGPIPES). Knighted, 1987.

Davies, [Henry] **Walford** (1869–1941), British musical educator – professor at University of Wales, and first widely popular BBC talker on music; also organist (St George's Chapel, Windsor) and composer of church music, etc. Knighted, 1922; Master of the King's Music, 1934.

Davis, Andrew [Frank] (b. 1944), British conductor; music director of the Toronto Symphony Orchestra, then (1989) of the BBC Symphony Orchestra and of Glyndebourne Opera.

Davis, Colin (b. 1927), British conductor, formerly clarinettist; conductor, BBC Symphony Orchestra, 1967; musical director Royal (Covent Garden) Opera, 1971–86. Knighted, 1980.

Davy, John (1763–1824), British composer of song 'The Bay of Biscay', much theatre music, etc.; also organist.

Davy, Richard (*c.*1467–*c.*1507), English composer of a Passion, motets, part-songs, etc.; organist of Magdalen College, Oxford, 1490–92.

de (Fr.), of. For names and phrases beginning thus, see next word – except for anglicized surnames, e.g. 'de la Mare'. (Italian names beginning 'de' are so listed.)

Dead March, any funeral march, especially 'The Dead March in Saul', i.e. from Handel's oratorio *Saul*, 1739.

Death and the Maiden (Ger., *Der Tod und das Mädchen*), title of song by Schubert (D531), 1817; hence nickname of Schubert's String Quartet in D minor, 1824, the second movement of which uses part of the song as a theme for variations.

Death and Transfiguration (Ger., *Tod und Verklärung*), symphonic poem by R. Strauss, first performed in 1890.

Death in Venice, opera by Britten, produced at Aldeburgh, 1973; based on the novel by Thomas Mann about a writer's homosexual passion and his death.

de Banfield, Raffaello (b. 1922), Italian composer; works include opera *Lord Byron's Love Letter* (libretto by Tennessee Williams), ballet *The Duel*.

Debussy, Claude-Achille (really named Achille-Claude) (1862–1918), French composer, also noted as critic; born near Paris, worked and died in Paris; visited Russia, 1881. Developed new outlook on harmony and musical structure, of which the name IM-PRESSIONISM reveals its kinship with contemporary visual art; he has affinity also with such poets as Verlaine and Baudelaire, whom he set. Was first pro- then anti-Wagner; his opera PELLÉAS AND MÉLISANDE is unlike any predecessor though seemingly indebted to Musorgsky for cultivation of natural speech-inflexions. Achieved

first marked success with THE AFTER-NOON OF A FAUN, 1894; had already composed cantata THE BLESSED DAM-OZEL. Also wrote IBERIA, THE SEA, NOCTURNES and other works for orchestra; two books of piano preludes (with picturesque titles) and other piano works including *Suite berga-masque* (see BERGAMASCA) and CHIL-DREN'S CORNER; a string quartet, violin sonata, cello sonata; music to KING LEAR and THE MARTYRDOM OF ST SEBASTIAN. See also CLAIR DE LUNE.

decani (Lat., of the dean), that section of the choir in a cathedral, etc., which is stationed on the south (i.e. dean's) side of the chancel; opposite of CAN-TORIS.

decrescendo (It., lessening), becoming softer.

Deering, see DERING.

Defesch, William (1687–?1757), Belgian organist, violinist, cellist and composer who settled in London, 1731; wrote Mass, oratorios, concertos, songs, etc.

degree, classification of a note with reference to its position in the scale. Thus the notes of the scale of C major (upwards, C–D–E–F–G–A–B–C) are called the first, second (etc.) degrees of the scale, returning eventually to the first degree, i.e. C. The alternative names for the first to seventh degrees (major or minor scale) are TONIC, SUPERTONIC, MEDIANT, SUBDOMI-NANT, DOMINANT, SUBMEDIANT, LEADING-NOTE. Other names are used in the TONIC SOL-FA system.

dehors (Fr. outside), sounding prominently – term applied to a melody, etc., which the composer intends should 'stand out' from its surroundings.

de Koven, [Henry Louis] **Reginald** (1859–1920), American composer, educated at Oxford and elsewhere in Europe. Wrote *The Canterbury Pilgrims* and other operas – including *Robin Hood*, for a London performance of which he composed the song 'Oh, Promise Me'; also operettas, ballets, piano music, songs, etc.

Delage, Maurice, [Charles] (1879–1961), French composer who studied with Ravel and travelled to the Far East; wrote *Four Hindu Poems* for voice with instrumental ensemble, *Seven Hai-kai* (French settings based on Japanese texts), a string quartet, etc.

Delalande, Michel Richard, see LALANDE.

de la Mare, Walter (1873–1956), poet and novelist. See CHANLER, GIBBS.

Delannoy, Marcel [François Georges] (1898–1962), French composer, formerly painter and architect, and mainly self-taught in music. Works include operas, ballets (among them a contribution to 'Jeanne's Fan'), two symphonies, string quartets, songs.

de Lara, Isidore (pen-name of Isidore Cohen) (1858–1935), British singer, concert organizer and composer of operas in English (including *The Light of Asia*, produced in 1892) and in French.

Delden, Lex van (1919–88), Dutch composer of chamber and choral music, children's ballets, *In memoriam* for orchestra (for the 1953 Dutch flood victims), seven symphonies, etc.; also critic.

Delibes (not Délibes) [Clément Phili-bert] **Léo** (1836–91), French composer, also organist, pupil of Adam. Works include ballets COPPÉLIA and SYLVIA (notably full of musical substance); LAKMÉ and other operas; also Mass, songs, etc.

Delius, Frederick (baptized Fritz Albert Theodor) (1862–1934), British composer of German descent; born in Bradford. Settled, 1889, in France, dying at his home at Grez-sur-Loing near Fontainebleau. Became blind and largely paralysed: FENBY, his amanuensis from 1928, took down some late compositions from dictation. Works include KOANGA, A VILLAGE ROMEO AND JULIET, and four other operas; choral-orchestral works including A MASS OF LIFE and REQUIEM; orchestral works including ON HEARING THE FIRST CUCKOO IN SPRING, BRIGG FAIR, *Paris* and two pieces called *Dance Rhapsody*; three violin sonatas, a violin and a piano concerto; many songs (English, French, German, Danish, Norwegian texts), etc.

Deller, Alfred [George] (1912–79), British counter-tenor, noted in works by Purcell and others written for his type of voice; Britten and others wrote specially for him. Also conductor and festival director.

Dello Joio, Norman (b. 1913), American composer (also pianist, organist, and teacher), pupil of B. Wagenaar and Hindemith; influenced by and makes use of Gregorian chant, e.g. in *New York Profiles* and *Variations, Chaconne and Finale* for orchestra. Has also written opera *The Trial at Rouen* (about Joan of Arc), ballets, a harmonica concerto, piano works, etc.

Del Mar, Norman [René] (b. 1919),

British conductor; conductor of BBC Scottish Orchestra, 1960–65. Author of a book on R. Strauss. CBE, 1975.

del Monaco, Mario (1915–82), Italian tenor, internationally known in opera (e.g. in title-role of Verdi's OTELLO) – at the Metropolitan, New York, from 1950.

Del Tredici, David (b. 1937), American composer of *Syzygy* (soprano, horn, tubular bells and chamber orchestra) and other settings of James Joyce, in addition to many settings of Lewis Carroll. Also university teacher.

De Luca, Giuseppe (1876–1950), Italian baritone, celebrated in opera, particularly Puccini. He was the first Sharpless in *Madam Butterfly*, 1914.

Delvincourt, Claude (1888–1954), French composer of mime-cantata *Lucifer*; dance-poem *The Offering to Siva*, a string quartet, etc.; director of the Paris Conservatory.

Demessieux, Jeanne [-Marie-Madeleine] (1921–68), French organist, pupil of Dupré; noted recitalist, visiting Britain from 1947. Also composer.

demisemiquaver, see THIRTY-SECOND-NOTE.

Demus, Jörg (b. 1928), Austrian pianist, eminent as soloist and song-accompanist (e.g. with Fischer-Dieskau).

Denisov, Edison [Vasilievich] (b. 1929), Russian composer who first trained as mathematician. Works (several becoming first known in the West) include opera *The Foam of Days*; concertos for piano, for flute, for cello, solo sonatas and duos.

Dent, Edward Joseph (1876–1957),

British musicologist, opera translator, professor of music at Cambridge and composer; made an arrangement of THE BEGGAR'S OPERA, edited various works by Purcell, etc. See also CAT'S FUGUE.

Denza, Luigi (1846–1922), Italian composer of 'Funiculì, funiculà' and about 500 other songs; also opera, etc. Settled in London, 1879, as a teacher; died there.

de Peyer, Gervase [Alan] (b. 1926), British clarinettist – principal clarinet, London Symphony Orchestra, 1955–71, also prominent as soloist and occasionally as conductor.

De Quincey, Thomas (1785–1859) British essayist and critic. See DIEREN.

der (Ger.), (1) the (masc. sing.); (2) of the (fem. sing.).

Dering, Richard (also Deering), (c.1580–1630), English organist, in service to Charles I's queen; composed church music, canzonets, fancies for viols, etc.; previously studied in Italy.

Dernesch, Helga (b. 1939), German soprano, prominent in Wagner's operas, etc. At Covent Garden from 1970. Has more recently sung mezzo-soprano roles.

des, of the (Fr., pl.; Ger., masc. and neut. sing.).

De Sabata, Victor (1892–1967), Italian conductor, active in opera (especially at La Scala, Milan) and in concerts, visiting Britain from 1947. Also composer of symphonic poems, operas, ballets, etc.

descant, (1) medieval term – see DISCANT. (2) additional part sung (sometimes improvised) above a given melody, e.g. above a hymn-tune; *descant recorder*, see RECORDER.

desk, an orchestral music-stand; in the strings of an orchestra each desk is shared by two players, so that *first desk only* is an instruction that the particular passage is to be played by the first *two* players only.

Després, Desprez, etc. see JOSQUIN.

Dessau, Paul (1894–1979), German composer; works include opera *The Trial of Lucullus* (libretto by Brecht), in which a piano with metal-covered hammers is used; also music to Brecht's plays, film music, orchestral works. Also conductor. Lived in France and USA, 1933–45.

Destinn, Emmy (originally Ema Kittlová) (1878–1930), Czech soprano who adopted a teacher's surname, latterly preferring the Czech form 'Destinnová'. Internationally distinguished in opera, especially Puccini.

détaché (Fr.), detached – an instruction to bow the violin, etc., in a particular way. It is the opposite of *lié* (bound) but does not imply STACCATO.

Deuteromelia, see PAMMELIA.

Deutsch, Otto Erich (1883–1967), Austrian musicologist. See SCHUBERT.

Deutscher Tanz, see GERMAN DANCE.

deutsches Requiem, Ein, see GERMAN REQUIEM.

Deutschland über Alles, see EMPEROR'S HYMN.

deux (Fr.), two.

development, the section of a movement (e.g. in SONATA-FORM) between the initial statement of themes and their final recapitulation, during which the themes are 'developed', i.e. expanded, modified, combined, broken up, etc.

Devienne, François (1759–1803), French composer of 12 operas, many concertos for bassoon and for flute (his own instruments), etc. Died insane.

devil in music, see TRITONE.

Devil's Trill, The, nickname for a violin sonata in G minor by Tartini, composed about 1714, and having a famous trill in the last of four movements; said to be modelled on a sonata played to Tartini by the Devil appearing in a dream.

De Vito, Gioconda (b. 1907), Italian violinist who made her London début in 1948 and settled there; won major international celebrity but retired in 1961.

de Waart, Edo, see WAART.

d'Hardelot, Guy (pen-name of Helen Rhodes, *née* Guy) (1858–1936), born at Hardelot, France – English composer of 'Because' and other genteelly sentimental and enormously successful songs.

Diabelli, Anton (1781–1858), Austrian composer (pupil of Haydn) and publisher. Wrote mainly for the piano, including a waltz on which 50 invited composers each wrote one variation, and Beethoven wrote 33 uninvited.

diabolus in musica, see TRITONE.

Dialectic, title of string quartet by A. Bush, 1929. (Title presumably with reference to dialectic as process of fruitful struggle between opposites, according to the Marxist beliefs professed by the composer.)

Dialogues of the Carmelites, The (Fr.,

Les Dialogues des Carmélites), opera by Poulenc, produced (in Italian) in Milan, 1957; libretto, by E. Lavery after a novel by Bernanos, narrates the martyrdom of a group of nuns in the French Revolution.

Diamond, David [Leo] (b. 1915), American composer, pupil of N. Boulanger in Paris. Works include eight symphonies, Concerto for two solo pianos, Jewish liturgical music.

diapason, the 'basic' tone of the organ, 'open' or 'stopped' according to whether the ends of the pipes are clear or plugged, the 'open' being the louder. Normally of eight-FOOT length: *double diapason*, of 16-foot length – see DOUBLE (2). (Other English uses of the term are obsolete, but see following entry.)

diapason normal (Fr.), a standard indication of pitch: A = 435 Hz. The international standard now accepted is different: see FREQUENCY.

diaphony, name sometimes given to simpler types of ORGANUM.

Diary of One Who Disappeared, The, usual English title for *Zápisník zmizeleho* (Cz., Diary of a disappeared [man]), song-cycle by Janáček for tenor, mezzo-soprano, three other voices and piano, first performed in 1921; occasionally presented as an opera.

diatonic, pertaining to a given major or minor key (opposite of CHROMATIC); so *diatonic scale*, any one of the major or minor scales; *diatonic harmony*, harmony made up predominantly from the resources of the prevailing key, without much use of notes outside its scale; similarly *diatonic discord*, discord arriving from

clashes within the key itself. Hence *diatonicism*, a pronounced use of diatonic harmony. See also PANDIATONIC(ISM).

Diaz, Alirio (b. 1923), Venezuelan guitarist, prominent as soloist in concerts and recitals; resident in Italy.

Dibdin, Charles (1745–1814), singer, composer, theatrical manager, publisher, author of novels and other literary works; in 1789 he instituted 'table entertainments' at which he recited, sang and accompanied. Composed 'Tom Bowling' and many other sea songs, and over 100 stage pieces including *Lionel and Clarissa*.

Dichterliebe, see POET'S LOVE.

Dichtung (Ger., poem); *symphonische Dichtung*, SYMPHONIC POEM.

Dickens, Charles (1812–70), British novelist. See BENTZON (J.), CHRISTMAS CAROL, CIKKER, GOLDMARK (K.), HULLAH, MACKENZIE.

Dickinson, Emily (1830–86), American poet. See ESCHER.

Dickinson, Peter (b. 1934), British composer, professor (1973–84) at University of Keele; also pianist, collaborating with his sister Meriel (b. 1940), mezzo-soprano. Works include an organ concerto, two string quartets (no. 2 with tape or offstage piano); several works (mainly for piano) based on ragtime and blues; church drama *The Judas Tree*.

diction, correct and clear enunciation in singing. (This is the recognized meaning in musical contexts, though the term primarily refers to literary skill in using words.)

didgeridoo, see DIDJERIDOO.

didjeridoo, didjeridu, Australian aboriginal wind instrument of trumpet type, made out of a tree trunk 4–5 ft long.

Dido and Aeneas, opera by Purcell (Z626), produced in London in 1689. Libretto by N. Tate, after Virgil's account of Dido's abandonment by Aeneas and her ensuing suicide. (Purcell's only fully sung stage work.) See CHACONNE.

Diepenbrock, Alphons (1862–1921), Dutch composer, mainly of vocal music – Mass, church music, songs (Dutch, German and French), etc. Also critic.

Dieren, Bernard van (1887–1936), Dutch-born composer and writer on music, resident in Britain from 1909. Cultivated an individual and often intricate idiom; wrote many songs and several unusual works, e.g. a symphony (with voices) on Chinese themes, and a setting for voices and piano of De Quincey's 'On Murder Considered as One of the Fine Arts'.

Dies Irae (Lat., Day of Wrath), a section of the Requiem Mass, the plainsong tune of which is quoted, e.g., in Berlioz's FANTASTIC SYMPHONY, Saint-Saëns's DANSE MACABRE, and various works of Rakhmaninov including *Rhapsody on a Theme of Paganini* for piano and orchestra.

Dies Natalis, setting by Finzi, 1940, of prose and poems by Traherne; for high voice and strings.

differential tone, see RESULTANT TONE.

dim., abbr. for (1) diminished (see DIMINISH as term in harmony); (2) *diminuendo,* i.e. becoming softer.

diminish, (1) to 'lessen' certain intervals; see DIMINISHED; (2) to subject a melody to DIMINUTION.

diminished, term applied to a type of INTERVAL regarded as a 'lessened' version of a certain other interval. In practice this is a useful term only for (1) *diminished fifth,* e.g. one semitone less than perfect fifth, and (2) *diminished seventh,* one semitone less than minor seventh. In effect the latter sounds as i.e. as major sixth; but it is distinctive by the intermediate harmony it is presumed to carry, namely otherwise (and various other notations); this chord is the *diminished-seventh chord* on C, elliptically referred to as *C diminished* (abbr. *C dim.*).

diminuendo (It., lessening), becoming gradually softer.

diminution, the treatment of a melody in such a way as to decrease (usually halving) the time-values of its notes (used, e.g., in some fugues).

d'Indy, Vincent, see INDY.

Dinner Engagement, A, comic opera by Berkeley, produced in Aldeburgh, 1954. Libretto by Paul Dehn, the dinner being given by (relatively) impoverished English nobility.

Dioclesian (properly *The Prophetess, or The History of Dioclesian*), play by T. Betterton for which in 1690 Purcell wrote incidental music (Z627).

discant, a developed form of the type of medieval part-writing called OR-

GANUM. The most reliable medieval theorists describe it as essentially a homophonic, measured style.

discord, see CONCORD (of which it is the opposite).

disjunct motion, see MOTION.

dissonance, discord (see CONCORD); *Dissonance Quartet,* nickname for Mozart's String Quartet in C, K465 (1785), opening with a passage in which there is a pronounced use of dissonance.

di Stefano, Giuseppe, see STEFANO.

Distler, Hugo (1908–42), German composer of church music, choral works, etc.; also organist.

Dittersdorf (Ditters originally his surname), **Carl Ditters von** (1739–99), Austrian violinist and composer, in service to various noble patrons; friend of Haydn and Mozart. Composed symphonies, string quartets, church music, etc.; also more than 40 operas, including the very successful *Doctor and Apothecary* and one based on *The Merry Wives of Windsor* (1796).

div., abbr. of DIVISI or 'divided'.

divertimento (It., an amusement), a not-too-serious work, usually for a small instrumental group, in several movements (e.g. by Mozart, Stravinsky).

divertissement (Fr., an amusement), (1) a musical paraphrase on familiar tunes, or some similar light instrumental work; (2) a danced entertainment of the type of BALLET (1), but being merely a suite of dances not unified by any fundamental idea or connecting story.

Divine Poem, The (Rus., *Bozhestvennaya poema*), orchestral work by Skrya-

bin, also called his Symphony no. 3. First performed in Paris, 1905. Illustrates the composer's theosophical ideas and has an explicit literary source. The three movements are entitled 'Struggles', 'Delights', 'Divine Play'. Cp. POEM OF ECSTASY, PROMETHEUS.

divisi (It.), divided – term used, e.g., of the first violins or other string group of the orchestra when they temporarily split into two or more smaller bodies playing different parts.

divisions, (1) obsolete term for VARIATIONS because the splitting of the time-values of notes was formerly a common way of making variations; (2) obsolete term for long, agile vocal runs, whether notated by the composer or introduced by the performer as an embellishment.

division viol, see VIOL.

Dixieland, name given to a style of jazz-playing based on the 'classic' jazz of the pre-1914 era in New Orleans – unsentimental, rather naïvely syncopated, and using small bands of a particular instrumental combination.

do, the note C (in Latin countries, and formerly elsewhere); cp. DOH.

Dobbs, Mattiwilda (b. 1925), American soprano of high range, the first black singer to win international reputation in opera – Covent Garden (1954), Glyndebourne, La Scala (Milan), etc.

dobro, type of guitar with a large circular metal resonator under the bridge.

Doctor Faust, opera by Busoni; completed after Busoni's death by Jarnach and produced in Dresden, 1925. Libretto by composer, on the Faust legend but not based on Goethe's drama.

Doctor Gradus ad Parnassum, see GRADUS AD PARNASSUM.

Doctor of Music, the highest musical degree (British, Commonwealth and American; not awarded elsewhere). Abbr. *D.Mus.*, *Mus.D.*, or *Mus.Doc.*

dodecaphonic (Gk., *dodeka*, 12), a misapplied term: linguistically it should mean (cp. MONOPHONIC) 'in 12 strands or parts', but it has been accepted as referring to the TWELVE-NOTE method of composition. Similarly *dodecaphony*, *-ist*, etc.

Dodgson, Stephen (b. 1924), British composer, pupil of R. O. Morris and others. Works include a symphony, piano quartet, pieces for guitar, including two concertos – see WILLIAMS, (J.).

doh, in TONIC SOL-FA, the spoken name for the first degree (tonic) of the scale, written **d**. See DO.

Dohnányi, Christoph von (b. 1929), German conductor, music director of the Cleveland Orchestra since 1984; occasionally stage director for opera. Grandson of the following.

Dohnányi, Ernö (he used the German form, Ernst von) (1877–1960), Hungarian pianist and composer of two piano concertos, *Variations on a Nursery Theme* (same as 'Twinkle, twinkle') for piano and orchestra, two symphonies, three operas, etc. More 'German' in style than his 'nationalist' Hungarian contemporaries, Bartók and Kodály. From 1948 resident in USA.

Doktor Faust, see DOCTOR FAUST.

dolce (It.), sweet(ly); *dolcezza*, sweetness.

dolente (It.), sorrowful(ly).

Doles, Johann Friedrich (1715–97), German composer of church music, songs, etc.; pupil of Bach, and appointed in 1756 as Bach's successor in his Leipzig post.

Dolly, suite of six children's pieces for piano duet by Fauré, 1893; orchestrated for ballet by Rabaud, 1896.

Dolmetsch, surname of a Swiss (Anglicized) family famous for the authentic interpretation of old music and for the revived manufacture of old instruments. The most famous members are Arnold Dolmetsch (1858–1940) and his son Carl (b. 1911), English (French-born) player chiefly of the recorder but also of violin and viols; CBE, 1954.

Domestic Symphony, see SYMPHONIA DOMESTICA.

dominant, the fifth note of the scale, in relation to the keynote: thus if the key is C (major or minor), the dominant is G. So *dominant seventh*, chord of the (minor) seventh on the dominant (in this case G, B, D, F) resolving normally on the TONIC chord (in this case C major or minor). So also *secondary dominant*, term sometimes encountered as translation of Ger. *Wechseldominante* (literally, 'exchange dominant'), meaning 'the dominant of the dominant', e.g. the note D in key C (major or minor).

Domingo, Plácido (b. 1941), Spanish tenor, brought up in Mexico, who made his first appearance at Metropolitan, New York, in 1968 and at Covent

Garden in 1971, winning highest international reputation. Is also, occasionally, conductor of opera and concerts.

domra, Russian plucked instrument, usually three-stringed, with convex back like a mandolin; made in several sizes and used for folk-music, etc. Cp. BALALAIKA.

Donatoni, Franco (b. 1927), Italian composer of biblical oratorio *The Book with Seven Seals,* four string quartets, a bassoon concerto, etc.; some of his work does homage to other composers, e.g. to Schoenberg in *Etwas ruhiger in Ausdruck* (Ger., Somewhat more Peaceful in Expression) for five instruments, the title being borrowed from a Schoenberg piano piece.

Don Carlos, opera by Verdi, produced in Paris, 1867. Libretto (in French) by F. J. Méry and C. du Locle, after Schiller: Don Carlos, the son of Philip II of Spain, is presented as the champion of liberty.

Don Giovanni, opera by Mozart (K527), produced (in Italian) in Prague, 1787. Original title, *Il dissoluto punito, o sia Il Don Giovanni* (The Rake Punished or, Don Giovanni). Libretto by L. da Ponte, dealing with some of the loves of the Spanish character better known as Don Juan, who is eventually dragged down to hell by a statue. See also DON JUAN, GAZZANIGA, STONE GUEST, ZAMPA.

Donizetti, Gaetano [Domenico Maria] (1797–1848), Italian composer; after 1844 suffered mental illness and paralysis. Composed more than 60 operas in a style of characteristic Italian lyricism but also with humour. Some are

in French (e.g. THE DAUGHTER OF THE REGIMENT) but most in Italian – including DON PASQUALE, THE LOVE POTION, LUCIA DI LAMMERMOOR. The theory that he was the grandson of a Scot named Don(ald) Izett has been discounted.

Don Juan, (1) ballet with music by Gluck, first performed in 1761; (2) symphonic poem by R. Strauss, first performed in 1889; after a poem by Lenau (1802–50).

Donne, John (1572–1631), English poet. See BENNETT (Richard Rodney), BRITTEN, TALMA.

Donohoe, Peter (b. 1953), British pianist who made London début in 1979 and came joint second at the Moscow Tchaikovsky Competition in 1982.

Don Pasquale, comic opera by Donizetti, produced (in Italian) in Paris, 1843. Libretto partly by the composer: Don Pasquale is an old man trapped into a fake marriage.

Don Quixote, symphonic poem by R. Strauss, first performed in 1898. After Cervantes, and styled 'Fantastic Variations on a Theme of Knightly Character'.

dopo (It.), after(wards).

Doppel (Ger.), double. See also DOPPELSCHLAG.

Doppelschlag (Ger.) = TURN (musical ornament).

doppio (It.), double; *doppio movimento,* at double the speed (of the preceding section).

Doráti, Antal (1906–88), Hungarian-born, American-naturalized conductor of Minneapolis Symphony Orchestra, 1949–60; later of the BBC

Symphony, Stockholm Philharmonic, (US) National Symphony and (1975–8) the Royal Philharmonic Orchestra. Was also a composer, and arranged the music of J. Strauss the younger for the ballet *Graduation Ball*.

Dorian mode, the MODE represented by the white keys of the piano beginning on D.

'Dorian' Toccata and Fugue, nickname for a certain Toccata and Fugue in D minor (not the familar one) by Bach, BWV 538; given because, although in fact in D minor, it was originally written without key-signature, as a work in the Dorian mode and ending on D would be.

Dostoyevsky, Feodor Mikhailovich (1821–81), Russian novelist. See BLACHER, FROM A HOUSE OF THE DEAD, JEREMIÁŠ (o.), PETROVICS, TAVENER.

dot, mark in musical notation (1) placed above note, indicating STACCATO; (2) placed after note, indicating that the time-value of the note is to be extended by half; similarly a *double dot* indicates that the time-value is to be extended by half as much again – e.g. ♩‥ = ♩♪♪ (But before the double dot was invented, by Leopold Mozart, the single dot might indicate prolongation by an amount greater than half, even by three-quarters – i.e. as much as the double dot now conveys; the performer deduced from the musical context which interpretation was intended.)

double, (1) twofold – so DOUBLE BAR; *double chant*, form of ANGLICAN CHANT covering two verses of a psalm for each repetition, instead of one; *double choir*, *double chorus*, choir with

a twofold multiplicity of voices (usually two choirs of four parts, making eight voice-parts in all); *double concerto*, concerto either with two solo instruments (e.g. Brahms's) or two orchestras (e.g. Martinů's); *double* COUNTERPOINT; DOUBLE-FLAT; *double fugue*, FUGUE with two subjects; DOUBLE-HANDED; *double* HORN; *double organ*, obsolete term for an organ with two manuals, or simply with one manual of full range; DOUBLE-SHARP. So also *double octaves*, *double thirds*, etc., octaves or thirds played (on a keyboard) simultaneously in both hands. (2) prefix meaning 'sounding (about) an octave lower'. (This meaning arises because a pipe doubled in length sounds an octave lower: see FOOT.) So DOUBLE-BASS; *double-*BASSOON; *double* DIAPASON. So also *double-bass clarinet*, *double-bass saxophone*, lowest and extremely rare members of the CLARINET and SAXOPHONE families. (3, verb) term alluding to (a) duplication of a melody by several performers: so, e.g., 'the voice-part is doubled by the clarinet and, an octave lower, by the bassoon'; (b) duplication of instruments by one player: so, e.g., 'Berlioz's *Fantastic Symphony* demands two flutes, the second doubling piccolo', i.e. the second player to play piccolo instead of flute when required. (4, Fr.), a variation, especially in the form of an ornamented version of the theme (cp. DIVISION). See also the following entries.

doublé (Fr.), a TURN (musical ornament).

double bar, double perpendicular line marking the end of a composition or of a major division of it; usually but not always placed coincidentally with the single bar-line, and sometimes equipped with 'repeat' marks

▤ – see REPEAT. See also BAR.

double-bass, the largest and lowest bowed stringed instrument of the orchestra – also used in jazz and dance bands (mainly pizzicato), and occasionally introduced into the military band for concerts; used occasionally in chamber music, very rarely solo. The standard modern instrument has four strings, and a compass from E just over an octave below the bass stave, upwards for nearly three octaves; but five-string instruments, with an extra string sounding B below bottom E, are also found. Though it belongs to the violin family, some players use bowing grip (as for viols).

double-flat, indication (notated ♭♭) of the lowering of the pitch of a note by two semitones. (Cp. FLAT.) Its use is necessitated by the 'grammar' of harmony, even though the resultant note, e.g. on the piano, will always have an alternative simpler name – e.g A♭♭ is G♮, i.e. G natural.

double-handed (of an instrumentalist), capable of playing two different instruments. (See DOUBLE, 3. But the term does not usually refer to a player skilled merely on different sizes of the 'same' instrument, e.g. flute and piccolo, but to such wider skill as will enable him e.g. to play in a light orchestra on, say, the violin or saxophone as required.)

double-sharp, indication (notated 𝄪) of the raising of the pitch of a note by two semitones. (Cp. SHARP.) Its use is necessitated by the 'grammar' of harmony, even though the resultant note,

e.g. on the piano, will always have an alternative simpler name – e.g. F𝄪 is G♮, i.e. G natural.

double-whole-note, the note ‖◌‖ or ⊏⊐ considered as a time-value. This is standard North American usage and should clearly be preferred to 'breve', still surviving in British use. The corresponding rest is notated.

Douglas, Barry (b. 1960), British pianist, the first from UK to win outright (see OGDON) the Moscow Tchaikovsky Competition (1986).

doux, douce(ment) (Fr.), sweet(ly).

Dowland, John (1563–1626), English lutenist and composer, serving the king of Denmark (1598–1606) and other such patrons; achieved international reputation and had his music published in eight capitals. Became Roman Catholic but later Protestant again. Works are chiefly solo songs with lute, and lute solos; also wrote *Lachrimae* ('seven passionate pavans ... for lute, viols, or violins'), etc. Father of Robert Dowland.

Dowland, Robert (1591–1641), English lutenist (at Charles I's court, succeeding his father, John Dowland), composer, and publisher of an international collection of AYRES.

down-beat, the downward motion of the conductor's stick or hand, especially as indicating the first beat of the bar; (term therefore also used for) the first beat of the bar, whether or not the piece is being 'conducted'. Cp. UP-BEAT.

down-bow, the motion of the bow of a stringed instrument when pulled by the player – the opposite (pushing) motion being an UP-BOW.

Downes, Edward [Thomas] (b. 1924), British conductor; on staff of Covent Garden, 1952–69, conductor of BBC Northern (later retitled BBC Philharmonic) Orchestra since 1980. Also translator of Russian opera.

Downes, Ralph [William] (b. 1904), British organist (noted in recital) and designer of organs, e.g. at the Royal Festival Hall, on which he gave his farewell recital in 1987. Worked in USA, 1928–35. Also composer.

Draghi, Giovanni Battista (1640–1710), Italian harpsichordist, composer of harpsichord pieces, songs, etc.; settled in London, becoming organist to Charles II's wife, and died there.

Dragonetti, Domenico (1763–1846), Italian double-bass player who won exceptional fame as a soloist; was also a composer for his instrument, and a friend of Beethoven; settled in London and died there.

dramatic (soprano, tenor, etc.), having powerful voice and a style suitable for forceful operatic roles.

drame (Fr.), drama; *drame lyrique*, lyric drama – term used, e.g., by Debussy to classify PELLÉAS AND MÉLISANDE.

dramma (It.), drama; *dramma per musica* (drama through music), term frequently used for 'opera' in the 17th and 18th centuries; *dramma giocoso*, comic drama, i.e. (in musical contexts) comic opera which nevertheless has one or more non-comic characters – applied by Mozart to DON GIOVANNI.

Drdla, František (1869–1944), Czech violinist and composer chiefly for his instrument, but also of operettas, songs, etc. Known as Franz Drdla.

Dream of Gerontius, The, oratorio by Elgar, first performed in Birmingham, 1900. Text, Cardinal Newman's poem (abridged) on a vision of the soul's fate after death.

Dreigroschenoper, Die, see THREE-PENNY OPERA.

Dresden, Sem (1881–1957), Dutch composer, pupil of Pfitzner. Works include two piano concertos, two violin concertos, cantatas (one with brass band), chamber music. Also writer on music, conductor, and director of The Hague Conservatory.

Dresden State Orchestra (or Dresdner Staatskapelle; see KAPELLE), German orchestra tracing its origins to the 16th century. Conductor since 1985, Hans Vonk; Sinopoli to succeed in 1992.

Drigo, Riccardo (1846–1930), Italian composer of songs, ballet *Harlequin's Millions* (source of popular 'Serenade'), etc.; also conductor, holding posts in St Petersburg and elsewhere.

droit(e) (Fr.), right, right hand; *main droite* or *MD*, with the right hand (e.g. in piano music).

drone, pipe(s) sounding note(s) of fixed pitch continuing as a permanent bass on various forms of BAGPIPE; hence, similar effect (*drone bass*) in other forms of music.

Druckman, Jacob [Raphael] (b. 1928), American composer, pupil of Copland and others. Works include several combining taped with 'live' music, also two string quartets, *Windows* for orchestra, etc.

drum, percussion instrument of many varieties, all having a skin or other membrane which is stretched over a hollow space and struck – usually with a stick, but cp. BONGO. The KETTLEDRUMS (also called 'timpani') and some TOM-TOMS are tuned to definite notes; most other drums (e.g. BASS, SNARE, TENOR drums) are not. So *drum-head*, the stretched membrane which is beaten; *drum-roll*, quick succession of strokes on the drum, the instrument's nearest approach to a sustained sound. See also following entries.

Drum Mass, nickname for Haydn's Mass in C, 1796 (Hob. XXII: 9), in which kettledrums are unusually prominent.

Drum-roll Symphony, nickname for Haydn's Symphony no. 103 in E♭ (Hob. I:103), opening with kettledrum-roll.

Dryden, John (1631–1700), English poet. See ALEXANDER'S FEAST, CLARKE, GRABU, INDIAN QUEEN, KING ARTHUR, ODE FOR ST CECILIA'S DAY.

dry recitative, see RECITATIVE.

Drysdale, Learmont (1866–1909), British composer of operas (one on Euripides' *Hippolytus*), cantatas, orchestral works, songs, etc., much of his music having Scottish associations.

du (Fr.), of the.

Dubois, [François Clément] Théodore (1837–1924), French composer of operas, church music, orchestral works, etc. Director of Paris Conservatory, 1896–1905, being obliged to resign after discriminating against the young Ravel.

Ducasse, Jean Jules Aimable Roger-, see ROGER-DUCASSE.

due (It.), two.

Duenna, The, opera (so-called, but more a play with music) with words by Sheridan, music by the elder and younger LINLEY (with some borrowings from other composers); produced in London, 1775. The plot (but not the music) was the basis for two operas entitled *The Duenna*, one by Gerhard (BBC radio production, 1949) and one by Prokofiev – libretto (in Russian) by composer and M. Mendelson-Prokofiev, produced in Prague, 1946. The latter is known in Russian as *The Betrothal in the Monastery* but Sheridan's title is also sanctioned.

duet, a combination of two performers (sometimes with accompaniment, as is usually implied, e.g., by *vocal duet*), or a work for such a combination; *piano duet*, two performers on one piano. See DUO.

duettino (It.), a little duet.

duetto (It.), duet.

Dufay, Guillaume (*c.* 1400–1474), Franco-Flemish composer, also singer – in Papal choir at Rome, 1428–37; also canon of the Church. In 1440s, in service to the court of Burgundy. Noted teacher, e.g. of Ockeghem. Works include Masses (one on L'HOMME ARMÉ), other church music (some with accompanying instruments), and chansons.

Dukas, Paul (1865–1935), French composer – also editor of old music, critic and teacher. Works – in a very clear texture, tinged with prevailing influences of IMPRESSIONISM – include opera *Ariadne and Bluebeard*, dance-poem THE PERI, descriptive orchestral work THE SORCERER'S APPRENTICE, and many piano works.

Is said to have been the first major French composer to write a piano sonata.

Duke, Vernon, see DUKELSKY.

Duke Bluebeard's Castle, see BLUE-BEARD'S CASTLE.

Dukelsky, Vladimir (1903–69), Russian-born composer (pupil of Glière) who settled in New York, 1922. Works include three symphonies and a piano concerto; also wrote, as Vernon Duke, 'April in Paris' and other dance-tunes, light theatre music, etc.

dulciana, type of soft organ stop.

dulcimer, (1) type of instrument (old, but still in use for traditional music, e.g. in Eastern Europe) in which strings stretched over a sound-board are struck with hammers; the Hungarian kind, sometimes seen in the concert-hall, is the CIMBALOM; (2) name given to an American three-string folk-instrument of zither type, (*Appalachian dulcimer*), with strings plucked by player's right hand.

Dumas, Alexandre (senior; 1802–70), French writer. See RAYMOND.

Dumas, Alexandre (junior; 1842–95), French novelist and dramatist. See TRAVIATA.

Dumbarton Oaks Concerto, Concerto in E♭ for 15 instruments by Stravinsky, 1938 – title taken from the Washington, DC estate of the patron who commissioned it, where it was also first performed. (Title-page of score prints 'Dumbarton Oaks 8-v-38' and then in larger type 'Concerto en mi♭', etc.: 'Concerto' is therefore the real title, 'Dumbarton Oaks' having no more claim to substantive use than has the date.)

dumka (Rus., Cz.; pl. *dumky*), a lament of Ukrainian folk-origin, a movement in which slow and fast tempos alternate – term used by Dvořák, e.g. *dumka* movements in his String Sextet and Piano Quintet. *Dumky Trio*, nickname for Dvořák's Piano Trio, op. 90, 1891, made up of six independent *dumka* movements in different keys.

dumky, see preceding entry.

dump (also *dumpe, dompe*, etc.), English title for a piece for lute or guitar, of which a few survive from around 1700; though the derivation of the word is not known, it apparently signifies a lament.

Dunayevsky, Isaac (1900–1955), Russian composer who also trained as violinist (pupil of Akhron); achieved chief success with popular Soviet songs. Also wrote operettas, ballets, a string quintet, etc.

Dunbar, William (*c.*1460–*c.*1514), Scottish poet. See CROWN IMPERIAL.

Dunhill, Thomas [Frederick] (1877–1946), British composer (pupil of Stanford), teacher and writer on music. Wrote operetta *Tantivy Towers* (words by A. P. Herbert), many songs, a symphony, chamber music, etc.

Duni, Egidio Romualdo (1708–75), Italian-born composer (pupil of Durante) who settled in France, 1757; and died there. Wrote chiefly opera, in both French and Italian: notable practitioner of the OPÉRA COMIQUE.

Dunstable (or Dunstaple), **John** (*c.*1390–1453 or later), English composer of European repute (also mathematician and astrologer); spent some time on the Continent. Works, displaying notable melodic invention within smoothly consonant contrapuntal style, include motets and other church music, and three-part secular songs.

duo (It.), two performers, or a work written for them; *duo-pianist* (US), member of a duo playing on two pianos (not two people on one piano).

duodecuple scale (Lat., *duodecim*, 12), a scale of 12 notes, i.e. the ordinary European scale considered as having 12 notes all of equal value, as in TWELVE-NOTE music. (This term avoids the use of CHROMATIC, which has harmonic implications foreign to 12-note practice.)

Duparc, Henri (style of name used by Marie Eugène Henri Foucques-Duparc) (1848–1933), French composer, pupil of Franck, prevented by illness from working after 1885. Noted for his 16 songs, some with optional orchestral accompaniments; wrote little else.

duplet, a pair of notes of equal time-value, written where the number of beats is not capable of simple division by 2 – e.g. two notes occupying a bar

of 3/8, written 𝅘𝅥𝅘𝅥 (One of the notes may, of course, be replaced by a rest.)

duple time, time in which the primary division is into 2 or 4 – e.g. 2/4, 4/4 – as distinct particularly from TRIPLE TIME (primary division into 3). Note especially that 6/4 indicates a bar of two dotted half-notes, i.e.   .
while 3/2 indicates a bar of three half-notes, i.e.   giving different accents although both total six quarter-notes.

Duplex-Coupler piano, see MOÓR.

du Pré, Jacqueline (1945–87), British cellist (married Daniel Barenboim, 1967). Studied with Tortelier and (after her London début, 1961) briefly with Rostropovich in Moscow. Incapacitated through multiple sclerosis from 1973. OBE, 1976.

Dupré, Marcel (1886–1971), French organist (pupil of Widor) and composer of many organ works, also two symphonies, etc. Noted recitalist. Director of the Paris Conservatory, 1954–6.

Dur (Ger., = MAJOR).

Durante, Francesco (1684–1755), Italian composer, mainly of church music; noted as theorist and teacher. Taught Pergolesi, Paisiello and others.

Durchführung (Ger., a through-leading) = DEVELOPMENT.

durchkomponiert (Ger., through-composed), term used of a work, especially a song, composed in a continuous form, not repeating itself in successive stanzas – opposite of STROPHIC. (Term also sometimes used to mean 'fully worked out', 'really composed', etc., as distinct from something that seems to proceed merely in patches.)

Durey, Louis (1888–1979), French composer, influenced by Satie; one of the group of SIX. Also critic. His works include chamber music, songs, unpublished opera. See PROGRESSIST.

Durkó, Zsolt (b. 1934), Hungarian composer, pupil of Petrassi in Rome. Works include *Hungarian Rhapsody* for two clarinets and orchestra; *Organisms* for violin and orchestra; two string quartets.

Dürrenmatt, Friedrich (b. 1921), Swiss

dramatist. See VISIT OF THE OLD LADY.

Duruflé, Maurice (1902–86), French organist and composer, pupil of Dukas and others. Works include a Requiem, organ pieces and three dances for orchestra, but he composed very sparingly.

Dusík, see DUSSEK.

Dussek (Western-Europeanized form of surname used by Jan Ladislav Dusík) (1760–1812), Czech pianist and composer. Wrote chiefly for the piano, but also chamber music, theatre music, etc. Pupil of C. P. E. Bach and friend of Haydn. Lived variously in Paris, Hamburg, London and elsewhere, dying near Paris.

Dutilleux, Henri (b. 1916), French composer of two symphonies, a piano sonata, two-piano works, ballet *The Wolf*, etc. Pupil of Büsser and others.

Dutoit, Charles [Edouard] (b. 19??), Swiss conductor, active in Europe before becoming music director of the Montreal Symphony Orchestra, 1977.

Dvořák, Antonín (1841–1904), Czech composer; 1866–73, viola-player in Czech National Theatre orchestra, conducted by Smetana, who influenced him; 1874, became friend of Brahms. Wrote cantata THE SPECTRE'S BRIDE for use in England, which he visited nine times (Mus.D., Cambridge, 1891). Director of Prague Conservatory, 1891; director of the National Conservatory in New York, 1892–5, composing the AMERICAN string quartet and the Symphony no. 9 in E minor (FROM THE NEW WORLD) at this time. Until after World War II this was known as no. 5 and the previous four symphonies were numbered in a chronologically wrong order; in addition there are four earlier symphonies of his which remained unpublished at the composer's death and were not numbered. Current practice is to number all chronologically – 1 in C minor (*The Bells of Zlonice*), 2 in B♭, 3 in E♭, 4 in D minor, 5 in F, 6 in D, 7 in D minor, 8 in G. Wrote also SLAVONIC DANCES and SLAVONIC RHAPSODIES in a Czech 'national' style which also appears in, but does not dominate, his other works. These include a piano concerto, violin concerto, the Cello Concerto in B minor (and another early cello concerto), cycle of three concert-overtures (see CARNIVAL); 10 operas including ARMIDA and THE RUSALKA; a Mass and a Requiem; four piano trios; 14 works for string quartet, a piano quintet, etc. (see AMERICAN QUARTET and DUMKA); piano pieces and many songs and part-songs.

Dykes, John Bacchus (1823–76), British composer of many hymn-tunes and other church music; was also Anglican clergyman.

dynamics, the gradations of loudness and softness in music.

Dyson, George (1883–1964), British composer of *The Canterbury Pilgrims* and other choral works; also of chamber music, church music, etc. Director of the RCM, 1937–52; knighted, 1941.

Dzerzhinsky, Ivan [Ivanovich] (1909–78), Russian composer (also pianist), pupil of Gnessin. Works include *Quiet Flows the Don* and *Virgin Soil Upturned* (from Sholokhov's novels), and other operas; also three piano concertos, orchestral works, theatre and film music, etc.

E

E, note of the scale. So *E* FLAT (E♭), DOUBLE-FLAT (E♭♭), NATURAL (E♮), SHARP (E♯), DOUBLE-SHARP (E𝄪); *E major*, *E minor*, etc. – see MAJOR. So also either (1) in the key of E♭ (major, understood), or (2) indication of a TRANSPOSING INSTRUMENT on which the note written C sounds as E♭ (and correspondingly with other notes) – e.g. the small *clarinet in E♭*, or (colloquially) an E♭ *clarinet*.

e (It.), and.

Eagles, see ECCLES (s.).

early music, a term identifying a past period of music which, characterized by instruments and musical conventions significantly different from those of today, supposedly requires historically appropriate interpretation; cp. AUTHENTIC.

Early Music Consort of London, see MUNROW.

East, Michael (*c.*1580–1648), English composer of madrigals (one in THE TRUMPHS OF ORIANA), anthems, viol music, etc.

Easter Oratorio (Ger., *Oster-Oratorium*). Work by Bach (BWV 249) for church performance (solo and choral singers with orchestra), composed about 1736 – or rather arranged by him from earlier work to secular text.

It is a short work in 10 numbers, not a full-length work as 'oratorio' usually signifies.

Eaton, John [Charles] (b. 1935), American composer of operas (one based on *The Tempest*), songs, instrumental music using a syn-ket (type of synthesizer).

Eben, Petr (b. 1929), Czechoslovak composer, also pianist, organist and teacher. Wrote many works for organ including two concertos; also a string quartet and oratorio *The Apologia of Socrates*.

Eberlin, Johann Ernst (1702–62), German organist and composer of church and organ music, etc.

Ebony Concerto, work by Stravinsky for clarinet (slang 'ebony stick') and dance band, augmented by harp; written for Woody Herman's band, and first performed in 1946.

Eccles, John (*c.*1668–1735), English composer of masque *The Judgement of Paris* to Congreve's words, also of much other stage music (see SEMELE), songs, etc. Master of the King's Band, 1700. Other members of the Eccles family were also musicians in the 17th and 18th centuries.

echo organ, a manual (and the apparatus it controls) found on certain

111

large organs, suitable for echo effects
– having soft stops, and sometimes
pipes at a distance from the main body
of pipes.

eclogue, short poem, especially a pastoral dialogue – term derived from
Virgil and sometimes taken over from
poetic to musical usage, e.g. as title of
the first movement of Ireland's *Concertino Pastorale* for strings, 1939. See
also ENCINA.

écossaise (Fr.), sort of COUNTRY DANCE
cultivated, e.g., by Beethoven and
Schubert. (Although meaning 'Scottish' it is apparently not of Scottish
origin, nor identical with SCHOTTISCHE.)

Edwards, Richard (1524–66), English
composer, also playwright and poet;
wrote words of madrigal 'In going to
my naked bed', and probably the
music of it – as he certainly did to
other verse of his own.

Egdon Heath, symphonic poem by
Holst, first performed in 1928 – after
Hardy's description of a Dorset landscape in *The Return of the Native*.

Egge, Klaus (1906–79), Norwegian
composer, pupil of Valen and others.
Works, sometimes making use of Norwegian folk-music, include two piano
concertos, five symphonies, and chamber music.

Egk, Werner (1901–83), German composer of operas, including *Peer Gynt*
(after Ibsen), *Irish Legend* (after Yeats),
The Government Inspector (after Gogol)
and *Betrothal in Santo Domingo*, and of
ballet *A Summer Day* (on themes of
Kuhlau and Clementi), orchestral
French Suite (based on Rameau), a
violin concerto, etc.; also conductor.
Mainly self-taught.

Egmond, Max [Rudolf] **van** (b. 1936),
Dutch bass, born in Dutch East Indies
(now Indonesia); internationally active career from early 1960s, with
specialization in baroque oratorio, etc.

Egmont, play by Goethe – for a revival
of which, in 1810, Beethoven wrote
incidental music, comprising overture
(in concert performance combined
with *Triumph Symphony* from the end
of the play), four entr'actes, two songs,
music for the heroine's death, and one
MELODRAMA (in the technical sense).

**Eichendorff, Joseph Karl Benedict,
Baron von** (1788–1857), German
poet. See LIEDERKRANZ/LIEDERKREIS; FOUR LAST SONGS.

Eichheim, Henry (1870–1942), American composer (also violinist) who
travelled in Japan, China, etc., and incorporated the effects of oriental music
– and sometimes oriental instruments
themselves – into such works as
Nocturnal Impressions of Peking and
Korean Sketch for chamber music.

Eighteen-Twelve (1812), concert-overture by Tchaikovsky, 1880, commemorating Napoleon's retreat from
Moscow and incorporating the 'Marseillaise', the Tsarist Russian national
anthem, and other material. Scoring
includes, optionally, cannon effects
and military band.

eight-foot (organ stop, etc.), see FOOT.

eighth-note, the note ♪ considered as
a time-value. This term is standard
North American usage and, as mathematically corresponding to the element of time-signature represented by
/8, should clearly be preferred to
'quaver', still surviving in British use.
The corresponding rest is notated 𝄾

Eight Songs for a Mad King, music-theatre piece (for actor-singer and six instrumentalists) by P. M. Davies, 1969; text by Randolph Stow with sayings of King George III.

ein, eine (Ger.), one, a. See next word of phrase and also the following entry.

Eine kleine Nachtmusik (Ger. A Little Night Music, i.e. a little serenade), work for strings – quintet or small orchestra – by Mozart, 1787 (K525). Cp. SERE-NADE.

Einem, Gottfried von (b. 1918), Swiss-born Austrian composer, pupil of Blacher in Berlin and formerly opera répétiteur. Has composed operas *Danton's Death*, *The Trial* (after Kafka) and THE VISIT OF THE OLD LADY, ballet *Princess Turandot*, four symphonies, Serenade for double string orchestra, chamber music, etc. See RICCI.

Einleitung (Ger.), introduction, prelude, etc.

Einstein on the Beach, opera by Glass with the theatre director Robert Wilson; produced (in English) at Avignon, 1974. Einstein appears as a violinist-onlooker who observes as an abstract action unfolds.

Eisler, Hanns (1898–1962), German composer, pupil of Schoenberg; in USA, 1933–48, then returned to (East) Germany. Works, many linked to his Marxist beliefs, include music to Brecht's play *Galileo*, *German Symphony* (to words by Brecht); chamber music; *Newspaper Cuttings* for voice and piano; film music (and a book on this in English, 1947).

Eisteddfod (Welsh), type of Welsh national music festival, or a local emulation of this – or, as in Australia,

any competitive music festival, no connection with ¬Wales being then implied. (Pl. *eisteddfodau* reserved for specifically Welsh contexts.)

Ek, Gunnar (1900–1981), Swedish composer. Works, some with themes from folk-music, include three symphonies, *Swedish Fantasy* for orchestra, choral works, songs, organ music.

el (Sp.), the. See next word of phrase.

Elder, Mark, [Philip] (b. 1947), British conductor; musical director of the English National Opera since 1979; conducted at Bayreuth, 1981.

Electra, see ELEKTRA.

electric, term used with reference to musical instruments in two senses: (1) where electricity is used to facilitate the use of mechanical parts, e.g. *electric action* on a pipe-organ, not affecting the quality of the note produced; (2) where the use of amplification or other process determines or affects the quality of sound – see ELECTRO-PHONIC. For *electric guitar*, *electric violin*, etc., also see ELECTROPHONIC.

electronic, (1) term used of a class of instruments – properly, only those with electron-tube tone-generators (e.g. some organs, also THEREMIN and MARTENOT), but in loose usage extended to other ELECTROPHONIC instruments; (2) term used of musical compositions, or an element in them or in their performance, which employs tape-recorded or instantly synthesized sound. (See the following entry.) *Live electronics* usually means that the electronic element in a work is not fixed in advance but subject to variable, purposeful operation somewhat like the performance of a conventional instrumental part.

electronic music, term applied not to every musical performance or experience involving electronic apparatus, but to a type of composition (from mid-1950s) in which musical elements are assembled under the composer's direction on recorded tape, the playback of the tape then functioning as performance, no written score being necessary. (A score or diagram or other readable instruction *may*, however, be made.) The original sound-sources may be taken from a conventional instrument, a street-noise, or whatever, and treated by tape-manipulation (this use of 'real' sources being formerly termed CONCRETE MUSIC), or may be themselves electronically produced under laboratory conditions. The process may be facilitated by voltage-controlled synthesizer (see SYNTHESIZER) and by computer. The eventual playback may be subject to modification under concert conditions (*live electronics*: see ELECTRONIC).

Electronic Poem (Fr., *Poème électronique*), title of electronic piece (recorded and assembled from 'real' rather than synthesized sounds) by Varèse, composed for the Brussels International Exhibition, 1958, where it was distributed over 425 loud-speakers.

electrophonic (word compounded from modern *electric* plus Gk. *phoné* 'sound' as in *monophony*, etc.), technical term embracing different classes of instruments of which the notes are transmitted through electronic circuits ending in transducers (e.g. loudspeakers). They may be divided into (1) *electro-acoustic*, in which the tone of a conventional instrument, or one slightly modified, is converted into electrical vibrations and then subjected to controlled amplification and modification, e.g. electric guitar (and bass guitar), electric violin, electric PIANO; (2) *electromechanical*, those with electrostatic, electromagnetic, or photo-electric tone-generators, e.g. Compton, HAMMOND and certain other electric organs; (3) *electronic*, those with electronic-tube tone-generators: see ELECTRONIC.

élégie, elegy (Fr., Eng.), a song of lamentation, especially for the dead, or an instrumental work of similar intention or mood.

Elegy for Young Lovers, opera by Henze, produced (in German) in Schwetzingen (Germany), 1961; the libretto (originally in English), by W. H. Auden and Chester Kallman, concerns a self-centred poet, writer of the 'Elegy' of the title.

Elektra, opera by R. Strauss, produced in Dresden, 1909. Libretto by H. von Hofmannsthal, after Sophocles, concerned with the heroine's part in avenging her murdered father, Agamemnon.

Elgar, Edward (1857–1934), British composer, all but self-taught; Roman Catholic, but was much associated with the Three Choirs Festival (based on Anglican cathedrals). The ENIGMA VARIATIONS and THE DREAM OF GERONTIUS established him, 1899–1900. Had already written song-cycle SEA PICTURES. Later wrote oratorios THE APOSTLES and THE KINGDOM (intended as the first two parts of an uncompleted trilogy); cantata THE MUSIC MAKERS; two symphonies, symphonic study FALSTAFF; overtures COCKAIGNE and IN THE SOUTH; recitation with orchestra CARILLON; *Introduction and Allegro for Strings*; a violin concerto, cello concerto, chamber music, etc. The *Severn Suite* for brass band is one of his few post-1919 works. Knighted, 1904; Order of Merit, 1911; Master of the King's Music, 1924; baronet, 1931. Evolved a forthright style which won recognition as 'national' (though not indebted to folk-song), and unashamedly wrote 'popular' works such as the five POMP AND CIRCUMSTANCE marches. See also PIZZICATO.

Elias, German title of Mendelssohn's ELIJAH.

Elijah, oratorio by Mendelssohn, first performed in Birmingham (to English translation of original German text), 1846. Words from the Bible.

Eliot, George (Mary Anne Evans) (1819–80), British novelist. See JOUBERT.

Eliot, T. S. (1888–1965), American, British-naturalized, poet. See MURDER IN THE CATHEDRAL, PIZZETTI, TOGNI.

Elisir d'amore, L', see LOVE POTION.

Elizalde, Federico (1907–79), Spanish composer and conductor (also pianist), born in the Philippines; studied under Bloch, Falla and others. Conducted dance bands and, later, symphony orchestras. Works include opera *Paul Gauguin*, a piano concerto and a violin concerto.

Ellington, Duke (professional name of Edward Kennedy Ellington) (1899–1974), American pianist, dance-band leader, and composer of dance music and also of concert works in, or indebted to, the jazz idiom.

Elman, Mischa (German spelling of Russia 'Misha') (1891–1967), violinist born in Russia who visited USA from 1908 and afterwards settled there (US citizen, 1923), maintaining high international reputation.

Eloy, Jean-Claude (b. 1938), French composer, pupil of Milhaud and Boulez, who taught in California, 1966–8. Works include *Equivalences* for 18 instruments; *Polychronies* for wind instruments, piano, harp, percussion; songs; *Shanti* for voices and instruments combined with electronic sound.

Elsner, Joseph [Xaver] (1769–1854), German-Polish composer of 27 operas, etc., and teacher of Chopin at Warsaw Conservatory.

embouchure (Fr., used also in English), the position and application of the lips to the mouthpiece of a wind instrument. (In French the word also means the mouthpiece itself.)

'Emperor' Concerto, nickname (not Beethoven's title) for Beethoven's Piano Concerto no. 5 in E♭, 1808. Origin uncertain.

Emperor Jones, opera by Gruenberg, produced in New York, 1933. Libretto by composer, after O'Neill's play: Jones is a black American railwayman who, after committing murder, becomes 'emperor' of a Caribbean island.

'Emperor' Quartet, nickname for Haydn's String Quartet in C (Hob. III: 77, also known as op. 76, no. 3), *c*.1799, of which the slow movement takes Haydn's own 'Emperor's Hymn' (see next entry) as a theme for variations.

Emperor's Hymn, patriotic hymn by Haydn, 1797 (Hob. XXVIa: 43), adopted as national anthem in Austria – and later (to words 'Deutschland über Alles') in Germany. See preceding entry. A similar tune is found in a Telemann suite, so Haydn's may be an adaptation.

empfindsamer Stil; Empfindsamkeit (Ger., expressive style; expressiveness), terms characterizing the music of certain German composers of the mid 18th century, e.g. Graun and C. P. E. Bach, with reference to their deliberate cultivation of specified emotions. An alternative translation is 'sensibility', as in Jane Austen's *Sense and Sensibility*.

enchaînez (Fr.), link (them) together – i.e. let the next movement follow its predecessor without a break.

Enchanted Lake, The (Rus., *Volshebnoye ozero*), symphonic poem by Lyadov, 1909 – descriptive, but with no explicit story.

Encina, Juan del (1468–1529), Spanish composer, and also (from 1519) priest – chiefly famous to his countrymen as poet and dramatist. Wrote eclogues (pastoral plays) with songs composed by himself.

encore (Fr., again), term used in English (though not in French) to mean 'perform it again', or, loosely, to mean 'perform some more'; hence (noun) a repetition or extra piece in response to such demand. (For the current French term, see BIS.)

Enescu, George (1881–1955), Romanian violinist and composer (also pianist and conductor) who used a French form of his name, Georges Enesco. Studied in Vienna, and later in Paris with Fauré and Massenet; afterwards mainly resident in France. Distinguished teacher, e.g. of Menuhin. Works include opera *Oedipus*, five symphonies, two *Romanian Rhapsodies* for orchestra, piano and violin solos.

Enfance du Christ, L', see CHILDHOOD OF CHRIST.

Enfant et les sortilèges, L', see CHILD AND THE SPELLS.

English Chamber Orchestra, a London chamber orchestra which adopted that name in 1960 (earlier the Goldsbrough Orchestra); it had no regular principal conductor until the appointment of Jeffrey Tate in 1985.

English Concert, see PINNOCK.

English fingering, see FINGERING.

English horn, woodwind instrument of oboe type, but standing a fifth lower than the oboe, and written as a TRANSPOSING INSTRUMENT a fifth higher than sounding; compass from the E below middle C upwards for about two and a half octaves. Used rarely before the 19th-century ROMANTICS but often thereafter in the orchestra – but still rarely in chamber music, as solo instrument, etc. More usually in Britain called 'cor anglais'; but the translated form 'English horn' is more sensible, is accepted American usage, and corresponds also to use in other languages – Italian *corno inglese*, etc. The Italian name was known before the French and the supposed derivation from *anglé* (angled) is wrong: the instrument seems to be called the French 'horn' because of its original curved shape (different from the modern type) and 'English' possibly because of its being known from England – Purcell in DIOCLESIAN specifies a 'tenor hoboy', i.e tenor oboe, though this is apparently a different instrument.

English National Opera, new name adopted in 1974 by the former Sadler's Wells Opera, which performs in English; see SADLER'S WELLS. Musical director since 1979, Mark Elder.

English Suite, title of six suites for harpsichord by Bach (BWV 806–11), composed in about 1725 – so called, apparently, because, like Purcell's suites and unlike Bach's own FRENCH SUITES, they have preludes for first movements.

enharmonic, description of the difference between, e.g., F♮ and E♯ or D♯ and E♭ – i.e. on the piano and other fixed-note instruments, a difference only of notation, not of pitch; and on other instruments, and voices, possibly a very small change of pitch also, as may be required to adjust to new harmony. Hence *enharmonic change*, the change of a note in a performer's part, e.g. from D♯ to E♭; and similarly, *enharmonic modulation*, involving such a change, as in the two top notes bracketed here:

Enigma Variations, usual name for Elgar's *Variations on an Original Theme, for Orchestra*, first performed in 1899; the word 'enigma' does not occur on the title-page but heads the actual music-type. Each variation 'portrays' a person identified in the score only by initials or a nickname – in one case by three asterisks. No. 9 ('Nimrod', i.e. a hunter; in German, *Jaeger*) depicts Elgar's friend A. J. Jaeger of Novello's, his publishers; no. 14 (finale), 'E.D.U',

which quotes some previous variations, represents the composer himself. The naming of the variations is not the only 'enigma': Elgar said that a well-known tune 'goes with' his theme: it has now been plausibly (but not indisputably) identified as 'Auld lang syne'. See also POTTER.

En Saga, see SAGA.

ensemble (Fr. together), (1) the quality of teamwork in performance ('their ensemble was poor'); (2) an item in opera for several soloists, with or without chorus; (3) a group of performers – the term implying a group of no fixed number, and not so numerous and regularly constituted as to deserve the name of orchestra or choir.

Entführung aus dem Serail, Die, see SERAGLIO.

entr'acte (Fr.), interval (US, intermission) in a play, opera, etc., or the music to be played in it: cp. ACT TUNE, INTERMEZZO.

entrée (Fr., entry), sub-division of an act, e.g. in 17th–18th century French ballet, roughly corresponding to a 'scene' in opera.

Entry of the Little Fauns (Fr., *Marche des petits faunes*), piece by Pierné forming part of his ballet *Cydalise and the Satyr*, produced in 1923.

Eötvös, Peter (b. 1944), Hungarian conductor and composer, prominent in conducting new works by Boulez and Stockhausen.

epicedium (Latinized form of Gk.), dirge; used by Purcell in *The Queen's Epicedium* (Z383), a Latin elegy for Queen Mary, 1695.

episode, a section in a piece of music considered to have a subordinate role; in particular, (1) in a RONDO, a contrasting section between recurrences of the main theme; (2) in a FUGUE, a section occurring between entries of the subject.

éponge (Fr.), sponge; *baguettes d'éponge*, drum-sticks with sponge head.

equali (old It. pl., equal), instrumental pieces for instruments of the same kind, especially funeral pieces for four trombones, e.g. by Beethoven (1812).

equal temperament, see TEMPERAMENT.

equal voices, voices of the same kind. (Hence a piece of music 'for equal voices', e.g. for three trebles, as in some school music.) Cp. EQUALI.

Erb, Donald [James] (b. 1927), American composer (pupil of N. Boulanger in Paris) and teacher. Works include *Fallout?* for narrator, chorus, string quartet, piano; *In no Strange Land* for tape, trombone, double-bass; String Trio for violins, electric guitar, cello.

Erbse, Heimo (b. 1924), German composer; also conductor and operatic stage director; pupil of Blacher. Works include two symphonies, ballet *Ruth*, chamber music.

Erickson, Robert (b. 1917), American composer, pupil of Krenek. Works include *General Speech* in which a solo trombonist articulates speech-like sounds into his instrument; *Pacific Sirens* for tape and 10–14 instruments.

Erkel, Ferenc (1810–93), Hungarian composer, also pianist and conductor. Wrote *Hunyadi László, Bánk Bán*, and other nationalistic Hungarian operas; also many songs, etc.

Erl-King, usual English title for Schubert's song *Erlkönig* (D328), composed in 1815, based on a Goethe ballad depicting Death snatching a child. The meaning of the title appears to derive from 'King of the Alders'.

ernst (Ger.), serious. (For Brahms's *Vier ernste Gesänge*, see FOUR SERIOUS SONGS.)

Ernst, Heinrich Wilhelm (1814–65), Moravian violinist; composer of concertos, etc., for his instrument.

'Eroica' Symphony, name given by Beethoven to his Symphony no. 3, 1803–4: 'Heroic Symphony to celebrate the memory of a great man', i.e. Napoleon. To him, as a liberator, the work was originally dedicated, the inscription being altered when Beethoven learnt with scorn that Napoleon had taken the title of Emperor. See also PROMETHEUS.

'Eroica' Variations, see PROMETHEUS.

Erwartung, see EXPECTATION.

Eschenbach (originally Ringman), **Christoph** (b. 1940), German pianist; prizewinner in international contest, Lucerne, 1962, thereafter prominent (US appearances from 1969). Henze's Piano Concerto no. 2 was written for him.

Escher, Rudolf (1912–80), Dutch composer (also critic), pupil of Pijper. Works include two symphonies; *Summer Rites at Noon* for two orchestras facing each other: *Songs of Love and Eternity* for chamber choir, based on poems of Emily Dickinson. Also poet and painter.

Eshpai, Andrey [Yakovlevich] (b. 1925), Russian composer, also pianist. Works include four symphonies, a piano concerto, violin concerto, over 30 film scores.

España (Sp., Spain), orchestral rhapsody by Chabrier, first performed in 1883, making exuberant use of Spanish tunes.

espansiva (It., expansive), title (*Sinfonia espansiva*) of C. Nielsen's Symphony no. 3, composed 1910–11.

Esplá, Oscar (1886–1976), Spanish composer of ballets, symphonic poems, a violin sonata, many piano works, etc. Lived mainly in Belgium, 1936–51, then returned to Spain; active in promoting modern music.

Esposito, Michele (1855–1929), Italian pianist, conductor and composer of *Irish Symphony*, overture to Shakespeare's *Othello*, chamber music, etc.; long resident in Dublin.

estampie (Fr.), an instrumental form (probably of dance origin) current in the 13th–14th centuries, having between four and seven sections (*puncta*, Lat. pl. of *punctum*) each of which is stated twice – with a different ending the second time.

Esther, oratorio by Handel; words by S. Humphreys, after Racine. Originally done as a masque (i.e. with action and costumes) in private, 1720, with the title *Haman and Mordecai*; expanded and given in concert form in London, 1732, thus becoming the first English oratorio.

estinto (It., extinct), as soft and still as possible.

et (Fr., Lat.), and.

ethnomusicology, the study of musical activity in relation to anthropological background – especially that of non-European cultures.

Etler, Alvin [Derald] (1913–73), American composer, pupil of Hindemith; was also oboist. Works include Concerto for brass quintet with string orchestra and percussion; Concerto for string quartet and orchestra.

Eton College Manuscript, a large choirbook in the Library of Eton College, dating from about 1500.

étouffez (Fr.), damp down, stop the tone, etc. – direction used, e.g., when the sound of a cymbal or harp-string is to be cut short.

étude, see STUDY.

etwas (Ger.), moderately, somewhat.

Eugene Onegin, see YEVGENY ONEGIN.

euphonium, brass instrument (mainly used in the brass band and military band), equivalent to the tenor TUBA; a TRANSPOSING INSTRUMENT in B♭.

eurhythmics, a system of expressing the rhythmical aspects of music by bodily movement, invented by JAQUES-DALCROZE, who set up an institute for this in Germany in 1910.

Euridice, see EURYDICE.

Euripides (480–406 BC), Greek dramatist. See ALKESTIS, BASSARIDS, DRYSDALE, IPHIGENIA, PACINI.

Euryanthe, opera by Weber, produced in Vienna, 1823. Libretto by H. von Chezy: the medieval heroine, whose reputation for chastity is challenged and vindicated, gives her name to the work.

Eurydice (*Euridice* is the Italian form), title of two of the earliest surviving operas: see CACCINI, PERI. The same legend inspired Monteverdi's ORPHEUS.

Evangelisti, Franco (1926–80), Italian composer who broke off studies in engineering to take up music. His works include *4!* (i.e. mathematical 'factorial four') for violin and piano; *Integrated Fields* (tape); and a theatrical piece with mimes, *The Box* (under German title *Die Schachtel*).

Evans, Geraint [Llewellyn] (b. 1922), British baritone, chiefly noted in opera (Papageno in THE MAGIC FLUTE, title-role of WOZZECK, etc.): Covent Garden début, 1948. Has occasionally worked as operatic stage director. Knighted, 1969.

Evening and Tempest, name given to one of a set of three symphonies by Haydn – see MORNING.

exercise, (1) vocal or instrumental study of no artistic value, e.g. a *five-finger exercise* for piano; (2) in the 18th century, a short keyboard work: D. Scarlatti's early sonatas were published under the Italian equivalent of this name; (3) the composition which candidates are obliged to write for certain university degrees in music.

Expectation (Ger., *Erwartung*), a 'monodrama' (i.e. stage piece for one character) by Schoenberg, composed in 1909 but not performed till 1924. In it a woman going to meet her lover finds his dead body.

exposition, (1) that part of a SONATA-FORM or similar movement in which the main themes are initially stated before they undergo DEVELOPMENT; (2) in a FUGUE, the initial statement of the subject by all the 'voices' in turn.

expressionism, term borrowed from painting and applied to literature, drama and music – involving the expression of the artist's state of mind by means of external symbols not necessarily in normal relation to each other. (The application of the term, e.g. to Schoenberg's music, alludes apparently to an extreme emotionalism and to a 'hard' sound, supposedly opposite to the IMPRESSIONISM of Debussy's muted, more liquid style.)

Exsultate, jubilate (Lat., Exult, rejoice), title of a solo motet by Mozart (K165), 1773, originally for castrato voice with orchestra; contains a celebrated 'Alleluia'.

extemporize = IMPROVISE.

extension organ = UNIT ORGAN.

extravaganza (It., *stravaganza*, Anglicized), 19th-century English type of stage entertainment with music, in the form of farce or burlesque, often harnessing new words to known tunes.

F

F, note of the scale. So *F* FLAT (F♭), DOUBLE FLAT (F♭♭), NATURAL (F♮), SHARP (F♯), DOUBLE SHARP (F𝄪); *F major, F minor*, etc. – see MAJOR. So also *in F*, either (1) in the key of F (major, understood), or (2) indication of a TRANSPOSING INSTRUMENT on which the note written C sounds as F, and likewise with other notes – e.g. *trumpet in F*, or (colloquially) an *F trumpet*. So also *F-clef*, clef indicating the position of the F below middle C – the BASS clef being now the only such clef used.

F, abbr. for (1) Fanna (in numbering Vivaldi's works, being superseded by Ryom's system – see VIVALDI); (2) Fellow, in musical diplomas or honours, e.g. FRAM (Fellow of the Royal Academy of Music).

f, symbol in TONIC SOL-FA notation for the fourth degree (subdominant) of the scale, pronounced FAH.

f, abbr. of *forte* (It., loud); hence, as indications of increasingly greater loudness, *ff*, *fff*, etc. – sometimes in even greater aggregations.

fa, the note F (in Latin countries, and formerly elsewhere); cp. FAH.

faburden (Old Eng.; literally 'false bass'), a style of improvised polyphony particularly associated with 15th-century English vocal music, adding an extra voice or voices above and below a given chant. (The cognate French term FAUX-BOURDON has a different meaning.)

Façade, a sequence of settings by Walton for reciter and small instrumental ensemble to poems by Edith Sitwell, first performed publicly in 1923. The selection of numbers (Walton wrote a total of more than 40) varied between this and subsequent performances; 21 settings were 'established' from a revival of 1942 and a further eight were given under the title *Façade 2* in 1977. Meanwhile the music had become well known in two orchestral suites and (1931) a ballet under the same title.

facile (Fr., It.), easy. So *facilità* (It.), ease, fluency; also a simplified version, e.g. of a solo passage written for virtuoso performers and now brought within more modest capacities.

fado, fadinho (Port.), type of Portuguese folk-song, mainly urban and properly having a particular rhythm and binary form.

Fagott, fagotto (Ger., It.), BASSOON.

fah, in TONIC SOL-FA, the spoken name for the fourth degree (subdominant) of the scale, written f. Cp. FA.

Fair at Sorochints, The, see SORO-CHINTSY FAIR.

121

Fairfax, Robert, see FAYRFAX.

Fair Maid of Perth, The (Fr., *La Jolie Fille de Perth*), opera by Bizet, produced in Paris, 1867. Libretto by J. H. Vernoy de St-Georges and É. Adenis, after Scott's historical novel of 15th-century Scotland.

Fair Maid of the Mill, The (Ger., *Die schöne Müllerin*), song-cycle by Schubert, 1823, to 20 poems by W. Müller about a fruitless courtship.

Fairy Queen, The, an adaptation of Shakespeare's *A Midsummer Night's Dream*, produced in 1692, for which Purcell wrote the music (Z629).

Fall, Leo (1873–1925), Austrian composer of *The Dollar Princess* and other operettas.

Falla, Manuel de (1876–1946), Spanish composer, also pianist. Won first major success with opera *Life is Short* (*La vida breve*), produced in 1913; later wrote ballets THE THREE-CORNERED HAT and LOVE, THE SORCERER. Much influenced by Spanish folk-music in these and other works – e.g. NIGHTS IN THE GARDENS OF SPAIN, and *Fantasia Bética* (i.e. Andalusian Fantasy) for piano; but less so in some other works including puppet opera MASTER PETER'S PUPPET SHOW, and a harpsichord concerto, the latter showing NEO-CLASSICAL tendency. From 1938 resident in Argentina, where he died: his opera *Atlantis* (Sp., *La Atlántida*) was completed after his death by E. Halffter.

false relation(s), English term of which the American equivalent is the more sensible – see CROSS-RELATION(S).

falsetto (It.), kind of singing (or speech) produced by adult males in a register higher than their normal utterance: this is the standard type of voice production used by the male ALTO or COUNTER-TENOR voice; it is sometimes specified (generally as comic effect, e.g. imitating women) in other voices.

falsobordone (It., false drone), type of harmonization of a psalm-tune, usually in four-part block chords; a variety is the ANGLICAN CHANT. (The cognate French term FAUXBOURDON has a different meaning.)

Falstaff, title of works by several composers, after Shakespeare, including (1) opera by Verdi, produced in Milan, 1893 – libretto by A. Boito, based on *The Merry Wives of Windsor*; (2) symphonic study by Elgar, first performed in 1913 – after *King Henry IV* and *King Henry V*. See also MERRY WIVES OF WINDSOR, SIR JOHN IN LOVE.

familiar style (also It., *stile familiare*), term probably originating in the 16th century to describe vocal music in which the voices move uniformly together from one syllable to the next and from one note-value to the next – e.g. in a conventional hymn in four parts, without contrapuntal independence such as might be found in a madrigal.

family, term used to group instruments of similar nature and tone-quality – even if there are significant differences in shape (e.g. the saxophone family) or even if they do not all carry the same name (e.g. the 'violin family' of violin, viola, cello and double-bass).

Fanciulla del West, La, see GIRL OF THE GOLDEN WEST.

fancy, term used in England in the 16th–17th centuries for FANTASY (2).

fandango (Sp.), Spanish dance in triple time, probably of South American origin; accompanied normally by guitar, castanets, etc.

fanfare, (1) a flourish for trumpets (or other instruments imitating them), usually by way of a proclamation or introduction; so *fanfare* TRUMPET, instrument designed for such ceremonial purpose; (2) (Fr.), a brass band.

Fanshawe, David [Arthur] (b. 1942), British composer and sound archivist whose extensive travels resulted in *African Sanctus* for chorus and orchestra (with extra African percussion) and other works including *Symphony of the Arabian Gulf*.

fantaisie, fantasia, Fantasie (Fr., It., Ger.), see FANTASY.

Fantastic Symphony (Fr., *Symphonie fantastique*), symphony by Berlioz, 1830, subtitled 'Episodes in the life of an artist' – with a programmatic basis derived from Berlioz's own despairing love for the actress Harriet Smithson.

fantasy (or, borrowed from Italian, *fantasia*), term of various musical meanings, but nearly always associated with the idea of the 'free' play of the composer's imagination, as distinct from adherence to 'set' forms. Notable senses are – (1) a mood-piece or character-piece of a 19th-century ROMANTIC kind, e.g. Schumann's *Fantasy Pieces* (Ger., *Fantasie-Stücke*) for piano, 1837; (2) a contrapuntal piece, normally in several sections, for one player (keyboard) or several (e.g. viols) current in the 16th and 17th centuries; an alternative name in this sense was 'fancy', and the spelling 'phantasy' was used when the form was revived in 20th-century English

chamber music; (3) a piece compounded of known tunes; so *fantasy on* ... e.g. an opera, i.e. built from tunes contained in the opera; (4) term used in the phrase *free fantasy* or *free fantasia* as a synonym for DEVELOPMENT, e.g. in SONATA-FORM.

farandole (Fr.), a dance of Provence, accompanied by pipe and tabor – properly in 6/8 time, which the so-called 'Farandole' in Bizet's THE WOMAN OF ARLES is not, though it is based on an authentic Provençal tune.

Farewell Symphony, nickname of Haydn's Symphony no. 45 (in the unusual key of F♯ minor), 1772 (Hob. I:45), in which the music of the last movement ends in such a way that the players may leave their stands one after the other, only two violins eventually remaining. (Or perhaps Haydn, as CONTINUO-player at the harpsichord, remained?) This is said to have been a hint to Haydn's patron, Prince Esterházy, that the orchestra deserved a holiday.

Farkas, Ferenc (b. 1905), Hungarian composer – and famous teacher of other Hungarian composers such as Ligeti. His works include *The Sly Students* and other operas, two masses, *Ricordanze* (It., *Remembrances*) for clarinet and string trio.

Farmer, John (*c*.1570–?, English organist and composer; moved from a Dublin organistship to London in 1599. Noted for madrigals; also wrote psalm-tunes, contrapuntal exercises, etc.

Farnaby, Giles (*c*.1565–1640), English composer, living in London. Wrote music for virginals, including pieces with picturesque titles, e.g. *A Toy*, *Giles Farnaby's Dream*; also canzonets, madrigals, psalm-tunes.

Farrant, Richard (*c.*1530–80), English organist (St George's Chapel, Windsor) and composer of anthems and other church music; also of songs for plays which he produced with choirboys.

farruca, energetic Andalusian dance – used, e.g., by Falla for the Miller's Dance in THE THREE-CORNERED HAT.

Farwell, Arthur (1872–1952), American composer (also teacher and critic), pupil in Europe of Humperdinck, Pfitzner and Guilmant; studied American Indian music and derived some influence from it. Composed symphonic, choral and chamber works, etc.

Fasch, Johann Friedrich (1688–1758), German composer of church cantatas, concertos (for violin, oboe, etc.) and other works.

Faschingsschwank aus Wien, see CARNIVAL JEST FROM VIENNA.

Fauré, Gabriel [Urbain] (1845–1924), French composer (also organist); director of the Paris Conservatory, 1905–20, teacher of Ravel and others. Cultivated delicately balanced idiom expressed mainly in small forms – wrote many piano solos, DOLLY for piano duet, numerous songs, including *La Bonne Chanson* and other song-cycles; also two piano quartets, and other chamber music. Also wrote a Requiem; orchestral works including PAVANE (with optional chorus); Ballade for piano and orchestra (originally for piano alone); incidental music to PELLÉAS AND MÉLISANDE, and other music for the French and English stage.

Faust, opera by Gounod, produced in Paris, 1859. Libretto by J. Barbier and M. Carré, after Goethe's drama. For other works on the Faust legend (all after Goethe, unless stated), see DAMNATION OF FAUST, DOCTOR FAUST, MEPHISTOPHELES, and the following entries. Incidental music has also been written to Goethe's play itself, e.g. by Diepenbrock.

Faust, opera by Spohr, produced in Prague, 1816. Libretto by J. K. Bernard – without reference to Goethe's *Faust*, at that time not complete.

'Faust', Episodes from Lenau's, two orchestral works by Liszt, first performed, 1861 – the second is the MEPHISTO WALTZ, no. 1. After a German poem on Faust by Lenau.

'Faust', Scenes from Goethe's, concert work by Schumann (overture and six other numbers) for soloists, chorus and orchestra, completed in 1853.

Faust Overture, A, orchestral work by Wagner, 1839, referring to Goethe's drama but intended for independent concert performance (originally conceived as the first movement of a symphony on Faust).

Faust Symphony, A, symphony by Liszt (with choral ending), after Goethe; first performed in 1857, revised in 1880. In three movements respectively on Faust, Gretchen and Mephistopheles, the final chorus however being non-Mephistophelian.

fauxbourdon (old Fr.), a medieval technique of adding one or more lines in counterpoint to a given chant, as in 15th-century French music. (The cognate English term FABURDEN refers to a similar but not identical practice; see also FALSOBORDONE.)

favola d'Orfeo, La, see ORPHEUS.

Fayrfax, Robert (1464–1521), English composer of motets, Masses and songs; organist of St Albans cathedral. As a member of the Chapel Royal, attended Henry VIII to his meeting with Francis I of France on the Field of the Cloth of Gold, 1520, when the English and French choirs sang together. Cp. SERMISY.

feierlich (Ger.), solemnly, exaltedly.

Feld, Jindřich (b. 1925), Czechoslovak composer, also violinist and writer on music; taught in Adelaide, Australia, 1968–70. Works include a bassoon concerto, cello concerto, children's opera *The Postman's Tale*.

Feldman, Morton (1926–87), American composer, pupil of Riegger and others, and influenced by association with Cage. Works, often in unusual notation allowing much choice to performers, include *The Swallows of Salangan* for chorus and 23 instruments, *The Viola in My Life* for viola with different co-participants.

Feldpartie, Feldpartita (Ger.), 'field suite', i.e. suite for open-air performance by a military band – cp. PARTITA. (Haydn wrote 10.)

feminine, term used in certain musical contexts to imply (unjustly?) relative weakness – so, e.g., the 'second subject' in SONATA-FORM is sometimes said to have feminine character as being less assertive than the first subject. So also *feminine cadence, feminine ending,* in which the final chord is reached on a 'weak' beat of the bar instead of a strong beat as usual – e.g. the end of 'The Vicar of Bray'. (Where the final chord on a weak beat merely repeats a chord first reached on a strong beat, e.g. at the end of 'What shall we do with the drunken sailor?', the ending still remains 'masculine'.)

Fenby, Eric [William] (b. 1906), British composer (overture *Rossini on Ilkla Moor,* etc.), who acted as amanuensis to the blind and paralysed Delius from 1928, taking down some of his late works from dictation. OBE, 1962. Also, latterly, conductor of Delius's works.

Ferencsik, János (1907–84), Hungarian conductor, with Budapest Opera from 1927; also principal conductor of Hungarian State Symphony Orchestra. He made his first London appearance in 1957.

Ferguson, Howard (b. 1908), Northern Irish composer, pianist and teacher, resident in London. Works include Partita for orchestra, five Bagatelles and other piano solos, songs. Also editor of old music.

fermata (It.), the PAUSE, ⌒.

Fernández, Oscar Lorenzo (1897–1948), Brazilian composer and conservatory director. Works, in an idiom recognized by his compatriots as national, include opera *Malazarte* (Master of the Evil Arts), and other music indebted to Brazilian folklore – e.g. *Batuque* (Brazilian dance) for orchestra; also chamber music, piano solos, songs, etc.

Ferneyhough, Brian (b. 1943), British composer who moved to Switzerland, 1969, and much of whose music has won prior acceptance outside Britain. Works include *Transit* for chamber orchestra and six amplified solo voices; four string quartets; a series of works called *Carceri di invenzione* (It., Dungeons of Invention). Many compositions present extreme difficulty in performance.

Ferrabosco, surname of Italo-English musical family, principally the two following.

Ferrabosco, Alfonso (1543–88), Italian composer of motets, madrigals, etc.; intermittently resident in London, for a time court musician to Elizabeth I, but returned finally to Italy, 1578. Father of the following.

Ferrabosco, Alfonso (1575–1628), English composer of Italian descent (son of preceding); court musician to James I, composer of ayres, fantasies for viols, music for masques, etc.

Ferrier, Kathleen (1912–53), British contralto – noted in recital (Bruno Walter accompanied her), oratorio and opera; many works of Britten, including the title-role of THE RAPE OF LUCRETIA, were written for her. CBE, 1953. Achieved unique reputation, particularly in Britain; died of cancer.

Ferroud, Pierre Octave (1900–36), French composer, pupil of Schmitt, killed in a motor accident in Hungary; also critic. Works include a symphony, piano solos, opera *Surgery* (i.e. dentistry, after a Chekhov story).

Fesch, William, see DEFESCH.

Festa, Constanzo (*c*.1490–1545), Italian composer of madrigals (perhaps the first Italian-born composer of them), and of church music; was a singer in the Papal Chapel.

Festin de l'araignée, Le, see SPIDER'S BANQUET.

Festing, Michael Christian (*c*. 1680–1752), English violinist and composer,

pupil of Geminiani, member of the King's band and director of the Italian Opera in London. Wrote cantatas, concertos, sonatas, etc.

Fêtes (Debussy), see NOCTURNES.

Feuermann, Emanuel (1902–42), Austrian-born cellist who settled in Germany and then, after the Nazi advent, in USA; his outstanding career was cut short by his early death.

Février, Henri (1875–1957), French composer of eight operas (including *Gismonda*, produced in Paris, 1918), songs, etc.; pupil of Massenet and Fauré.

f-hole, name given to a hole approximately in the shape of an *f*, of which there are two cut in the belly of a violin, etc., for the sake of the sound.

Fibich, Zdeněk (1850–1900), Czech composer (also conductor and critic) who studied in Leipzig and Paris. Composed operas, including *The Tempest* (after Shakespeare); MELODRAMAS (in the technical sense); many piano works; symphonic poems; orchestral piece *At Twilight*, of which the well-known POEM is a movement.

fiddle, (1) colloquial term for the violin; (2) term for the whole range of small, bowed, non-fretted stringed instruments (including not only the violin but also its medieval predecessors such as the rebec, and various folk-instruments); (3) term used to identify particular instruments of this range, e.g. the Norwegian *Hardanger fiddle* (with its SYMPATHETIC strings; see TVEITT). Thus Mahler's direction, in the Scherzo of his Symphony no. 4, that a solo violin with its strings tuned a tone higher than normal is to play 'like a fiddle' – Ger., *wie ein Fidel* – refers to the imitation of folk idiom. So also (referring to (1) above) *bass fiddle*, colloquial term for the double-bass (but see GRAINGER for an eccentric use). See also following entry.

Fiddle Fugue, nickname for an organ fugue in D minor by Bach (BWV 539), arranged from an earlier (1720) version for violin solo.

Fidel (Ger.), see FIDDLE.

Fidelio, or Married Love (Ger., *Fidelio, oder Die eheliche Liebe*), Beethoven's only opera, with libretto by J. Sonnleithner. Produced in Vienna, 1805; revised version, 1806; further-revised version, 1814, with new overture now known as *Fidelio*. See also GAVEAUX and LEONORA. ('Fidelio' is the male name assumed by the heroine, Leonora, in her rescue of her husband from prison.)

Field, John (1782–1837), Irish pianist and composer, pupil of Clementi in London; settled in St Petersburg in 1803, toured Europe from there, and died in Moscow. Invented the name and style of the NOCTURNE, taken over by Chopin. His work, admired e.g. by Schumann and Liszt, includes 20 nocturnes for piano, seven piano concertos, and chamber music.

Fielding, Henry (1707–54) British novelist. See TOM JONES.

Fiery Angel, The (Rus., *Ognenny Angel*), opera by Prokofiev, composed 1919–27, first staged in Venice, 1955; libretto by the composer, after Bryusov's novel, involves witchcraft and religious hysteria in the 16th century. (The opera is also known as *The Flaming Angel, The Angel of Fire,* etc.)

fife, term historically meaning a kind of high-pitched wooden flute, usually without keys; but today's military 'drum and fife' band includes low-pitched flutes as well as high ones – none, however, identical with the orchestral flute and piccolo.

fifteenth, organ stop of DIAPASON tone sounding two octaves above the note played – i.e. 15 steps (of the diatonic scale) above, counting both the extreme notes.

fifth, an interval in melody or harmony, reckoned as taking five steps in the (major or minor) scale – counting the bottom and top notes. A *perfect fifth* is the distance, e.g., from C up to G; a semitone less gives the *diminished fifth* (e.g. C up to G♭), and a semitone more gives the *augmented fifth* (e.g. C up to G♯). (For *consecutive fifths* and *hidden fifths,* 'prohibited' intervals in certain types of composition, see CONSECUTIVE.)

'Fifths' Quartet, nickname for Haydn's String Quartet in D minor (no. 2 of op. 76, 1797–8; Hob. III:76), because of the opening melodic leaps of a fifth. The minuet movement is known as the 'Witches' Minuet' (Ger., *Hexenmenuett*) due to its eerie character.

Figaro, see MARRIAGE OF FIGARO. (As a character, he also occurs in THE BARBER OF SEVILLE.)

Figlia del reggimento, La, title given (in Italian usage) to Donizetti's French opera THE DAUGHTER OF THE REGIMENT.

figure, a short musical phrase, especially one that is recognizable and repeated.

figured bass, a standardized notation for CONTINUO, practised especially in the 17th and 18th centuries, and also used today, e.g. in academic training and as a kind of harmonic shorthand. Figures with a bass-note indicate the distance above that bass-note of the other notes which are to be sounded. E.g. if the key is C major, and the bass-note is C, the figure 5 would indicate G, and 5♯ would indicate G♯; but the choice of the particular octave in which this G or G♯ is to be placed is left to the musicianship of the performer. Various abbreviations and other conventions are also used. (The CHORD-SYMBOLS used in modern pop music, though similar in being a kind of shorthand, are not the same. They are named after chords – major, minor, augmented, etc. – irrespective of which note of these chords comes in the bass; *figured-bass symbols* are invariably relative to a particular bass-note.)

Fille du régiment, La, see DAUGHTER OF THE REGIMENT.

fin (Fr.), end.

final, (1, Eng.) the note on which the modal scale ends (see MODE), analogous to the keynote of the major or minor scale; (2, Fr.) = FINALE.

finale (It., final; but used in English as follows), (1) the last movement of a work in several movements; (2) an ensemble ending an act of an opera – so *first finale, second finale,* etc., referring to Acts I, II, etc.

fine (It.), end – term sometimes occurring in the middle of music as notated, in conjunction with some instruction at the end of the music-type to go back to an earlier point and proceed from there to the point where *fine* occurs.

Fine, Irving (1914–62), American composer, pupil of N. Boulanger in Paris; also conductor. Works include Toccata Concertante for orchestra, Partita for wind quintet.

Fingal's Cave, see HEBRIDES.

Finger, Gottfried (or Godfrey) (*c.* 1660–1730), Moravian composer who worked in England under James II's patronage until 1702, then in Germany; wrote operas and other stage music, some of it in English, and various instrumental pieces.

fingerboard, the part of a stringed instrument over which the strings are stretched, the player's fingers pressing the strings down to select the length of vibrating string required to produce a particular note.

fingering, (1) the use of the fingers in playing an instrument; (2) the indication on paper of which fingers are to be used for which notes – so (in piano-playing) *Continental fingering,* numbering the thumb as 1 and the other fingers as 2–5, as opposed to (obsolete) *English fingering,* in which the thumb was signified by + and the other fingers as 1–4.

Finlandia, orchestral work by Sibelius, first performed in 1900 – of patriotic intent but not using folk-music as material.

Finney, Ross Lee (b. 1906), American composer, pupil of N. Boulanger in Paris and Berg in Vienna; also conductor and university teacher. Works include four symphonies, eight string quartets, and *The Nun's Priest's Tale* (Chaucer) for chorus, solo singers (including folk-singer with electric guitar) and small orchestra.

Finnissy, Michael (b. 1946), British composer, also pianist. Works include seven piano concertos (no. 7 with wind quintet); *Pathways of Sun and Stars* for orchestra; opera *The Undivine Comedy*.

Finzi, Gerald (1901–56), British composer, mainly of vocal works including *Let Us Garlands Bring* (song-cycle to poems by Shakespeare) and DIES NATALIS (high voice and strings). Also wrote a clarinet concerto, etc.

fioritura (It., a flowering; pl. *-re*), 'decoration' of a melody by ornaments – sometimes added by the performer, e.g. in 17th- and 18th-century Italian opera.

fipple, the obstructive block of wood which canalizes the air in the instrumental species called the *fipple flute* – of which the chief example is the RECORDER.

Firebird, The (Rus., *Zhar Ptitsa*), ballet (after a Russian fairy-tale) with music by Stravinsky, produced in Paris, 1910; source of orchestral suite of 1911, and of revised versions of this in 1919 and 1945. See also LYADOV.

Fireworks Music (otherwise *Music for the Royal Fireworks*), suite by Handel for wind band, performed in 1749 at the official London celebration of the Peace of Aix-la-Chapelle. Afterwards Handel added string parts. The frequently performed 20th-century orchestral arrangement is by Harty.

Firsova, Elena (b. 1950), Russian composer whose music first gained prominence outside USSR. Works include three string quartets; Shakespeare settings for voice and organ; chamber opera *A Feast in Time of Plague* (after Pushkin).

first, term implying in an orchestra (e.g. *first trombone*) a position of leadership as well as (usually) a part higher in pitch; but in a choir (e.g. *first basses*) implying only a higher-pitched part, not leadership. See also following entries.

first inversion, see INVERSION.

first-movement form, term sometimes used for SONATA-FORM.

first subject, see SONATA-FORM.

Fischer, Edwin (1886–1960), Swiss pianist, also conductor (and simultaneous conductor-pianist, particularly in Bach); noted teacher, and also writer on music.

Fischer, Friedrich Ernst, see FISHER (F.E.).

Fischer, Johann Kaspar Ferdinand (1670–1746), German composer of music for organ (including 20 preludes and fugues in 20 different keys – before Bach's WELL-TEMPERED CLAVIER) and for harpsichord.

Fischer-Dieskau, Dietrich (b. 1925), German baritone, of unsurpassed authority from the 1950s in recitals of German song; had also a very large operatic repertory. From the 1970s he also occasionally appeared as conductor.

Fišer, Luboš (b. 1935), Czechoslovak composer of *Fifteen Prints after Dürer's Apocalypse* for orchestra; Requiem for soprano, baritone, chorus and orchestra; four piano sonatas, much music for film and television.

Fisher, F. E. (full name and dates unknown), a possibly British composer, also violinist and cellist, active in London between 1748 and 1773. Works include trio-sonatas (two violins and keyboard continuo). May be identical with Friedrich Ernst Fischer, a German composer known to have worked in Holland.

Fistoulari, Anatole (b. 1907), Russian-born conductor ('prodigy' conductor at seven) who has worked much in England and USA, but served in French army in World War II; much associated with ballet. British citizen since 1948.

Fitelberg, Grzegorz (1879–1953), Polish composer (of a symphony, violin sonatas, etc.), and conductor of Polish Radio Symphony Orchestra; father of Jerzy Fitelberg.

Fitelberg, Jerzy (1903–51), Polish composer of two piano concertos, two violin concertos, five string quartets, etc.; from 1940 resident in USA, dying there. Shows influence of Stravinsky.

Fitzgerald, Edward (1808–83), British poet. See LEHMANN (Liza).

Fitzwilliam Virginal Book, early 17th-century English collection of 297 pieces for keyboard by various (mainly English) composers in manuscript; named after Viscount Fitzwilliam (1745–1816), into whose hands it came. Published, 1899. See VIRGINAL.

Five, The, see MIGHTY HANDFUL.

Flagello, Nicolas (b. 1928), American composer, pupil of Pizzetti in Rome; is also pianist, violinist, viola-player, oboist. Works include *The Passion of Martin Luther King* for soloists, chorus

and orchestra; several one-act operas; *Burlesca* for flute and guitar.

flageolet, obsolete high six-holed wind instrument (similar to recorder but with different arrangement of finger-holes and thumb-holes), used e.g. in Handel's RINALDO; *double flageolet,* instrument of two such pipes side by side, often seen in 'pastoral' illustrations. The terms *flageolet-notes* (Eng.), *flageolets* (Fr.), *Flageolette* (Ger.), meaning HARMONICS on a stringed instrument, refer to the supposed resemblance of these thin-sounding notes to those of the flageolet.

Flagstad, Kirsten [Malfrid] (1895–1962), Norwegian dramatic soprano internationally celebrated for stage performances of Wagner's heroines and in recital, particularly in German and Norwegian songs.

flam, two-note figure in side-drum playing, in the rhythm ♪ . – *open flam* or *closed flam* according to whether the first or second note falls on the accented beat.

flamenco (Sp.), type of Spanish, particularly Andalusian, song (*cante flamenco*), with various sub-types named after districts – *malagueña, sevillana,* etc.; often danced to. (The term is properly applied only to songs of more recent origin than the *cante* HONDO, and is less predominantly sad.) So also *flamenco style* in guitar-playing, indicating a suitably forceful style different (and with different finger technique) from the 'classical' style.

Flaming Angel, The, see FIERY ANGEL.

Flanagan, William (1923–69), American composer, also critic. Composed songs, *Narrative* for orchestra, music to plays by Albee (who also collaborated on libretto for Flanagan's one-act opera, *Bartleby*); committed suicide.

flat, term indicating a lowering in pitch – either (1) indeterminately, as when a singer is said to sing flat, by mistake; or (2) precisely by a semitone, as represented by the sign ♭; so 'B♭' (B flat), the note a semitone lower than B♮ (B natural); so also, e.g., C♭ – a notation which is sometimes called for through adherence to the 'grammar' of music, though on, e.g., the piano the note is identical with B♮ (B natural). So DOUBLE-FLAT; *flat keys,* those having flats in their key-signatures; *in three flats,* in the key of E♭ major or C minor, the key-signature of which is three flats (and similarly with other keys); *flattened seventh* (US, *flatted seventh*), the lowering of the seventh degree of the scale by a semitone. See also FLAT TWENTY-FIRST.

Flatterzunge (Ger.), flutter-tongue (see TONGUE).

flat twenty-first, in a MIXTURE stop on the organ, a rank sounding three octaves less one tone above the note struck. (The interval of three octaves less one tone equals twenty-one steps of the diatonic scale with the top note flattened.)

Flaubert, Gustave (1821–80), French novelist. See HERODIAS.

flautando, flautato (It.), direction to player of the violin, etc., to move the bow over the fingerboard in order to produce a thin, special tone supposedly like that of a flute (It., *flauto*).

flautist (US, flutist), player of the flute.

flauto (It., pl. *-i*), flute (in the widest sense). Since the period of Haydn this has meant the ordinary side-blown FLUTE, i.e. the transverse flute (*flauto traverso*); its small size is the *flauto piccolo,* or little flute – commonly called PICCOLO. However, in preceding periods *flauto* alone may indicate the RECORDER or other end-blown flute – Bach, for instance, writes *flauto traverso* in full (or just *traverso*) when he wants not the recorder but the side-blown flute; similarly *flauto piccolo* in Bach (the word *traverso* omitted) is thought to mean a flageolet, the piccolo of modern usage having not yet been invented. For *flauto d'amore,* see under FLUTE.

flebile (It.), tearful, plaintive.

Flecker, James Elroy (1884–1915), British poet. See HASSAN.

Fledermaus, Die (Ger., The Bat), operetta by J. Strauss the younger, produced in Vienna, 1874 – Strauss's most successful stage work. Libretto by C. Haffner and R. Genée: the 'bat' has the flimsiest connection with the plot, being merely the fancy-dress costume used by one of the characters on a previous occasion.

Fleisher, Leon (b. 1928), American pianist (first American to win the Queen Elisabeth Competition in Brussels, 1952) whose career was interrupted when he lost the use of his right hand in 1956. Thereafter he played left-hand concertos as well as conducting, and later attempted to resume playing with both hands.

flexatone, instrument which is a kind of superior version of the 'musical SAW'; like the saw, it has a steel blade, which is put under varying tension (by thumb-pressure) to produce different notes, but it is shaken (not bowed) to make it vibrate. A part for it, imitating an Armenian folk-instrument, occurs in Khachaturian's Piano Concerto (first published in 1937; but a newer edition omits it). Other composers making occasional use of it have included Schoenberg (Variations for orchestra).

flicorno, name of a family of brass instruments similar to SAXHORN family, used in Italian military bands.

fliegende Holländer, Der, see FLYING DUTCHMAN.

Flies, J. Bernhard, see WIEGENLIED.

Flight of the Bumble-bee, The, orchestral interlude occurring in Rimsky-Korsakov's opera *The Legend of Tsar Saltan* (1900), in which a prince turns into a bee and stings his villainous aunts. Has been arranged and misarranged as a virtuoso display for various solo instruments.

Flood, The, 'musical play' by Stravinsky for singers, speakers and orchestra, produced on American television, 1962; text from the York and Chester miracle plays. See also NOYE'S FLUDDE.

florid, term descriptive of melody that is full of ORNAMENTS – whether such are written in by the composer or, as common e.g. in 17th- and 18th-century Italian opera, intended to be added at the taste of the performer.

Flothuis, Marius (b. 1914), Dutch composer, influenced by Pijper but mainly self-taught; also critic. Has written concertos for piano, violin, flute, horn; Capriccio for string orchestra; a string quartet, songs, etc.

Flotow, Friedrich von (1812-83),

German composer who studied in Paris, and worked there and in Vienna and elsewhere. Wrote operas in French, Italian and German – the German ones including MARTHA and *Alessandro Stradella* (see STRADELLA). Composed also ballets, chamber music, etc.

flourish, (1) a FANFARE; (2) decorative musical figuration.

Floyd, Carlisle (b. 1926), American composer, also university teacher; works include operas *Susannah, Wuthering Heights, The Passion of Jonathan Wade* and *Markheim*; piano pieces, etc.

flue-pipe, organ pipe into which the air is made to enter directly, as into a flute or recorder (not striking a vibrant tongue or REED, as in a reed-pipe).

Flügel (Ger., wing), a grand piano (i.e. a wing-shaped piano) or a harpsichord so shaped. See also FLUGELHORN.

flugelhorn, type of brass instrument with valves, made in various sizes. (Properly *Flügelhorn*, in German, but in British brass-band usage spelt and pronounced with simple 'u'.) The one used in British brass bands is the alto in Bb, having the same compass as the cornet in Bb; neither this nor other sizes of the instrument are commonly found in other types of musical combination, but one occurs in Vaughan Williams's Ninth Symphony. Cp. SAXHORN.

flute, (1) general name for various types of woodwind instruments without reeds, including nose-blown and other primitive instruments; *English flute, German flute*, old English names for the vertical-blown and cross-blown instruments now respectively called RECORDER and simply 'flute' – see next definition; (2) a type of cross-blown woodwind instrument (see preceding definition) coming into standard use in the 16th century and mechanically improved since then (now sometimes made of metal, not wood); used in the orchestra and military band, also occasionally as solo instrument and in chamber music. Compass from middle C upwards for about three octaves. Other sizes of this instrument in current use are (a) the PICCOLO; (b) the various sizes used in a military 'drum and fife' band; (c) the *alto flute*, pitched a fourth or fifth lower than the standard instrument, and sometimes miscalled the *bass flute* – specified in some works by e.g. Ravel and Stravinsky, and functioning as a TRANSPOSING INSTRUMENT in G. A true bass flute, an octave below the standard instrument, has also been made since 1910 but is not used in the standard orchestra. Long obsolete is the *flûte d'amour* or *flauto d'amore* (Fr., It.), pitched a minor third below the standard flute. The *concert flute* is a name for the standard-sized flute to distinguish it from other sizes; (3, obsolete usage, e.g. 17th-century) RECORDER.

flûte-à-bec (Fr., beaked flute) = RECORDER.

flutter-tongue, see TONGUE.

Flying Dutchman, The (Ger., *Der fliegende Holländer*), opera by Wagner, produced in Dresden, 1843; libretto by composer; about the legendary accursed sailor redeemed by love.

Foerster, Josef Bohuslav (1859–1951), Czech composer who worked for some time in Hamburg and Vienna; also critic. Composed Masses, religious cantatas, a biblical opera; also other operas (one based on *The Merchant of Venice*), five symphonies, songs and choral works.

Foldes (originally Földes), **Andor** (b. 1913), Hungarian pianist, pupil of E. Dohnányi, naturalized American in 1948; sometimes directs his own concerto performances, and is also a composer.

Folía, La (Sp., also *La follia*, It.), the name originally of a dance ('The Folly') of Portuguese origin, and hence the name of a particular tune used for the dance. This tune enjoyed an extraordinarily wide currency during the 16th–18th centuries, more especially as the subject of variations. It is best known from a set of variations written on it by Corelli in a sonata for violin and continuo, 1700.

folk-music, -song, -tune, terms implying that the work concerned has been transmitted aurally among 'the people' from one generation to the next, and can be ascribed to no particular composer. As this definition suggests, (1) a folk-song must be, or have been, 'popular', but not every 'popular' song is a folk-song; (2) folk-song has special importance to a 'primitive' population or to a depressed class, where music does not generally take a written form; (3) because of aural transmission, a folk-song is likely to exist in several differing versions. Folk-song, although 'national' in character, has tended to show wide international similarities: in particular it has preserved the MODES longer than normal 'composed' music. But it is arguable that certain 'composed' and written-down songs, e.g. Stephen Foster's, have in a sense become folk-songs – i.e. they have been transmitted aurally, they circulate in several versions, and the composer's name is unknown to many who know the songs. Note that (1) the above definition of folk-songs, etc., does not necessarily coincide with the use of parallel words in other languages: e.g. *Volkslied* (Ger.) takes in a wider variety of traditional popular song; (2) the post-1945 revival of what is called 'folk' admits many new songs (in traditional style) by named composers, who are often performers also.

Fontane di Roma, see FOUNTAINS OF ROME.

foot, unit of length used to measure the length of a vibrating air-column: hence, a measure of pitch – because, e.g., an air-column eight feet long vibrates twice as fast as an air-column 16 feet long, and so sends out a note one octave higher. Hence – *eight-foot C*, the C two lines below the bass stave, sounded by a vibrating air-column (e.g. an open organ-pipe) approximately eight feet long; *16-foot C*, the C below this; *four-foot C*, the C above eight-foot C, and so on in proportion. So organ stops are classified by what sound will issue if the note representing *eight-foot* C is struck. An *eight-foot stop* will sound the note itself; a *16-foot stop* will sound the note an octave below, a *32-foot stop* the note two octaves below; a *four-*, *two-*, *one-foot stop* will sound the note one octave, two octaves, three octaves, respectively above eight-foot C. These stops will have similar effects on all other notes, and thus by simultaneous use of several stops the player can sound a melody in various octaves at choice. (This terminology is sometimes used, by analogy, of other instruments, as when a double-bass is said

to provide '16-foot tone' to a cello part, i.e. doubling the cello part an octave below.)

Foote, Arthur William (1853–1937), American organist and composer of cantatas (one on Longfellow's *Hiawatha*), orchestral suites, organ and piano works, etc. Also teacher and writer of textbooks.

Force of Destiny, The (It., *La forza del destino*), opera by Verdi, produced (in Italian) at St Petersburg, 1862. Libretto by F. M. Piave – a tale of tragic intrigue in which a curse takes its long-range effect.

Ford, Thomas (*c*.1580–1648), English lutenist and composer of ayres (with lute), madrigals, anthems, dances, etc.; musician to Charles I.

Forest, Jean Kurt (1909–75), German composer (also violinist, viola-player and conductor). He worked in East Berlin. Compositions include opera *The Flowers of Hiroshima*, ballet *Romeo, Juliet and the Darkness*, chamber music, over 250 songs.

forlana, forlane (It., Fr.), old Italian dance in 6/8 time.

form, the layout of a piece of music considered as a succession of sections. A simple song may thus be said to have a *form* consisting of, say, one line, another line, the first line repeated, then another line; while a more involved piece may be said to have a *form* corresponding to one of various basic types – see, e.g., BINARY, TERNARY, FUGUE, PASSACAGLIA, RONDO, SONATA-FORM, VARIATIONS; or such a piece may be said to be 'free' in form, i.e. unrelated to such a 'set' type. Note that *form* as thus conventionally defined takes in only the 'horizontal' aspects of music and not the 'vertical' (harmony, counterpoint), and does not fully deal with rhythm; it would be better (and more analogous to terminology in, e.g., painting) if *form* were to be defined as taking in these also, i.e. as concerned with the totality of significant relationships between notes. See also MOMENT (2).

formalism, a supposed fault in composition for which Russian composers – Prokofiev and Shostakovich, among others – were denounced by Soviet officialdom in 1948; the implication is that the music concerned was deficient in communicative content, overemphasizing 'form'. There was usually an added implication that the music was over-discordant and uncritically pursued modernity for its own sake.

Forqueray, Antoine (1671–1745), French bass-viol player, chamber musician to Louis XIV, and composer. His son Jean-Baptiste-[Antoine] (1699–1782) was also a bass-viol player and composer.

Forster, E. M. [Edward Morgan] (1879–1970), British novelist. See BILLY BUDD.

forte, fortissimo (It.), loud, very loud (abbr. *f*, *ff*; quite commonly *fff* and even greater aggregations are used to indicate still greater loudness).

fortepiano, an early Italian name meaning the same as PIANOFORTE. Its use in English to denote the late 18th-century piano is arbitrary and affected. (*Fortepiano* is, however, the standard Russian word for the normal instrument.)

Fortner, Wolfgang (1907–87), German composer (also conductor and teacher). Works include Lutheran church music; Latin oratorio *The Sacrifice of Isaac* (with 40 solo instruments including 'jazz trumpets' and 'jazz trombones'); concertos for various instruments; organ works; opera *Blood Wedding* (after Lorca's play).

'Forty-Eight, The', or **'Forty-Eight Preludes and Fugues',** see WELL-TEMPERED CLAVIER.

Forza del destino, La, see FORCE OF DESTINY.

Foss (originally Fuchs) **Lukas** (b. 1922), German-born American composer, also pianist and conductor. After opera *The Jumping Frog of Calaveras County* (after Mark Twain), two piano concertos, etc., he adopted a more radical technique in such works as *Cello Concert* for cello, orchestra and tape, and *Echoi* for clarinet, cello, percussion and piano.

Foster, Stephen [Collins] (1826–64), American composer, almost entirely self-taught. Composed mainly songs to his own words, including 'The Old Folks at Home', 'Camptown Races' and other 'plantation songs' (i.e. of the black-faced minstrel-show type) which became among the world's best-known songs – often with some alteration of the original tunes; also 'drawing-room' songs, e.g. 'Jeanie with the Light Brown Hair'. Died poor and an alcoholic.

Fountains of Rome (It., *Fontane di Roma*), an orchestral work by Respighi in four sections each 'depicting' a different fountain; first performed, 1917. Cp. PINES OF ROME.

Four Boors, The, see SCHOOL FOR FATHERS.

four-foot (organ stop, etc.), see FOOT.

Four Last Songs, title actually bestowed by R. Strauss on his set of songs with orchestra, 1948, to texts by Eichendorff and Hesse.

Fournier, Pierre (1906–86), French cellist, internationally prominent as soloist and in chamber music; latterly resident in Switzerland.

fourniture (Fr.) = FURNITURE (organ stop).

Four Saints in Three Acts, opera (in four acts) by V. Thomson, produced in Hartford, Conn., 1934, with an all-black cast. Libretto by Gertrude Stein, with saints (far more than four) and without normal 'plot'.

Four Seasons, The (It., *Le quattro stagioni*), a set of four concertos by Vivaldi (op. 8, nos. 1–4; RV 269, 315, 293, 297), published in 1725, for violin and orchestra, 'depicting' birds, storms, falls on the ice, etc., as indicated on score. See also SEASONS.

Four Serious Songs (Ger., *Vier ernste Gesänge*), song-cycle, based on biblical texts, for bass and piano by Brahms, 1896, his last work but one. The piano accompaniment has been orchestrated, e.g. by Sargent.

Four Temperaments, The, (1) title of Symphony no. 2, 1902, by C. Nielsen (Dan., *De fire temperamenter*), each of the 'temperaments' having one movement; (2) title of Hindemith's Theme and Variations for piano and strings, 1940, each 'temperament' taking charge for one variation. (The reference is to the types of 'temperament' – choleric, phlegmatic, melancholic, sanguine – thought in medieval times to be the dominant factor in a person's character.)

fourth, an interval in melody or harmony, reckoned as taking four steps in the (major or minor) scale, counting the bottom and top notes. Hence, *perfect fourth*, the distance, e.g., from C up to F; one semitone more gives the *augmented fourth*, e.g. C up to F♯. The *diminished fourth*, one semitone less than the perfect, is little used, being virtually equivalent – e.g. on the piano – to the major THIRD: but note its inclusion, as F♯–B♭, in the so-called 'mystic chord' which SKRYABIN compounded entirely of various fourths.

Fox, Virgil [Keel] (1912–80), American organist, whose concerts with lighting effects drew massive audiences to a classical repertory.

fractional tone = MICROTONE.

Fra Diavolo, or The Inn at Terracina (Fr., . . . *ou L'Hôtel de Terracine*), comic opera by Auber, produced in Paris, 1830. Fra Diavolo (It., Brother Devil), is a character modelled on a celebrated Italian brigand and renegade monk who died in 1806.

Françaix, Jean (b. 1912), French composer (also pianist), pupil of N. Boulanger and others; had a piano suite published at age nine. Works, cultivating clarity (and often brevity) of style, and influenced by Stravinsky, include a piano concertino (1934) and concerto (1936); a symphony for strings; *Beach* and other music for ballet; Serenade for 12 instruments (also used as ballet with title *À la Françaix*), chamber music; operas.

Francesca da Rimini, (1) 'symphonic fantasy' by Tchaikovsky, first performed in 1877 – after Dante, who narrates her tragic love for Paolo and her fate in hell (Tchaikovsky originally intended an opera on this subject; (2) title of operas on this subject by Goetz, Rakhmaninov, Zandonai and others.

Francescatti, Zino (originally René-Charles) (b. 1902), French violinist (father Italian-born); made public appearances from age five, performing in Britain with Ravel as pianist, 1926. Eminent concerto-player and recitalist.

Francis of Assisi, St (1181/2–1226). See SPIES.

Franck, César [Auguste] (1822–90), Belgian composer, son of a German mother; studied at Paris Conservatory and settled in Paris in 1844. Was also organist (eventually at the church of Ste Clotilde, Paris) and noted teacher. Exponent of cyclic form (use of the same theme in more than one movement or section of a work), e.g. in Symphonic Variations for piano and orchestra, violin sonata. Also evolved notably individual harmonic language, much given to CHROMATICISM. Other works include a symphony; symphonic poems; a piano quintet and other chamber music; piano and organ works; many songs; religious cantatas including *The Beatitudes*; four operas (one unperformed and unpublished).

Franck, Melchior (c. 1579–1639), German composer of church music, dance-music for instrumental ensembles, etc.

Francœur, François (1698–1787), French violinist, court musician and composer of operas, ballets, violin sonatas, etc.

Frankel, Benjamin (1906–73), British composer whose works include several with Jewish allusions, e.g. violin concerto in memory of 'the six million', i.e. Jews whose deaths were caused by the Nazis; also eight symphonies and a posthumously performed opera *Marching Song*, etc.

Franz, Robert (pen-name of Robert Franz Knauth) (1815–92), German composer, chiefly of more than 250 songs – also of church music, etc. Through deafness and a nervous disease, ceased to compose in 1868.

Fraser-Simson, Harold (1878–1944), British composer of musical comedy *The Maid of the Mountains*, children's songs to A. A. Milne's poems, etc.

Frauenliebe und -leben, see WOMAN'S LOVE AND LIFE.

Frederick the Great [Friedrich II] (1712–86), King of Prussia, amateur flautist and composer – especially of music with prominent flute parts. While C. P. E. Bach was in his service, J. S. Bach visited him in 1747 and later dedicated to him THE MUSICAL OFFERING. See QUANTZ.

free-bass accordion, see ACCORDION.

free counterpoint, see COUNTERPOINT.

Freedman, Harry (b. 1922), Polish-born Canadian composer; also oboist and jazz clarinettist. Works include *Tangents* for orchestra, ballet *Rose Latulippe*, Toccata for soprano and flute.

free fantasia, name sometimes given to the DEVELOPMENT section of a movement, e.g. in SONATA-FORM.

Freire, Nelson (b. 1944), Brazilian pianist who studied in Vienna. Pursued career in Latin America, then in Europe (from 1964) and USA.

Freischütz, Der (Ger., The Marksman with Magic Bullets), opera by Weber, produced in Berlin, 1821, with libretto by F. Kind; the rustic hero is involved in black magic.

French horn, see HORN.

French overture, see OVERTURE.

French sixth, type of 'augmented sixth' chord (see AUGMENTED) distinguished by the intermediate intervals of the chord – e.g. (reading upwards) D♭, F, G, B. (Cp. GERMAN SIXTH, ITALIAN SIXTH – the reason for the names is not known.)

French Suite, title given to each of six suites for harpsichord by Bach, composed in about 1722 (BWV 812–17); unlike Bach's ENGLISH SUITES they have no preludes, but the supposition that they represent a characteristically French style has not been universally accepted.

Freni (originally Fregni), **Mirella** (b. 1935), Italian soprano, noted in French, Italian and other opera; at Covent Garden from 1961, La Scala (Milan) from 1962.

frequency, term in acoustics for the number of complete vibrations undergone by an air-column or a resonating body in one second. The unit of measurement (one cycle per second) is the Hertz, abbreviated Hz. As frequency increases, the pitch of the note sounded is raised, so pitch can be defined by frequency; by international agreement, 1939, the A commonly-used for tuning (i.e. that above middle C) is fixed at 440 Hz. See PITCH.

Frescobaldi, Girolamo (1583–1643), Italian composer and organist – at Antwerp, then (1608–28) at St Peter's, Rome, where a presumably over-enthusiastic chronicler reports an audience of 30,000 listening to him. Wrote toccatas, fugues, ricercari, etc., for organ and harpsichord, influencing German and other music; also motets, madrigals, etc.

fret, name given to each of the strips of wood or metal fixed on the fingerboard of, e.g., a guitar, viol, lute (but not the violin family). The player presses the finger against a fret to shorten the length of string vibrating. So *fretted* instruments, those fitted with frets.

fretta (It.), haste; *non in fretta,* not hurrying the pace. Cp. AFFRETTANDO.

Frick, Gottlob (b. 1906), German bass, well known in Wagner's operas, with international career – Covent Garden 1951, Metropolitan Opera 1962.

Fricker, Peter Racine (1920–90), British composer, from 1964 resident in California as university professor. Works include five symphonies (no. 5 with organ); two violin concertos (no. 1 with chamber orchestra, no. 2 properly *Rapsodia concertante*); four string quartets; a wind quintet; songs and piano works.

Friedman, Ignaz (1882–1948), Polish-born pianist of world-wide celebrity, said to have given 2,800 concerts; settled in Sydney, 1940.

Friml, Rudolf (1879–1972), Czech composer who settled in USA, 1906, and won success with *Rose Marie* and other musical plays; also composer of a piano concerto, etc., and himself a pianist.

Froberger, Johann Jacob (1616–67), German organist and composer for organ and harpsichord; pupil of Frescobaldi; visited England, 1622.

frog, North American equivalent of British NUT, from Ger., *Frosch.*

'Frog' Quartet, nickname of Haydn's String Quartet in D (Hob. III:49, also known as op. 50, no. 6), 1787, with a 'croaking' theme in the finale.

From a House of the Dead (Cz., *Z Mrtvého domu*), opera by Janáček, produced in Brno (posthumously), 1930; text by composer, after Dostoyevsky's novel of a Siberian prison-camp. (Also known as *From the House of the Dead*, the Czech language having no definite or indefinite article.)

From Bohemian Fields and Groves, see MY COUNTRY.

From My Life (Cz., *Z mého života*), sub-title of the first of Smetana's two string quartets; in E minor, 1876. The high E in the finale depicts 'the fatal whistling in my ear in the highest register which in 1874 announced my deafness'. The quartet has been arranged for full orchestra by G. Szell – first performed in 1941 in this version.

From the New World (Cz., *Z noveho svéta*), subtitle of Dvořák's Symphony in E minor, composed in USA and first performed in New York, 1893; no. 9, but formerly called 'no. 5' (see DVOŘÁK). Some of its tunes allude to idioms of US black folk-music, but without any direct quotation.

frottola (It., pl. *-e*), light Italian song for several voices with the melody at the top, flourishing about 1500; set to poems of varying metres, of which successive stanzas were sung to repetitions of the same music.

Frühbeck de Burgos, Rafael (b. 1933),

Spanish conductor of German parentage (surname properly Frühbeck; 'de Burgos' an addition from his birthplace). Conductor of Spanish National Orchestra, 1962–78, and (concurrently) of Montreal Symphony Orchestra 1975–7.

Frumerie, Gunnar de (1908–87), Swedish pianist and composer; works include Symphonic Variations (on a Swedish folk-tune), two piano concertos, two violin concertos, opera, piano solos. Sometimes wrote in classic dance-forms – saraband, etc.

Fry, Christopher (b. 1907), British poet and playwright. See PARADISE LOST.

Fry, William Henry (1813–64), American composer – opera *Leonora*, 1845, sometimes called the first notable American opera. (It is unconnected with the plot of FIDELIO.) Also a critic.

Frye, Walter (15th century), English composer apparently attached to the court of Burgundy; no biographical detail is known.

fuga, Fuge (It., Ger.) = FUGUE. (The original Italian word means 'flight'.)

fugato (It.), literally 'fugued', i.e. suggestive of the style of FUGUE though not actually constituting a fugue.

fughetta (It.), a little FUGUE.

fugue, a type of contrapuntal composition for a given number of PARTS or 'voices' (so called, whether the work is vocal or instrumental), hence *fugue in three voices, a four-part fugue,* etc. The essential feature of a fugue is the entries of all the voices successively in IMITATION of each other. The opening entry is in the tonic key and is

fuguing tune

called the 'subject'; the imitative entry of the next voice, in the dominant, is called the 'answer'; similarly with the entries of subsequent voices (if any) alternately. Commonly there are several complete entries of all voices (with the order changed) in the course of a fugue; the complete entries are separated by 'episodes'. Commonly also each voice having announced the subject or answer passes to another fixed thematic element called the 'countersubject' – the countersubject being heard in the first voice simultaneously with the answer in the second voice, etc. But the great masters of fugue such as Bach (see, e.g., ART OF FUGUE, WELL-TEMPERED CLAVIER) do not confine the fugue to a strict pattern, though time-wasting academic theorists have done so. For a further distinction, see ANSWER. See also preceding and following entries.

fuguing tune, type of 18th-century American hymn-tune, practised and perhaps originated by Billings – in which there is occasional primitive IMITATION between parts.

Fuleihan, Anis (1900–70), Cyprus-born American composer; settled in USA, 1914. Also pianist and conductor. Works include a two-piano concerto; THEREMIN concerto; *Three Cyprus Serenades* for orchestra; ballets; chamber works; songs in English and French. After World War II, became director of the Beirut (Lebanon) Conservatory.

full anthem, anthem (in the Anglican Church) sung by the full choir throughout, without soloists.

full orchestra, an orchestra with the four usual- sections (strings, woodwind, brass, percussion) and of normal concert-hall strength.

full organ, direction that the organ should be played at full strength. Owing to the construction of the instrument and of the human ear, this does not necessarily imply the use of all the stops.

full score, see SCORE.

fundamental, fundamental note, the primary or 'parent' note of the HARMONIC SERIES.

funebre, funèbre (It., Fr.), of a funeral. So *marcia funebre, marche funèbre*, funeral march.

Funeral March of a Marionette (Fr., *Marche funèbre d'une marionette*), work of humorous intent by Gounod – piano solo and piano duet versions published in 1873, orchestral version later.

'Funeral March' Sonata, nickname for Chopin's Piano Sonata in B♭ minor, completed in 1839, having a funeral march as its third movement.

fuoco (It.), fire; *con fuoco*, with fire.

für (Ger.), for.

furiant (Cz.), quick dance with changing rhythms – though some of Dvořák's movements so entitled do not change in rhythm. (The word is not connected with 'fury'.)

furniture, type of MIXTURE stop on the organ.

Furtwängler, Wilhelm (1886–1954), German orchestral and operatic conductor, achieving eminence with Berlin Philharmonic and Vienna Philharmonic Orchestras, and making first London appearance in 1924. Accusations of Nazi complicity muted his post-1945 activities. Also composer of three symphonies, etc.

Futurism, attempt, particularly by the Italian poet Marinetti and by Russolo, at 'a great renovation of music through the Art of Noises' – first mooted in 1909 and persisting in Italy at least until the 1920s. Special 'noise instruments' (e.g. exploders, thunderers and whistlers) were invented, composed for, and performed on.

Fux, Johann Joseph (1660–1741), Austrian composer of 18 operas, much church music, etc.; organist; and especially known as theorist and author of a highly influential treatise on counterpoint called GRADUS AD PARNASSUM.

fz (abbr. of It., *forzando*), less frequently encountered equivalent of *sf* – see SFORZANDO.

G

G, note of the scale. So G FLAT (G♭), DOUBLE-FLAT (G♭♭), NATURAL (G♮), SHARP (G♯), DOUBLE-SHARP (G𝄪); *G major*, *G minor*, etc. – see MAJOR. So also *in G*, either (1) in the key of G (major, understood), or (2) indication of a TRANSPOSING INSTRUMENT on which the note written C sounds as G (and correspondingly with other notes) – e.g. *horn in G* (obsolete), *alto flute in G*; note, however, that the bass trombone is sometimes spoken of as being 'in G' because G is its FUNDAMENTAL, but the music for it is written at the pitch at which it sounds, So also *G-clef*, clef indicating the position of G above middle C, i.e. the TREBLE clef; *G-string*, string of an instrument tuned to the note G, especially the lowest string of a violin. (For the so-called *Air on the G string* see AIR.)

G, abbr. for Graduate (in musical diplomas, e.g. GRSM – Graduate of the Royal Schools of Music).

Gabrieli, Andrea (*c.*1510–86), Italian composer, pupil of Willaert at St Mark's, Venice, where he later became chief organist. Works include motets, madrigals, organ pieces. Pupils included Giovanni Gabrieli (his nephew).

Gabrieli, Giovanni (*c.* 1555–1612), Italian composer, pupil of his uncle (Andrea Gabrieli) whom he succeeded as chief organist of St Mark's, Venice, 1585. Works include *Sacred Symphonies* and other church music for voices with instruments, often using antiphonal groups; music for instrumental ensembles; organ works. Teacher of Schütz.

Gaburo, Kenneth [Louis] (b. 1926), American composer who studied in Italy with Petrassi; also teacher (in California, 1968–75) and founder of his own choral group cultivating audience-participation, etc. Works include *Shapes and Sounds* for orchestra; *Mouthpiece* for trumpet, with visual projections; opera *The Widow*.

Gade, Niels Vilhelm (1817–90), Danish composer (opera, choral works, eight symphonies, overture *Echoes from Ossian*, etc.) and conductor. Studied at Leipzig and was much influenced by Mendelssohn, though Danish 'national' traits exist in his earlier works.

gagaku (Jap.), the orchestral music traditionally associated (since the eighth century) with the Japanese court, using wind, strings and percussion.

Gagliano, Marco da (1582–1643), Italian composer, also priest. Wrote *Daphne* and other operas, as well as church music, etc.

gaillard (Fr.) = GALLIARD.

Gál, Hans (1890–1987), Austrian-born composer and musicologist resident in Scotland from 1938; lecturer at Edinburgh University, 1945. Works include four symphonies, a piano concerto and a violin concerto.

galant (Fr., Ger.), courtly – term used of a mid-18th-century style distinguished by formal elegance and clarity (rather than by intense feeling), practised e.g. by J. C. Bach and influencing e.g. Mozart.

Galantieren, galanteries (Ger., Fr.), in the classical SUITE, those numbers (e.g. minuet, polonaise) whose inclusion was optional, not obligatory.

Galilei, Vincenzo (*c*.1520–91), Italian composer of vocal and instrumental music; lutenist; musical theorist; contributor to the current of ideas from which opera eventually resulted. Father of the astronomer Galileo Galilei.

galliard, lively dance at least as old as the 15th century, usually but not always in 3/2 time; often contrasted with, and sometimes built from the same musical material as a PAVAN (which is slower); obsolete, but revived e.g. by Vaughan Williams in JOB.

Galli-Curci, Amelita (1882–1963), Italian soprano, prominent in opera in Chicago (from 1916) and New York; recordings of her coloratura singing won wide fame.

galop, a 19th-century ballroom dance in quick 2/4 time.

Galuppi, Baldassare (1706–85), Italian composer, chiefly of operas, but also of harpsichord sonatas, etc.

Visited London and St Petersburg; in service at St Mark's, Venice, from 1748. (Browning's poem 'A Toccata of Galuppi's' refers to him; but the exact work is unidentified, if not imaginary.)

Galway, James (b. 1939), British flautist, the most celebrated woodwind soloist of his generation; Rodrigo and other composers wrote for him.

gamba (It., leg), (1) abbr. for *viola da gamba*; (2) organ stop imitating this instrument's tone. See VIOL.

gamelan, Indonesian instrumental ensemble using string, wind and – notably – varied percussion instruments.

gamme (Fr.), scale.

gamut, (1) compass, range (also metaphorically); (2, various obsolete senses) the G at the bottom of the bass clef; the written system of HEXA-CHORDS; the musical scale (like French *gamme*).

ganz (Ger.), whole, complete(ly); hence *Ganze*, abbreviation of GANZE-TAKTNOTE.

Ganz, Rudolph (1877–1972), Swiss-born composer of orchestral and other music who settled in USA; also conductor (of the St Louis Symphony Orchestra, 1921–7).

Ganzetaktnote (Ger.), WHOLE-NOTE, semibreve – literally meaning a note lasting a whole bar or measure.

gapped, (of a scale) having some intervals of more than a tone's distance, unlike the normal major or minor scales; e.g. the PENTATONIC scale.

García, Manuel [del Popolo Vicente Rodríguez] (1775–1832), Spanish tenor for whom Rossini wrote the role of Almaviva in *The Barber of Seville*. His opera company toured to USA and Mexico, 1825–8. The singers Maria Malibran and Pauline Viardot-Garcia were his daughters.

Gardelli, Lamberto (b. 1915), Italian-born conductor who conducted opera in Sweden, 1946–55, and took Swedish nationality; London appearances from 1966. Is also composer.

Garden, Mary (1874–1967), American (Scottish-born) soprano, famous as the first Mélisande in Debussy's PELLÉAS AND MÉLISANDE, 1912; later director of the Chicago Civic Opera.

Gardiner, H[enry] Balfour (1877–1950) British composer who trained in Germany. Composed little, but works include a symphony, *Shepherd Fennel's Dance* (after T. Hardy) for orchestra, piano pieces. Was also noted promoter of music by other British composers. See following entry.

Gardiner, John Eliot (b. 1943), British conductor, great-nephew of the preceding, specialist in Monteverdi and French opera. Conductor of the Lyons Opera, 1983–8.

Gardner, John [Linton] (b. 1917), British composer, formerly teacher at RAM. Works include a symphony, piano concerto; operas *The Moon and Sixpence* and *The Visitors*; church music including *Five Hymns in Popular Style*. CBE, 1976.

Gaskell, [Mrs] **Elizabeth** (1810–65), British novelist. See COOKE (Arnold).

Gaspard de la nuit, set of three piano pieces of Ravel, 1908; the title (Gaspard of the Night) was taken from a

set of prose-ballads by A. Bertrand, subtitled 'Fantasies in the manner of Rembrandt and Callot'. No. 1 is 'Ondine' (water-nymph seducing young men to their death); no. 2, 'Le Gibet' (The Gibbet); no. 3, 'Scarbo' (name of a diabolic creature).

Gasparini, Francesco (1668–1727), Italian composer of more than 50 operas, also of oratorios, church music, etc.; pupil of Corelli.

Gassmann, Florian Leopold (1729–74), Bohemian composer of operas, chamber and orchestral music; pupil of 'Padre Martini'; worked at court in Vienna.

'Gastein' Symphony, supposedly lost symphony written by Schubert at Gastein (Austria), 1825 (D849); possibly identical to the Symphony no. 9 in C. The Sonata in C for piano duet (see GRAND DUO) was formerly believed to be an arrangement of it.

Gastoldi, Giovanni Giacomo (*c*.1550–*c*.1622), Italian composer of balletts (which influenced those of Morley, etc.) and of madrigals and church music, etc.; was himself singer, then director of music at Milan Cathedral.

Gatty, Nicholas Comyn (1874–1946) British composer of six operas (including *The Tempest* and *Macbeth*, after Shakespeare), chamber music, etc.; also critic.

Gaultier, Denis (*c*.1603–72), French lutenist and composer for the lute, developing a style of ornamentation which influenced others' keyboard style.

Gauntlett, Henry John (1805–76), British lawyer and church musician; composer of 'Once in Royal David's

City' and many other hymns (apparently thousands).

Gaveaux, Pierre (1760–1825), French composer (also tenor); wrote about 30 operas including *Leonora, or Wedded Love* (see LEONORA) to a libretto which was the principal source of the libretto of Beethoven's FIDELIO.

gavotte, old dance in 4/4 time beginning on the third beat of the bar; sometimes (but not always) a constituent of the baroque SUITE, and occasionally revived in modern times – e.g. by Prokofiev in his CLASSICAL SYMPHONY.

Gay, John (1685–1732), English poet and playwright, particularly known for having written the words of THE BEGGAR'S OPERA to popular tunes of the day. See also ACIS AND GALATEA.

Gayaneh, ballet with music by Khachaturian, produced in 1942 – named after its collective-farm heroine, the virtuous wife of a villain. Contains the 'Sabre Dance'.

Gazza ladra, La, see THIEVING MAGPIE.

Gazzaniga Giuseppe (1743–1818), Italian composer; his many operas include a *Don Giovanni* (1787), which was the immediate predecessor of Mozart's.

Gebrauchsmusik, see UTILITY MUSIC.

Gedackt, Gedact, end-stopped type of organ pipe of soft tone. (The term means 'covered'; in modern German, *gedeckt*.)

Gedda, Nicolai (b. 1925), Swedish-born tenor of Russian and Swedish descent, prominent in opera and operetta in many languages (Covent Garden début, 1954) and on records.

Geige (Ger., pl. *-en*), fiddle, violin.

Geisha, The, operetta by S. Jones, produced in London, 1896. Libretto, set in Japan, by 'Owen Hall' (i.e. J. Davis) and H. Greenbank. It was afterwards produced in many countries and languages, apparently helping to set a fashion for oriental operatic subjects.

'Geister' Trio, see GHOST TRIO.

Geminiani, Francesco (1687–1762), Italian violinist, composer (violin sonatas, trios and works of CONCERTO GROSSO type, etc.), and author of a famous treatise on violin-playing. Pupil of Corelli. After 1714 lived partly in England, and died in Dublin.

gemshorn, soft-toned organ stop usually of four-FOOT pitch.

Genée, [Franz Friedrich] **Richard** (1823–95), German conductor (especially at Vienna), composer of many operettas and librettist of others – see e.g. FLEDERMAUS.

general pause (abbr. GP), a rest of one or more bars for all performers – i.e. complete silence. Note that this does not correspond to the usual English meaning of 'pause' – see PAUSE, English and German meanings.

Gentle Shepherd, The, ballad opera set to traditional airs selected by the librettist Allan Ramsay and produced in Edinburgh, 1729. One of the first BALLAD OPERAS. It has a conventional pastoral plot.

Genzmer, Harald (b. 1909), German composer of a symphony, concertos for various instruments (one for TRAUTONIUM), a septet with harp, two piano sonatas, etc. Influenced by Hindemith.

Gerhard, Roberto (1896–1970), Spanish composer, resident in Britain from 1938; pupil of Pedrell and Schoenberg. Composed opera THE DUENNA (after Sheridan, for radio); four symphonies; a setting of Edward Lear's 'The Akond of Swat' for mezzo-soprano and two percussionists; *Concerto* for eight instruments (including accordion) without orchestra, etc.

German, Edward (pen-name of German Edward Jones) (1862–1936), British composer; also violinist and theatre conductor. Wrote MERRIE ENGLAND, TOM JONES and other operettas, and music to various plays including Shakespeare's *Henry VIII* and Anthony Hope's *Nell Gwyn* (dances from these becoming popular in their own right). Also composed two symphonies, *Welsh Rhapsody*, etc., and completed Sullivan's *The Emerald Isle*. Knighted, 1928.

German Dance, type of slow waltz, cultivated e.g. by Mozart and Schubert.

German flute, obsolete name for the ordinary (cross-blown) flute, as distinct from the RECORDER, formerly known as the 'English flute'.

Germani, Fernando (b. 1906), Italian organist (also composer and music-editor); held post at St Peter's, Rome, 1948–59, and is a much-travelled recitalist.

German Requiem, A (Ger., *Ein deutsches Requiem*), work for soloists, chorus and orchestra by Brahms; first complete performance, 1869. Texts from Luther's translation of the Bible; title of the work therefore distinguishes it from the Roman Catholic Requiem set to a liturgical Latin text.

German sixth, type of 'augmented sixth' chord (see AUGMENTED) distin-

guished by the intermediate intervals of the chord – e.g. (reading upwards) D♭, F, A♭, B. (If the B is re-named C♭ then the chord becomes also a 'minor seventh' chord, i.e. the dominant seventh in the key of G♭ – an ambiguity useful in modulation.) Cp. FRENCH SIXTH, ITALIAN SIXTH – the reason for the names is not known.

Gershwin, George (1898–1937), American pianist and composer of many popular songs; extended his range (especially in applying jazz idioms to concert works) in RHAPSODY IN BLUE (1924), a piano concerto, *Cuban Overture,* AN AMERICAN IN PARIS, opera PORGY AND BESS, piano preludes. (The orchestration of *Rhapsody in Blue* is by F. Grofé; of the other works, by Gershwin himself.) Studied with R. Goldmark but was mainly self-taught. Died after an unsuccessful brain operation.

Gervaise, Claude (16th century), French viol-player, composer of dance music and chansons; in service to French court.

Ges (Ger.), G flat.

Gesang (Ger.), song, hymn. So *Lobgesang* (Mendelssohn) = HYMN OF PRAISE. Stockhausen's title, *Gesang der Jünglinge,* literally 'Hymn of the Youths' (1956), refers to the book of the Apocrypha traditionally known as the Song of the Three Children – see SONG.

Geschöpfe des Prometheus, Die, see PROMETHEUS.

gestopft (Ger.), stopped (notes on the horn). See STOP.

Gesualdo, Carlo (*c.*1560–1613), Italian prince who was also a composer and lutenist; wrote madrigals employing very adventurous and 'prophetic' harmony, and also songs to religious words, etc. Gained notoriety by having his wife and her lover assassinated in 1590.

Geteilt (Ger., in older spelling *getheilt*), divided: see DIVISI.

Gevaert, François Auguste (1828–1908), Belgian theorist (author of treatises on orchestration, etc.), director of the Brussels Conservatory, composer and musical editor.

Gewandhaus Orchestra, orchestra of Leipzig taking its name from its hall ('Cloth House'); Kurt Masur has been its principal conductor since 1970.

Ghedini, Giorgio Federico (1892–1965), Italian composer of operas including BILLY BUDD and *The Happy Hypocrite* (after Max Beerbohm); concertos for string orchestra, church music, etc.; also editor of old Italian music.

Ghelderode, Michel de (1898–1962), Belgian dramatist, writing in French. See GREAT MACABRE.

Ghiaurov, Nicolai (b. 1929), Bulgarian bass who studied in Moscow; noted in Russian and other types of opera – La Scala (Milan) since 1959, Covent Garden since 1962.

'Ghost' Trio, nickname (from 'mysterious' slow movement) for Beethoven's Piano Trio in D, op. 70, no. 1 (1808).

Gianni Schicchi, one-act comic opera by Puccini, produced in New York, 1918 – along with THE CLOAK and SISTER ANGELICA, two other one-act operas which precede it and with which it forms Puccini's *Triptych*

(It., *Trittico*). Libretto by G. Adami: Schicchi, a medieval Florentine rogue mentioned by Dante, is the hero.

Giannini, Vittorio (1903–66), American composer of operas *The Taming of the Shrew* (after Shakespeare), *Beauty and the Beast*; also symphonies and *Frescobaldiana* for orchestra, based on Frescobaldi's organ works.

'Giant' Fugue, nickname for a fugal chorale prelude in D minor by Bach contained in Part III of the CLAVIERÜBUNG (BWV 680) – from the giant-like strides of a figure in the pedals.

Giardini, Felice de (1716–96), Italian violinist, opera manager and composer, long resident in London; collaborated with Avison in oratorio *Ruth*. Died in Moscow.

Giazotto, Remo, see ALBINONI.

Gibbons, Christopher (1615–76), English composer of fantasies and dances for strings, church music and (with Locke) music for the masque CUPID AND DEATH. Private organist to Charles II, organist of Westminister Abbey. Son of Orlando Gibbons.

Gibbons, Orlando (1583–1625), English composer, also virginalist and organist; his father, William, brothers, Edward, Ellis and Ferdinando, and son, Christopher (see preceding entry), were also musicians. Choirboy at King's College, Cambridge; later organist of Chapel Royal and Westminster Abbey. Works include about 40 anthems and other church music; madrigals and part-songs ('The Silver Swan', etc.); IN NOMINES and other works for viols; keyboard pieces (see PARTHENIA).

Gibbs, [Cecil] **Armstrong** (1889–

1960), British composer of songs, many to poems by de la Mare; also of comic opera *The Blue Peter*, waltz *Dusk*, church music, etc.

Gibson, Alexander (b. 1926), Scottish conductor – of Scottish National Orchestra, 1959–84; musical director, Scottish Opera, from its foundation, 1962, until 1987. Knighted, 1977.

Gide, André (1869–1951), French writer. See PERSEPHONE.

Gielen, Michael [Andreas] (b. 1927), German conductor-composer. In Argentina 1940–50; since then has held various conducting posts in Europe and USA (music director, Cincinnati Symphony, 1980–86). Works include *One Day Stood Out* – described as a 'pentaphony' for piano, five solo instruments and five groups of five musicians each; Variations for 40 instruments.

Gieseking, Walter [Wilhelm] (1895–1956), German pianist (though born in France). Made début in 1912 and afterwards toured widely; of high international reputation, particularly in French music. Was also composer.

giga (It.) = JIG.

Gigli, Beniamino (1890–1957), Italian tenor; made début in 1914. Had operatic career but later maintained his exceptional celebrity chiefly by recitals of operatic excerpts, etc., and by records.

Gigout, Eugène (1844–1925), French organist and composer, especially for organ; pupil of Saint-Saëns.

gigue (Fr.) = JIG.

Gilbert, Henry Franklin Belknap (1868–1928), American composer,

pupil of MacDowell; made use of various indigenous American melodies – e.g. Creole in ballet *The Dance in Place Congo*.

Gilbert, [Sir] W. S. [William Schwenck] (1836–1911) British dramatist. See GONDOLIERS, GRAND DUKE, HMS PINAFORE, IOLANTHE, MIKADO, PATIENCE, PINEAPPLE POLL, PIRATES OF PENZANCE, POP, PRINCESS IDA, RUDDIGORE, SAVOY OPERAS, SORCERER, TRIAL BY JURY, UTOPIA LIMITED, YEOMEN OF THE GUARD.

Gilels, Emil [Grigoryevich] (1916–85), Russian pianist who won international awards in Vienna (1936) and Brussels (1938) and gained widespread celebrity after World War II.

Giles, Nathaniel (*c.*1558–1634), English organist (of the Chapel Royal, 1596) and composer of madrigals and much church music.

Gilles, Jean (1668–1705), French composer chiefly of church music, including a famous Requiem; was himself church musician, originally as choirboy.

Gillis, Don (1912–78), American composer (also trumpeter, trombonist, teacher and conductor); works include 10 symphonies and *Symphony No. 5½* (also called *A Symphony for Fun* and used for ballet).

Gilson, Paul (1865–1942), Belgian composer, also teacher and critic. Works include two Flemish operas, *Fantasy on Canadian Themes* for orchestra, many songs.

gimel, see GYMEL.

Ginastera, Alberto (1916–83). Argentinian composer of music which often has nationalist characteristics –

e.g. ballet *Panambí* (based on an American-Indian legend), *Argentinian Concerto* for piano and orchestra; other works include overture to Goethe's *Faust*, operas *Don Rodrigo* and *Bomarzo*. Lived in USA 1945–6.

Gioconda, La, opera by Ponchielli, produced in Milan, 1876. Libretto by Boito, after Victor Hugo. 'La Gioconda', literally 'the joyful girl', is the name of a street-singer, the heroine. Act III contains the 'Dance of the Hours' (ballet music). The opera is unrelated to da Vinci's portrait or to D'Annunzio's play (1898), similarly named.

giocoso (It.), merry, playful, humorous.

Gioielli della Madonna, I, see JEWELS OF THE MADONNA.

Giordanello, see following entry.

Giordani, Giuseppe (1743–98), Italian composer of operas, ballets, church music, concertos, songs, etc. – the song 'Caro mio ben' (My very dear one) is ascribed to him. Never left Italy, but was formerly confused with Tommaso Giordani (no relation). Known also as Giordanello.

Giordani, Tommaso (*c.* 1730–1806), Italian composer (no relation of Giuseppe Giordani) who worked in Dublin (where he died) and London. Composed or contributed items to more than 50 operas, Italian and English; wrote songs for Sheridan's *The Critic* on its first production.

Giordano, Umberto (1867–1948), Italian composer of ANDRÉ CHÉNIER, *Fedora* and other operas of the Italian 'realistic' kind (see VERISMO).

Giovanni da Cascia (also known as 'da Firenze', of Florence) (14th century), Italian composer of madrigals (in the older sense), *caccie* (see CACCIA), etc.; held court post at Verona.

Gipsy Baron, The (Ger., *Der Zigeunerbaron*), operetta by J. Strauss the younger, produced in Vienna, 1885. Libretto by I. Schnitzer. The hero is a young Hungarian landowner regarded by the gipsies as their chief – and eventually made a real baron. See RÁKÓCZI MARCH.

Gipsy Princess, The, English title commonly used for *Die Csárdásfürstin* (Ger., Princess Csárdás), operetta by Kálmán, produced in Vienna, 1921.

Girl of the Golden West, The, opera by Puccini, produced in New York, 1910. Set in California at the time of the Gold Rush. The Italian title *La Fanciulla del West* omits 'golden'; the English title is taken from the play by D. Belasco upon which the opera libretto was based by G. Civinini and C. Zanganini.

Gis, Gisis (Ger.), G sharp, G double-sharp.

Giselle, or The Wilis (Fr., ... *ou les Wilis*), ballet with music by Adam, produced in Paris, 1841. The Wilis are the spirits of maidens who die before their intended marriages.

gittern, old English name for a type of guitar (not the same as CITTERN).

Giuliani, Mauro [Giuseppe Sergio Pantaleo] (1781–1829), Italian guitarist and composer of three guitar concertos, chamber works with guitar, songs with a choice of guitar or piano accompaniment, etc. Active in Paris, Vienna and elsewhere.

Giulini, Carlo Maria (b. 1914), Italian

149

conductor of great distinction in concerts and opera; music director of La Scala (Milan), 1953–6; first appeared at Covent Garden, 1958. He was music director of the Los Angeles Philharmonic Orchestra, 1978–84.

Giulio Cesare, see JULIUS CAESAR.

giusto (It.), strict, just proper; hence such expressions as *allegro giusto*, meaning either (1) allegro with a special attention to keeping a strict beat, or (2) a moderate (neither too fast nor too slow) allegro.

Glagolitic Mass, Mass by Janáček for chorus, organ and orchestra, 1926. Glagolitic is an obsolete Slav alphabet; the form of Mass associated with it has patriotic Czech associations.

Glanville-Hicks, Peggy (1912–90), Australian-born composer who studied in Europe but whose main career was in USA, where she lived 1942–59. Works include a piano concerto, chamber music, operas. Also critic.

Glasser, Stanley (b. 1926), South African composer, pupil in London of Seiber and Frankel; teacher at London University. Works include *The Chameleon and the Lizard* (text in Zulu); Sinfonietta Concertante for orchestra; chamber music.

glass harmonica, obsolete instrument consisting of glass vessels of various sizes, rubbed with damped finger (or operated mechanically) – written for, e.g., by Mozart. Also called the 'musical glasses'. Invented by Benjamin Franklin, 1763.

Glass, Philip (b. 1937), American composer (see MINIMALISM) who studied with N. Boulanger in Paris and also with R. Shankar; created own ensemble, chiefly amplified electronic music, for performing his concert works (e.g. *Koyaanisquatsi*, American–Indian word for 'life out of balance', which won wider-than-classical popularity). He also composed operas including EINSTEIN ON THE BEACH and AKHNATEN.

Glazunov, Alexander [Konstantinovich] (1865–1936), Russian composer of eight symphonies (all by 1906), plus one (1909) unfinished, first performed in Moscow, 1948; concertos for piano (2), for violin, for saxophone; CARNIVAL overture; ballets including THE SEASONS, piano pieces, songs, etc. He cultivated a Romantic idiom without the musical 'nationalism' of his teacher, Rimsky-Korsakov. Became director of the St Petersburg (later Leningrad) Conservatory but left in 1928 and settled in Paris, where he died.

Glebov, Igor, see ASAFIEV.

glee, short choral composition, properly in several sections and for unaccompanied male voices; flourished in Britain about 1650–1830. (Cp. PART-SONG.) Hence *glee club* – term used in US for choir (traditionally all-male) cultivating short works of various types.

gli (It.), the (masc. pl.).

Glière, Reinhold [Moritzovich] (1875–1956), Russian composer of Belgian descent; pupil of Arensky, Taneyev and Ippolitov-Ivanov; professor at the Moscow Conservatory. Works include *Shah-Senem* (based on folk-music of Azerbaijan) and other operas; *The Red Poppy* and other ballets; three symphonies (no. 3, *Ilya Murometz*); a concerto for coloratura soprano and orchestra; chamber music; many songs and piano pieces.

Glinka, Mikhail Ivanovich (1804–57), Russian composer, the first whose music won general acceptance outside Russia; shows various 'nationalist' traits in his works. Regarded therefore as the 'father' of Russian music. Studied piano with Field; visited Italy and Germany before bringing out operas A LIFE FOR THE TSAR (1836) and RUSLAN AND LYUDMILA; made other trips abroad later, dying in Berlin. Also composed *Jota aragonesa* and other works in imitation-Spanish style; chamber music for strings and for wind; many piano pieces and songs.

glissando (mock-It. from Fr. *glisser*, to slide), sliding up and down the scale, i.e. making a quick uninterrupted passage up or down the scale, e.g. on the piano, harp, xylophone, trombone. The effect of PORTAMENTO on stringed instruments is not the same, since it implies only the smooth linking of two notes, not the deliberate sounding of the notes in between.

Globokar, Vinko (b. 1934), Yugoslav composer (born in France) who studied in both Yugoslavia and France – and also in Germany with Berio. Is also trombonist, for whom Berio wrote no. 5 of his SEQUENCES. Works include *Explanation of Dreams* for four choruses; *Fluid* for nine brass and three percussion.

Glocke(n) (Ger.), bell(s) – referring, in orchestral scores, to tubular bells. (See BELL.)

Glockenspiel (Ger., play of bells), percussion instrument of tuned metal bars giving small bell-like sound: played with keyboard or (more usually) small hammers held in hand. (The term is also used, though more rarely, for a chime of real bells played mechanically or by hand, i.e. a CARILLON.)

Gloria [in excelsis Deo] (Lat., Glory [to God in the highest]), see MASS. A number of composers, e.g. Poulenc, Walton, have set this text separately.

Gloriana, opera by Britten, produced in London, 1953, in honour of the coronation of Queen Elizabeth II. Libretto by W. Plomer; 'Gloriana' is Elizabeth I.

glotte, coup de, see COUP DE GLOTTE.

Glover, Jane [Alison] (b. 1949), British conductor who became known first as a musicologist; conducted at Glyndebourne from 1981 and became artistic director of London Mozart Players, 1984.

Gluck, Christoph Willibald [von] (1714–87), German composer, born in Bavaria but possibly of Bohemian origin; travelled much – London, 1745; Paris, 1773–9, where his followers opposed those of Piccinni; settled and died in Vienna. Was consciously an operatic reformer, stressing importance of subordinating music to dramatic needs – and also dispensing with 'dry RECITATIVE'; his ALKESTIS (1767) has a famous preface expounding his ideas. This opera, like its predecessor ORPHEUS, was originally in Italian; both were later revised with French texts. Other operas include IPHIGENIA IN AULIS, IPHIGENIA IN TAURIS and ARMIDA, all in French. Wrote in all more than 45 stage works including ballet *Don Juan*; also instrumental pieces, etc.

Glyndebourne, a small opera house in the Sussex countryside founded by John Christie, the owner of the estate in which it stands. International short summer seasons there opened in 1934. Music director from 1989 (succeeding Haitink), Andrew Davis.

Gnecchi, Vittorio (1876–1954), Italian composer of operas, including *La Rosiera*, 1910, with an early use of quarter-tones.

Gnessin, Mikhail Fabianovich (1883–1957), Russian composer, pupil of Rimsky-Korsakov and Lyadov; travelled in Western Europe and Palestine. He composed many works with Jewish associations including operas *The Youth of Abraham* and *The Maccabees*; also symphonic poems, chamber music, Jewish folk-song arrangements, etc.

Gobbi, Tito (1913–84), Italian baritone, made début in 1938; celebrated in opera (such roles as Rigoletto, Falstaff, Scarpia in TOSCA, etc.) and appeared in many films. Also opera producer.

Godard, Benjamin Louis Paul (1849–95), French composer, also violinist. Works include *Jocelyn* (from which the well-known 'Berceuse' comes) and seven other operas; also orchestral works, over 100 songs, etc.

Godowsky, Leopold (1870–1938), Polish-born pianist who became American, 1891; made and performed many virtuoso-style transcriptions of famous orchestral and other works. Was also composer, e.g., of the *Triakontameron* (30 piano pieces each composed on a different day).

God save the King (Queen), British national anthem; author and composer unknown, though a keyboard piece by Bull (in the minor key) has some relationship to the tune. Generally adopted in the mid 18th century. (Tune also set to various other words – e.g. US, 'My country, 'tis of thee', 1831.)

Goedicke, Alexander Fedorovich (1877–1957), Russian pianist, teacher, and composer of operas, three symphonies, etc.

Goehr, Alexander (b. 1932), British (German-born) composer, pupil of R. Hall and (in Paris) of Messiaen. Professor of music at Cambridge since 1976. Works include symphonies; *Romanza* for cello and orchestra; operas ARDEN MUST DIE and *Behold the Sun*; a triptych of 'music-theatre' pieces. His father was the conductor and composer Walter Goehr (1903–60).

Goethe, Johann Wolfgang von (1749–1832), German poet and novelist. See BALLAD, BOULANGER (L.), DAMNATION OF FAUST, DOCTOR FAUST, ERL-KING, FAUST, JELINEK, KLEBE, MEPHISTOPHELES, MIGNON, PROMETHEUS, REUTTER, WERTHER, WOLF, ZIMMERMANN.

Goetz, Hermann (1840–76), German composer of opera THE TAMING OF THE SHREW, a symphony, piano concerto, chamber music, songs, etc.; settled in Switzerland and died there.

Gogol, Nikolay [Vasilievich] (1809–52), Russian dramatist. See EGK, MARTINŮ, SEARLE, VOLKONSKY.

Goldberg, Szymon (b. 1909), Polish-born violinst long resident in Holland (where he directed his own chamber orchestra) and latterly in England and USA; noted teacher.

Goldberg Variations, usual name for Bach's 30 variations for harpsichord (with two keyboards) on an original theme, 1742 (BWV 988); written for his pupil, J. G. Goldberg, whose noble patron required music as a solace for insomnia. See QUODLIBET.

Golden Cockerel, The (Rus., *Zolotoy petushok*), Rimsky-Korsakov's last opera; at first banned by censorship, then produced (only after the composer's death) in Moscow, 1909. Libretto by V. I. Bielsky, after Pushkin: title from a magic 'weathercock' which gives warning of danger to the city. The work is a satire on stupid despotism.

Golden Sonata, nickname (not the composer's) for Purcell's Sonata in F for two violins, viola da gamba and continuo (Z810), no. 9 of a set of 10 published posthumously in 1697. (The set is called *Sonatas of Four Parts*, but see PURCELL.)

Goldmark, Karl (1830–1915), Austro-Hungarian composer who trained in Vienna and eventually settled there. Works include operas (*The Cricket on the Hearth*, after Dickens; *The Winter's Tale*, after Shakespeare; etc.); two symphonies, one called RUSTIC WEDDING; two violin concertos; piano music, and songs. Uncle of Rubin Goldmark.

Goldmark, Rubin (1872–1936), American composer, nephew of preceding; pupil of Dvořák, teacher of Gershwin. Wrote orchestral works – one on *Hiawatha* – chamber music, piano pieces, etc.

Goldoni, Carlo (1707–93), Italian dramatist. See HANUŠ, SCHOOL FOR FATHERS, WORLD OF THE MOON.

Goldschmidt, Berthold (b. 1903), German-born composer (pupil of Schreker) and conductor, resident in England since 1935. Works include opera *Beatrice Cenci* (after Shelley); ballet *Chronica*; a piano concerto.

Goldsmith, Oliver (1728–74), Irish writer. See LEHMANN (Liza).

Golliwogg's Cakewalk, see CHILDREN'S CORNER.

Gombert, Nicolas (*c.*1495–*c.*1560), Flemish (Netherlandish) composer, in service to the (Holy Roman) Emperor Charles V, with whom he travelled widely; he is thought to have been a pupil of Josquin. Wrote more than 70 chansons, also Masses, motets, etc.

Gomes, [Antonio] **Carlos** (1836–96), Brazilian composer of operas, some in Italian, others in Portuguese; the former include *The Guarani* (*Il Guarany*), the hero being a member of the American–Indian people of that name.

Gondoliers, The, or The King of Barataria, operetta by Sullivan, produced in London, 1889. Libretto by W. S. Gilbert (his last successful collaboration with Sullivan). Title from the heroes, two Venetian boatmen who despite their own egalitarian views find themselves jointly reigning as king.

gong, circular percussion instrument of bronze, made in various sizes, usually with a turned-down rim; sometimes of definite and sometimes of indefinite pitch. (This is a broad, ethnomusicological definition, but in modern orchestral usage there is a tendency to reserve *gong* for the various-sized instruments with definite pitch and TAM-TAM for those with indefinite.) The gong was possibly first used in the Western orchestra by Gossec in 1791; the earliest known mention is sixth-century Chinese.

Goodall, Reginald (1901–90), British conductor, celebrated in Wagner, especially for English National Opera productions in London and on recordings. Knighted, 1985.

Goodman, Benny (originally Benjamin David) (1909–86), American clarinettist who became eminent in the jazz sphere (led his own band from 1933) and afterwards became noted soloist with orchestra, chamber-music player, etc.; Copland's Clarinet Concerto and Bartók's CONTRASTS were written for him.

Goossens, [Aynsley] **Eugene** (1893–1962), British conductor and composer (also violinist), son and grandson of conductors of the same name (of Belgian descent). Active in USA, then (1947–56) conservatory director in Sydney, Australia. Wrote operas *Judith* and *Don Juan de Mañara*, two symphonies, piano pieces, etc. Brother of Léon Goossens (and also of Sidonie and Marie Goossens, harpists). Knighted, 1955.

Goossens, Léon [Jean] (1897–1988) British oboist, noted soloist for whom concertos and other works were written by Vaughan Williams and others. CBE, 1950. See preceding.

gopak, Russian folk-dance in quick 2/4 time. (In English sometimes also written as 'hopak'.)

Gordon, Gavin [Muspratt] (1901–70), Scottish bass singer, actor, opera producer – and composer e.g. of THE RAKE'S PROGRESS and other ballets.

Górecki, Henryk [Mikolaj] (b. 1933), Polish composer of three symphonies (no. 3, *A Symphony of Sorrowful Songs*); a harpsichord concerto; *Genesis* for soprano and instrumental ensemble.

Goss, John (1800–1880), British organist (St Paul's Cathedral, London,

1838) and composer, chiefly of church music. Knighted, 1872. No relation of John Goss (1894–1952), English baritone.

Gossec, François Joseph (1734–1829), Belgian composer, from 1751 living in France (where he died); also musical organizer and teacher. Wrote symphonies, pioneering in form in France; also many operas and ballets, chamber music, works for outdoor performance celebrating the French Revolution, etc. Innovator in orchestration and the massed use of instruments.

Gotovac, Jakov (1895–1982), Yugoslav composer of *Ero the Joker* and other operas, choral works, songs with orchestra and with piano, etc.; made use of folk-music idiom. Was also conductor. Studied in Vienna.

Götterdämmerung, see RING.

Gottschalk, Louis Moreau (1829–69), American pianist, the first such to win international standing as a virtuoso. Also composer of virtuoso-style piano pieces, some in a 'Creole' style foreshadowing RAGTIME; also of two operas and various orchestral works.

Goudimel, Claude (*c.*1510–72), French composer at first of Roman Catholic church music; then, after becoming a Protestant, of psalm-tunes, etc., for Protestant use. Also wrote secular songs. Killed in the 'St Bartholomew' massacre of Protestants.

Gould, Glenn [Herbert] (1932–82), Canadian pianist who made his début with the Toronto Symphony Orchestra at 14, later toured widely (European début with Karajan in Berlin, 1957) – but from mid-1960s very seldom appeared in concerts, preferring only to record. Also composer, conductor and lecturer.

Gould, Morton (1913–82), American composer and conductor (also pianist). Associated with 'popular' music, but works include three symphonies, Concerto for tap dancer, and four *American Symphonettes* (*sic*) from no. 2 of which comes 'Pavanne' (*sic*).

Gounod, Charles [François] (1818–93), French composer, pupil of Halévy and others at the Paris Conservatory, where he won the 'Rome Prize' and so spent three years in Rome; afterwards church organist in Paris. At one time intended to become a priest. Had great success with opera FAUST, 1857. Also conductor; first conductor of what is now Royal Choral Society, during the years 1870–75 spent in London. Later concentrated on religious music, e.g. oratorio THE REDEMPTION. Other works include opera ROMEO AND JULIET and 12 other operas; nine Masses and other church music; many songs; three symphonies; several miscellaneous pieces including his *Meditation* on the first prelude of Bach's THE WELL-TEMPERED CLAVIER (the so-called AVE MARIA), and the FUNERAL MARCH OF A MARIONETTE. Cultivated an immediately effective style, often chromatically spiced, which has declined in favour since his death.

Gow, Nathaniel (1763–1831), Scottish musician (son and father of other musicians); was trumpeter, violinist, publisher, song-composer, etc. Wrote tune of song 'Caller Herrin'', the words being fitted later.

Goyescas (Sp., Goya-esque works), (1) two sets of piano pieces (seven in all) by Granados, suggested by Goya's paintings and first performed in 1914; (2) opera by Granados, produced in New York in 1916, partly based on the preceding and having a plot of love and killing in a Goya-esque setting; libretto (in Spanish) by F. Periquet.

Gozzi, Carlo (1722–1806), Italian dramatist. See TURANDOT.

GP, abbr. of GENERAL PAUSE.

Grabu, Louis (d. after 1694), French violinist and composer; Master of the King's Music to Charles II, 1665; composer of music to Dryden's *Albion and Albanius* and other stage works.

grace (verb), to decorate a melody, particularly to add such decorations (see ORNAMENT) as an accomplishment in the act of performance; hence *grace* (noun, somewhat obsolete), an ornament. A *grace-note* is a note forming such an addition to a melody, being considered as a decoration even though it may be actually written down by the composer rather than originated by the performer.

Gradus ad Parnassum (Lat., Steps to Parnassus – the mountain sacred to the Muses), (1) a treatise on counterpoint by Fux, 1725; (2) a collection of piano studies by Clementi, 1817. It is to the latter that Debussy pays humorous homage in 'Doctor Gradus ad Parnassum' (see CHILDREN'S CORNER).

Graener, Paul (1872–1944), German composer of operas (one about W. F. Bach), orchestral works, etc.; also conductor. Lived in London 1896–1908.

Grainger, Percy Aldridge (1882–1961), Australian-born composer and pianist; lived 1900–1915 in London and thereafter in USA (naturalized). Pupil in Germany of Busoni; friend of Grieg. Collected and edited English folk-music and based some compositions on it. Also wrote choral works, many short orchestral pieces (e.g. *Country Gardens, Handel in the Strand*); usually published his work in several different (and often unconventional) instrumental versions. Used deliberately Anglicized vocabulary, e.g. 'louden' (crescendo), 'middle-fiddle' (viola), 'bass fiddle' – to mean cello, not double-bass, which term he retained. See also LONDONDERRY AIR.

Granados [y Campina], **Enrique** (1867–1916), Spanish composer (pupil of Pedrell), also pianist and conductor; his seven operas include GOYESCAS, partly based on piano works of the same name. Wrote also other piano music, orchestral works and songs, cultivating Spanish 'nationalist' idiom. Died when the ship on which he was returning from New York was torpedoed by a German submarine.

gran cassa (It.) = BASS DRUM.

grand chœur (Fr.) = FULL ORGAN.

Grand Duke, The, or The Statutory Duel, operetta by Sullivan – his last (unsuccessful) collaboration with W. S. Gilbert as librettist – produced in London, 1896. The Grand Duke appears to lose his title through a type of duel with playing-cards.

Grand Duo, name given to a sonata in C by Schubert (D812; 1824) for piano duet. See GASTEIN SYMPHONY.

Grande Messe des Morts (Fr., Grand Requiem Mass), title given by Berlioz to his setting of the Latin text of the REQUIEM, using an exceptionally large orchestral accompaniment; first performed in 1837.

Grandi, Alessandro (*c.*1577–1630), Italian composer of madrigals, etc.; also church musician. Died at Bergamo of the plague.

grand jeu (Fr.) = FULL ORGAN.

Grand Macabre, Le, see GREAT MACABRE.

grand opera, imprecise term sometimes meaning all-sung opera (without spoken dialogue), sometimes referring specifically to French spectacular opera using historical plots such as WILLIAM TELL (Rossini) and THE HUGUENOTS (Meyerbeer); also used by laymen to distinguish 'serious' opera from, e.g., operetta.

grand piano, see PIANO.

graphic notation, term describing certain post-1950 types of musical notation, especially those which pictorialize the action required of the performer, or which represent duration by comparative length of a printed line or other visual symbol.

Grappelli (originally Grappelly), **Stephane** (b. 1908), French violinist famous as a jazz musician and in recordings and performances with Menuhin from the mid-1970s.

Graun, Carl Heinrich (1703/4–59), German composer (also tenor singer), musical director to Frederick II of Prussia from 1740. Earlier influenced by Lotti at Dresden, and later himself visited Italy. Wrote Italian and German operas, chamber music, and church music including notably successful cantata *The Death of Jesus* – see PASSION.

grave (It., heavy, grave), in slow tempo.

gravicembalo (It., corruption of *clavicembalo*), harpsichord.

grazia, grazioso (It.), grace, graceful(ly).

great, usual abbreviation for GREAT ORGAN.

Great C-Major Symphony, name for Schubert's Symphony no. 9 in C (D944) (in some editions called no. 7 – see SCHUBERT), completed in 1828 but never performed in the composer's lifetime. The title distinguishes the symphony from the shorter no. 6 in the same key, and alludes both to its quality and its unusual length: it takes nearly an hour in performance.

Great Fugue (Ger., *Grosse Fuge*), fugue by Beethoven for string quartet, op. 133 (1825), originally designed as last movement of Quartet in B♭, op. 130; but Beethoven gave this work a new finale and issued the fugue separately.

Great Macabre, The (Fr., *Le Grand Macabre*), opera by Ligeti, produced in Stockholm, 1978. Libretto, after a play by Ghelderode, is a comic satire on death and sexuality.

great organ (or simply *Great*), chief and most powerful division of an organ (a manual and the equipment controlled by it). No connection with *Great Organ Mass* (see the following).

Great Organ Mass, nickname for Haydn's Mass in E♭, 1774 (Hob. XXII:4), with an important organ part. Better called *Great Mass with Organ*, avoiding suggestion of a connection with 'great organ'. Cp. LITTLE ORGAN MASS.

great service, see SERVICE.

Grechaninov, Alexander Tikhonovich (1864–1956), Russian composer (pupil of Rimsky-Korsakov) resident in France from 1925, in USA from 1939. Works include operas, five symphonies, many songs, music for children, and *Missa oecumenica*, 1944, designed to embrace musically both Eastern and Western Christianity.

Greek, opera by Turnage, produced in Munich, 1988; libretto – adapted from Berkoff's play by the composer and Jonathan Moore – applies the Oedipus legend to modern lower-class city life.

Greek Passion, The, opera by Martinu, produced in Zurich, 1961; libretto (in English) founded on Kazantzakis's novel *Christ Recrucified*, enacting the Passion in modern times.

Greene, Graham (1904–91), British novelist. See OUR MAN IN HAVANA.

Greene, Maurice (1696–1755), English composer of songs, church music, etc.; also organist.

Greensleeves, old English tune mentioned by Shakespeare and found with several sets of words and in several old musical arrangements (see CUTTING); *Fantasia on Greensleeves*, orchestral work by Vaughan Williams adapted from his opera SIR JOHN IN LOVE.

Gregorian chant, type of PLAINSONG associated with Pope Gregory I (otherwise St Gregory; *c.*540–*c.*604) which became standard in the Roman Catholic Church.

Gregorian tone, name given to each of eight melodies of Gregorian chant (each in a different MODE) prescribed by the Roman Catholic Church for the

Psalms. TONUS PEREGRINUS is additional to these.

Gretchaninov, see GRECHANINOV.

Grétry, André Ernest Modeste (1741–1813), Belgian composer who studied in Italy and in 1767 settled in France (where he died). Was one of the chief composers of OPÉRA COMIQUE: he wrote dozens of works of this type, including *Zémire and Azor* (based on the tale of Beauty and the Beast) and *Richard Cœur de Lion*. The latter is the source of an aria quoted in Tchaikovsky's THE QUEEN OF SPADES as an evocation of this period.

Grieg, Edvard Hagerup (1843–1907), Norwegian composer whose Scottish great-grandfather's name was Greig; also pianist, particularly as accompanist to his wife (and cousin) Nina, who sang his songs. Encouraged by Ole Bull, went to study in Leipzig; later, pupil of Gade in Copenhagen. Became 'nationalist' in music. At Ibsen's request, wrote music for PEER GYNT. Wrote an early symphony; works also include a piano concerto, HOLBERG SUITE for strings, music to Bjørnson's *Sigurd Jorsalfar* (see HOMAGE MARCH); choral works; *Bergliot* (text by Bjørnson) for reciter and orchestra; three violin sonatas, many songs and piano works, various Norwegian folk-music arrangements. Often visited Britain; Hon.D.Mus., Cambridge, 1894.

Griffes, Charles Tomlinson (1884–1920), American composer – pupil of Humperdinck in Germany, but mainly influenced by French IMPRESSIONISM. Overworked, through poverty, and died of pneumonia. Composed *The Pleasure Dome of Kubla Khan* (after Coleridge) for orchestra; music to a Japanese mime play; THE WHITE PEACOCK for piano (later orchestrated) and other piano music.

Grigny, Nicolas de (1672–1703), French organist whose *First Organ Book* (he died young and did not publish another) was copied out in admiration by Bach; it contains music for the Mass, hymns, fugues, etc.

Griller Quartet, British string quartet founded in 1928, led by Sidney Griller; it disbanded in 1961.

Grimm, Jacob Ludwig Karl (1785–1863) and Wilhelm Karl (1786–1859), German folklorists and writers. See CLEVER GIRL, HANSEL AND GRETEL, HUMPERDINCK.

Grisi, Giulia (1811–69), Italian soprano, one of the most famous opera singers of her day in Paris and London. Her sister Giuditta Grisi (1805–40) was a mezzo-soprano.

grosse caisse (Fr.) = BASS DRUM.

Grosse Fuge (Ger.) = GREAT FUGUE.

Grosses Orchester (Ger.) = FULL ORCHESTRA.

Grosse Trommel (Ger.) = BASS DRUM.

Grossi, Carlo (c.1634–1688), Italian composer active in Venice c.1655–c.1680, also church singer at St Mark's there; wrote vocal and instrumental music for church use, also operas and chamber music.

ground, term sometimes used for GROUND BASS.

ground bass, bass pattern which is persistently repeated while upper parts proceed; hence, e.g., in 17th-century England 'DIVISIONS on a ground', i.e.

a piece in variation-form constructed by this means. Cp. CHACONNE.

Grove, George (1820–1900), British musical scholar (also engineer, biblical commentator, magazine editor, etc.), first director of the Royal College of Music (1883–94); founder and first editor (1879–89) of *Grove's Dictionary of Music and Musicians*. Knighted, 1883.

Groven, Eivind (1901–77), Norwegian composer of choral music, symphonic poems, etc.; strongly influenced by Norwegian folk-music (on which he was an authority). Disliking the use of the 'tempered scale' (see TEMPERAMENT), he invented an organ 'with automatically controlled non-tempered intervals'.

Groves, Charles [Barnard] (b. 1915), British conductor – of Royal Liverpool Philharmonic Orchestra, 1963–77; music director of English National Opera, 1978–9. Knighted, 1973.

Grovlez, Gabriel [Marie] (1879–1944), French pianist, conductor and composer of songs, two operas, etc.

Gruber, H[ans] **K**[arl] (b. 1943), Austrian composer of deliberately outrageous pieces such as *Frankenstein!!*, styled 'a pandemonium' for baritone and orchestra, and *Demilitarized Zones* for brass band.

Gruenberg, Louis (1884–1964), Russian-born American composer and pianist (brought to USA at age two); piano pupil of Busoni in Vienna. Much influenced by jazz and Negro music: his works include EMPEROR JONES and other operas, also a violin concerto, symphonic poems, *Jazzberries* for piano.

Gruenthal, Joseph, see TAL.

Grumiaux, Arthur (1921–86), Belgian violinist, pupil of Enescu in Paris, and an internationally celebrated performer (especially in Mozart) from about 1950. See HASKIL. He was created a Belgian baron, 1973.

Grümmer, Elisabeth (1911–86), German soprano noted in opera and concerts; at Covent Garden from 1951, Bayreuth from 1957.

gruppetto (It.) = TURN (type of ornament).

Guadagni, Gaetano (*c.*1725–1792), Italian male alto (castrato), later soprano. Worked with Handel in London and was Gluck's first Orpheus, 1762.

Guarneri, Guarnerius, Italian family (the second name is the Latinized form) of 17th- and 18th-century makers of violins, etc. The founder, Andrea Guarneri, was a pupil of Amati. Giuseppe Antonio Guarneri (1698–1744) is known as Giuseppe Guarneri del Gesù.

Guarneri Quartet, American string quartet founded in 1964, led by Arnold Steinhardt; recorded with Arthur Rubinstein.

Guarnieri, [Mozart] **Camargo** (b. 1907), Brazilian composer, pupil of Koechlin in Paris, also conductor. Works, often making use of Brazilian folk-music, include four symphonies, five piano concertos; chamber music.

Gubaidulina, Sofia (b. 1931), Russian composer who in the 1980s won marked attention in the West. Compositions include a piano concerto (*Introitus*), violin concerto (*Offertorium*), a symphony entitled *Stimmen . . . ver-*

stummen (Ger., Voices . . . Made Dumb), with one section for conductor alone.

Gui, Vittorio (1885–1975), Italian conductor who in 1928 founded in Florence the orchestra from which eventually arose the *Maggio Musicale* (Musical May) Festival there. Noted conductor of opera, e.g. at Glyndebourne from 1952; was also composer.

Guido d'Arezzo (*c*.990–*c*.1050), Italian monk (long resident in Arezzo; hence the name) and musical theorist. Inventor of two devices greatly facilitating the practice of music: (1) the names 'ut', 're', 'mi', etc. (ancestors of modern 'do', 're', 'mi') as indication of the relative positions of the notes of the scale – 'ut' to be either G, C or F, bottom notes of the HEXACHORDS then used; (2) the 'Guidonian hand', an aid to memory whereby the tips and joints of the fingers are given the names of the various notes.

Guillaume Tell (Fr.), see WILLIAM TELL.

Guilmant, Félix Alexandre (1837–1911), French organist in Paris and composer of two 'symphonies' for organ and orchestra, many organ solos for recital and church use.

Guion, David [Wendel Fentress] (1895–1981), American pianist (pupil of Godowsky), composer, and arranger of *Turkey in the Straw* and other traditional American tunes.

Guiraud, Ernest (1837–92), French (American-born) composer (eight operas, one unfinished and completed by Saint-Saëns) and teacher. Wrote recitatives for Bizet's CARMEN; arranged the second suite from Bizet's *L'Arlésienne* (see WOMAN OF ARLES); revised

THE TALES OF HOFFMANN, left unfinished by Offenbach.

guitar, plucked, fretted string instrument: it exists in various types of which the principal one came to other European countries from Spain and is therefore sometimes called *Spanish guitar*; now normally with six strings, with compass from E below the bass stave upwards for more than three octaves. This type (now also called *classical guitar*) enjoyed revival in the 20th century (see SEGOVIA), calling forth concertos by Villa-Lobos and others; it is also (rarely) used in chamber music (e.g. Schoenberg, *Serenade*). The *electric guitar* and four-stringed *electric bass guitar* (see ELECTRIC) are chiefly used in pop music, etc.; in pop circles *acoustic guitar* (primarily meaning non-electric) customarily demands a bulkier instrument than the Spanish guitar. See also DOBRO and STEEL GUITAR.

Gulda, Friedrich (b. 1930), Austrian pianist who occasionally added jazz works to the classics in recital; also composed for jazz ensemble and occasionally played flute and saxophone.

Gundry, Inglis (b. 1905), British composer, pupil of Vaughan Williams and others; works include *The Partisans*, *Avon* and other operas, ballet, orchestral and chamber music, songs.

Gung'l, Joseph (1810–89), Austro-Hungarian bandmaster and composer of marches, dances, etc.: visited USA, 1849.

Guridi, Jesús (1886–1961), Spanish (Basque) composer, using Basque themes; studied in Paris and elsewhere. Works include operas, organ music, folk-song arrangements.

Gurlitt, Cornelius (1820–1901), German pianist, organist, and composer of much educational piano music; also opera. Great-uncle of Manfred Gurlitt.

Gurlitt, Manfred (1890–1973), German conductor and composer of operas (one on the WOZZECK story used by Berg), orchestral and chamber works, etc. Settled in Japan, 1939. Great-nephew of Cornelius Gurlitt.

Gurney, Ivor [Bertie] (1890–1937), British composer (also poet) who won distinction for songs, some to his own words. Also composed piano and orchestral music. Became insane, 1922.

Gurrelieder, see SONGS OF GURRE.

gusla (also *gusle*), ancient Slavonic one-string bowed instrument, distinct from the following.

gusli, Russian instrument of zither type used in folk-music; 'played' by Sadko in Rimsky-Korsakov's opera of that name, the effect being simulated in the orchestra.

gut (Ger.), good, well, markedly.

Guy, Barry (b. 1947), British double-bassist and composer, active in jazz and ensembles of modern music. Works include *Incontri* (It., Encounters) for cello and orchestra; three string quartets; *Statements II* for amplified double-bass, unaccompanied.

Guy-Ropartz, Joseph, see ROPARTZ.

gymel (from Lat. *gemellus*, twin), type of 13th–15th-century vocal music in two PARTS, making considerable use of thirds and sixths, and chiefly practised in England.

Gymnopédies, see SATIE.

Gyrowetz (Germanized form of Czech name 'Jirovec'), **Adalbert** (1763–1850), Bohemian composer, some of whose symphonies (he wrote more than 40) were performed under Haydn's name in Paris. Visited London, 1789–92; court conductor at Vienna from 1804. Composed German and Italian operas, MELODRAMAS, about 45 string quartets, church music, etc.

H

H, German note-symbol; see B.

Haas, Monique (1906–87), French pianist, internationally noted; her husband was the composer MIHALOVICI.

Hába, Alois (1893–1973), Czech composer (pupil of Novák and Schreker), sometimes using quarter-tones with special instruments to play them – and also, less frequently, using sixth-tones; works include operas, orchestral and chamber music, songs with guitar, solos for ordinary piano and for quarter-tone piano. Brother of Karel Hába.

Hába, Karel (1898–1972), Czech violinist, viola-player and composer, pupil of his brother Alois Hába; sometimes used quarter-tones. Works in normal tonal system include a violin concerto, cello concerto, septet.

habanera, Cuban dance with singing introduced into Spain. The word comes from Habana (i.e. Havana), Cuba; whence the French equivalent term, *havanaise*. (For the example in Bizet's *Carmen*, see YRADIER.) The spelling 'habañera' is mistaken.

Hacker, Alan [Ray] (b. 1938), British clarinettist, also conductor; pioneered the revival of the BASSET-CLARINET in Mozart's works.

Hadley, Henry Kimball (1871–1937), American composer and conductor who studied in Vienna; works include operas, four symphonies (no. 2, *The Four Seasons*), choral works, more than 100 songs.

Hadley, Patrick [Arthur Sheldon] (1899–1973), British composer of *La Belle Dame Sans Merci* and other choral works, orchestral and chamber music, incidental music for Sophocles' *Antigone*, etc. Professor at Cambridge, 1946–63.

Haebler, Ingrid (b. 1926), Austrian pianist (celebrated interpreter of Mozart, Schubert, etc.) who appeared at various international festivals (Salzburg from 1954).

Haefliger, Ernst (b. 1919), Swiss tenor eminent in oratorio and opera – Salzburg Festival, 1949, Glyndebourne, 1956, etc.

Haendel, Georg Friederich, see HANDEL.

Haendel, Ida (b. 1923), Polish-born violinist resident in Canada since 1962; was child prodigy (London, 1937). CBE, 1991.

'Haffner' Serenade, nickname of a serenade composed by Mozart, 1776 (K250), for a marriage in the Haffner family of Salzburg. See also 'HAFFNER' SYMPHONY.

'Haffner' Symphony, nickname for Mozart's Symphony no. 35 in D (K385), arranged from a serenade (not that of the preceding entry) written for the Haffner family of Salzburg in 1782.

Hageman, Richard (1882–1966), Dutch-born composer who settled in USA, 1907; also operatic and concert conductor. Works include opera and many songs, such as 'Do not go, my love' (text by Tagore).

Hahn, Reynaldo (1874–1947; the birth-date 1875 is mistaken), French composer, Venezuelan-born, who went to Paris in infancy, entered Conservatory there at 11 (pupil of Massenet and others), and became conductor. Wrote operas (one on *The Merchant of Venice*), operettas, music for plays (including Sacha Guitry's *Mozart*), chamber music, songs (including 'If my songs had only wings').

Haieff, Alexei (b. 1914), Russian-born composer resident in New York from age 17; pupil of N. Boulanger and others. Works, showing some influence of Stravinsky, include a piano concerto, three symphonies, chamber music, ballet *Beauty and the Beast*.

hairpins, colloquial name for the signs < and > indicating respectively crescendo and diminuendo.

Haitink, Bernard [Johan Herman] (b. 1929), Dutch conductor, principal conductor of the Concertgebouw Orchestra of Amsterdam, 1961–88, and, 1967–79, of the London Philharmonic Orchestra; music director at Glyndebourne, 1978–87, then at Covent Garden. Hon. KBE, 1977.

Halb(e) (Ger.), half: *Halbe, Halbenote* = HALF-NOTE, minim.

Hale, see LA HALE.

Halévy, (original surname Levy) Jacques François [Fromental Elias] (1799–1862), French composer: was a pupil of Cherubini in Paris and also studied in Italy. Works include THE JEWESS and more than 30 other operas, usually of a spectacular kind – mostly in French, but one in Italian based on Shakespeare's *The Tempest*. Also composed ballets (see MANON LESCAUT), cantatas, etc. After his death, his daughter married his ex-pupil Bizet.

half-close = imperfect CADENCE.

Halffter [Escriche], Ernesto (b. 1905), Spanish composer of partly German descent, resident in Portugal; also conductor. Works include his Sinfonietta; opera *The Death of Carmen*; chamber music. See also FALLA. Brother of Rodolfo Halffter.

Halffter, [Escriche] Rodolfo (1900–1987), Spanish composer of partly German descent, resident in Mexico; also writer on music. Works include a violin concerto, ballets, piano solos. Brother of Ernesto Halffter.

half-note, the note ♩ considered as a time-value. This term is standard North American usage and, as mathematically corresponding to the element of time-signature represented by /2, should clearly be preferred to 'minim', still surviving in British use. The corresponding rest is noted ▬

Hälfte, die (Ger., the half), direction indicating that a passage is to be played by only half the normal number of instruments, e.g. half the first violins.

Halka, opera by Moniuszko, produced in Vilna, 1854. Regarded as the chief

Polish national opera. Libretto by W. Wolski. Named after the humbly born heroine who drowns herself when her aristocratic lover leaves her with child.

Hall, Richard (1903–80), British composer of five symphonies, organ works, etc. Noted teacher in Manchester, e.g. of Goehr.

Halle, Adam de la, see LA HALE.

Hallelujah Chorus, the chorus consisting mostly of the one repeated word 'Hallelujah', at the end of Part II of Handel's MESSIAH. (This is what the term now refers to, though other works have similar choruses.)

'Hallelujah' Concerto, nickname for Handel's Organ Concerto in B♭ (no. 3 of his second set, published in 1740), because it contains a phrase also occurring in the 'Hallelujah Chorus'.

Hallé Orchestra, orchestra founded in Manchester in 1858 by the German-born pianist and conductor Carl Halle, 1819–95, who became Sir Charles Hallé. Barbirolli was its conductor, 1943–70; James Loughran, 1971–83; Stanislaw Skrowaczewski, 1984–91.

halling (Norw.), a Norwegian acrobatic solo dance for men, in 2/4 time, cultivated by Grieg and other Norwegian composers.

Halm, see KINSKY.

Halvorsen, Johan (1864–1935), Norwegian composer, also violinist and conductor; married a niece of Grieg. As a young violinist, worked in Aberdeen. Compositions – strongly influenced by Grieg – include two symphonies, a violin concerto, stage music.

Haman and Mordecai, see ESTHER.

Hambraeus, Bengt (b. 1928), Swedish composer and organist; till 1972 he worked for Swedish Radio, then took university post in Montreal. Works include *Rota* for three orchestras and tape; *Interferences* for organ; choral music.

Hamerik, Asger (1843–1923), Danish composer, pupil of Gade and Berlioz; in USA 1872–98. Works include seven symphonies (no. 6 *Spirituelle*, i.e. light), four operas, two choral trilogies. Father of Ebbe Hamerik.

Hamerik, Ebbe (1898–1951), Danish composer and conductor. Studied with his father (Asger Hamerik) and abroad. Works include *The Travelling Companion* (after Hans Andersen) and other operas; orchestral *Variations on an Old Danish Folk-Tune*; woodwind quintet.

Hamilton, Iain (b. 1922), British composer, pupil of Alwyn. Originally apprenticed as engineer. Works include four symphonies; a concerto and other works for clarinet; *Sonata notturna* for horn and piano; cantata *The Bermudas* (text by Marvell); also operas including *The Catiline Conspiracy, The Royal Hunt of the Sun* (after Peter Shaffer's play) and *Anna Karenina* (after Tolstoy's novel). Professor, Duke University, North Carolina, 1962–71.

Hamlet, title of various works after Shakespeare, including (1) opera by A. Thomas, produced in Paris, 1868 (libretto, J. Barbier and M. Carré); (2) symphonic poem by Liszt, 1858, composed as a prelude to the play; (3) overture-fantasia by Tchaikovsky, 1888; (4) incidental music by Tchaikovsky to the play, 1891 – shortened version of the preceding plus other movements adapted from his earlier works; (5) opera by Searle, produced in Hamburg, 1968.

'Hammerklavier' Sonata, nickname for Beethoven's Piano Sonata in B♭, op. 106 (1815–19). The nickname has small justification: the word is merely an ostentatiously German substitute (hammer-keyboard) for the Italian 'pianoforte', and this was not the only sonata to which Beethoven applied it.

Hammerstein, Oscar, II (1895–1960), American librettist and lyricist. See RODGERS.

Hammond, Joan [Hood] (b. 1912), New Zealand-born soprano; spent early years in Australia; made operatic début in Vienna, then appeared (1938) in London, continuing to specialize in operatic music. Created Dame, 1974.

Hammond organ, type of ELECTRONIC organ, usually with two manuals and pedal keyboard; invented in USA, 1934. (Trade name, after its inventor, Laurens Hammond.)

Handel, George Frideric (form of name adopted in England, by Georg Friederich Händel or Haendel) (1685–1759), composer; born in Halle, Germany; first visited England in 1710, and was naturalized there in 1727. Precocious musical activity, at first against his father's wish. Violinist in Hamburg Opera orchestra, 1703. Visited Italy, 1706–10. Wrote Italian operas for London, including RINALDO (his first there), ALCINA, BERENICE, JULIUS CAESAR, ORLANDO and XERXES. 'Invented' English biblical oratorio with ESTHER, 1732; other oratorios include SAUL, ISRAEL IN EGYPT, MESSIAH, SAMSON, JUDAS MACCABAEUS, SOLOMON, SUSANNA, THEODORA and (last) JEPHTHA. (See ORATORIO.) Other vocal works include ACIS AND GALATEA, SEMELE and ALEXANDER'S FEAST; four coronation anthems including ZADOK THE PRIEST. See also CHANDOS ANTHEMS. Noted harpsichordist and organist; played his organ concertos as intermissions in oratorio. Wrote for orchestra his WATER MUSIC, FIREWORKS MUSIC and works of CONCERTO GROSSO type (for strings alone and for wind and strings); composed also THE HARMONIOUS BLACKSMITH (later so called), other harpsichord pieces etc. Worked within the prevailing style of his time, based on Italian vocal line. Made some unacknowledged 'borrowings' from other composers, and also reused parts of his own works. Became partially blind, 1751; totally so, 1753. Died in London. (See also KERLL).

hand-horn, the 'natural' HORN (i.e. without valves): incapable of a continuous scale, it could produce only the notes of the HARMONIC SERIES, plus a few others obtained by inserting the hand in the bell.

Handl, Jacob (1550–91), Austrian church musician working finally in Prague; composer of motets, Masses, etc.

Hansel and Gretel (Ger., *Hänsel und Gretel*), opera by Humperdinck, produced in Weimar, 1893. Libretto by A. Wette, the composer's sister, after the brothers Grimm: the two children of the title defeat a witch. (The spelling and pronunciation 'Hansel' without the German *ä* has become standard in English.)

Hans Heiling, opera by Marschner, produced in Berlin, 1833. Libretto by E. Devrient (originally written for Mendelssohn). Named after a gnome king who unsuccessfully courts a human woman.

Hanslick, Eduard (1825–1904), Austrian music critic, author of influential treatise *The Beautiful in Music*; champion of Brahms and opponent of Wagner, who pilloried him as Beckmesser in THE MASTERSINGERS.

Hanson, Howard (1896–1981), American composer; worked in Rome, 1921–4, as recipient of an American prize; from 1924, director of the Eastman School of Music, Rochester, NY. Also conductor. Works, some alluding to his Swedish descent, include seven symphonies (no. 1 *Nordic*, no. 4 *Requiem* – in memory of his father; no. 5 *Sinfonia sacra*), a piano concerto, opera, chamber music, songs.

Hanuš, Jan (b. 1915), Czechoslovak composer of *The Servant of Two Masters* (after Goldoni), *The Torch of Prometheus* and other operas; also of four symphonies, a wind quintet, etc.

Harbison, John (b. 1938), American composer. Works include *Ulysses' Raft* for orchestra; cantata *Flight into Egypt*; opera *The Winter's Tale* (after Shakespeare).

Hardanger fiddle (Norw., *hardingfele*), see FIDDLE.

Hardenberger, Håkan (b. 1961), Swedish trumpeter and cornetist for whom Birtwistle and others have composed specially.

Hardy, Thomas (1840–1928), British novelist and poet. See EGDON HEATH, GARDINER, MULDOWNEY, HODDINOTT.

harm., direction to stringed instruments that certain notes are to be played as 'harmonics'. See HARMONIC (noun).

harmonic (adjective), (1) relating to harmony; hence the *harmonic minor* scale (see MINOR) used in harmonizing; hence also the HARMONIC SERIES (see below), the series of tones (*harmonic tones*) from which the system of harmony has historically sprung; (2) relating to the HARMONIC SERIES itself; hence, e.g., the *harmonic flute* stop on an organ, producing four-FOOT tone from an eight-FOOT pipe pierced at half-length – i.e., using the second tone of the HARMONIC SERIES.

harmonic (noun), = harmonic tone (see preceding entry), i.e. one of the tones of the HARMONIC SERIES. The lowest such tone, or 'fundamental', is called the *first harmonic*, the next lowest the *second harmonic*, etc. But in such phrases as 'playing in harmonics' on stringed instruments, the allusion is to harmonics with the exclusion of the first – since the first is the 'normal' sound requiring no special directions. To obtain these harmonics other than the first, it is necessary to set the string vibrating not as a whole length but in fractional parts of its length. (See HARMONIC SERIES.) A violinist, etc., does this by placing a finger lightly at a given point of a vibrating string: when the string is an open string (i.e. not otherwise fingered) then the result is called a *natural harmonic*, but when the string is a stopped string (one finger used for stopping and another for 'lightly placing') then the result is an *artificial harmonic*. The harmonics obtainable on the harp (also by 'lightly placing' the finger on a vibrating string) are in this sense 'natural' harmonics.

harmonic series, the set of tones (called *harmonic tones* or simply *harmonics*) produced by a vibrating string or air-column, according to whether this is vibrating as a unit through its whole length or in aliquot parts ($\frac{1}{2}$, $\frac{1}{3}$, $\frac{1}{4}$, etc.). Vibration of the whole length gives the lowest ('fundamental') tone, or 'first harmonic'. The other tones, or 'upper partials', i.e. the second, third, fourth, and higher harmonics, are at fixed intervals above the fundamental – an octave above it, then a perfect fifth above that, and so on, decreasingly, ad infinitum. E.g. if the fundamental is the C in the bass stave, the series will begin as follows:

in the simplest instance, 'blowing harder' on a tin-whistle to produce a higher octave means the use of the second harmonic; (3) every note of normal musical instruments consists not of a 'pure' tone (like that of a tuning-fork) but of a blend of the 'fundamental' and certain upper partials, the precise blend differing between instruments. In fact this difference in blend determines the difference between tone-colours of instruments.

harmonica, name given to various types of musical instruments – especially, today, to the instrument also called 'mouth-organ', i.e. small

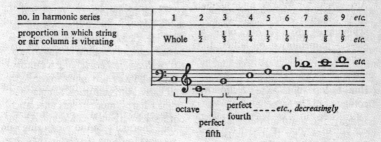

(Not all of these, however, correspond exactly to the notes as tuned in modern European scales.) The importance of the series lies in the following points (among others); (1) the basic technique of brass instruments is to produce the various harmonics by varying the mode of blowing; on, e.g., a bugle this one harmonic series yields all the notes available, while on, e.g., a trumpet and trombone the range is made more complete by use of valves and slide respectively; (2) the use of the upper partials also forms an important device in string-playing (see preceding entry); and those tones are used also on woodwind instruments –

wind instrument with metal reeds (one to each note), made in various sizes, most often with range upwards from about middle C, the superior models having chromatic compass. The instrument has mainly been used informally, e.g. by children, but works by e.g. Milhaud and Vaughan Williams have been written for Larry Adler, its most notable exponent. (Cp. REED ORGAN.) The name was also given to an instrument consisting of musically tuned glasses (now obsolete); see GLASS HARMONICA.

harmonie (Fr.), (1) harmony; (2) wind band (not a purely brass band, which in

Fr. is *fanfare*). Also in German, in both senses; hence the two following entries.

Harmoniemesse, German name (see preceding entry) for Haydn's WIND-BAND Mass.

Harmoniemusik (Ger.), music for wind instruments (see HARMONIE).

Harmonious Blacksmith, The, nickname for a set of variations for Handel's suite for harpsichord in E (1720). Although the regular strokes of the theme may suggest a blacksmith's hammering, the nickname is not Handel's and originated after his death.

harmonium, small portable instrument of the REED-ORGAN family, in which pedals actuate a bellows which drives air through the reeds. Mainly used as a substitute in humble circumstances for the organ as an accompaniment to hymns, etc.; very occasionally elsewhere, e.g. in some *Bagatelles* (with two violins and cello) by Dvořák.

harmony, the simultaneous sounding of notes in a way that is musically significant. (COUNTERPOINT is concerned with the simultaneous combination of melodies, not individual notes; but counterpoint and harmony represent overlapping types of relationships between notes, and a composer considers both relationships together.)

Harnoncourt, Nicolaus (b. 1929), German conductor, cellist and musicologist; distinguished for his work in reviving baroque music with authentic instruments, observing historical style (see CONCENTUS); he also works with 'normal' orchestras.

Harold in Italy, work by Berlioz, 1834, for viola and orchestra – but called a 'symphony'. After Byron's *Childe*

Harold. Written for Paganini, who wanted a viola work for himself, but rejected by him as giving the soloist too little prominence.

harp, plucked stringed instrument of ancient origin, of which the chief modern development (*double-action harp*, from early 19th century) now has a compass from B below the bass clef upwards for nearly seven octaves. It is much used in orchestral music, less frequently in chamber music, solos and for the accompaniment of voices. Its strings in their basic position give the scale of C♭ major (i.e. for practical purposes, B major) which is modified by the use of seven pedals – one raising all the notes C♭ to either C♮ or C♯ as desired, the other pedals doing similarly for all the D♭'s, all the E♭'s, etc. Despite the pedal action, the basic tuning of the harp is thus DIATONIC; a *chromatic harp* (giving a CHROMATIC scale) was also in use in the 19th and early 20th centuries. Simpler and smaller harps, more or less after ancient models, are also still found, e.g. in accompanying Irish and Welsh folksong (*Celtic harp*). See also AEOLIAN HARP and HARP STOP.

Harper, Edward (b. 1941), British composer of *Hedda Gabler* (after Ibsen) and other operas; symphony; Double Variations for oboe, bassoon and wind band. Also university lecturer.

Harper, Heather [Mary] (b. 1930), British soprano, active in opera (Covent Garden from 1962; Bayreuth from 1967) and in concert (Henry Wood Promenade Concerts since 1957). CBE, 1965.

'Harp' Quartet, nickname for Beethoven's String Quartet in E♭, op. 74 (1809) with harp-like pizzicato arpeggios in the first movement. It is a somewhat absurd nickname, because it might be taken for a descriptive name: on the analogy of e.g. 'piano quartet', a 'harp quartet' ought to be a work for harp and three bowed instruments.

harpsichord, keyboard instrument with strings plucked mechanically – as distinct from the piano, in which the strings are struck, and from CLAVICHORD, where the process is again different. Prominent *c.*1550–1800 as solo and ensemble instrument and revived after 1900 for new works (e.g. a concerto by Falla) and for performing old music authentically. Two manuals are commonly found, and are actually required sometimes for contrast, e.g. in Bach's ITALIAN CONCERTO; there may (rarely) be a pedal keyboard too, as on the organ. The player has little control of tone-quality by means of touch, but has at his disposal certain STOPS and COUPLERS. Cp. SPINET and VIRGINALS.

harp stop, a contrivance on a harpsichord damping the strings so that the resulting tone resembles the rather thin tone of the harp.

Harrell, Lynn (b. 1944), American cellist who made London début in 1975 and has a distinguished international career. Son of the baritone Mack Harrell (1909–60).

Harris, Roy (originally Leroy Ellsworth Harris) (1898–1981), American composer; took no professional training until after he was 20, but later studied with N. Boulanger in Paris; held various university teaching posts. Works include 15 symphonies of which no. 4 (*Folk-Song*) is for chorus and orchestra, incorporating various traditional tunes. Other works include

concertos for piano, for two pianos, for accordion; *Elegy and Paean* for viola and orchestra (with electrically amplified piano).

Harris, William Henry (1883–1973), organist of St George's Chapel and composer of church music, cantatas, etc. Knighted, 1954.

Harrison, Lou (b. 1917), American composer of opera *Rapunzel* (after William Morris), a Mass, three orchestral suites, works for percussion instruments alone, pieces for classical Korean court orchestra, ballets, etc.; pupil of Cowell and Schoenberg. Also critic and formerly dancer.

Harsányi, Tibor (1898–1954), Hungarian composer, pupil of Kodály, but resident in Paris from 1923 and predominantly French in musical outlook. Works include a symphony, violin concerto, nonet, stage works.

Hartmann, Johan Peter Emilius (1805–1900), Danish composer of operas including *Little Kirsten* (after Hans Andersen), ballet *A Folk-Tale* (with Gade, his son-in-law), symphonic poems on Nordic subjects, choral works, etc. Director of the Copenhagen Conservatory.

Hartmann, Karl Amadeus (1905–63), German composer. Dissociated himself from the Nazis. Pupil of Scherchen and Webern. Works include eight symphonies, two string quartets, 'pacifist' opera *Simplicius Simplicissimus*. Also organizer of notable concerts of modern music in Munich ('Musica Viva').

Harty, [Herbert] Hamilton (1879–1941), British conductor, born in Northern Ireland; conductor of the Hallé Orchestra, 1920–33, and composer of *Irish Symphony*, a violin concerto, cantata *The Mystic Trumpeter*, many songs, etc. Also pianist and organist. Made orchestral arrangements of excerpts from Handel's FIREWORKS MUSIC and WATER MUSIC which became standard. Knighted, 1925.

Harvey, Jonathan [Dean] (b. 1939), British composer (also Sussex University teacher), pupil in USA of Babbitt. Works include *Persephone Dream* for orchestra; *Round the Star and Back* for piano 'and a few other instruments capable of a reasonable blend'; *Cantatas I–VII* on various authors and with various scoring.

Harwood, Basil (1859–1949), British cathedral organist and composer of church music, cantatas, an organ concerto, etc.

Háry János, opera by Kodály, produced in Budapest, 1926; orchestral suite drawn from this, first performed in 1927. The opera contains traditional Hungarian tunes, and the libretto (by B. Paulini and Z. Harsányi) concerns the folk-hero whose name forms the title (in Hungarian fashion, i.e. with surname first).

Haskil, Clara (1895–1960), Romanian pianist, naturalized Swiss in 1949; noted in Mozart. A regular partner of GRUMIAUX, she died in Belgium.

Hasler, Hans Leo, see HASSLER.

Hassan, play by Flecker to which Delius wrote incidental music, 1920, including a well-known 'Serenade'.

Hasse, Johann Adolph (1699–1783), German composer, also tenor singer; pupil of Porpora and A. Scarlatti in Italy. Wrote dozens of Italian operas, one on the libretto afterwards used by Mozart in THE CLEMENCY OF TITUS; also church music, harpsichord works, etc. Director of the Dresden Court Opera; afterwards lived mainly in Vienna and in Venice, where he died.

Hassler (also Hasler), **Hans Leo** (1562–1612), German composer, pupil of A. Gabrieli in Venice; also organist at various churches and courts. Wrote church music, organ works, German songs including the original tune made familiar by Bach as the 'Passion' chorale 'O sacred head'.

Hatton, John Liptrot (1809–86), British singer, pianist, organist, theatre conductor and composer of 'Simon the Cellarer', 'To Anthea', and about 300 other solo songs; also of part-songs, church music, stage music, etc.

Haubenstock-Ramati, Roman (b. 1919), Polish-born composer, resident in Israel 1950–57, later in Paris and Vienna. Works include electronic music; *Interpolation* for flute and recorded tape; *Recitative and Aria* for harpsichord and orchestra; *Credentials* or *Think, Think, Lucky* (text from Beckett's *Waiting for Godot*) for voice and eight instrumentalists – whose written parts are divided into square 'fields' which can be played vertically or horizontally.

Hauer, Josef Matthias (1883–1959), Austrian composer who arrived at a form of TWELVE-NOTE technique independently of Schoenberg and seemingly a little before him (from 1912; books 1925, 1926); he postulated 44 combinations (called tropes) of the 12 notes of the octave. Works, using this method, include a piano concerto, violin concerto, chamber music, cantata *The Way of Humanity*.

Haunted Ballroom, The, ballet with music by G. Toye, produced in London, 1934.

Haussmann, Valentin (?–c.1612), German composer who assembled a collection of German and Polish dances which he published as *The Garden of Venus*; also composed part-songs, church music, etc.

hautbois (Fr.), oboe – the actual word (literally meaning 'loud wood') from which 'oboe', really an Italian word, is derived.

hautboy, obsolete English term (from preceding entry) for oboe (and, earlier, for the shawm). An alternative spelling was 'hoboy'.

havanaise (Fr.) = HABANERA.

Hawaiian guitar, see STEEL GUITAR.

Haydn, surname of two composers, brothers (below). The surname alone alludes to the first.

Haydn, [Franz] **Joseph** (1732–1809), Austrian composer (not, despite some writers, of Croatian descent). Born in Rohrau; cathedral choirboy in Vienna; became pupil of Porpora; married an unappreciative wife, 1760. Took post with Hungarian noble family of Ester-házy, 1761–90, first at Eisenstadt (Austria) then at Eszterháza (Hungary). Achieved European reputation there, especially for his symphonies and string quartets; he established the now 'classical' concept of both these types. Visited Britain in 1791–2 and 1794–5 – presenting in London the last 12 (see SALOMON) of his 104 catalogued symphonies (for a previous set see PARIS), and also other works; received honorary Oxford degree. Handel's oratorios in London influenced him towards his own THE CREATION and THE SEASONS, written on his return to Vienna, where he died. Nicknames have been give to many of his symphonies (see BEAR, CLOCK, DRUM-ROLL, FAREWELL, HEN, HORN SIGNAL, HUNT, IMPERIAL, LAMENT-ATION, LAUDON, LONDON, MARIA THERESA, MILITARY, MIRACLE, MORNING, MOURNING, OXFORD, PAS-SION, PHILOSOPHER, QUEEN, ROXO-LANE, SCHOOLMASTER, SURPRISE) and to his Masses (see DRUM MASS, GREAT ORGAN, LITTLE ORGAN, NELSON MASS, WIND-BAND MASS), in which he characteristically combines cheer-fulness and devotion. Wrote also two cello concertos (see KRAFT, A.), various other concertos, about 80 string quartets (see EMPEROR, FIFTHS, FROG, LARK, RAZOR, TOST), 125 trios with BARYTON; more than 20 Italian and German operas (e.g. ARMIDA, THE WORLD OF THE MOON, *Deceit Outwitted* – It., *L'Infedeltà delusa*); songs, some in English; EMPEROR'S HYMN; THE SEVEN LAST WORDS, etc. (Very prolific throughout unusually long career.) See TOY SYMPHONY for a work mistakenly ascribed to him. Brother of Michael Haydn. Six string quartets listed as Haydn's op. 3 are now thought to be not by him but by Hoffstetter. His works are indexed by 'Hob.' numbers, after the catalogue by Anthony van Hoboken, published from 1957.

Haydn, [Johann] **Michael** (1737–1806), Austrian composer of much church music, also of symphonies, chamber music, operas, etc. (See TOY SYMPHONY.) Also organist. In service to the Archbishops of Salzburg from 1762, dying in Salzburg. Brother of Joseph Haydn.

Head, Michael (1900–1976), British singer, pianist and composer – especially of songs which he sang to his own accompaniment.

head voice, that 'register' of the voice which gives the feeling to the singer of vibrating in the head – i.e. the higher register, contrasted with CHEST VOICE.

Hebrides, The, overture by Mendelssohn, born of his visit there, 1829; later revised, and first performed 1832 in London. (Also called *Fingal's Cave*.)

Heckelclarina, instrument of the clarinet type invented by the German firm of Heckel for the playing of the 'shepherd's pipe' part in Act III of Wagner's TRISTAN AND ISOLDE – now more usually played on the English horn.

Heckelphone, bass instrument of the oboe type (see OBOE) made by the German firm of Heckel; an octave lower in pitch than the oboe; used e.g. by R. Strauss and, under the name 'bass oboe', by Delius.

Heger, Robert (1886–1978), German composer of symphonic poem *Hero and Leander*, a violin concerto, cantata *Song of Peace*, etc.; influenced by R. Strauss. Also conductor.

Heifetz (original forename Yosif), **Jascha** (German spelling of Russian 'Yasha'), Russian-born violinist, boy prodigy; first appeared in USA, 1917, becoming naturalized there, 1925; continued touring with immense reputation. Commissioned violin concertos from Gruenberg and Walton.

Heiller, Anton (1923–79), Austrian composer and organist; works –

mainly church music, apart from a chamber symphony – include five Masses, a Te Deum, many motets.

Heine, Heinrich (1797–1856), German poet. See LIEDERKRANZ/LIEDERKREIS, POET'S LOVE.

Heininen, Paavo (b. 1938), Finnish composer of operas *The Damask Drum* and *The Knife*, also of three piano concertos, a cello concerto, etc.

Heldenleben, Ein, see HERO'S LIFE.

Heldentenor, see HEROIC TENOR.

helicon, form of tuba passing round the player's body, e.g. the SOUSAPHONE. (Rare in Britain, common in USA.) The name is from its helical (i.e. spiral) shape, not from the ancient Mt Helicon, sacred to the Muses.

Heller, Stephen (1813–88), Hungarian pianist and composer chiefly for the piano – sonatas, fantasies, studies, pieces with 'romantic' titles, etc.

Hely-Hutchinson [Christian] **Victor** (1901–47), South African pianist, conductor, teacher and composer, who worked from 1926 in England; BBC Music Director, 1944–7. Works include *A Carol Symphony* (based on Christmas Carols) and chamber music.

hemidemisemiquaver, see SIXTY-FOURTH-NOTE.

hemiola, hemiolia (the former term is commoner, the latter more correct, from Gk., one-and-a-half), term implying the ratio 3:2. In current usage it mainly refers to the rhythmic change resulting when a pulse of 2×3 is temporarily replaced by 3×2, or vice versa – e.g. when ♩.♩.| is replaced by ♩♩♩|

Hendricks, Barbara (b. 1948), American soprano, resident in Paris since 1977, noted internationally in opera and concert; performed Mimì in the filmed version of *La Bohème*, 1988.

Henkemans, Hans (b. 1913), Dutch composer, pupil of Pijper and influenced by Debussy; also pianist. Has written works for piano and for piano and orchestra; also a symphony, flute concerto, etc.

Henriques, [Valdemar] Fini (1867–1940), Danish composer, pupil of Svendsen; also violinist, pupil of Joachim. Works include operas, ballet *The Little Mermaid* (after Hans Andersen), two symphonies, piano solos.

Henry, Pierre (b. 1927), French composer, pupil of Messiaen and others, active from 1950 in Paris in pioneering 'concrete music' (tape-recorded process later subsumed in ELECTRONIC MUSIC). Several of his taped works, e.g. *Symphony for a Lonely Man*, were choreographed as ballets by Maurice Béjart.

Henry V (1387–1422), King of England, amateur composer. The vocal compositions bearing the name 'Roy Henry' in the OLD HALL MANUSCRIPT are usually considered to be by him; a case has also been made for Henry IV.

Henry VIII (1491–1547), King of England, amateur composer, some of whose vocal music survives; but the motet 'O Lord, the maker of all thing', formerly attributed to him, is really by W. Mundy.

Henschel, George (originally Isidor Georg Henschel) (1850–1934), baritone, pianist, composer and conductor. German-born, was naturalized British, 1890, and knighted, 1914.

Conductor of the newly founded Boston Symphony Orchestra, 1881–4; as singer accompanying himself, broadcast and recorded until his 70s. Composed two operas, songs in German and English, much piano music, etc.

Hensel, Fanny, see MENDELSSOHN [BARTHOLDY], FANNY.

'Hen' Symphony, nickname for Haydn's symphony no. 83 in G minor (Hob. I: 83), 1786, one of the PARIS symphonies – the nickname presumably bestowed by someone who eccentrically detected a hen's clucking in the oboe figure of the first movement.

Henze, Hans Werner (b. 1926), German composer (pupil of Fortner) resident in Italy since 1953; also conductor and opera producer. Works include operas *Boulevard Solitude* (see MANON), *King Stag*, *The Prince of Homburg*, ELEGY FOR YOUNG LOVERS, THE BASSARIDS, THE YOUNG LORD and WE COME TO THE RIVER; cantata *Novae de infinito Laudes* (Lat., New praises of the infinite) with words by Giordano Bruno; *Undine* and other ballets; seven symphonies; *Ode to the West Wind* (after Shelley) for cello and orchestra; *Dance Marathon* (suite from ballet) for jazz band and symphony orchestra; secular oratorio *The Raft of the Medusa*.

Herbert, [Sir] A. P. [Alan Patrick] (1890–1971), British writer. See DUNHILL.

Herbert, Victor (1859–1924), Irish-born composer (also cellist, conductor) who settled in New York, 1886, and wrote many successful operettas including *Naughty Marietta* and *Babes in Toyland*; also operas, two cello concertos, etc.

Herbig, Günther (b. 1931), German conductor; held posts in East Germany and elsewhere before becoming music director of the Toronto Symphony Orchestra in 1990.

Her Foster-daughter, see JENÚFA.

Hérodiade, see HERODIAS.

Herodias (Fr., *Hérodiade*), opera by Massenet, produced in Brussels, 1881. Libretto by P. Milliet and 'Henri Grémont' (i.e. G. Hartmann), after a tale by Flaubert: a variation of the story of Salome, who here begs for John the Baptist's life to be saved and afterwards kills herself. Cp. SALOME.

heroic tenor, tenor capable of 'heavy' dramatic roles in opera, especially (as translation of Ger. *Heldentenor*) in Wagner.

Hérold, [Louis Joseph] **Ferdinand** (1791–1833), French composer of ZAMPA, *The Pré aux Clercs* (referring to a famous duelling-ground) and many other operas; also two symphonies, etc. Also pianist and opera chorus-master.

Hero's Life, A (Ger., *Ein Heldenleben*), symphonic poem by R. Strauss, 1898, with autobiographical connotation – the section 'The Hero's Works of Peace' quoting some of Strauss's previous compositions.

Herrick, Robert (1591–1674), English poet. See LAWES (Henry).

Herrmann, Bernard (1911–75), American composer, pupil of B. Wagenaar and others; also conductor, especially for radio. Works include a symphony, violin concerto, opera *Wuthering Heights*, cantata *Moby Dick*, a string quartet, and music for *Citizen Kane* and other films.

Hertel, Johann (1727–89), German composer of at least 36 symphonies, also concertos, chamber music, Italian and German opera, and church music.

Hervé (pen-name of Florimond Ronger) (1825–92), French composer of operettas, many parodying historical subjects or literary works (one on *The Knights of the Round Table*); also of ballets, a symphony with voices based on *The Ashanti War*, many songs, etc.

Herz, Henri (really Heinrich) (1803–88). Austrian pianist-composer who settled in Paris and wrote eight piano concertos and other works in brilliant 'virtuoso' style. Contributor to the HEXAMERON.

Heseltine, Philip, see WARLOCK.

Hess, Myra (1890–1965), British pianist, pupil of Matthay, who promoted and directed National Gallery Concerts in London during World War II; created Dame, 1941; celebrated for her piano transcription of a chorale from Bach's church cantata no. 147, under the name 'Jesu, joy of man's desiring'.

Hesse, Hermann (1877–1962), German author. See FOUR LAST SONGS.

Heure espagnole, L', see SPANISH HOUR.

hexachord, obsolete (11th–17th centuries) grouping of notes not by octaves (eight notes) but by sixes – Greek *hex*, 6. The 'hard', 'natural' and 'soft' hexachords ascended respectively from G, C, and F, using what are now the white notes of the piano. Cp. GUIDO D'AREZZO.

Hexameron, variations contributed by

Liszt, Thalberg, Herz, Pixis, Czerny and Chopin on a march from Bellini's THE PURITANS, 1831, with linking passages by Liszt. (From Greek for 'six days' – cf. *Decameron*, 10 days – alluding to the six composers. Cp. also GODOWSKY.)

Hexenmenuett, see FIFTHS QUARTET.

Hiawatha, three cantatas by Coleridge-Taylor, first performed together in 1900: *Hiawatha's Wedding Feast, The Death of Minnehaha, Hiawatha's Departure*. Words from Longfellow's *Hiawatha*, narrative poem of American-Indian life. See also GOLD-MARK (R.).

hidden fifths, see CONSECUTIVE.

Hildegard of Bingen (1098–1179), German abbess, composer and poet. Wrote a cycle of vocal settings of 77 poems arranged according to the liturgical calendar.

Hill, Alfred (1870–1960), Australian composer, also violinist and conductor; studied in Leipzig; spent some time in New Zealand and used Maori folklore for cantata *Hinemoa* and song 'Waiata Poi', etc. Also composed 17 string quartets, *Overture of Welcome* (players of orchestra entering successively), etc.

Hill, Edward Burlingame (1872–1960), American composer and teacher; works include three symphonies, a violin concerto, *Music for English Horn and Orchestra*.

Hiller, Ferdinand (1811–85), German pianist (pupil of Hummel), conductor, teacher and composer – many piano pieces, also operas and three symphonies.

Hiller, Johann Adam (1728–1804),

German composer (also flautist and singer) and conductor; cantor at St Thomas's, Leipzig (Bach's old position). Wrote church music, instrumental works and *The Devil is at Large* (*Der Teufel ist los*) – the first of that type of opera known as SINGSPIEL.

Hiller, Lejaren [Arthur] (b. 1924), American composer (pupil of Sessions and Babbitt) who first worked as research chemist; became a pioneer (in late 1950s) of the application of computers to the techniques of composition. Collaborated with Cage in *HPSCHD* for 1–7 harpsichords and 1–51 tapes. Also wrote *Machine Music* for piano, percussion and tape, as well as seven string quartets, etc.

Hilton, John (*c*.1560–1608), English organist (of Trinity College, Cambridge) and composer of anthems, madrigals, etc. Contributor to THE TRIUMPHS OF ORIANA. See also next entry.

Hilton, John (1599–1657), English organist (of St Margaret's, Westminster) and composer of church music, 'Ayres or Fa-Las' (in this case, works of BALLETT type), etc. Was also compiler and part-composer of *Catch that Catch Can* – a collection of rounds, catches and canons, etc. He was possibly a son of the John Hilton who died in 1608.

Himmel, Friedrich Heinrich (1765–1819), German composer of operas (in German and Italian), church music, piano works, etc.

Hindemith, Paul (1895–1963), German composer – formerly violinist and viola player (soloist in first performance of Walton's Viola Concerto, 1929); teacher in Berlin from 1927. Banned by Nazis as musically 'degenerate' (though not Jewish); taught in

Turkey from 1933, settled in USA, 1939. Noted teacher and theoretician. Composed for almost every type of musical medium, and (in his earlier period) much music of deliberately functional intent (see UTILITY MUSIC), e.g. for pianola, and a musical game for children; his piano work LUDUS TONALIS is also didactic. His earlier work was in a dissonant idiom verging on atonality, e.g. in the works labelled CHAMBER MUSIC (*Kammermusik*); later he adopted an 'advanced' but strictly tonal idiom. He composed the operas MATHIS THE PAINTER (on the life of the painter Grünewald) and *The Harmony of the World* (on the life of the astronomer Kepler): he based a symphony on each of these. Other works include operas *There and Back* (see PALINDROME) and CARDILLAC; *Nobilissima Visione* and other ballets; *Symphonic Metamorphoses of Themes of Weber* (see METAMORPHOSIS); a Symphony in E♭ and many other orchestral works; THE FOUR TEMPERAMENTS for piano and strings; *Funeral Music* for viola and strings, on the death of George V; six string quartets, many sonatas for various instruments; songs including cycle *The Life of Mary* (*Das Marienleben*; see also REQUIEM).

Histoire du soldat, L', see SOLDIER'S TALE.

HMS Pinafore, or The Lass that Loved a Sailor, operetta by Sullivan, produced in London, 1878. Libretto by W. S. Gilbert, with the action aboard an English warship.

Hob., abbr. for 'Hoboken' in numbering Haydn's works: see HAYDN.

Hoboken, Anthony van (1887–1983), Dutch musicologist. See HAYDN.

hoboy, see HAUTBOY.

hocket (Fr., *hoquet*, hiccup), in medieval church music, the insertion of rests into vocal parts, even in the middle of words – often for expressive purposes.

Hoddinott, Alun (b. 1929), Welsh composer of seven symphonies, a clarinet concerto, *Four Welsh Dances*, chamber music, operas including *The Beach of Falesá* and *The Trumpet Major* (based on Hardy's novel), oratorio *Job*, etc. Professor at Cardiff (1967–87) and formerly festival director there.

hoe-down, an American folk-dance included in Copland's ballet, RODEO.

Høffding, Finn (b. 1899), Danish composer and teacher. Has written opera *The Emperor's New Clothes* and orchestral work *It's a True Story*, both after Hans Andersen; also four symphonies, other operas, wind quintet, *Dialogues* for oboe and clarinet, etc.

Hoffmann, Ernst Theodor Amadeus (1776–1822), German Romantic novelist and essayist, influencing e.g. Schumann; also composer of opera *Undine* and other works – and adopting the forename 'Amadeus' in homage to Mozart, replacing 'Wilhelm'. Hero of Offenbach's THE TALES OF HOFFMANN.

Hoffmeister, Franz Anton (1754–1812), Austrian composer of 66 symphonies, much chamber music, nine German operas, etc.; was also important publisher – of Haydn, Beethoven, etc.

Hoffstetter (incorrectly Hofstetter), **Romanus** (1742–1815), Austrian monk and composer who is now believed to have written six string quartets formerly ascribed to Haydn (as op. 3). He also wrote three viola concertos, church music, etc.

Hofhaimer, Paul (1459–1537), Austrian organist (also organ-builder) and composer, in service to the (Austrian) Emperor Maximilian I – based mainly at Innsbruck, but travelling widely. Was given noble rank – exceptional for a musician. His compositions include German part-songs, organ pieces, church music.

Hofmann, Josef (really Józef Kazimierz Hofmann) (1876–1957), Polish-born pianist, pupil of Anton Rubinstein; composer of symphony, five piano concertos, and other works – some under the name 'Michel Dvorsky'. Public performer from the age of six; first visited USA in 1887, later becoming naturalized and dying there.

Hofmannsthal, Hugo von (1874–1929), Austrian poet, playwright and librettist; see ARABELLA, ARIADNE ON NAXOS, ELEKTRA, ROSENKAVALIER.

Hofstetter, see HOFFSTETTER.

Hogwood, Christopher (b. 1941), British harpsichordist and conductor, founding director of the Academy of Ancient Music (see ACADEMY); also director of the St Paul (Minnesota) Chamber Orchestra.

Hohlflöte (Ger., hollow-sounding flute), type of eight-FOOT organ stop in wood or metal.

Hoiby, Lee (b. 1926), American composer, pupil of Menotti; has written *Summer and Smoke* and other operas, also a piano concerto, etc.

Holberg, Ludvig (1684–1754), Norwegian dramatist. See HOLBERG SUITE, MASQUERADE.

Holberg Suite, suite composed by Grieg for piano, then arranged for strings (1884); bicentenary tribute, in the form of a pastiche of old dance-movements, to Ludvig Holberg (above).

Holborne, Anthony (?–1602), English composer who published a book of dances and other music for consort (1599) and composed and arranged other works for lute, etc.

Holbrooke, Joseph (on some scores 'Josef') [Charles] (1878–1958), British composer of operatic trilogy *The Cauldron of Annwen* and other operas; orchestral variations on 'Three Blind Mice'; *Byron* and other symphonic poems. Also pianist, conductor and polemical writer on music.

Hölderlin, Johann Christian Friedrich (1770–1843), German poet. See ANTIGONE.

Höller, Karl (1907–87), German composer of *Variations on a Theme of Sweelinck* and other orchestral works in somewhat conservative style; also chamber music, etc.

Höller, York [Georg] (b. 1944), German composer of opera *The Master and Margarita* (after Bulgakov), two piano concertos, electronic music; directs the West German Radio's electronic-music studio in Cologne.

Holliger, Heinz (b. 1939), Swiss oboist and director of chamber-music ensemble. Noted virtuoso in modern works (written for him by Stockhausen, Berio and others). He is also a composer (pupil of Boulez): works include *The Magic Dancer* for two speakers, two dancers, orchestra and tape. Wife is Ursula Holliger, harpist.

Hollins, Alfred (1865–1942), British organist (blind from birth) and composer for his instrument; earlier a pianist, playing concertos, etc.

Holmboe, Vagn (b. 1909), Danish composer, pupil of Toch, Høffding, and others; influenced by Bartók. Works include 20 string quartets, 12 symphonies and 13 'chamber concertos'.

holograph, see AUTOGRAPH.

Holst, (originally von Holst), **Gustav** [Theodore] (1874–1934), British composer of partly Swedish descent, pupil of Stanford, at various times pianist, trombonist, teacher (especially at Morley College, London), and conductor – of Boston Symphony Orchestra, 1922. Interested in oriental philosophy, and made various settings of the Hindu scriptures in his own translations. Bold harmonic experimenter, e.g. in polytonality; finally cultivated a markedly austere style, e.g. in EGDON HEATH for orchestra. Other works include operas *At the Boar's Head* (after Shakespeare's *Henry IV*), THE PERFECT FOOL and SAVITRI; also THE PLANETS for orchestra; ST PAUL'S SUITE for strings; choral HYMN OF JESUS and a *First Choral Symphony* (words by Keats; there is no second); music for military and brass band; songs (four for voice and violin), etc. Father of Imogen Holst.

Holst, Imogen (1907–84), British musical educationist, conductor and composer (overture, folk-song arrangements, songs, etc.); collaborator with Britten. Author of books on her father (preceding entry).

homage, hommage (Eng., Fr.), terms used by a composer especially in the expression 'homage to' (or *hommage à*) another composer, usually implying a quotation from that other composer's work or an evocation of his style. So Falla's *Homage* (Sp. *Homenaje*) for guitar, inscribed 'For the grave of Debussy'. Cp. also ULYSSES.

Homage March, (1) by Wagner (Ger., *Huldigungsmarsch*), originally for military band, 1864 (for King Ludwig II of Bavaria), later orchestrated; (2) by Grieg, from his incidental music to Bjørnson's play *Sigurd the Crusader*.

Homage to the Queen, ballet with music by M. Arnold, produced in London to celebrate the coronation of Elizabeth II, 1953.

Homenaje, see HOMAGE.

Homer (*c.* 700 BC), Greek poet. See DALLAPICCOLA, KING PRIAM, LOGOTHETIS, ULYSSES.

Home, Sweet Home, see BISHOP, who composed it.

Homme armé, L' (Fr., The Armed Man), title of a popular song (possibly originating in a polyphonic chanson, and possibly composed by Busnois) which was used by Dufay, Palestrina and more than 25 other composers of the 15th, 16th and 17th centuries as a CANTUS FIRMUS in their Masses. Such Masses are accordingly known by this name.

homophony (from Gk. for 'same-sounding'), term used as opposite of POLYPHONY – i.e. signifying that (as for instance in an English hymn-tune) the PARTS move together, presenting only a top-melody and chords beneath, as distinct from the contrapuntal interplay of different melodies simultaneously. So also *homophonic*; and cp. MONOPHONY.

hondo (Sp., deep), term used in the expression *cante hondo* (deep song), type of sad Andalusian song characteristically using some intervals smaller than a semitone.

Honegger, Arthur (1892–1955), Swiss composer, though born in France and largely resident there. Pupil of Widor and d'Indy. Was one of the SIX (a group of composers) but developed his own distinctive style, often heavily dissonant and with marked declamatory elements. Collaborated with Ibert in opera *The Eaglet* (*L'Aiglon*); other stage works include ANTIGONE, KING DAVID, JUDITH, JOAN OF ARC AT THE STAKE. Composed five symphonies – no. 2 for strings plus optional trumpet, no. 3 *Liturgical*, no. 5 *Di tre re* – see RE. Other works include three 'symphonic movements' – PACIFIC 231, *Rugby* and no. 3 (non-programmatic); *Dance of the Goat* for flute; piano solos; French and British film music; *Christmas Cantata* (in English, French, German, and Latin).

Hook, James (1746–1827), British organist and composer – working in both capacities at Marylebone and Vauxhall Gardens, London, 1774–1820; wrote musical plays, concertos, sonatas, cantatas, catches and over 2,000 songs including 'The Lass of Richmond Hill'.

hopak, see GOPAK.

Hopkins (surname changed from Reynolds in boyhood), **Antony** (b. 1921), British composer, pianist, conductor and radio commentator on music. Works include operas *Lady Rohesia* and *Three's Company*; ballet *Café des Sports*.

Hopkins, Gerard Manley (1844–89), British poet. See WELLESZ.

Hopkinson, Francis (1737–91), American statesman, writer and amateur composer – e.g. of the song 'My Days Have Been So Wondrous Free', the first published composition by a native-born American.

Horenstein, Jascha (Ger. spelling of Rus. 'Yasha', dim. of Jacob) (1898–1973), Russian-born, Vienna-trained conductor, noted in Bruckner and Mahler; settled in Switzerland.

horn, (1) type of wind instrument descended from primitive use of an animal's horn for blowing through. The term now applies especially to the coiled brass orchestral instrument which was developed (particularly in France, whence the name *French horn*) from the earlier *hunting horn* or *hand-horn*. This earlier instrument, without valves or keys, yielded to the player only the notes of the HARMONIC SERIES, like a bugle, plus a few obtainable by the insertion of the hand in the bell of the instrument. The particular harmonic series sounded depended on the length of the instrument's tube: from about 1700 CROOKS were inserted into the instrument to vary the length of the tube and thus to make the harmonic series available at various different pitches. But only from about 1850 did the modern horn, with VALVES to secure a chromatic range of notes, become standard. It is normally today a TRANSPOSING INSTRUMENT in F, with compass from B below the bass staff upwards for about three and a half octaves; also used is the *double horn*, which can be switched from a horn in F (as normal) to a horn in high B♭. Orchestral horn parts assume that the odd-numbered players specialize in the higher notes, the even-numbered in lower: four horns are usually specified in scores, modern orchestral practice often reinforcing them with a fifth; but since Wagner composers have on occasion specified six or eight. The instrument is also standard in the military (not the brass) band; a few concertos have been written for it, e.g. by R. Strauss, or for its valveless predecessor, e.g. by Mozart. (2) term used colloquially in the brass band to mean not the above instrument (not used in the brass band) but the tenor SAXHORN; and used as jazz slang to mean a trumpet, a trombone, even a saxophone. (3) *English horn*, see under ENGLISH.

Horn, Charles Edward (1786–1849), British singer and composer of many songs including 'Cherry Ripe'; also of oratorios and music for plays. Settled in USA, 1833, dying there. Son of Karl Friedrich Horn.

Horn, Karl Friedrich (1762–1830), German-born pianist, organist, composer of piano music, etc.; settled in England, 1782, and died there. An early participant in the 19th-century revival of Bach. Father of C. E. Horn.

Horne, Marilyn (b. 1934), American mezzo-soprano active in opera (La Scala, Milan, 1969; Metropolitan, New York, 1970); formerly a celebrated Carmen, she sang (on the sound-track) the title-role in film *Carmen Jones*, 1964. Later she won celebrity in Rossini's coloratura mezzo-soprano roles.

Horneman, Christian Emil (1841–1906), Danish composer of opera *Aladdin*, orchestral and piano music, songs, etc.

hornpipe, lively English dance formerly (e.g. in Purcell) with three beats in the bar, now (as in the well-known 'Sailor's Hornpipe' and as in Sullivan's RUDDIGORE) with two beats in the bar. So named because originally accompanied by pipe made from animal's horn.

Horn Signal, Symphony with the, nickname for Haydn's Symphony no. 31 in D, 1765 (Hob. I: 31) – from the slow movement with its horn calls. Four horns are used instead of the two normal at that period.

Horovitz, Joseph (b. 1926), Austrian-born composer-conductor-pianist resident in England since 1938; pupil of Jacob and N. Boulanger. Works include *Alice in Wonderland* and other ballets; one-act operas, clarinet concerto, euphonium concerto (with brass band).

Horowitz, Vladimir (1903–89), pianist, born in Russia; début, 1922. Went to USA, 1928, and settled there, earning highest reputation. Contracted nervous ailment; ceased to give concerts, 1950, though continued to make records; resumed occasional (much-prized) concerts, 1965, continuing into his 80s. Married Toscanini's daughter, Wanda.

Horsley, Charles Edward (1822–76), British pianist, organist and composer especially of oratorios (pupil of Mendelssohn); went to Australia, 1862, and later to USA, where he died.

hot, lively, exciting (of jazz, etc.) – international but now faded term (Joe Daniels and his Hot Shots, Quintette du Hot Club de France, etc.).

Hotter, Hans (b. 1909), German baritone (formerly church organist) noted in Wagner (e.g. as Sachs in *Die Meistersinger*); also opera producer, e.g. of THE RING at Covent Garden. Has also conducted.

Hotteterre, Jacques Martin (1674–1763), French player of the flute (and other instruments), the most famous member of a family of instrumentalists and instrument-makers. Composer of music for flute (and other instruments), and author of a famous instructional treatise, he is regarded as the founder of the French flute tradition.

House of the Dead, see FROM A HOUSE OF THE DEAD.

Hovhaness, Alan (b. 1911), American composer of Armenian descent; also conductor and organist. Works, much influenced by ancient Middle Eastern music, mainly have Armenian titles; they include a piano concerto (with strings) entitled *Lousadzak* (The Coming of Light), 51 symphonies, *And God Created Great Whales* for humpbacked-whale solo (on tape) and orchestra.

Howells, Herbert [Norman] (1892–1983), British composer (pupil of Stanford), teacher and former cathedral organist. Compositions include choral works to religious texts – Requiem, HYMNUS PARADISI, *Missa Sabrinensis* (Lat., Severn Mass), etc.; also orchestral works, a piano concerto, music for piano solo, for brass band, etc. CH, 1972.

Hubay, Jenö (1858–1937), Hungarian violinist, also composer. A child prodigy, he became pupil of Joachim and Vieuxtemps; director of the Budapest Conservatory, 1919–34.

Huber, Klaus (b. 1924), Swiss composer (also violinist), pupil of Blacher in Berlin. Has written chiefly oratorios and other religious works – among them *The Angels' Address to the Soul*, for tenor, flute, clarinet, horn and harp.

Huberman, Bronislav (1882–1947), Polish violinist, internationally noted; in 1936 he organized the Palestine Symphony Orchestra (which became the Israel Philharmonic).

Hucbald (*c*.840–*c*.930), French monk, supposed author of a musical treatise in Latin about the MODES, DIAPHONY, etc.

Hudson, George (*c*.1620–72), English violinist and composer, in service to Charles II; wrote part of the music to THE SIEGE OF RHODES.

Hughes, Arwel (b. 1909), British composer and conductor; works include opera *Menna* (on a Welsh legend) and other works of Welsh inspiration. His son, Owain Arwel Hughes (b. 1942), is also a conductor.

Hughes, Ted (b. 1930), British poet. See CROSSE.

Hugh the Drover, or *Love in the Stocks*, opera by Vaughan Williams, produced in London, 1924. Libretto by H. Child: the scene is a Cotswold village at the time of the Napoleonic Wars. Styled 'a Romantic ballad opera', but see BALLAD OPERA.

Hugo, Victor (1802–85), French writer. See GIOCONDA, MAZEPPA, PANTOUM, RIGOLETTO, RUY BLAS.

Huguenots, The (Fr., *Les Huguenots*), Meyerbeer's most successful opera, produced in Paris, 1836. Libretto by E. Scribe and E. Deschamps, culminating in the St Bartholomew Massacre of French Protestants, 1572.

Hullah, John Pyke (1812–84), British composer of songs including 'O that we two were maying', opera *The Village Coquettes* (libretto by Dickens), etc.; singing-teacher and writer of textbooks.

Hume, Tobias (*c*.1569–1645), English composer, also professional soldier, known as Captain Hume. Wrote dances and other music for viols; also songs including 'Fain would I change that note'.

Humfrey (or Humphrey), **Pelham** (1647–74), English composer who studied in France and Italy and was in service to Charles II. Wrote music to plays including Shakespeare's *The Tempest*, also church music, vocal solos and duets, etc. One of Purcell's teachers.

Hummel, Johann Nepomuk (1778–1837), Austrian pianist (pupil of Mozart) and composer (pupil of Haydn and others), touring extensively as performer. Wrote concertos and other works for piano, and also operas, church music, etc.

Humoreske, humoresque (Ger., Fr., the latter also used as Eng.), type of instrumental composition supposedly of a wayward or capricious nature – term used e.g. by Schumann and Dvořák.

Humperdinck, Engelbert (1854–1921), German composer; friend and assistant to Wagner; also teacher (for some time in Spain) and critic. Composed operas including HANSEL AND GRETEL and *King's Children* (Ger., *Königskinder*); also incidental music to various plays, choral works, *Moorish Rhapsody* for orchestra, etc.

Humphrey, Pelham, see HUMFREY.

Hungarian Fantasia, see HUNGARIAN RHAPSODY.

Hungarian Rhapsody, title given by Liszt to each of 19 piano pieces in Hungarian-gipsy style – nos. 1–15 were composed by 1852, and others about 30 years later. Some were afterwards orchestrated, and on no. 14 is based Liszt's *Hungarian Fantasia* (properly *Fantasia on Hungarian Popular Themes*) for piano and orchestra, 1852.

Hunt, The, nickname for Haydn's Symphony no. 73 in D, 1781 (Hob. I: 73) – from the music of the horns and oboes in the finale, a movement originally taken from one of Haydn's operas.

Hunter, Rita [Nellie] (b. 1933), British soprano, noted in principal Wagner roles from 1970 with the (former) Sadler's Wells Opera, now the English National Opera; first appearance at the Metropolitan, New York, 1972. CBE, 1980. Settled in Australia.

hunting-horn, instrument used for giving signals while hunting, from which evolved the orchestral HORN.

'Hunt' Quartet, nickname for Mozart's String Quartet in B♭, K458 (1784), because the opening suggests hunting-horns.

hurdy-gurdy, term applied wrongly to any instrument worked by turning a handle (e.g. BARREL-ORGAN, STREET PIANO) and correctly only to one such instrument, a kind of portable, mechanical viol called in French *vielle*. One hand turns a handle actuating a rosined wheel which acts as a bow; the other hand stops the strings not directly (as on a violin) but by means of a tiny piano-like keyboard. In addition there are one or two freely vibrating strings, giving a DRONE bass. Mozart and others wrote for this instrument.

Hurford, Peter [John] (b. 1930), British organist (also composer and editor);

founded an organ festival at St Albans, where he was organist at the abbey church, 1958–78. OBE, 1984.

Hurlstone, William Yeates (1876–1906), British composer of *Variations on a Swedish Air* for orchestra, also a sonata for clarinet and piano, chamber music, etc.

Hurník, Ilja (b. 1922), Czechoslovak composer, also pianist. Works include opera *The Lady and the Robbers*; *Sonata da camera* for flute, oboe, cello and harpsichord; *Moments musicaux* for 11 wind instruments.

Husa, Karel (b. 1921), Czechoslovak composer and conductor, resident in USA since the mid-1950s. Works include *Evocations of Slovakia* for clarinet, violin and cello; concertos for saxophone, for trumpet and for organ.

hydraulis, hydraulos (Gk., water-pipe), also called water-organ; ancient instrument, cultivated in Greek and Roman eras, precursor of the organ. Water was used to maintain a constant pressure on the air fed to the pipes.

hymn, a song of praise to a deity, saint, etc.; particularly (in Protestant churches) that which has words specially written, not taken directly from the Bible, and is sung congregationally. Also an extended composition to words supposedly of a hymn-like nature – see following entries – or an instrumental composition suggesting a vocal hymn.

Hymn of Jesus, The, work for two choruses, semi-chorus and orchestra by Holst, 1917; text from the apocryphal Acts of St John.

Hymn of Praise (Ger., *Lobgesang*), symphonic cantata by Mendelssohn, first performed in 1840. One choral movement (religious text) is preceded by three orchestral ones and the whole is numbered as Mendelssohn's Second Symphony.

Hymn to St Cecilia, setting for unaccompanied chorus by Britten (who was born on St Cecilia's Day) of a poem by W. H. Auden, 1942. See also ODE FOR ST CECILIA'S DAY and CECILIA.

Hymn to the Sun, an aria sung by the Queen of Shemakha in Rimsky-Korsakov's opera THE GOLDEN COCKEREL.

I

I., abbr. for International (e.g. ISCM, International Society for Contemporary Music).

i (It.), the (pl.) – see next word of phrase.

Iberia, (1) four sets each of three piano pieces by Albéniz, representing various parts of Spain; first complete performance in 1909 (five of the pieces were later orchestrated by Arbós); (2) orchestral work by Debussy, first performed in 1910, being the second part of his IMAGES for orchestra. It is in three movements suggestive of aspects of Spain.

Ibert, Jacques [François Antoine] (1890–1962), French composer, pupil of Fauré; director of the French Academy in Rome from 1937. Collaborated with Honegger in opera The Eaglet (L'Aiglon). Other works include Angélique and other operas; symphonic poem after Wilde's The Ballad of Reading Jail; orchestral suite Ports of Call (Escales); Divertissement, arranged from his music to the play The Italian Straw Hat; Concertino da camera for alto saxophone and 11 instruments; The Little White Donkey and other piano works.

Ibsen, Henrik Johan (1828–1906), Norwegian dramatist. See BRUNS-WICK, EGK, GRIEG, HARPER, PEER GYNT, SAEVERUD.

idée fixe, term used by Berlioz, e.g. in the FANTASTIC SYMPHONY, for what is usually called MOTTO THEME.

idiophone, term used in the scientific classification of instruments to mean 'self-sounding', e.g. cymbals, xylophone, whether hit, rattled, stroked, etc. (But drums, in which a membrane is stretched and an air-space is fully or partly enclosed, are MEMBRANO-PHONES.)

Idomeneo, see IDOMENEUS.

Idomeneus, King of Crete, or Ilia and Idamantes, opera by Mozart (K366), produced in Munich (in Italian), 1781. Libretto by G. B. Varesco: a story of love and sacrifice taking place after the Trojan War, Idamantes being the son of Idomeneus and the lover of Ilia. (The story is based on Virgil, the usual title Idomeneo being an Italianization of the king's Latin name.)

idyll, literary term for a peaceful, pastoral work – transferred to music e.g. in Wagner's SIEGFRIED IDYLL.

Ifigenia, see IPHIGENIA.

Iliev, Konstantin Nikolov (b. 1924), Bulgarian composer who studied with A. Hába in Prague and has written five symphonies, Tempi concertanti for string quartet and string orchestra, etc. Also conductor – of the Sofia Philharmonic Orchestra, 1956–72.

Illuminations, Les, cycle of nine songs by Britten, 1939, for high voice and strings, to French poems by Rimbaud evocative of various sights and sounds.

illustrative music, music describing, evoking, or otherwise alluding to a non-musical source, e.g. a poem, novel, play, picture, landscape, or an explicit emotional experience. (The more usual but confusing term for this is PROGRAMMATIC MUSIC.)

Images, title given by Debussy to two series of works – (a) two sets each of three piano pieces (1905, 1907), and (b) three orchestral works of which IBERIA was completed in 1908, *Dances of Spring* (*Rondes de Printemps*) in 1909, and *Gigues* (originally *Gigues tristes*, i.e. Sad Jigs) in 1912 – the orchestration of *Gigues* being by Caplet.

Imai, Nobuko (b. 1942), Japanese viola-player; she took part in the première of Tippett's Triple Concerto, 1980, with Pauk and Kirshbaum.

Imbrie, Andrew Welsh (b. 1921), American composer, pupil of Sessions; has written three symphonies (and a chamber symphony), four string quartets, a violin concerto, opera *Christmas in Peebles Town* (or *Three against Christmas*), etc. Teaches at University of California, Berkeley.

imitation, a composers' device in partwriting: one voice repeats (if not literally, then at least recognizably) a figure previously stated by another voice. CANON and FUGUE employ imitation according to strict and regular patterns.

Immortal Hour, The, opera by Boughton, produced in Glastonbury, Somerset, 1914. Libretto by composer, based on Celtic legend as drawn from plays and poems of 'Fiona Macleod' (i.e. William Sharp).

Imperial (Fr., *L'Impériale*), nickname for Haydn's Symphony no. 53 in D (Hob. I: 53), about 1780 – presumably named, somewhat arbitrarily, from its 'Largo maestoso' opening.

Imperial Mass, another nickname for Haydn's NELSON MASS.

Impresario, The (Ger., *Der Schauspieldirektor*), play with overture and other music by Mozart (and usually classed as one of his operas), produced in Vienna, 1786 (K486). Words by G. Stephanie, satirizing the relationships of impresario and female singers.

impressionism, term borrowed from painting (applied e.g. to Monet, Degas, Whistler) and used to describe the works e.g. of Debussy and Ravel in so far as they seem to interpret their titles not in a narrative or dramatic way (like the ROMANTICS) but as though an observer were recording the impression on him at a given point. See also EXPRESSIONISM.

impromptu, short piece of music (usually for piano) seeming to suggest improvisation. Examples by Voříšek antedate those by Schubert and Chopin. Britten called the slow movement of his revised Piano Concerto (1945) an impromptu, and Walton based on it his *Improvisations on an Impromptu by Benjamin Britten* (1970).

improvisation, see IMPROVISE and preceding entry.

improvise (or 'extemporize'), to perform according to spontaneous fancy, not from memory or from written copy – though often a performer improvises 'on' (i.e. round about) a given tune. Hence *improvisation*: this term is sometimes also used as title of an actual written-down piece presumably intended to convey the roving spirit of genuine improvisation, whether the source is musical or not (see BOULEZ).

in, term with various musical usages including (1) indication of a conductor's beat – so e.g. *in 2*, meaning that two beats will be actually given to each bar, although the composer may have indicated two or four or six, etc.; (2) indication of the division of forces in an orchestra – so e.g. *in 4*, applied to the violas, would indicate that the viola-players are to be divided into four sections each playing a different PART; (3) indication of key, e.g. *symphony in C minor*; (4) indication of (a) the basic key in which a wind instrument is pitched, and sometimes also of (b) the transposition it consequently requires (see TRANSPOSING INSTRUMENT). Only usage can show whether or not the additional meaning (b) is implied. E.g. *horn in F* means not only that the instrument is basically pitched in F (if blown, without depressing any valves, it will produce a HARMONIC SERIES basically related to the key of F major), but also that it is a TRANSPOSING INSTRUMENT sounding a fifth lower than written – the note written as C sounds as F, etc. Thus here both the meanings (a) and (b) are implied. But a bass trombone is sometimes said to be *in G* because of its basic harmonic series, though it is not a transposing instrument, being written at the pitch it sounds.

Inbal, Eliahu (b. 1936), Israeli conductor, pupil of Celibidache (in Italy); since 1974 conductor of the Hesse (Frankfurt) Radio Symphony Orchestra.

incidental music, that which is intended to be used intermittently to heighten the performance of a play. (The term is not generally applied to film.)

incipit (Lat., it begins), the first few bars of a musical work, used e.g. in a bibliographical compilation to identify the piece.

Incoronazione di Poppea, L', see CORONATION OF POPPAEA, THE.

Incredible Flutist, The, ballet with music by Piston, first performed in 1938, the 'flutist' (US form) being a charmer of snakes and human beings. A concert suite drawn from it was first given in 1940.

indeterminacy, the principle, employed by some composers from the 1950s, of leaving elements of the performance either to pure chance (see ALEATORY), or to the decision of the performer. For examples, see BERIO, HAUBENSTOCK-RAMATI, STOCKHAUSEN.

Indian Queen, The, opera by Purcell (Z630), produced in London, 1695 (the last of its five acts is partly by D. Purcell). It was an adaptation, with music, of a play by Dryden and R. Howard on the rivalry of Mexicans and Peruvians – 'Indian' thus meaning American-Indian.

Indy, [Paul Marie Théodore] **Vincent d'** (1851–1931), French composer, pupil and follower of Franck; enthusiast for Wagner; joint founder of the

Schola Cantorum (a Paris musical academy, originally for the study of church music), 1894. Works include *Fervaal* and five other operas; SYMPHONY ON A FRENCH MOUNTAINEER'S SONG and three other symphonies; orchestral variations *Istar* (after a Babylonian epic); a triple concerto for flute, cello, piano and orchestra; much chamber music.

inequality, a modern name for a convention in performing (chiefly) 18th-century music by which a pair of notes printed as of equal duration is sounded long–short; the convention originated in French music (*notes inégales*, unequal notes) and the extent of its proper application to other music is disputed.

Inextinguishable, The, see UNQUENCHABLE (title of symphony by Carl Nielsen).

Ingegneri, Marc' Antonio (*c*.1545–1592), Italian composer, choirmaster of Cremona Cathedral; teacher of Monteverdi. Works include Masses and other church music (some formerly attributed to Palestrina) and madrigals.

Inghelbrecht, Désiré Émile (1880–1965), French conductor and composer of ballet *El Greco*, chamber music, *La Nursery* for piano duet, etc.

inglese (It.), English. For *corno inglese* see ENGLISH HORN.

in modo di (It.), in the manner of.

In Nature's Realm, alternative English name for Dvořák's overture AMID NATURE.

In nomine, type of 16th- and 17th-century English polyphonic instrumental composition based on a section of the Benedictus of Taverner's Mass *Gloria*

tibi Trinitas, at the words 'in nomine'. Transcriptions of this passage were made for viols, lute and keyboard, and later composers up to Purcell gave the name 'In nomine' to works based both on Taverner's composition and directly on the plainsong melody ('Gloria tibi Trinitas') on which Taverner's Mass itself is based.

instrument, musical, an object (other than the organs of the body) used for the production of musical sound by the application of mechanical energy – or, as in ELECTROPHONIC instruments, by the application of electrical impulses. Non-electrophonic instruments are classified scientifically as AEROPHONES, CHORDOPHONES, IDIOPHONES and MEMBRANOPHONES, but the usual practical classification is into *wind*, *strings* and *percussion* (in which, respectively, vibrations are set up in an air-column, a string and a membrane or other surface). Wind instruments are divided, e.g. in the orchestra, into WOODWIND and BRASS (between which there is a difference in method of sound-production, more important than differences in materials used). Note that this classification is one of practical convenience and is not technically exhaustive: the piano, for instance, uses strings but is also 'percussive' in mechanism – and yet is not normally spoken of as a stringed or percussion instrument. See also next entry.

instrumentation, the writing of music for particular instruments – term used particularly with reference to a composer's necessary knowledge of what is practicable, and what sounds well, on different instruments. Cp. ORCHESTRATION, which properly applies to scoring for groups and not

187

primarily to the qualities of individual instruments.

Intendant (Ger.), superintendent, administrative director – especially of an opera house or other theatre.

interlude, piece of music inserted between other pieces (e.g. organ passage between the verses of a hymn) or between non-musical events, e.g. between the acts of a play. (Occasionally also used as a musical title without such implications, e.g. in A. Bush's *Lyric Interlude* for violin and piano, 1944.)

intermède (Fr.) = INTERMEZZO.

intermezzo (It.), something 'in the middle', hence (specifically musical meanings) – (1) instrumental piece in the middle of an opera, e.g. that performed while the stage is left empty in Mascagni's CAVALLERIA RUSTICANA; (2) short concert-piece – term used e.g. by Brahms for some piano works; (3, obsolete) short comic opera, e.g. Pergolesi's THE MAID AS MISTRESS, originally played between the acts of an early 18th-century serious opera. See also the following entry.

Intermezzo, opera by R. Strauss, produced in Dresden, 1924. Libretto by composer, based on an episode (i.e. 'intermezzo' in a non-musical sense) in his own life, and having as hero an opera-conductor whose peace is interrupted when his wife suspects him of infidelity.

International(e), socialist anthem composed by P. Degeyter (1848–1932), till 1944 also the national anthem of the USSR; its title refers to an international socialist organization.

interrupted cadence, see CADENCE.

interval, the 'distance' between two notes, in so far as one of them is higher or lower than the other. Thus the interval from C to the G above it is a 'fifth', to the A above it a 'sixth', etc. (These are calculated by counting upwards, and by including in the count the notes at both extreme ends.) The names 'fifth', 'sixth', etc., are themselves further defined – see PERFECT, MAJOR, MINOR, AUGMENTED, DIMINISHED. Intervals above an octave ('eighth') are called *compound intervals*, being 'compounded' of so many octaves plus a smaller interval. Thus the interval from C to the next G above it but one (12 notes, counting the extremes) is called a 12th and is a compound interval made of an octave (C–C) and a fifth (C–G).

In the South, concert-overture by Elgar, subtitled 'Alassio', the Italian town where he composed it (1904). The word 'Moglio' above a clarinet phrase in the score is the name of a nearby village.

In the Steppes of Central Asia, usual English title for the work actually entitled simply 'In Central Asia' (Rus., *V srednei Azii*), an 'orchestral picture' by Borodin, 1880, representing the approach and passing of a caravan; composed to accompany a *tableau vivant*.

Intimate Letters (Cz., *Listy duverne*), title (referring to a love-affair) of Janáček's Quartet no. 2 (1928).

intonation, tuning (of pitch); thus a singer's or violinist's intonation is praised if the notes are pitched with a high degree of precision. See also JUST INTONATION.

intrada (from Sp. *entrada*, entry), a preliminary piece – term used especially *c.* 1600 for the opening number (in pompous, festive style) of a suite of dances.

introduction, (1) term often used for the shorter, slower first part of a mainly allegro movement, as in a symphony or in Elgar's *Introduction and Allegro* for strings (1905); (2 = It., *introduzione*), the opening choral number of an act in many 19th-century Italian operas.

invention, name given by Bach to a type of short keyboard work in two-part counterpoint; 15 of these are included in his *Little Clavier Book* (Ger. *Clavierbüchlein*), 1720, for the instruction of his son W. F. Bach. The term has also been applied by Bach's editors to similar pieces in three-part counterpoint in the same collection (called by Bach himself 'symphonies') and has been occasionally used also by later composers.

inversion, see INVERT.

invert, to turn upside-down; thus (1) a chord not in its 'root position' is said to be in one or other *inversion* – see POSITION (3); (2) two melodies in counterpoint may be mutually *inverted* by the upper becoming the lower and vice versa (counterpoint capable of making sense under this treatment is called *invertible counterpoint* and forms the stuff of, e.g., FUGUE); (3) a single melody may be *inverted* by being performed 'upside-down', i.e. with all its successive intervals applied in the opposite direction. Thus an upward interval of a major third (say D–F♯) when inverted would be replaced by a downward interval of a major third (D–B♭), or by an upward interval of a minor sixth which would produce the same note (D–B♭) though in a higher

octave. A melody so inverted is called the *inversion* of the original – often abbreviated to *I* in the theory of TWELVE-NOTE technique.

Invisible City of Kitezh, The, workable abbreviation for 'The Legend of the Invisible City of Kitezh and of the Maid Fevronia' (Rus., *Skazkanie o nevidimom gradie Kitezhe i devie Fevronie*), opera by Rimsky-Korsakov, produced in St Petersburg, 1907. Libretto by V. I. Belsky, combining two Russian legends – of the miraculous rescue of Kitezh from the Tartars, and of St Fevronia.

Invitation to the Dance (not 'to the Waltz'), piano piece by Weber (Ger., *Aufforderung zum Tanz*), in the form of a waltz with slow introduction and slow epilogue, 1819. Orchestrated e.g. by Berlioz and by Weingartner; used for the ballet *Le Spectre de la rose*, 1911.

Iolanta, see YOLANDE.

Iolanthe, or The Peer and the Peri, operetta by Sullivan, produced in London and New York on the same day, 1882. Libretto by W. S. Gilbert, on the interaction of Fairyland and the House of Lords. The term 'Peri', usefully borrowed for the title-pun, is derived from Persian mythology: cp. THE PERI, PARADISE AND THE PERI.

Ionian mode, the MODE which may be represented by the white keys of the piano from C to C.

Iphigenia in Aulis, operas after Euripides by several composers including (1) Gluck (Fr., *Iphigénie en Aulide*), with libretto by F. L. L. du Roullet, indebted to Racine; produced in Paris, 1774; (2) Cherubini (It., *Ifigenia in Aulide*), with libretto by F. Moretti;

produced in Turin, 1788. The plot of these operas has its sequel in *Iphigenia in Tauris*.

Iphigenia in Tauris, operas after Euripides (see also preceding entry) by various composers including (1) Gluck (Fr., *Iphigénie en Tauride*) with libretto by N. F. Guillard; produced in Paris, 1779; (2) Piccinni, with libretto by A. du C. Dubreuil; produced in Paris, 1781. (Supporters of Gluck and Piccinni clashed over the two operas.)

Ippolitov-Ivanov, Mikhail [Mikhailovich] (1859–1935), Russian composer, pupil of Rimsky-Korsakov; director of the Moscow Conservatory. Studied folk music, e.g. of Georgia, and wrote orchestral *Caucasian Sketches*, and other regionally titled works – also two symphonies, operas, many songs, etc. Completed Musorgsky's unfinished opera *The Marriage*.

IRCAM, acronym for the Institut de Recherche et de Co-ordination Acoustique/Musique, established in Paris, 1977, under Pierre Boulez as a laboratory for composition, exploring acoustical and electronic phenomena relating to music.

Ireland, John [Nicholson] (1879–1962), British composer, pupil of Stanford; also pianist and organist. Published no opera, no ballet, no symphony, but a piano concerto and various orchestral works including A LONDON OVERTURE; a sonata and many other works for piano; many songs, including 'Sea Fever'; cantata *These Things Shall Be*; three piano trios, etc.

Iris, opera by Mascagni, produced in Rome, 1898. Libretto, set in Japan, by L. Illica – the joint librettist, later, for Puccini's MADAM BUTTERFLY.

Irving, Robert [Augustine] (b. 1913), British conductor, especially of ballet; at Covent Garden, then from 1958 with New York City Ballet.

Isaac, Heinrich (*c.*1450–1517), Flemish (Germanized) composer, holding posts with the Medici and other noble families, and living in Austria and Italy; died in Florence. Composed church music; instrumental works; songs in French, Italian, German and Latin: the well-known tune 'Innsbruck', which he harmonized, was probably not his own composition.

Ishii, Kan (b. 1921), Japanese composer, pupil of Orff in Munich (also conductor). Works include operas, ballets, symphonic poem *Yama*, stage and film music. Brother of the following.

Ishii, Maki (b. 1936), Japanese composer (brother of preceding) who studied in West Berlin, and later took up residence there. Some works have Japanese titles (*Kyō-Sō* for percussion groups and orchestra. *La-Sen II* for cello solo); some use Japanese instruments (*Nucleus* for biwa, harp, shakuhachi and flute).

Islamey, fantasy for piano by Balakirev, evoking an 'oriental' atmosphere and prompted by a visit to the Caucasus; first performed in 1869. Orchestrated by Casella, 1908.

Isle of the Dead, The, a picture by the German painter Arnold Böcklin (1827–1901), which inspired Rakhmaninov's symphonic poem of the same name (1909) and a few other musical works.

isorhythmic (from Gk., equal-rhythmed), term applied to certain medieval motets, e.g. by Machaut, of which the rhythms are repeated according to a strict scheme not corresponding to repetition in the melody.

Isouard, Nicolas (or Nicolò) (1775–1818), Maltese-born composer who wrote operas in Italian and, after settling in Paris in 1799, in French, with great success – see CINDERELLA.

Israel in Egypt, oratorio by Handel, with words from the Bible, first performed in London, 1739; predominantly choral, it includes famous double (i.e. eight-part) choruses. Incorporates unacknowledged 'borrowings' from KERLL.

Israel Philharmonic Orchestra, orchestra based in Tel-Aviv (founded in 1936 as the Palestine Symphony Orchestra); music director since 1977, Mehta. Cp. HUBERMAN.

istesso tempo, L' (It.), at the same tempo, i.e. preserving the same pace although the unit of beat may have changed – say from 2/4 to 6/8 in which case the old ♩ and the new ♩. would have the same duration.

Istomin, Eugene (b. 1925), American pianist, noted as trio-partner of Isaac Stern and Leonard Rose. Married Casals' widow, the cellist Marta Casals (née Montañez).

Ištván, Miloslav (b. 1928), Czechoslovak composer of *Rhythms and Antirhythms* for two pianos and two percussion instruments; *Dodekameron* for 12 instruments; *Odyssey of a Child of Lidice* (site of Nazi massacre) for piano; etc.

Italiana in Algeri, L', see ITALIAN WOMAN IN ALGIERS, THE.

Italian Caprice, orchestral work by Tchaikovsky, composed in 1879 in Italy, based on tunes heard there. (Original title *Capriccio italien* is bastard Italian-plus-French.)

Italian Concerto, usual title given to Bach's *Concerto in the Italian Style* (BWV 971) for harpsichord, published in 1735 (see CLAVIERÜBUNG). Though for a solo instrument, it maintains the form and style then associated with the term CONCERTO, the necessary element of contrast being available through use of the harpsichord's two manuals.

Italian overture, see OVERTURE.

Italian Serenade, work by Wolf for string quartet, 1887; he later made an arrangement for orchestra and intended to add two more movements to this.

Italian sixth, type of 'augmented sixth' chord (see AUGMENTED) distinguished by having a major third (and no other note) between the notes forming the sixth – e.g. (reading upwards) D♭, F, B. (Cp. FRENCH SIXTH, GERMAN SIXTH.) The reason for the names is not known.

Italian Song-book (Ger., *Italienisches Liederbuch*), Wolf's song-settings, 1890–96, of 46 Italian poems in German translation.

Italian Symphony, Mendelssohn's Symphony no. 4 in A major and minor; commemorating a visit to Italy, and first performed in 1833. See SALTARELLO.

Italian Woman in Algiers, The (It., *L'Italiana in Algeri*), comic opera by Rossini, produced in Venice, 1813. Libretto by A. Anelli, the heroine easily outwitting the oriental despot who holds her prisoner.

Italienisches Liederbuch, see ITALIAN SONG-BOOK.

Iturbi, José (1895–1980), Spanish conductor and pianist (sometimes simultaneously). Lived in USA; held conductor's post in Rochester (NY), 1935–44. Several film appearances.

Ivanhoe, Sullivan's only 'serious' opera, produced in London, 1891. Libretto by J. R. Sturgis, after Scott's novel. (See also MARSCHNER.)

Ivan Susanin, see LIFE FOR THE TSAR, A.

Ivan the Terrible, (1) opera by Bizet, with libretto by A. Leroy and H. Trianon about the Russian Tsar; composed in 1865, withdrawn, thought lost, recovered in 1944 and produced in Württemberg, 1946; (2) title sometimes given to Rimsky-Korsakov's opera THE MAID OF PSKOV.

Ives, Charles [Edward] (1874–1954), American composer of music which, all written before 1920, anticipates later devices, e.g. POLYTONALITY, POLYRHYTHM, quarter-tones. Was organist and choirmaster and had business career, his work being little recognized until his CONCORD piano sonata was played in 1939 and his Symphony no. 3 in 1946. Works include five symphonies, *Three Places in New England* for orchestra, and songs.

Ives (or Ive or Ivy), **Simon** (1600–1662), English composer and church organist, more than 100 of whose instrumental and vocal works survive.

Iwaki, Hiroyuki (b. 1932), Japanese conductor, pupil of Karajan; principal conductor of NHK Symphony Orchestra (Japan) and, since 1974, of Melbourne Symphony Orchestra.

J

jack, the vertical strip of wood carrying the plectrum that plucks the string of a harpsichord, virginals, etc.; as the finger-key is depressed, the jack moves up and the string is plucked.

Jackson, William (1730–1803), British organist and composer of church music; also of operas, harpsichord pieces, etc. Was organist of Exeter Cathedral and is known as 'Jackson of Exeter'.

Jackson, William (1815–66), British organist and composer (church music, glees, etc.); active in Yorkshire and known as 'Jackson of Masham'.

Jacob, Gordon [Percival Septimus] (1895–1984), British composer, pupil of Stanford and C. Wood; noted also as teacher and as authority on orchestration. Works include *Passacaglia on a Well-known Theme* (Oranges and Lemons) and concertos for various instruments. CBE, 1968.

Jacobi, Frederick (1891–1952), American composer, also conductor; pupil of Bloch and others; studied American-Indian music and wrote a string quartet and other works making use of it; also a symphony, Jewish liturgical music, etc.

Jacobs, René (b. 1946), Belgian counter-tenor, prominent in various baroque ensembles; also conductor.

Jacopo da Bologna (14th century), Italian composer of madrigals (in the earlier sense) and other vocal works.

Jahreszeiten, Die, see SEASONS.

Jamaican Rumba, piece for two pianos by Benjamin, published in 1938 after a visit to Jamaica; arranged also for many other combinations.

James, Henry (1843–1916), American novelist. See ARGENTO, TURN OF THE SCREW.

jam session, informal improvised performance by jazz musicians.

Janáček, Leoš (1854–1928), Czech composer; also choral conductor; studied Czech folk-song and speech which greatly influenced his musical idiom. Works include JENŮFA, KATYA KABANOVA, THE CUNNING LITTLE VIXEN, THE MAKROPOULOS AFFAIR, FROM A HOUSE OF THE DEAD and four other operas; GLAGOLITIC MASS and many other choral works; Sinfonietta, *Taras Bulba* and other orchestral works; two string quartets (see INTIMATE LETTERS); song cycle THE DIARY OF ONE WHO DISAPPEARED; folk-song arrangements. Visited Britain in 1926.

Janequin, Clement, see JANNEQUIN.

janissary music, term for the effect

produced by using triangle, cymbals and bass drum, e.g. in Mozart's overture to THE SERAGLIO – imitating Turkish music as played by the janissaries (infantry forming the Sultan's bodyguard).

Jannequin (also spelt Janequin), **Clément** (*c*.1485–1558), French composer of long dramatic CHANSONS in four parts with, e.g., representation of bird-song; also of other songs, and Masses and other church music. Possibly a pupil of JOSQUIN.

Janowitz, Gundula (b. 1937), German soprano, noted in opera; sang at Vienna State Opera from 1960 but not at Covent Garden until 1976.

Janowski, Marek (b. 1939), Polish-born German conductor; music director of Royal Liverpool Philharmonic Orchestra, 1983–6.

Jaques-Dalcroze, Émile (1865–1950), Swiss (Austrian-born) inventor of EURHYTHMICS; also composer of operas, etc.

Jarnach, Philipp (1892–1982), Spanish (Catalan) composer (French-born) with a German mother; trained chiefly in Paris; taught in Zurich, Berlin, etc. Studied also with Busoni and completed Busoni's unfinished DOCTOR FAUST. He himself composed *Sinfonia brevis* and other orchestral works, unaccompanied violin sonatas, etc.

Järnefelt, Armas (1869–1958), conductor and composer, Finnish-born, naturalized Swedish in 1910. Introduced Wagner's music to Finland. Works included PRAELUDIUM and *Berceuse* for orchestra, choral music, songs. His sister married Sibelius.

Järvi, Neeme (b. 1937), Soviet-Estonian conductor, music director of Scottish National Orchestra, 1984–8.

jazz, term used at least from 1914 for a type of American popular music originating among blacks of New Orleans and taken over also by whites: also applied generally to various types of dance music indebted to this (though purists reserve the term for such music as retains the original flavour and the original basis of improvisation). The jazz idiom, characterized by certain syncopations over strongly reiterated rhythms, influenced e.g. Stravinsky, Walton and Milhaud, as well as many American composers. See BLUE NOTE, BLUES, RAGTIME.

Jeanne d'Arc au bûcher, see JOAN OF ARC AT THE STAKE.

Jeans, Susi (b. 1911), Austrian-born organist and harpsichordist, resident in England, specializing in old music; originally Susi Hock, she married the physicist Sir James Jeans (author of book *Science and Music*).

Její Pastorkyňa, see JENŮFA.

Jelinek, Hanns (1901–69), Austrian composer, mainly self-taught but studied briefly with Schoenberg, Berg and Schmidt. Compositions include *Symphonia brevis* for orchestra, *Twelve-note Primer* for piano, song-setting (with orchestra) of Goethe's *Prometheus*.

Jemnitz, Alexander (Hungarian form, 'Sándor') (1890–1963), Hungarian composer, conductor and writer on music; pupil of Reger and Schoenberg. Works include *Overture for a Peace Festival*; a harp sonata; various piano and organ works.

'Jena' Symphony, name given to symphony found at Jena, Germany, in 1909; wrongly conjectured to be an early work of Beethoven's, it is known to be by J. F. Witt.

Jenkins, John (1592–1678), English composer in service to various noble families. Wrote fantasies for viols, songs and rounds; also sonatas and suites for combinations of violins, viols and continuo.

Jensen, Adolf (1837–79), German pianist and composer, particularly of piano music and songs; also of an opera, cantatas, etc. Pupil of Liszt.

Jenůfa, opera by Janáček, produced in Brno, 1904. Libretto by composer, after a play by G. Preissova; originally titled *Her Foster-daughter* (Cz., *Její Pastorkyňa*). Named after the heroine, whose illegitimate baby is drowned by Jenůfa's foster-mother.

Jephtha, (1) Latin oratorio (originally entitled *Jefte*) by Carissimi (words from the Bible) for six voices and continuo, composed by 1650; one of the earliest oratorios – each 'character' sings, and there is a narrator; (2) oratorio by Handel, first performed in London, 1752; words by T. Morell, after the Bible.

Jeremiáš, Jaroslav (1889–1919), Czech composer of oratorio *Jan Hus*, etc.; pupil of Novák and brother of Otakar Jeremiáš.

Jeremiáš, Otakar (1892–1962), Czech composer, pupil of Novák, brother of preceding. Works include opera *The Brothers Karamazov* (after Dostoyevsky); cantata *Songs of My Country*, Choral Fantasia (with orchestra), etc. Also conductor.

Jeritza (originally Jedlitzka), Maria (1887–1982), Czech soprano celebrated in opera in Vienna and, from 1921, at the Metropolitan Opera, New York.

Jerusalem, Siegfried (b. 1940), German tenor, formerly orchestral bassoonist; prominent in Wagner, appearing at Bayreuth Festival from 1977.

Jesu, joy of man's desiring, see HESS.

Jeux d'enfants, see CHILDREN'S GAMES.

Jewels of the Madonna, The (It., *I gioielli della Madonna*), opera by Wolf-Ferrari, produced in Berlin (in German), 1911. Libretto originally in Italian, by E. Golisciani and C. Zangarini. Blood-and-thunder plot, like CAVALLERIA RUSTICANA, and likewise containing a popular orchestral intermezzo.

Jewess, The (Fr., *La Juive*), opera by Halévy, produced in Paris, 1835. Libretto by E. Scribe (originally written for Rossini); the 'Jewess', executed by order of a 15th-century Cardinal, turns out to be the Cardinal's own daughter.

Jew's harp, primitive instrument held in the mouth, having a strip of metal 'twanged' (i.e. set vibrating) by the finger, the different notes being elicited by altering the shape of the cavity of the mouth. (Reason for the name unknown; apparently not corruption of 'jaw's harp'.)

jig, type of dance usually in 6/8 or 12/8 time; often constituting the last movement of an 18th-century suite, in which it was usually structured in BINARY form.

jingling johnny, obsolete military-band percussion instrument shaped like a tree or pavilion (hence other name, 'Chinese pavilion') and hung with bells which were shaken.

Jirák, Karel Boleslav (1891–1972), Czech composer, pupil of Novák; also conductor. Works include six symphonies, *Overture to a Shakespearean Comedy*, seven string quartets, many song-cycles, etc. Resident in USA from 1947.

Joachim, Joseph (1831–1907), Hungarian violinist and composer, living mainly in Germany; visited Britain aged 13 and many times thereafter. Friend of Brahms, whose Violin Concerto is dedicated to him; he himself composed three violin concertos, overtures to *Hamlet* and *King Henry IV*, etc. See also GRAND DUO (Schubert), which he orchestrated.

Joan of Arc at the Stake (Fr., *Jeanne d'Arc au bûcher*), play by P. Claudel with some spoken parts (including Joan's) and some sung; music by Honegger – his most widely performed stage work. Produced at Basle, 1938.

Job, (1) oratorio by C. H. H. Parry (words from the Bible), first performed in 1892; (2) 'masque for dancing' (in effect a ballet) with music by Vaughan Williams, produced in London, 1931 (after Blake's illustrations to the Book of Job); (3) opera (but called a 'mystery play') by Dallapiccola, after the Bible, produced in Rome, 1950.

Jocelyn, opera by Godard, produced in Brussels, 1888. Libretto by P. A. Silvestre and V. Capone, after Lamartine: Jocelyn is a seminarist tempted by earthly love. The work is now remembered by the leading tenor's 'Berceuse'.

Jochum, Eugen (1902–87), German

conductor celebrated in German and Austrian symphonic music; held posts in Berlin, Munich, Amsterdam (see CONCERTGEBOUW); appointed 'conductor laureate' of London Symphony Orchestra, 1975.

jodel, see YODEL.

Johannes-Passion, see ST JOHN PASSION.

Johnny Strikes Up (Ger., *Jonny spielt auf*), opera by Křenek, in a jazz-influenced style; produced in Leipzig, 1927. Libretto by composer; Johnny is a black jazz violinist.

John of Fornsete, English 13th-century monk, conjecturally the composer of SUMER IS ICUMEN IN.

John of the Cross, St [Juan de la Cruz] (1542–91), Spanish poet and mystic. See BEECROFT.

Johnson, Anthony Rolfe, see ROLFE JOHNSON.

Johnson, Graham (b. 1950), British pianist, born in Rhodesia; prominent as an accompanist to singers, he founded the Songmakers' Almanac (vocal group) in 1976.

Johnson, Hunter (b. 1906), American composer of ballet *Letter to the World*, a symphony, piano concerto, piano sonata, etc.

Johnson, John (*c.*1540–1595), English lutenist and composer of songs and lute music; attached to the court of Elizabeth I.

Johnson, Robert (*c.*1500–1554), Scottish priest and composer who fled to England from religious persecution; wrote Latin motets, English church music, also secular vocal works and music for viol consort.

Johnson, Robert (*c*.1583–1633), English lutenist, serving Charles I and James I; composed solo songs (including two from *The Tempest*), catches, viol music, etc.

Johnson, Robert Sherlaw (b. 1932), British composer – also pianist, Oxford University teacher, and author of a book on Messiaen. Works include two string quartets; *Asterogenesis* and other works for piano; *Festival Mass of the Resurrection*.

Johnston, Ben[jamin Burwell] (b. 1926), American composer (pupil of Milhaud), also pianist. Works include nine string quartets; *Auto Mobile* – a 'sound environment' on tape for a car exhibition; *One Man* for trombonist who also plays percussion (using his feet).

Joio, Norman Dello, see DELLO JOIO.

Jolas, Betsy (b. 1926), French composer (also pianist and organist), pupil of Messiaen and Milhaud in Paris – and also studied in USA. Works include *Points of the Dawn* for contralto and 13 wind instruments; *States* for violin and six percussionists; Sonata for 12 solo voices.

Jolie Fille de Perth, La, see FAIR MAID OF PERTH.

Jolivet, André (1905–74), French composer, pupil of Varèse and others; one of the former group called 'Young France'. Works include three symphonies (and a symphony for strings); Concertino for piano and trumpet; works for MARTENOT; piano solos; oratorio *The Truth About Joan [of Arc]*. Musical director of the Comédie Française, Paris, 1945–60. See LESUR.

Jomelli, Niccolò (1714–74), Italian composer, pupil of Leo; wrote oratorios, church music, etc., but especially operas – apparently more than 80. Was a pioneer of the use of the orchestral crescendo. Much admired in Germany, and was court music director in Stuttgart, 1753–69.

Jones, Daniel (b. 1912), British composer of 12 symphonies (he was apparently the first composer from Wales to have a symphony performed), 9 string quartets, opera *The Knife*, oratorio *St Peter*, music to *Under Milk Wood* (dramatic poem by his friend Dylan Thomas); also of a sonata for three kettledrums; etc. OBE, 1968.

Jones, Gwyneth (b. 1936), British soprano (formerly mezzo-soprano); sang at Covent Garden from 1963, and at the Bayreuth Festival from 1966. Created Dame, 1986.

Jones, Philip (b. 1928), British trumpeter, founding director of Philip Jones Brass Ensemble (1951–87), the first such brass group to sustain a long and distinguished reputation.

Jones, Robert (*c*.1570–*c*.1615), English lutenist, in service to various patrons; composed songs with lute, madrigals – one in THE TRIUMPHS OF ORIANA. (An earlier Robert Jones sang in the English Chapel Royal in 1520.)

Jones, Sidney (1861–1946), British composer of THE GEISHA and other operettas; also conductor.

Jongen, Joseph (1873–1953), Belgian composer of symphonic poems, a piano concerto, a quartet for saxophones, piano and organ works, etc. Director of the Brussels Conservatory, 1920–39. Brother of Léon Jongen.

Jongen, Léon (1885–1969), Belgian

composer and pianist; director of the Brussels Conservatory from 1939, succeeding his brother Joseph Jongen. Works include operas, *Rhapsodia belgica* for violin and orchestra, piano solos.

jongleur (Fr., juggler), medieval wandering minstrel who was singer, instrumentalist (chiefly on a form of fiddle), acrobat, juggler, etc.

Jonny spielt auf, see JOHNNY STRIKES UP.

Jonson, Ben (1573–1637), English poet and dramatist. See ANTHEIL, BURT, CASTIGLIONI.

Joplin, Scott (1868–1917), American composer and pianist whose ragtime compositions for piano had a revived vogue in the 1970s; also composed operas *A Guest of Honour* (lost) and *Treemonisha* (not staged till 1972).

Joseph, opera by Méhul, produced in Paris, 1807; libretto by A. Duval, after the Bible.

Josephs, Wilfred (b. 1927), British composer of Requiem for baritone, chorus and orchestra (text is the KADDISH); nine symphonies; two piano sonatas; music for child performers; opera *Rebecca*; etc. He was a dentist before becoming a full-time musician.

Joshua, oratorio by Handel (words by T. Morell, after the Bible), first performed in London, 1748.

Josquin (*c.*1440–1521), in full Josquin des Prez (and other spellings, 'Josquin' being properly a diminutive forename). Flemish composer, pupil of Ockeghem, and singer at the Papal Church in Rome. Composed Masses, motets (one on the STABAT MATER text), chansons, etc. His work is not-

able for an expressiveness new at that time – see MUSICA RESERVATA.

Josten, Werner (1885–1963), composer, German-born, who settled in USA, 1920. Works include ballets, choral and orchestral works, two pieces for strings and piano called *Concerto sacro* – prompted by Grünewald's altar-painting at Isenheim (cp. MATHIS THE PAINTER).

jota, northern Spanish dance in quick triple time, traditionally with castanets.

Joubert, John (b. 1927), South African composer who studied in London under H. Ferguson and others; university teacher at Hull, then Birmingham (1962). Works include opera *Silas Marner* (after George Eliot); cycle of Latin unaccompanied motets *Pro Pace* (for peace); two symphonies; *Threnos* for harpsichord and 12 solo strings; church music.

Joyce, Eileen (1912–91), Australian pianist who settled in Britain, gaining much popularity in concertos – e.g. at the Proms from 1942.

Joyce, James (1882–1941). Irish writer. See CAGE, DEL TREDICI, MIHÁLY, PISK, SEARLE, SZYMANOWSKI, ULYSSES.

Jubilate [Deo], Latin name for Psalm 100, as used in church services (in English, 'O be joyful in the Lord') and as occasionally set for concert and ceremonial purposes, as an expression of rejoicing.

Judas Maccabaeus, oratorio by Handel (words by T. Morell, after the Bible), first performed in London, 1747.

Judenkünig, Hans (*c.*1450–1526), German lutenist and composer for his instrument who died in Vienna.

Judith, works based on the Apocryphal Book, including – (1) Latin oratorio (*Juditha Triumphans* – Judith Triumphant) by Vivaldi, 1716; (2) English oratorio by Thomas Arne (words by I. Bickerstaffe), first performed in London, 1761; (3) oratorio by C. H. H. Parry, first performed in 1888; (4) opera by Honegger, produced in Monte Carlo, 1926 – expanded from his music to a play by R. Morax, 1925.

juggler, see JONGLEUR.

Juilliard Quartet, American string quartet founded in 1946 in association with the Juilliard School of Music, New York, with Robert Mann as leader; though with some changes of membership, it has sustained a first-class reputation.

Juive, La, see JEWESS, THE.

Julius Caesar, operas in Italian (entitled *Giulio Cesare*) by (1) Handel, produced in London, 1724 – properly *Giulio Cesare in Egitto,* i.e. in Egypt; libretto by N. Haym; (2) Malipiero, produced in Genoa, 1936; libretto by composer, after Shakespeare.

junge Lord, Der, see YOUNG LORD.

Jungfernquartette, see RUSSIAN QUARTETS.

'Jupiter' Symphony, nickname given in many different countries to Mozart's last symphony, no. 41 in C (K551): the name has no authority, only convenience. The dates of composition of this and the two preceding symphonies span less than seven weeks in 1788.

Jurinac, Sena (short for Srebenka) (b. 1921), Yugoslav soprano who appeared with Vienna State Opera (from 1944), at Glyndebourne (from 1949), etc.

just intonation, the tuning of an interval in its 'pure' form according to the HARMONIC SERIES, not a tempered interval (see TEMPERAMENT); hence a general system of tuning, which must incorporate at least five such 'pure' tunings within the octave. (It is not possible to construct a diatonic scale in which both the major third and the perfect fifth are 'pure'.) Such a tuning is theoretically accessible to voices, bowed string instruments, etc., in which the pitch of the notes is not mechanically fixed. Some modern American composers, e.g. Partch, have had other instruments specially constructed to be tuned to 'pure' intervals.

K

K, abbreviation for (1) 'Köchel' in numbering the works of W. A. MOZART; (2) KIRKPATRICK in numbering D. Scarlatti's works.

Kabalevsky, Dmitri [Borisovich] (1904–87), Russian composer, pupil of Myaskovsky, also pianist and writer on music. Composed operas including *Colas Breugnon* and *The Family of Taras* (based on a story of the Nazi occupation of Russian territory); three piano concertos and other concertos for violin and cello; four symphonies, songs, piano pieces.

Kabeláč, Miloslav (1908–79), Czechoslovak composer (also conductor), wrote an *Improvisation on Hamlet* and other orchestral works; *Ricercari* for 1–6 percussionists; several works for speaker(s) and orchestra; choral music.

Kabos, Ilona (1893–1973), British pianist, Hungarian-born, noted teacher in London and New York; married to Kentner, 1931–45.

Kaddish, Jewish mourners' prayer, in Aramaic (similar to Hebrew); set in Bernstein's Symphony no. 3 and Josephs's Requiem.

Kadosa, Pál (1930–83), Hungarian composer and pianist. Works include eight symphonies, four piano concertos, songs.

Kafka, Franz (1883–1924), German-Czech writer. See EINEM.

Kagel, Mauricio (b. 1931), Argentinian composer who moved to West Germany in 1957. Works, many including electronics and theatrical elements, include *On Stage* (Fr., *Sur scène*) for speaker, mime, singer and three instrumentalists; *Match* for three players on two cellos, with percussion; *Improvisation Added* for three organists.

Kaiserquartett (Ger.), see EMPEROR QUARTET.

Kajanus, Robert (1856–1933), Finnish conductor, friend and champion of Sibelius; also composer of symphonic poems, etc.

Kalabis, Viktor (b. 1923), Czechoslovak composer, formerly also radio music executive; works include five symphonies, Symphonic Variations, a piano concerto and a cello concerto, Sonata for violin and harpsichord.

Kalevala, the Finnish national epic poem. See SIBELIUS.

Kalinnikov, Vassily Sergeyevich (1866–1901), Russian composer of two symphonies, songs, stage music, etc.

Kalkbrenner, Frédéric (originally Friedrich Wilhelm Michael) (1785–1849), German-born pianist who studied and settled in Paris; noted performer and teacher; also composer of three piano concertos, many studies, etc.

Kalliwoda, Johann Wenzel (or, in Czech, Jan Václav Kalivoda), (1801–66), Bohemian violinist and composer of seven symphonies and other orchestral works formerly often performed; also of opera, string quartets, church music, etc.

Kálmán, Emmerich (1882–1953), Austro-Hungarian composer, particularly of operettas including THE GIPSY PRINCESS; latterly lived in France and USA, and died in Paris.

Kalomiris, Manolis (1883–1962), Greek composer, also critic and conservatory director in Athens. Works include operas, three symphonies (two with chorus, one with narrator), songs.

Kaminski, Heinrich (1886–1946), German composer of music to religious texts using modal style; also of opera, Concerto for Orchestra, *Triptych* for voice and organ, etc.

Kaminski, Joseph (1903–72), Polish-born Israeli violinist and composer who emigrated to Palestine, 1936; works include Concertino for trumpet and *Comedy Overture*.

Kammer (Ger.), chamber; hence *Kammermusik, Kammersymphonie*, etc. (See under CHAMBER.)

Kanawa, Kiri Te, see TE KANAWA.

Kantor, see CANTOR.

Kapelle (Ger.), chapel; hence, the musical establishment of a prince's private chapel; hence again, any established musical institution, e.g. an orchestra. See following entry, also CAPPELLA.

Kapellmeister (Ger., chapel-master), musical director, originally of a prince's private chapel; term later used also for a 'resident conductor', e.g. of an orchestra. Hence *Kapellmeistermusik*, 'conductor's music', (abusive term for) empty music composed by someone who has a conductor's familiarity with mere technique, but has nothing more.

Karajan, Herbert (originally Heribert) **von** (1908–89), Austrian conductor, also stage and film director for some of his own opera performances. Despite his former Nazi party membership he made his London début in 1947, and in 1955 became conductor of the Berlin Philharmonic Orchestra, resigning only three months before his death. In a career of unsurpassed international fame he recorded all Beethoven's symphonies four times.

Karelia, overture and orchestral suite by Sibelius, 1893; evocative of the province of Karelia in the south of Finland.

Karg-Elert (real name Karg), **Sigfrid** (1877–1933), German composer, also pianist and organist; now known chiefly for his many organ works. Wrote also a symphony, string quartets, many songs, etc.

Karr, Gary [Michael] (b. 1941), American double-bass player, the most celebrated solo exponent of his instrument; commissioned works from Henze and others.

Kasemets, Udo (b. 1919), Canadian composer who emigrated from Soviet Estonia, 1951; also pianist, organist, conductor, critic and director of various concert series in Canada.

Works include some for conventional sized groups of instruments, others for variable groups (e.g. *Cascando* for 1–128 performers), others for mixed media with speech, film, etc.

Kastalsky, Alexander Dmitrievich (1856–1926), Russian composer, pupil of Tchaikovsky and Taneyev; active in church music before and after the 1917 Revolution. Also composed patriotic choral works, opera, etc.

Kát'a Kabanová, see KATYA KABANOVA.

Katchen, Julius (1926–69), American pianist who, as a child prodigy, withdrew from career in US, later making European début in Paris, 1946; much admired as a soloist, he also occasionally conducted from 1959. Died in Paris from leukemia.

Katerina Izmailova, opera by Shostakovich, produced in Leningrad, 1934, under the title 'Lady Macbeth of the Mtsensk District'; new title was first used in a Moscow production later in the same year. Libretto by A. G. Preis and the composer (after a story by Leskov), centring on a woman who kills her husband and father-in-law. The work was banned under Stalin and brought out in a revised version in Moscow, 1963.

Katya Kabanova (in Czech properly spelt *Kát'a Kabanová*), opera by Janáček, produced in Brno, 1921. Named after the tragic heroine, whose husband is mother-ridden: libretto by composer, after V. Cervinka's translation of Ostrovsky's Russian play *The Storm*.

Kay, Ulysses [Simpson] (b. 1917), American composer, pupil of Hanson and Rogers: works include operas, a symphony, three string quartets.

Kazantzakis, Nikos (*c*.1883–1957), Greek writer. See GREEK PASSION.

kazoo, children's musical instrument into which one hums to produce an effect rather superior to that of comb-and-paper.

Kb., abbr. for Ger. *Kontrabass*, i.e. double-bass.

Keal, Minna (originally Minnie Nirenstein) (b. 1909), British composer who, previously almost unknown, had her Symphony no. 1 (written at the age of 76) performed at the Proms in 1989.

Keats, John (1795–1821), English poet. See CASTIGLIONI, HOLST.

keen (Ir., *Caoine*), an Irish funeral song accompanied by wailing; to wail thus.

Keiser, Reinhard (1674–1739), German composer; also director of the Hamburg Opera, and afterwards worked for some time in Copenhagen. Wrote about 50 operas, some with mixed German and Italian words; more than anyone else, established Hamburg as an opera centre. Also composed oratorios, a 'St Mark' PASSION, etc.

Kelemen, Milko (b. 1924), Yugoslav composer, pupil in Paris of Messiaen and Milhaud; has worked much in Germany. Compositions include opera *The Plague*, a bassoon concerto, *Equilibriums* for two orchestras.

Keler-Béla (pen-name of Adalbert von Keler) (1820–82), Hungarian violinist, bandmaster, conductor, and composer chiefly of dances and marches.

Kell, Reginald [Clifford] (1906–81), British clarinettist, noted as soloist and director of his own ensemble; resident mainly in USA, 1948–71.

Kelley, Edgar Stillman (1857–1944), American composer (also organist and critic) who studied in Germany. Studied Chinese music and wrote an orchestral suite on Chinese themes. Other works include the symphony *Gulliver* (after Swift), operettas, string quartets.

Kelly, Michael (1762–1826), Irish tenor, friend of Mozart; took part in the first performance of THE MARRIAGE OF FIGARO; was himself the composer of music for many London stage pieces.

Kempe, Rudolf (1910–76), German conductor; director of the Munich Opera, 1952–4; noted Wagner conductor at Covent Garden; principal conductor, Royal Philharmonic Orchestra, 1961–75.

Kempff, Wilhelm (b. 1895), German pianist, formerly director of a musical academy at Stuttgart; also composer. Continued performing until his 80s.

Kennan, Kent [Wheeler] (b. 1913), American composer, pupil of Pizzetti in Italy. Works include a symphony; *Night Soliloquy* for flute (with piano or with orchestra or with other accompaniment); Sonata for trumpet and piano; choruses. Also university teacher and writer of music textbooks.

Kennedy, Nigel (b. 1956), British violinist who plays jazz as well as concertos, etc.; also viola-player.

Kent bugle, see OPHICLEIDE.

Kentner, Louis (originally Lajos) [Philip] (1905–87), pianist born in Karvinna (then in Hungary, now in Czechoslovakia) who studied in Budapest and settled in England, 1935; partner of Menuhin (his brother-in-law) in recitals. See KABOS.

Kerl, Johann Caspar, see KERLL.

Kerle, Jacob van (*c*.1531–91), Flemish composer of church music, long in service to the Bishop of Augsburg; his work was performed with approval at the Council of Trent, 1562–3, when propriety in church music was discussed. Died in Prague.

Kerll (also Kerl), **Johann Caspar** (1627–93), German organist and composer, chiefly in Munich and Vienna. Studied in Italy, wrote Italian operas – also church music, etc. Handel 'borrowed' some of his music and incorporated it into, e.g., ISRAEL IN EGYPT.

Kern, Jerome [David] (1885–1945), American composer of many popular songs of marked individuality – especially in *Show Boat* and other musical plays, and in films of a similar nature. Composed also a few other works including *Portrait of Mark Twain* for orchestra.

Kertesz, István (1929–73), Hungarian-born, German-naturalized conductor; musical director of Cologne Opera House and (1965–8) principal conductor of the London Symphony Orchestra.

Ketèlbey, Albert [William] (1875–1959), British composer of *In a Monastery Garden* and other popular light orchestral pieces; also theatre conductor.

Ketting, Piet (1905–84), Dutch pianist and composer (pupil of Pijper; also influenced by Schoenberg). Works include a symphony, string quartets, settings of Shakespeare and other songs.

kettledrum, cauldron-shaped drum originally from the Orient, and originally smaller and more delicate-sounding than now; in modern form, tuned to a definite pitch, normally by handles on the rim. Two such drums were normal in the symphony orchestra up to Beethoven, and later composers have used three or (rarely) more. The drum rests on a stand, the skin facing upwards; the tone-quality may be varied according to the drumsticks used and the point of impact. A cloth on the drum may be used to give the effect of a mute. Mechanically tuned drums, using pedals, and commonly called 'pedal drums', have also come into wide use in the 20th century; they (1) make tuning quicker, allowing rapid changes in the middle of a movement, and (2) allow the use of glissando (drum struck, then pedal depressed – e.g. in Bartók's Concerto for Orchestra). The kettledrum is standard also in the mounted military band – one slung each side of a horse. (In all contexts *kettledrum* is preferable to *timpani*, the Italian term: this is a plural form of which the singular is not commonly used in English, though *timpano* is valid in Italian.)

Keuris, Tristan (b. 1946), Dutch composer whose visits to USA inspired *To Brooklyn Bridge* for 24 solo voices and instrumental ensemble; also wrote Concerto for saxophone quartet and orchestra, two string quartets, etc.

key, (1) a lever, e.g. on piano, organ, or a woodwind instrument, depressed by finger or foot to produce a note. (2) a classification of the notes of a scale, the most important note being called the *keynote* and the others functioning in relation to it. If the keynote is C, then the key may be either C major or C minor, according to whether the major or minor scale is used basically in the music concerned (see MAJOR); notes outside the 'basic' scale are said to be foreign to the key. The sharps and flats appertaining to the key are displayed in a KEY-SIGNATURE; other sharps, flats and naturals occurring 'casually' in the music are written as ACCIDENTALS. The major and minor keys were the only two types of note-ordering generally used in Western music between approximately 1600 and 1900; earlier, the MODES prevailed, and later certain composers began to dispense with key altogether (see ATONAL).

keyboard, a continuous arrangement of keys – see KEY (1) – either for the fingers, as on the piano, or for the feet, as on the *pedal keyboard* of an organ. So also *keyboard of light*, instrument throwing colours on a screen in Skryabin's PROMETHEUS. The term *keyboard* is also used as a general term for *a keyboard instrument* – especially in such contexts as 'Bach's keyboard works' where the works may be suitable for more than one type of keyed instrument.

key-bugle, see OPHICLEIDE.

keyed bugle, see OPHICLEIDE.

keyed trumpet, see TRUMPET.

keynote, see KEY (2).

key-signature, the indication in written music of the number of sharps or flats in the prevailing key, such indication normally being placed at the beginning of each line of music (or at any point when the key-signature is changed). Thus flat-signs on the lines or spaces in the staff denoting B, E and A indicate that these notes are to be played as B♭, E♭ and A♭ – unless an indication to the contrary is given by an ACCIDENTAL. Thus the key of E♭ major or C minor is indicated, since only these have all these three notes flat (and no others). It is the 'natural' form of the minor scale which is used to determine key-signature. See MAJOR.

Khachaturian, Aram [Ilich] (1903–78), Soviet-Armenian composer, pupil of Gnessin and Myaskovsky; aged 20 before he began professional study. Works, often influenced by Armenian folk-music, include a piano concerto (originally with a part for FLEXATONE, imitating an Armenian folk-instrument), a violin concerto, cello concerto, three symphonies; ballets GAYANEH and *Spartacus*; music to Lermontov's play MASQUERADE; choral, piano and chamber works. For 'Sabre Dance' see GAYANEH.

khorovod (Rus.), type of traditional Russian round dance with singing; one of the sections (based on a Russian folk-tune) of Stravinsky's THE FIREBIRD is so named.

Khovanshchina, see following entry.

Khovansky Affair, The (Rus. *Khovanshchina*), unfinished opera by Musorgsky; as completed by Rimsky-Korsakov, it was produced in St Petersburg, 1886. A later completion, more faithful to the composer's harmonic originality, was made by Shostakovich. Libretto, by Musorgsky and V. V. Stassov, about the princes of the Khovansky family at the time of Peter the Great.

Khrennikov, Tikhon [Nikolayevich] (b. 1913), Russian composer, pupil of Shebalin, also pianist; works include

three symphonies, two piano concertos, operas. As secretary-general of the Union of Soviet Composers, he took part in denouncing Prokofiev and other musicians for FORMALISM in 1948, and remained in his post through the 1980s.

Kienzl, Wilhelm (1857–1941), Austrian composer encouraged by Liszt and associated with Wagner; composed operas including *The Preacher* (*Der Evangelimann*), and also many piano pieces and songs.

Kikimora, work by Lyadov styled a 'legend for orchestra' and published in 1910. Kikimora is a malevolent goblin – the name is etymologically related to Fr. *cauchemar*, nightmare.

Kiladze, Grigori Varfolomeyevich (1902–62), Russian (Georgian) composer who worked in manual trades as a young man; later pupil of Shcherbachev and others. Works, some influenced by Georgian folk-music, include operas, ballets, *Heroic Symphony* and other orchestral works.

Kilpinen, Yrjö (1892–1959), Finnish composer enjoying a state grant to enable him to compose; he wrote hundreds of songs in Finnish, Swedish and German, also other works including a suite for bass viol and piano.

Kim, Young-Uck (b. 1947), Korean violinist who studied in USA and settled there; soloist with major orchestras from age 15.

Kinderscenen, see SCENES OF CHILDHOOD.

Kindertotenlieder, see SONGS ON THE DEATH OF CHILDREN.

King, Charles (1687–1748), English composer of church music, organist of

St Paul's Cathedral, London; pupil of Blow and Clarke.

King, Robert (active 1678–1726), English composer of songs, stage music, etc.; member of Charles II's band, 1680.

King, William (1624–80), English organist, priest and composer of church music and songs.

King Arthur, or The British Worthy, opera by Purcell (Z628), with libretto by Dryden, produced in London, 1691. In the convention then prevalent, it is only partly musical: King Arthur and some other leading characters do not sing.

King Christian II, play by G. Paul for which Sibelius wrote incidental music, 1898; concerns the 16th-century Danish king.

King David (Fr., *Le Roi David*), 'dramatic psalm' by Honegger – basically an oratorio with spoken narration. Words by R. Morax, after the Bible. First performed, as a stage work, in Mézières, Switzerland, 1921.

Kingdom, The, oratorio by Elgar, first performed in 1906; text from the Bible. See APOSTLES.

King Lear, play by Shakespeare, music for which includes overture by Berlioz, 1831; overture and incidental music by Balakirev, 1861; incidental music by Debussy, 1904, only two fragments surviving; opera by Reimann (*Lear*, 1978). Verdi also planned, but never completed, an opera based on the play.

'King of Prussia' Quartets, an alternative name for Mozart's set of PRUSSIAN quartets.

King Priam, opera by Tippett, produced in Coventry, 1962. Libretto, by the composer, treats the Homeric story of Greek and Trojan leaders.

King Roger (Pol., *Król Roger*), opera by Szymanowski, produced in Warsaw, 1926. Libretto by composer and J. Iwaskiewicz, about Roger II, 12th-century king of Sicily.

King Stephen, play by A. von Kotzebue for which Beethoven wrote the overture and incidental music, 1811. It refers to Stephen I of Hungary, canonized in 1083.

King Thamos (Ger., *Thamos, König in Aegypten* – i.e. in Egypt), play by Baron T. P. von Gebler for which Mozart wrote incidental music, 1773, revised and added to in 1779.

Kinsky, Georg (1882–1951), German musicologist. See BEETHOVEN.

Kipnis, Alexander (1891–1978), Russian-born bass resident in USA, with high reputation in Russian and German songs; father of Igor Kipnis (b. 1930), harpsichordist.

Kirbye, George (*c.*1565–1634), English composer of madrigals (one in THE TRIUMPHS OF ORIANA), motets, viol pieces, etc.

Kirche (Ger.), church; so *Kirchenmusik* (church music), etc.

Kirchner, Leon (b. 1910), American composer, pupil of Bloch, Schoenberg and Sessions; works include two piano concertos, a piano sonata, three string quartets. Is also pianist.

Kirkby, Emma (b. 1949), British soprano who made London début in 1974; became celebrated in baroque music, particularly for an almost vibrato-less tone which set a new model.

Kirkpatrick, Ralph (1911–84), American harpsichordist (also performer on piano and clavichord) whose biography of D. Scarlatti (1953) incorporated a catalogue of Scarlatti's works which has become standard. Thus these works are referred to by their 'Kirkpatrick' or 'K' or 'Kk' numbers. (This has superseded the LONGO numbering.)

Kirnberger, Johann Philipp (1721–83), German violinist, composer and important theorist; pupil of Bach.

Kirshbaum, Ralph (b. 1946), American cellist, resident in London since 1971. Prominent in concertos, including Tippett's Triple Concerto (see IMAI).

kit, very small type of violin formerly used by dancing-masters.

kitchen department, humorous term for the percussion section of an orchestra.

Kitezh, see INVISIBLE CITY OF KITEZH.

kithara, ancient Greek plucked string instrument of lyre type, with a squared-off box resonator at the foot.

Kjerulf, Halfdan (1815–68), Norwegian composer who studied in Leipzig. His works, including choruses, male voice quartets and songs, were among the first to bring the flavour of Norwegian folk-song into the concert-hall.

Klang (Ger.), sound; so *Klangfarbenmelodie* (sound-colour melody), a term proposed by Schoenberg, and used by him and by Webern, indicating a succession of notes produced in different instrumental sounds (whether or not at the same pitch); i.e. the change of tone-colour stands for the differentiation which, in normal melody, is effected by a change of pitch.

Klavier (Ger., in older spelling *clavier*), a keyboard, hence a keyboard instrument, particularly harpsichord or piano. For Bach's *Das wohltemperierte Klavier*, see WELL-TEMPERED CLAVIER. See also following entries.

Klavierauszug (Ger.), a piano 'reduction' – i.e. the score of an orchestral or similar work arranged for piano.

Klavierübung, see CLAVIERÜBUNG.

Klebe, Giselher [Wolfgang] (b. 1925), German composer, pupil of Blacher and others. Works include four symphonies, one of them for 42 strings; sonatas for violin and for two pianos; *Roman Elegies* (text by Goethe) for reciter with instruments; operas *The Robbers* (based on Schiller's play), *Alkmene, Figaro Seeks a Divorce* (sequel to THE MARRIAGE OF FIGARO), *Jacobowsky and the Colonel* (after Franz Werfel's play).

Kleiber, Carlos (b. 1930), German-born conductor who emigrated in boyhood with his father, Erich Kleiber (below), to Argentina; established European celebrity from the 1970s and became Austrian citizen.

Kleiber, Erich (1890–1956), conductor, Austrian-born, who rejected the Nazi régime and took Argentinian citizenship, 1938. Noted in opera (at Covent Garden 1950–53). Father of Carlos Kleiber (above).

klein (Ger.), little; *kleine Flöte* (little flute), piccolo; *kleine Trommel* (little drum), side drum. See also next entry.

kleine Nachtmusik, Eine, see EINE KLEINE NACHTMUSIK.

Klemperer, Otto (1885–1973), conductor, German-born (also composer of six symphonies, Mass, etc.), internationally noted in opera and concerts. Expelled by the Nazis (as a Jew), he became an American citizen, then (1970) an Israeli citizen. He was named principal conductor of the Philharmonia (later New Philharmonia) Orchestra, London, 1959. Also opera stage-director.

Klenovsky, Nikolai Semenovich (1857–1915), Russian composer of ballets, choral music, etc.; also conductor. Pupil of Tchaikovsky. Not to be confused with the following.

Klenovsky, Paul, the pseudonym under which Henry Wood made an orchestral arrangement (1929) of Bach's organ Toccata and Fugue in D minor.

Klien, Walter (b. 1928), Austrian pianist who has recorded all Mozart's solo piano works, all Schubert's sonatas, etc. Also studied composition with Hindemith.

Klopstock, Friedrich Gottlieb (1724–1803), German poet. See RESURRECTION SYMPHONY.

Knaben Wunderhorn, Des, see YOUTH'S MAGIC HORN.

Knappertsbusch, Hans (1888–1965), German conductor with long tenures at the Bavarian State Opera (1922–36) and Vienna State Opera (1936–50).

Knight, Joseph Philip (1812–87), British clergyman who composed 'Rocked in the cradle of the deep' and other songs.

Knipper, Lev [Konstantinovich] (1898–1974), Russian composer, pupil of Glière and, in Berlin, of Jarnach. Works include operas (one on Voltaire's Candide), 14 symphonies and Turkmenian Suite for orchestra, a violin concerto, popular choruses.

Knorr, Iwan (1853–1916), German composer of operas, chamber music, etc.; teacher in Leipzig of Quilter and C. Scott.

Knot Garden, The, opera by Tippett, first performed in London, 1970. Libretto by composer in contemporary domestic setting but with allusion to Shakespeare's The Tempest.

Knussen, Oliver (b. 1952), British composer (wrote operas Where the Wild Things Are and Higglety-Pigglety-Pop) and conductor, especially of modern works.

Koanga, opera by Delius, produced (in German) in Elberfeld, 1904; revised after Delius's death by Beecham and Edward Agate and produced in London, 1935. Libretto by C. F. Keary, Koanga being an African chief transported as a slave to America. See also BANJO and CALINDA.

Köchel, Ludwig von (1800–1877), Austrian scholar. See MOZART (W. A.).

Kodály, Zoltán (1882–1967), Hungarian composer. Collected and edited Hungarian folk-songs, partly in collaboration with Bartók; developed a strongly national idiom based on these songs. He constructed a system of music education which bears his name, and achieved a national status as composer, particularly with his PSALMUS HUNGARICUS and his opera HÁRY JÁNOS. Other works include

Concerto for Orchestra, a symphony, DANCES OF GALÁNTA, variations on the Hungarian folk-song 'The Peacock', and other orchestral works; *Dances of Marosszek* for piano (afterwards orchestrated); Missa Brevis, and other choral works; chamber music, songs, etc.

Koechlin, Charles (1867–1950), French composer, pupil of Massenet and Fauré; also writer of textbooks, etc. Works include a symphony, symphonic poems *The Law of the Jungle* and *The Bandar-Log* (both after Kipling's *The Jungle Book*), and other orchestral pieces; three string quartets, songs, piano solos.

Kogan, Leonid [Borisovich] (1924–82), Russian violinist who won first prize in Brussels international competition, 1951, and thereafter toured widely – British début, 1955; American, 1958.

Köhler, [Christian] **Louis Heinrich** (1820–86), German composer of much educational piano music, and of opera and other works; also pianist and conductor.

Kokkonen, Joonas (b. 1921), Finnish composer of five symphonies, a cello concerto, three string quartets, opera *The Last Temptations*, etc.; is also pianist, and was formerly music critic.

Kolisch Quartet, Vienna-based string quartet, 1922–39, led by Rudolf Kolisch (1896–1978), which pioneered works by Schoenberg and Berg.

Kollo (originally Kollodziewski), **René** (b. 1937), German tenor who, after beginning his career in light entertainment, won celebrity in Wagner (at Bayreuth Festival from 1969).

Kol Nidrei (Heb., All the vows), work for cello and orchestra by Bruch, published in 1881, 'after Hebrew melodies'. The title refers to a prayer associated with the annual Jewish Day of Atonement.

Kondrashin, Kirill [Petrovich] (1914–81), Russian conductor of Moscow Philharmonic, 1960–75); left USSR and became conductor of the Concertgebouw Orchestra of Amsterdam, 1979.

Kontarsky, Aloys (b. 1931) and **Alfons** (b. 1932), German pianists, celebrated since late 1950s as piano duo, especially in modern works. They are brothers: a third brother, Bernhard (b. 1937), is a pianist and conductor.

Kontrabass (Ger.), double-bass; similarly *Kontrabassposaune*, double-bass trombone, etc.

Kontrafagott (Ger.), double-bassoon.

Konzertmeister (Ger.), leader of an orchestra, (US) concert-master.

Koopman, Ton (b. 1944), Dutch harpsichordist and organist; formed the Amsterdam Baroque Orchestra in 1977.

Korbay, Francis Alexander (really Ferencz Sándor Korbay) (1846–1913), Hungarian singer, also pianist, who settled and taught in London (dying there); arranged Hungarian gipsy songs, with English words.

Korchmarev, Klementy Arkadievich (1899–1958), Russian composer of operas (including *Ten Days That Shook the World*, based on the 1917 Russian Revolution), piano music, choral symphony *Holland* (on Dutch revolutionary poems), etc.

Korean temple block, see TEMPLE BLOCK.

Kornett (Ger.) = CORNET(T), in both senses.

Korngold, Erich Wolfgang (1897–1957), Austrian-born composer, naturalized in USA, 1943. Child prodigy: at age 13, wrote piano sonata played by Schnabel. Later works include *The Dead City* and other operas, a violin concerto, piano (left-hand) concerto; also much film music – in Hollywood after 1935. Was also conductor.

Kósa, György (1897–1984), Hungarian composer (also pianist, pupil of Bartók and Dohnányi). Works include nine symphonies, eight string quartets, Easter Oratorio, opera *Tartuffe* (after Molière).

Kostelanetz, André (1903–80), conductor, Russian-born, who settled in USA, 1922, and, with his own orchestra, won fame chiefly in succulent arrangements of light music. Married the French-American soprano Lily Pons (1898–1976).

koto, a Japanese plucked stringed instrument of the zither type, usually with 13 strings, placed horizontally and played by three plectrums worn on the thumb and two fingers.

Kotónski, Wlodzimierz (b. 1925), Polish composer who studied in Paris and worked in electronic music at Cologne. Works include *Study on One Cymbal Stroke* (tape); Trio for flute, guitar and percussion; *Sirocco* for orchestra.

Kotzwara (Germanized form of original name Koczwara), **Franz** (*c.*1750–91), Czech-born violinist, double-bass player and composer who settled in London; committed suicide there. His imitative fantasia *The Battle of Prague*, for piano with optional additional instruments, formerly enjoyed great popularity.

Koussevitzky, Serge (form of name used by Sergey Alexandrovich Kusevitsky) (1874–1951), Russian-born conductor (previously double-bass player) who settled in USA; conductor of the Boston Symphony Orchestra, 1924–49. Encouraged young composers, partly by means of the Koussevitzky Music Foundation, which continues after his death. See ODE.

Koutzen, Boris (1901–66), Russian-born American composer, pupil of Glière; works include a violin concerto, *Fanfare, Prayer and March* for orchestra, etc. Also violinist.

Kovacevich, see BISHOP-KOVACEVICH.

Koven, Reginald de, see DE KOVEN.

Kozeluch (Germanized form of original name Kozeluh), **Leopold** (1747–1818), Czech composer who settled in Vienna; was one of the precursors of the 'classical' symphonic style (i.e. that of Haydn), and one of the first to compose specifically for the piano as distinct from the harpsichord. Wrote also operas, oratorio *Moses in Egypt*, etc.

Kraft, Anton (1749–1820), Bohemian-Austrian cellist and composer, member of Haydn's orchestra at Eszterháza. Composed chiefly cello music; Haydn's Cello Concerto in D was, for a time, attributed to him.

Kraft, William (b. 1923), American composer, also percussionist and conductor. Works include *Configurations* for four percussionists and jazz orchestra, song-cycle *Silent Boughs* for soprano and string orchestra.

Krakowiak, Polish dance in quick 2/4 time from the Cracow region.

Kraus, Alfredo (b. 1927), Spanish tenor of Austrian descent; achieved highest distinction in Italian opera repertory at Covent Garden, etc.

Kraus, Lili (1903–86), Hungarian pianist who took New Zealand nationality, then American; noted in Mozart; resumed career after Japanese internment during World War II.

Krause, Tom (b. 1934), Finnish baritone, noted for concert and operatic performances in many languages; sang at Glyndebourne from 1963.

Krauss, Clemens (1893–1954), Austrian conductor, director of opera in Vienna, Berlin and Munich successively; friend and noted interpreter of R. Strauss; joint librettist (with the composer) of Strauss's opera CAPRICCIO; was married to Viorica URSULEAC.

Krebs, Johann Ludwig (1713–80), German organist and composer of church music, keyboard works, etc.; a favourite pupil of Bach.

Krein, Alexander Abramovich (1883–1951), Russian composer of ballet, patriotic cantatas, etc., and also of works with Jewish associations – e.g. operas *The Youth of Abraham* and *The Maccabees*. Brother of the following.

Krein, Grigory Abramovich (1879–1955), Russian composer, pupil of Glière and (in Leipzig) of Reger. Works include two piano concertos, much chamber music. Brother of the preceding.

Kreisler, Fritz (1875–1962), Austrian violinist of enormous fame; also composer of string quartet, operettas and especially of violin pieces some of which he fathered on various 17th- and 18th-century composers (admitting his hoax in 1935). See PUGNANI.

Kreisleriana, cycle of piano pieces by Schumann, 1838, dedicated to Chopin – referring to the character of the eccentric musician Kreisler, created in the writings of E. T. A. HOFFMANN.

Krejči, Iša (1904–68), Czech composer, pupil of Novák and Jirák; works include opera *The Uproar at Ephesus* (after Shakespeare's *The Comedy of Errors*), Sinfonietta, a nonet and other chamber music.

Kremer, Gidon (b. 1947), Soviet-Latvian violinist, prominent in new music; mainly resident in the West, he founded the Lockenhaus Festival in Austria which became established in the late 1980s.

Krenek, Ernst (b. 1900), Austrian-born composer of partly Czech descent, resident in the USA since 1938; US citizen, 1954. Pupil of Schreker; married (formerly) to Mahler's daughter Anna. Discarded the Czech spelling (Křenek) of his name. Showed jazz influence in very successful opera JOHNNY STRIKES UP, 1927; later operas include *The Life of Orestes* and *The Golden Ram*. Has also written five symphonies, four piano concertos, Symphonic Elegy (for strings, in memory of Webern), and various works with specifically American associations – orchestral variations on the folk-tune 'I wonder as I wander', choral *Santa Fé Time-table* (on names of railway stations), etc. Has also made use of electronic music. Is also teacher and writer of textbooks, e.g. on Ockeghem.

Kreutzer, Conradin (1780–1849), German pianist, conductor and composer of *The Night-camp in Granada* and other operas.

Kreutzer, Rodolphe (1766–1831), French violinist and composer of 19 violin concertos, over 40 operas, etc.; friend of Beethoven. See following entry.

Kreutzer Sonata, nickname for Beethoven's Sonata in A (1803) for violin and piano, dedicated to Rodolphe Kreutzer.

Křička, Jaroslav (1882–1969), Czech composer of operas, overture to Maeterlinck's *The Blue Bird*, song-cycles, etc.; also conductor. Was 'involuntarily retired' in Czechoslovakia, 1945.

Krieger, Johann Philipp (1651–1725), German composer, partly trained in Italy. Wrote Masses and other church music, instrumental suites, etc., as did his brother Johann (1652–1734).

Krips, Josef (1902–74), Austrian conductor, prominent in London orchestral life after World War II; principal conductor, London Symphony Orchestra, 1950–54.

Kronos Quartet, American string quartet founded in 1973 by its leader, David Harrington; it plays modern works almost exclusively.

Kubelík, [Jeronym] Rafael (b. 1914), Czech conductor; left post-1945 Communist Czechoslovakia; naturalized Swiss, 1973. Music director of Covent Garden Opera, 1955–8; of Metropolitan Opera, New York, 1972–4. Also composer. His father was the violinist Jan Kubelík (1880–1940); married the soprano Elsie Morison (b. 1924).

Kubik, Gail [Thompson] (1914–84), American violinist, conductor and composer – pupil of Piston and N. Boulanger. Works include three symphonies, two violin concertos (no. 1 withdrawn), cantata *In Praise of Johnny Appleseed,* music for film cartoon *Gerald McBoing Boing.*

Kuhlau, Friedrich (1786–1832), German flautist and composer who settled in Denmark and wrote Danish operas, keyboard works, etc. Died in Copenhagen.

Kuhnau, Johann (1660–1722), German composer and organist, Bach's immediate predecessor in Leipzig. Wrote harpsichord works including so-called *Biblical Sonatas,* which are early examples of ILLUSTRATIVE MUSIC; also motets and other church music.

Kullak, Theodor (1818–82), German composer of much educational piano music; also of piano concerto, etc.

Kunst der Fuge, Die, see ART OF FUGUE.

Kurtag, György (b. 1926), Hungarian composer who studied in Paris, 1957–8, and did not start numbering his works (op. 1, etc.) until after that. Works include *Messages of the late Miss R. V. Trusova* (Russian text) for soprano and instrumental ensemble; duos for violin and cimbalom; *The Little Predicament* for piccolo, trombone and guitar.

Kuula, Toivo (1883–1918), Finnish composer of cantatas, orchestral music, etc., in a Finnish national style; also conductor. Pupil of Busoni and Sibelius. Was shot dead in a street fight.

Kvapil, Jaroslav (1892–1958), Czech

composer of four symphonies, cantata *The Lion-hearted* (on movement for Czechoslovak independence in World War I), etc., also pianist and organist.

Kyrie eleison (Gk.), Lord have mercy [on us], part of the Mass, often referred to simply as 'Kyrie'.

L

L, abbr. for (1) Licentiate (in musical diplomas, e.g. LRAM – Licentiate of the Royal Academy of Music); (2) London (as in LPO, LSO – London Philharmonic Orchestra, London Symphony Orchestra); (3) LONGO (in numbering D. Scarlatti's works; but see KIRKPATRICK).

l, symbol in TONIC SOL-FA notation for the sixth degree (submediant) of the scale, pronounced *lah*.

l' (Fr., It.), the.

la, the note A (in Latin countries, and formerly elsewhere); cp. LAH.

la (Fr., It., Sp.), the.

Lablache, Luigi (1794–1858), Italian bass of French and Irish descent, celebrated in opera, singing in the first performance of Donizetti's *Don Pasquale*, 1843.

Lac des cygnes, Le, see SWAN LAKE.

Ladmirault, Paul Émile (1877–1944), French composer of piano works, operas, church music, etc.; his music often has specifically Breton associations.

Lady Macbeth of the Mtsensk District, see KATERINA IZMAILOVA.

Lady Nevill's Book, see MY LADY NEVILL'S BOOK.

lah, in TONIC SOL-FA, the spoken name for the sixth degree (submediant) of the scale, written l. Cp. LA.

la Hale, Adam de (or Halle) (*c*.1230–*c*.1286), French minstrel (TROUVÈRE) known as 'The Hunchback of Arras'. Works include motets, secular songs, and *Robin and Marion* (Fr., *Le Jeu de Robin et de Marion*), a comic play with music. He died in Naples.

lai, see LAY.

Lajtha, László (1892–1963), Hungarian composer (also pianist) who worked in France and Switzerland. Followed Bartók in collecting and editing Hungarian folk-music. Works include nine symphonies, 10 string quartets, ballets; also writer on music.

Lakmé, opera by Delibes, produced in Paris, 1883. Libretto by E. Gondinet and P. Gille, the title-role being that of the daughter of a Brahmin priest, in love with a British officer.

Lalande, Michel Richard de (1657–1756), French composer and organist; worked at the French court from 1683, becoming master of the French Chapel Royal from 1714; celebrated for church music, he also wrote operas. (The surname is also encountered as Delalande.)

Lalo, [Victor Antoine] Édouard

(1823–92), French composer, also
viola-player; composed little until his
40s. Works include SPANISH SYM-
PHONY (*Symphonie espagnole*) and other
works for violin and orchestra; opera
The King of Ys (*Le Roi d'Ys*), ballet *Nam-
ouna*; chamber music and songs.

Lambert, Constant (1905–51), British
conductor (particularly of ballet), composer, arranger (e.g. of ballet COMUS),
and writer on music. Works – influenced by jazz in, e.g., THE RIO GRANDE
and a piano concerto – also include
Summer's Last Will and Testament (baritone, chorus and orchestra); *Horo-
scope* and other ballets; songs; film
music.

lament, a piece of music signifying grief
especially at a death; and, specifically,
a type of piece for bagpipes played at
Scottish clan funerals.

Lamentations, the biblical Lamentations of the prophet Jeremiah, traditionally sung (in plainsong or to other
settings) in Roman Catholic churches
in the week before Easter. See also
THRENI.

'Lamentation' Symphony, nickname
for Haydn's Symphony no. 26 in D
minor, composed about 1767–8 (Hob.
I: 26); so called because certain
themes resemble plainsong melodies
sung in Roman Catholic churches in
the week before Easter (see preceding
entry). Sometimes the form 'Lamenta-
tione' – bastard Latin-cum-Italian – is
encountered.

Lamoureux Orchestra, a Paris orchestra founded in 1881 by its conductor,
Charles Lamoureux (1834–99), and remaining important after his death.

lancers, a type of QUADRILLE which
became popular in the second half of
the 19th century.

Landi, Steffano (*c*.1586–1639), Italian
composer of church music and operas;
also singer in the Papal choir.

Landini, Francesco [or Landino]
(*c*.1335–97), Italian organist, lutenist
and composer (also poet); blind from
early childhood. Wrote concerted
vocal music of various kinds, and was
an exponent of ARS NOVA. Born, lived
and died in Florence. See the following.

Landino, alternative form of LANDINI'S
surname; *Landino sixth*, a type of
cadence characteristically found in his
music. In this the leading-note falls to
the submediant before rising from that
note to the tonic; i.e. the sixth degree
of the scale is inserted between the
seventh and the eighth. Thus this
term does not refer to 'a sixth' in the
harmonic sense but to the melodic insertion of the sixth degree of the scale.

Ländler (sing. or pl.), type of dance in
triple time originating in rural Austria
and being a slow variant of the
waltz. Beethoven and Schubert wrote
examples.

Land of Hope and Glory, see POMP
AND CIRCUMSTANCE.

Landowska, Wanda (1877–1959),
Polish-born harpsichordist and authority on old music, etc.; long resident
in France, then from 1941 in USA.
Falla's Harpsichord Concerto was written for her.

Landré, Guillaume [Louis Frédéric]
(1905–68), Dutch composer, pupil of
his father (below) and of Pijper.
Works, favouring CYCLIC FORM, include four symphonies and a *Sinfonia
sacra* in memory of his father, a violin
concerto, much chamber music; also
opera *Jean Lévecq* (after Maupassant's
'The Return'), etc. Also critic.

Landré, Willem (form of name used by Guillaume Louis Frédéric Landré) (1874–1948), Dutch composer of French descent, father of Guillaume Landré (above). Wrote operas, cantatas, *Little Suite on the Notes E–F* for orchestra, etc. Also critic.

Langlais, Jean [François Hyacinthe] (b. 1907), French composer (pupil of Dukas) and organist, blind from infancy; has written mostly for organ (including three concertos) but also orchestral and other works.

Lanier (or **Laniere**) **Nicholas** (1588–1666), English composer, the most prominent of a musical family of that surname. Master of the King's Music to Charles I and Charles II; Italian-influenced, he is said to have introduced the recitative to England. Was also singer and painter. Composed songs, some for masques.

Lanner, Joseph [Franz Karl] (1801–43), Austrian violinist, orchestra-leader, and composer of over 200 waltzes and other light music; the chief rival of Johann Strauss the elder.

Laparra, Raoul (1876–1943), French composer primarily of Spanish-influenced music, e.g. opera *La Habanera*; he was his own librettist. Killed in an air-raid near Paris.

Lara, Isidore de, see DE LARA.

largamente (It.), broadly – a term usually denoting a spacious and deliberate style rather than a clear indication of slow tempo. Cp. LARGO, from which it is derived.

large, the note of the largest time-value in the notation which grew up in the Middle Ages and gave rise to the present notation. It was divisible into either two or three LONGS.

larghetto (It., a little largo), direction indicating a speed not quite as slow as LARGO.

largo (It., broad), slow; but see LARGAMENTE. For the aria referred to as 'Handel's Largo', see XERXES.

Lark Ascending, The, 'romance' by Vaughan Williams for violin and orchestra after a poem by Meredith; composed in 1914 but not performed till 1921.

'Lark' Quartet, nickname of Haydn's String Quartet in D, op. 64, no. 5, composed *c.*1790–92 (Hob. III: 63) – named from the high-soaring violin part at the opening.

Larrocha, Alicia de (b. 1923), Spanish pianist who was a child prodigy but became internationally prominent only in the mid-1960s; directs an academy in Barcelona.

Larsson, Lars-Erik (1908–86), Swedish composer, pupil of Berg in Vienna; also conductor and critic. Works include concertos for violin, for cello, for saxophone; piano sonatas; Missa Brevis for chorus; opera *The Princess of Cyprus*; etc.

la Rue, Pierre de (*c.*1460–1518), Flemish (Netherlandish) composer of 36 known Masses, also of chansons, etc.; in service to the court of Burgundy.

Lasso, Orlando di, see LASSUS.

lassú (Hung.), the slow section of a CSÁRDÁS.

Lassus, Roland de (Italianized form, Orlando di Lasso) (*c.*1532–94), Flemish composer. Choirboy in Mons, his birthplace; afterwards choirmaster at the church of St John Lateran, Rome, and then worked in Antwerp before taking service at the Bavarian court in

Munich. He settled there (travelling to Italy, however) and died in Munich. His works, all for two or (usually) more voices, number more than 2,000 and include madrigals and similar works to French, German and Italian poetry, as well as much religious music – Masses, motets, miscellaneous biblical settings in Latin, settings of various texts in Italian, etc.

lauda, laude (It.), a song of praise; *lauda spirituale* or *laude spirituale* (pl., *laudi spirituali*), type of Italian religious song for several voices, having its own distinctive poetry and sung (14th–18th centuries) by a religious confraternity called the *laudisti*. This type of work is reckoned a forerunner of ORATORIO.

Lauda Sion (Lat., Praise, O Zion), a Roman Catholic hymn (SEQUENCE) for the feast of Corpus Christi, sung either to traditional plainsong or to other settings.

laudi, see LAUDA.

'Laudon' Symphony, nickname for Haydn's Symphony no. 69 in C (Hob. I: 69), 1778–9, composed in honour of the Austrian field-marshal so named.

lavolta, English name for a dance popular in Elizabethan times, featuring a leap (It., *volta*). One is included in Britten's GLORIANA.

Lawes, Henry (1596–1662), English composer in service at court; celebrated in a sonnet by Milton, having set Milton's COMUS. Wrote coronation anthem for Charles II, songs (some to poems by Herrick), church music; collaborated in the music to THE SIEGE OF RHODES, the first English opera, 1656. Brother of William Lawes.

Lawes, William (1602–45), English composer of masques, songs, music for viols and violins, etc.; pupil of J. Cooper, Musician to Charles I; killed while fighting on Royalist side in the Civil War. Brother of Henry Lawes.

lay (English equivalent of Fr., *lai*), 13th-century French narrative poem set to music. The term is also encountered for a purely instrumental work of that period, and in certain more general references (e.g. in Chaucer) it simply means 'a song'.

Lazarof, Henri (b. 1932), Bulgarian-born American composer who uses this French spelling of his name; pupil of Ben-Haim in Jerusalem and of Petrassi in Rome. Works include a viola concerto, a cello concerto, Concerto for piano and 20 instruments, Octet for wind, *Asymptotes* for flute and vibraphone.

le (Fr. masc. sing., It. fem. pl.), the.

lead, see LEADER.

leader, the directing member of an ensemble, e.g. a string quartet or a pop group. But as applied to an orchestra, *leader* in Britain means the principal violinist (US, concertmaster) as the chief performer, whereas in USA it is an alternative term for conductor. Similarly with 'to lead'.

leading-motive, English equivalent term for Ger. *Leitmotiv* (not-*motif*) – a musical theme used (particularly in Wagner's operas) recurrently to denote an object, an aspect of character, etc.

leading-note, the seventh degree of the major scale, so called because it seems to lead upwards to the TONIC a semitone above it. In the minor scale this note (e.g. B♮ in the key of C minor) is commonly used in ascending but not in descending. See MAJOR.

leading seventh, term which is in fact an abbreviation for 'chord of the minor seventh built on the leading-note' – e.g., in C major, the chord B, D, F, A (reading upwards). This is characteristically produced on the harmonica, by sucking.

Lear, Edward (1812–88), British writer. See GERHARD, PETRASSI.

Lebègue, Nicolas Antoine (*c*.1631–1702), French organist and composer of works for organ, for harpsichord, and for voices; in service to Louis XIV.

Leclair, Jean Marie (1697–1764), French violinist and composer – and, in his 20s, a ballet-master. For a time played in the Paris Opéra orchestra, and himself wrote opera and ballets as well as 12 violin concertos and other violin music. Visited Holland to meet Locatelli, and shortly after a second visit there was murdered near his home in Paris.

Lecocq, Alexandre Charles (1832–1918). French composer, also organist. From 1868 successful with dozens of operettas including *Madame Angot's Daughter* (*La Fille de Mme Angot*), from which the ballet *Mam'-zelle Angot* (1947) is derived, and *Giroflé-Giroflà*.

ledger line, short line written above or below the staff to accommodate notes outside the staff – as in the following: (This is the correct

spelling, but 'leger line' is also encountered.)

Lees, Benjamin (b. 1924), American composer, born in China. Works include three symphonies; Concerto for string quartet and orchestra; cantata *Visions of Poets*.

Leeuw, Ton de (b. 1926), Dutch composer, pupil of Messiaen (in Paris) and Badings; also pianist and critic. Works include a piano concerto; two symphonies; orchestral *Funeral Music for Willem Pijper*; radiophonic oratorio *Job*; opera *The Dream*; chamber works.

Lefanu, Nicola (b. 1947), British composer, daughter of Maconchy, pupil in Italy of Petrassi; also teacher. Works include opera *Dawnpath*; *Farne* for orchestra; *Antiworld* (based on Russian texts) for dancer, two voices and three instruments.

Lefébure-Wély, Louis James Alfred (1817–69), French organist, performing from age eight, and composer chiefly of organ works.

le Gallienne, Dorian (1915–63), Australian composer, pupil in England of Howells, Benjamin and Jacob. Works include Sinfonietta, incidental music to plays, piano solos, songs. Also critic.

legato (It., bound together), smoothly, not STACCATO – as a direction for performance.

Legend of the Invisible City of Kitezh and of the Maid Fevronia, The, see INVISIBLE CITY OF KITEZH.

léger (Fr., light), *légèrement*, lightly; *musique légère*, light music.

leger line, see LEDGER LINE.

leggero, leggeramente (It.), light, lightly. (The spellings 'leggiero', 'leggieramente' are obsolete in Italian, though still found in the scores of ill-informed composers and publishers.)

leggiero, leggieramente, see preceding.

legno (It.), wood; *bacchetta di legno*, (instruction to drummer to use) wooden-headed drum-stick; *col legno*, with the wood – instruction to string-player to hit the string with the back of the bow instead of with the hair, producing a dry and rather grotesque sound, e.g. in Saint-Saëns's DANSE MACABRE).

Lehár, Ferencz (Germanized as Franz, but surname not Léhar) (1870–1948), Hungarian composer, for a time violinist and military bandmaster; wrote a violin concerto, etc., but mainly many successful Viennese operettas including *The Count of Luxembourg*, *Frederica*, *The Land of Smiles*, THE MERRY WIDOW.

Lehmann, Lilli (1848–1929), German soprano, celebrated in opera and for a repertory of more than 600 songs. Helped to organize early Salzburg festivals.

Lehmann, Liza (form of name used by Elizabetta Nina Mary Frederika Lehmann) (1862–1918), British soprano and composer. Works include *In a Persian Garden* (words from Fitzgerald's translation of Omar Khayyám) and other song-cycles, and opera *The Vicar of Wakefield* (after Goldsmith). See BEDFORD.

Lehmann, Lotte (1888–1976), operatic and concert soprano, German-born, naturalized in USA; also novelist and autobiographer.

Leibowitz, René (1913–72), French (Polish-born) composer, conductor, and noted theoretician, pupil of Ravel,

Schoenberg and Webern. Works include piano and choral music; Chamber Symphony; *The Explanation of Metaphors* for speaker, two pianos, harp and percussion.

leicht (Ger.), (1) light; (2) easy.

Leiferkus, Sergey (b. 1946), Russian baritone who sang opera in his native Leningrad from 1972; a much admired visiting singer in the West, beginning with the Wexford Festival, 1983.

Leigh, Walter (1905–42), British composer of light opera *The Jolly Roger* and other theatre music, Concertino for harpsichord and strings, etc.; pupil of Hindemith. Killed in action in Libya.

Leighton, Kenneth (1929–88), British composer, pupil of Petrassi in Rome. Works include three piano concertos; concertos for violin, viola, cello, organ; a piano trio; Mass; opera *Columba*. Also teacher at Edinburgh University, pianist and conductor.

Leinsdorf, Erich (b. 1912), American conductor, born and trained in Vienna; conducted opera at the Metropolitan, New York, from 1938; conductor of the Boston Symphony Orchestra, 1962–9.

Leitmotiv, see LEADING-MOTIVE.

le Jeune, Claude (*c.*1530–1600), French composer of Protestant church music (including psalm-settings), chansons, etc.; held court appointment under Henri IV.

Lekeu, Guillaume (1870–94), Belgian composer, pupil of Franck and d'Indy. Works include a piano quartet and cello sonata, both completed by d'Indy after Lekeu's early death from typhoid; also orchestral *Fantasy on two Angevin Airs*, etc.

Lemare, Edwin Henry (1865–1934), British organist who performed much in USA and died in Los Angeles; composed much organ music including two solo 'symphonies'.

Lemminkäinen's Homecoming, orchestral work by Sibelius referring to one of the heroes of the Kalevala (Finnish national epic); it is no. 4 of four pieces about Lemminkäinen, no. 3 being THE SWAN OF TUONELA.

Lenau, Nikolaus (1802–50), Austrian poet. See FAUST, EPISODES FROM LENAU'S.

Léner Quartet, Austro-Hungarian string quartet (active 1918–48) led by Jenö Léner; particularly celebrated in recordings of the 1930s.

Leningrad Philharmonic Orchestra, Russian orchestra founded in 1921; conductor from 1988, Temirkanov.

'Leningrad' Symphony, nickname for Shostakovich's Symphony no. 7, glorifying the spirit of besieged Leningrad and partly composed there, 1941.

lent, lento (Fr., It.), slow.

Lenya (also spelt Lenja), **Lotte** (1898–1981), Austrian-born actress and singer, famous in works by her husband, Kurt Weill, e.g. *The Threepenny Opera*. Refugees from the Nazis, they emigrated to USA.

Lenz, Jakob [Michael Reinhold] (1751–92), German playwright. See SOLDIERS.

Leo, Leonardo (1694–1744), Italian composer working in Naples. His comic operas, some in Neapolitan dialect, are considered (with Pergolesi's) pioneers of their type. Wrote, or contributed numbers to, about 70 operas in all; other works include oratorios, church music, harpsichord pieces.

Leoncavallo, Ruggero (1857–1919), Italian composer of PAGLIACCI (Clowns), his only successful opera, 1892. Before this worked as café pianist, etc. Was encouraged by Wagner and, acting as his own librettist, wrote various other operas including LA BOHÈME which failed where Puccini's on the same subject succeeded. Other works include operettas, symphonic poem *Serafita*.

Leonhardt, Gustav (b. 1928), Dutch organist and harpsichordist, director of his own ensemble in historically oriented performances of baroque music.

Léonin (also Leoninus, *Lat.*), French composer active about 1163–90 as church musician in Paris: wrote a cycle of two-part organa (see OR- GANUM) for all the principal church feasts of the year.

Leonora, form generally used in English for Ger. 'Leonore' or Fr. 'Léonore', as in the following: (1) the name of the heroine of Beethoven's opera FIDE- LIO – hence Beethoven's *Leonora Overtures* nos. 1, 2 and 3 (the numbering, formerly thought chronologically deceptive, is now considered correct). Each of these was in its time intended as the overture to the opera, but all were eventually superseded for this purpose by the overture now actually called *Fidelio*. The 'Leonora' overtures are now heard as concert pieces; and no. 3, the best-known, is also sometimes performed (without authority from Beethoven) as an orchestral interlude during the opera. In modern use 'Leonora' as a title sometimes distinguishes the rare revival of Beethoven's earliest (1805) version of the opera – but this distinction also has no authority, all Beethoven's versions having been staged originally as *Fidelio*. (2) title of the opera by Gaveaux (*Leonora, or Wedded Love*), produced in Paris in 1798, from the libretto of which (by J. N. Bouilly) the plot of Beethoven's FIDELIO derives. See also PAER. (3) name used (with reference to Beethoven's use) in the title of Liebermann's opera *Leonora 40/45* (produced in Basle, 1952, with libretto by composer) in which, as in FIDELIO, love triumphs over officialdom, this time in World War II. (4) see FRY.

Leonore; Leonore 40/45, see preceding entry. (The name is the German form of Leonora.)

Leppard, Raymond (b. 1927), British conductor, formerly Cambridge University teacher; prominent in revival of early baroque opera (Monteverdi and Cavalli) in his own editions, especially at Glyndebourne since 1962. Conductor of BBC Northern Symphony Orchestra, 1973–80, though mainly resident in USA from 1977. CBE, 1983.

Lermontov, Mikhail Yurevich (1814–41), Russian poet and novelist. See MASQUERADE.

Leroux, Xavier Napoléon (1863–1919), French composer, pupil of Massenet; also critic. Works include opera *The Tramp* (*Le Chemineau*) using French peasant songs; also other operas, church music, songs, etc.

les (Fr.), the.

Leschetizky, Theodor (Germanized form of Teodor Leszetycki) (1830–1915), Polish piano teacher mainly active in St Petersburg and Vienna; developed a famous 'method', and

taught Paderewski and other noted pianists. Also composer of operas, piano solos, etc.

Leskov, Nikolay Semeonovich (1831–95), Russian writer. See KATERINA IZMAILOVA.

lesson, English term used in 17th–18th centuries for a short keyboard piece or a set of such pieces (i.e. a SUITE). No teaching purpose is implied. Cp. EXERCISE.

le Sueur, Jean François, see the following.

Lesueur, Jean François (1760–1837), French composer who wrote church music using orchestra and then, when this met with disapproval, wrote spectacular operas and French Revolutionary pieces using enormous forces. In court service to Napoleon and then to Louis XVIII. Taught Berlioz and Gounod.

Lesur, Daniel [Jean Yves] (b. 1908), French composer of orchestral music, *The Inner Life* for organ, piano solos, songs, opera *Andrea del Sarto*, etc. Also pianist and organist. With Baudrier, Jolivet and Messiaen, he formed the 'Young France' group, and collaborated with Jolivet in a ballet, *The Child and the Monster*.

Let's Make an Opera!, Britten's 'entertainment for young people' (his own description) produced at Aldeburgh, 1949. It incorporates a miniature opera, *The Little Sweep* – about a maltreated boy chimney-sweep of the mid 19th century – most of the roles in which are for children. This opera is rehearsed in the first section of the 'entertainment' and performed, with the audience's vocal participation, in the second. Libretto by Eric Crozier.

221

Leveridge, Richard (c.1670–1758), English bass singer and composer chiefly of songs (including 'The Roast Beef of Old England') and stage music, etc.

Levine, James (b. 1943), American conductor; music director, Metropolitan Opera, since 1975; also pianist, often directing concertos from the keyboard.

Lewis, Anthony [Carey] (1915–83), British composer, conductor and authority on 17th- and 18th-century English music. Pupil of N. Boulanger. Formerly with BBC, then professor at Birmingham University; 1968–82, principal of RAM. Knighted, 1972.

Lewis, Richard (1914–90), British tenor noted in opera (Glyndebourne, Covent Garden, etc.) and oratorio. Created the part of Troilus in Walton's TROILUS AND CRESSIDA. CBE, 1962.

Lewkovitch, Bernhard (b. 1927), Danish composer, also Roman Catholic choirmaster and organist; works include Masses, motets, five piano sonatas. Also critic.

Ley, Henry George (1887–1962), British organist and composer (songs, church music, etc.); Precentor (i.e. musical director) of Eton College, 1926–45.

l.h., left hand (e.g. in piano-playing).

Lhévinne, Josef (1874–1944) and **Rosina** (1880–1976), Russian-born American pianists, husband and wife, who became outstanding teachers, e.g. at the Juilliard School, New York.

Liadov, see LYADOV.

Liapunov, see LYAPUNOV.

libretto (It., booklet), the text of an opera – or sometimes of an oratorio or other non-stage work. Plural *libretti* (It.) or *librettos* (Anglicized).

licenza (It.), licence, freedom: *con alcuna licenza* (or *con alcune licenze*, plural), with some freedom(s) as to performance, or as to the construction of a work (when it is not tied to a 'strict' pattern).

Lidholm, Ingvar [Natanael] (b. 1921), Swedish composer who studied in London with Seiber, 1954, and was formerly conductor and Swedish Radio executive. Works include *Mutanza* (It., Mutation) and other works for orchestra; the scena *Nausicaa Alone* for soprano, chorus, orchestra; television opera *The Dutchman*; chamber music; Concertino for flute, oboe, English horn and cello (without orchestra).

Lie, Sigurd (1871–1904), Norwegian composer, also violinist and conductor, who before dying of tuberculosis wrote a symphony, many songs, violin sonata, etc.

Liebermann, Rolf (b. 1910), Swiss composer of *Leonora 40/45* (see LEONORA), *School for Wives* and other operas; also of Concerto for jazz band and symphony orchestra, etc. Was also conductor and critic – but chiefly known as administrator of Hamburg State Opera, 1959–72, then of Paris Opera till 1980.

Liebeslieder-Walzer, see LOVE-SONG WALTZES.

Liebestraum (Ger., a dream of love; pl. *-träume*), title given by Liszt to his piano arrangements (1850) of three of his songs. No. 3 is the well-known one.

lieblich (Ger.), lovely; *lieblich Gedackt* (organ stop), same as GEDACKT.

Lied (Ger., pl. *Lieder*), song; specifically, in the non-German-speaking world, the type of song with piano composed by, e.g., Schubert, Schumann and Wolf. The term is dubiously applied also to songs not in German but of a similar kind, e.g. by Grieg. For the term *Lieder recital* instead of 'song recital' there is no excuse unless the programme is exclusively of German song. See also the following entries.

Lieder eines fahrenden Gesellen, see SONGS OF A WAYFARER.

Liederkranz, Liederkreis (Ger.) = song-CYCLE. *Liederkreis* is used as the actual title of two cycles by Schumann (op. 24, op. 39 – both 1840), to poems by Heine and by Eichendorff.

Lied(er) ohne Worte, see SONGS WITHOUT WORDS.

Liedertafel (Ger., song-table – referring to origin in drinking-gatherings), male-voice choir in German or German-descended communities, e.g. in USA and South Australia.

Lied von der Erde, Das, see SONG OF THE EARTH.

Lier, Bertus van (1906–72), Dutch cellist, conductor (pupil of Scherchen), critic, teacher and composer (pupil of Pijper). Works include three symphonies, *The Dyke* for orator and orchestra, stage music, unaccompanied cello sonata.

Life for the Tsar, A (Rus., *Zhizn za Tsarya*), opera by Glinka, produced in St Petersburg, 1836; libretto, by G. F. Rosen, based on a 17th-century patriotic subject. The composer's or-iginally intended title was *Ivan Susanin* (after the peasant hero), a title which was generally adopted under the Soviet régime to 1989, with an altered libretto not extolling the Tsar; the Bolshoi Theatre re-introduced the original libretto and the 'Tsarist' title in 1989.

ligature, (1) a symbol in medieval musical notation which combines one or more notes in succession; (2) in standard notation, a slur-mark indicating a group of notes all sung to the same syllable (term sometimes also used in instrumental music when the SLUR indicates that notes are to be phrased together); (3) on the clarinet, saxophone, etc., the metal band which secures the reed to the mouthpiece.

Ligeti, György (b. 1923), Hungarian composer who left Hungary in 1956, taking Austrian nationality and becoming professor in Hamburg, 1973–89. Works include opera THE GREAT MACABRE; music-theatre pieces *Adventures* and *New Adventures* (using a meaningless language); *Atmospheres* and *Lontano* (It., Distant) for orchestra; *Articulation* for recorded tape; *Symphonic Poem* for 100 metronomes.

light, term applied to music supposedly not requiring the listener's full concentration; *light orchestra*, orchestra providing this. So also *light opera*, imprecise non-technical term sometimes used by laymen in opposition to 'grand opera' (also imprecise), and not clearly distinguishable from 'operetta'.

Lighthouse, The, opera by P. M. Davies, produced in Edinburgh, 1980; libretto, by the composer, deals with a true story of the unexplained disappearance of three lighthouse-keepers.

Lilburn, Douglas [Gordon] (b. 1915), New Zealand composer, partly trained in London. Works include *Aotearoa* (Maori name for New Zealand) for orchestra, three symphonies, a string trio and other chamber music, piano solos.

Lill, John [Richard] (b. 1944), British pianist, joint winner (with Vladimir Krainev) of the Moscow Tchaikovsky Competition, 1970. He has specialized in Beethoven. OBE, 1978.

Lily of Killarney, The, opera by Benedict, produced in London, 1862 (and long a favourite in Britain); libretto by J. Oxenford and D. Boucicault, after the latter's play *The Colleen Bawn*.

Lincoln Portrait, work for narrator and orchestra by Copland, on the sayings of Abraham Lincoln; first performed in 1942.

Lind, Jenny (originally Johanna Maria) (1820–87), Swedish soprano who won European fame in opera but gave up opera for concerts at age 29; made celebrated US tour managed by Barnum, 1850–51. Settled in UK, she became in her 60s a celebrated teacher at Royal College of Music.

linear counterpoint, term – senseless, because all counterpoint is a matter of lines – sometimes used for a type of 20th-century counterpoint (e.g. Stravinsky's) held to be musically valid through the value of the separate lines themselves and not through their mutual harmonization.

linke Hand (Ger.), left hand.

Linley, Thomas (1733–95), British composer, especially for the stage; composed the song 'Here's to the Maiden' for Sheridan's *The School for Scandal*. Was also singing-teacher and concert-promoter. Father of Elizabeth Ann Linley, singer, who married Sheridan. See also next entry.

Linley, Thomas (1756–78), British composer of opera *The Cady of Baghdad*, etc., and with his father (see preceding entry), of music for Sheridan's THE DUENNA. In boyhood, studied in Italy, met Mozart there and became his firm friend; met early death by drowning.

'Linz' Symphony, nickname for Mozart's Symphony no. 36 in C, K425, composed in Linz and first performed there in 1783.

Lipatti, Dinu (diminutive of Constantin) (1917–50), Romanian pianist, also composer; illness restricted his career, but his recordings continued after his death to win much admiration.

lira (It.), (1) LYRE; (2) the VIELLE in its medieval sense (bowed string instrument, not the hurdy-gurdy); (3) term used in various compound names, e.g. *lira da braccio* (. . . for the arm), type of bowed string instrument developed in the late 15th century, with a less pronounced 'waist' than that of the violin; *lira da gamba* (for the leg), a larger relation of this; *lira organizzata*, superior type of hurdy-gurdy (with organ-like pipes) composed for by Haydn.

Liszt, Ferencz (Germanized as Franz) (1811–86), Hungarian pianist and composer. As child prodigy pianist, visited France and Britain. Lived with the Countess d'Agoult, 1833–44, one of their children (Cosima) later becoming Wagner's wife. From 1848 lived with the Princess Sayn-Wittgenstein, whose eventual effort to secure a divorce from her husband failed; Liszt separated from her in 1861, never married, and in 1865 took minor orders in the Roman Catholic Church and was referred to as 'the Abbé Liszt'. He revisited London in 1886. He consistently aided new composers from Berlioz to Grieg, and made Weimar a highly important centre when he was court musical director there, 1848–59. His piano works include a sonata (pioneering one-movement form), also DANTE SONATA, 20 HUNGARIAN RHAPSODIES, MAZEPPA (also for orchestra), and other pieces with allusive titles; and many operatic paraphrases, transcriptions of other composers' work, etc. Arranged Schubert's WANDERER FANTASY in a version for piano and orchestra. Also composed THE PRELUDES, ORPHEUS, HAMLET, DANTE SYMPHONY, FAUST SYMPHONY, *Episodes from Lenau's 'Faust'* (see FAUST), etc., for orchestra; four MEPHISTO WALTZES; MALEDICTION for piano and orchestra; VIA CRUCIS and other church works; more than 70 songs in French, German, Italian, Hungarian and English (e.g. on Tennyson's 'Go not, happy day'); and much else. See also LIEBESTRAUM. Was a bold harmonic innovator, especially in late years. His 'Hungarian' music is chiefly of a gipsy, not an authentically peasant, character.

litany, an extended form of Christian prayer for help, often set to music; and the term is sometimes used allusively in the titles of instrumental pieces.

Litolff, Henry Charles (1818–91), French pianist, composer and publisher; he was born in London of an Alsatian father and settled eventually in Paris. He wrote operas, piano solos and five works for piano and orchestra, each termed a 'symphony-concerto' (*concerto symphonique*), from the fourth of which comes the well-known Scherzo.

Little Night Music, A, see EINE KLEINE NACHTMUSIK; SONDHEIM.

Little Organ Book (Ger., *Orgelbüchlein*), a compilation by Bach (1717) of 46 chorale preludes for the organ.

Little Organ Mass, nickname for a Mass in B♭ by Haydn, composed in 1778 (Hob. XXII: 7) – short in length and, like the GREAT ORGAN MASS, with a solo organ part.

'Little Russian' Symphony, see UKRAINIAN SYMPHONY.

Little Slippers, The (Rus., from Ukrainian, *Cherevichki*), opera by Tchaikovsky, produced in Moscow, 1887, with libretto by Y. P. Polonsky (a revision of the earlier *Vakula the Smith*), based on Gogol's comic plot of village life. See also CHRISTMAS EVE.

Little Sweep, The, see LET'S MAKE AN OPERA!

lituus (Lat.), ancient Roman cavalry trumpet – straight, with small upturned bell. There are various later exceptional uses of the word, Bach in his Cantata no. 118 (*c.*1737) specifying two *litui*, apparently tenor trumpets.

Liverpool Philharmonic Orchestra, see ROYAL LIVERPOOL PHILHARMONIC ORCHESTRA.

Liviabella, Lino (1902–64), Italian composer of opera *The Shell* (*La Conchiglia*), after R. L. Stevenson's *The Bottle Imp*; also of symphonic poems, etc.

Lloyd, Charles Harford (1849–1919), British organist (e.g. of the Chapel Royal) and composer of church and organ music, cantatas, etc.

Lloyd, George (b. 1913), British composer of *John Socman* and other operas based on British history or legend; also of 12 symphonies, cantata *The Vigil of Venus*, etc.

Lloyd, Jonathan (b. 1948), British composer of four symphonies, cantata *Toward the Whitening Dawn*, etc.

Lloyd, Robert [Andrew] (b. 1940), British bass, particularly well known in opera at Covent Garden from 1972; sang title-role of *Boris Godunov* there and (1990) at Kirov Theatre, Leningrad.

Lloyd-Jones, David [Mathias] (b. 1934), British conductor, artistic director of Opera North from its inception, 1978, until 1990. Edited (and translated and conducted) Musorgsky's *Boris Godunov*, 1975.

Lloyd Webber, Andrew (b. 1948), British composer whose musicals have won prodigious international success. The early ones, in collaboration with Tim Rice as librettist, include *Jesus Christ Superstar*. Later musicals include *The Phantom of the Opera*. He also composed a Requiem (1984). His brother is Julian Lloyd Webber (b. 1951), cellist.

Lobgesang, see HYMN OF PRAISE.

Locatelli, Pietro (1695–1764), Italian violinist and composer, pupil of Corelli in Rome, settled in Amsterdam and died there. Works include sonatas, studies and other works for violin; also trios, works of CONCERTO GROSSO type, etc.

Lock, see LOCKE.

Locke (also Lock), **Matthew** (*c*.1622–77), English composer in service to Charles II, 1661; also author of pamphlet defending his own 'modern' style. Wrote music for the masque CUPID AND DEATH (with C. Gibbons); also opera THE SIEGE OF RHODES (with others), songs, church music, works for violins and viols. Apparently not the composer of the music to MACBETH long attributed to him.

loco (It., place), indication that music is to be performed at the pitch written, cancelling the instruction *8va sopra* (i.e. *ottava sopra*) or *8va bassa* indicating that music is to be played respectively an octave higher or an octave lower than written.

Locrian mode, a MODE that could be represented by the white keys of the piano beginning on B, if it were not rejected as unusable in practice. (Unlike the other MODES, it would not include a note a perfect fifth upward from its 'final', B.)

Loder, Edward [James] (1813–65), British composer of operas including *The Night Dancers, Raymond and Agnes*; songs including 'The Brooklet' (translation of the poem set by Schubert as 'Wohin?' in THE FAIR MAID OF THE MILL), string quartets, etc.

Loeffler, Charles Martin [Tornow] (1861–1935), Alsatian-born violinist-composer who spent boyhood partly in Russia (his orchestral *Memories of My Childhood* has Russian musical elements) and settled in USA, 1881. Composed other orchestral works including *A Pagan Poem* (after Virgil) with piano, English horn and three trumpets; also cantatas, chamber music, songs, etc.

Lœillet, Jean-Baptiste (1680–1730), Belgian composer, flautist, oboist and harpsichordist, who worked much in London and died there. Wrote music for flute, recorder and other instruments, and helped to popularize the flute (a new instrument compared to the recorder) in England.

Loewe, [Johann] Carl Gottfried (1796– 1869), German composer, also organist; visited London, 1847. Noted for songs, especially ballads on dramatic poems, e.g. 'Edward' and 'Erl-King' (see BALLAD, 2); wrote also operas, oratorios, piano music, etc. Had a six-week trance in 1864 and died after a similar attack.

Logothetis, Anestis (b. 1921), Greek (Bulgarian-born) composer, naturalized Austrian. Works include Labyrinth for any soloists, any chamber orchestra; Styx for orchestra of plucked stringed instruments; ballet Odysseus. Uses his own form of graphic notation.

Logroscino, [Bonifacio] Nicola (1698 – after 1765), Italian composer active in Naples; wrote dozens of comic operas including Trick for Trick (Inganno per inganno). Was also organist and composer of church music.

Lohengrin, opera by Wagner, produced in Weimar, 1850; libretto by composer. Lohengrin, Knight of the Holy Grail with personal swan-drawn transport, is incidentally the son of PARSIFAL.

Löhr, Hermann [Frederic] (1872– 1943), British composer of 'Where My Caravan Has Rested' and other popular English drawing-room songs.

London Classical Players, an orchestra of period instruments (early 19th cen-

tury) founded in 1978 by its conductor, Roger Norrington.

Londonderry Air, Irish folk-tune which was first brought into print in 1855; it has since been variously arranged (e.g. by Grainger as 'Irish Tune from County Derry') and given various words ('Danny Boy', etc.).

London Mozart Players, a chamber orchestra conducted by its founder, Harry Blech, from 1949 to 1984, with specialization in Haydn and Mozart; the repertory has expanded under his successor, Jane Glover.

London Overture, A, orchestral work by Ireland, 1936; has a prominent phrase said to originate from a bus-conductor's intonation of 'Piccadilly!'

London Philharmonic Orchestra, an orchestra founded by Beecham in 1932, but becoming self-governing in 1939. Principal conductor, 1979–83 (succeeding Bernard Haitink), Georg Solti, then (1983) Klaus Tennstedt, from 1990 Franz Welser-Möst.

London Sinfonietta, British chamber orchestra founded in 1968, specializing in modern music; it has no fixed conductor.

'London' Symphony, nickname for Haydn's last symphony, no. 104 in D (Hob. I: 104), first performed in 1795 during Haydn's second visit to London. A curious nickname, because all Haydn's last 12 symphonies were written for London and first performed there. See also next entry.

London Symphony, A, title of Vaughan Williams's Symphony no. 2 (but, in conformity with his practice, not numbered by him), first performed in 1914; revised version first performed in 1920. Quotes the Big Ben chimes and is an evocation of London. See NOCTURNE. (See also preceding entry.)

London Symphony Orchestra, an orchestra founded in 1904, self-governing from the beginning; principal conductor, 1979–87, Claudio Abbado, then Michael Tilson Thomas, from 1988.

long, obsolete time-value of a note, in the system of notation which grew up in the Middle Ages and was superseded by the present one; a long could equal either a half or a third of a LARGE and was itself divisible into either two or three 'breves'.

Long, Marguerite (1874–1966), French pianist who championed Debussy and Ravel; duo-partner with Jacques THIBAUD. In 1943 they founded an international competition which still bears their names.

Longfellow, Henry Wadsworth (1807–82), American poet; see FOOTE, HIAWATHA.

Longo, Alessandro (1864–1945), Italian pianist and composer who supervised the publication of a complete edition of D. Scarlatti's keyboard works, these being referred to as 'Longo No. . . .' or 'L. . . .' (followed by a number). This numbering has been superseded by that of KIRKPATRICK.

Lopatnikoff, Nikolai [Lvovich] (1903–76), Estonian-born composer who studied in St Petersburg, Berlin (pupil of Toch) and elsewhere; lived in Britain, 1933–9, then in USA – naturalized American, 1944. Works include three symphonies, two piano concertos, opera *Danton* (after Büchner).

Lorca, Federico García (1899–1936), Spanish poet and dramatist. See FORTNER, NONO, OHANA, RIETI, SZOKOLAY.

Lorengar, Pilar (b. 1921), Spanish soprano; sang at Glyndebourne, 1956, then from 1958 regularly with German Opera, West Berlin, with other appearances at La Scala, Covent Garden, etc.

Loriod, Yvonne (b. 1924), French pianist, noted especially in performing the works of Messiaen (her husband) and other modern French composers; is also herself a composer.

Lortzing, [Gustav] **Albert** (1801–51), German composer, almost entirely of operas and operettas, with his own librettos; his TSAR AND CARPENTER (*Zar und Zimmermann*) is still popular in Germany. Also conductor and, on occasion, tenor singer.

Los Angeles, Victoria de (real name originally Victoria Gomez Cima; married surname Magriñá; b. 1923), Spanish soprano noted in opera (from 1950 at Covent Garden and the Metropolitan, New York) and recital, sometimes accompanying herself on the guitar in Spanish traditional songs.

Lotti, Antonio (*c*.1667–1740), Italian composer of church music, oratorio, etc.; also of opera. Was church singer and organist, becoming chief organist of St Mark's, Venice, from 1704 until his death.

loud pedal, misleading name for the sustaining pedal – see PIANO.

Loughran, James (b. 1931), Scottish conductor – of Hallé Orchestra, 1971–83.

Louise, opera by G. Charpentier, produced in Paris, 1900. Libretto by composer; 'realistic' opera (cp. Italian VERISMO) which put the slums of Paris on the stage. The heroine is a seamstress.

Louis Ferdinand, Prince (form of name used by Prince Friedrich Christian Ludwig of Prussia) (1772–1806), amateur composer of chamber music, etc.; praised by Beethoven, who dedicated to him his Piano Concerto no. 3.

loure (Fr.), a type of rustic French bagpipe; and hence a French dance, usually in moderate 6/4 time. Hence also *louré* (derived from a technique of bagpipe-playing), a kind of bowing on the violin, etc., in which several notes are taken in one stroke of the bow but are slightly detached from one another.

louré, see preceding entry.

Lourié, Arthur Vincent (1892–1966), Russian-born composer who settled first in France (1921), then in USA (1941). Works, some with Roman Catholic allusions, include *Kormchaya* (Rus., Helmswoman, i.e. the Virgin Mary) for orchestra; string quartets; settings of poems by Tolstoy and Mayakovsky.

Love for Three Oranges (Rus., *Lyubov k trem apelsinam*), opera by Prokofiev, produced in French in Chicago, 1921. Libretto, in Russian, by composer, after an Italian play by Gozzi: a satirical fable, some of the actors impersonating an audience, the main action being thus 'a play within a play'. The prince who loves the three oranges finds his princess in the third. An orchestral suite drawn from this includes the march that is also well known in concert.

Love in a Village, opera with music collected and arranged by T. Arne, produced in London, 1761; the music is by 16 other composers as well as Arne himself, the work being a PASTICCIO. Modern revivals include one with the music edited by Arthur Oldham (b. 1926), produced in Aldeburgh, 1952.

Love Potion, The (It., *L'Elisir d'amore*), comic opera by Donizetti, produced in Milan, 1832. Libretto by F. Romani; the elixir or love potion is a quack-doctor's dose of cheap wine.

Love-song Waltzes (Ger., *Liebeslieder-Walzer*), a set of 18 waltzes by Brahms 'for piano duet and [four] vocal parts ad lib', 1869; 15 more, called *New Love-song Waltzes* (1875), were designated as 'for four voices and piano duet'.

Love, the Magician, see next entry.

Love, the Sorcerer (Sp., *El Amor brujo*), ballet with music by Falla, first performed in 1915, later revised; written for a ballerina who can sing as well as dance. A suite for orchestra (properly with contralto) is drawn from it. (Title commonly translated 'Love, the Magician'; *brujo* is actually a 'male witch', and the ballet is about a girl malevolently haunted by a dead lover.)

Lualdi, Adriano (1885–1971), Italian composer of operas including *The Moon of the Caribbees* (after Eugene O'Neill) with some unorthodox orchestration – e.g. 'the two lowest strings of a double-bass, untuned'; also of string quartet, songs, etc. Director of the Florence Conservatory, 1947–56; also music critic.

Lübeck, Vincenz (1654–1740), German organist (latterly in Hamburg), composer of chorale preludes and other works for organ, and of cantatas, etc.

Luca, Giuseppe De, see DE LUCA.

Lucas, Leighton (1903–83), British conductor – noted in ballet and in French music; also composer (film music, a Latin Requiem Mass, orchestral works, etc.).

Lucia di Lammermoor, Lucy of Lammermoor, opera by Donizetti, produced in Naples, 1835. Libretto by S. Cammarano, after Scott; set in Scotland about 1700. After slaying her husband the heroine has a famous 'mad scene'.

Lucier, Alvin (b. 1931), American composer, particularly for non-standard resources, e.g. *Music for Solo Performer* where three electrodes are attached to the scalp to pick up 10-cycle alpha waves from the brain, this signal being then amplified and used to activate resonances; also of *Composition for Pianist and Mother* (pianist, actress), etc.

Ludus Tonalis (Lat., The Play of Notes), piano work by Hindemith, first performed in 1943. It comprises a prelude, 12 fugues separated by 11 interludes, and a postlude which is the INVERTED (upside-down) version of the prelude. (Intended as studies in both composition and piano technique.)

Ludwig, Christa (b. 1924), German mezzo-soprano (formerly soprano); sang at Vienna State Opera from 1955, at the Metropolitan, New York, from 1959.

Luening, Otto (b. 1900), American composer who studied in Munich and in Zurich (pupil of Busoni); was also flautist and conductor. Has made much use of electronic music – e.g. *Fantasy in Space* (flute on tape) and, composed jointly with Ussachevsky, *Poem in Cycles and Bells* for tape and orchestra; earlier, wrote three string quartets, Serenade for three horns and strings, opera *Evangeline*, etc.

Luigini, Alexandre [Clément Léon Joseph] (1850–1906), French violinist, conductor, and composer of orchestral piece called *Egyptian Ballet* and other light orchestral music; also of operas, etc.

Luisa Miller, opera by Verdi, produced in Naples, 1849. Libretto by S. Cammarano, after Schiller; the setting is the Tyrol, and the three acts are respectively headed Love, Intrigue and Poison.

Lully, Jean-Baptiste (originally Giovanni Battista Lulli) (1632–87), Italian-born composer who was taken in boyhood to France and first worked there as a scullion, then as a violinist. Went into service of Louis XIV, 1652; naturalized French, 1661; achieved the supreme musical position at court, 1662. Himself a dancer, collaborated with Molière in comedy-ballets including LE BOURGEOIS GENTILHOMME; from 1673 wrote operas including AL-KESTIS and ARMIDA. Wrote also church music, dance music, etc., and established the 'French OVERTURE'. A brilliant intriguer; obtained a monopoly of opera production in France; made a fortune by speculation; injured his foot with the long staff he used for beating time on the floor, and died of the resulting abscess.

Lulu, opera by Berg, with libretto by

composer; almost completed, but only Acts I and II (of three) published; first staged in Zurich, 1937. Completed by Friedrich Cerha, first performed in Paris, 1979. Its heroine typifies female sexuality.

Lumbye, Hans Christian (1810–74), Danish composer of galops and other dance music, etc., and conductor of such works in Copenhagen.

Lumsdaine, David (b. 1931). Australian composer, pupil of Seiber in London. Works include cantata *Annotations of Auschwitz*, *Looking-glass Music* for brass quintet and tape, *Kangaroo Hunt* for piano and percussion.

lungo, lunga (It.), long.

Lupo, Thomas (early 17th century), English composer of Italian origin; wrote fantasies and dance-music for viols, anthems, etc.

Lupu, Radu (b. 1945), Romanian pianist who won international competition at Leeds, 1969, and settled in Britain.

lur (Dan.), prehistoric large bronze trumpet of which several specimens have been found, chiefly in Denmark.

lusingando, lusinghiero (It.), flatteringly, i.e. alluringly.

lustig (Ger.), cheerful.

lustigen Weiber von Windsor, Die, see MERRY WIVES OF WINDSOR.

lustige Witwe, Die, see MERRY WIDOW.

lute, fretted stringed instrument plucked with the fingers (or, in the case of some earlier types, with a plectrum), much in use 1400–1700 for solos, song accompaniment and ensembles; it had isolated orchestral use even as late as Bach's ST JOHN PASSION, 1723. Since 1950 it has been extensively revived for the playing of old music. The sizes of lutes differed, and also the tuning; but a regular feature was the tuning of strings in pairs (called 'courses') in unison or octaves. Hence *lutenist* (more rarely *lutanist*), a player of the lute. Larger types are called ARCHLUTES.

luth (Fr.), lute; *luthier*, lute-maker – and hence, today, a maker of stringed instruments in general.

Luther, Martin (1483–1546), German Protestant leader; he was skilled in music (as singer, flautist, and lutenist) and is thought to have written the music to hymns – e.g. 'A Stronghold Sure' (*Ein' feste Burg*). He certainly wrote the words of hymns and intended a treatise in praise of music. See REFORMATION SYMPHONY.

luthier, see LUTH.

Lutosławski, Witold (b. 1913), Polish composer whose music has moved from traditional to advanced West European models. Works include three symphonies, Concerto for Orchestra, a cello concerto; also *Woven Words* (Fr., *Paroles tissées*) for tenor with chamber orchestra, and a series of works each called *Chain*. See also PAGANINI.

Lutyens, [Agnes] Elisabeth (1906–83), British composer, daughter of Sir Edwin Lutyens, architect. Works include *Infidelio* and other operas; ballet *The Birthday of the Infanta* after Oscar Wilde; unaccompanied motet on German philosophical text by Wittgenstein; a horn concerto; a viola concerto; six Chamber Concertos for various instrumental groups; 12 string quartets; songs in English and

French; film music. Also wrote auto-biography. CBE, 1969.

Luxon, Benjamin [Matthew] (b. 1937), British baritone, formerly tea-cher of physical education; prominent in Britten's and other operas (title-role in televised première of Britten's *Owen Wingrave*, 1971); his recitals have included informal folk-songs with banjo accompaniment. CBE, 1986.

Lvov, Alexis Feodorovich (1798– 1870), Russian composer of operas, much church music, and the pre-Rev-olutionary Russian National Anthem – quoted in Tchaikovsky's overture *1812* (see under EIGHTEEN-TWELVE).

Lyadov, Anatol Konstantinovich (1855–1914), Russian composer of symphonic poems BABA YAGA, THE ENCHANTED LAKE and KIKIMORA, and other works for orchestra and for piano in Russian nationalist style; also collector and arranger of folk-songs, and conductor. Was originally invited to compose the music for THE FIRE-BIRD, but owing to his characteristic dilatoriness Stravinsky undertook it.

Lyapunov, Sergey Mikhailovich (1859–1924), Russian pianist and composer in 'nationalist' style; friend of Balakirev, and collector of folk-songs. Wrote two symphonies, two piano concertos, piano solos, etc.

Lydian mode, the MODE represented by the white keys on the piano begin-ning on F.

lyra, see the following entry.

lyre, (1) general name for a type of plucked stringed instrument in which the strings are fixed to a cross-bar be-tween two arms; (2) ancient Greek in-strument (Gk., *lyra*) of this type, rounded off at the foot (cp. KITHARA). See also LIRA.

lyric, (1, strictly) relating to vocal per-formance with the lyre, i.e. sung; hence *lyric drama*, occasional syn-onym for opera (especially in French, as *drame lyrique*); hence also *the lyric stage*, i.e. the operatic stage; (2, of a poem) not epic, not dramatic, but fairly short and expressing the writer's own feelings; hence (term taken over from poetry into music) *Lyric Piece* (Grieg), *Lyric Suite* (Berg), etc.; (as vocal description, e.g. *lyric sop-rano, lyric tenor*), term indicating inter-mediate vocal 'weight' between light and 'dramatic' (heavy) – see also SPINTO; (4, *lyrics,* as noun) the words of a song in a musical, etc.; so *lyricist,* writer of such lyrics.

M

M, abbr. for Master (in certain university degrees; e.g. M.MUS., Master of [or 'in'] Music).

m, symbol in TONIC SOL-FA for the degree (mediant) of the scale, pronounced *me*.

ma (It.), but.

Ma, Yo-Yo (b. 1955), Chinese cellist, born in France, giving public performances from age five; after moving with parents to New York, he performed on television in 1963, studied with Leonard Rose and achieved international eminence as soloist.

Maazel, Lorin [Varencove] (b. 1930). American conductor, born in France, also violinist, music director of the Cleveland Orchestra, 1972–82, of the Vienna State Opera, 1982–4, and of the Pittsburgh Symphony Orchestra since 1986.

Macbeth, (musical works after Shakespeare, including) (1) opera by Verdi, produced in Florence, 1847, and revised for Paris, 1865; libretto by F. M. Piave and A. Maffei; (2) symphonic poem by R. Strauss, first performed in 1890; (3) opera by Bloch, produced in Paris, 1910; libretto by E. Fleg; (4) incidental music (formerly ascribed to Locke) written for a production of the play in a distorted version, 1674; the true composer is unidentified.

McCabe, John (b. 1939), British composer who studied in Manchester and Munich; also pianist and director of the London College of Music. Works include *The Chagall Windows* for orchestra; *Notturni ed Alba* (It., Nocturnes and Dawn) for soprano and orchestra; *Miniconcerto* for organ, percussion and audience ('485 penny-whistles'); piano and organ solos.

McCormack, John (1884–1945), Irish-born tenor who studied in Italy, made Covent Garden début in 1907, but later appeared chiefly in concert; enormously popular. Became US citizen, 1917; created a papal Count, 1928.

MacCunn, Hamish (1868–1916), British composer, many of whose works are on Scottish subjects including opera *Jeanie Deans*; concert-overtures *Land of the Mountain and the Flood* and *The Ship o' the Fiend*; cantatas, songs, etc. Was also conductor.

MacDowell, Edward [Alexander] (1860–1908), American composer, also pianist. Trained in France and Germany. Wrote many short piano pieces, somewhat after Grieg's manner, winning him wide popularity; also two piano concertos, *Hamlet and*

Ophelia and other symphonic poems, songs, etc. The MacDowell Colony – a peaceful working-place for composers and other artists, in New Hampshire – was organized in his memory.

McEwen, John Blackwood (1868–1948), British composer of 17 string quartets (no. 6, *Biscay*), orchestral works including *Grey Galloway* (no. 2 of three 'Border Ballads'), a viola concerto, etc. Principal of the RAM, 1924–36; knighted, 1931.

Macfarren, George Alexander (1813–87), British composer of church music, many operas (one on Robin Hood), oratorios, overtures to *Hamlet* and other plays, etc. Principal of the RAM 1876–87; professor at Cambridge; knighted, 1883. Totally blind in later life.

Mácha, Otmar (b. 1922), Czechoslovak composer of opera *Lake Ukereve*, *Variants* for orchestra, oratorio *The Testament of Comenius*.

Machaut (also Machault), **Guillaume de** (*c.*1300–77), French composer – also poet and priest, latterly Canon of Rheims. Considered the chief exponent of ARS NOVA in France. His Mass for four voices is almost the earliest surviving polyphonic Mass. Composed also other vocal music to religious and secular texts, some to a very intricate scheme of construction (see ISO-RHYTHMIC, a term applying to some of his work).

McIntyre, Donald [Conroy] (b. 1934), New Zealand bass-baritone celebrated in Wagner roles such as Wotan; sang at Bayreuth Festival, 1967–81.

Mackenzie, Alexander [Campbell] (1847–1935), British violinist, conductor, principal of the RAM (1888–1924), and composer. Works include *Colomba, The Cricket on the Hearth* and other operas; many vocal works of all types; three orchestral Scottish rhapsodies. Knighted, 1895.

Mackerras [Alan] **Charles** [Maclaurin] (b. 1925), Australian conductor (born in USA); resident in Britain since 1947. Conductor of Sydney Symphony Orchestra, 1982–5; musical director of Welsh National Opera since 1986. Arranger of Sullivan's music for the ballet PINEAPPLE POLL. Knighted, 1979. See NATHAN.

Macleod, Fiona (pseudonym of William Sharp) (1855–95), Scottish poet. See WHITE PEACOCK.

Maconchy, Elizabeth (b. 1907), British composer; studied under Vaughan Williams, and also in Prague. Works include *And Death Shall Have No Dominion* for chorus and brass: 12 string quartets and other chamber music; a symphony for double string orchestra; songs, ballets, operas. See LEFANU.

McPhee, Colin (1901–64), American (Canadian-born) composer, pupil of Varèse; lived in Bali, became authority on its music, and composed orchestral work *Tabuh-Tabuhan* based on Balinese musical systems; also piano solos, Concerto for piano and eight wind instruments etc. Was also writer and teacher.

Madam Butterfly (It., *Madama* . . .), opera by Puccini, produced in Milan, 1904 (February); successful only in a revised version three months later. Libretto by G. Giacosa and L. Illica, after D. Belasco's (American) play: the Japanese heroine is deserted by an American naval lieutenant. See SAMISEN.

Maderna, Bruno (1920–73), Italian

composer and conductor. Works include Concerto for two pianos and chamber orchestra; *Serenata* for 11 instruments; and various pieces involving tape and (sometimes) theatrical action, e.g. *Hyperion* (composite piece with flute as main performer). Was a leading conductor of modern music.

Madetoja, Leevi Antti (1887–1947), Finnish composer of operas, three symphonies, recitations with piano, etc.; pupil of Sibelius and d'Indy; also conductor and critic.

madrigal, (1) 16th–17th-century type of contrapuntal composition for several voices, originating in Italy but flourishing also in England – mostly self-contained in vocal texture, but some later examples (e.g. by Monteverdi) having independent instrumental accompaniment. The words are usually secular, chiefly amorous, though some *madrigali spirituali* (sacred) exist; (2) term used also for the Italian forerunner of the above type, from the 14th century (after which the term fell out of use until revived as above); (3) term used also in various looser senses – e.g. the so-called madrigals in operettas by Sullivan and German, which pay homage to an older manner without reviving it.

Maelzel, Johann Nepomuk (1772–1838), see METRONOME.

maestoso (It.), majestic, dignified.

maestro (It.), title traditionally given in Italy to recognized conductors and composers (and used, particularly in USA, as a loose honorific for conductors). The *maestro al cembalo* was the musician who in the 18th century and thereabouts directed concerts or operas while playing the harpsichord; so also *maestro di cappella*, the musical director of a chapel of a prince's establishment, etc. (but not used today in such a wide sense as its German equivalent, KAPELLMEISTER). *Il maestro di cappella* is the title of Cimarosa's solo cantata satirizing a conductor: see THE MUSICAL DIRECTOR.

maestro di musica, see MUSIC MASTER.

maggiore (It.), major.

Magic Flute, The (Ger., *Die Zauberflöte*), opera by Mozart, produced in Vienna, 1791 (K620); libretto by E. Schikaneder, perhaps aided by C. L. Gieseke. The flute secures the passage of the hero through danger to enlightenment; the opera is one of Masonic and humanistic symbolism.

Magnificat, the hymn of the Virgin Mary as given in St Luke (Latin name, from first word of the Vulgate translation); used in Roman Catholic and Anglican services, the musical setting in the latter being often combined with a setting of the NUNC DIMITTIS. Hence Vaughan Williams's *Magnificat*, concert-setting of the words of the hymn, plus additional text, first performed in 1932.

Mahagonny, see RISE AND FALL OF THE CITY OF MAHAGONNY.

Mahler, Gustav (1860–1911), Austrian (Bohemian-born) composer; also noted conductor – Vienna Opera, 1897–1907. Jewish, but became Roman Catholic. Attended Bruckner's university lectures and admired him, but was never a direct pupil; his own music – intensely expressive and chromatically inclined – is incidentally regarded as the forerunner of Schoenberg's and thus of TWELVE-NOTE music. Most of his works have a literary or other non-musical link. Wrote nine completed symphonies notable for their length, the large forces used, highly individual orchestration, and some employment of PROGRESSIVE TONALITY. Nos. 2 (RESURRECTION), 3 and 8 (SYMPHONY OF A THOUSAND) employ vocal soloists and chorus, no. 4 a soprano soloist. No. 10, left unfinished, was completed by Deryck Cooke and first performed entire in this form in 1964. The SONG OF THE EARTH, though formally a song-cycle with orchestra, is also of symphonic dimensions. Wrote also cycles SONGS OF A WAYFARER and SONGS ON THE DEATH OF CHILDREN both with orchestra, and other songs; little else. See ADAGIETTO, YOUTH'S MAGIC HORN, TITAN.

Mahomet II, see SIEGE OF CORINTH.

Maid as Mistress, The (It., *La serva padrona*), comic opera by Pergolesi, produced in Naples, 1733 (as 'intermezzo' between the acts of a serious opera). Libretto by G. A. Federico. Prodigiously successful musical setting of light-hearted intrigue; in France, set off a rivalry between champions of Italian and French opera (the so-called 'War of the Buffoons') after Pergolesi's death.

Maiden Quartets, see RUSSIAN QUARTETS.

Maid of Orleans, The, opera by Tchaikovsky, produced in St Petersburg, 1881. Libretto by composer after Schiller's play about Joan of Arc. (Text in Russian; the French title, *Jeanne d'Arc*, is not appropriate except in French contexts.)

Maid of Pskov, The (Rus., *Pskovi-*

tianka), opera by Rimsky-Korsakov, produced in St Petersburg, 1873; libretto by composer. Also called *Ivan the Terrible*, the 16th-century Tsar being one of the chief characters.

maîtrise (Fr.), a choir school attached to a church.

maj., abbr. for major (scale, etc.).

major, minor, terms contrasting with one another and having various musical applications – (1) Scales. The *major* SCALE of C (i.e. treating the note C as its point of repose) is –

C D E F G A B C

(and the same notes descending). The *minor* scale is divided for theoretical purposes into three types, of which the *natural minor* scale of C is:

C D E♭ F G A♭ B♭ C

(and the same notes descending). The *melodic minor* scale of C differs in its ascending and descending forms:

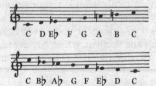

C D E♭ F G A B C

C B♭ A♭ G F E♭ D C

The *harmonic minor* scale of C is

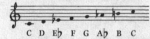

C D E♭ F G A♭ B C

(and the same notes descending). Similarly with scales beginning on the other notes; i.e. all major scales are internally alike, the distances (INTERVALS) between successive notes being the same, although the note of starting differs. All scales belonging to one of the three types of minor scales are, similarly, alike.

(2) Keys. The KEY of C *major* is that in which the notes of the scale of C major are treated as 'normal', other notes entering only for special purposes. The key of C *minor* bears a like relation to the scale of C minor; but, though there are three types of minor scale, there is only one type of minor key (the three types of scale corresponding to different aspects of it). The KEY-SIGNATURE of a minor key is determined by the *natural minor* scale (above); e.g. for C minor it is three flats (B♭, E♭, A♭)

(3) Chords. A *major* or *minor* chord is one which, being built out of the major or minor scale, may serve to identify that scale. More particularly, the *common chord of C major*, or just *chord of C major*, or *C-major triad* means the notes C, E, G – as contrasted with the *common chord of C minor* (*chord of C minor*, *C-minor triad*), C, E♭, G.

(4) Intervals. The INTERVALS second, third, sixth and seventh are classified as either *major* or *minor*, the latter a semitone less than the former. Thus, measuring upwards from C, the major and minor intervals (in that order) are – second, C–D, C–D♭; third, C–E, C–E♭; sixth, C–A, C–A♭, seventh, C–B, C–B♭. Likewise, of course, measured upwards or downwards from any other note.

Makropoulos Affair, The (Cz., *Věc Makropulos*), opera by Janáček, produced in Brno, 1926; libretto by composer, after Čapek's play about an elixir of eternal life administered to a woman called Makropoulos (this is the normal English spelling of such Greek names, though the Czech spelling is different). Also known as *The Makropoulos Case*; but, although the opera is concerned with a lawsuit, no legal 'case' is referred to in the original title.

Mal (Ger.), time (in the sense of *1. Mal*, first time, etc.).

malagueña (Sp.), dance originating in Málaga, marked by singing; also instrumental piece of similar nature.

Malcolm, George [John] (b. 1917), British harpsichordist, pianist, conductor, church musician and composer of *Variations on a Theme of Mozart* for four harpsichords; 1947–59, Master of the Music at Westminster (Roman Catholic) Cathedral. CBE, 1965.

Malcuzyński, Witold (1914–77), Polish-born pianist, pupil of Paderewski; resident successively in France, USA and Switzerland.

Malediction, name applied to a Liszt piano concerto, composed apparently in the early 1840s but not published till after his death. In fact Liszt gave the name only to the opening theme of the work.

Malgoire, Jean-Claude (b. 1940), French conductor, best known in recordings of baroque opera using authentic instruments.

Malibran, Maria [Felicia] (1808–36), French soprano, daughter of the Spanish tenor Manuel García; though dying so young, she was internationally celebrated in opera (London and New York débuts, 1825).

malinconia (It.), melancholy.

Malipiero, Gian Francesco (1882–1973), Italian composer of operas including JULIUS CAESAR and (after Pirandello) *The Fable of the Changeling Son*; 11 symphonies, and also a 'symphony' in one movement and a *Symphony of the Zodiac*; chamber music (including *Dialogues* of various voices and instruments); many songs, etc. Director of the Venice Conservatory, 1939–52; noted as historian and editor of Monteverdi, Vivaldi and other old Italian composers. Uncle of the following.

Malipiero, Riccardo (b. 1914), Italian composer and critic, formerly pianist and cellist; nephew of preceding. Works include *Concerto breve* for ballerina and orchestra, various other concertos, operas *Minnie la candida* and *La Donna è mobile* (quotation from RIGOLETTO).

Mallarmé, Stéphane (1842–98), French poet. See AFTERNOON OF A FAUN.

Mallet, David (*c*.1705–65), Scottish poet and dramatist. See ALFRED.

mambo (Sp.), Afro-Cuban dance in 4/4 time; developed in the 1940s, it became internationally popular.

Mamelles de Tirésias, Les, see BREASTS OF TIRESIAS.

Ma mère l'oye, see MOTHER GOOSE.

Mancinelli, Luigi (1848–1921), Italian composer of operas (one on *A Midsummer Night's Dream*), etc.; noted opera conductor, much at Covent Garden.

mandola, mandora, obsolete lute-like stringed instrument, from which the MANDOLIN developed.

mandolin (also spelt 'mandoline'), plucked stringed instrument of Italian origin, now usually of eight strings tuned in pairs (to the same four notes as a violin) and played with plectrum. Much used in informal music-making and operatic simulations of this, e.g. in the Serenade in Mozart's *Don Giovanni* and in Verdi's *Otello*; but used also as concerto instrument (Vivaldi), in Mahler's Symphony no. 7, etc.

Manfred, works based on Byron's verse drama – (1) overture and 15 numbers (including background music for speech) by Schumann, composed for stage performance and first given in 1852; (2) symphony by Tchaikovsky, first performed in 1886 – not numbered among his other symphonies.

Manfredini, Francesco [Onofrio] (1684–1762), Italian violinist, church musician and composer of orchestral works (some of CONCERTO GROSSO type), trio-sonatas, etc. Father of the following.

Manfredini, Vincenzo (1737–99), Italian composer who took court post in Russia (and died there); composed operas, ballets, harpsichord sonatas, etc. Pupil of his father (preceding).

Mann, Thomas (1875–1955), German writer. See DEATH IN VENICE, ROSENBERG.

mannerism, a term borrowed from art history, identifying a supposed tendency to give more value to a strikingly individual feature of a piece (e.g. a succession of unusual chords) than to an overall direction of form; it is sometimes applied to Gesualdo's music.

Mannheim school, name given by early 20th-century historians to a group of mid-18th-century composers centred at the court of Mannheim (Germany), held to be historically significant for (1) the cultivation of a type of symphony forerunning the classical (Haydn–Mozart) type; (2) refinement of orchestral technique – the clarinet and the controlled orchestral crescendo supposedly making here their first entry into this type of music. The founder of the school is generally considered to be J. W. Stamitz, a Bohemian; the other members (including F. X. Richter) were all either Bohemian or Austrian, except for Toeschi, an Italian.

Manon, opera by Massenet, produced in Paris, 1884. Libretto by H. Meilhac and P. Gille. Named after the heroine, eventually condemned for prostitution; based on Prévost's novel *Manon Lescaut,* as were also Balfe's opera *The Maid of Artois* (1836) and Henze's *Boulevard Solitude.* See also the following.

Manon Lescaut, title of various works based on Prévost's novel (see also preceding entry), including (1) ballet with music by Halévy, 1830; (2) opera by Auber, produced in Paris, 1856 (libretto by E. Scribe); (3) opera by Puccini, produced in Turin, 1893 (libretto by M. Praga, D. Oliva and L. Illica – though the process of writing it was so involved that the title-page names no librettist).

manual, a keyboard played with the hands – especially on the organ, as opposed to a pedal-keyboard; hence *manualiter,* bogus-Latin term for 'to be played on the manuals'.

Maometto II, see SIEGE OF CORINTH.

maraca, Latin-American percussion instrument used in dance bands, etc., and occasionally elsewhere – e.g. in Varèse's *Ionization.* It is a gourd filled with dried seeds which rustle when the instrument is shaken – or is made of other materials to produce the same effect. Usually as a pair – in plural, *maracas.*

Marais, Marin (1656–1728), French bass-viol player; also composer (pupil of Lully) writing operas, music for viols, a Te Deum, etc.

Marbeck (also Merbecke, etc.), **John** (*c.*1510–1585), English composer of Mass, motets and (especially) *The Book of Common Prayer Noted*; i.e. the first musical setting of the Anglican prayer-book. Was also organist at St George's, Windsor; compiler of the first biblical concordance in English, and theological writer; condemned to death for heresy in 1543 but pardoned.

marcato (It.), marked; *marcato il basso,* the bass to be played in a prominent manner.

Marcello, Alessandro (1684–1750), Italian composer of cantatas, concertos, etc. An oboe concerto of his, which Bach transcribed for keyboard, was formerly misattributed to other composers.

Marcello, Benedetto (1686–1739), Italian composer – also violinist, singer, writer, translator and civil servant. Works include operas, oratorios, and a famous setting of Italian paraphrases of the Psalms. See preceding entry.

march, a piece for marching, slow (usually 4/4) or quick (usually 2/4 or 6/8); transferred from military to other uses. See also MARCHE, MARCIA.

Marchal, André (1894–1980), French organist, from 1945 at St Eustache, Paris; noted recitalist, touring Europe, USA, Australia; blind from birth.

Marchand, Louis (1669–1732), French organist and composer, chiefly for the organ and harpsichord. Toured in Germany; but the story that he left Dresden rather than face a challenge to compete at the organ with Bach is not authenticated.

marche (Fr.), march: *Marche militaire*, French title used by Schubert for each of three marches for piano duet (D733), composed before 1824 – no. 1 being the famous one.

marcia (It.), march; *alla marcia*, in march-like style – term usually applied to 4/4, 2/4 or 6/8 rhythms (see MARCH).

Marenzio, Luca (1554–99), Italian composer, wrote more than 200 madrigals, very successful and having much influence in England. Wrote also a Mass and other church music, but, exceptionally for an Italian of that period, never held a church appointment. Worked for a time in Warsaw, but mainly in Rome.

'Maria Theresa', nickname for Haydn's symphony no. 48 in C (Hob. I: 48), composed in 1772 – in honour of the Empress of Austria. (Usually called 'Maria Theresia', a variant spelling of her name.)

marimba, percussion instrument of African origin; the standard Central American form, now well known in concert use, is a sort of large, deeper-toned XYLOPHONE (with wooden slabs) played with soft-headed sticks. Milhaud wrote a concerto (1947) for marimba and vibraphone (one player). The *marimbaphone* (or *steel marimba*) is a patented instrument, similar but with metal instead of wooden slabs. See also XYLORIMBA.

marimbaphone, see preceding.

marine trumpet, see TRUMPET MARINE.

Marinuzzi, Gino (1882–1945), Italian conductor and composer of operas, symphonic poems, etc.; editor of old Italian music. His son, of the same name (b. 1920), is also a composer and conductor.

Maritana, opera by W. V. Wallace, produced in London, 1845; libretto by E. Fitzball. Named after its Spanish gipsy heroine.

Markevitch, Igor (1912–83), Russian composer and conductor who settled in Paris; pupil of N. Boulanger. Works include Sinfonietta, ballets, a cantata on Milton's *Paradise Lost*. Held conducting posts in Paris and Moscow, then (1973) with Orchestra of Santa Cecilia Academy, Rome.

Marlowe, Christopher (1564–93), English dramatist. See TALMA.

Marriage of Figaro, The (It., *Le nozze di Figaro*), comic opera by Mozart (K492), produced in Vienna (in the original Italian), 1786. Libretto by L. da Ponte, based on a comedy by Beaumarchais – sequel to that on which the libretto of Rossini's THE BARBER OF SEVILLE is based. Figaro, formerly a barber whose successful intrigues resulted in Count Almaviva's marriage, is now the Count's personal servant. (See also DITTERSDORF, KLEBE.)

Marriner, Neville (b. 1924), British conductor, originally violinist; founder-director of the Academy of St

Martin-in-the-Fields (see ACADEMY) and (1979–86) conductor of the Minnesota Orchestra. Knighted, 1985.

Marsalis, Wynton (b. 1961), American trumpeter, admired both in jazz and the classical repertory, sometimes 'multi-tracking' when recording works for more than one trumpet.

Marschner, Heinrich August (1795–1861), German composer – also conductor, for a time assistant to Weber. Composed German Romantic operas including *The Vampyr, The Templar and the Jewess* (after Scott's *Ivanhoe*), and HANS HEILING; also songs, male chorus, orchestral works, etc.

Marseillaise, La, French national anthem of which Rouget de Lisle (1760–1836) wrote both tune and words in 1792; so named because it was associated with the body of volunteers from Marseilles who sang it on entering Paris.

Marsh, Roger (b. 1949), British composer of Serenade for amplified double-brass and 15 strings; *Jesters (for sicks)* for six woodwind; music-theatre pieces.

Marteau sans maître, Le, piece by Boulez for contralto and six instruments, 1957 (text by R. Char); title implies verbal assonance between *marteau* and *maître* (Fr., hammer, master).

martelé, martellato (Fr., It.), hammered, i.e. strongly accented – as applied e.g. to the piano, and to a certain manner of bowing the violin and other stringed instruments.

martenot, convenient English name for the instrument otherwise called 'Martenot Waves' (Fr., *Ondes Martenot*),

after its French inventor, Maurice Martenot (1898–1980). It is an ELECTRONIC instrument sounding only one note at a time, played with a keyboard. Brought out in 1928, it has achieved occasional usage as a solo and orchestral instrument – e.g. by Honegger in JOAN OF ARC AT THE STAKE and Messiaen in TURANGALÎLA.

Martha, or Richmond Fair (Ger., *Martha, oder Der Markt von Richmond*), opera by Flotow, produced in Vienna, 1847. Libretto by F. W. Riese: under the name of Martha, the aristocratic heroine lets herself be bound as a servant (in jest) at the hiring fair at Richmond (presumably Surrey). The opera incorporates 'The Last Rose of Summer' (see MOORE, T.).

Martin, Frank (1890–1974), Swiss composer who worked much in Holland; was also pianist and harpsichordist. In *The Drugged Wine* (Fr., *Le Vin herbé*) for voices and instruments he used the legend on which also Wagner's TRISTAN AND ISOLDE is based. Other works include *Petite Symphonie Concertante* (i.e. Little Sinfonia Concertante) for harpsichord, harp, piano and two string orchestras; operas THE TEMPEST (Ger., *Der Sturm*), after Shakespeare, and *Monsieur de Pourceaugnac*, after Molière; oratorios *Golgotha* and *The Mystery of the Nativity*; various orchestral and chamber works; *Six Monologues from Everyman* (voice with piano accompaniment, later orchestrated).

Martinelli, Giovanni (1885–1969), Italian tenor, celebrated in opera – particularly at the Metropolitan, New York. He sang at least 36 roles.

Martini, Giovanni Battista (known as

Padre (Father) Martini) (1706–84), Italian priest, mathematician and composer of music for church and stage, etc. Author of learned musical treatises; teacher of Mozart and other distinguished composers.

Martini, Giovanni Paolo (name used by Johann Paul Aegidius Schwartzendorf) (1741–1816), known as 'Martini the German' (It., *Martini il Tedesco*), German organist and composer who settled in France. Now remembered for his song 'Plaisir d'amour' (Fr., Pleasure of Love); wrote also operas, church music, works for military band, etc.

Martini, 'Padre', see MARTINI (G. B.).

Martini il Tedesco, see MARTINI (G. P.).

Martino, Donald [James] (b. 1931), American composer, pupil of Babbitt, Dallapiccola and others. Works include a piano concerto; *Strata* for bass clarinet; *Augenmusik* (Ger., Eye-music) for 'actress, *danseuse* or uninhibited percussionist and electronic tape'.

Martinon, Jean (1910–76), French conductor, giving London concerts from 1946; held posts in Chicago, Paris and elsewhere, then from 1974 at The Hague (Residentie Orchestra). Also composer of four symphonies, two violin concertos, etc.

Martinů, Bohuslav (1890–1959), Czech composer, formerly violinist: resident from 1932 chiefly in France, also in USA; pupil of Suk and Roussel. Works include COMEDY ON THE BRIDGE, *Julietta, The Marriage* (English libretto by the composer, after Gogol's play), *The Greek Passion* (after Kazantzakis's novel *Christ Recrucified*) and other operas; six symphonies; a 'double concerto' for two string orch-

estras, piano and kettledrums; concertos for piano, for two pianos, for violin, for two violins; symphonic poems *Tumult* (Fr., *La Bagarre*) and *Half-time* (referring to a soccer match); seven string quartets and other chamber music (see THEREMIN).

Martin y Soler, Vicente (1754–1806), Spanish composer of Italian operas (including *Una coša rara*, quoted by Mozart in DON GIOVANNI), Russian operas, church music, etc. Died in St Petersburg, where he held a court post.

Martirano, Salvatore (b. 1927), American composer, pupil of Dallapiccola in Florence. Works include *L's GA* (i.e. Lincoln's Gettysburg Address) for gas-masked politico, helium bomb, three cine projectors and tape – the helium being inhaled by the performer to change the vocal sound; also *Contrasts* for orchestra, *Cocktail Music* for piano etc.

Marton, Eva (b. 1943), Hungarian soprano with international career – Metropolitan Opera, New York, from 1976. Noted in 'heavy' roles such as R. Strauss's Elektra.

Martucci, Giuseppe (1856–1909), Italian pianist, composer (two symphonies, two piano concertos, etc.), arranger of old Italian music, conductor, director of Naples Conservatory.

Martyrdom of St Magnus, The, chamber opera by P. M. Davies, produced at Kirkwall, Orkney, 1977; libretto by composer, after George Mackay Brown.

Martyrdom of St Sebastian, The (Fr., *Le Martyre de St Sébastien*), mystery-play by D'Annunzio for which Debussy wrote incidental music, 1911.

Marx, Joseph (1882–1964), Austrian

composer of many songs (some with orchestral accompaniment) in the German Romantic tradition; also of a piano quartet, a 'Romantic Piano Concerto', etc.

marziale (It.), martial.

Masaniello, name often given to Auber's opera, *The Dumb Woman of Portici* (Fr., *La Muette de Portici*), produced in Paris, 1828. Libretto by E. Scribe and G. Delavigne. Masaniello, a revolutionary leader, is the hero; Auber avoided using his name for the title because another opera of that title (by Carafa) had appeared two months earlier. The other title referred to the principal female character; she is dumb, and the part is traditionally taken by a dancer.

Mascagni, Pietro (1863–1945), Italian composer, pupil of Ponchielli. His CAVALLERIA RUSTICANA won an operatic competition in 1889 and scored a success which he never afterwards matched in other operas including *L'Amico Fritz* (Friend Fritz), IRIS and *The Masks* (*Le maschere*). He followed the full-blooded Italian operatic manner of the time – see VERISMO. Other works include a symphony, Requiem; was also conductor and conservatory director.

mask, old English spelling of MASQUE, now occasionally revived for a work of dramatic or allegorical significance: cp. MASK OF ORPHEUS, MASK OF TIME.

Maskarad, Maskarade, see MASQUER-ADE.

Masked Ball, A (It., *Un ballo in maschera*), opera by Verdi, produced in Rome, 1859. Libretto by A. Somma, on a plot based on the assassination of Gustav III of Sweden, 1792. But to comply with censorship the action was incongruously changed to Boston (Mass.). Some later productions have switched the action to Italy – or reverted to the historical Swedish setting.

Mask of Orpheus, The, see ORPHEUS.

Mask of Time, The, concert work for solo singers, chorus and orchestra by Tippett, on texts written and compiled by the composer; first performed in 1984.

Mason, Daniel Gregory (1873–1953), American composer of three symphonies (no. 3, *A Lincoln Symphony*), piano music, etc.; pupil of d'Indy. Also writer on music. Grandson of the following.

Mason, Lowell (1792–1872), American organist, composer (especially of hymns) and educationalist. Grandfather of the preceding.

masque, type of English stage entertainment (related to opera and ballet), cultivated chiefly in the 17th century and intended for aristocratic audiences: it incorporated vocal and instrumental music, dancing and spectacle. For examples see COMUS, VENUS AND ADONIS, ALFRED. Anachronistically and confusingly, Vaughan Williams's JOB is styled 'a masque for dancing'. See also MASK.

Masquerade, (1) opera by C. Nielsen (Dan., *Maskarade*), produced in Copenhagen, 1906; libretto by V. Andersen after Holberg, involving an 18th-century masked ball; (2) play by Lermontov (Rus., *Maskarad*) for which Khachaturian wrote incidental music, 1939, from which a suite is drawn; it deals with the licentious life of the Russian aristocracy in the early 19th century.

Masque of Comus, see COMUS.

Mass, form of religious service, which, though occasionally found in other ecclesiastical contexts, is chiefly important as the principal service of the Roman Catholic Church; High Mass is sung, Low Mass said. The musical setting of the 'Proper' of the Mass, varying with the occasion, has normally been left to the traditional plainsong – except for the REQUIEM MASS, to which new settings have been frequently composed. The unvarying part, called the 'Ordinary' or 'Common' of the Mass and consisting of five sections (Kyrie, Gloria, Credo, Sanctus with Benedictus, and Agnus Dei), has been frequently set in the Latin text which was in universal use until the decrees of the Second Vatican Council took effect in the 1970s. Such settings of the Ordinary are usually called simply (e.g.) Mass in C (Beethoven's early setting) – or they may have titles or nicknames (e.g. Haydn's NELSON MASS) for ease of identification. Bach's so-called 'Mass in B minor' was not so named by him (nor is it preponderantly in B minor); see MISSA. See also the following entries.

Mass, title of a 'theatre piece for singers, players and dancers' by Bernstein (produced in Washington, 1971) which is *about* a celebration of the Mass and combines the traditional Latin text with other matter by Stephen Schwartz.

Massenet, Jules Émile Frédéric (1842–1912), French composer, pupil of A. Thomas. Wrote 27 operas, in a mellifluous and sometimes rather 'lightweight' style including MANON, *The Cid,* WERTHER, CINDERELLA and *Our Lady's Juggler* (*Le Jongleur de Notre Dame*). Other works include ballets, incidental music to plays, orchestral suites, a piano concerto, about 200 songs.

Mass of Life, A, work by Delius for four solo singers, chorus and orchestra; first performed complete in 1909. Text from Nietzsche's *Thus Spake Zarathustra*: not a Mass, but a kind of pagan counterpart to one.

Master of Music, degree awarded at some universities, ranking between Bachelor and Doctor of Music.

Master of the King's (or Queen's) Music, title of a British court post, dating from Charles I's time, and now carrying a small salary and no fixed duties. It formerly implied the directorship of the sovereign's private band. (The spelling 'musick' has no authority today.) The post has been held since 1975 by Malcolm Williamson (succeeding Bliss).

Master Peter's Puppet Show (Sp., *El retablo de maese Pedro*), opera by Falla, first staged in Paris, 1923 (after an earlier performance in Seville in concert version). Libretto by composer, after an episode from *Don Quixote.* Uses three human characters plus marionettes.

Mastersinger (Ger., *meistersinger,* sing. and pl.), title given to members of a German guild of musicians, flourishing in the 14th–16th centuries; they were by origin merchants, etc., not aristocrats like the earlier MINNE-SINGERS. *The Mastersingers* (or *Die Meistersinger*) is commonly used as a short title for THE MASTERSINGERS OF NUREMBERG.

Mastersingers of Nuremberg, The (Ger., *Die Meistersinger von Nürnberg*), comic opera by Wagner, produced in Munich, 1868. Libretto by composer, dealing with a medieval guild (see preceding entry) and serving incidentally as a platform for some of Wagner's own views on art. See HANSLICK.

Mather, Bruce (b. 1939), Canadian composer (also pianist and university teacher), pupil of Milhaud and Messiaen in Paris. Works include song-cycle on poems of Rilke for voice and guitar; *Shades* for orchestra; Sonata for two pianos.

Mathias, William [James] (b. 1934), British composer, also pianist and professor (University of North Wales). Works include some with Welsh connections, also a clarinet concerto, three string quartets, etc.

Mathis the Painter (Ger., *Mathis der Maler*), (1) opera by Hindemith, produced in Zurich, 1938 (scheduled for Berlin, 1934, but banned by Nazis); libretto by composer, alluding to the painter Grünewald (early 16th century) and his altar-piece at Isenheim; (2) title of a symphony by Hindemith, drawn from the opera (the first movement is the overture); first performed in 1934, in advance of the opera.

Matin, Le, see MORNING.

Matrimonio segreto, Il, see SECRET MARRIAGE.

Matsudaira, Yoritsune (b. 1907), Japanese composer, pupil of A. Tcherepnin. Works include *Metamorphosis* (on an old Japanese melody) for soprano and orchestra, a two-piano concerto, piano solos and songs.

Matthäus-Passion, see ST MATTHEW PASSION.

Matthay, Tobias (1858–1945), British

pianist, and famous piano teacher, evolving a method of his own; also composer. His pupils included Myra Hess.

Mattheson, Johann (1681–1764), German organist, harpsichordist, singer, and composer of operas, church cantatas, keyboard music, etc.; also noted writer on music.

Matthews, Colin (b. 1946), British composer, pupil of Maw. Works include *Fourth Sonata* (orchestral), string quartets, *Shadows in the Water* for tenor and piano.

Matthews, David (b. 1943), British composer, brother of preceding; his works include three symphonies, five string quartets.

Matthews, Denis (1919–88), British pianist, noted in Beethoven, and writer on music; professor at Newcastle University, 1972–84; CBE, 1975. He committed suicide.

mattinata (It.), morning song.

Matton, Roger (b. 1929), Canadian composer (pupil of N. Boulanger in Paris); also university teacher. Works include a saxophone concerto, a two-piano concerto, *Brazilian Dance* for two pianos or orchestra.

Maupassant, Guy de (1850–93), French novelist. See ALBERT HERRING, LANDRÉ (G.).

Maurel, Victor (1848–1923), French baritone, among the most famous of his day; created Iago in Verdi's *Otello*, 1886.

Maw, Nicholas (b. 1935), British composer of operas *One Man Show* and *The Rising of the Moon*; *Scenes and Arias* (concert work for three female singers and orchestra on old French texts); *Odyssey* for orchestra (one movement, 90 mins.); *Essay* for organ; two string quartets, etc.

Maxwell Davies, Peter, see DAVIES ('Maxwell' is a middle name, not a surname).

Mayakovsky, Vladimir (1893–1930), Russian poet. See LOURIÉ.

Mayr, Richard (1877–1935), Austrian bass-baritone who took part in the first performances of Mahler's Symphony no. 8 and in early performances of R. Strauss's operas.

Mayuzumi, Toshiro (b. 1929), Japanese composer, trained in Tokyo and Paris. Works include *Bacchanal* for orchestra, Divertimento for 10 instruments, *Tonepleromas 55* for wind and percussion instruments and musical saw.

Mazeppa, (1) works by Liszt for piano (final version, 1847) and for orchestra (founded on the former, 1851) – alluding to the story (from Byron and Victor Hugo) that Mazeppa survived his punishment of being lashed naked to a wild horse, and became a Cossack chief; (2) opera by Tchaikovsky, produced in Moscow, 1884, with libretto by composer and V. P. Burenin, after Pushkin – alluding to Mazeppa's later treason to Peter the Great. Mazeppa (1664–1709) is a historical character.

mazurka, Polish country dance in 3/4 or 3/8 time; brought by Chopin (he wrote at least 55) into concert music.

m.d., right hand (in piano-playing etc.; Fr., *main droite*; It., *mano destra*).

me, in TONIC SOL-FA, the spoken name for third degree (mediant) of the scale, written m. See MI.

Meale, Richard (b. 1932), Australian composer of opera *Voss* (based on Patrick White's novel), orchestral work *Clouds Now and Then*, etc.

mean-tone temperament, see TEMPERAMENT.

measure, see BAR. (Also a term, used poetically, for a dance, etc.).

Medea (Fr., *Médée*), opera by Cherubini, produced in Paris, 1797. Libretto by F. B. Hoffman, about the sorceress of Greek legend who kills her own children as an act of vengeance.

mediant, name for the third degree of the scale, e.g. E in C major – so called because it stands midway between the tonic (or keynote) and dominant, i.e. between the first and fifth degrees. Cp. SUBMEDIANT.

Medium, The, opera by Menotti, produced in New York, 1946. Libretto by composer, about a fake spiritualistic medium. Also filmed, with the score slightly altered, 1951.

Medtner, Nicolas (properly Nikolay Karlovich Metner) (1880–1951), Russian composer-pianist of German descent. Left Russia, 1921, and in 1936 settled in England, where he died. Works, conforming generally to traditional structures and a Romantic idiom, include three piano concertos, numerous songs in Russian and German, many piano solos (several entitled *Fairy Tales*).

Mefistofele, see MEPHISTOPHELES.

Mehta, Zubin (b. 1936), Indian conductor (formerly violinist and pianist) who studied in Vienna and won an international conducting competition in Liverpool, 1958. Music director, Los Angeles Philharmonic Orchestra

1962–76; music adviser, Israel Philharmonic Orchestra, since 1968, later music director; music director, New York Philharmonic Orchestra, 1978–90.

Méhul, Étienne [Henri Nicolas] (1763–1817), French composer, encouraged by Gluck to write for the stage. Operas include *Joseph* and *The Two Blind Men of Toledo*; wrote also ballets, symphonies, patriotic (French Revolutionary) music etc.

Meistersinger von Nürnberg, Die, see MASTERSINGERS OF NUREMBERG.

Melba, Nellie, stage name (from her birthplace, Melbourne) of Helen Porter Mitchell (1861–1931), Australian soprano who settled in Britain and won unsurpassed operatic fame; first sang at Covent Garden in 1888. Created Dame, 1918.

Melchior, Lauritz (originally Lebrecht Hommel) (1890–1973), Danish-born singer who won fame in Wagner; became US citizen, 1947.

melisma (Gk., song; pl. *melismata*), a group of notes sung to a single syllable. (Term also sometimes applied more loosely to any florid vocal passage in the nature of a cadenza.) *Melismata* is also the title of a collection of English vocal pieces published by T. Ravenscroft in 1611.

Mellnäs, Arne (b. 1933), Swedish composer, pupil of Blacher in Berlin. Has produced several electronic works on tape (including *Kaleidovision* for a television ballet) as well as *Capricorn Flakes* for piano, harpsichord and vibraphone, *Aura* for orchestra, etc.

mellophone, type of brass instrument shaped similarly to an orchestral

HORN and used as a kind of 'poor relation' to it (e.g. occasionally in dance bands), being easier to play. Named presumably from 'mellow', it is also called the 'tenor cor'.

melodic minor, see MINOR.

mélodie (Fr.), (1) melody; (2) a song.

melodrama, term of which the current English sense (a sensational and sentimental play) is a debased meaning. As used in this book, and generally in musical contexts, it refers to the dramatic use of spoken words against a musical background – whether throughout a musical work (as in certain 18th-century examples) or forming part of a work, as in the gravedigging scene in Beethoven's FIDELIO. But note that the Italian form *melodramma* means simply opera.

melodramma, see preceding entry.

melody, a succession of notes varying in pitch and having a recognizable musical shape. Thus the three 'dimensions' of music are often thought of as (1) melody, (2) rhythm, (3) harmony and counterpoint. The term is also used as title for certain rather simple pieces – e.g. *Melody in F*, the almost sole survivor of Anton Rubinstein's piano solos, being no. 1 of *Two Melodies*, op. 3 (1853).

melos, ancient Greek word (from which 'melody' is derived), sometimes used to indicate a primal musical surge; borrowed for the names of the Melos Ensemble of London, founded 1950, and the following (but note also the leader's name).

Melos Quartet of Stuttgart, German string quartet founded in 1965, with Wilhelm Melcher as leader.

Melville, Herman (1819–91), American novelist. See BILLY BUDD, MENNIN.

membranophone, term used in the scientific classification of instruments for those in which a stretched skin (or something similar) is set in vibration, by stick or otherwise – drums, etc.

Mendelssohn, name by which the composer J. L. F. Mendelssohn Bartholdy and his family (see following two entries) are customarily known. Mendelssohn was their original surname, Bartholdy being added by the composer's father.

Mendelssohn [Bartholdy], Fanny Cäcilie (also in the French form, Cécile) (1805–47), German (amateur) pianist and composer, valued consultant of her brother (see next entry). Six of her songs were published as his, and she also wrote part-songs, piano solos, a piano trio. Married W. Hensel, painter, 1829.

Mendelssohn [Bartholdy], [Jacob Ludwig] Felix (1809–47), German composer; a grandson of the Jewish philosopher Moses Mendelssohn, but brought up as a Lutheran. Brother of the preceding. Noted pianist and organist; also conductor, head of Leipzig Conservatory (1843), and amateur painter. Born in Hamburg; boy prodigy, composing the overture to A MID-SUMMER NIGHT'S DREAM at 17 (the other music to it later). Visited Scotland, 1829 (see SCOTTISH SYMPHONY and HEBRIDES), and afterwards revisited Britain nine times, conducting the first performance of ELIJAH in 1846. Other works include operetta Son and Stranger; oratorio ST PAUL; five symphonies (no. 2 HYMN OF PRAISE, no. 3 SCOTTISH, no. 4 ITALIAN, no. 5 RE-

FORMATION; RUY BLAS and other overtures; two piano concertos; Violin Concerto in E minor (a youthful concerto in D minor, left in MS, was resuscitated by Menuhin); string octet (the Scherzo later scored for orchestra) and other chamber music; SONGS WITHOUT WORDS and other piano solos; organ works; songs. Combined Romantic ardour with a classical decorousness of form; but did not fulfil all his early promise and in the 20th century suffered a decline in popularity.

Mengelberg, Willem (1871–1951), Dutch conductor, unique in 50-year conductorship of Concertgebouw Orchestra of Amsterdam, 1895–1945; champion of Mahler and R. Strauss. Disgraced for support of Nazi wartime occupation of Holland, he died in Switzerland.

Mennin, Peter (originally Mennini) (1923–83), American composer, pupil of B. Rogers and Hanson. Wrote seven symphonies, Concertato [sic] for orchestra (inspired by Melville's Moby Dick), cantata The Christmas Story, two string quartets, piano pieces, etc. Head of Juilliard School of Music, New York, from 1963.

meno (It.), less; meno mosso, less moved, i.e. slower. Sometimes composers unhelpfully omit mosso and write, e.g. poco meno (really 'a little less') for 'a little slower'.

Menotti, Gian-Carlo (b. 1911), Italian composer living mainly in USA since 1928, but latterly in Scotland. Won international success as composer of operas with his own librettos. These include AMELIA GOES TO THE BALL, with libretto originally in Italian, and successors, nearly all in English – including *The Old Maid and the Thief*, THE MEDIUM, THE TELEPHONE, THE CONSUL, AMAHL AND THE NIGHT VISITORS (for television) and '*Goya*' (written for Plácido Domingo); also *The Unicorn, the Gorgon and the Manticore*, sung off-stage, mimed on-stage; has also written a piano concerto, etc. Acts as stage director for his operas, and directed the film of THE MEDIUM. Founder-director of music festival at Spoleto, Italy, 1958.

mensural notation, i.e. 'measured' or 'proportioned' notation, a system such as that in current use in which relative time-values of notes are mainly indicated by their visual shape. But the term is usually restricted to the early stages of the system (*c.*1250–1600), with visual shapes not the same as later ones, and a different set of guiding conventions.

menuet, Menuett (Fr., Ger.) = MINUET.

menuetto, term often written in scores by German-speaking composers under the impression that it is the Italian (correctly *minuetto*) for 'minuet'.

Menuhin, Yehudi (b. 1916), American-born violinist (British citizen, 1985), famous since boyhood; pupil of Enescu and others. Commissioned Bartók's unaccompanied Violin Sonata and in 1952 resuscitated an early MS concerto by Mendelssohn. Also viola player and conductor, chief musical figure of the Bath Festival and musical director of its chamber orchestra, 1959–68. Hon. KBE, 1965 ('Sir Yehudi' on naturalization); OM, 1987. His sisters are the pianists Hephzibah (1920–81) and Yaltah (b. 1921) Menuhin. See also KENTNER.

Mephisto (abbr. for Mephistopheles), name used by Liszt in four *Mephisto Waltzes* of which no. 1 (see FAUST) is the well-known one. Nos. 1 and 2, written for orchestra, were transcribed both for piano solo and for piano duet; no. 3 is for piano; no. 4 (unfinished, not published till 1952) is also for piano.

Mephistopheles (It., *Mefistofele*), opera by Boito, produced in 1868; libretto by the composer, after Goethe's *Faust*.

Mer, La, see SEA.

Merbecke, see MARBECK.

Mercadante, [Giuseppe] **Saverio** [Raffaele] (1795–1870), Italian composer of about 60 operas, including *The Horatii and the Curiatii*; was also church musician and (1840) director of the Naples Conservatory. Became totally blind in 1862 but continued to compose.

Mercure, Pierre (1927–66), Canadian composer who studied in Paris, active in organizing modern music events in Montreal. (Killed in a car accident.) Works include electronic pieces on tape or for tape-plus-live performance; also *Kaleidoscope* for orchestra, *Dissidence* (three songs) for soprano and piano, etc.

Meredith, George (1828–1909), British poet and novelist. See LARK ASCENDING.

Merikanto, Aare (1893–1958), Finnish composer of opera *Juha*, three symphonies, four violin concertos, etc.

Merrie England, the most popular operetta by German, produced in London, 1902. Libretto by B. Hood – introducing Queen Elizabeth I, Essex, etc.

Merrill, Robert (b. 1919), American baritone who sang with the Metropolitan Opera, New York, in more than 700 performances from 1945.

Merry Widow, The (Ger., *Die lustige Witwe*), first and most popular operetta by Lehár, produced in Vienna, 1905. Libretto by V. Leon and L. Stein, concerning romantic and diplomatic intrigue.

Merry Wives of Windsor, The (Ger., *Die lustigen Weiber von Windsor*), the most successful opera by Nicolai, produced in Berlin, 1849. Libretto by S. H. Mosenthal, after Shakespeare. (Another German opera so titled, by Dittersdorf, had appeared in 1796; Verdi's FALSTAFF and Vaughan Williams's SIR JOHN IN LOVE are founded on the same play.)

Merulo (real surname Merlotti), **Claudio** (1533–1604), Italian composer of music for stage and church: noted organist (at St Mark's, Venice) and composer for the organ.

messa (It.), (1) a placing or putting – see next entry; (2) Mass (=Lat., MISSA). So *Messa da Requiem*, title used (e.g. by Verdi) for a musical setting of the REQUIEM.

messa di voce (It., placing of the voice), the steady swelling and decreasing of vocal volume in one long-held note.

Messager, André [Charles Prosper] (1853–1929), French composer of *Mirette*, *Monsieur Beaucaire* (both in English), *Véronique* and other operettas, and of ballets (including *The Two Pigeons*), piano duets, etc. Also distinguished opera conductor, e.g. of the first performances of Debussy's PELLÉAS AND MÉLISANDE, which is dedicated to him. Pupil of Saint-Saëns.

Messe (Fr., Ger.), MASS.

Messiaen, Olivier [Eugène Prosper Charles] (b. 1908), French composer, and also organist and writer on music. Member of the former 'Young France' group. Influenced by Indian music, and cultivates great rhythmical complexity – see TURANGALÎLA. Uses almost literal orchestral imitation of bird-song in various works including *The Awakening of the Birds* for piano and orchestra. Has also written various works with Roman Catholic associations, including church music, *Visions of the Amen* for two pianos. *Twenty Looks at the Child Jesus* for one piano; also songs, organ works, QUARTET FOR THE END OF TIME, etc. See LORIOD.

Messiah (not *The Messiah*), oratorio by Handel, first performed in Dublin, 1742. Words selected from the Bible by C. Jennens.

mesto (It.), sad.

metà (It.), half.

Metamorphoses (Ger., *Metamorphosen*), work for 23 solo strings by R. Strauss, inscribed 'In Memoriam', quoting the funeral march from Beethoven's EROICA SYMPHONY and being apparently a dirge for lost Germany. First performed in 1946.

metamorphosis, term used to describe the way a composer may change a theme – altering tempo and rhythm, even notes, but preserving something essential and recognizable. This device has its obvious use in ILLUSTRATIVE MUSIC, and is also used elsewhere, e.g. in some symphonies (Franck's, Elgar's no. 1). Hindemith wrote an orchestral piece called *Symphonic Metamorphoses of* [in English references usually mistranslated as *on*] *Themes of Weber* (1943).

Metastasio, Pietro (1698–1782), Italian poet and dramatist. See CLEMENCY OF TITUS.

meter, American spelling of METRE.

metre, term used in prosody to cover the relationship between accented and unaccented beats, and sometimes similarly used in music – e.g. 3/8 and 6/8 being described as different kinds of *metres*. Usually the term RHYTHM is so defined as to cover this relationship along with others; but some writers define rhythm and *metre* as mutually exclusive, *metre* concerned with the basic unvarying pulse (as above) and rhythm with the actual time-patterns of notes effected by the composer with reference to this basic pulse. The usage *common metre*, etc., with reference to hymns, alludes to the verse, not to the music. See also next entry.

metrical, of METRE; so (referring to the verse, not the music) *metrical psalm*, a psalm translated and versified in a regular syllabic metre, and thus singable to an ordinary hymn-tune.

metronome, apparatus for sounding an adjustable number of beats per minute. The standard one is that patented in 1814 by J. N. Maelzel (1772–1838) who stole the invention from D. N. Winkel. There are also other types including electrical. A composer wishing for 60 quarter-note (crochet) beats in one minute writes 'MM [Maelzel's Metronome] ♩= 60'. Metronome marks for early works are added by modern editors. See also LIGETI.

Metropolitan Opera House (New York), the principal opera house of the United States, opened in 1883, re-housed in 1966. James Levine has been music director since 1975.

Meyer, Kerstin [Margareta] (b. 1928), Swedish mezzo-soprano well-known in opera; in 1960 first appeared at Covent Garden and at the Metropolitan (New York), in 1962 at the Bayreuth Festival.

Meyerbeer, Giacomo (originally Jakob Liebmann Meyer Beer) (1791–1864), German composer of opera in Italian, German and especially French – including ROBERT THE DEVIL, THE HUGUENOTS, *The Prophet, The African Woman* (*L'Africaine*). These are noted for spectacle and for a striking use of the orchestra. Visited Italy; settled in Paris, 1826, and died there, but was also active in Berlin from 1842 as musical director to the King of Prussia. Wrote also church music, marches, songs, etc.

Meyerowitz, Jan (originally Hans-Hermann) (b. 1913), German-born composer resident in USA since 1946; pupil of Casella and Respighi in Rome. Works include *The Barrier, Esther* and other operas; also a symphony subtitled 'Midrash Esther' (referring to Jewish biblical commentary), chamber music, etc.

mezzo, mezza (It.), half. So *mezza voce*, at half voice, i.e. with restricted tone; *mezzo-forte* (abbr. *mf*), midway between loud and soft; *mezzo-soprano*, type of female voice halfway between soprano and contralto range. The form *mezzo-contralto* is sometimes encountered, supposedly meaning a little lower than mezzo-soprano.

mf, see MEZZO.

m.g., left hand (in piano-playing, etc.; Fr., *main gauche*).

mi, the note E (in Latin countries, and formerly elsewhere); cp. ME. For *mi contra fa,* see TRITONE.

Miaskovsky, see MYASKOVSKY.

Michelangeli, Arturo Benedetti (b. 1920), Italian pianist, touring widely; first heard in Britain in 1946. Noted also as teacher. (His surname is really a double one, Benedetti Michelangeli, but in English-speaking use he is commonly referred to only as Michelangeli.).

Michelangelo [Michelagniolo Buonarroti] (1475–1564), Italian poet, sculptor and painter. See BRITTEN.

Mickiewicz, Adam (1798–1885), Polish poet. See BALLADE.

microtone, an interval smaller than a semitone. (An alternative name is 'fractional tone'.) QUARTER-TONES have been systematically exploited by A. Hába and other Czechs, and have also had occasional use in more 'orthodox' contexts, e.g. the string parts of Bloch's chamber music; see also CARRILLO (whose experiments in this field have extended to much smaller intervals) and OHANA.

Midday, name given to one of a set of three symphonies by Haydn: see MORNING.

middle C, the note C found at approximately the middle of the piano keyboard. It is commonly tuned to 261.6 Hz. (See FREQUENCY.)

Midi, Le, title of one of a set of three symphonies by Haydn: see MORNING.

Midsummer Marriage, The, opera by Tippett produced in London, 1955. Libretto by composer, applying ancient myth to modern characters (and having parallels to Mozart's THE MAGIC FLUTE). A set of *Ritual Dances* for chorus and orchestra is drawn from this.

Midsummer Night's Dream, A, play by Shakespeare which has had various musical treatments. Mendelssohn composed an overture in 1826 (when he was 17), and other incidental music including the celebrated 'Wedding March' in 1842. Incidental music to the play has also been written by Orff (1939). Britten's opera of the same title (produced at Aldeburgh, 1960) has Shakespeare's actual text (abbreviated by the composer and Peter Pears) as its libretto. See also FAIRY QUEEN, MIGNON.

Mighty Five, The, an alternative English term for THE MIGHTY HANDFUL.

Mighty Handful, The, English translation of Rus. *moguchaya kuchka,* term invented by Stasov, later applied to Balakirev, Borodin, Cui, Musorgsky and Rimsky-Korsakov. These five Russian composers took up a consciously 'nationalist' standpoint in music, drawing much on Russian history, literature, folk-music and folk-lore generally.

Mignon, opera by A. Thomas, produced in Paris, 1866. Libretto by J. Barbier and M. Carré, after Goethe's *Wilhelm Meister.* The soprano air 'I am Titania' occurs with reference to a performance (within the action of the opera) of *A Midsummer Night's Dream.*

Mignone, Francisco (1897–1986), Brazilian composer who studied in

Italy. Works include opera *The Diamond Broker* (incorporating a dance called 'Cogada' which is also given as a concert work); symphonic poem *Four Churches*; piano solos. Some of his works are indebted to Brazilian folk-lore.

Migot, Georges Elbert (1891–1976), French composer, pupil of d'Indy and Widor. He composed oratorios, 13 symphonies and *Sinfonia da chiesa* (It., Church Symphony) for 85 wind instruments, solo works for piano and for harpsichord, etc. He was also a writer on music.

Mihalovici, Marcel (1898–1985), composer, Romanian-born, who studied with d'Indy in Paris and settled there. Works include opera *Krapp* (after Beckett's *Krapp's Last Tape*), five symphonies, *Concerto quasi una fantasia* for violin and orchestra, chamber music. Wife was the pianist Monique Haas.

Mihály, András (b. 1917), Hungarian composer, also conductor. Works include three symphonies, opera *Together and Alone*, *Chamber Music* (on texts by James Joyce) for voice and piano.

Mikado, The, or The town of Titipu, operetta by Sullivan, produced in London, 1885; libretto by W. S. Gilbert. Set in an imaginary Japan, it was its creators' most successful work and has been subjected to various adaptations; filmed versions appeared in 1938 and 1966.

Mikrokosmos (Gk., Microcosm), piano work by Bartók, composed between 1926 and 1937; it consists of 153 small pieces in the nature of technical studies, progressively arranged.

Milán, Luis (*c.*1500–*c.*1561), Spanish player of the VIHUELA (Spanish form of lute), and composer of music for it; also composer of songs with vihuela accompaniment in Spanish, Portuguese and Italian – including one of the first pubished books of songs for a single voice with accompaniment, 1536.

Milhaud, Darius (1892–1974), French composer, one of the group of composers called the SIX. Associated with various important literary figures, especially Claudel (opera CHRISTOPHER COLUMBUS, and other works) and Cocteau (ballets, etc.). Visited Brazil and USA and was influenced by jazz as early as 1922–3 (ballet THE CREATION OF THE WORLD) and also by Latin-American music (see SAUDADES; SCARAMOUCHE). Very prolific, his other works include operas *Bolivar* and *David*; 18 symphonies; 18 string quartets, of which nos. 14–15 can be played separately or together; Jewish liturgical music; many songs. In USA during World War II, and frequently afterwards.

military band, a band of brass and woodwind (not brass alone – see BRASS BAND) with percussion, maintained by armies, etc., principally for performing on the march. The instruments and numbers vary considerably between countries and to a lesser extent within them. A British band of a large mid-20th-century type typically used flute, piccolo, oboe, clarinets, bassoons, saxophones, horns (orchestral), cornets (sometimes trumpets), trombones, euphoniums and tubas, plus percussion, with a double-bass often added when not on the march. Cp. CONCERT BAND.

Military Symphony, nickname for

Miller, Arthur

Haydn's Symphony no. 100 in G (Hob. I: 100; first performed in 1794, on Haydn's visit to London), having 'military band' effects from bass drum, cymbals and triangle.

Miller, Arthur (b. 1915), American dramatist. See WARD (R.), ROSSELLINI.

Millöcker, Karl (1842–99), Austrian composer of *The Beggar Student* and many other operettas; also of piano pieces, etc. Active also as theatre conductor.

Milne, A. A. [Alan Alexander] (1882–1956), British writer and poet. See FRASER-SIMSON.

Milner, Anthony [Francis Dominic] (b. 1925), British composer; pupil of R. O. Morris, Seiber and others. Has written chiefly vocal music including unaccompanied Mass, cantata *The City of Desolation*, and other works with Roman Catholic associations; also three symphonies, Variations for orchestra, an oboe quartet, songs. In addition he is a university teacher, and a writer on music.

Milnes, Sherrill [Eustace] (b. 1935), American baritone, eminent in opera; first appearance at the Metropolitan (New York), 1965, at Covent Garden, 1971. Has also conducted operatic recordings.

Milstein, Nathan [Mironovich] (b. 1904), Russian-born American violinist, pupil of Auer and Ysaÿe; eminent soloist, and also arranger of violin pieces.

Milton, John (*c.* 1563–1647), English composer, father of the poet (below). Contributed a madrigal to THE TRIUMPHS OF ORIANA and wrote other vocal music, fantasies for viols, etc.

Milton, John (1608–74), English poet. See COMUS, CREATION, LAWES (Henry), MARKEVICH, MASQUE, PARADISE LOST, WOOD (Hugh).

mime, acting without speech; a stage piece consisting of such (sometimes given with music).

min., abbr. for minor (scale, etc.).

minacciando (It.), threatening.

Mines of Sulphur, The, opera by Richard Rodney Bennett, produced in London, 1965; libretto, by Beverley Cross, is a ghost-story. The title is metaphorical and a quotation from Shakespeare's *Othello*.

miniature score, see SCORE.

minim, see HALF-NOTE.

minimalism, a compositional tendency evolving from the 1960s, particularly evident in the work of such American composers as Riley, Glass and Adams; short units of basic harmony and rhythm are cumulated by repetition with little variation.

Minkus, Léon (really Aloisius Ludwig Minkus) (1826–1917), Austrian-born composer who settled in Russia but died in Vienna; composed mainly ballets, including *Don Quixote*.

Minnesinger (Ger., sing. and pl.; also as English word), type of minstrel flourishing in guilds in 12th- and 13th-century Germany. By social origin these singers were aristocratic; the MASTERSINGERS who flourished afterwards were of the merchant class.

Minnesota Orchestra, American orchestra founded in 1903 as Minneapolis Symphony Orchestra, taking its present name in 1986; conductors have included Doráti (1949–60), Marriner (1979–86), and currently De Waart.

minor, term opposed to 'major' and applied to scales, keys, chords and intervals; for all these usages see MAJOR.

minore (It.), minor (in the above sense); the word is often used in a 'theme and variations' to label a minor-key variation of a major-key theme.

minstrel, (1) general term applied in modern usage to a type of medieval musical performer, usually singing to his own accompaniment, and usually belonging to a guild or other recognized company; in medieval times such performers were classed more particularly (see, e.g., JONGLEUR, MASTERSINGER, MINNESINGER, TROUBADOUR, TROUVÈRE); (2) term applied to a black-faced (imitation-Negro) entertainer such as were organized into troupes in USA in the 1830s and later elsewhere. Debussy's *Minstrels*, in his second book of piano preludes, refers to these.

Mintz, Shlomo (b. 1957), Russian-born violinist who went as a child to Israel; gave New York début recital in 1973. Adviser to the Israel Chamber Orchestra.

minuet, minuetto (Eng., It.), dance in triple time of French rustic origin, 'promoted' to court use and becoming widely fashionable in the 18th century. It forms the standard third movement of the 'classical' (Haydn–Mozart) sonata, symphony, string quartet, etc., later developing with Beethoven into the SCHERZO. It is normally in AABA form, the 'B' being in contrast and called 'trio' because of the French custom (long since dropped) of writing it in only three parts. See BOCCHERINI.

Minute Waltz, nickname for Chopin's Waltz in D♭, op. 64, no. 1 (published in 1847) – bestowed evidently by someone too insensitive to realize that it can be played in one minute only if taken too fast.

Miracle, The, nickname for Haydn's Symphony no. 96 in D (Hob. I: 96) – because, when Haydn directed its first performance in London in 1791, a chandelier was supposed to have fallen on a vacant space in a crowded hall, hitting no one. This account is now known to be false.

Miraculous Mandarin, The (Hung., *A csodálatos mandarin*), one-act mime-play with music by Bartók (scenario by M. Lengyel), composed 1919; produced in Cologne, 1926; source of a concert suite first performed in 1928. The mandarin, though stabbed and hanged by robbers, refuses to die until the robbers' woman yields herself to him.

Mireille, opera by Gounod, produced in Paris, 1864. Libretto by M. Carré, after a Provençal poem. (The name is that of the heroine.) It has a tragic ending, but Gounod also provided a happy ending as an alternative.

mirliton (Fr.) = KAZOO.

mirror canon, mirror fugue, a canon or fugue in which two or more PARTS appear on paper simultaneously both the right way up and upside down – i.e. as if a mirror lay between them, making one the reflection of the other. (The use of the term for a piece that can be played backwards – i.e. as if a mirror could be put at the end – is sometimes encountered but is not correct.)

Mirzoyan, Edvard [Mikhailovich] (b.

255

1921), Soviet-Armenian composer of cantatas (one called *Soviet Armenia*), *Introduction and Perpetuum Mobile* for violin and orchestra, a trombone concerto, etc.

Miserere, the name in the Roman Catholic Church for Psalm 50 (51 in the Hebrew and English Bibles), often set by composers; see ALLEGRI. A setting is incorporated into Act IV of Verdi's IL TROVATORE.

missa (Lat.), Mass. So – *Missa brevis*, either (1) a setting of the Mass in unusually concise musical form, or (2) a setting of the Kyrie and Gloria only, in obsolete Lutheran usage; *Missa parodia* (erroneous term), see PARODY; *Missa sine nomine* (Mass without a name), Mass of entirely original material, not based on a plainsong or secular tune (term used in the 15th and 16th centuries, when the latter was the common practice, the Mass then taking the name of its source). So also *Missa solemnis*, term sometimes used by composers for a lengthy and exalted setting of the Mass – and now particularly associated with Beethoven's Mass in D (first performance, St Petersburg, 1824), so entitled. See also next entry.

Missa Papae Marcelli, a Mass by Palestrina dedicated to Marcellus II, who became Pope in 1555.

misura (It.), a measure (in various senses); *senza misura*, not in strict time (e.g. of a passage in which bar-lines are omitted).

mit (Ger.), with.

Mitropoulos, Dmitri (1896–1960), Greek-born American conductor, also pianist and composer; gave premières of works by Hindemith, Copland, Barber (opera *Vanessa*) and other composers. Conductor of New York Philharmonic Orchestra, 1949–57.

mixed chorus, mixed voices, etc., a body comprising both male and female (adult) voices.

Mixolydian mode, the MODE represented by the white notes on the piano from G to G.

mixture, type of organ-stop simultaneously sounding two or more of the higher tones (other than octaves) of the HARMONIC SERIES. A stop sounding two such tones is said to be a mixture of two 'ranks' (and so forth); and the number of ranks is indicated in organ specifications by roman figures. The *mixture* is used in conjunction with 'normal' stops to add richness to the tone.

MM, see METRONOME.

M.Mus., abbr. of Master of Music (degree between 'Bachelor' and 'Doctor' of Music, awarded at some universities).

modal, of the old MODES. See next entry.

mode, name for each of the ways of ordering the notes of a scale. Thus in references to major and minor keys (see MAJOR), the terms *major mode* and *minor mode* may be met. But the chief use of the word is in reference to non-major, non-minor scales prevalent in Western art-music before 1600 and still encountered in other music. The accepted older modes (as played on the white notes of the modern piano) were:

> D – D, called Dorian, numbered I
>
> E – E, called Phrygian, numbered III

F – F, called Lydian, numbered V

G – G, called Mixolydian, numbered VII

plus two more introduced in the 16th century:

A – A, called Aeolian, numbered IX

C – C, called Ionian, numbered XI

– these two foreshadowing the minor and major keys respectively. A melody in the Dorian mode will end on D, in the Phrygian on E, etc. This note is called the 'final'.

The modes detailed above are called the *authentic modes*: this implies that the compass of the melody shall be within the octave marked (D to D for the Dorian, etc.). The *plagal modes* are formed from the same notes but have a compass that puts the final in the middle: e.g. in the plagal mode corresponding to the Dorian, the melody will still end on D but will have a compass from A to A. Accordingly it is called 'Hypodorian' and given the number II; the other plagal modes likewise take the prefix *hypo-* (from the Greek for 'under') and take the even number following that of the corresponding authentic mode. Hence Hypophrygian, mode IV (E is final, with the range B to B).

Note that (1) the modal system thus links the *kind* of scale with the *pitch* of a scale – unlike the key-system, where major and minor scales are merely relative, to be applied at any pitch; but, of course, a modern composer using a mode can transpose it to any pitch (by the use of what are, on the piano, black notes); and before 1600 composers did this to a limited extent; (2) the names of the modes are taken from ancient Greek names, but do not correspond to Greek usage.

moderato (It.), at a moderate pace. It is also used after another tempo-direction, e.g. *allegro moderato*, implying 'a moderate allegro', i.e. that the word 'allegro' is not to be taken in an extreme sense.

modinha, type of Portuguese (and hence Brazilian) popular song mainly flourishing in the 18th and 19th centuries.

modo (It.), manner; *in modo di*, in the manner of.

modulate, to change from one key to another in the course of a composition – such a change being accomplished by 'continuous' musical means (i.e. not simply by starting afresh in another key) and having a definite validity in the structural organization of the music. Hence *modulation* and *style modulation* (see under STYLE).

modulator, diagram used for instructional purposes in TONIC SOL-FA, for practice in sight-reading and modulation.

Moeran, Ernest John (1894–1950), British composer, pupil of John Ireland. Works include a symphony, Sinfonietta, a violin concerto, cello concerto, chamber music, piano solos, many songs and folk-song arrangements. Was himself a collector of Norfolk folk-songs.

Moffo, Anna (b. 1932), American soprano who made her operatic début in Italy, 1956; first sang at Covent Garden in 1964 as Gilda in *Rigoletto*.

Mohaupt, Richard (1904–57), composer, German-born (also conductor), who settled in USA, 1939, but returned to Europe, 1955, and died in Austria. Works include opera *The Host-*

ess of Pinsk (based on Napoleon's invasion of Russia); *Town Piper Music* (after a painting by Dürer) for orchestra; a violin concerto.

Moïse, see MOSES.

Moiseiwitsch (German transliteration of Rus. 'Moiseivich'), **Benno** (1890–1963), Russian-born pianist who settled in Britain during World War I and was naturalized in 1937. Toured much and won celebrity in romantic music.

Molière [Jean Baptiste Poquelin] (1622–73), French dramatist. See ARIADNE ON NAXOS, BOURGEOIS GENTILHOMME, CHARPENTIER (M.-A.), KÓSA, LULLY.

Molinari-Pradelli, Francesco (b. 1911), Italian conductor, prominent in opera – La Scala, Milan, from 1946; Covent Garden from 1955.

Molinaro, Simone (c.1565–1615), Italian lutenist and composer of lute music, madrigals and church music; director of music at Genoa Cathedral.

Molique, [Wilhelm] **Bernard** (1802–69), German violinist and composer of six violin concertos, eight string quartets, etc.; lived in London, 1849–66.

moll (Ger.), minor – in the sense *D-moll*, D minor, etc.

Molloy, James Lyman (1837–1909), Irish amateur composer of 'Love's Old Sweet Song' and similar popular Victorian songs; London barrister by profession.

Molter, Johann [Melchior] (1696–1765), German composer of 167 symphonies, and of concertos for clarinet, for one and two trumpets, etc.

molto (It.), much, very; so, e.g., *allegro molto* or (more rarely) *allegro di molto*, very fast.

moment, (1) see the following entry; (2) a structural concept in composition devised by Stockhausen; a 'moment' is a normally brief segment of a composition with its own musical characteristic. Occurrences within each 'moment' may be held more important than the succession between moments, and such a succession may indeed be indeterminate, as in Stockhausen's work entitled *Moments* (Ger., *Momente*) for soprano, four choirs and 13 instruments, 1964. Hence *moment-form* as description of such a work.

Moment Musical (Fr., pl. *Moments musicaux*), title given by Schubert to each of a set of six short pieces for piano, completed 1828 (D780), and afterwards used similarly by other composers.

Mompou, Federico (1893–1987), Spanish pianist and composer, mainly for the piano but also of songs; he lived at different periods in Barcelona and Paris.

Monaco, Mario Del, see DEL MONACO.

Monckton, Lionel (1861–1924), British composer of *The Country Girl* and other musical comedies, etc.; collaborated with H. Talbot in *The Arcadians*.

Moniuszko, Stanisław (1819–72), Polish composer who is regarded as the chief 19th-century composer of his country, after Chopin – especially through his opera HALKA. Wrote other operas in a Romantic style recognized as 'national', and also many songs and much church music. Was also conductor, and formerly organist; studied in Berlin.

Monk, William Henry (1823–89), English organist and composer of 'Abide with Me' and other hymns, etc.; editor of *Hymns Ancient and Modern*, 1861.

Monn, Georg Matthias (1717–50), Austrian organist, and composer of the first extant symphony in four movements, with a minuet, 1740 (anticipating the Haydn–Mozart type). Also composed concertos, chamber music, church music, etc.

monochord, scientific instrument consisting of a single string with a movable bridge, used (since the time of Ancient Egypt) for showing how, by altering the ratios in which the string is vibrating, different notes may be produced. These are the notes of the HARMONIC SERIES. A musical instrument based on this principle is the TRUMPET MARINE.

monodic, see MONODY.

monodrama, stage piece for one character, e.g. Schoenberg's EXPECTA-TION (Ger., *Erwartung*). Berlioz's *Lélio* is also so styled because it has only one actor – though many other performers (musicians, not actors).

monody (from Gk. for 'single song'), term used to describe the melody-and-CONTINUO style of writing (e.g. in early 17th-century Italian opera) in contrast to the earlier polyphonic style when all parts were held as of equal importance (none simply as accompaniment). So also *monodic*.

monophony (from Gk. for 'single sound'), term used of music with a single line of melody (with neither harmonic support nor other melodies in counterpoint). It is sometimes used also even when a simple accompani-ment is present, provided that the melody is self-sufficient. So also *monophonic*. (Cp. HOMOPHONY, POLY-PHONY.)

monothematic, having only a single theme.

Monsigny, Pierre Alexandre (1729–1817), French composer, of a noble family. Wrote successful operas of the OPÉRA-COMIQUE type, including *Rose and Colas*, *The Deserter* and *Philemon and Baucis*. Ceased to compose in middle life, with the rise of Grétry.

Monte, Philippe de (1521–1603), Flemish composer. Visited Italy and (briefly) England. Chapel music director to the Hapsburg emperors at Vienna and at Prague, where he died. Composed madrigals and similar works (more than 1,200 surviving), and also Masses, motets, etc.

Montéclair, Michel Pinolet de (1667–1737), French composer of operas, chamber music, etc.; in early life a church chorister, and afterwards player of double-bass and other stringed instruments in Paris.

Montemezzi, Italo (1875–1952), Italian composer of *The Love of the Three Kings* and other operas; also orchestral works, Elegy for cello and piano, etc.

Monteux, Pierre (1875–1964), French conductor, active in Paris where in 1913 he gave the first (riot-provoking) performance of Stravinsky's *The Rite of Spring*. Later he was conductor of the Boston Symphony Orchestra (1919–24), Paris Symphony Orchestra (1929–35), San Francisco Symphony Orchestra, London Symphony Orchestra (1961).

Monteverdi, Claudio (1567–1643),

Italian composer, notable in the history of opera, harmony and orchestration. Choirboy at his birthplace, Cremona; afterwards held various state and church musical positions in Mantua and elsewhere – finally in Venice, where he died. Became a priest, 1632. His operas (usually considered history's first major operas) include ORPHEUS, THE RETURN OF ULYSSES and (when he was 75) THE CORONATION OF POPPAEA – known in various modern editions. Some other operas are lost. Wrote also more than 250 madrigals (some with independent instrumental parts – see MADRIGAL), including a few 'madrigali spirituali' (to religious words); Masses, two settings of the Magnificat, VESPERS and other vocal works with varying accompaniment – and often with 'daringly' expressive harmony. Wrote no purely instrumental works.

Montreal Symphony Orchestra, Canadian orchestra which adopted that title (and its French equivalent) in 1953. Conductor since 1977, Charles Dutoit.

Montsalvatge, Xavier [Bassols] (b. 1912), Spanish composer. Works include opera *Babel 1948*; *Five Invocations to the Crucified* for soprano and 12 instruments; *Concerto breve* for piano and orchestra; songs and piano solos.

Moog, Robert (b. 1934), inventor of SYNTHESIZER named after him.

Moonlight Sonata, nickname (not Beethoven's, and fitting only the first movement) for Beethoven's Piano Sonata in C♯ minor, op. 27, no. 2 (1801).

Moór, Emanuel (1863–1931), Hungarian pianist, composer (operas,

eight symphonies, etc.), conductor and inventor of what he called the Duplex-Coupler piano (1921) with two keyboards tuned an octave apart. Settled in Switzerland and died there.

Moore, Douglas [Stuart] (1893–1969), American composer; pupil of d'Indy, N. Boulanger and Bloch. Works (several alluding to American history and legend) include operas *The Devil and Daniel Webster* and THE BALLAD OF BABY DOE; also composed two symphonies, chamber music, works for amateur performers, etc.

Moore, Gerald (1899–1987), British pianist who created a new dignity for the art of the song-accompanist, retiring in 1967 but continuing to write and lecture. CBE, 1954.

Moore, Thomas (1779–1852), Irish poet who wrote (to Irish traditional tunes) the words of 'The Last Rose of Summer' (see MARTHA) and 'The Minstrel Boy', etc. See also PARADISE AND THE PERI.

Morales, Cristóbal (*c.*1500–1553), Spanish composer, also priest. For a time was singer in the Papal Chapel in Rome, afterwards holding cathedral music posts in Spain. Composed Masses, motets and other church music; also a few madrigals.

morality, description ('a morality' instead of 'an opera') given by Vaughan Williams to his stage work THE PILGRIM'S PROGRESS, with allusion to medieval 'morality plays' on religious subjects.

morbido (It.), gentle, delicate (not 'morbid'). So *morbidezza*, delicacy, etc.

morceau (Fr.), a piece (of bread, music, etc.).

mordent, musical ornament which in its standard form (following the original meaning, 'biting') consists of the rapid alternation of the main note with a subsidiary note a step below. In this form it is also called a *lower mordent*, having the sign ⩗. Its variant, the *inverted mordent* (also called *upper mordent*), having the sign ⩘ , consists of the alternation of the main note with a subsidiary note a step above. In the baroque period, however, the sign ⩘ implied a short trill (Ger., *Pralltriller*), from the note above, thus:

Moreau, Jean Baptiste (1656–1733), French composer of church music, stage works, songs, etc. Teacher of both singing and composition, and held a court post under Louis XIV.

morendo (It.), dying – direction aimed not at the performer but at the music, which is to lose force and (if necessary) speed.

Mörike, Eduard Friedrich (1804–75), German poet. *Mörike Songs* (Ger., *Mörike-Lieder*) is the usual name for a set of 53 songs by Wolf (1888) to his verse. Wolf also wrote four earlier settings of Mörike.

Morley, Thomas (1557/8–1602), English composer, pupil of Byrd; organist of St Paul's Cathedral, London, and member of the Chapel Royal. Writer of textbook, *A Plain and Easy Introduction to Practical Music*. His setting of 'It was a lover and his lass' from Shakespeare's *As You Like It* may have been for the original production of the play (1599). He also wrote Latin and English church music, madrigals, BAL-

LETTS (he introduced this form to England), canzonets for two and more voices, solo songs with lute, pieces for viols and for keyboard. Editor of and contributor to THE TRIUMPHS OF ORIANA.

Morning; Midday; Evening and Tempest, titles given respectively to Symphonies nos. 6–8 by Haydn, *c*.1761 (Hob. I: 6–8). The music has illustrative intent, though no explicit clues are given. Haydn affixed the titles in French, the international 'polite' language of the time – *Le Matin, Le Midi, Le Soir et la tempête*, the last being also known sometimes simply as *Le Soir*.

Morning Heroes, 'symphony' by Bliss – work for orator, chorus and orchestra, on texts by various authors, in memory of the composer's brother and others killed in World War I. First performed in 1930.

Moross, Jerome (1913–83), American composer of *Gentlemen, Be Seated!* and other operas; Sonata for double-bass and piano; film music, etc.

morris, type of English folk-dance associated with Whitsuntide and historically performed by men, the dancers wearing bells; traditionally accompanied by PIPE and TABOR.

Morris, William (1834–96), British poet and artist. See HARRISON.

Morton, Robert (*c*.1430–*c*.1476), English composer of chansons, etc.; in service to the court of Burgundy.

Moscheles, Ignaz (1794–1870), German-Bohemian pianist and composer (eight piano concertos, etc., now hardly ever performed); friend of Beethoven, teacher of Mendelssohn.

Resident in England as teacher (and also conductor), 1826–46.

Mosè in Egitto, see MOSES.

Moses, opera by Rossini, originally in Italian (*Mosè in Egitto*, i.e. Moses in Egypt), produced in Naples, 1818, with libretto by A. N. Tottola; revised and enlarged version in French (*Moïse*), produced in Paris, 1827, with libretto by G. L. Balochi and V. J. E. de Jouy.

Moses and Aaron (Ger., *Moses und Aron*), opera by Schoenberg. The libretto, by the composer, exists complete, but he finished the music of only the first two (out of three) acts. The work was first performed posthumously on the Hamburg radio station, 1954, and first staged in Zurich, 1957.

Mosolov, Alexander Vasilievich (1900–1973), Russian composer (also pianist), pupil of Glière. Won wide notice with orchestral piece *Iron Foundry*, 1928, incorporating a metal sheet, shaken. Other works include six symphonies, a harp concerto, operas.

mosso (It.), moving, animated.

Mossolov, a frequently encountered (but strictly mistaken) spelling for the Russian composer MOSOLOV.

Moszkowski, Moritz (1854–1925), Polish-German pianist and composer, dying in poverty in Paris. Composed sets of Spanish dances for piano duet; also the symphony *Joan of Arc*, a piano concerto, operas, etc.

motet, (1, normal current use) type of church choral composition, usually in Latin, to words not fixed in the liturgy – corresponding in the Roman Catholic service to the ANTHEM (in English) in the Anglican service; (2, exceptionally) type of work related to the preceding but not exactly conforming to it – e.g. Parry's *Songs of Farewell* (designated by the composer as *motets*) which are choral and 'serious' but not ecclesiastical; (3, medieval use) a polyphonic vocal composition based on a 'given' tenor part, over which the upper voice or voices (up to three) moved at a faster rate. In the French secular motet the upper parts commonly had different texts from the Latin tenor and might be in the vernacular (hence *polytextual motet*).

Mother Goose (Fr., *Ma mère l'oye*), suite by Ravel for piano duet, 1908, orchestrated and given as ballet, 1912. It consists of five movements, based on fairy-tales by Perrault.

motif (Fr.), term sometimes used in English for LEADING-MOTIVE and sometimes simply for 'theme', etc.; better avoided because of its ambiguities.

motion, term used to describe the course upwards or downwards of a melody or melodies. A single melody is said to move by *conjunct motion* or *disjunct motion* according to whether a note moves to an adjacent note or to some other note (i.e. by a 'step' or by a 'leap'). Apart from this, two melodies move by *similar motion* (in the same direction, i.e. up or down together), or by *contrary motion* (one up, one down), or by *oblique motion* (one remaining on the same note, the other not). *Parallel motion* is 'similar motion' of such a kind that the parts not only move up and down together, but do so 'in parallel', preserving the same interval between them.

Motiv, motive (Ger., Eng.), a short recognizable melodic or rhythmic figure

– term used especially to indicate the smallest possible subdivision in musical analysis: one THEME possibly having several *motives*. But the term LEADING-MOTIVE conveys a larger type of unit and a different meaning.

moto (It.), movement; *con moto*, with movement; *moto perpetuo* (perpetual motion), title given to a rapid piece, usually having repetitive note-patterns – also (Lat.), *perpetuum mobile*.

Mottl, Felix [Josef] (1856–1911), Austrian conductor, arranger of orchestral music – e.g. from Gluck's stage works – and composer of three operas.

motto, motto theme, theme which, in the course of a piece of music, recurs (perhaps transformed) in the manner of a quotation – e.g. in Berlioz's FAN-TASTIC SYMPHONY (where it is called *idée fixe*) and in Tchaikovsky's Symphony no. 5. The device is related to METAMORPHOSIS of themes.

Motu Proprio (Lat.), a type of decree issued by the Pope; in musical contexts referring particularly to that of Pius X, 1902, emphasizing the prime value of plainsong and Palestrina-period polyphony for the Roman Catholic Church, and curbing tendencies towards the employment in church of secular-style compositions, orchestral instruments, women's voices, etc.

'Mourning' Symphony, nickname for Haydn's Symphony no. 44 in E minor, *c*.1772 (Hob. I: 44). Haydn wanted its slow movement to be played at his own funeral service.

Moussorgsky, see MUSORGSKY.

mouth music, English equivalent for Gaelic *port á beul*, type of wordless but articulated singing used to accompany Scottish Highland dancing when no instrument is available. Known in Ireland as 'lilting'.

mouth-organ, see HARMONICA.

Mouton, Charles (1626–after 1700), French lutenist and composer of music for his instrument (and of church music). Held court post at Turin.

Mouton, Jean (*c*.1459–1522), French composer of Masses and other church music, also CHANSONS; in service at the French court. Pupil of JOSQUIN, and teacher of Willaert.

mouvement (Fr.), (1) motion; *mouvement perpetuel = moto perpetuo* (see MOTO); *au mouvement, premier (1er) mouvement = a tempo, tempo primo* (see TEMPO); so also *mouvementé*, with movement; (2) a MOVEMENT in the sense below.

movable doh, description of systems of sight-reading, etc., in which (e.g. in TONIC SOL-FA) *doh* represents the keynote, *ray* the note above, etc., whatever the key. (Opposite to systems wherein, as in Continental SOLFEG-GIO, *do* is C, *re* is D, etc., whatever the key.)

movement, the primary self-contained division of a large composition – usually each having a separate indication of speed, hence the name. A large composition without any such division is said to be 'in one movement'. The word is used as a title in Stravinsky's *Movements* for piano and orchestra (short work in five sections, 1958–9).

movimento (It.), motion (not 'movement' in the preceding sense); *doppio movimento*, at double the preceding speed.

Mozart, [Johann Georg] **Leopold** (1719–87), German violinist and author of a famous violin 'method'; composer (see TOY SYMPHONY); and father of the following. Settled in Salzburg, Austria.

Mozart, Wolfgang Amadeus (christened Joannes Chrysostomus Wolfgangus Theophilus) (1756–91), Austrian composer, born in Salzburg. His father (see above) took him and his sister on tour to Paris, London, etc., chiefly as harpsichord prodigies, in 1763–6. He had already begun to compose (including opera BASTIEN AND BASTIENNE); by 1773, he had thrice visited Italy and had entered the service of the Prince Archbishop of Salzburg. Disliked this and left it after a quarrel, 1781, settling in Vienna. Visited Prague (where DON GIOVANNI and THE CLEMENCY OF TITUS were produced), Berlin and elsewhere; died, poor, in Vienna, of typhus. Other operas include IDOMENEUS, THE SERAGLIO, THE IMPRESARIO, THE MARRIAGE OF FIGARO, COSÌ FAN TUTTE, THE MAGIC FLUTE. Wrote also 21 concertos for piano, one for clarinet and various others, more than anyone else establishing classical concerto form. (Four further, juvenile piano concertos are arrangements of others' music.) His symphonies (including those nicknamed HAFFNER, LINZ, PRAGUE, PARIS, JUPITER) have been numbered up to 41, but some of these are spurious and some other works of this kind are not so numbered. Composed various serenades (see HAFFNER, EINE KLEINE NACHTMUSIK); A MUSICAL JOKE; 24 string quartets (some nicknamed, e.g. PRUSSIAN QUARTETS), one clarinet quintet, six string quintets and other chamber works; sonatas for violin and for harpsichord (or piano); Requiem (unfinished, completed by Süssmayr), 17 Masses, some works for Masonic use, isolated arias with orchestra and songs with piano. Some works are misattributed to him (see WIEGENLIED). His compositions are indexed by 'K' numbers, referring to the catalogue made by Ludwig von Köchel (published in 1862).

Mozart and Salieri, opera by Rimsky-Korsakov, produced in Moscow, 1898 – a setting of Pushkin's dramatic poem, based on the (false) notion that Salieri poisoned Mozart.

Mozartiana, suite by Tchaikovsky, 1887 – orchestration of three piano works and the motet *Ave Verum Corpus* (Hail, True Body) by Mozart.

Mravinsky, Yevgeny [Alexandrovich] (1903–88), Russian conductor, for 50 years associated with the Leningrad Philharmonic Orchestra; gave premières of five Shostakovich symphonies.

m.s., left hand (in piano-playing, etc.; It., *mano sinistra*).

MS, MSS, manuscript(s).

Mudarra, Alonso de (*c.*1510–80), Spanish composer of music for the VIHUELA (Spanish lute) – fantasias, dance music, etc.

Mudge, Richard (1718–63), British clergyman and composer, known for a set of six concertos (of CONCERTO GROSSO type).

Muette de Portici, La, see MASANIELLO.

Muffat, Georg (1653–1704), German organist and composer, possibly of Scottish descent. Studied in Paris and Rome; wrote keyboard music, works of CONCERTO GROSSO type, etc. Father of the following.

Muffat, Gottlieb (1690–1770), German composer of suites for harpsichord, fugues and other works for organ; himself an organist, in service to the court at Vienna.

muffle, to cover the surface of a drum with a cloth, producing an effect analogous to that of a MUTE.

Muldowney, Dominic (b. 1952), British composer (also conductor); his teachers include Birtwistle. Works include *Music at Chartres* for chamber orchestra; *The English Soldier's Tale* for the same ensemble (including actors and dancer) as Stravinsky's – see SOLDIER'S TALE; much music composed or arranged for National Theatre productions.

Mulè, Giuseppe (1885–1951), Italian cellist, and composer of opera, music to Greek plays, symphonic poems, etc.

Mulliner Book, a MS collection of English pieces (mainly for keyboard instrument, but a few for cittern and gittern) made by Thomas Mulliner and apparently dating approximately from 1550 to 1575; published in modern notation in 1951 and reckoned one of the most valuable sources of its period.

multimedia, term applied to mixtures of musical, visual, poetic and other events as practised by such composers as Berio and Lejaren Hiller, mainly from the early 1960s – often incorporating electronic means and excluding traditional 'mixtures' such as opera and ballet.

multi-serialism, see SERIES.

Mumma, Gordon (b. 1935), American composer who uses the term 'cyber-

sonics' to indicate the use of computer-type electronics in his work – e.g. *Swarm* for violin, concertina, bowed cross-cut saw and cybersonic modification. Other works include *Gestures II* for two pianos.

Munch (originally **Münch**), **Charles** (1891–1968), French conductor who gave many first performances. Conductor of the Boston Symphony Orchestra, 1949–62; founded the Orchestre de Paris, 1967.

Mundy, John (c.1555–1630), English composer of church music, madrigals (one included in THE TRIUMPHS OF ORIANA), pieces for viols, etc. Organist of St George's Chapel, Windsor. Son of the following.

Mundy, William (c.1529–1591), English composer of anthem 'O Lord, the maker of all thing' (sometimes wrongly attributed to Henry VIII) and other anthems, Latin motets, etc. Singer in the Chapel Royal but perhaps a secret Roman Catholic. Father of the preceding.

Munrow, David [John] (1942–76), British player of the recorder, crumhorn and other medieval (and later) instruments; founder-director of the Early Music Consort of London, 1967. He inspired a wide enthusiasm for EARLY MUSIC.

Muradely, Vano (1908–70), Russian composer, pupil of Shcherbachev and Myaskovsky. Works include *Symphony in Memory of Kirov*, choral works, opera *The Great Friendship* (1947) – this work touching off the denunciation by Soviet officialdom in 1948 of Muradely and other composers (including Prokofiev and Shostakovich) for FORMALISM and other alleged faults.

Murder in the Cathedral, opera by Pizzetti, produced in Milan, 1958; libretto (*Assassinio nella cattedrale*) a shortened Italian version of T. S. Eliot's play about Thomas à Becket.

murky bass, term of unknown origin, signifying (particularly in 18th-century music) a left-hand keyboard part proceeding in alternating notes an octave apart.

Murrill, Herbert [Henry John] (1909–52), British composer of opera *Man in Cage*, two cello concertos (no. 2 on a Catalan folk-song and dedicated to Casals), etc. Director of music, BBC, from 1950 until his death.

Mus., abbr. for Music – especially in university degrees, etc.; B.Mus., D.Mus. – bachelor, doctor of music.

Musard, Philippe (1793–1859), French violinist, conductor, composer of quadrilles, etc.; gave early successful promenade concerts in Paris and (1840 and afterwards) in London.

musette, (1) French type of bagpipe fashionable in Louis XIV's time through the cultivation of 'pastoral' ideal; used in the opera orchestra by Lully; (2) type of gavotte with a drone bass suggesting this instrument.

Musgrave, Thea (b. 1928), British composer, pupil of N. Boulanger in Paris; works include a clarinet concerto, viola concerto and a horn concerto; *The Five Ages of Man* for chorus and orchestra with optional brass band; operas *The Voice of Ariadne*, A CHRISTMAS CAROL, *Mary Queen of Scots*.

music, (1) 'an arrangement of, or the art of combining or putting together, sounds that please the ear' (*Chambers Essential English Dictionary*, 1968); (2, as in 'Master of the Queen's Music') an old English name for a band of musical performers. See also following entries.

musica ficta (Lat., 'false' or 'feigned' music), the principle, current from *c*.1350 to *c*.1650, by which performers added accidentals to certain notes. The practice was necessary (*causa necessitatis*) to avoid forbidden intervals (such as the augmented fourth or octave), but was also used to create sweeter-sounding intervals (*causa pulchritudinis*). The term is also used today to describe the addition of such accidentals by the editor of a printed edition.

musical (noun, as abbr. for *musical play*), term for the type of light stage entertainment (largely American-influenced) which succeeded the older MUSICAL COMEDY in the mid 20th century.

musical box, toy in which pins on a rotating cylinder 'pluck' the teeth of a comb which, being of different lengths, emit different notes; several sets of pins allow several tunes.

musical comedy, type of English and American light entertainment, prominent in later 19th and early 20th centuries – related to OPERETTA, but often less unified musically and using more than one composer. See MUSICAL.

Musical Director, The (It., *Il maestro di cappella*), short piece by Cimarosa in comic-opera style, composed *c*.1790, in which a baritone impersonates a conductor guiding an orchestra; it does not appear to have been intended for dramatized stage performance.

musical glasses = GLASS HARMONICA.

Musical Joke, A (Ger., *Ein musikalischer Spass*), work for strings and two horns by Mozart, 1787 (K522), satirizing clumsy composition.

Musical Offering (Ger., *Musikalisches Opfer*), work by Bach, 1747 (BWV 1079), of 13 pieces in various contrapuntal forms, dedicated to Frederick the Great of Prussia, and all using a theme given by Frederick to Bach on his visit to court that year.

musical saw, see SAW.

musica reservata (Lat., 'reserved' music), a term in use approximately 1550–1625, whose meaning is still obscure. It is assumed to refer to a central aspect of the style or performance of music in this period or earlier (particularly that of Josquin and Lassus). The likelihood is that it involved some musical expression of the verbal text; the use of chromaticism; or some aspect of performing practice, particularly performance by soloists. Or perhaps the music was, by its subtlety, reserved for connoisseurs.

Musica Transalpina, the first printed collection of Italian (i.e. transalpine) madrigals with English words; it had great influence on English music. Edited by Nicholas Yonge in two volumes, 1588 and 1597, the composers including Palestrina, Marenzio and Lassus.

music-drama, term used by Wagner of his operas after *Lohengrin*, the term 'opera' itself being thought to be inadequate or inappropriate to his intended new type of drama set to continuously expressive music based on LEADING-MOTIVES (as distinct from the old division into operatic 'numbers').

Music for the Royal Fireworks, see FIREWORKS MUSIC.

Music Makers, The, work for contralto, chorus, and orchestra, by Elgar, first performed in 1912. Text, A. Shaughnessy's poem. In this score Elgar quotes some of his own earlier works.

Music Master, The (It., *Il maestro di musica*), one-act comic opera satirizing the singing-master's profession; the music was formerly ascribed to Pergolesi, but in fact is not by him – apparently an altered version of *Orazio*, opera mainly by Auletta, with libretto by A. Palombo, produced in Naples, 1737 or earlier.

musicology, musical scholarship – 20th-century word useful in such contexts as 'to study musicology', implying an academic discipline different from that in 'to study music'. So also *musicologist* (usually implying someone whose activity is more 'learned' than that of a mere critic), *musicological*, etc. See also ETHNOMUSICOLOGY.

music-theatre, term of two quite distinct meanings, both post-1950: (1) opera production in a 'realistic' or 'truthful' manner as supposedly distinct from traditional type sacrificing all else to vocal display; (2) a genre of concert works for which a semi-staged presentation is needed, e.g. works by Kagel and P. M. Davies (EIGHT SONGS FOR A MAD KING).

Musik, musikalisch (Ger.), music, musical; *Musikalischer Spass*, see MUSICAL JOKE; *Musikalisches Opfer*, see MUSICAL OFFERING.

Musikwissenschaft (Ger.) = MUSICOLOGY.

musique (Fr.), music; *musique concrète*, see CONCRETE MUSIC.

Musorgsky, Modest Petrovich (1839–81), Russian composer; at first army officer, later a civil servant, but studied briefly as a young man with Balakirev. (Both were members of THE MIGHTY HANDFUL, the group of five 'nationalist' composers.) Expressed sympathy with 'the people' and showed it in various works including his masterpiece, the opera BORIS GODUNOV. Evolved, partly from Russian speech-inflexion, a highly individual musical idiom misunderstood by many contemporaries – Rimsky-Korsakov's 'correcting' (misleadingly) much of his work after his death and fathering on him a piece called *Night on the Bare Mountain* (see ST JOHN'S NIGHT ON THE BARE MOUNTAIN). His other works include unfinished operas THE KHOVANSKY AFFAIR, SOROCHINTSY FAIR and *The Marriage*; also PICTURES AT AN EXHIBITION for piano (orchestrated by others); many songs including SONGS AND DANCES OF DEATH. Died after alcoholic epileptic fits.

Mussorgsky, a frequently encountered (but strictly less accurate) transliteration of the name MUSORGSKY.

Mustel organ, keyboard instrument of the AMERICAN ORGAN type, invented by V. Mustel (1815–90).

muta (It.), change (imperative) – indicating that a player has to transfer from one instrument to another, or a drummer has to change the tuning of a drum (e.g. *muta la in si*, change A to B).

mutano (It., they change), term used as the plural of MUTA.

mutation stop, organ stop sounding not the note struck but one of its HARMONIC SERIES other than the octave – e.g. a stop called '12th' sounding the twelfth note above.

mute, a contrivance to reduce the volume of an instrument and/or modify its tone – on bowed instruments, a prolonged damper placed at the bridge; on brass instruments, an object of wood, metal, or fibre (there are various types) placed in the bell. To depress the SOFT PEDAL of a piano or to MUFFLE a drum is also in effect to apply a mute. (So also *to mute*, as verb.)

Müthel, Johann Gottfried (1718–85), German composer of keyboard works, pupil of J. S. Bach; organist at Lutheran Church in Riga, where he died.

Muti, Riccardo (b. 1941), Italian conductor of (New) Philharmonia Orchestra, 1973, and of Philadelphia Orchestra, 1980; also musical director of La Scala, Milan, since 1986.

Mutter, Anne-Sophie (b. 1963), German violinist whose precocious gifts were encouraged by KARAJAN; she made her British début in 1977.

Myaskovsky, Nikolay [Yakovlevich] (1881–1950), Russian composer, pupil of Glière and Rimsky-Korsakov, and others. One of the most prolific modern composers of symphonies – he wrote 27 (no. 19 is for wind band, no. 27 was performed posthumously). Wrote also symphonic poem *Nevermore* (after Poe), a violin concerto, piano solos, songs, etc. Denounced by Soviet officialdom in 1948 for FORMALISM, etc., along with Prokofiev, Shostakovich and others.

My Country (Cz., *Má Vlast*), cycle of six symphonic poems by Smetana, composed 1874–9 (after he had become deaf): (1) 'Vyšehrad' (an ancient citadel); (2) 'Vltava' (river); (3) 'Šárka' (Bohemian Amazon leader); (4) 'From Bohemian Fields and Groves' (Cz. *Z Českych Luhů a Hájů*; (5) 'Tábor' (city associated with the Hussites); (6) 'Blaník' (legendary sleeping-place of dead Hussite heroes).

My Lady Nevill's Book, a MS collection of 42 keyboard pieces by Byrd, 1591 (published in 1926).

Mysliveček, Josef (1737–81), Bohemian composer of Italian operas, and also of symphonies, etc.; called *il divino Boemo* (It., the divine Bohemian). Mozart admired him. He died in poverty in Rome.

mystic chord, see SKRYABIN.

N

N, abbr. for New (in orchestras' names, etc.): NPO, NYPO – New Philharmonia Orchestra, New York Philharmonic Orchestra.

Nabokov, Nicholas (originally Nikolay) (1903–78), Russian-born composer who lived much in France and died in USA. Works include opera on Shakespeare's *Love's Labour's Lost* and *Sinfonia biblica* for orchestra. Cousin of the writer Vladimir Nabokov.

Nabucco (It., abbr. of 'Nabucodnosor', i.e. Nebuchadnezzar), opera by Verdi, produced in Milan, 1842. Libretto by T. Solera, after the biblical story of the Israelites' captivity in Babylon.

nach (Ger.), to, after; so, e.g., *E nach G* (instruction to kettledrummer), 'change the tuning of the drum from E to G'.

Nachez, Tivadar (1859–1930), Hungarian violinist, editor of violin music, composer of a violin concerto, etc. Settled in France and died in Switzerland.

Nachschlag (Ger., after-stroke), (1) the two extra notes which conventionally close a TRILL; (2) an extra note (printed in small type) coming after a main note and robbing that main note of some of its time-value – see SPRINGER.

Nachtanz (Ger.), 'after-dance', i.e. a quick dance normally used to follow a slow one, e.g. a galliard following a pavan.

Nachtmusik (Ger.), serenade (literally, 'night music') – not a normal musical term, but used in Mozart's EINE KLEINE NACHTMUSIK.

nail fiddle, nail harmonica, nail violin, alternative names for a freak 18th-century instrument with nails of graduated sizes that were stroked with a violin-bow.

nakers, old English name, deriving from Arabic through French, for the small oriental KETTLEDRUM (normally played in pairs) brought from the Middle East to Europe in the 13th century.

Name-day (Ger., *Namensfeier*), concert-overture by Beethoven, 1814, celebrating the name-day of Francis II, Emperor of Austria.

Namensfeier, see preceding entry.

Nänie (Ger.), see NENIA.

Nápravník, Eduard (1839–1916), Czech composer of four operas, four symphonies, etc.; settled in Russia, 1861, becoming a leading conductor and dying there.

Nardini, Pietro (1722–93), Italian violinist and composer of nine violin concertos, chamber music, etc.; held court posts. A leading pupil of Tartini.

Nares, James (1715–83), British composer of church music, glees, harpsichord pieces, etc.; also organist.

Narvaez, Luis de (c.1500–after 1550), Spanish player of VIHUELA (Spanish lute-like instrument) and composer of variations and other works for it; also of church music.

Nathan, Isaac (1790–1864), British singer and composer – of stage works, songs to words by his friend Byron, etc. Settled in Australia, 1841, and died there. CHARLES MACKERRAS is a descendant.

nationalism, nationalist, terms applied to music which (usually through elements derived from folk-music) suggests supposed national characteristics. The terms are particularly applied to the work of such 19th-century composers as Smetana, Liszt, Balakirev and Grieg, with the implication of national 'emancipation' from the domination of German-Austrian musical concepts.

Natra, Sergiu (b. 1924), Romanian-born Israeli composer; works include *Song of Deborah* (in Hebrew) for mezzo-soprano and chamber orchestra; sonatinas for trombone, for trumpet and for oboe.

natural, (1, of a note or key) not sharp or flat – designated by the sign ♮; (2, of a horn, trumpet, etc.) not having valves, keys, or any other mechanism, and so producing only the notes of the HARMONIC SERIES as determined by the length of the tube; (3) a type of 'harmonics' in string-playing – see HARMONIC. See also next entry.

naturale (It., natural), direction that a voice or instrument which has been performing in an 'abnormal' way (e.g. falsetto, muted) should return to its 'natural' manner of performance.

Naumann, Johann Gottlieb (1741–1801), German composer who studied in Italy with Tartini and G. B. Martini, and won wide fame in his day, especially with operas – mostly in Italian, but three in Swedish and one in Danish for Stockholm and Copenhagen. Also wrote symphonies, Masses, oratorios, etc.

Navarra, André [Nicolas] (1911–88), French cellist, internationally prominent; teacher in France, Germany and Italy.

Naylor, Bernard (1907–86), British composer of choral works, *Sonnets from the Portuguese* (E. B. Browning) for voice and string quartet, etc. Pupil of Vaughan Williams, Holst and Ireland; spent two periods as conductor in Canada. Son of Edward Naylor (1867–1934), organist, composer and musicologist.

Neapolitan sixth, a type of chord – in key C, it comprises the notes (reading upwards) F, A♭, D♭; and correspondingly in other keys. The reason for the name is uncertain – cp. ITALIAN SIXTH, but note that the *Neapolitan sixth* is always relative to the prevailing key, whereas an *Italian sixth* is formed irrespective of it. The term *Neapolitan harmony* is sometimes found as indicating (especially in 18th-century music) a pronounced use of this chord.

Neel, [Louis] Boyd (1905–81), British conductor. Qualified originally in medicine, but turned to music, founding

Boyd Neel String Orchestra in London in 1933. Dean of the Royal Conservatory of Music, Toronto, 1953–71.

Negro Quartet, see AMERICAN QUARTET.

Negro spiritual, see SPIRITUAL.

'Nelson' Mass, nickname for Haydn's Mass in D Minor, 1798 (Hob. XXII: 11), because it is supposed to signalize joy at Nelson's victory in the Battle of the Nile.

nenia (Gk.), a dirge; Brahms used the German form *Nänie* for a choral setting of Schiller, 1881; Birtwistle's *Nenia on the Death of Orpheus* (1970) is for soprano and instrumental ensemble.

neo-, prefix (from Gk. for 'new') used, in classifying musical styles, to indicate the re-adopting (real or supposed) of apparently outmoded characteristics, suitably modified for a new era. So, e.g., NEO-CLASSICAL (see below); *neo-modal*, referring to the 20th-century revival of the old MODES; *neo-Romantic*, referring to the inclination of some composers to Romanticism even after the 20th-century reaction against it.

neo-classic(al), neo-classicism, terms used of a trend in musical style manifesting itself particularly in the 1920s. Its characteristics include: preference for small rather than large instrumental forces; use of CONCERTO GROSSO technique; emphasis on contrapuntal values; avoidance of 'emotionalism'. In the hands of Stravinsky, Hindemith, and others this had analogies with Bach's rather than Mozart's (the so-called 'Viennese-classical') period, and might be better

labelled *neo-baroque*. See BAROQUE, CLASSIC(AL).

Nesterenko, Yevgeny [Yevgenyevich] (b. 1938), Russian bass who won operatic prominence in the West, beginning wih the Bolshoi Opera's visit to Milan, 1973.

neum(e), generic name for each of the various signs in medieval musical notation (superseded by modern staff notation) showing the note(s) to which a syllable of vocal music was to be sung. As surviving in plainsong notation, the *neums* give precise indication of pitch; but, originally, from the seventh century, they were only approximate reminders of the shape of the melody.

Neumann, Vaclav (b. 1920), Czechoslovak conductor; music director of the Stuttgart Opera, 1970–73, chief conductor of the Czech Philharmonic Orchestra 1968–90.

Neusiedler, Hans (1508–63), German lutenist and composer of lute music – fantasies, dances, song-arrangements, etc.

Nevin, Ethelbert Woodbridge (1862–1901), American composer of 'The Rosary' (sold 6 million copies in 30 years) and other popular sentimental songs; *Narcissus* and other piano pieces, etc. His brother Arthur Finley Nevin (1871–1943) was also a composer and a researcher in American-Indian music.

Newman, John Henry [Cardinal] (1801–90), British writer. See DREAM OF GERONTIUS.

new music, term with two special historical meanings – (1) in the early 17th century, the type of newly expressive music then being pioneered – see CACCINI; (2) in the period 1850–1900, the music of Liszt, Wagner and their followers as opposed to that of, e.g., Brahms (supposedly more 'traditional' in outlook).

New Philharmonia Orchestra, London orchestra which in 1964 succeeded the disbanded Philharmonia Orchestra (founded in 1945); it reverted to the original title (see PHILHARMONIA) in 1977.

'New World' Symphony, see FROM THE NEW WORLD.

New York Philharmonic Orchestra, orchestra which was called the New York Philharmonic Symphony Orchestra when established in 1928 from a merger of the older New York Philharmonic and New York Symphony Orchestras, but which currently uses the simpler title. Music director 1978–90, Zubin Mehta (succeeding Boulez).

Nibelung's Ring, The, see RING.

Nicholson, Richard (c.1570–1639), English organist and composer of madrigals (e.g. one in THE TRIUMPHS OF ORIANA), anthems and songs. The first professor of music at Oxford, 1627.

Nicholson, Sydney [Hugo] (1875–1947), British organist, composer (chiefly of church music), and founder of what is now the Royal School of Church Music; knighted, 1938.

Nicolai, [Carl] **Otto** [Ehrenfried] (1810–49), German composer and conductor; studied in Italy and wrote Italian operas as well as (in German) THE MERRY WIVES OF WINDSOR; also choral and orchestral works, etc. Founder-conductor of the Vienna Philharmonic Concerts (i.e. of the present-day Vienna Philharmonic Orchestra), 1842; in 1847 went as director of the court opera and the cathedral choir to Berlin, where he died of a stroke.

Nicolet, Aurèle (b. 1926), Swiss flautist, for whom solo works have been written by Ligeti, Takemitsu and others.

Nielsen, Carl [August] (1865–1931), Danish composer, reckoned his country's greatest and influencing many younger Danish composers; director of the Royal Conservatory, 1930; also conductor, and formerly violinist. In 1891–2 he composed his Symphony no. 1, probably the first ever to begin in one key and end in another (see PROGRESSIVE TONALITY) – a principle much evident in his succeeding five symphonies (no. 2 THE FOUR TEMPERAMENTS, no. 3 *Sinfonia espansiva* – see ESPANSIVA – no. 4 THE UNQUENCHABLE) and other works. These include concertos for flute, for clarinet and for violin; operas *Saul and David* and MASQUERADE; chamber music (see SERENATA); organ work *Commotio*.

Nielsen, Riccardo (b. 1908), Italian composer of a violin concerto, opera *The Incubus*, chamber music, works for one and two pianos, etc.

niente (It.), nothing, so *a niente*, to nothing – term used e.g. after sign >, indicating that the sound is gradually to die away entirely.

Nietzsche, Friedrich Wilhelm (1844–1900), German philosopher. See BIZET, MASS OF LIFE, REQUIEM, THUS SPAKE ZARATHUSTRA.

Nigg, Serge (b. 1924), French composer, pupil of Messiaen. Works include symphonic poems *Timur* and *For a Captive Poet*; two piano concertos.

Nigger quartet, see AMERICAN QUARTET.

nightingale, imitative toy instrument used in the TOY SYMPHONY mistakenly ascribed to Haydn.

Night on the Bare Mountain, see ST JOHN'S NIGHT ON THE BARE MOUNTAIN.

Nights in the Gardens of Spain (Sp. *Noches en los jardines de España*), 'symphonic impressions' by Falla for piano and orchestra in three movements; first performed in 1916.

Nikisch, Arthur (1855–1922), Hungarian conductor, pre-eminent in his day; from 1895 he conducted both the Gewandhaus Orchestra (Leipzig) and the Berlin Philharmonic, and was well known too in Boston and London.

Nilsson, [Märta] Birgit (b. 1918), Swedish soprano, internationally known as Brünnhilde in Wagner's RING, in the title-role of Puccini's TURANDOT, etc. Retired from public performance in 1986.

Nilsson, Bo (b. 1937), Swedish composer, self-taught; works include *Essays* for orchestra, *Reactions* for four percussionists, *Quantities* for piano.

Nilsson, Christine (originally Kristina) (1843–1921), Swedish soprano who established highest operatic fame in Paris (from 1864), London and New York.

Nin [y Castellanos], Joaquin (1879–1949), Spanish pianist, editor of old Spanish music, composer of stage works, pieces for violin and for piano, etc. Born and died in Cuba. Father of the following.

Nin-Culmell, Joaquin [Maria] (b. 1908), American composer, born in Berlin, son of preceding. Also pianist, conductor and university teacher. Works include a piano concerto, piano quintet, Mass (in English).

nineteenth, a MUTATION stop on the organ producing a note at the interval of a 19th (two octaves and a fifth) above the note touched.

ninth, an interval of nine steps (counting the bottom and top notes), e.g. from C upwards for an octave and a whole-tone to D (*major ninth*) or for an octave and a semitone to D♭ (*minor ninth*). So, e.g., a *chord of the dominant ninth*: in the key of F major this would be (reading upwards) C, E, G, B♭, D, since the dominant of F major is C, the B is flat according to the scale of F major, and the note D indicates the interval of the major ninth from C.

Ninth Symphony (Beethoven), see CHORAL SYMPHONY.

Nixon in China, opera by Adams, produced in Houston (Texas), 1987; libretto, by Alice Goodman, deals semi-satirically with US president Richard Nixon and other real-life figures.

nobile, nobilmente (It.), noble, nobly.

Noble, Thomas Tertius (1867–1953), British organist who lived much in USA, and died there; composer of church music, etc.

Noces, Les, see WEDDING.

Noches en los jardines de España, see NIGHTS IN THE GARDENS OF SPAIN.

nocturne, a night-piece: (1, generally, in Italian, *notturno*) 18th-century composition of SERENADE type for several instruments in several movements; (2) short lyrical piece, especially for piano, in one movement – a sense originated by Field and adopted by Chopin; (3) term applied at the composer's fancy – e.g. to the third movement of Vaughan Williams's A LONDON SYMPHONY, which is headed 'Scherzo (Nocturne)', and in Britten's song-cycle with orchestra (1958) entitled *Nocturne*. See also next entry.

Nocturnes, a set of three orchestral pieces by Debussy, first performed complete in 1901 – (1) 'Clouds'; (2) 'Fêtes'; (3) 'Sirens'. The last has a wordless female chorus.

node, a stationary point on a vibrating string or air-column – the vibrations taking place in opposite directions on either side of it.

noël (Fr., Christmas), a Christmas carol, or an instrumental piece in the same spirit (often, in the 17th and 18th centuries, for keyboard or instrumental ensemble).

noire (Fr., black) = QUARTER-NOTE, crotchet.

non (Fr., It.), not.

nonet, a composition for nine instruments or nine voices; if the former, it will probably be in some regular several-movement form – as QUARTET.

non-harmonic note (US, non-harmonic tone), term used in the theory of harmony for a note that is not part of the chord with which it sounds, and therefore needs its own 'explanation' – e.g. it may be a PASSING-NOTE or APPOGGIATURA.

Nono, Luigi (1924–90), Italian composer, pupil of Scherchen. Works,

often with many percussion instruments, include *Epitaph for Federico García Lorca* (for speaker, singers and orchestra); *Encounters* (*Incontri*) for 24 instruments; cantata *On the Bridge of Hiroshima* for soprano, tenor and orchestra; opera *Intolerance* (title changed from original *Intolerance 1960*). Many of his texts were linked to his Communist beliefs. His visit to Moscow in 1962 significantly brought young Soviet composers into open contact with West European modernism.

Norcombe, Daniel (b.1576, d. before 1626), English lutenist and composer who contributed a madrigal to THE TRIUMPHS OF ORIANA. (An English viol-player of the same name active in Brussels as late as 1647 is a different person.)

Nordheim, Arne (b. 1931), Norwegian composer (formerly also critic). Works include *Dinosaurus* for accordion with accordion sounds on tape; Partita for viola, harpsichord and percussion. He takes part in 'live electronics' performances as used in several of his own compositions.

Nordraak, Richard (1842–66), Norwegian composer of what is now the Norwegian national anthem; despite his short life, he exerted great influence (e.g. on Grieg) in the direction of a Norwegian national style of music.

Nørgård, Per (b. 1932), Danish composer and teacher. Works include oratorio *Babel* (with four soloists – clown, rock singer, cabaret artist, conductor); *Voyage into the Golden Screen* for chamber ensemble; *Constellations* for 12 solo strings or 12 string groups.

Norma, opera by Bellini, produced in

Milan, 1831. Libretto by F. Romani. Named after the heroine, a young Druid priestess torn between love and duty.

Norman, Jessye (b. 1945), American soprano, appearing at the West Berlin Opera from 1969, Covent Garden from 1972; also noted recitalist.

Norrington, Roger [Arthur Carver] (b. 1934), British conductor, formerly tenor; with his London Classical Players he won fame for performances of Beethoven and Berlioz using instruments of the period.

Northern Sinfonia, chamber orchestra based in Newcastle-on-Tyne, established in 1961. Principal conductor, 1982–9, Richard Hickox, followed by Heinrich Schiff.

nota cambiata (It., exchanged note), a device in counterpoint by which an 'extra' NON-HARMONIC NOTE is used on an accented beat. Instead of (a) below, in which the B is an auxiliary note between the two C's, the use of *nota cambiata* (b) gives the extra note D, which is thought of as a substitute for the B (hence the idea of 'exchange'). The leap from B to an accented D, both non-harmonic notes, is the essential feature; or it might have been from D to B. (The US term is simply *cambiata*.)

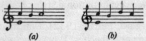

(a)   (b)

notation, the writing down of music – whether by symbols (as in ordinary STAFF notation), by letters (as in TONIC SOL-FA), or by a graphic representation of how an instrument should be fingered to produce particular notes (as in TABLATURE).

note, (1) a single sound of a given pitch and duration; (2) a written sign for the preceding; (3) a lever depressed by the performer on the piano, organ, etc., to produce a sound of particular pitch. The US term for the first of these is TONE.

note-cluster, see CLUSTER.

note-row (US, *tone-row*), in TWELVE-NOTE music, the order in which the composer chooses to arrange the 12 notes comprised within the octave, this order serving as the basis for the particular composition.

notes inégales (Fr., unequal notes), see INEQUALITY.

notturno, see NOCTURNE.

Novák, Vítězslav (1870–1949), Czechoslovak composer, pupil of Dvořák; director of the Prague Conservatory, 1919–22, and long a professor there. Works include symphonic poems, a piano concerto, three string quartets, cantata THE SPECTRE'S BRIDE, operas, ballets, Slovak folk-song arrangements.

novelette, Novellette (Eng., Ger.), title for a short instrumental piece supposedly the equivalent of a romantic tale – term apparently first used by Schumann, 1848 (for a piano work).

Novello, Ivor (real name, David Ivor Davies) (1893–1951), British playwright, actor and composer of music for his own plays – e.g. *The Dancing Years*, *King's Rhapsody* – as well as of song 'Keep the home fires burning', etc. Son of the choral conductor Clara Novello-Davies.

Nowowiejski, Feliks (1877–1946), Polish composer of the oratorio *Quo Vadis?* (after Sienkiewicz's novel), operas, organ music, etc.; also conductor.

Noye's Fludde, work of operatic type (though intended for church performance with participation of the audience in traditional hymns) by Britten, first performed in Orford (Suffolk), 1958. Title is ancient spelling of 'Noah's Flood'; text is adapted from the Chester miracle play. See also FLOOD.

Nozze di Figaro, Le, see MARRIAGE OF FIGARO.

number, a self-contained item in an opera, a musical, etc. (so called because each such piece is separately numbered 1, 2, etc., in the written score); hence *number-opera,* an opera in which this separation into self-contained items is followed, as distinct from those operas (e.g. Wagner's work from *Tristan and Isolde* onwards) where a whole act is written out without internal divisions and thus without possible pause.

Nunc Dimittis, text from St Luke (named from its opening words, 'Now lettest thou thy servant depart', in Latin translation) forming part of the Roman Catholic and Anglican evening service; for the latter, composers have commonly written a MAGNIFICAT and Nunc Dimittis as a unified work.

nut, (1) on a stringed instrument, the ridge over which the strings pass between the pegs and the fingerboard; *movable nut,* contrivance placed on the fingerboard of, e.g., a ukulele, having the effect of shortening all strings equally and thus raising their pitch at choice, to facilitate playing in various keys; (2) on the bow of, e.g., a violin, the device at the heel by which the tension of the bow-strings can be regulated.

Nutcracker, The (Rus., *Shchelkunchik*), ballet with music by Tchaikovsky, produced in St Petersburg, 1892 – some months after the concert suite drawn from it had already been performed. On a fairy-tale, with a battle between the Nutcracker and the King of Mice. See CELESTA.

Nyman, Michael (b. 1944), British composer of opera *The Man Who Mistook His Wife for a Hat,* much film music, etc.

Nystroem, Gösta (1890–1966), Swedish composer, pupil of d'Indy in Paris – where, himself a painter, his artistic outlook was influenced by Picasso, Braque, etc. Works include six symphonies (no. 3 *Sinfonia del mare,* i.e. of the sea), a viola concerto, Sinfonia Concertante for cello and orchestra; songs, some with orchestra.

O

o (It.), or; *o sia*, see OSSIA.

obbligato (It., obligatory), term used of an instrument with a compulsory, unusual and special role – e.g. 'song with flute obbligato' (where *obbligato* is really an adjective qualifying 'flute'). It should be noted (1) that, by contrast, 'flute ad lib' would imply optional, not compulsory, use of the instrument; (2) that occasionally the word *obbligato* is encountered actually meaning 'ad lib' – quite wrongly; (3) that the spelling is not 'obligato'.

Oberon, or The Elf-King's Oath, opera by Weber, produced in London, 1826; libretto, in English, by J. R. Planché. The story, a romance set in the days of Charlemagne, has nothing to do with the exploits of Oberon in *A Midsummer Night's Dream*. See also VRA-NICKÝ (P.).

obligato, mis-spelling for OBBLIGATO.

oblique motion, see MOTION.

oboe, woodwind instrument blown through a double reed and having a compass from the B♭ below middle C upwards for more than two and a half octaves; standard in the orchestra, and used also in the military band, in chamber music and as solo instrument. *Oboe d'amore*, similar instrument of slightly lower pitch and less pungent tone, written for, e.g., by Bach and (exceptionally in modern times) by Ravel (BOLERO) and R. Strauss; *oboe da caccia* – literally 'hunting oboe', though it is not clear why – predecessor of the ENGLISH HORN, the present 'contralto' to the oboe's soprano. The lowest members of the oboe family are two different instruments each with compass approximately an octave below the oboe – the (French) *baritone oboe*, blown through a side tube like the bassoon, and the (German) HECKELPHONE, sometimes called (e.g. in Delius's scores) *bass oboe*. The oboe's predecessor is the SHAWM.

Obraztsova, Elena [Vasilyevna] (b. 1937), Russian mezzo-soprano; performed in opera at the Bolshoi Theatre while still a student; sang at Metropolitan Opera, New York, 1976. She teaches at the Moscow Conservatory.

Obrecht (latinized as Obertus), **Jacob** (*c.*1450–1505), Netherlandish composer who worked mainly in Flanders, but also visited Italy and died of plague there. Wrote Masses, motets and secular songs, showing some emotional characteristics foreshadowing the expressive art of JOSQUIN.

ocarina, small keyless flute-like instrument (invented *c.*1860) with holes for fingers; mainly used as a toy, but featuring in Irving Berlin's score (1950) for the musical *Call Me Madam*. The body is shaped like an egg – or, counting the protruding mouthpiece, rather like a goose, thus possibly suggesting the name (from It. *oca*, goose?).

O'Casey, Sean (1884–1964), Irish dramatist. See SIEGMEISTER.

Ockeghem (or Okeghem), **Jean de** (*c*.1410–97), Flemish composer, in service to the French court; also visited Spain. Of great influence; called 'the Prince of Music' in his own day; his pupils included JOSQUIN. Wrote Masses and motets, sometimes choosing a secular tune as CANTUS FIRMUS; wrote also French chansons.

octave, the interval that is considered as having eight (Lat. *octo*) steps, counting both the bottom and top notes; according to standard notation, notes an octave apart from each other have the same letter-names, the note an octave above A being also called A, etc. This naming corresponds to the fact that notes an octave apart seem to the ear like the same note sounded at different pitches, not like entirely different notes. Strictly, the interval from A to the next A above is the *perfect octave*; from A up to A♭ and from A up to A♯ are respectively the *diminished* and *augmented octave*. Thus also *double octave*, two octaves; *at the octave*, (performed) an octave higher than written; *in octaves*, (performed) with each note doubled one or more octaves above or below; *octave coupler*, device on organ or harpsichord whereby the note struck is doubled an octave higher (sometimes called *super-octave coupler*, to distinguish from *sub-octave coupler* doubling at the octave

below); *octave key*, finger-lever on woodwind instruments giving player access to a higher octave. For *consecutive octaves* see CONSECUTIVE.

octet, composition for eight instruments or eight voices; if the former, it will probably be in some regular several-movement form – as QUARTET. Also a group of eight performers.

octobass, a huge, bowed stringed instrument, larger and pitched lower than a double-bass, invented in 1849. It failed to win acceptance.

octuor (Fr.), octet.

ode, (1) musical setting of a poem itself called 'ode', such a setting often having a ceremonial nature – see the following; (2) term exceptionally used in music with some vaguer significance: Stravinsky's work in memory of Koussevitsky's wife, 1943, is entitled *Ode: Elegiacal Chant*.

Ode for St Cecilia's Day, (1) title of four choral works by Purcell, two of 1683 (Z329 and 334), another (Z339) probably of that date, another (Z328) of 1692; Z329 is in Latin, the others in English; (2) title of a setting by Handel of Dryden's poem of the same title, first performed in London, 1739. See also HYMN TO ST CECILIA.

Ode to Napoleon, work by Schoenberg, 1942, for speaker (whose part is rhythmically notated at approximate pitch), strings and piano; text, by Byron, expresses loathing of despotism.

Odo of Cluny (879–942), French monk, appointed Abbot of Cluny in 927; he was a noted composer and teacher, and various writings on music are ascribed to him.

Oedipus Rex (Lat., King Oedipus),

'opera-oratorio' by Stravinsky – intended for stage presentation with restricted movement, but first performed as a concert work in Paris, 1927. The text is a Latin translation by J. Daniélou of a script by Cocteau suggested by Sophocles' Greek tragedy. See also PARTCH.

Offenbach, Jacques (1819–80), French composer born in Cologne, Germany – the family originally hailing from Offenbach-am-Main; his father's original surname was Eberst (other versions are not substantiated). He was taken to Paris in boyhood and remained there, attaining tremendous success as composer of nearly 90 French operettas including LA BELLE HÉLÈNE and ORPHEUS IN THE UNDERWORLD, often satirizing contemporary manners, and in a sprightly musical style which became standard for this type of work. Also wrote opera THE TALES OF HOFFMANN. Had early career as cellist, and later managed his own theatres; dubiously said to have encouraged J. Strauss the younger to write operetta. Visited England and USA.

offertoire (Fr.) = OFFERTORIUM.

offertorium, offertory (Lat., Eng.), a plainsong or polyphonic setting of biblical works (in Latin) occurring after the Credo in the Mass of the Roman Catholic Church while the Eucharist is being prepared and offered. Organ music supplementing or replacing this is also so called.

Ogdon, John [Andrew Howard] (1937–89), English pianist, joint winner in 1962 of the International Tchaikovsky Competition at Moscow (see ASHKENAZY); known for performance of Busoni's Piano Concerto and

other unusual works. Also composer, e.g. of preludes for piano.

Ohana, Maurice (b. 1914), French composer of Spanish descent, born in Casablanca and resident in Paris; works include choral settings of Spanish verse (some by Lorca) and a guitar concerto. Some other works use a zither with tuning of one-third of a tone.

Ohlsson, Garrick (b. 1948), American pianist, the first American to win the Chopin International Competition at Warsaw (1970).

ohne (Ger.), without.

Oistrakh, David [Fedorovich] (1908–74), Russian violinist to whom Shostakovich's violin concertos are dedicated, and who became among the best-known Soviet artists in the West. Also, from the 1960s, conductor. Father of the following.

Oistrakh, Igor [Davidovich] (b. 1931), Russian violinist, pupil of his father (preceding), internationally prominent after winning the Wieniawski Competition in Poland in 1952.

Okeghem, Jean de, see OCKEGHEM.

Old Hall Manuscript, a collection of 14th–15th-century church music found at St Edmund's College, Old Hall, Herts, and published 1933–9.

oliphant, medieval horn made of elephant's tusk or of gold, a symbol of high dignity (e.g. that of knighthood).

Oliver, Stephen (b. 1950), English composer, pupil of Leighton and R. Sherlaw Johnson. Full-length opera TOM JONES came after many youthful dramatic pieces including three 'mini-operas' (*c.*10 minutes each). Has also written a symphony, etc., and much incidental music for plays, including Royal Shakespeare Co.'s *Nicholas Nickleby*.

Oliveros, Pauline (b. 1932), American composer making much use of electronics and quasi-theatrical presentations. Works include Trio for flute, piano and page-turner; *To Valerie Solanas and Marilyn Monroe in Recognition of their Desperation* for orchestra, chorus, electronics, lights.

Omar Khayyám (*c*.1050–1123), Persian poet. See LEHMANN (Liza).

Ondes Martenot, see MARTENOT.

O'Neill, Eugene (1888–1953), American playwright. See EMPEROR JONES, LUALDI.

O'Neill, Norman (1875–1934), British composer of much theatre music, including the incidental music to Barrie's *Mary Rose*; also theatre conductor. In addition he wrote orchestral works, chamber music, etc.

On Hearing the First Cuckoo in Spring, piece by Delius for small orchestra, first performed in 1913; it introduces a Norwegian folk-song, and the cuckoo is discreetly impersonated by a clarinet.

Onslow, George (1784–1853), French composer (mother French, father British); lived for a while in London but settled in France and died there. Wrote 35 string quartets and other chamber music which won fashionable success in England and France; also operas, etc.

op., abbr. of OPUS.

open, (1, of a string) allowed to vibrate throughout its full length, not 'stopped' by a finger pressed on it; (2, of a pipe) not stopped at the end – e.g. the *open diapason* of the organ, contrasted with the 'stopped diapason'; (3, of the notes of the orchestral horn) not 'stopped' by the placing of the hand firmly inside the bell.

open form, term used to describe certain compositions (from the 1950s) in which the performer has the option of varying the sequence of component sections or may begin at any point and continue in circular fashion until reaching that point again. See CYCLE (Stockhausen).

Oper (Ger.), opera – also in the sense of 'opera company'; so *Staatsoper*, State Opera.

opera, (1, obsolete) = OPUS; (2) a company performing opera as defined below; so *Vienna State Opera*, etc.; or an opera house itself, e.g. the 'Opéra' (building) in Paris, opened in 1875; (3, principal meaning) type of drama in which all or most characters sing and in which music constitutes a principal element having its own unity. The first works properly so classified are those arising in Italy about 1600 (see, e.g., CACCINI, PERI). Various synonyms or near-synonyms for the term *opera* are to be met, their precise significance often depending on historical context: see, e.g., MUSIC-DRAMA, MUSIC-THEATRE. The apparent subdivisions of opera (see following entries) have seeming inconsistencies which are similarly to be resolved only by their differing historical contexts.

opera-ballet, stage work giving approximately equal importance to opera and ballet, especially those written by Lully, Rameau and others in 17th- and 18th-century France.

opéra bouffe (Fr.), type of light, often satirical opera or operetta, e.g. the operettas of Offenbach. Term taken from, but not historically quite the same as, OPERA BUFFA.

opera buffa (It.), comic opera, particularly the 18th-century Italian kind as represented by Pergolesi's THE MAID AS MISTRESS. Cp. OPERA SERIA.

opéra comique (Fr.), term literally signifying comic opera, but having two special meanings – (1) in the 18th century, a type of French comic opera with spoken dialogue, e.g. by Philidor and Monsigny, less lofty in ideas and style than the current serious operas (generally on heroic or mythological subjects); (2) in the 19th century, any opera with spoken dialogue, whether comic or not – Gounod's FAUST and Bizet's CARMEN (in their original versions, without recitatives) being so classifiable. (The Paris theatre called the 'Opéra-Comique' originally observed this distinction.)

opera-oratorio, term applied by Stravinsky to his OEDIPUS REX, intended to be presented on the stage but in a static manner remote from ordinary theatrical practice.

opera seria (It.), term literally signifying 'serious opera', opposite to OPERA BUFFA, but used particularly for a specific type of opera flourishing in the 18th century and lingering up to, e.g., Rossini's SEMIRAMIS (1823). This type is characterized by (1) Italian libretto, (2) heroic or mythological plot, (3) much formality in music and action, (4) often, leading roles for CASTRATO singers.

operetta (It., little opera), term used for an opera of a light type whether full-length or (like some of Offenbach's) in one act. The term is virtually synonymous with 'light opera'; see also MUSICAL COMEDY.

opérette (Fr.) = operetta.

ophicleide, bass instrument made of metal and with keys; used in the orchestra (e.g. by Berlioz, Mendelssohn, early Verdi) as an improvement on the SERPENT, but superseded about 1850 by the tuba, on which instrument the parts intended for the ophicleide are now normally played. The 'key bugle' (or 'keyed bugle', or 'Kent bugle') was an instrument of related type, but roughly of bugle size and pitch; it had some use in early 19th-century bands before the advent of the cornet.

opus (Lat., a work; abbr. *op.*), term used, with a number, for the enumeration of a composer's works supposedly in the order of their composition; if an 'opus' comprises more than one piece, then a subdivision may be used (e.g. 'opus 40, no. 2'). Occasionally the letters *a* and *b* are used to indicate different but equally valid versions of the same work: see ST ANTHONY VARIATIONS. But confusion arises because various composers have (a) failed to number their works, (b) numbered only some and not others, (c) allowed their works to appear with numbers not representing their real order of composition – e.g. Dvořák, to satisfy a publisher's desire to present early works as recent ones.

oratorio, (1) type of musical composition (originating about 1600 in performances at the Oratory of St Philip Neri in Rome, hence the name) consisting of an extended setting of a religious text set out in more or less dramatic form – usually for soloists, chorus and orchestra: originally requiring scenery, costumes and action, but later customarily conceived and given in concert form; (2) term used also for a type of work similar to the above but on a non-religious – though usually 'elevated' – subject; e.g. Handel's SEMELE, Tippett's A CHILD OF OUR TIME and certain Soviet-Russian works to patriotic texts.

Orchésographie, title of a French treatise on dancing (an important source in music history), 1589.

Orchester (Ger.) = orchestra.

orchestra a numerous mixed body of instrumentalists. As a more or less stable institution, the orchestra originated in early 17th-century opera, being afterwards continually modified (obsolete instruments being replaced by new ones), enlarged and re-systematized. So *symphony orchestra*, standard large orchestra of 19th and 20th centuries, able to play symphonies, etc. – as opposed, e.g., to *chamber orchestra* (small size) or *string orchestra* (strings only). The term *theatre orchestra* customarily indicates not an opera orchestra (which is ideally of 'symphonic' size) but a smaller orchestra used for musicals, etc., commonly including saxophones. A combination of wind instruments only, or any combination for dancing to, is commonly called not an orchestra but a band. Note that *philharmonic orchestra*, unlike *symphony orchestra*, is not a type of orchestra: see PHILHARMONIC. Although composers may vary both the kind and numbers of instruments used (variety being especially noticeable in the percussion section), the forces standardized by the requirements of symphonic music in the late 19th century and most of the 20th are:

(a) woodwind:	3 flutes, 1 doubling piccolo
	3 oboes, 1 doubling English horn
	3 clarinets, 1 doubling bass clarinet
	3 bassoons, 1 doubling double-bassoon
(b) brass:	4 (sometimes 6) horns
	3 trumpets
	3 trombones (2 tenor, 1 bass)
	1 tuba
(c) percussion:	3 kettledrums (1 player)
	snare-drum, bass-drum, cymbals, gong, triangle, xylophone, vibraphone, etc. (2 or more players)
(d) unclassified:	2 harps
	1 piano
(e) strings:	first violins (about 14)
	second violins (about 14)
	violas (about 12)
	cellos (about 10)
	double-basses (about 8)

Such works as Tchaikovsky's Symphony no. 6 (1893), Elgar's Symphony no. 1 (1908), Bartók's Concerto for Orchestra (1944) and Shostakovich's Symphony no. 15 (1972) could all be encompassed by these forces. The order given above is that observed in conventional modern printing of a score, except that there is no standard order in percussion.

Orchestra of the Age of Enlightenment, London-based orchestra which began giving concerts in 1986, using 18th-century type instruments for music of that period. Self-governing, it has no permanent conductor.

orchestration, the art of writing suitably for an orchestra, band, etc.; or of scoring for these a work originally designed for another medium. So *orchestrate, orchestrator.*

orchestre (Fr.), orchestra; Orchestre de Paris, see the following.

Orchestre de Paris, French orchestra founded in 1967; Barenboim, conductor from 1975, was succeeded by Bychkov, 1990.

Ord, Boris (first name really Bernhard) (1897–1961), English organist, harpsichordist and conductor; director of music, King's College, Cambridge, 1929–57.

ordre (Fr.), an equivalent of SUITE, e.g. in Couperin's keyboard works.

Orefice, Giacomo (1865–1922), Italian composer of operas (e.g. one on Chopin's life using Chopin's music), symphony, chamber music, etc.

Orfeo, see ORPHEUS.

Orff, Carl (1895–1982), German composer, chiefly for the stage; also noted musical educator: a specially devised educational range of percussion instruments bears his name and his own music is also conspicuous for its use of percussion (see STONE CHIMES). Works include operas *The Clever Woman* (*Die Kluge*), *The Moon, Oedipus the Tyrant,* ANTIGONE and others; incidental music to *A Midsummer Night's Dream*; scenic choral works CARMINA BURANA, *Catulli Carmina* (Lat., Songs of Catullus), *Trionfo di Afrodite* (It., Triumph of Aphrodite) – these last three grouped as *Trionfi* (Triumphs).

organ, (1) historically, a keyboard instrument in which wind is blown by a bellows through pipes to sound the notes; made in various sizes down to the medieval 'portative', i.e. portable, carried by the player. (See also POSITIVE.) Tone is varied by the selection and combination of different stops (see STOP; FOOT) on different keyboards; a pedal keyboard, originating in Germany before 1500, has gradually become standard as well as up to five (very rarely more) manual keyboards. These five are called CHOIR, GREAT, SWELL, SOLO and ECHO (reading upwards), but it is common to find only two (Great, Swell) or three (Choir, Great, Swell). The 19th and 20th centuries have not only brought technical improvements, e.g. electricity to work the bellows, but have also much increased the power and variety of organs – not necessarily with comparable artistic gain. *Extension organ* or *unit organ,* type of organ built for economy of space and expense; for its principle see UNIT. See also THEATRE ORGAN. (2) term of each component tone-producing part of the instrument described above – e.g. the *Great Organ, Pedal Organ,* meaning the Great and Pedal keyboards plus the pipes controlled by them and the appropriate machinery. (3) a keyboard instrument imitating the traditional organ, but with the sound generated and amplified not by air pressure through pipes, but by electromechanical or electronic devices; see ELECTROPHONIC. A *computer organ* is one in which the electronic system uses a computerized digital process. See also REED-ORGAN.

organistrum = HURDY-GURDY.

organology, (rare term for) the study of musical instruments in general (not just the organ).

organ-point = PEDAL-point.

organum (Lat.), a medieval form of PART-writing (from the ninth century) based on a plainsong which was harmonized by the addition of one, two, or three (usually parallel) parts.

Orgel (Ger.) = organ; so Bach's *Orgel-büchlein* − see LITTLE ORGAN BOOK.

orgue (Fr.) = organ.

Orlando, Italian opera by Handel, produced in London, 1733. Libretto by G. Bracciotti, after Ariosto's 16th-century epic poem, *Orlando Furioso* (i.e. Mad Orlando). Remarkable for its operatic depiction of the hero's madness.

Ormandy (original surname Blau), **Eugene** (1899–1985), Hungarian-born conductor (originally violinist). Settled in USA 1920; succeeded Sto-kowski as conductor of Philadelphia Orchestra, 1936–80.

Ormindo, opera by Cavalli, produced in Venice, 1644. Libretto by Giovanni Faustini: the title-role is that of a prince of Tunis.

ornament, one or more notes considered as an embellishment of a melody, either − (1) inserted by the performer (e.g. the opera-singer in Handel's time) from his or her knowledge of current conventions, without specific written instructions from the composer − see APPOGGIATURA; (2) conveyed by a sign or abbreviation, e.g. ∼ (TURN), *tr* ∿ (TRILL), or by notes in small type (see, e.g., ACCIAC-CATURA); or (3) written in full or ordin-

ary notation, even when it could have been conveyed by a sign − as, e.g., the turn written out in full by Wagner and Bruckner. Also as verb − to *orna-ment* a melody in performance, etc.

Ornstein, Leo (b. 1892), Russian-born pianist and composer who settled in USA, 1906. Works include a piano concerto, chamber music, *Hebraic Fantasy* for violin and piano (written and performed in celebration of Albert Einstein's 50th birthday, 1929).

Orphée (Fr.), see various titles beginning ORPHEUS.

Orpheus, title of operas by various composers including − (1) Monteverdi, (one of the first of all operas), produced in Mantua, 1607; libretto by A. Striggio (*La favola d'Orfeo*, The Story of Orpheus); (2) Gluck, produced in Vienna, 1762, with Italian libretto (*Orfeo ed Euridice, Orpheus and Eury-dice*) by R. da Calzabigi; revised version in French, produced in Paris, 1774. Birtwistle's version is entitled THE MASK OF ORPHEUS. See also following entries.

Orpheus, symphonic poem by Liszt, 1854 − Orpheus, tamer of the beasts, symbolizing the power of art.

Orpheus, ballet with music by Stravinsky, produced in New York, 1948 − based on story of Orpheus's quest for Eurydice, and his death.

Orpheus Britannicus (Lat., the British Orpheus, i.e. Purcell), title of two posthumous volumes of Purcell's songs; a selection of 18 of these was arranged by Britten.

Orpheus in the Underworld (Fr., *Orphée aux enfers*; i.e. in Hades), operetta by Offenbach, produced in Paris, 1858 (revised, expanded version, 1874). Libretto by H. Crémieux and L. Halévy, satirizing modern times under cover of guying the old legend. It quotes, satirically, the famous aria 'Che farò' from Gluck's ORPHEUS.

Orr, Robin (name used by Robert Kemsley Orr) (b. 1909), British composer, pupil of Casella in Siena, N. Boulanger in Paris. Works include Prelude and Fugue for string quartet, opera *Full Circle*. Professor at Cambridge, 1965–75. CBE, 1972.

Orrego Salas, Juan [Antonio] (b. 1919), Chilean composer of *Five Castilian Songs* for voice and chamber orchestra – also of cantata *America, we do not invoke your name in vain* (in Spanish), four symphonies, opera *Widows*, etc. University teacher in USA.

Ortiz, Cristina (b. 1950), Brazilian pianist, naturalized British in 1977; the first woman to win the Van Cliburn Competition in Texas (1969).

Ortiz, Diego (*c*.1510–*c*.1570), Spanish composer who was in service to the Spanish viceroy in Naples and later to Philip II of Spain; wrote a famous treatise on instrumental variation-technique as well as vocal polyphonic works – Magnificats, motets, etc.

O salutaris hostia (Lat., O saving victim), latter part of a Roman Catholic hymn, sung to its own plainsong melodies or to later composed settings.

Osborne, Nigel (b. 1948), British composer and university teacher; works include *I am Goya* for baritone and instrumental ensemble, opera *The Electrification of the Soviet Union*.

ossia (It., from *o sia*, or it may be), (1) term used to introduce an alternative version of a musical passage, e.g. an editor's correction of an old composer's text which appears to be in error, or a composer's own simpler alternative for a passage difficult to perform; (2) term used to introduce the alternative title of an opera, etc. – for an example see OTELLO (Rossini).

ostinato (It., obstinate), a persistently repeated musical figure or rhythm; so *basso ostinato*, a bass having this characteristic – i.e. a GROUND BASS. (The term *pizzicato ostinato* in the third movement of Tchaikovsky's Symphony no. 4, exceptionally means only 'persistent pizzicato', not implying repetition.)

Ostrčil, Otakar (1879–1935), Czech composer of operas, symphonic poems, etc.; in later works was influenced by Mahler. Also opera conductor.

Otello, form of name used by Italians for the character called Othello by Shakespeare: title of operas (based on Shakespeare's play) (1) by Rossini, produced in Naples, 1816, with libretto by B. de Salsa (*Otello, ossia Il Moro di Venezia*; Othello, or The Moor of Venice); (2) by Verdi, produced in Milan, 1887, with libretto (*Otello*) by A. Boito. See also OTHELLO.

ôtez (Fr.), take off (imperative); *ôtez les sourdines*, take off the mutes.

Othello, concert-overture by Dvořák, 1892, after Shakespeare; see CARNIVAL. See also OTELLO.

ottava (It., sometimes written 8va.), octave; so *all'ottava*, at the octave (higher); *ottava bassa*, an octave lower.

ottavino (It.), the modern Italian name for the small flute, elsewhere called PICCOLO (itself signifying 'little' in Italian).

Otterloo, [Jan] Willem van (1907–78), Dutch conductor (and composer of orchestral music); conductor of the Residentie Orchestra of The Hague, 1949–73; he also worked in Sydney and Melbourne.

ottoni (It.), brass instruments.

Our Man in Havana, opera by Malcolm Williamson, produced in London, 1963; libretto by Sidney Gilliat after Graham Greene's novel, bitterly satirizing espionage and 'security'.

Ours, L', see BEAR (Haydn).

Ouseley, Frederick [Arthur] Gore (1825–89), English organist, composer of church music, etc., professor at Oxford, clergyman and baronet (succeeding his father).

Ousset, Cécile (b. 1936), French pianist who achieved international prominence rather later in life than is common; British début, 1980.

ouverture, Ouvertüre (Fr., Ger.) = OVERTURE.

overblow, to blow a woodwind instrument harder, in such a way that its notes are 'stepped up' from those of its 'basic' pitch. In most such instruments the notes are 'stepped up' first of all by an octave (this representing, in the HARMONIC SERIES, the distance from the first to the second harmonic), and such instruments are said to *overblow an octave*. In the clarinet, however, the second harmonic is missing and the notes are 'stepped up' not by an octave but by a 12th: it is therefore said to *overblow a twelfth*.

overstrung, description of pianos in which the strings are set at two different levels, crossing – this affording greater length of string for a given size of instrument.

overtone, name for any notes of the HARMONIC SERIES except the first (fundamental).

overture, (1) piece of orchestral music preceding an opera or oratorio – since Gluck, usually musically allusive to what follows; (2) similar piece preceding a play; (3) since Mendelssohn's HEBRIDES, also a type of one-movement orchestral work composed for the concert hall, and usually having a title revealing a literary, pictorial, or emotional clue. (This last type is specifically called *concert-overture*.) So *French overture*, 17th–18th century form of (1) above, in two movements, slow-fast (sometimes with final return to slow tempo); *Italian overture*, in three movements, quick-slow-quick (the form from which the symphony evolved).

Owen, Wilfred (1895–1918), British poet. See WAR REQUIEM.

'Oxford' Symphony, nickname for Haydn's Symphony no. 92 in G (Hob. I: 92), performed when Haydn visited Oxford University in 1791 to receive an honorary doctorate; but composed in 1789 without this purpose in mind.

Ox Minuet (Ger., *Ochsenmenuett*), minuet attributed to Haydn, but really by his pupil, I. X. von Seyfried (1776–1841), who introduced it into an opera of the same name, compiled mainly from Haydn's works. (Haydn was supposed to have received an ox as payment for this minuet.)

Ozawa, Seiji

Ozawa, Seiji (b. 1935), Japanese conductor, pupil of Karajan in Berlin; music director of Toronto Symphony Orchestra, 1965–70, of San Francisco Symphony Orchestra, 1969–76, of Boston Symphony Orchestra since 1973.

P

p, abbr. of *piano* (It., soft); hence, as indications of increasing degrees of softness, *pp*, *ppp*, etc. – sometimes in even greater aggregations.

Pachelbel, Johann (1653–1706), German organist and composer of keyboard music (including preludes on Lutheran chorales), church music, etc. Teacher of Bach's elder brother Johann Christoph, who in turn was the teacher of Bach himself in his boyhood.

Pachmann, Vladimir [de] (1848–1933), Russian pianist who specialized in Chopin and was famous for eccentric behaviour at the keyboard.

Pacific 231, 'symphonic movement' by Honegger, first performed in 1924. Named after an American railway engine – but 'I have not aimed to imitate the noise of an engine, but rather to express in terms of music a visual impression and physical enjoyment' (Honegger).

Pacini, Giovanni (1796–1867), Italian composer of more than 80 operas including *The Youth of Henry V*, after Shakespeare; also of church music, *Dante Symphony*, etc.

Paderewski, Ignacy [Jan] (1860–1941), Polish pianist, pupil of Leschetizky in Vienna, and composer of operas, a piano concerto, symphony, piano solos (including Minuet in G), songs, etc. Also statesman: first Prime Minister of the newly created state of Poland, 1919 (he resigned after ten months). Died in New York.

Paer, Ferdinando (1771–1839), Italian composer who became musical director to Napoleon, and settled in Paris, 1807. (In France the spelling 'Paër' is used.) Wrote more than 40 operas including a *Leonora* (in Italian) on the plot which had already served Gaveaux and which was to serve Beethoven in FIDELIO.

Paganini, Niccolò (1782–1840), Italian violinist, called by Schumann 'the turning-point of virtuosity'; enormously successful – though, with the subsequent advance in the general level of performers' skill, his feats are no longer regarded as freakishly difficult. Was also guitarist (wrote three string quartets with guitar part) and viola-player: he commissioned, but never played, Berlioz's HAROLD IN ITALY. Compositions include at least six violin concertos (no. 2 in B minor contains the BELL RONDO); a set of variations for violin called THE CARNIVAL OF VENICE; and 24 Capricci (i.e. studies) for unaccompanied violin. One of the latter, in A minor, is the source of (1) Brahms's *Studies in Piano*

Technique: Variations on a Theme of Paganini, 1866; (2) Rakhmaninov's *Rhapsody on a Theme of Paganini* for piano and orchestra (also in variation-form), 1934; (3) Blacher's orchestral *Variations on a Theme of Paganini*, 1947; (4) Lutosławski's *Variations on a Theme of Paganini* for two pianos, 1941. Liszt, Schumann, Busoni and others also transcribed his works for piano. The intense, 'demonic' quality of some of his music led to legends of his being inspired by the Devil, etc. Died in Nice.

Pagliacci (It., Clowns), opera by Leoncavallo, produced in Milan, 1892. Libretto by composer – on the interaction between a play and the real tragic 'drama' lived by the players.

Paik, Nam June (b. 1932), Korean composer who studied in Germany and later worked in New York and Los Angeles. His works include *Étude for Pianoforte* involving among other things 'the destruction of two pianos, cutting John Cage's necktie, and shampooing him without warning'; also other action-pieces, a cello sonata, etc.

Paine, John Knowles (1839–1906), American organist and composer (two symphonies, cantatas, etc.) who studied in Germany and later founded the musical faculty at Harvard.

Paisiello, Giovanni (1740–1816), Italian composer who worked in St Petersburg (Catherine the Great's court), Paris (under Napoleon) and Naples, where he died. Wrote more than 100 operas, including a very successful BARBER OF SEVILLE (before Rossini's); also symphonies, church music, etc. Befriended and influenced Mozart.

Palestrina, Giovanni Pierluigi da (1525–94), Italian composer who took the name Palestrina from his native town, near Rome. Was a choirboy, and spent all his musical life in service of the Church; also proved an able businessman. Became choirmaster of the Julian Chapel at St Peter's, Rome, and later held other high positions. Much honoured in his lifetime, he was described on his coffin as 'Prince of Music'. After his first wife died he entered the priesthood, but abandoned it and remarried. Apart from a few madrigals his works are all Latin church music for unaccompanied choir – nearly 100 Masses (including MISSA PAPAE MARCELLI and a Mass on L'HOMME ARMÉ), motets, a Stabat Mater, psalms, etc. Posthumous veneration of him led to various fanciful legends; see next entry.

Palestrina, opera by Pfitzner, produced in Munich, 1917. Libretto by Pfitzner, about the composer – but on the basis of the fiction that Palestrina, by composing his MISSA PAPAE MARCELLI at direct angelic inspiration, persuaded the ecclesiastical Council of Trent (1545–63) not to ban polyphonic music.

palindrome, a literary name for a word or phrase which reads the same backwards as forwards, e.g. 'Was it a cat I saw?'; hence a similar construction in music, usually involving not note-for-note reversal but a reversed order of sections of a piece, e.g. in Hindemith's opera *There and Back* (where a revised sequence occurs in both the music and the stage action).

Pallavicino, Carlo (*c.*1630–1688), Italian composer, chiefly of opera; worked much, and died, in Dresden.

Palmgren, Selim (1878–1951), Finnish composer who studied in Germany and Italy with Busoni and others; also pianist and conductor; taught in USA, 1923–6. Works include many short piano pieces with 'picturesque' titles (e.g. *Night in May*) and some of Finnish nationalist significance; also five piano concertos, operas, etc.

Pammelia, a collection of English rounds, catches, etc., for voices, published by T. Ravenscroft in 1609. Named from Greek for 'all-honey', and succeeded by *Deuteromelia* (also 1609; Gk., *deutero-*, second).

pandiatonic(ism), term coined (from Gk., *pan*, all) by the American musicologist Nicolas Slonimsky to indicate the pronounced use in chord-formation of all seven degrees of the DIATONIC scale. Examples of such use are the ADDED SIXTH in jazz and the chord C–E–G–B at the beginning of Delius's ON HEARING THE FIRST CUCKOO IN SPRING.

pandora (also *bandora*), name given to many varieties of plucked instrument – especially a type of large, wire-strung CITTERN used in the 16th–17th centuries as a continuo instrument.

pan-pipes, a series of simple short vertical pipes fixed side by side in order to give a scale when blown – an ancient, medieval and 'folk' instrument. Papageno, as a 'child of Nature', plays one in Mozart's THE MAGIC FLUTE.

pantomime (from Gk. for 'all-imitating'), (1) a play in dumb-show, a mime-play – either as a self-contained work or (as in Ravel's DAPHNIS AND CHLOE, where the story of Pan and Syrinx is mimed) as an episode in a larger work; (2) type of English stage-entertainment presented at Christmastime, loosely founded on a fairy-story or similar traditional source, interspersed with songs and formerly ended with a harlequinade.

pantonal(ity), see ATONAL.

pantoum (Fr.), type of quatrain of Malayan origin introduced into French verse by Hugo and used by Ravel to describe what is in effect the Scherzo (second of four movements) of his Piano Trio, 1914.

Panufnik, Andrzej (b. 1914), Polish composer of ten symphonies (no. 3, *Sinfonia sacra*), *Universal Prayer* for mezzo-soprano, baritone, chorus and orchestra (text by Pope), Polish folksong settings, etc.; also conductor. Left Poland in protest against political regimentation and came to Britain, 1954 (naturalized 1961); conductor, City of Birmingham Symphony Orchestra, 1957–9. Knighted 1991.

Papillons (Fr., Butterflies), 12 short dance pieces by Schumann, op. 2 (1829–31); thematically connected with Schumann's CARNIVAL.

Papineau-Couture, Jean (b. 1916), Canadian composer and university teacher. Works include *Landscape* for eight narrators, eight singers and instrumental ensemble; a symphony, two string quartets, etc.

Paradies (or Paradisi), [Pietro] **Domenico** (*c*.1707–91), Italian harpsichordist, composer of operas, etc., as well as of harpsichord works. Lived for many years as teacher in London.

Paradis, Maria Theresia von (1759–1824), Austrian pianist (for whom Mozart wrote a concerto), also organist, singer and composer of three operas and other works; blind from childhood. Performed as pianist in Paris and London.

Paradise and the Peri (Ger., *Das Paradies und die Peri*), cantata by Schumann, 1843, with German text translated from part of T. Moore's *Lalla Rookh*. The Peri here is a good spirit of Persian mythology, seeking readmittance to Heaven; cp. THE PERI and IOLANTHE.

Paradise Lost, opera by Penderecki, produced in Chicago, 1978; libretto by Christopher Fry, after Milton's poem. See also CONSTANT and MARKEVICH.

Paradisi, Domenico, see PARADIES.

parallel motion, see MOTION.

parameter, vague term (distorted from precise mathematical use) applied from the 1950s to such basic elements of a composition as pitch, loudness, duration and timbre – especially where such elements are subjected to a mathematical order, as in 'total serialism' (see SERIES).

paraphrase, an alternative term for 'fantasy' in the sense of a virtuoso solo based on a well-known work – e.g. Liszt's *Rigoletto: Concert Paraphrase* for piano, based on Verdi's opera of that name.

parergon (Gk., accessory work), term used by R. Strauss in his *Parergon to the Symphonia Domestica* (see SYMPHONIA DOMESTICA) for piano (left hand) and orchestra, 1925, partly based on the same material as the other work.

Paris, Orchestre de, see under ORCHESTRE

'Paris' Symphonies, a set of six symphonies by Haydn (Hob. I: 82–7) composed in 1785–6, mainly for a series of concerts in Paris: no. 82 is nicknamed THE BEAR, no. 83 THE HEN, no. 85 THE QUEEN.

'Paris' Symphony, nickname for Mozart's Symphony no. 31 in D (K297), composed in Paris for a performance there, 1778.

Parker, Horatio [William] (1863–1919), American composer and organist; pupil of Rheinberger in Germany. Wrote *Hora Novissima* and other oratorios; also two operas, symphony, organ concerto, etc. D. Mus., Cambridge (England), 1902.

parlando, parlante (It., speaking) – either as a literal instruction (e.g. in opera), or as a direction in song indicating a near appoach to a speaking tone.

parody, properly (in music as in literature) a work, or part of it, which makes an exaggerated or distorted use of an identifiable model, with humorous intent. But the term is also misleadingly employed to denote a composer's straightforward (non-humorous) imitation or adaptation of his own or someone else's work, e.g. especially the *parody mass* (or, Lat., *missa parodia*) of the 16th–17th centuries, based on a pre-existing motet. This term is a later (musicologists') usage, not stemming from the period.

Parry, [Charles] **Hubert** [Hastings] (1848–1918), British composer of unison song 'Jerusalem', many solo settings of notable English verse, five symphonies, oratorios (see JOB, JUDITH), much chamber music, etc. Also writer on music, director of the

Royal College of Music (1894–1918), professor at Oxford (1900–1908). Knighted, 1898; baronet, 1903. No relation of the following.

Parry, Joseph (1841–1903), British composer of hymn-tune 'Aberystwyth' (sung to 'Jesu, lover of my soul') and other hymns; also of operas, oratorios, orchestral works, etc. Became professor at Aberystwyth. No relation of the preceding.

Parsifal, opera by Wagner, produced in Bayreuth, 1882; libretto by composer, the hero being the 'simpleton without guile' who restores a sacred spear to the Knight of the Holy Grail (see also LOHENGRIN). Wagner described the work as a *Bühnenweihfestspiel*, approximately a 'sacred-festival play'.

part, (1) the music of a particular performer in an ensemble – the *tenor part*, the *flute part*, etc.; *score and parts*, expression contrasting the score (containing the music of all performers) with the music written separately for individuals; hence – (2) an individual 'strand' of music, whether or not it is actually performed by one or more; a *fugue in four parts* or *four-part fugue*, etc.; so also PART-SONG, PART-WRITING; (3) a section e.g. of an oratorio (corresponding to an act in opera), a complete evening's work being divided into *parts* so that intervals can be made.

Pärt, Arvo (b. 1935), Soviet-Estonian composer of a 'St John' Passion, three symphonies, etc.; emigrated in 1988, settling in West Berlin.

Partch, Harry (1901–74), American composer, self-taught, inventor of a

series of string and percussion instruments tuned in JUST INTONATION and using microtones ('cloud-chamber bowls', 'bamboo marimba', 'quadrangularis reversum', etc.) for which his music is composed – *Windsong, Water, Water* (theatrical work with voices), *And on the Seventh Day Petals Fell in Petaluma*, etc. His other works include a setting of Sophocles' *Oedipus Rex*.

parte (It.) = PART (1, 2); *colla parte*, with the (solo) part, i.e. the accompanying instrument(s) accommodating the soloist to allow some licence of tempo.

Parthenia (Gk., maidenhood), fanciful title given to the first book of keyboard music ever printed in England, 1611, containing pieces by Bull, Byrd and O. Gibbons. Full title, *Parthenia, or the Maidenhead of the first music that ever was printed for the virginals*. A succeeding volume was called *Parthenia inviolata* (a pun on 'unviolated' and 'set for viol') – being for keyboard and bass viol.

partial, name given to each of the notes of the HARMONIC SERIES, the lowest or 'fundamental' being the *first partial* and the others (numbered upwards consecutively) *upper partials*.

partie (Fr.) = (1) PART (in all senses); (2) PARTITA.

partita (It.), suite or set of variations – term used much in the 18th century, occasionally revived since. See also FELDPARTIE.

partition, Partitur (Fr., Ger.) = SCORE.

Partos, Oedoen (1907–77), Israeli viola-player and composer, Hungarian-born, who settled in Palestine, 1938;

works include *In Memoriam* (Heb., *Yizkor*) for viola and orchestra, and a choral fantasy on Yemenite Jewish themes.

part-song, (literally) any song written for several vocal PARTS, without independent accompaniment, as distinct from a solo or unison song; but the term is particularly applied (1) to English songs from the early 16th century onwards, in which the vertical (harmonic) aspect prevails over the horizontal (contrapuntal) one, and the top part most frequently has the melody (unlike the madrigal); (2) to English choral pieces of similar texture to the above, written in the 19th and 20th centuries.

part-writing, the laying-out of a composition so that each part (see PART 2) progresses euphoniously. (The US term is 'voice-leading', introduced as translation of Ger. *Stimmführung* by immigrant musicians unaware of the established English term.)

pas (Fr.), step (in dancing, etc.); *pas d'action*, ballet scene of a dramatic nature; *pas seul, pas de deux*, etc., dance for one person, for two, etc.

pasodoble (Sp., double step), modern Spanish dance in quick 2/4 time – used, in a spirit of parody, in Walton's FAÇADE.

Pasquini, Bernardo (1637–1710), Italian organist, harpsichordist and composer of operas, harpsichord sonatas, etc.

passacaglia (It.), instrumental piece (originally a dance) in which a theme stretching over several bars is continually repeated, usually but not necessarily always in the bass. Cp. CHACONNE: the two terms, though of different origin, are now often used almost interchangeably, except that *passacaglia* seems never to have been applied to a vocal work.

passage, a section of a musical composition – sometimes, not always, with the implication of not having much structural importance (e.g. when a piece is said to contain 'showy passage-work' for a soloist's display).

passamezzo (It., also *pass'e mezzo*, i.e. 'pace and a half'), Italian dance, similar to the pavan, known from the 16th century; the music for it often conformed to one of two standardized harmonic patterns.

Passereau, Pierre (active 1509–47), French composer of whom a motet and some chansons (in the style of Jannequin) survive.

passing-note, in harmony, a note which forms a discord with the chord with which it is heard, but which is 'justified' because it is melodically placed between two notes which are not discordant. E.g. the D in the two examples below: the melody appears merely to be 'passing' on the discordant D between the two notes E and C, both concordant. When, however, the discordant note occurs between two repetitions of the same concordant note, a different term is used: see AUXILIARY NOTE.

Passio (Lat.) = PASSION, in the sense of the following entry.

Passion, a musical setting of the biblical story of the suffering (Lat., *passio*) and death of Jesus, properly to be sung in churches in the week before Easter. Works of this character exist as Latin motets (e.g. by Davy and Rore), but the term is usually reserved for larger works written in the vernacular tongue – notably those in German by Bach (ST JOHN PASSION, ST MATTHEW PASSION) and earlier by Schütz. These have a semi-dramatic form, individual singers taking the parts of Jesus, Judas, etc. The so-called *Passion chorale* (see CHORALE) is the hymn 'O Haupt voll Blut und Wunden' (usually translated 'O Sacred Head'), originally by Hassler, which Bach used prominently in both his Passions as part of the (non-biblical) commentary made by soloists and chorus on the story: other hymn-tunes are similarly incorporated. See also the following entry, and CHILD OF OUR TIME, GRAUN, PÄRT, PEPPING, ROCHBERG.

Passion, or (It.) *La Passione*, nickname for Haydn's Symphony no. 49 in F minor, 1768 (Hob. I:49). The reference is apparently to the Christian *Passion* (see preceding), perhaps for a performance at Passiontide.

pasticcio (It., a pie), operatic work with music drawn for the purpose from works by different composers – as commonly in the 18th century; see, e.g., LOVE IN A VILLAGE. The term might well be extended to include a piece compiled from different works by the same composer, e.g. VIENNA BLOOD.

pastiche (Fr.), (1) PASTICCIO; (2) a piece composed deliberately in the style of another composer.

pastoral, (1) term or nickname for music evoking (e.g. by instrumentation or verbal label) a rustic subject – usually as adjective (see following

entries) but also as noun; (2) obsolete term for a stage entertainment with a rustic setting – e.g. Handel's ACIS AND GALATEA.

'Pastoral' Sonata, nickname (not the composer's) for Beethoven's Piano Sonata in D, op. 28, 1801: the last movement may seem to suggest a dance to a rustic bagpipe.

Pastoral Symphony, (1) Beethoven's own title for his Symphony no. 6 in F, first performed in 1808. Title goes on: '. . . or Memories of Life in the Country (the expression of feeling, rather than painting)' – the five movements having allusive titles (e.g. no. 2, 'By the Brook', incorporating imitations of quail, cuckoo and nightingale); (2) title of an orchestral interlude in Handel's MESSIAH, referring to the shepherds to whom Christ's birth was announced, and said to be based on an Italian folk-melody heard by Handel (cp. PIFFERO) – this not being a SYMPHONY in the modern sense; (3) title (*A Pastoral Symphony*) of Vaughan Williams's Symphony no. 3 (but, in conformity with his practice, not numbered by him – first performed in 1922); it has a wordless high voice in the last movement.

pastourelle (Old Fr., shepherdess), type of poetic dialogue (and the music associated with it) between a shepherdess and a knight aiming to seduce her; current in 13th-century France and earlier. The term was later revived for works making sophisticated allusion to pastoral life.

Pathetic Sonata, title given by Beethoven (in French, as *Sonate pathétique*) to his Piano Sonata in C minor, op. 13, composed about 1798.

Pathetic Symphony, name (authorized by composer) for Tchaikovsky's Symphony no. 6, 1893.

pathétique (Fr.), see preceding entries.

Patience, or Bunthorne's Bride, operetta by Sullivan, produced in London, 1881. Libretto by W. S. Gilbert. Patience, the dairymaid heroine of this satire on 'aestheticism', does not become the bride of the poet Bunthorne – nor does anyone.

Patterson, Paul (b. 1947), British composer of a Requiem (in memory of President Kennedy); *Time-piece* for male voices, etc. Teacher at Royal Academy of Music.

patter-song, type of comic song (especially in opera) dependent for its effect on the rapid enunciation of syllables – usually a solo, though Sullivan has a patter-trio in RUDDIGORE.

Patti, Adelina (originally Adela Juana Maria) (1843–1919), Spanish-born Italian soprano who made her operatic début at 16 in New York, later settling in Britain; one of the most famous performers of her period.

Pau, Maria de la, see TORTELIER.

Pauk, György (b. 1936), Hungarian-born violinist, naturalized British in 1967; recital partner with Peter Frankl; performs major modern works (see IMAI).

Pauke(n) (Ger.), kettledrum(s); *Paukenmesse*, see DRUM MASS; *Sinfonie mit dem Paukenschlag* (Symphony with the Drum-stroke), see SURPRISE SYMPHONY; *Sinfonie mit dem Paukenwirbel*, see DRUM-ROLL SYMPHONY.

Paul Bunyan, operetta by Britten, with text by W. H. Auden, on the subject of an American legendary lumberman hero; first performed, New York 1941, then suppressed by the composer until 1976 (when publication and radio and stage performances took place).

Paulus, see ST PAUL.

pausa (It.) = REST (not the English PAUSE, = It. *fermata*).

pause (Eng.), (1) the sign ∩ Its meaning is that the note or rest so marked must be held longer than normally, to an extent determined by the performer's discretion, though the composer may add the words 'short' or 'long' in various languages as an additional indication; (2) term used in the phrase GENERAL PAUSE. See also next entry.

Pause (Ger.), (1) a PAUSE (as in English, above); (2) a REST; (3) an interval (in a concert, etc.).

pavan, pavane (Eng., Fr.), slow stately dance dating at least from the 16th century, and mentioned in Shakespeare; it was often followed by the quicker GALLIARD. Fauré's work so entitled (1887) is for orchestra and optional chorus; Ravel's *Pavan for a Dead Infanta* (Fr., *Pavane pour une Infante défunte*) was composed for piano in 1899 and later orchestrated. (Note that *pavan*, accented on first syllable, is the authentic English form.) See also GOULD (M.), and PASSAMEZZO.

Pavarotti, Luciano (b. 1936), Italian tenor, eminent in opera: Covent Garden from 1963; La Scala, Milan, from 1966. Twenty-five years later he was still a major box-office star.

pavillon (Fr.), the 'bell' (extremity opposite to the mouthpiece) of a horn, trumpet, etc. (Named from its pavilion-like shape.) So, as direction to brass-players, *pavillons en l'air*, with the bells held high up so as to increase the volume. But for *pavillon chinois* (i.e. Chinese), see JINGLING JOHNNY.

Paz, Juan Carlos (1901–72), Argentinian composer of *Three Jazz Movements* and other works for piano, *Continuity* for orchestra, etc. Also writer on music.

Pearl-Fishers, The (Fr., *Les Pêcheurs de perles*), opera by Bizet, produced in Paris, 1863. Libretto by E. Cormon and M. Carré: the scene is set in Ceylon, though the characters are called Indians.

Pears, Peter [Neville Luard] (1910–86), British tenor, much associated with Britten – who wrote for him the leading tenor parts in his operas and other works (e.g. PETER GRIMES, SERENADE, WAR REQUIEM). Internationally distinguished also in Bach, etc.; also writer on musical subjects, editor, etc. (See MIDSUMMER NIGHT'S DREAM.) Knighted, 1978.

Pearsall, Robert Lucas (calling himself de Pearsall) (1795–1856), British composer, chiefly of vocal music – madrigals in 16th-century style, partsongs, Anglican and Roman Catholic church music, etc. Settled in Switzerland and died there.

Pearson, Henry Hugo, see PIERSON.

Pêcheurs de perles, Les, see PEARL-FISHERS.

ped., abbr. for pedal: (1, in piano music) instruction that the sustaining pedal is to be depressed until a point when its release is indicated; (2, in organ music) indication of music to be played on the pedal keyboard.

pedal, (1, in harmony) a note sustained below (i.e. at the foot of) changing harmonies: this is called a *pedal* or *pedal point* or *pedal bass*. If it is thus sustained but not in the bass it is an *inverted pedal* (cp. INVERT, 1); (2) the lowest ('fundamental') note of the HARMONIC SERIES, especially with reference to the playing of brass instruments; (3) a foot-operated lever – see HARP, HARPSICHORD, KETTLEDRUM, ORGAN, PIANO. See also following entries.

pedal-board, a keyboard played with the feet – such as is normally found on the organ, rarely on harpsichord, clavichord and piano (see PEDAL-PIANO).

pedal clarinet, see CLARINET.

pédalier (Fr.) = (1) PEDAL-BOARD, (2) PEDAL-PIANO.

pedal-piano, a piano fitted with a pedal keyboard in addition to its ordinary one – used by organists for home practice, but also written for expressly, e.g. by Schumann and Alkan.

pedal point, see PEDAL (1).

Pedrell, Felipe (1841–1922), Spanish musicologist, editor of old Spanish music; teacher of Falla, Granados and others, and composer of operas, church music, symphonic poems, etc.

Pedrotti, Carlo (1817–93), Italian composer, mainly of operas; also conductor of a much admired orchestral concert series (1868–82) in Turin. He committed suicide.

Peer Gynt, play by Ibsen (named after its boasting folk-hero) for which Grieg wrote incidental music for the original production, 1876: two orchestral suites are drawn from this. An opera by Egk (1938) is also based on the play, as is a ballet with music by Schnittke (1989). Incidental music to the play has also been written by Saeverud (1948).

Peerson, Martin (*c.*1571–1651), English composer of church music and other vocal music and also works for viols and for keyboard, etc.: master of the choristers at St Paul's, London.

Peeters, Flor (1903–86), Belgian organist, pianist, musical editor, composer of an organ concerto, songs, etc.; was created a Belgian baron in 1971.

Pelléas and Mélisande (Fr., *Pelléas et Mélisande*), play by Maeterlinck, 1892 (named from its ill-fated medieval lovers) – source of (1) opera by Debussy, almost a word-for-word setting of the play, produced in Paris, 1902; (2) incidental music to the play composed by Fauré, 1898, and by Sibelius, 1905; (3) symphonic poem by Schoenberg, composed 1902–3, first performed in 1905.

Penderecki, Krzysztof (b. 1933), Polish composer who has travelled widely to supervise (and sometimes conduct) his own music. His compositions include Canon for 52 string instruments and tape, *De natura sonoris* (Lat., Of the Nature of Sound) for orchestra, operas *The Devils of Loudun* and PARADISE LOST; also various works for voices and orchestra on religious texts – Stabat Mater, 'St Luke' Passion, etc.

penillion (Welsh, pl.), a type of traditional Welsh singing, in which verses (either given or improvised) are sung in counterpoint to a well-known melody played on the harp. Term used also as title of an orchestral work by Grace Williams, 1955, based on the musical ideas of traditional penillion.

penny-whistle, see TIN-WHISTLE.

pentatonic (from Gk., *pente*, five), term used of a scale comprising only five notes – particularly that represented by the five black keys of the piano (or other notes in the same position relative to each other). This form of pentatonic scale is widely used in folk-music of many countries – Scottish, Chinese, Afro-American (e.g. 'Swing Low, Sweet Chariot'), etc.

Pentland, Barbara [Lally] (b. 1912), Canadian composer, pupil of Copland and others; formerly university teacher. Works include four symphonies, three string quartets, piano pieces.

Pépin, [Jean-Joséphat] **Clermont** (b. 1926), Canadian composer, pupil of Honegger, Jolivet and Messiaen in Paris. Works include ballet *The Gates of Hell*, four symphonies, four string quartets.

Pepping, Ernst (1901–81), German composer, chiefly of Protestant church music – unaccompanied motets, a *St Matthew* PASSION, etc.; also of works for orchestra, for piano and for organ.

Pepusch, Johann Christoph (also known in England as John Christopher) (1667–1752), German-born composer (also organist) who settled in London about 1700, and died there. Arranged the music for the original production of THE BEGGAR'S OPERA; also composed other stage music, church music, concertos, etc., and wrote theoretical treatises.

per (It.), by, through, for, etc.; *per archi*, for strings; *dramma per musica*, drama through music, i.e. opera.

Perahia, Murray (b. 1947), American pianist who settled in London; became a director of the Aldeburgh Festival.

He directs Mozart concertos from the keyboard.

percussion, collective name for instruments in which (usually) a resonating surface is struck by the player – in most cases directly by hand or stick, but sometimes through leverage as in the type of bass-drum used in dance bands, operated by a pedal. The piano and celesta come technically within this definition of percussion instruments but are not conventionally so classified: however, the piano is sometimes said to be 'employed as a percussion instrument' (i.e. for percussive rather than melodic effect) in such 20th-century works as Stravinsky's THE WEDDING; and see ORFF. Percussion instruments as used today in the symphony orchestra, dance band, etc., may be tuned to a definite pitch (see, e.g., KETTLEDRUM, tubular BELL, GLOCKENSPIEL, XYLOPHONE, VIBRAPHONE, MARIMBA) or may be of indefinite pitch, e.g. TRIANGLE, GONG, CASTANETS, WHIP, RATTLE, ANVIL and the following drums – SNARE DRUM, TENOR DRUM, BASS DRUM, TABOR, TAMBOURINE, BONGO; the TOM-TOM may be of definite or indefinite pitch; the normal CYMBALS are of indefinite pitch but the 'ancient cymbal' or CROTALE is not. Instruments that are shaken rather than struck, e.g. MARACA, RATTLE, are also placed within the percussion section of an orchestra, as are certain freak instruments, e.g. motor-horn, iron chains, when (exceptionally) employed. In listing the members of an orchestra, a common but absurd British practice gives 'timpani [i.e. kettledrums] and percussion' as though these were mutually exclusive; the reason is that the kettledrummer counts as the senior player, the other players taking any other instruments specified.

perdendosi (It., losing itself; accent on second syllable), direction for performance indicating 'softer and softer until dying away'.

perfect, (1) term used to describe the intervals of a fourth, fifth and eighth (octave) in their 'standard' dimensions – e.g. C up to F, to G, and to C respectively. They become DIMINISHED if lessened by a semitone and AUGMENTED if enlarged by a semitone; (2) type of cadence: see CADENCE; (3) term used in the phrase *perfect time*, meaning (in medieval music) triple time; (4) term used in the phrase *perfect pitch*: see PITCH.

Perfect Fool, The, opera by Holst, produced in London, 1923. Libretto by composer. The work parodies the operatic manner of other composers; the title refers not to any of them, however, but to the simpleton hero.

performance practice, 20th-century term (translated literally from Ger. *Aufführungspraxis*) for the body of conventions and knowledge that a performer must apply in order to interpret a composer's notation and instructions. The term implies the recognition that such notation and instructions are insufficient in themselves and require the study of their historical context.

Pergolesi, Giovanni Battista (1710–36), Italian composer, also violinist and church organist; wrote serious and comic operas, among the latter the enormously successful THE MAID AS MISTRESS (*La serva padrona*). (Imported into France, it provoked a quarrel between supporters of French and Italian opera – the so-called 'War of the Buffoons'.) Died of tuberculosis. Afterwards, in order to capitalize on his popularity, many works not his were ascribed to him and sometimes still are – among them the opera THE MUSIC MASTER, concertinos for strings, the songs 'Se tu m'ami' (used by Stravinsky in PULCINELLA) and 'Tre giorni son che Nina'. Authentic works include a STABAT MATER for (male) soprano and alto with orchestral accompaniment.

Peri, Jacopo (1561–1633), Italian composer who wrote the first real operas to be staged, *Daphne* (1597, lost) and *Eurydice* (1600); also composed other operas (some in collaboration with other composers), ballets, madrigals, etc. Was a priest in service to the Medici family. See CAMERATA.

Peri, The (Fr., *La Péri*), ballet with music by Dukas – the score being described as a 'dance-poem' – produced in Paris, 1912. The Peri is here a good female spirit of Persian mythology: cp. PARADISE AND THE PERI; IOLANTHE.

Perlman, Itzhak (b. 1945), Israeli violinist, son of Polish émigré parents; contracted polio at age four and so plays seated. Trained in New York and made début there in 1963; appeared in London from 1968.

Perosi, Lorenzo (1872–1956), Italian priest and composer who won short-lived success (especially in Italy) with a series of New Testament oratorios, more than 30 Masses, etc. Suffered from mental illness.

Pérotin [Latinized as Perotinus], French composer active in the early 13th century; composed liturgical music showing a high degree of structural organization, in the style later known as ARS ANTIQUA.

perpetual canon, see CANON.

perpetuum mobile, see MOTO.

Persephone, stage work by Stravinsky for speaker, singers and orchestra (styled MELODRAMA); produced in Paris, 1934. Libretto in French, based on the Greek myth, by A. Gide.

Persichetti, Vincent (1915–87), American composer, pupil of Roy Harris; also pianist, conductor, writer on music, and music publishing executive. Works include nine symphonies (no. 6 is for wind-band); Concerto for piano duet and orchestra; ballet *King Lear*; sonatas for violin alone and for cello alone.

Perti, Giacomo [Antonio] (1661–1756), Italian composer of operas, oratorios ('Abraham the conqueror of his own feelings', etc.), Masses, etc.; for 60 years director of music at the church of San Petronio in Bologna.

pesante (It.), heavily.

Peter and the Wolf (Rus., *Petya i volk*), 'musical tale for children' by Prokofiev, first performed in 1936; a narrator's words are illustrated by the orchestra.

Peter Grimes, opera by Britten, produced in London, 1945. Libretto by M. Slater, after Crabbe's poem. 'The Borough'; named after its misanthropic fisherman hero.

petit(e) (Fr.), little; *petite flûte*, PICCOLO.

Petrarch [Francesco Petrarca] (1303–74), Italian poet. See BARTOS, VICTORY.

Petrassi, Goffredo (b. 1904), Italian composer, formerly choirboy. Works include operas *The Spanish Screen* (*Il Cordovano*) and *Death in the Air*; ballets

Portrait of Don Quixote and *Orlando's Madness*; seven concertos for orchestra; *Choir of the Dead* and other choral works including *Nonsense* (title in English) on poems by Edward Lear in Italian translation; piano works, songs, etc.

Petri, Michala (b. 1958), Danish recorder-player who began international career in her teens, playing modern as well as baroque works with her mother, Hanne Petri (b. 1929), as accompanist.

Petrovics, Emil (b. 1930), Yugoslav-born composer who studied in Hungary and lives there; conservatory teacher and operatic administrator in Budapest. Works include operas *C'est la guerre* (Fr., That's War – text in Hungarian), and *Crime and Punishment* (after Dostoyevsky); also a flute concerto, Sinfonia for strings, etc.

Petrushka, ballet with music by Stravinsky, produced in Paris, 1911. The suite drawn from it was revised in 1947. Petrushka is a traditonal Russian puppet figure: 'Pétrouchka', the French transliteration of his name, is suitable only for French usage.

petto, voce di = CHEST VOICE.

Petzold (also Pezel), Johann Christoph (1639–94), trumpeter and violinist, employed as municipal musician at Leipzig and Bautzen; composer and publisher of suites and other works for wind ensemble.

Peyer, Gervase de, see DE PEYER.

Pezel, see PETZOLD.

pezzo (It., pl. *-i*), a piece, a play, a musical work, etc.

Pfitzner, Hans [Erich] (1869–1949),

German composer, born in Moscow; also pianist, conductor and writer – attacking Busoni and modernism generally, from a traditionalist German-Romantic standpoint. Works include PALESTRINA and other operas, a piano concerto, violin concerto, chamber music, songs (some with orchestra).

Phantasie, phantasy (Ger., Eng.), see FANTASY.

Philadelphia Orchestra, American orchestra established in 1900; Stokowski, whose conductorship (1912–38) made it famous, was succeeded by Eugene Ormandy, followed by Riccardo Muti (1980–92), then Wolfgang Sawallisch.

Philharmonia Orchestra, British orchestra founded in 1945 under private management; it was succeeded in 1964 by the self-governing New Philharmonia Orchestra, which itself dropped the 'New' in 1977. Giuseppe Sinopoli has been principal conductor since 1984.

philharmonic (from Gk., 'friendly to harmony'), term used as title of various orchestras and other musical bodies. Note that *philharmonic orchestra* merely identifies a particular orchestra; it does not also stand for a type of orchestra, as 'symphony orchestra' does; see ORCHESTRA. *Old Philharmonic pitch* and *New Philharmonic pitch* are two standards of PITCH, both now obsolete.

Philidor, surname of a French musical family of whom the most important is François André [Danican] Philidor (1726–95), composer especially of operas (see OPÉRA COMIQUE) including TOM JONES; also of a Requiem for

Rameau, etc. He was also noted as a chess-player. Died in London.

Philips, Peter (1560/1–1628), English composer of madrigals, motets, pieces for virginals, etc.; also organist. A Roman Catholic, he worked mainly in the Low Countries (then under Spanish rule) and died probably in Brussels.

Phillips, Montague [Fawcett] (1885–1969), English composer best known for his light music (operetta *The Rebel Maid*, many songs); also wrote a symphony, two piano concertos, etc.

Philosopher, The, nickname for Haydn's Symphony no. 22 in E♭, 1764 (Hob.I:22), perhaps because it has a grave first movement instead of the customary lively one.

Phoebus and Pan, commonly used title for *The Contest Between Phoebus and Pan* (Ger., *Der Streit zwischen Phoebus und Pan*), cantata by Bach, *c.*1729 (BWV 201) satirizing (in the character of Midas) a hostile music critic. In the 20th century it has sometimes been performed as an opera.

phrase, a small group of notes forming what is recognized as a unit of melody; so *to phrase* and *phrasing*, terms used in regard to a performer's correctly observing the division of a melody into phrases. So also *phrase-mark*, a line linking written notes and indicating that they belong to one phrase.

Phrygian cadence, see CADENCE.

Phrygian mode, the MODE represented by the white keys of the piano, beginning on E.

piacere, a (It.), at pleasure, i.e. (in performance) at the performer's discretion, especially as meaning that strict time need not be observed.

piacevole (It.), agreeably, pleasantly, easily.

piangendo (It., weeping). plaintive(ly).

pianino, a small upright piano.

pianissimo (abbr. *pp*), very softly, superlative of PIANO (1).

piano (It.), (1) soft, abbr. *p*; so *pianissimo* or *pp*, very soft. (2) common English word for the keyboard instrument called in Italian *pianoforte* (literally soft-loud) – the shorter term being more convenient than the longer, and no worse English. The instrument, distinguished e.g. from harpsichord and clavichord by having its strings struck with hammers, was invented shortly after 1700 (see also FORTEPIANO), and by 1800 had almost displaced the harpsichord. The modern piano is iron-framed and normally has 88 keys: it is either 'upright' (i.e. the strings are vertical) or 'grand' (i.e. they are horizontal). It has a 'sustaining pedal' (wrongly called 'loud pedal') operated by the right foot to prolong the sound by holding off the dampers; and a 'soft pedal' (left foot) lessening the volume by causing fewer than the normal number of strings to be struck or by bringing the hammers nearer the strings before they start their movement. On a minority of pianos, there is also a centre pedal enabling selected notes to be sustained independently of others. An obsolete early form of piano is the *square piano* (oblong, box-like in shape, horizontally strung) sometimes miscalled SPINET (really quite a different instrument). Used universally as a solo, accompanying and chamber-music instrument, it has also been used (particularly in the 20th century) as an ordinary member of the orchestra and in the manner of a special percussion instrument (see, e.g., Stravinsky's THE WEDDING). Certain mid-20th-century composers, particularly under the influence of Cage, have used the piano as a repository of differing sounds – the strings being 'doctored' (cp. PREPARED PIANO), plucked by hand, or used (e.g. by Xenakis) as resonators for the sounds of brass instruments played over them. Pianos have also been constructed with double keyboards (see MOÓR), with quarter-tone tuning, etc., but none of these have become standard. The term *electric piano* is applied to various instruments which more or less imitate piano tone, whether by electronically generated sound or by amplification of the sound of vibrating metal bars (see ELECTRO-PHONIC). See PEDAL-PIANO, STREET PIANO, and the following entries.

piano-accordion, see ACCORDION.

pianoforte, Italian name for the instrument more commonly called *piano* in English. The name literally means 'soft-loud', alluding to the much greater possibilities of grading volume than on the harpsichord. See PIANO.

pianola, see PLAYER-PIANO.

piano organ, see STREET PIANO.

piano quartet, see QUARTET.

piano quintet, see QUINTET.

piano score, see SCORE.

piano trio, see TRIO.

Piatigorsky, Gregor (1903–76), cellist, Russian-born, who settled in USA, becoming naturalized in 1942; internationally noted as soloist and teacher. Composed and arranged works for cello.

pibroch (Gael., *piobaireachd*), type of

Scottish Highland bagpipe music, in a kind of elaborate variation-form.

Picardy third or (Fr.) *tierce de Picardie*, the major third used at the end of a piece otherwise in the minor key, converting the expected minor chord into a major one. The effect was common up to the mid 18th century; its occasional subsequent use tends to the effect of archaism.

Piccinni (or Piccini), Nicola (1728–1800), Italian composer of more than 100 operas including *The Good Girl* (*La buona figliola*), after Richardson's *Pamela*; also of oratorios, church music, etc. Lived partly in Paris, and died there. His Paris supporters clashed with those of Gluck: both composers wrote an opera on IPHIGENIA IN TAURIS.

piccolo, small flute pitched an octave above the standard flute, used in the orchestra and military band. (The name is from It. *flauto piccolo*, small flute, but the current It. term is *ottavino*, from the word for octave.) For *piccolo trumpet* see TRUMPET.

Pick-Mangiagalli, Riccardo (1882–1949), Czech-born composer partly of Italian descent; naturalized Italian. Became director of Milan Conservatory. Works include operas, ballets, piano pieces.

Pictures at an Exhibition (Rus., *Kartinki s vistavki*, literally 'Pictures *from* an exhibition'), piano work by Musorgsky, 1874, giving a musical 'reproduction' of 10 pictures by the Russian artist Victor Hartmann; a 'Promenade' is used as an introduction and linking passage. Of orchestral versions of the work, the standard one is by Ravel.

Pierné, [Henri Constant] **Gabriel** (1863–1937), French organist, conductor, and composer of *The Children's Crusade* for children's choir and orchestra, orchestral suites, operas, ballets – including *Cydalise and the Satyr*, from which comes the ENTRY OF THE LITTLE FAUNS.

Pierrot Lunaire (Fr., Moonstruck Pierrot), cycle of 'three times seven' songs by Schoenberg for voice (using SPEECH-SONG), flute (also piccolo), clarinet (also bass-clarinet), violin (also viola), cello and piano, to poems translated into German from the French of Albert Giraud – first performed in 1912.

Pierson (originally Pearson), **Henry Hugo** (1815–73), British composer who, after resigning from his Edinburgh professorship, settled in Germany in the mid-1840s. Died there. Wrote notable songs and part-songs (including 'Ye Mariners of England'), also German operas, English oratorio *Jerusalem*, etc.

pifa, see PIFFERO.

pifferaro, a player on the PIFFERO.

piffero, rustic Italian wind instrument of the SHAWM family, to whose characteristic music Handel apparently alludes in writing the word *pifa* above the music of the PASTORAL SYMPHONY in *Messiah*.

Pijper, Willem (1894–1947), Dutch composer (the most prominent of his generation), also writer on music; pupil of J. Wagenaar. Works include three symphonies and the piece called *Six Symphonic Epigrams*; five string quartets (no. 5 unfinished) and other chamber music; opera *Halewijn*, music to plays, piano pieces, Dutch folk-song

arrangements, etc. Also influential as a teacher.

Pilgrim's Progress, The, opera (but, instead, styled 'A Morality') by Vaughan Williams, produced in London, 1951. Libretto by composer, after Bunyan. It incorporates the composer's earlier one-act opera, *The Shepherds of the Delectable Mountains* (London, 1922).

Pilkington, Francis (*c.*1565–1638), English composer, also clergyman. Composed madrigals (e.g. one in THE TRIUMPHS OF ORIANA), songs with lute, lute solos, etc.

Pineapple Poll, ballet with music adapted by Mackerras from the Gilbert and Sullivan operettas, produced in London, 1951. The story is based on one of Gilbert's 'Bab Ballads'.

Pines of Rome (It., *Pini di Roma*), orchestral work by Respighi, in four linked movements, referring to the pines of four Roman sites; first performed in 1924. The score includes a nightingale (on a gramophone record). Cp. FOUNTAINS OF ROME.

Pinkham, Daniel (b. 1923), American composer, pupil of Piston, Copland, and others; also organist, harpsichordist and church musician. Works include three symphonies, Stabat Mater and other choral music.

Pinnock, Trevor [David] (b. 1946), British harpsichordist and conductor who founded the English Concert in 1972 as his personal ensemble; it won admiration for performances of music from the Bach–Handel period.

Pinsuti, Ciro (1829–88), Italian composer of more than 200 songs; also of opera *The Merchant of Venice* (after Shakespeare), piano works, etc. Taught for many years in London.

Pinto, George Frederick (1785–1806), British composer of songs, piano sonatas, duets for two violins, etc.; also pianist and violinist.

Pinza, Ezio [Fortunato] (1892–1957), Italian bass who settled in USA; after noted operatic career (Metropolitan Opera, New York, from 1926), appeared in films, Broadway musicals, etc.

pipe, a hollow cylinder or cone in which air vibrates, e.g. in an organ or a blown wind instrument; (term also used for) type of simple wind instrument itself composed only of such a cylinder or cone without mechanism – e.g. the three-holed pipe used in English folk-dancing with the TABOR, and the *bamboo pipes* (of various sizes, mainly used educationally).

Pipkov, Lubomir [Panayatov] (1904–74), Bulgarian composer, pupil in Paris of N. Boulanger and Dukas; also pianist and conductor (music director of the Sofia Opera, 1944–7).

Pique Dame, German translation (not French, which would be *La Dame de Pique*) of the original title of Tchaikovsky's opera THE QUEEN OF SPADES. It has no claim to use in English-speaking countries.

Pirandello, Luigi (1867–1936), Italian dramatist and novelist. See MALIPIERO (G. F.), WEISGALL.

Pirates of Penzance, The, or The Slave of Duty, operetta by Sullivan, produced in Paignton (Devon), 1879, for reasons of copyright: 'official' first performance in New York the next day. Libretto by W. S. Gilbert: the pirates are all 'noblemen who have gone wrong'.

Pisador, Diego (*c.*1508–after 1557), Spanish VIHUELA-player and composer of music for his instrument; he took minor orders in the Church but did not become a priest.

Pisk, Paul Amadeus (1893–1990), Austrian composer (pupil of Schoenberg) who settled in USA as university teacher; also musicologist. Works include *Three Ceremonial Rites* for orchestra, song-settings with words by James Joyce and others.

piston = VALVE (on brass instruments). Hence in French *piston* is also used as an abbreviation for *cornet-à-pistons*, i.e. the ordinary cornet.

Piston, Walter [Hamor] (1894–1976), American composer, pupil of N. Boulanger in Paris; professor at Harvard, author of important textbooks. Works include eight symphonies, a violin concerto, five string quartets, ballet THE INCREDIBLE FLUTIST.

pitch, the property according to which notes appear to be (in the conventional phrase) 'high' or 'low' in relation to each other – a property scientifically determined by the frequency of vibrations of the sound-producing agent (see FREQUENCY). So *concert pitch* is the standard of pitch to which instruments are normally tuned for performance. By international agreement of 1939, the tuning-note A (directly above middle C) was fixed at a frequency of 440 Hz; this makes middle C 261.6 Hz, and the C higher 523.2 Hz (i.e. twice the frequency of the octave below, as is the invariable rule). But in scientific investigation it is found mathematically convenient to suppose this C to have a frequency of 512 Hz (i.e. 2^9). In former centuries, pitch had wide variations according to period and place. *Absolute pitch* or *perfect pitch*, term for the faculty possessed by those who on hearing a note can identify it by name: it would be better to call this not *absolute pitch* but *an absolute sense of pitch*, etc. – though in fact such a faculty of identification is really not absolute but relative (to the nearest whole-tone, semitone, etc.). See also the following entries.

pitch-class, theorists' term, consequent on the practice of serial composition (see SERIES), for all notes of the same name in whatever octave – e.g. the *pitch-class* C includes middle C and all other notes called C.

pitch-pipe, small wind instrument employed to give correct starting pitch to singers or by which to tune instruments.

più (It.), more; *più lento*, slower.

piuttosto (It.), rather, somewhat.

Pixis, Johann Peter (1788–1874), German pianist, composer of piano music, operas, etc., contributor to the HEXAMERON.

pizz., abbr. for PIZZICATO.

Pizzetti, Ildebrando (1880–1968), Italian composer of *The Daughter of Jorio*, *Deborah and Jael*, MURDER IN THE CATHEDRAL, and other operas; also of incidental music for plays, a piano concerto, cello concerto, *Prelude to Another Day* and other orchestral works, choral works, chamber music, etc. Also writer on music and noted teacher.

pizzicato (It., pinched), direction that notes on bowed string instrument are to be plucked, not bowed; abbr. *pizz.* So *pizzicato tremolando*, direction used

by Elgar in his Violin Concerto to make the orchestral string-players 'thrum' rapidly with the fingers across the strings. Bartók sometimes required a *pizzicato* so forcible as to cause the string to snap back against the fingerboard, e.g. in his String Quartet no. 4. See also OSTINATO.

plagal cadence, see CADENCE.

plagal modes, see MODE.

plainchant, plainsong, type of medieval church music which in its final form called GREGORIAN CHANT became standard in Roman Catholic use. It consists of a single line of vocal melody (properly unaccompanied) in 'free' rhythm, not divided into regular bar-lengths; it has its own system of notation. (The ritual music of the Greek church – called 'Byzantine music' – and of the Jewish synagogue, though of a somewhat similar type, is not called plainsong.)

Planets, The, orchestral suite by Holst, first performed complete in 1920. Its seven movements treat their subjects from an astrological viewpoint; the last, 'Neptune, the Mystic', uses two three-part female choruses, wordless and unseen.

Planquette, Robert (1848–1903), French composer of *The Bells of Corneville* and other operettas.

plainsong, see PLAINCHANT.

Plath, Sylvia (1932–63), American poet and novelist. See TURNAGE.

player-piano, general name for a piano fitted with the type of mechanism usually known by such trade names as 'Pianola'. By this mechanism the keys are depressed not by the fingers but by air-pressure supplied by bellows and pedals, or electrically: the air-pressure is applied through perforations on an unwinding paper roll, such perforations being arranged so that a composition is played. There is, of course, no need for the perforations to be restricted to the normal number of notes playable by two (or four) hands. Sometimes the perforations are made mechanically from an actual performance by an eminent pianist, the player-piano then reproducing (within limits) this actual performance: for this reason the alternative name *reproducing piano* is sometimes used.

plectrum, small piece of wood, metal, or other material used to pluck the strings of a lute, mandolin, banjo, etc.; also the part of the mechanism of the harpsichord which performs an analogous function.

plein(e) (Fr.), full; *plein jeu* (full play), either (1) a type of MIXTURE stop on the organ, or (2) FULL ORGAN.

Pleyel, Ignaz Joseph (1757–1831), Austrian pianist, violinist, composer (symphonies, chamber music, etc.), pupil of Haydn and founder of the piano-making firm of Pleyel in Paris. Died in Paris.

pneuma (Gk., breath), a type of florid passage sung to a single vowel in plainsong.

pochette (Fr., pocket), small-size violin (small enough to be kept in a long pocket) formerly used by dancing-masters: same as KIT.

pochetto, pochettino (It.), very slightly. (Diminutives of POCO.)

pochissimo (It.), very slightly. (Superlative of POCO.)

poco (It.), slightly. Note the difference in correct Italian between *un poco crescendo* (with a little increase in volume) and *poco crescendo* (with little increase in volume) – i.e. the difference between 'a little' and just 'little' (with its negative sense) in English. But in musical contexts the usage is often loose and the sense is usually 'a little', even without the *un*.

Poe, Edgar Allan (1809–49), American writer. See MYASKOVSKY, RAKHMANINOV, VIOZZI.

poem, poema, poème (Eng., It., Fr.), term which was brought into music by Liszt in the expression SYMPHONIC POEM and which has since been somewhat extended (cp. DANCE-POEM); usually implies music based on a narrative. See also following entries.

Poem, title of (1) a movement from Fibich's orchestral piece, *At Twilight* (Cz., *V. Podvečer*), 1893; (2) work for violin and orchestra, in one movement, by Chausson, 1896 (Fr., *Poème*).

poema, poème, see POEM.

Poem of Ecstasy, The, Rus., *Poema ekstasa*), orchestral work by Skryabin (on 'joy in creative activity') first performed in New York, 1908. Cp. DIVINE POEM and PROMETHEUS.

Poem of Fire, see PROMETHEUS.

Poet and Peasant (Ger., *Dichter und Bauer*), play to which Suppé wrote the overture and other incidental music.

Poet's Love (Ger., *Dichterliebe*), song-cycle by Schumann, 1840, to 16 poems by Heine.

Pogorelich, Ivo (b. 1958), Yugoslav pianist who trained in Moscow (and married his teacher); noted for individualistic interpretation. Settled in London.

poi (It.), then; *scherzo da capo, e poi la coda*, repeat the scherzo and then go on to the coda.

point, (1) the end of the bow opposite to that held by the hand; (2) see PEDAL, 1 (for *pedal-point; organ-point* is the same thing); (3, verb) see POINTING.

point d'orgue (Fr., organ-point), (1) pedal-point (see PEDAL, 1); (2) the PAUSE, ⌒ ; (3) the place in the music – generally a pause on the second inversion of the tonic chord – at which a cadenza in a concerto begins.

pointillist(e), term borrowed from painting (where it refers to the use of separate dots of pure colour instead of mixed pigments) and applied to music where the notes seem to be disposed in isolated 'dots' rather than in normal melodic curves – e.g. certain music of Webern.

pointing, in Anglican chant, the allotting of syllables to the notes on which they are to be sung.

polacca (It.) = POLONAISE.

'Polish' Symphony, nickname for Tchaikovsky's Symphony no. 3, 1875; it has a finale in POLONAISE rhythm but has no other no claim to the name.

polka, a dance in 2/4 time for couples, originating in the 19th century in Bohemia.

Pollini, Maurizio (b. 1942), Italian pianist, pupil of Michelangeli; winner of international Chopin competition in Warsaw, 1960; known for modern as well as classical-virtuoso repertory.

Polly, ballad opera with words by John Gay and musical arrangements by Pepusch – a sequel to THE BEGGAR'S OPERA. It was published in 1729, but banned from the London stage as subversive of authority and not produced till 1777. A modern musical arrangement was made by F. Austin (London, 1922).

polo, type of Spanish dance, with song.

polonaise (Fr., 'Polish'), a stately Polish dance in 3/4 time, dating from the 16th century, if not earlier – its use for concert pieces goes back at least to Bach. Among Chopin's examples are some of an ardent, even martial, nature, apparently expressing patriotic sentiments.

Polovtsian dances, see PRINCE IGOR.

polymetre, polymetrical, terms which may refer to a composer's simultaneous use of different types of METRE or simply to the use of different metres successively in the course of a single movement.

polyphonic, see next entry.

polyphony, term literally meaning (from Gk.) any simultaneous sounding of different notes – and correctly used e.g. in reference to instruments: *polyphonic synthesizer* (see SYNTHESIZER). But, as more commonly used, it implies the presence of counterpoint – opposite of HOMOPHONY, where melodic interest is virtually confined to one 'line' of music, the other sounds acting as accompaniment. Hence historical references to the *polyphonic period*, imprecise term usually indicating a period from about the 13th to the 16th or early 17th centuries, ending with (e.g.) Palestrina, Lassus and Byrd. (The style of such a later composer as Bach is also polyphonic, but there the polyphony is governed by the harmonic scheme, whereas in the earlier period the polyphony supposedly 'comes first' and gives rise to the harmony.)

polyrhythm, the systematic exploitation of several rhythms performed simultaneously – especially in African music and in European music of the 20th century, sometimes with the aid of mechanical devices. But there are earlier European examples, notably Mozart's three different simultaneous dance-rhythms in DON GIOVANNI.

polytonal, see next entry.

polytonality, the simultaneous use of more than one key (an effect used systematically e.g. by Holst, Milhaud). Where only two keys are involved the more precise term is 'bitonality'. See TONALITY.

pommer, see SHAWM.

Pomp and Circumstance, title of five military marches by Elgar: nos. 1–4 composed in 1901–7, no. 5 in 1930. Title is a quotation from Shakespeare's *Othello*. Elgar adopted part of no. 1 in his *Coronation Ode* (1902) with the words 'Land of Hope and Glory'.

Ponce, Manuel (1882–1948), Mexican composer who studied in Italy and Germany, and (at the age of 40) under Dukas in Paris. Works include *Southern Concerto* (Sp., *Concierto del sur*) for guitar and chamber orchestra; a violin concerto (using in the second movement his own well-known song 'Estrellita'); orchestral and piano works, etc.

Ponchielli, Amilcare (1834–86), Italian composer of LA GIOCONDA (from which the 'Dance of the Hours' comes) and other operas; also cantatas (one in memory of Garibaldi), etc. Was also church musician.

ponticello (It.), the bridge of a violin or other stringed instrument; *sul ponticello* (literally, 'on the bridge'), instructions to play with the bow as close to the bridge as possible, for the production of a special kind of 'nasal' or 'metallic' tone-quality.

Poot, Marcel (1901–88), Belgian composer of operas, three symphonies, symphonic poem *Charlot* (i.e. Charlie Chaplin), chamber music, etc. Director of the Brussels Conservatory, 1949–66. Pupil of Dukas and others.

pop, abbr. for 'popular' (originally adjective, hence noun). In older usage it carries the straightforward meaning of 'appealing to a wide audience' – e.g. 'classical Monday Pops' (W. S. Gilbert, *The Mikado*, referring to a London concert series). See also BOSTON POPS ORCHESTRA. Since the 1950s, however, it has usually referred to a non-classical, commercially promoted type of American-derived song, whether delivered by solo or group vocalists. *Pop* in this sense has assumed the role of a popular alternative to the classical tradition of composition and performance. Hence *pop groups* (performers), *pop festivals*, etc. See ROCK; see also JAZZ (which, as a separate and older growth from similar musical sources, is not generally included in *pop*) and FOLK-MUSIC.

Pope, Alexander (1688–1744), English poet. See PANUFNIK, WALOND.

Popp, Lucia (b. 1939), Czech-born

Austrian soprano, active in opera – Salzburg Festival, 1963, Covent Garden, 1966, etc.

Popper, David (1843–1913), Austrian cellist, born in Prague, composer of many works for his instrument.

popular, see POP.

Porgy and Bess, the only full-length opera by Gershwin, produced in Boston, 1935. Libretto by D. Heyward and I. Gershwin (the composer's brother). Written for a black cast on a story about blacks – Porgy (crippled) and Bess are lovers. Has stylistic borrowings from spirituals and jazz, but no actual folk-songs are incorporated: references to it as a 'folk opera' should thus be treated cautiously.

Porpora, Niccolò Antonio (1686–1768), Italian composer; in London, his operas rivalled Handel's in popularity. Was also church musician and, especially, singing-teacher; one of the most famous ever. Haydn, as a young man, was for a time his pupil, accompanist and valet.

port á beul, see MOUTH MUSIC.

Porta, Costanzo (1528/9–1601), Italian composer and Franciscan monk; working at Padua, Ferrara and elsewhere, he wrote in a contrapuntal style that was much admired. A distinguished teacher of other composers.

portamento (It.), the 'carrying' of a sound – e.g., on a voice or a stringed instrument, the transition from one note to another higher or lower without any break in the sound.

portando (It.), carrying; *portando la voce,* PORTAMENTO (in singing).

portative, a portable organ, especially that which in medieval and Renais-

sance times could be placed on a table or carried in procession.

port de voix (Fr., carrying of the voice) = PORTAMENTO, in singing. The term is also used for certain 'ornaments' in French music from the 17th century and later.

Porter, Cole (1891–1964), American composer of popular songs – many for musical plays (e.g. *The Gay Divorce, Kiss Me Kate,* etc.), and films. Pupil of d'Indy. Also writer of words to his own songs.

Porter, [William] Quincy (1897–1966), American composer, pupil of d'Indy (in Paris), Bloch and others; also viola-player, and professor at Yale. Works include a viola concerto, a two-piano concerto, two symphonies, 10 string quartets.

Porter, Walter (*c.*1588–1659), English composer of motets, madrigals, etc.; also lutenist and singer (boy chorister at Westminster Abbey, then tenor). He was probably a pupil of Monteverdi.

Portsmouth Point, concert-overture by Walton, 1925, after a drawing by Rowlandson of a cheerful quayside scene.

Posaune (Ger.), trombone (in standard musical use: but also 'trumpet', e.g. in the biblical phrase 'the last trumpet').

positif (Fr.) = CHOIR-ORGAN.

position, (1, in string-playing) term used to specify how far along the finger-board the left hand should rest in order to play a given passage – *first position* being that nearest the pegs; *second,* etc., progressively further away; (2, in trombone-playing) term specifying how far the slide should be pushed out (*first position* the least extended); (3, in harmony) the 'layout' of a chord, determining which note comes at the bottom. E.g., with the chord consisting of the notes, C, E, G, B♭ (i.e. the dominant-seventh chord in key F) – if the note C (regarded as the 'root' of the chord) is at the bottom, then the chord is in *root position*; if E is at the bottom then it is in the 'first inversion'; if G is at the bottom, the 'second inversion'; if B♭, the 'third inversion'. It is solely what note is at the bottom that determines these 'positions'; the order of the upper notes is irrelevant.

positive, type of small organ with a single manual (usually without pedal), in use from 10th to 17th century (and revived in mid 20th); too large to be carried (in contrast to the POR-TATIVE), it was 'positioned' (hence its name) on the floor or on a table.

possibile (It.), possible; term used ellip-tically, e.g. *dim. possibile* or even > *possibile* – meaning that the sound is to be diminished to the faintest pos-sible (not 'diminish as rapidly as pos-sible').

post-horn, brass instrument of simple design – a long tube, made without valves or keys, and so able to produce only the notes of one HARMONIC SERIES. Built in various shapes (often, however, in a straight unbent tube) and formerly used by postillions for signalling. The well-known *Post-Horn Galop* (composed by the cornettist Koenig, 1844), for post-horn solo with accompaniment, skilfully uses the instrument's limited range of notes.

postlude, a final piece – opposite of PRE-LUDE, and an equally imprecise term, but much less commonly found.

post-Romantic(ism), terms applied to musical styles seeming to continue on ROMANTIC lines even after the orig-inal 'wave' of Romanticism in music apparently reached its climax in Wagner. The allusion is particularly to the employment of large forces and the linking of music to an emotional message and philosophical or similar ideas (e.g. in Mahler).

pot-pourri (Fr.), term used in a musical sense for a medley of tunes with little formal cohesion between them.

Potter, [Philip] **Cipriani** [Hambly] (1792–1871), English composer of nine symphonies, piano works includ-ing a set of variations entitled *The Enigma*, ('in the style of five eminent artists') etc.; as a student he was advised by Beethoven in Vienna. Prin-cipal of the Royal Academy of Music, 1832–59.

Poule, La, see HEN SYMPHONY.

Poulenc, Francis (1899–1963), French composer, member of the former group of THE SIX; influenced by Satie; composed in a transparent, mellifluous, sometimes witty style. Also pianist, noted particularly as ac-companist to Pierre Bernac. Works in-clude a piano concerto, two-piano con-certo, Concerto for organ with strings and kettledrums; piano solos, songs, Mass; opera THE CARMELITES, opera-burlesque *The Breasts of Tiresias*; ballets – including *Les Biches* (produced in Britain as *The House Party*), based on popular-song idiom.

Pousseur, Henri (b. 1929), Belgian composer of electronic music and other works including *Your Faust* (Fr., *Votre Faust*), a 'variable operatic fan-tasy', which has engendered other pieces; also a quintet (clarinet, bass clarinet, piano, violin, cello) in memory of Webern, *Mobile* for two pianos, etc.

Powell, Mel (b. 1923), American composer, also pianist, university teacher and writer on music; formerly active in jazz. Works include *Analogs 1–4* (tape), *Stanzas* for orchestra, *Filigree Setting* for string quartet.

Powers, Anthony (b. 1953), British composer of *Nymphéas* (after Monet's paintings) for 12 instruments, also a piano sonata, etc.

Praeludium (Lat.), prelude; the well-known orchestral work so entitled is by Järnefelt, first heard in Britain in 1909. See also PUGNANI.

Praetorius, Latinized name of several German musicians, before 1700. The most important is Michael Praetorius (c.1571–1621), composer, organist, writer on music.

'Prague' Symphony, nickname for Mozart's Symphony no. 38 in D (K504), first performed in Prague, 1787.

Pralltriller, see MORDENT.

Pré, Jacqueline du, see DU PRÉ.

precentor, eccesiastical musical dignitary – in an Anglican cathedral, the cleric in charge of the vocal music, to whom the organist is technically subordinate.

Preciosa, German play on a gipsy subject by P. A. Wolff (produced in 1821), to which Weber wrote the overture and other music.

precipitato, precipitoso (It.), impetuously.

pre-classic(al), term used of composers (e.g. C. P. E. Bach, J. C. Bach) whose style is considered later than baroque and leading to the 'Viennese-CLASSICAL' style of Haydn and Mozart.

prelude, properly a piece preceding something – e.g. preceding a fugue, or forming the first number of a suite, or forming the orchestral introduction to an act of an opera; but the term is also used for a short self-contained piece, for piano – whether quite abstract, e.g. Chopin's and Rakhmaninov's, or illustrative, e.g. Debussy's. See also following entries.

Prélude à l'après-midi d'un faune, see AFTERNOON OF A FAUN.

Preludes, The (Fr., *Les Préludes*), symphonic poem by Liszt, taking its title from a poem by Lamartine, but originally the overture to an unpublished choral work and having no connection with the poem. Composed in 1848, revised several times, given final form in 1854. Liszt's prefatory note suggests that life is a series of preludes to the hereafter. (Thus 'prelude' is not used here in its musical sense.)

preparation, a device in harmony by which the impact of a discord is softened: the actual note which, in a chord, causes that chord to be discordant, is sounded first in the preceding chord where it does not form a discordant element. Thus a discord is said to be *prepared* – or, if the impact is not 'softened' in this way, *unprepared*.

prepare, (1, in harmony) see preceding entry; (2) to 'set' an instrument ready to produce a particular effect, e.g. double-basses in an orchestra may be instructed to *prepare low* E♭, i.e. to let down to E♭ their lowest string which is normally tuned to E♮; see also the following entry.

prepared piano, a piano in which the strings are 'doctored' with various objects (cp. PREPARE, 2) in order to produce tone-qualities other than normal, sometimes with the addition of unusual techniques of playing – e.g. reaching over the keyboard and plucking the strings by hand. Its originator was CAGE.

pressez (Fr.), increase speed.

prestissimo (It.), very fast. (Superlative of PRESTO.)

presto (It.), fast. In the period of Mozart, this approximates to the meaning 'as fast as possible'; later composers have tended to convey this meaning by *prestissimo*.

Preston, Simon [John] (b. 1938), British organist and university teacher (Christ Church, Oxford, 1970–81, then Westminster Abbey till 1987); also harpsichordist and conductor.

Prêtre, Georges (b. 1924), French conductor, eminent in opera; conducted at Covent Garden (*Tosca* with Callas), 1965; music director of Paris Opera, 1970–71.

Previn, André (originally Andreas Ludwig Priwin) (b. 1929), German-born conductor and pianist who was brought up in Los Angeles and acquired American nationality in 1943. Principal conductor of Houston (Texas) Symphony Orchestra, 1967–9, of London Symphony Orchestra, 1968–79; music director, Royal Philharmonic Orchestra, 1985–7. Also composer (pupil of Castelnuovo-Tedesco): has written a guitar concerto, piano pieces, etc.

Prévost, Abbé [Antoine François Prévost d'Exiles] (1697–1753), French writer. See MANON, MANON LESCAUT.

Prey, Hermann (b. 1929), German baritone, active in opera (Metropolitan, New York, 1960) but more widely known as recitalist in German song. In 1976 he founded an annual Schubert festival at Hohenems, Austria.

Price, Leontyne (b. 1927), American soprano, eminent in opera; sang in USA and Europe as Bess in Gershwin's *Porgy and Bess*, 1952–5; first appeared at Covent Garden, 1958; Metropolitan, New York, 1961.

Price, Margaret [Berenice] (b. 1941), British soprano who made her début in 1962 with the Welsh National Opera; later appeared at Covent Garden (from 1963), in German opera-houses, etc., with a speciality in Mozart. CBE, 1982.

prick-song, old English term for music that was 'pricked', i.e. written down, as distinct from traditional or improvised music.

Priestley, J. B. [John Boynton] (1894–1984), English novelist and dramatist. See BLISS.

Prigioniero, Il, see PRISONER.

prima, prima donna, see following entry.

primo, prima (It.,: masc., fem.), first. So *primo*, the top part in piano duets: *prima donna*, the chief woman singer in the cast of an opera, etc. (overuse of this term giving rise to *prima donna assoluta*, the 'absolutely chief' woman); *primo uomo*, the chief male singer in an opera, etc.; *prima vista*, first sight (as in sight-reading); *tempo primo*, with the same tempo as at first;

come prima, as at first; *prima volta*, first time.

Primrose, William (1903–82), British viola-player (originally violinist), resident in USA from 1937. Various works were written for him, including Bartók's Viola Concerto. CBE, 1953.

Prince Igor (Rus., *Knyaz Igor*), opera by Borodin, produced in St Petersburg, 1890. Libretto by composer. The work was left unfinished, and after Borodin's death was completed and scored by Rimsky-Korsakov and Glazunov. Named after its 12th-century Russian warrior hero, captured by the Polovtsians – whose dances occur in Act II.

Prince of the Pagodas, The, ballet (on a fairy-tale subject) with music by Britten; produced in London, 1957.

Princess Ida, or Castle Adamant, operetta by Sullivan, produced in London, 1884. Libretto by W. S. Gilbert. Styled 'a respectful operatic per-version of Tennyson's *Princess*' – to which poem the libretto alludes by quotation and parody. The Princess heads a women's university.

principal, (1) leading player of a particular instrument (e.g. *principal horn*) in an orchestral section; (2) a singer who takes main parts in an opera company – thus *principal tenor* does not mean the chief tenor, but any tenor who has attained the standing of a 'principal'; (3) an organ stop of the open DIAPASON type but sounding an octave higher; (4) see following entry.

principale (It.), name used of a type of 17th- and 18th-century trumpet part – see TRUMPET.

Prisoner, The (It., *Il prigioniero*), opera by Dallapiccola, produced in Florence, 1950 (previously on Turin radio); libretto by the composer, after a short story by Villiers de l'Isle Adam, 'Torture by Hope'.

Pritchard, John [Michael] (1921–89), British conductor active in opera at Glyndebourne (musical director, 1969–77), Covent Garden and abroad; was conductor of the Royal Liverpool Philharmonic Orchestra, then (1962–6) of the London Philharmonic Orchestra. Chief conductor BBC Symphony Orchestra, 1982–9. Knighted, 1983.

Prodaná Nevěsta, see BARTERED BRIDE.

programmatic music, programme music, music interpreting a story, picture etc. A better term – because self-explanatory, and avoiding the confusion with 'concert programmes' etc. – is ILLUSTRATIVE MUSIC.

progression, motion from one note or chord to the next, in accordance with a musically logical plan.

progressive tonality, a musicologists' (rather than composers') term for the systematic plan of beginning a movement in one key and ending it in another, as in certain works by, e.g., Mahler and C. Nielsen.

Prokofiev, Sergey [Sergeyevich] (1891–1953), Russian composer; also pianist. Pupil of Rimsky-Korsakov and others. Lived abroad from 1918 until settling again in Russian in 1934; his style then became more straightforward and 'popular' – e.g. in PETER AND THE WOLF and Violin Concerto no. 2. None the less, some of his later works, e.g. his Symphony no. 6, were officially condemned for FORMALISM in 1948, along with works by other leading Soviet composers, and his last opera, *The Story of a Real Man*, was publicly produced only after his death, 1960. His previous operas include THE FIERY ANGEL, THE DUENNA and WAR AND PEACE. Also composed seven symphonies (no. 1, CLASSICAL SYMPHONY), five piano concertos, two violin concertos, a cello concerto, a concertino (see ROSTROPOVICH), Sinfonia Concertante for cello and orchestra; CINDERELLA, ROMEO AND JULIET and other ballets; songs, patriotic cantatas (e.g. ALEXANDER NEVSKY); nine piano sonatas (see Svyatoslav RICHTER), two violin sonatas and other instrumental works; film music. See also LOVE FOR THREE ORANGES.

prolation, in medieval musical notation, the division of the whole-note (semibreve) into either three smaller time-units (*major prolation*) or two (*minor prolation*).

Promenade Concert, the accepted British misnomer (since the audience do not now walk about) for a concert at which some members of the audience stand. Henry Wood's London series of Promenade Concerts began in 1895, more than 50 years after the first of this type.

Prometheus, Greek legendary figure alluded to in various musical works including (1) *The Creatures of Prometheus* (Ger., *Die Geschöpfe von Prometheus*), ballet for which Beethoven wrote the music (including overture), 1801. A theme from this was used by Beethoven in his Variations for piano in E♭ (1802), sometimes called the 'Eroica' Variations, because the theme was also used in the 'EROICA' SYMPHONY. Beethoven also used it in no. 7 of 12 *Country Dances* for orchestra,

1802. (2) song-settings of Goethe's poem 'Prometheus', e.g. by Schubert (1819) and Wolf (1889). (3) *Prometheus – The Poem of Fire* (Rus., *Prometei – Poema Ognya*), symphonic poem by Skryabin, with chorus ad lib and properly with a KEYBOARD of light; first performed, without this, in 1911.

prompt (in operatic performance), to supply cues to a singer – not merely, as in a play, when the performer forgets, but often supplying verbal and musical cues in anticipation throughout a performance.

Prophetess, The, see DIOCLESIAN.

proportional notation, proportionate notation, see GRAPHIC NOTATION.

Prout, Ebenezer (1835–1909), British organist, conductor and composer; chiefly known as writer of musical textbooks which are ridiculed as pedantic by those ignorant of them.

'Prussian' Quartets, name (not the composer's) for a set of string quartets by Mozart, intended for the use of Friedrich Wilhelm II, King of Prussia, who was a good cellist; only three were actually written (K575, 589, 590), 1789–90.

psalm, properly (from Gk.) a hymn sung to a harp; applied almost exclusively to the contents of the Old Testament Book of Psalms, for which various settings (see e.g. METRICAL PSALM) exist for religious use – also a number of concert settings. (See PSALMUS HUNGARICUS.) So PSALMODY.

psalmody, the study, etc., of the psalms; or an arrangement of psalms for singing.

Psalmus Hungaricus (Lat., Hungarian

Psalm), work for tenor, chorus and orchestra by Kodály, 1923, based on Psalm 55 in a 16th-century Hungarian translation.

psalter, volume containing the Book of Psalms, often with music.

psaltery, ancient and medieval stringed instrument, plucked like a lyre and of similar shape, but with a soundboard at the back of the strings.

Pskovitianka, see MAID OF PSKOV.

Puccini, Giacomo [Antonio Domenico Michele Secondo Maria] (1858–1924), Italian composer, pupil of Bazzini and Ponchielli. In youth a church musician. Works almost entirely operatic, including (in this order) MANON LESCAUT (1893), LA BOHÈME, TOSCA, MADAM BUTTERFLY, THE GIRL OF THE GOLDEN WEST; a 'triptych' (It., *trittico*) – THE CLOAK, SISTER ANGELICA, GIANNI SCHICCHI – intended to form a single bill; TURANDOT (1924, unfinished). Became one of history's most successful opera-composers through a gift for strong melody wedded to forceful dramatic plots (see VERISMO): was also an original harmonist and orchestrator.

Pugnani, Gaetano (1731–98), Italian violinist and composer of violin sonatas, operas, etc.; the *Praeludium and Allegro*, formerly said to be arranged from Pugnani by Kreisler, was admitted by Kreisler in 1935 to be entirely the latter's own work.

Pugno, [Stéphane] **Raoul** (1852–1914), French pianist, organist, composer of operas, ballets, etc. Died in Moscow.

Pulcinella, ballet with music by Stravinsky (including songs), produced in Paris, 1920. Based on music said to be by Pergolesi – but see PERGOLESI.

Pult (Ger.), desk – in the sense of an orchestral music-stand shared e.g. by two string-players; so *1. Pult,* first desk, i.e. instruction that a passage is to be played only by the first two players of that section.

Punch and Judy, opera by Birtwistle, produced in Aldeburgh, 1968. Libretto by S. Pruslin reinterprets the traditional puppet-play.

punta (It.), point; *punta d'arco,* (with the) point of the bow.

Purcell, the surname alone indicates Henry Purcell – below.

Purcell, Daniel (*c.*1663–1717), English composer of much stage music (see INDIAN QUEEN), also cantatas, etc. Also organist. Brother of Henry Purcell.

Purcell, Henry (1659–95), English composer; boy chorister; pupil of Humfrey and of Blow, whom he succeeded as organist of Westminster Abbey in 1679. Said to have died through a cold caused by being locked out of his own house at night. Wrote short opera DIDO AND AENEAS for a Chelsea girls' school; also semi-operas (music not altogether predominant) including THE FAIRY QUEEN, KING ARTHUR, DIOCLESIAN, THE INDIAN QUEEN and music for various plays. Other works include ODES FOR ST CECILIA'S DAY and other cantatas; songs (see ORPHEUS BRITANNICUS and EPICEDIUM; keyboard works; TRIOSONATAS (some described as in three parts and some as in four, but identical in scoring), including the GOLDEN SONATA; anthems (including BELL ANTHEM) and other church music. His subtlety of rhythm (especially in the treatment of English words) and harmony has contributed to his high repute in the 20th century; he notably influenced Holst, Britten and others. For the *Trumpet Voluntary* misattributed to him, see CLARKE. See also WELDON. Purcell's work is indexed by 'Z' numbers, referring to the thematic catalogue made by Franklin Zimmerman in 1963.

Puritans, The (It., *I Puritani*, originally *I Puritani di Scozia* – The Puritans of Scotland, though the action takes place in England), Bellini's last opera, produced in Paris (in Italian), 1835. Libretto by C. Pepoli, based ultimately on Scott's *Old Mortality*; See also HEXAMERON.

Pushkin, Alexander (1799–1837), Russian writer. See BORIS GODUNOV, BRITTEN, FIRSOVA, GOLDEN COCKEREL, MAZEPPA, MIGHTY HANDFUL, MOZART AND SALIERI, QUEEN OF SPADES, RUSALKA, RUSLAN AND LYUDMILA, YEVGENY ONEGIN.

Puyana, Rafael (b. 1931), Colombian harpsichordist, pupil of Wanda Landowska in USA. Resident in Paris; has had international career since mid-1950s.

puzzle canon, see CANON.

Q

quadraphonic, quadrophonic (hybrid coinage from Latin for 'square' plus Gk. *phoné*, sound), term applied to sound emitted from four fixed points, usually by loudspeakers.

quadrille, type of square-dance very popular in the 19th century – in four sections of 32 bars each, plus a final section. Operatic and other popular tunes were commonly adapted for the music. The 'lancers' is a type of quadrille.

quadruple counterpoint, see COUNTER-POINT.

quadruplet, a group of four notes (or notes and rests) of equal time-value, written where a group of three, five, or some other number of notes is suggested by the time-signature. E.g. a four-note group occupying a bar of 3/4 time, written

quail, toy instrument imitating a quail used e.g. in the TOY SYMPHONY formerly ascribed to Haydn.

Quantz, Johann Joachim (1697–1773), German composer and flautist; taught Frederick the Great to play the flute, and remained in his service from 1741 until death. Wrote about 300 concertos for one or two flutes, many flute solos; also hymns, songs, etc. Author of a treatise on flute-playing.

quarter-note, the note ♩ considered as a time-value. This is standard North American usage and, as mathematically corresponding to the element of time-signature represented by /4, should clearly be preferred to 'crotchet' still surviving in British use. The corresponding rest is notated 𝄽 or ⊺

quarter-tone, half a semitone – an interval not used in Western music until the 20th century, and then only exceptionally, e.g. by Hába and other Czech composers (making use of special quarter-tone pianos) and by Bloch as an occasional melodic subtlety in string-writing. See also MICROTONE.

quartet, (1) a performing group of four instrumentalists or singers: where the instruments are unspecified (e.g. Juilliard Quartet) a string quartet is assumed – two violins, viola, cello; a *piano quartet* consists of piano, violin, viola, cello. (2) a piece for four performers; if instrumental, and actually entitled 'Quartet', it will probably have the character of a SONATA for four performers, in several movements. See following entries.

Quartet for the End of Time (Fr., *Quatuor pour la fin du temps*), work by Messiaen (composed in a German prisoner-of-war camp and first performed there, 1941) for violin, clarinet, cello and piano.

Quartet Movement, name used for a movement by Schubert (D703), in C minor (1820) intended for a string quartet that was never completed.

Quartetto Italiano, an Italian quartet founded in 1945 (known as the Nuovo Quartetto Italiano until 1951), led by Paolo Borciani. Played an extensive repertory from memory; disbanded in 1986.

Quartettsatz (Ger.), = preceding.

quasi (It.), almost, as if, approximating to.

Quasimodo, Salvatore (1901–68), Italian poet. See BILLY BUDD.

Quatro rusteghi, I, see SCHOOL FOR FATHERS.

quatuor (Fr.) = quartet; *Quatuor pour la fin du temps*, see QUARTET FOR THE END OF TIME.

quaver, see EIGHTH-NOTE.

Queen, The (Fr. *La Reine*), nickname of Haydn's Symphony no. 85 in B♭ (one of the PARIS SYMPHONIES), composed in 1785–6 (Hob. I:85) and so called perhaps because Queen Marie Antoinette liked it. Its slow movement consists of variations on a French song.

Queen of Spades, The (Rus., *Pikovaya Dama*), opera by Tchaikovsky, produced in St Petersburg, 1890. Libretto by Modest Tchaikovsky (the composer's brother) after Pushkin. *The Queen of Spades* is the nickname of an old Countess, with allusion to her former uncanny luck at cards. See GRÉTRY.

Quiet City, suite by Copland for trumpet, English horn and strings, first performed in 1941; taken from incidental music to a play so named.

Quiet Place, A, opera by Bernstein, produced in Houston, Texas, 1983, with libretto by Stephen Wadsworth; originally written as a sequel to *Trouble in Tahiti* (1952, libretto by the composer), it was later adapted to incorporate the earlier piece (in two flashbacks). Mocks modern urban domesticity: 'Tahiti' figures only as part of the title of a film which the heroine describes.

Quilter, Roger (1877–1953), British composer, trained in Germany. Wrote chiefly song-settings of Shakespeare, Herrick and other distinguished poets.

quint, organ stop sounding a note a fifth (Lat., *quintus*) higher than the key depressed. It is with the aid of this stop on the pedals that the effect of a 32-ft stop is produced even without 32-ft pipes – see ACOUSTIC BASS.

quintadena, quintatön, types of organ stop which sound not only the note of the key depressed, but also the note a 12th (i.e. an octave plus a fifth) higher.

quintet, (1) a performing group of five instrumentalists or singers; a *string quintet* adds an extra viola or cello to the standard string QUARTET, and a *piano quintet* usually adds a piano to this standard string quartet – but see TROUT QUINTET for an exception; (2) a piece for five performers; if instrumental, and actually entitled 'Quintet', it will probably have the character of a SONATA for five performers in several movements.

quintuor (Fr.), = quintet.

quintuplet, group of five notes (or notes and rests) of equal time-value, written where a group of three, four or some other number of notes is suggested by the time-signature. E.g. a five-note group occupying a bar of 4/4 time, written 𝅘𝅥𝅘𝅥𝅘𝅥𝅘𝅥𝅘𝅥

quodlibet (Lat., *quod libet*, what is desired), piece containing several popular tunes put together in unusual and (usually) ingenious fashion – such as that which ends Bach's GOLDBERG VARIATIONS, incorporating two well-known tunes of his day.

R

R., abbr. for (1) as in *r.h.*, right hand (in piano music, etc.): (2) Royal, as in names of some British institutions, e.g. RAM (Academy of Music), RCM (College of Music), RCO (College of Organists), RNCM (Northern College of Music), RPO (see ROYAL PHILHARMONIC ORCHESTRA); (3) Ryom, especially in the form RV (Ger., *Verzeichnis* = index), in numbering Vivaldi's works: see VIVALDI.

r, symbol in TONIC SOL-FA for the second degree (supertonic) of the scale, pronounced *ray*.

Rabaud, Henri [Benjamin] (1873–1949), French composer, pupil of Massenet and others; also conductor, and (1920–41) director of the Paris Conservatory. Works include *Mârouf, the Cobbler of Cairo* and other operas (one based on Synge's *Riders to the Sea*), symphonic poems, songs, film music. He orchestrated Fauré's DOLLY.

Rachmaninov, see RAKHMANINOV (the spelling which is consistent with the standard transliteration of other Russian names).

Racine, Jean (1639–99), French poet and dramatist. See AURIC, CHARPENTIER (M.-A.), ESTHER, IPHIGENIA IN AULIS

racket(t), double-reed wind instrument of various sizes cultivated in the 16th–18th centuries; a late variety was sometimes called the 'sausage bassoon'. (The name is of uncertain derivation but does not mean 'noise'.)

Rácóczy March, see RÁKÓCZI MARCH (correct spelling).

Radetzky March, march by Johann Strauss the elder, 1848, named after an Austrian field-marshal and coming to symbolize the Hapsburg monarchy.

Raff, [Joseph] **Joachim** (1822–82), Swiss composer, disciple of Liszt, some of whose works he scored for orchestra. Prolific composer of symphonies with allusive titles (no. 1 *To the Fatherland*, no. 3 *In the Forest*, etc.), chamber music, operas, etc.; best known for a CAVATINA (violin and piano). Was also pianist and critic.

rag, see RAGTIME.

rāg (Hindi), the approximate equivalent in Indian music of a scale – but the term also has connotations of mode, melodic shape and even ornamentation.

ragtime, name given to an early type of jazz, particularly associated with piano-playing, with characteristic syncopations; e.g. *Maple Leaf Rag* (Joplin). In vogue *c*.1890-1920, revived in

1970s. Stravinsky's *Ragtime for 11 instruments* and *Piano-Rag Music* (alluding to this type of work) date from 1918 and 1919 respectively.

Raimondi, Pietro (1786–1853), Italian composer, also opera director and church musician (at St Peter's, Rome, 1851). Works include three oratorios (on the Old Testament subject of Joseph) which could be, and in 1852 were, performed simultaneously.

Raimondi, Ruggero (b. 1941), Italian bass, celebrated in opera, particularly as Mozart's Don Giovanni (on stage and in 1979 film version).

'Raindrop' Prelude, nickname for Chopin's Prelude in D♭, op. 28, no. 15 (1839), on the supposition that the repeated note A♭ (G♯) represents persistent raindrops.

Rainier, Priaulx (1903–86), South African composer – resident in Britain; she studied with N. Boulanger in Paris. Works include a cello concerto, string quartet, *Barbaric Dance Suite* for piano, *Cycle for Declamation* (unaccompanied high voice, on a text by Donne).

Rake's Progress, The, (1) ballet with music by G. Gordon, produced in London, 1935; (2) opera by Stravinsky, produced in Venice, 1951; libretto by W. H. Auden and C. Kallman. Both works are derived from Hogarth's series of paintings (1735).

Rakhmaninov, Sergey Vassilievich (1873–1943), Russian composer and pianist. (The spellings 'Rachmaninoff', etc., are inconsistent with the now standard system of transliteration from Russian.) Wrote his Piano Prelude in C♯ minor at age 20. Left Russia, 1918, disliking the Soviet régime, and lived mainly in Switzerland and in USA, where he died. Nevertheless he conspicuously aided the Russian anti-Nazi effort in World War II. He always maintained a Russian outlook and wrote in an emotional (and sometimes melancholy) Romantic style. Works include four piano concertos, *Rhapsody on a Theme of Paganini* for piano and orchestra (see PAGANINI), many piano solos (including transcriptions from other composers) and some two-piano works; also three symphonies, symphonic poem THE ISLE OF THE DEAD, three operas, choral work *The Bells* (after Poe), songs (see VOCALISE).

Rákóczi March, a Hungarian march dating from the early 19th century (composer unknown) but named after Prince Ferenc Rákóczi II, leader of a Hungarian revolt against the Austrians, 1703–11; has Hungarian patriotic associations. Best known from the orchestral arrangement by Berlioz included in his DAMNATION OF FAUST; it also enters into Johann Strauss's THE GIPSY BARON.

rall, abbr. for the following.

rallentando (It.), slowing down.

Rameau, Jean Philippe (1683–1764), French composer – also organist, harpsichordist and writer of an important *Treatise on Harmony* and other theoretical works. At 50, he began his succession of more than 20 operas and opera-ballets, including *The Courtly Indies* (*Les Indes galantes*) and *Castor and Pollux*. His champions and those of Pergolesi clashed in the so-called 'War of the Buffoons' (Fr., *Guerre des bouffons*). Other works include chamber music; dance-music and other pieces for harpsichord; cantatas and church music.

Rampal, Jean-Pierre [Louis] (b. 1922), French flautist, well known as soloist in 18th-century chamber music, etc.; Poulenc, Jolivet and others have written works specially for him.

Ramsay, Allan (1686–1758), Scottish poet – see GENTLE SHEPHERD.

Randegger, Alberto (1832–1911), Trieste-born conductor, composer (operas, Masses, etc.), and singing-master who in 1854 settled in London; died there.

Rands, Bernard (b. 1935), British composer, pupil of Dallapiccola, Boulez, Maderna; has held various university posts in UK and USA. Works include *Canti del Sole* (Songs of the Sun) for tenor and orchestra, and a series of pieces each called *Espressione* for piano(s).

Rangström, Ture (1884–1947), Swedish composer, largely self-taught; several of his works are associated with Strindberg, whom he knew. Works include four symphonies (no. 1 *In Memoriam August Strindberg*), three operas, more than 50 songs with orchestra.

rank, a set of organ pipes – term used particularly of MIXTURE stops.

Rankl, Karl (1898–1968), Austrian-born composer (pupil of Schoenberg) and conductor, resident in Britain from 1939. Musical director of Covent Garden Opera, 1946–51; works include eight symphonies, opera *Deirdre of the Sorrows* (not produced).

rant (perhaps a corruption of *coranto*; see COURANTE), term applied to a wide range of 17th-century English dances.

ranz des vaches, type of Swiss tune

(name means 'cow-rank') sounded vocally or on an alphorn to call the cows; incorporated e.g. into Rossini's overture to WILLIAM TELL, Beethoven's PASTORAL SYMPHONY (last movement), and (satirically) Walton's FAÇADE.

Rape of Lucretia, The, opera by Britten, produced at Glyndebourne, 1946. Libretto by R. Duncan. The main tragedy, set in Rome, is commented on by a male and female 'chorus' (one performer each) standing outside the temporal dimension of the plot.

rappresentazione (It.), a representation, a staged action; hence *rappresentativo*, of the stage, in stage style. For *La rappresentazione di anima e di corpo*, see REPRESENTATION.

rapsodia, rapsodie (It., Fr.) = RHAPSODY; *Rapsodie espagnole*, see SPANISH RHAPSODY.

rasch (Ger.), quick.

Rascher, Sigurd (b. 1907), German saxophonist, whose concert performances from the 1930s established the alto saxophone as a solo instrument. Glazunov was among the composers who wrote concertos for him.

Rasiermesser Quartet, see RAZOR QUARTET.

Rasoumoffsky, Rasumovsky, variant spelling of 'Razumovsky', the standard transliteration of this Russian name into English. See RAZUMOVSKY QUARTETS.

Rathaus, Karol (1895–1954), Polish-born composer who studed in Vienna, taught in Berlin, and in 1934 settled in London and afterwards in USA. Works include three symphonies, five string quartets.

Ratsche (Ger.) = RATTLE.

Rattle, Simon (b. 1955), British conductor; worked at Glyndebourne and with London Sinfonietta; from 1980, principal conductor, City of Birmingham Symphony Orchestra, vastly enhancing its prestige.

rattle, ratchet-toothed noise-making device which is occasionally used as an orchestral percussion instrument, e.g. in R. Strauss's TILL EULEN-SPIEGEL.

Rauzzini, Venanzio (1746–1810), Italian castrato singer and composer of vocal works in Italian and English, etc.; settled in London and then (1780) in Bath; died there. Noted teacher.

Ravel, [Joseph] **Maurice** (1875–1937), French composer; pupil of Fauré and others at the Paris Conservatory. Failed in three attempts for the French Rome Prize, and was unfairly barred (although he had already had works published and performed) from a fourth try. (See DUBOIS.) Notable for IMPRESSIONIST technique (more clear-cut, however, than Debussy's), mastery of orchestration, and innovations in exploiting the sonorities of the piano. Piano works include two concertos (one for left hand), a sonatina, suites GASPARD DE LA NUIT and *Mirrors* (including 'AL-BORADA del gracioso'); also (all later transcribed for orchestra) *Pavan for a Dead Infanta* (see PAVAN), *Valses nobles et sentimentales* (see VALSE) and *The Grave of Couperin* (see TOMBEAU). Other works include BOLERO, SPANISH RHAPSODY and LA VALSE for orchestra; MOTHER GOOSE (for piano duet, later orchestrated); operas THE SPANISH HOUR and THE CHILD AND THE SPELLS; ballet DAPHNIS AND CHLOE; a

septet including harp (also called *Introduction and Allegro*); a violin sonata (see TZIGANE); songs, some with orchestra (see CHANSON, SHÉHÉRA-ZADE). He orchestrated Musorgsky's PICTURES AT AN EXHIBITION. Visited England (Hon. D. Mus., Oxford, 1928) and USA; died in Paris. Refused the Legion of Honour.

Ravenscroft, Thomas (*c*.1582–*c*.1635), English composer of psalm-tunes, etc.; collector and editor of popular songs and rounds, published in PAMMELIA (with sequel *Deuteromelia*) and MELIS-MATA; author of a musical treatise.

ravvivando (It.), reviving, i.e. returning gradually to a previous faster tempo.

Rawsthorne, Alan (1905–71), British composer – mainly self-taught, having studied dentistry first; also studied piano. Works, almost entirely instrumental, include three symphonies, Symphonic Studies, two piano concertos, three string quartets, ballet *Madame Chrysanthème*, film music.

Raxach, Enrique (b. 1932), Spanish-born composer who took Dutch citizenship, 1969; works include *The Looking Glass* for organ, *Inside Outside* for orchestra and tape (titles in English).

ray, in TONIC SOL-FA, the spoken name for the second degree (supertonic) of the scale, written r. Cp. RE.

Raymond, or The Queen's Secret, opera by A. Thomas, produced in Paris, 1851. Libretto by A. de Leuven and J. B. Rosier, based on the elder Dumas's story *The Man in the Iron Mask*.

Razor Quartet, name for Haydn's String Quartet in F minor, op. 55, no. 2

(Hob. III:61). When Haydn was visited in 1787 by the English publisher Bland, he exclaimed that he would 'give his best quartet for a good razor', and (Bland having supplied the razor) this is it.

Razumovsky Quartets, name for Beethoven's three String Quartets, op. 59 (in F, E minor, and C), 1806–7, dedicated to Count Andreas Razumovsky, Russian ambassador in Vienna – and, in compliment to him, using a traditional Russian tune in the first two, and perhaps (though it is not identifiable) in no. 3.

re, the note D (in Latin countries, and formerly elsewhere); cp. RAY. Honegger's Symphony no. 5, first performed in 1951, is subtitled *Di tre re* – of the three D's – referring to the quietly emphatic note D ending each of the three movements.

Read, Gardner (b. 1913), American composer; works include four symphonies, opera *Villon*, piano and organ music. Also teacher, radio commentator, and writer on music.

Reading Rota, see SUMER IS ICUMEN IN.

real, term used in opposition to 'tonal' in special senses; for *real answer* and *real fugue* see ANSWER, for *real sequence* see SEQUENCE.

realism, stylistic term at least two meanings – (1) the use in opera of characterization and stories based on contemporary life as it is actually observed (not forgetting 'life in the raw'), as distinct from 'remote' subjects and 'refined' treatment: in this sense the term indicates a correspondence with the literary outlook e.g. of Zola, and is used e.g. of Italian opera

of the Puccini–Mascagni type (see VERISMO); (2) ('socialist realism'), the stance considered 'correct' for creative artists under Soviet officialdom up to the 1980s – showing optimism, sympathy with 'the people', a desire to be comprehensible, an avoidance of such deviations as FORMALISM, etc..

realize, to work out in full and artistically such music as was originally left by its composer in a sparsely notated condition. E.g. a 17th- or 18th-century piece might originally have a CONTINUO bass-line, might require ornaments (originally left to performers' taste), and might need written directions for performance in order to make it now intelligible: such a phrase as 'Britten's realizations of Purcell' covers all these functions. Though lacking the advantage of being self-explanatory, *realize* is superior to 'arrange' in this context since it avoids the implication of arbitrary alteration.

rebec(k), a bowed instrument of Arab origin, current in Europe in the 13th–16th centuries; generally pear-shaped with three strings; regarded as a forerunner of the violin and later surviving as a folk-instrument.

Rebikov, Vladimir Ivanovich (1866–1920), Russian composer of operas, orchestral suites, many piano pieces, etc. Made use of WHOLE-TONE scale and other harmonic novelties. Studied partly in Berlin, settled in southern Russia and taught and organized there; died in Yalta.

recapitulation, a section of a composition which repeats (in something like their original shape) themes which were originally presented in an earlier section but have interveningly undergone 'development'. The term is particularly used in the scheme of construction called SONATA-FORM, and variants of it.

recit., abbr. for RECITATIVE.

récit (Fr.) = SWELL (ORGAN).

recital, a musical performance, usually by soloists or duettists, rarely by larger combinations.

recitative, type of speech-like singing which is written in ordinary notation but in which a certain freedom in rhythm (and sometimes also in pitch) is allowed in performance; used particularly in opera, oratorio, etc. as preliminary to a song (so *recitative and air*, etc.) and for dialogue. Its two chief kinds are *accompanied recitative* (It., *recitativo accompagnato* or *stromentato*) with normal orchestral accompaniment, and *dry recitative* (*recitativo secco*) which, e.g. in 18th-century Italian opera, had merely an accompaniment of 'punctuating' chords from a harpsichord (the bass-line sometimes also reinforced by other instruments). (The word is commonly pronounced to rhyme with 'thieve', probably on the mistaken supposition that it is French; as it is only English, it might well be made as English-sounding as 'narrative'.) Cp. SPEECH-SONG.

recitativo, see preceding entry.

recorder, type of woodwind instrument, without reed, much used in 16th–18th centuries but ousted by the more powerfully toned 'ordinary' flute, which it resembles except for being blown at the end and held downwards instead of crosswise. The recorder itself was formerly known as the 'English flute'; and in the usage of

Bach's period the term 'flute' actually meant 'recorder' unless some such word as 'transverse' was added to indicate the other instrument. The recorder has been extensively revived in the 20th century, (a) to play the old music written for it; (b) as an inexpensive and relatively easy instrument for schoolchildren, etc. Some later composers, e.g. Rubbra and Berio, have also written for it. It is currently employed chiefly in five sizes named as follows – sopranino; descant (English) or soprano (Continental); treble (English) or alto (Continental); tenor; and bass. Two sizes of still lower pitch, the great bass and the double-bass (or contrabass) are also found. The size most often encountered is the descant, though nearly all old solo music is for the treble.

recte et retro (Lat., right way and backwards), the use of a theme performed normally, in counterpoint with that same theme performed backwards.

Redemption, The, oratorio by Gounod (words, in English, compiled from the Bible by the composer) first performed in Birmingham, 1882.

Redford, John (?–1547), English composer, organist (St Paul's Cathedral, London), poet and playwright; works include motets and organ music. The attribution to him of the anthem 'Rejoice in the Lord Alway' (not Purcell's version, i.e. BELL ANTHEM) is mistaken, but the true composer is unknown.

reduction, an edition enabling music to be played by fewer performers – particularly *piano reduction* (of an orchestral score).

reed, a vibrating 'tongue' of thin cane

or metal, used to set the air-column vibrating in certain types of mouth-blown wind instruments, certain organ pipes, etc. The reed may beat freely (e.g. in the harmonica, i.e. mouth-organ), or against a surface, as does the single reed of a clarinet; or two reeds may beat against each other, e.g. the double reed of an oboe. So *reed stop* on an organ, controlling pipes which have reeds. See also REED-ORGAN.

reed-organ, (1) general name for types of keyboard instrument using free-beating REEDS (one for each note) and no pipes, e.g. HARMONIUM, AMERICAN ORGAN; (2) name sometimes also used (by extension from the preceding) to cover generally various other instruments working on the same principle but not organ-like in appearance – e.g. ACCORDION, HARMONICA (mouth-organ).

reel, quick dance for two or more couples – found chiefly in Scotland, Ireland, Scandinavia and North America.

Refice, Licinio (1883–1954), Italian composer chiefly of motets, Masses and other religious music; also of symphonic poems with chorus. Was also priest and church musician.

'Reformation' Symphony, descriptive name given by Mendelssohn to his Symphony no. 5, 1830. The first and fourth (last) movements respectively quote the 'Dresden Amen' and the chorale 'A Stronghold Sure' (*Ein' feste Burg*) respectively of Roman Catholic and Lutheran associations. See LUTHER.

refrain, part of a song that recurs (both words and music) at the end of each stanza.

regal, type of small portable keyboard instrument of REED-ORGAN type (15th–17th centuries); in church it was employed to regulate the singing (Lat., *regolare* – hence the name). Some models could be folded shut like a book and so were named *bible-regal*. In some later models, short pipes were added, taking the instrument strictly out of the reed-organ class.

Reger, Max (1873–1916), German composer – also pianist, organist, conductor and teacher. Works include *Variations on a Theme of Mozart* and other orchestral works; much chamber music; piano and organ pieces; songs.

register, (1) a set of organ pipes controlled by one particular stop; so *to register* a piece for the organ is to select the stops appropriate to it; (2) part of an instrument's compass appearing to have a distinct tone-quality of its own, e.g. the CHALUMEAU register of the clarinet; (3) a part of the compass of the voice giving its own distinctive sensation to the singer – see CHEST VOICE, HEAD VOICE.

Reich, Steve (b. 1936), American composer, director of his own unique ensemble comprising mainly percussion and electronic keyboards. Studied African drumming, Javanese gamelan music and Jewish cantillation, and evolved a repetitively patterned music of his own, in what came to be called MINIMALIST style. Works include *Drumming* (for drums and other instruments), *Vermont Counterpoint* for 11 flutes.

Reicha, Antonín (1770–1836), Bohemian composer and teacher, friend of Beethoven; settled in Paris, becoming professor at the Conservatory in

1818. Himself a flautist, he composed 24 wind quintets as well as operas, symphonies, piano works, etc.

Reichardt, Johann Friedrich (1752–1814), German composer, musical director at the Prussian court; also writer on music. Wrote some notable German songs; also operas, incidental music to plays, etc.

Reimann, Aribert (b. 1936), German composer (pupil of Blacher and Pepping), also well known as piano accompanist to singers. Works include operas *A Dream Play* (after Strindberg) and *Lear* (after Shakespeare's KING LEAR); songs and choral settings; a cello concerto.

Reine, La, see QUEEN.

Reinecke, Carl [Heinrich Carsten] (1824–1910), German composer, pianist, conductor, writer on music; works include operas, four piano concertos, wind octet.

Reiner, Fritz (in Hungarian form, Frigyes) (1888–1963), Hungarianborn conductor, naturalized American in 1928; held important European and US posts, including conductorship of the Chicago Symphony Orchestra from 1953.

Reinken, Johann Adam (or Jan Adams) (1623–1722), German organist and composer; Bach several times walked long distances to hear him in Hamburg.

Reizenstein, Franz (1911–68), German-born composer and pianist who settled in Britain 1934 – pupil of Hindemith (in Germany) and Vaughan Williams. Works include cantata *Voices of Night*, a cello concerto, two piano concertos and many piano solos.

Rejoice in the Lord Alway, (1) anthem by Purcell – see BELL ANTHEM; (2) anthem by an unknown 16th–century composer: see REDFORD.

related, term used as a measure of one key's harmonic nearness to (or distance from) another. Hence, e.g., G major is more nearly related to D major (a difference of only one sharp in the key-signature, meaning that the modulation between them is of the simplest kind) than either is to A♭ major. The use of the term categorically (as when two keys are spoken of as *related*, and another two as *not related*) is inadvisable, since all keys are related at a greater or lesser remove, and the historical evolution of harmony has been to lessen the difficulty of transition between them. See also RELATIVE.

relative, term used to indicate the fact that a common key-signature is shared by one major and one minor key: e.g. E minor is termed the *relative minor* of G major, and G major as the *relative major* of E minor, both having a key-signature of one sharp, and modulations between them being accordingly of a simple kind.

Reményi, Ede (originally Eduard Hoffmann) (1828–98), Hungarian violinist who toured with Brahms as his pianist-partner in 1885; also composer.

reminiscence-motive, a recurring theme in an opera, identified with a character or emotion, etc. (but not necessarily subject to musical transformation as a Wagnerian LEADING-MOTIVE may be).

Renaissance (Fr., rebirth), term used by historians of visual arts to identify the rediscovery and reapplication of 'classical' (ancient Greek and Roman as opposed to Christian) images and values in the 14th–16th centuries and the emergence of a more individualistic and worldly art; analogously used by music historians to denote a period of style between 'medieval' and BAROQUE – from early 15th century (e.g. Dunstable, Dufay) to early 17th.

repeat (noun), a section of a composition consisting of a repetition of a previous section. To save the space of writing out the passage again, such a repetition is indicated by pairs of dots (called *repeat marks*) and a double bar.

On reaching these the performer repeats from the previous pair of dots or (if there is none) from the beginning.

répétiteur (Fr., also used in Eng.), the member of the musical staff of an opera company who coaches the singers and may also be employed as prompter in performance (see PROMPT).

répétition (Fr.), rehearsal; *répétition générale*, final (dress) rehearsal.

repiano, see RIPIENO.

Representation of the Soul and the Body, The (It., *La rappresentazione di anima e di corpo*), musical and dramatic work composed by Cavalieri, staged in Rome, 1600 – and regarded both as an early example of opera and (because it is a narrative work of a religious and allegorical nature) a progenitor of oratorio.

reprise (Fr., also used in Eng.), a 're-taking-up', particularly a return to the first section of a composition after an intervening and contrasting section, or (in an operetta or musical, etc.) the further occurrence of a song which has already been heard.

reproducing piano, See PLAYER-PIANO.

Requiem, (1, also *Requiem Mass*) the Roman Catholic Mass for the dead, in Latin, beginning with the word 'requiem' (repose); sung to plainsong or in settings by various composers – many appropriate to concert rather than liturgical use, e.g. Berlioz's (see GRANDE MESSE DES MORTS) and Verdi's (1874) in memory of the writer Alessandro Manzoni, 1785–1873); (2) a choral work similarly appropriate to the commemoration of the dead but with a different text – e.g. Brahms's (1866–8), based on biblical texts, called *A German Requiem* (as opposed to Latin), and Delius's (1914–16) on a pantheistic, non-biblical text by H. Simon; (3) term occasionally used allusively in other musical contexts – for Britten's *Sinfonia da requiem* see SINFONIA. Hindemith's choral work *When Lilacs Last in the Dooryard Bloom'd* (1946, on a text by Whitman) is subtitled 'Requiem for those we loved'.

resolution, the progression from a discord to a concord or to a less acute discord; so *to resolve* a discord.

Respighi, Ottorino (1879–1936), Italian composer, pupil of Rimsky-Korsakov in Russia; also conductor, teacher, and editor of old Italian music. Works include orchestral suites THE BIRDS, *Botticelli Triptych*, FOUNTAINS OF ROME, PINES OF ROME; nine operas, two violin concertos, many songs.

rest, the notation of an absence of sound in a performer's part for a length of time corresponding to a given number of beats or bars. So *eighth-note (quaver) rest, two bars' rest,* etc.

resultant tone, name given to either of two acoustical phenomena: (a) when two loud notes are sounded, another note may sometimes also be heard, lower in pitch, which corresponds to the difference in vibration between the original two and is called 'differential tone'; (b) another note, higher than the original two, may also be heard corresponding to the sum of their vibrations ('summational tone'). For a practical use of the former see ACOUSTIC BASS.

'Resurrection' Symphony, nickname for Mahler's Symphony no. 2 (1894): its final movement, with soprano and alto soloists and choir, is a setting of German words by Klopstock (1724–1803) on the subject of (Christian) resurrection.

Retablo de maese Pedro, El, see MASTER PETER'S PUPPET SHOW.

retardation, see SUSPENSION.

retenu (Fr.), held back (as to speed).

Rethberg, Elisabeth (originally Lisbeth Sättler) (1894–1976), German-born soprano who settled in USA and sang 30 roles at the New York Metropolitan Opera from 1922.

retrograde, term used of a theme when performed backwards – a device prominently used e.g. in the Middle Ages, in Bach's THE ART OF FUGUE, and in TWELVE-NOTE technique. In this last, both *retrograde* and *retrograde inversion* are standard procedures, the

latter meaning that the theme is turned upside-down as well as played backwards (see INVERT).

Return of Lemminkäinen, The, see LEMMINKÄINEN'S HOMECOMING.

Return of Ulysses, The (It., *Il ritorno di Ulisse in patria,* The Return of Ulysses to his Homeland), opera by Monteverdi, produced in Venice, 1640; libretto by G. Badoaro, after Homer's *Odyssey.*

Reubke, Julius (1834–58), German pianist and composer, pupil of Liszt. Compositions, published after his early death, include an organ sonata on Psalm 94 (alluding to the psalm's call for vengeance).

Reutter, Hermann (1900–1985), German composer – also pianist, particularly song-accompanist. Works include operas (one based on Thornton Wilder's *The Bridge of San Luis Rey*), choral works (texts by Goethe and others), four piano concertos.

'Revolutionary' Study, nickname for Chopin's Study in C minor, op. 10, no. 12 (1831) supposedly expressing his patriotic anger at the news of the fall of Warsaw to the Russians.

Revueltas, Silvestre (1899–1940), Mexican violinist, conductor and composer of symphonic poems on Mexican subjects for orchestra, three string quartets, songs, etc. Studied partly in USA; worked in Spain on the Republican side in the Civil War.

Reyer, Ernest (pen-name of Louis Étienne Ernest Rey) (1823–1909), French composer (operas, cantatas, etc.) and critic, follower and champion of Wagner.

Reynolds, Roger (b. 1934), American

composer who has worked in Paris, Cologne and Tokyo; works include *Ping* for flute, piano, harmonium, bowed cymbal, tam-tam, film, slides, tape and electronic equipment; *Masks* for chorus and orchestra.

Rezniček, Emil Nikolaus von (1860–1945), Austrian composer and conductor who settled in Germany and died there. Works, mainly before 1920, include *Donna Diana* and other operas (one based on the TILL EULENSPIEGEL tale), four symphonies, Mass, Requiem.

rfz., abbr. for RINFORZANDO.

rhapsody, title (not in itself denoting a particular musical form) used in the 19th and 20th centuries for a work generally in one continuous movement and usually suggestive of some kind of romantic 'inspiration'. Thus the basis may be some already existing theme(s): e.g. Liszt's HUNGARIAN RHAPSODIES, Delius's BRIGG FAIR (using an English folk-tune), Rakhmaninov's *Rhapsody on a Theme of Paganini* (see PAGANINI). Or no such allusiveness may be implied – e.g. Brahms's Rhapsodies for piano, his ALTO RHAPSODY (voices and orchestra), and the following.

Rhapsody in Blue, work for piano and dance-band orchestra by Gershwin (the first notable concert work by a jazz composer in the jazz idiom), first performed in 1924, later arranged for piano and symphony orchestra. Orchestration for both versions was by Grofé. See preceding.

Rheinberger, Josef [Gabriel] (1839–1901), German organist – child prodigy, holding church post at age seven – pianist, conductor and composer of many organ works. Also composed operas, Masses, chamber music, etc. Distinguished teacher of organ and composition.

Rheingold, Das, see RING.

'Rhenish' Symphony, name given to Schumann's Symphony no. 3 in E♭ (1850): the fourth of its five movements was prompted by the composer's witnessing the installation of a cardinal in Cologne (on the Rhine).

Rhinegold, The, see RING.

rhythm, that aspect of music concerned not with pitch but with the distribution of notes in time and their accentuation. (See also METRE.) Hence such phrases as a *strongly marked rhythm* or (by ellipsis) a *strong rhythm*; *two-beat rhythm* (accent on every other beat); a *five-bar rhythm* (each five bars making a regular rhythmic unit); *waltz rhythm* (accent on the first of every three beats, at waltz pace); *free rhythm*, rhythm not determined by the regular incidence of bar-lines but arrived at by the performer according to the natural or conventional flow of the notes (as in plainsong). So also *a sense of rhythm*, implying a performer's ability to convey the rhythmic element of a composition intelligibly; *rhythm section* of a dance band or jazz group, collective term for those instruments more concerned with giving the beat than with melody – e.g. piano, drums and other percussion, guitar(s), double-bass.

Ricci, Ruggiero (b. 1918), American violinist who made first tour of Europe in 1932; eminent as soloist (e.g. in Paganini's works) and in concertos – gave first performances of those by von Einem and Ginastera.

Ricciarelli, Katia (b. 1946), Italian soprano eminent in Italian operatic roles (Covent Garden from 1974).

Rice, Elmer (1892–1967), American playwright. See STREET SCENE.

ricercar(e) (It., to search), type of contrapuntal instrumental composition current in the 16th–18th centuries, usually in the strictest style of IMITATION.

ricercata, same as preceding entry.

Richards, [Henry] Brinley (1817–75), British pianist and composer of song 'God Bless the Prince of Wales', etc.

Richardson, Samuel (1689–1761), English writer. See PICCINNI.

Richter, Franz Xaver (1709–89), see MANNHEIM SCHOOL.

Richter, Karl (1926–81), German conductor, noted in Bach's choral work. Also organist – at St Thomas's, Leipzig, 1949–51 – and harpsichordist.

Richter, Svyatoslav [Teofilovich] (b. 1915), Russian pianist, formerly opera coach. Played in USA 1960, Britain 1961, and won highest international reputation; Prokofiev's Piano Sonata no. 9 was dedicated to him.

riddle canon, see CANON.

Riders to the Sea, opera by Vaughan Williams, produced in London, 1937: almost a word-for-word setting of Synge's play about an Irish fishing family. See also RABAUD.

Riegger, Wallingford (1885–1961), American composer who studied and conducted in Germany. Wrote many works for Martha Graham's and other dance companies; also three symphonies, Concerto for piano and wind,

three string quartets, *Study in Sonority* for 10 violins (or any multiple of 10), *Music for Brass Choir* (in 26 independent parts).

Rienzi, or The Last of the Tribunes (Ger., . . . *der Letzte der Tribunen*), opera by Wagner, produced in Dresden, 1842. Libretto by composer, after Bulwer-Lytton's novel: the hero is a historical 14th-century Italian patriot.

Ries, German family of musicians, the most important being Ferdinand Ries (1784–1838), friend of Beethoven, pianist, violinist, conductor, and composer of three operas, six symphonies, etc.

Rieti, Vittorio (b. 1898), Egyptian-born Italian composer, pupil of Respighi and others; settled in USA, 1940. Works include opera *Don Perlimplin* (based on Lorca's play), various ballets (including *Night Shadow*, with music arranged from Bellini), five symphonies, Triple Concerto (piano, violin, cello).

riff, in jazz and its derivatives a short, tuneful phrase subjected to repetition and possible harmonic variation; hence Bernstein's orchestral *Prelude, Fugue and Riffs,* 1955.

Rifkin, Joshua (b. 1944), American pianist, also university professor, Bach scholar and conductor. In the 1970s he became well known as a pianist for his revival of Scott Joplin's ragtime music.

rigadoon, rigaudon (Eng., Fr.), old French dance of a lively nature in 2/4 or 4/4 time.

Rigoletto, opera by Verdi, produced in Venice, 1851. Libretto by F. M. Piave, after Hugo's *Le Roi s'amuse*: title taken not from its romantic tenor role but from its baritone hero, a tragic court jester. 'La donna è mobile' (Woman is fickle), its most famous aria, has itself been taken as an opera title by R. Malipiero.

Rihm, Wolfgang (b. 1952), German composer of *Jakob Lenz* and other operas, also of five string quartets, etc.

Riley, Terry [Mitchell] (b. 1935), American composer (also saxophonist) whose works prominently use keyboards, electronics and indeterminate structures: *In C* for any number of instruments; *A Rainbow in Curved Air* for electronic keyboard instruments, etc.

Rilke, Rainer Maria (1872–1926), German poet. See CASANOVA, MATHER.

Rimbaud, Arthur (1854–91), French poet. See ILLUMINATIONS.

Rimsky-Korsakov, Nikolay Andreyevich (1844–1908), Russian composer, also conductor; member of the 'nationalist' group of composers called THE MIGHTY HANDFUL. In early life was naval officer, and picked up much of his musical technique *after* being appointed professor at the St Petersburg Conservatory, 1871. Author of a textbook on orchestration with examples entirely from his own work. Wrote operas including THE MAID OF PSKOV, THE SNOW-MAIDEN, SADKO, MOZART AND SALIERI, *The Legend of Tsar Saltan*, THE INVISIBLE CITY OF KITEZH and the GOLDEN COCKEREL (this last banned for its 'seditious' satire until after his death). Other works include three symphonies (no. 2, *Antar*), RUSSIAN EASTER FESTIVAL overture, suite SCHEHERAZADE,

SPANISH CAPRICE, a piano concerto, folk-song arrangements. His orchestrations and revisions of other composers' works, though now challenged by more 'faithful' editors, were of historical importance – see, e.g., BORIS GODUNOV, THE KHOVANSKY AFFAIR, PRICE IGOR, THE STONE GUEST.

Rinaldo, the first opera written by Handel for London; produced there in 1711. Libretto, in Italian, by G. Rossi, ultimately after Tasso's *Jerusalem Delivered*, of which epic of the Crusades Rinaldo is a hero. (The opera has a famous march 'borrowed' in THE BEGGAR'S OPERA.) See also ARMIDA (she is a pagan enchantress whom Rinaldo opposes).

rinforzando (It., reinforcing), direction that volume is to be suddenly increased on a particular note or chord or a small series of these; abbr. *rinf.*, *rfz.*

Ring, The, usual short title for *The Nibelung's Ring* (Ger., *Der Ring des Nibelungen*), series of four operas by Wagner – called by him a trilogy 'with a preliminary evening'. The complete cycle of four was first performed complete in Bayreuth, 1876, but the first two parts had already been given separately – *The Rhinegold* (*Das Rheingold*), Munich, 1869; *The Valkyrie* (*Die Walküre*), Munich, 1870; *Siegfried*; *Twilight of the Gods* (*Götterdämmerung*). These form a single developing musical structure and unfold a continuous plot: libretto by composer, after old German legends. The 'Nibelung' of the title (member of a race of dwarfs) is Alberich, the first possessor of the magic ring.

Rio Grande, The, work by Lambert for

chorus, orchestra and piano solo, first performed in 1928; it uses jazz idioms and jazz percussion instruments. Setting of a poem by Sacheverell Sitwell.

ripieno (It., replenished), term indicating (e.g. in the old CONCERTO GROSSO) the full body of performers as distinct from the solo group; so also indicating an additional 'filling-in' part. In the brass band the *ripieno cornets* (usually corrupted in writing and speech to *repiano cornets*) are those used to supplement the 'solo' (i.e. first) cornets.

Rise and Fall of the City of Mahagonny (Ger., *Aufstieg und Fall der Stadt Mahagonny*), opera by Kurt Weill, produced in Leipzig, 1930. Libretto by Brecht: 'Mahagonny' is the city of material pleasure and the opera bitterly satirizes 'capitalist' morality. An earlier version of the work was produced at Baden-Baden in 1927.

rit., abbr. for the following (or for RITE-NUTO).

ritardando (It.), becoming slower.

ritenuto (It.), held back (as to tempo) – effectively the same as RITARDANDO.

Rite of Spring, The (Rus., *Vesni svyashchenni* – literally *Spring, the Sacred*), ballet with music by Stravinsky, produced in Paris, 1913 – and occasioning a riot between its champions and its opponents. The title was then translated for French audiences as *Le Sacre du printemps*, but there is no point in the use of this outside French-speaking countries.

ritmo (It.), rhythm; *ritmo di tre battute*, in a rhythm of three bars (i.e. three bars are treated as forming a rhythmical unit).

ritornello (It., little return), a recurring passage, e.g. an instrumental passage always occurring between the verses of a song; so also a passage for full orchestra (without soloist) in a baroque or later concerto, thought of as 'coming round again' even though the material may not all be literally repeated. Hence *ritornello form*, as of a movement based on such recurrences (in various keys), e.g. the opening movement of the classical concerto.

Ritorno di Ulisse in Patria, Il, see RETURN OF ULYSSES.

Ritual Dances, see MIDSUMMER MARRIAGE.

Roberton, Hugh [Stevenson] (1874–1952), British choral conductor – founder and conductor of Glasgow Orpheus Choir, 1906–51; also composer and arranger of vocal music.

Robert the Devil (Fr., *Robert le Diable*), opera by Meyerbeer, produced in Paris, 1831. Libretto by E. Scribe: the hero is a son of the devil by a human woman.

Robeson, Paul [Leroy] (1898–1976), American bass of international repute, the most famous black performer of his day; specialized in spirituals and was also stage and film actor.

Rocca, Lodovico (1895–1986), Italian composer, pupil of Orefice; wrote operas including *The Dybbuk* (based on a Hebrew play), also symphonic poems, cantata *Ancient Inscriptions* (text from Greek epigrams), chamber music, etc.

Rochberg, George (b. 1918), American composer, pupil of Menotti. Works include several with Jewish references, e.g. choral psalm-settings in Hebrew; six symphonies (no. 3 *A 20th-century*

Passion, with voices); a violin concerto; *Contra mortem et tempus* (Lat., Against Death and Time) for violin, flute, clarinet and piano.

rock, type of popular music (originating from *rock 'n' roll*) which from US roots has spread over the Western world since about 1950 – based on solo voice and guitars (mainly electric), and mainly diffused by sound-recording. *Rock 'n' roll* is now applied only to a sub-type, with particular rhythmic and other features. Fusions with other popular music are indicated by such terms as *folk-rock* and *jazz-rock*. The term POP overlaps but is not used synonymously, 'pop' denoting a more commercialized, more juvenile and more easily assimilable product than 'rock'.

rock 'n' roll (i.e. *rock and roll*, bodily movement of response), see preceding.

rococo, term originally alluding to fancy rock-work (Fr., *rocaille*) and applied in visual art to the predominantly diverting – rather than elevating – style of e.g. Watteau (1684–1721) and to related styles in architecture. It has been borrowed by writers on music and applied e.g. to F. Couperin (1668–1733): in all cases the allusion is to a decorative and light art-style succeeding the massiveness and constructive ingenuity of BAROQUE.

Rodeo, or The Courting at Burnt Ranch, ballet with music by Copland, produced in 1942. Set in the Wild West and musically alluding to some traditional American songs.

Rodgers, Richard (1902–79), American composer of light music, especially of musicals in collaboration with the writer Oscar Hammerstein – e.g. *Oklahoma!*, *The Sound of Music*.

Rodrigo, Joaquin (b. 1901), Spanish (blind) composer, pupil of Dukas in Paris. Works include *Aranjuez Concerto* (Sp., *Concierto de Aranjuez* – Aranjuez is a Spanish town) and *Fantasy for a Gentleman*, both for guitar and orchestra; other concertos for piano, violin, cello, harp; songs.

Roger-Ducasse, Jean Jules Aimable (1873–1954), French composer, pupil of Fauré. Works include mime-drama *Orpheus*, three motets, symphonic poems, piano solos. Completed and orchestrated the Rhapsody for saxophone and orchestra which Debussy left unfinished at his death.

Rogers, Benjamin (1614–98), English organist and composer of church music – including the Latin hymn still sung at dawn on May Day from the tower of Magdalen College, Oxford, where he was organist – and also chamber and keyboard music.

Rogers, Bernard (1893–1968), American composer, pupil of Bloch – also of Frank Bridge in London and N. Boulanger in Paris. Composer of opera *The Warrior*, five symphonies and other orchestral works, religious choral works, *Pastorale* for 11 instruments.

Rogg, Lionel (b. 1936), Swiss organist, famous for his Bach recordings, who has toured widely; also composer and professor at Geneva Conservatory.

Rohrflöte, Rohr flute (Ger., Eng.), type of organ stop, the pipes being plugged at the end but having a thin tube (*Rohr*, reed) through the plug.

Roi David, Le, see KING DAVID.

Roland-Manuel (form of name used by Roland Alexis Manuel Lévy) (1891–1966), French composer of

335

operas, oratorio *Joan of Arc*, ballets, etc.; pupil of Roussel and Ravel. Also writer on music.

Roldán, Amadeo (1900–1939), Cuban composer (born in Paris of Cuban parents), also conductor in Havana. Works include ballet *La Rebambaramba* with orchestra including indigenous Cuban instruments; *Black Dance* for voice, two clarinets, two violas, percussion.

Rolfe Johnson, Anthony (b. 1940), British tenor, widely known in Handel oratorio and in opera; occasionally directs performances.

roll, a very rapid succession of notes on a drum, approximating to a continuous sound. The technique varies between types of drum: on the snaredrum each hand gives a double stroke.

Roman, Johan Helmich (1694–1758), Swedish composer of church music, 21 symphonies, etc.; studied in London and was influenced by Handel.

Roman Carnival (Fr., *Le Carnaval romain*), overture by Berlioz, 1844, on material from his opera BENVENUTO CELLINI.

romance, romanza, Romanze, respectively the French (and English), Italian and German forms of a term used with wide and vague musical significance. The slow middle movement of Mozart's Piano Concerto in D minor, K466 (1785), is headed 'Romanze' (an early use); Mendelssohn's *Songs without Words* are called in French *Romances sans paroles* (*romance* in French may simply signify any solo song); Vaughan Williams frequently employed *romance* and *romanza* as the

titles of slow movements, and his single-movement work (1951) for harmonica with strings and piano is called Romance. A quality of intimacy and tenderness is often implied. The term now bears no direct relation to the following entry, despite the common origin of the words.

Romantic(ism), terms alluding to an artistic outlook discernible in European literature towards the end of the 18th century, and taken over to describe a supposedly similar outlook in music, principally in the 19th century. One of its literary aspects, that of harking back to the Middle Ages, is rarely found in musical contexts – apart from Bruckner's 'Romantic' Symphony (no. 4 in E♭, 1874), a nickname bestowed after the composer's description of the opening in terms of a scene of medieval chivalry. Another literary aspect, that of cultivation of the supernatural, is evident e.g. in Weber but not in other composers supposedly no less typed as Romantic, e.g. Chopin. The main musical implication is that the composer is more concerned with the vivid depiction of an emotional state (often linked with a narrative or some other extra-musical element) than with the creation of aesthetically pleasing structures. (Such structures must, however, be the result if not the aim of any successful method of composition.) The attempt at more and more 'vividness' led to (a) a trend to the evocation of 'extreme' emotions, (b) an expansion of orchestral resources for this purpose. Romanticism is thus contrasted with CLASSICISM; it is also, less clearly, differentiated from IMPRESSIONISM. Composers such as Stravinsky, disclaiming a connection between music and the portraying of emotions, are said to be *anti-Romantic*. For a late variety of Romanticism see POST-ROMANTIC.

romanza, Romanze, see ROMANCE.

Romberg, Andreas Jakob (1767–1821), German violinist, conductor, and composer of violin concertos, string quartets, etc.; also of a *Toy Symphony* (not the famous one). Cousin of the following.

Romberg, Bernhard (1767–1841), German cellist and composer, cousin of the preceding.

Romberg, Sigmund (1887–1951), Hungarian-born composer of operettas (*New Moon, The Student Prince, The Desert Song*, etc.) and other music, resident in USA from 1909.

Romeo and Juliet, play by Shakespeare, source of many operas and other musical works, including (1) opera by Gounod, produced in Paris, 1867; libretto (*Roméo et Juliette*) by J. Barbier and M. Carré; (2) opera by Sutermeister, produced in Dresden, 1940; libretto (*Romeo und Julia*) by composer; (3) ballet with music by Prokofiev, produced in Brno, 1938 (two orchestral suites have been drawn from it); (4) 'dramatic symphony' by Berlioz, with solo and choral voices, 1839; (5) overture-fantasy by Tchaikovsky, 1869–70. See also VILLAGE ROMEO AND JULIET, ZANDONAI, ZINGARELLI.

Ronald, Landon (form of name used by Landon Ronald Russell) (1873–1938), British pianist (accompanist to Melba), composer (song 'Down in the Forest', etc.), and conductor, noted in early orchestral recordings. Son of Henry Russell. Knighted, 1922.

rondeau (Fr.), a musical (and/or poetic) form suggestive of a circle or of recurrence; in particular (1) a 13th–15th-century vocal form where certain sections of both verse and music recur; (2) a 17th-century and later instrumental form in which the opening section recurs at intervals – in which sense, the term was taken into Italian (and wider) usage as RONDO.

rondel (Fr.), variant spelling of RONDEAU (1).

rondo (properly spelt, in It., *rondò*, itself an Italianized form of Fr. *rondeau*), a form of composition, especially an instrumental movement, in which one section recurs intermittently (the French spelling *rondeau* was used e.g. by Bach). By Mozart's time the rondo had evolved into a standard pattern and was much used, e.g., for the last movement of a sonata or concerto. A simple rondo is built up in the pattern of ABACADA ... (etc.), where A represents the recurring section (called *rondo-theme*) and B, C, D ... represent contrasting sections called 'episodes'. (The rondo-theme can undergo some variation in its reappearances.) A combination of this with SONATA-FORM led to what is called the *sonata-rondo* (used e.g. by Mozart, Beethoven) in which the first episode (B) is originally in a key other than the tonic but later reappears in the tonic key (like the 'second subject' in sonata-form). Occasionally in Italian opera (e.g. Mozart, Rossini), *rondò* is used to designate an aria in which a slow section is succeeded by a faster one (without an implication of recurrence); the reason for this is obscure.

Rooley, Anthony (b. 1944), British

lutenist, joint founder and later sole director of the Consort of Musicke, one of the most successful early-music ensembles.

root, the lowest note of a chord when that chord is in what is regarded as its 'basic' position – e.g. for the chord of C major (C, E, G) the root is C, which is regarded as the basic note on the chord (the other notes being built up from it by thirds). In the case of complex chords, analysis may indicate a root which is not actually sounded. (See POSITION, 3.)

Ropartz, Guy (form of name used by Joseph Marie Guy-Ropartz) (1864–1955), French composer of operas, five symphonies, organ and piano music, etc.; pupil of Massenet, Franck and others.

Rore, Cyprian (or Cipriano) **de** (1516–65), Flemish composer who worked in Italy (and died there); pupil of Willaert in Venice, then held various church and court posts. Wrote notable madrigals; also church music, instrumental fantasies, etc. See PASSION.

Rorem, Ned (b. 1923), American composer of many songs and song-cycles; *Miss Julie* (after Strindberg) and other operas; three symphonies, 11 studies for 11 players etc. Pupil of V. Thomson and Copland. Lived in Paris, 1949–55. Also writer.

rosalia, name sometimes given to a 'real SEQUENCE' (because it occurred at the beginning of an old Italian popular song, 'Rosalia mia cara').

Rosamunde, Princess of Cyprus (Ger., *... Fürstin von Cypern*), play by Helmine von Chézy, 1823, for which Schubert wrote three entr'actes, two ballet pieces and various vocal numbers. The piece now known as the overture to *Rosamunde* was originally written for an earlier stage piece, *The Magic Harp*; the overture actually used at the first performance of *Rosamunde* was that already written for ALFONSO AND ESTRELLA and is still known by that name.

rose, see SOUND-HOLE.

Rose, Leonard (1918–84), American cellist, principal cellist of New York Philharmonic, 1943–51, thereafter prominent as soloist and teacher.

Rose Cavalier, The, see ROSEN-KAVALIER.

Roseingrave, English family of musicians, the most important of whom is Thomas Roseingrave (1688–1766), organist and composer of an opera, Italian cantatas, English church music, organ and harpsichord pieces, etc.; in Italy he became acquainted with A. and D. Scarlatti. Latterly lived in Ireland and died there.

Rosen, Charles (b. 1927), American pianist, pupil of Moriz Rosenthal; New York début, 1951. Also writer of books on the Vienna classics and on Schoenberg, etc.

Rosenberg, Hilding [Constantin] (1892–1985), Swedish composer, also conductor; studied in Germany and France. Works include eight symphonies – no. 4, *The Revelation of St John*, with chorus; concertos for violin, viola, cello, trumpet; ballet *Orpheus in Town*; tetralogy of stage oratorios after Thomas Mann's *Joseph and his Brethren*; 12 string quartets, piano solos, etc.

Rosenkavalier, Der, opera by R. Strauss, produced in Dresden, 1911.

Libretto by H. von Hofmannsthal. The 'Cavalier of the Rose' is the ceremonial bearer of a rose from a gentleman to his betrothed – the bearer in this case winning the girl for himself instead.

Rosenmüller, Johann (*c*.1620–84), German composer who worked for a time in Italy. Wrote Masses and other church music, suites of instrumental dances, etc.

Rosenthal, Manuel (b. 1904), French composer, pupil of Ravel; also conductor, especially in France and (1946–51) in USA. Works include symphonic suite *Joan of Arc*, operettas, oratorio *St Francis of Assisi*. He orchestrated some of Ravel's piano music.

Rosé Quartet, a Viennese string quartet founded in 1882 by Arnold Rosé, famous for first performances of works by Schoenberg and Webern. Nazi anti-semitism forced Rosé's emigration, and the end of the quartet, in 1938.

Roses from the South (Ger., *Rosen aus dem Süden*), waltz by Johann Strauss the younger – from his operetta *The Queen's Lace Handkerchief*, 1880.

Rosetti, Francesco, see RÖSSLER.

Rossellini, Renzo (1908–82), Italian composer of ballets including *A Tale of Winter* (not after Shakespeare's *The Winter's Tale*), operas including *A View from the Bridge* (after Arthur Miller's play), orchestral works, and music to films directed by his brother (Roberto Rossellini), etc.

Rosseter, Philip (*c*.1568–1623), lutenist and composer of ayres with lute and other accompaniment, music for broken consort, etc. Active at Queen Elizabeth's court.

Rossetti, Dante Gabriel (1828–82), British poet, see BLESSED DAMOZEL, CITTERN.

Rossi, Luigi (1598–1653), Italian singer, organist and composer – e.g. of opera *Orpheus*, the first Italian opera to be heard in Paris, 1647; also of solo cantatas, etc.

Rossi, Salomone (*c*.1570–*c*.1630), Italian composer – Jewish, but exempted from the stigma of wearing the yellow badge otherwise then compulsory for Jews in Italy; colleague of Monteverdi at the court of Mantua. Wrote Italian madrigals, Hebrew psalms, etc.; notably pioneered the form of TRIO-SONATA.

Rossi-Lemeni, Nicola (1920–91), Italian bass singer, Turkish-born (mother Russian, father Italian); began operatic career (specializing in Russian opera) in Italy; later sang in New York (1951), London, etc. From 1965 also operatic stage director.

Rossini, Gioachino (in modern spelling Gioacchino) [Antonio] (1792–1868), Italian composer, born in Pesaro. His operas appeared in various Italian cities; he visited England in 1823–4, and after 1829 lived partly in Paris, where he died. Successful in opera from 1810, although THE BARBER OF SEVILLE (1816) was at first a failure. Other operas include THE SILKEN LADDER, TANCRED, THE ITALIAN WOMAN IN ALGIERS, OTELLO, CINDERELLA, THE THIEVING MAGPIE, ARMIDA, MOSES, SEMIRAMIS, COUNT ORY, WILLIAM TELL (1829, in French, after which success he lived for nearly 40 more years but wrote no more operas). Other works include STABAT MATER and a few other church works; a few songs and duets (among them the collection SOIRÉES MUSICALES) and piano pieces, etc. For an arrangement, see FANTASTIC TOY-SHOP. Exploiter of the orchestral crescendo, and noted in his day for 'noisy' effects.

Rössler (or Rösler), **Franz Anton** (1750–92), German (Bohemian-born) composer of a Requiem, two oratorios, more than 30 symphonies, etc. He Italianized his name (presumably for reasons of fashion) as Antonio Rosetti and on modern programmes is sometimes designated 'Rös[s]ler-Rosetti.' He has been confused with another Antonio Rosetti (1740–?), mainly a theatrical composer.

Rostand, Edmond (1868–1918), French dramatist. See ALFANO, DAMROSCH, HAMILTON.

Rostropovich, Mstislav [Leopoldovich] (b. 1927), Russian cellist held in highest international esteem; also pianist (accompanist to his wife, Galina Vishnevskaya, soprano), composer and conductor. He was much associated with Prokofiev, whose Cello Concertino he completed after the composer's death. Left USSR, 1975; music director of National Symphony Orchestra, Washington, DC (USA) since 1977.

rota (Lat., wheel), term sometimes used for ROUND, particularly the famous SUMER IS ICUMEN IN, sometimes called the 'Reading Rota', because its conjectural composer, John of Fornsete, was a monk of Reading Abbey.

Rota, Nino (1911–79), Italian composer of operas including *The Two Shy People* (*I due timidi*) originally for radio; also of three symphonies; chamber music, songs (some to texts by Tagore), much film music, etc. Pupil of Pizzetti and Casella.

Rothenberger, Anneliese (b. 1924), German soprano, active at the Vienna State Opera from 1957; her wide repertory included operetta.

Rothwell, Evelyn, see BARBIROLLI.

Rouet d'Omphale, Le, see OMPHALE'S SPINNING-WHEEL.

roulade (Fr., a 'rolling'), non-technical term often applied to an extravagant display of notes, especially in operatic singing.

round, type of short vocal 'perpetual CANON' in which the voices, entering in turn, all sing the same melody at the same pitch (or at the octave). 'London's Burning' is a familiar example. See ROTA.

Rousseau, Jean-Jacques (1712–78), Swiss philosopher resident in France: author of THE SOCIAL CONTRACT, etc. Also wrote on various aspects of music. Championed Italian, as against French, opera (in the 'War of the Buffoons') and himself composed opera *The Village Soothsayer* (Fr., *Le Devin du village*) in demonstration of his views; also composed songs.

Roussel, Albert (1869–1937), French composer; had naval career until 1893, then studied with d'Indy and others. After visiting India wrote some works in an Eastern-influenced style, including opera-ballet *Padmavati*. His later works, some with NEO-CLASSICAL traits, include four symphonies, an orchestral suite in F, comic opera *Aunt Caroline's Will*, ballets THE SPIDER'S BANQUET and BACCHUS AND ARIADNE; also chamber works, piano pieces, songs, etc.

rovescio, al (It.), in reverse. This may refer to either (1) a passage that can be performed backwards, or (2) a type of CANON in which an upward interval in the original voice becomes a downward interval (of the same distance) in the imitating voice, and vice versa.

Roxolane, La, nickname for Haydn's Symphony no. 63 in C, composed about 1777 (Hob.I:63), named after a French song which is used in it as the subject of variations.

Royal Concertgebouw Orchestra, see CONCERTGEBOUW.

Royal Liverpool Philharmonic Orchestra, an orchestra which became full-time in 1943; its parent society dates from 1849. The title 'Royal' was granted in 1956. Conductor, 1983–6 (succeeding David Atherton), Marek Janowski, then Libor Pešek since 1987.

Royal Opera House, see COVENT GARDEN.

Royal Philharmonic Orchestra, a London orchestra founded by Beecham in 1946. It has no present link with the Royal Philharmonic Society (founded 1813). Music director from 1987, Vladimir Ashkenazy.

Rozhdestvensky, Gennady [Nikolayevich] (b. 1931), Russian conductor who took his mother's surname (father was the conductor Nikolai Anosov, 1900–1962). Principal conductor, Bolshoi Theatre, Moscow, 1965–70; 1978–81, conductor of BBC Symphony Orchestra.

Rózsa, Miklós (b. 1907), Hungarian composer who studied in Leipzig, then resided in Paris, London and (from 1940) USA, later becoming naturalized there. Composed much film music (especially for MGM in Hollywood, 1948–62) and also two violin concertos, a viola concerto, etc.

rubato (It., robbed), to be performed with a certain freedom as to time, for the purpose of giving the music suitable expression. As a noun ('he played with too much rubato') it is really short for *tempo rubato*.

Rubbra, Edmund [Charles] (1901–86), British composer, pupil of Vaughan Williams, Holst and others; also pianist, particularly as member of piano trio; teacher at Oxford University. Works include 11 symphonies, Sinfonia Concertante for piano and orchestra, a piano concerto, viola concerto; two Masses – one Anglican, one for the Roman Catholic Church, which Rubbra entered in 1948. CBE, 1960. See also CAVATINA.

Rubini, Giovanni Battista (1794–1854), Italian tenor celebrated in operas by Bellini and Donizetti, setting a model in style.

Rubinstein, Anton Grigorevich (1829–94), Russian pianist of great distinction, and composer of *The Demon* and other operas, six symphonies, five piano concertos, etc. Now hardly known except for a few songs and piano pieces including MELODY IN F. Brother of N. Rubinstein, below; no relation of Arthur Rubinstein.

Rubinstein, Arthur (1886–1982), pianist, Polish-born, naturalized American 1946; internationally known virtuoso, said to have played in every country except Tibet. Pupil of Leschetizky. Composer of some piano music, etc. No relation of the other

Rubinsteins. (The spelling Arthur, not Artur, was preferred by him.) Hon. KBE, 1977.

Rubinstein, Nikolay Grigorevich (1835–81), Russian pianist, founder and principal of Moscow Conservatory, and composer of piano music, etc. Brother of the more famous Anton Rubinstein (preceding).

Ruddigore, or The Witch's Curse, operetta by Sullivan, produced in London, 1887. Libretto by W. S. Gilbert: the plot, with 'Ruddigore' as the name of a family of 'bad baronets', parodies Victorian melodrama. The original spelling was 'Ruddygore', soon changed because thought offensive.

Rudhyar, Dane (pen-name of Daniel Chennevière) (1895–1985), French-born composer who settled in USA, 1917; also writer and painter. His musical works, mostly linked to occultist beliefs, include symphonic poems (*To the Real, The Surge of Fire*, etc.), piano pieces, songs.

Rue, Pierre de la, see LA RUE.

Ruffo, Titta (originally Ruffo Cafiero Titta) (1877–1953), Italian baritone with a long and celebrated operatic career, 1898–1931.

Ruggles, Carl (form of name adopted by Charles Sprague Ruggles) (1876–1971), American composer, also painter. He completed only a few works – of a pioneering modern nature including *Angels* for six trumpets, symphonic poems *Men and Mountains* and *Sun-Treader*, and a piano concertino.

Rührtrommel (Ger., rolling drum) = TENOR DRUM (not snare-drum).

Ruins of Athens, The, overture and incidental music (including a Turkish March) by Beethoven for a play by Kotzebue, produced for the opening of the German Theatre at Pest (Hungary), 1812.

Rule, Britannia!, see ALFRED.

rumba, Cuban dance in 8/8 time (3 + 3 + 2) which became established in ballroom dancing in USA and Europe about 1930. Occasional use in concert music – see JAMAICAN RUMBA.

Rusalka, a water-sprite in Slavonic legend. *The Rusalka* is thus the title of operas by (1) Dargomizhsky, produced in St Petersburg, 1856; libretto by composer, after Pushkin; (2) Dvořák, produced in Prague, 1901; libretto by J. Kvapil.

Ruslan and Lyudmila, opera by Glinka, produced in St Petersburg, 1842. Libretto by V. Shirkov and others, after Pushkin: named after the two lovers, eventually united despite the powers of magic.

Russell, Henry (1812–1900), British singer, organist, and composer of 'A Life on the Ocean Wave' and other songs: father of Landon RONALD.

Russian Easter Festival Overture (Rus., *Voskresenaya uvertyura*, i.e. Resurrection Overture), work by Rimsky-Korsakov, 1888, based on Russian Orthodox Church melodies and showing finally 'the unbridled pagan-religious merry-making on the morn of Easter Sunday'.

Russian Quartets, name for Haydn's six String Quartets, op. 33, of 1783 (Hob.III:33); they are dedicated to the Grand Duke Paul of Russia. They are also known as 'Gli Scherzi' from the character of their minuet movements (see SCHERZO), or the 'Maiden Quartets' (Ger., *Jungfernquartette*) for a reason unknown.

Russolo, Luigi (1855–1947), Italian composer (also painter) who in 1913–14 demonstrated his own invention of 'noise-instruments' in compositions of his own (now lost) – see FUTURISM.

'Rustic Wedding' (Ger., *Ländliche Hochzeit*), title of symphony by K. Goldmark, 1876; five illustrative movements, no. 1 a wedding march.

Rustle of Spring, no. 3 of six piano pieces (published 1909) by Sinding – formerly very popular, almost the only work of his to be heard.

Rute (Ger., rod), indication in German-language scores that a drummer is to use a (birch or wire) brush instead of the normal stick.

Ruy Blas, play by Victor Hugo for which Mendelssohn wrote an overture and a chorus for a production in Leipzig, 1839.

Ryom, Peter (b. 1937), Danish musicologist. See VIVALDI.

Rysanek, Leonie (b. 1926), Austrian soprano who won distinction at the Vienna State Opera; appeared also at the Bayreuth Festival (1951–68) and at the New York Metropolitan Opera, etc.

Rzewski, Frederic [Anthony] (b. 1938), American composer whose music often expounds a socialist message, e.g. in 36 variations for piano entitled *The People United will Never be Defeated.* Also pianist, prominent in performing other modernist work including Stockhausen's.

S

s, symbol in TONIC SOL-FA for the fifth degree (dominant) of the scale, pronounced *soh*.

Sabata, Victor De, see DE SABATA.

Sacchini, Antonio [Maria Gasparo] (1730–86), Italian composer who lived in London, 1773–81, and later in Paris, where he died. Wrote about 40 operas, at first in Italian, then in French and influenced by Gluck's reforms. Also composed church music, string quartets, etc.

sackbut, an early form of trombone, revived in mid-20th-century reconstructions of early music. (The name is also used in older biblical translations for an instrument which is not identified with the trombone.)

Sacred Service, title usual in English for Bloch's setting of a Jewish Sabbath morning service (1933) for baritone, chorus and orchestra. The Hebrew title is *Avodath hakodesh*, and the text follows a US 'Reformed' Jewish use.

Sacre du printemps, Le, see RITE OF SPRING.

Sadko, opera by Rimsky-Korsakov, produced in Moscow, 1898 – partly based on a symphonic poem of the same name by the composer, 1867. Libretto by the composer and V. I. Belsky: Sadko is a bard, the setting is

10th-century, and the story is legendary in character. The work is styled an *opera-bylina* (from a type of old Russian saga).

Sadler's Wells, a London theatre dating from the late 17th century; reopened 1931 for a repertory of plays and operas, plays being shortly dropped and ballet added. Sadler's Wells Opera at first retained its name on moving to the London Coliseum in 1968, then became the ENGLISH NATIONAL OPERA.

Saeverud, Harald [Sigurd Johan] (b. 1897), Norwegian composer of nine symphonies, 50 *Little Variations* (on a theme three bars long) and other works for orchestra; incidental music to Ibsen's *Peer Gynt*; many piano pieces, including *Ballad of Revolt* (also orchestrated).

Saga, A (Swe., *En Saga*), symphonic poem by Sibelius, 1892, revised in 1901. It alludes to the nature of the Scandinavian sagas in general.

Saint . . . (Titles beginning 'Saint' or 'St' are all listed here, but saints as people are listed by their commonly used names, e.g. Cecilia under C.)

St Anne, English hymn-tune, probably by Croft, published in 1708; now usually sung to the words 'O God, our help in ages past'. By mere coincidence an organ fugue in E♭ by Bach opens with the same notes: this is therefore known in Britain as the 'St Anne' Fugue.

'St Anthony' Variations, work by Brahms for orchestra, 1873, also issued by the composer for two pianos. Brahms took the theme from a FELD-PARTITA in B♭ by Haydn, and called it *Variations on a Theme of Haydn*; but it has since been found that the theme itself (called the 'St Anthony' Chorale) was not Haydn's own but was borrowed by him for the occasion. The present name is thus now preferred.

'St John' Passion, properly *The Passion According to St John* (Ger., *Johannespassion*), a setting by Bach (BWV 245) for solo voices, chorus and orchestra of the Passion narrative from St John's Gospel, with interpolations; first performed in 1723. See PASSION and ST MATTHEW PASSION. For other settings, see BÖHM (G.), PÄRT.

St John's Night on the Bare Mountain (Rus., *Ivanova noch na lisoi gore*), orchestral work by Musorgsky, alluding to a 'witches' sabbath'; it took various forms, originating in 1867 and eventually was used as an introduction to Act III of the opera SOROCHINTSY FAIR. This last version was revised and altered by Rimsky-Korsakov, and it is his version (1908, usually called *Night on the Bare Mountain* or *Night on Bald Mountain*) that is usually performed. It is misleading to pass this off as Musorgsky's, particularly since Musorgsky's original has itself now become known.

'St Matthew' Passion, properly *The Passion According to St Matthew* (Ger., *Matthäuspassion*), a setting by Bach

(BWV 244) for solo voices, chorus and orchestra of the passion narrative from St Matthew's Gospel, with interpolations; first performed in 1729. Cp. PASSION, ST JOHN PASSION.

St Paul, oratorio by Mendelssohn (Ger., *Paulus*), first performed in Düsseldorf, 1836; text from the Bible.

St Paul's Suite, work for string orchestra by Holst, 1913 – written for the orchestra of St Paul's Girls School, Hammersmith (London), where he taught. Incorporates the DARGASON in the last movement.

Saint-Saëns, [Charles] **Camille** (1835–1921), French composer, pupil of Halévy and Gounod; able pianist from early childhood; also organist. Works include SAMSON AND DELILAH and other operas; symphonic poems on Liszt's lines, e.g. *Omphale's Spinning-wheel*; three symphonies (no. 3 with organ), DANSE MACABRE and other works for orchestra; five piano concertos, three violin concertos, two cello concertos, THE CARNIVAL OF ANIMALS for two pianos and orchestra; chamber music, church music, many songs. Frequently visited Britain in his exceptionally long and prolific career. Hon. Mus. D., Cambridge, 1893.

Salas, Juan Orrego, see ORREGO SALAS.

salicet, salicional, organ stop of soft tone with some resemblance to orchestral stringed instruments.

Salieri, Antonio (1750–1825), Italian composer who lived mainly in Vienna, and died there: Beethoven and Schubert were among his pupils. He intrigued against Mozart, but the supposition that he poisoned Mozart is false. Wrote mainly Italian operas (including a *Falstaff*, after Shakespeare's *The Merry Wives of Windsor*), but also six Masses, a PASSION oratorio in Italian, two piano concertos, etc.

Sallinen, Aulis [Heikki] (b. 1935), Finnish composer (and formerly manager of the Finnish Radio Symphony Orchestra). Works include operas *The Red Line* and *The King Goes Forth to France*, violin concerto, cello concerto, four symphonies, five string quartets.

salmo (It., pl. *-i*), psalm.

Salome, opera by R. Strauss, produced in Dresden, 1905. Libretto a German translation of Oscar Wilde's French play – after the New Testament, but incorporating the medieval idea that Salome was in love with John the Baptist.

Salomon, Johann Peter (1745–1815), German-born violinist and concert organizer who settled in London (dying there); brought Haydn to England and commissioned what are now called the *Salomon Symphonies*.

Salomon Symphonies, the 12 symphonies (Hob. I: 93–104) commissioned from Haydn by J. P. Salomon (above) for Haydn's visits to England, 1791–2 and 1794–5. They were Haydn's last symphonies: see CLOCK, DRUM-ROLL, LONDON, MIRACLE, SURPRISE

Salón México, El, work by Copland, first performed in Mexico City, 1937; based on the composer's impressions of a Mexican dance-hall, and incorporating some traditional Mexican tunes.

Salonen, Esa-Pekka (b. 1958), Finnish conductor, also composer, formerly horn-player; made London début in 1983, appointed conductor of the Los Angeles Philharmonic Orchestra from 1992.

saltarello, salterello, type of Italian dance: in its most common meaning, a lively dance incorporating jumps, the music similar to TARANTELLA but not so smoothly flowing. The finale of Mendelssohn's ITALIAN SYMPHONY is so styled. The preferred modern Italian spelling is *salterello*, but Mendelssohn wrote *saltarello*, as did older Italian composers also.

Salzedo, Carlos (1885–1961), French-born harpist resident in USA; innovator in harp technique and composer of works for his instrument.

Salzman, Eric (b. 1933), American composer, pupil of Sessions, Babbitt and (in Italy) Petrassi; also critic and organizer of concerts. Works, many incorporating electronics, visual images, etc., include *The Nude Paper Sermon*, described as 'Tropes for actor, Renaissance consort, chorus and electronics'.

Samazeuilh, Gustave [Marie Victor Fernand] (1877–1967), French composer of symphonic poems, chamber works, Serenade for guitar, etc.; also critic. Pupil of Chausson, d'Indy and Dukas.

Saminsky, Lazare (1882–1959), composer and conductor (pupil of Lyadov and Rimsky-Korsakov), Russian-born, resident in USA from 1920. Works include five symphonies, music for Jewish worship, opera-ballet *Jephtha's Daughter*. Was also writer, particularly on modern and Jewish music, and synagogue music director.

samisen, Japanese lute-like, plucked-string instrument: the application of this term to a gong-like percussion instrument in Puccini's MADAM BUTTERFLY is an error.

Sammartini, Giovanni Battista (*c.*1700–1775), Italian composer and organist (brother of the following), teacher of Gluck. Among his works (said to number 2,000) are various symphonies and string quartets pioneering the style later developed e.g. by Haydn and Mozart.

Sammartini, Giuseppe (1695–1750), Italian oboist and composer (brother of preceding) who settled in London, taking a post with the Prince of Wales.

Samson, oratorio by Handel (text from poems by Milton) first performed in London, 1743. Cp. SAMSON AND DELILAH.

Samson and Delilah (Fr., *Samson et Dalila*), opera by Saint-Saëns, produced (in German) in Weimar, 1877. Libretto by F. Lemaire. At first barred, because of its biblical subject, from stage presentation in Britain and performed only in concert.

Sanctus (Lat., Holy), part of the Mass, beginning with a threefold assertion of that word.

Sand, George [Aurore Dudevant] (1804–76), French writer. See CHOPIN.

Sándor, György (b. 1912), pianist, Hungarian-born, who trained in Budapest (where he also had lessons in composition from Kodály) and settled in USA, 1939. Noted in Bartók and Kodály.

Sanz, Gaspar (1640–1710), Spanish guitarist whose manual of instruction

for the instrument (1674) is the source of many pieces favoured by later players.

Sappho (sixth century BC), Greek poet. See PACINI.

saraband, sarabande (Eng., Fr.), dance coming to the rest of Europe from Spain, and forming a regular constituent of the old SUITE; it is slow and in 3/2 time.

Sarasate [y Navascues], **Pablo Martin Melitón** (1844–1908), Spanish violinist (among the most famous virtuosos of his time), who toured widely; composed many works for his instrument, including a fantasy (with orchestra) in gipsy style called *Zigeunerweisen* (see ZIGEUNER). See also SPANISH SYMPHONY.

sardana (Sp.), a national dance of Catalonia, properly to pipe-and-drum accompaniment.

Sardou, Victorien (1831–1908), French dramatist. See TOSCA.

Sargent, [Harold] **Malcolm** [Watts] (1895–1967), British conductor; also pianist and organist. Conductor of BBC Symphony Orchestra, 1950–57, of the Royal Choral Society, 1928–67; chief conductor of the Proms, 1948–66. Arranger and orchestrator of traditional and other music. Revived, at the Proms, the authentic tune of 'Rule, Britannia!' (see ALFRED); see also FOUR SERIOUS SONGS. Knighted, 1947.

Šárka, see MY COUNTRY.

sarod, Indian plucked instrument; it generally has 4–5 melody strings, 3–5 drone strings and 11 or more SYMPATHETIC strings.

sarrusophone, double-reed instrument, classified as woodwind though made of brass; invented by a French bandmaster named Sarrus, 1856, and made in various sizes. The second largest (*double-bass sarrusophone*) has been stipulated in the orchestra to replace the double-bassoon, e.g. by Saint-Saëns and Delius (although the parts are now usually given back to double-bassoon). Various sizes have been used in some Continental military bands.

Sarti, Giuseppe (1729–1802), Italian composer who travelled much, wrote more than 70 operas (in Italian, French, Danish and Russian), and died in Berlin. Other works include church music and harpsichord sonatas. In DON GIOVANNI Mozart uses an air from Sarti's *Between Two Litigants* (It., *Fra due litiganti*) as part of the hero's supper-music.

Satie, Erik [Alfred Leslie] (1866–1925), French composer; for a time worked as café pianist, etc., and at 39 became a pupil of Roussel and d'Indy. Influenced younger composers (see SIX) towards a cool, clear style and away from the lushness sometimes associated with IMPRESSIONISM. Most of his piano solos and duets have eccentric titles, e.g. *Gymnopédies* (name derived from an ancient Greek festival) and *Three Pear-shaped Pieces*; several of these were orchestrated by Poulenc and others. Wrote also ballets, including *Relâche* (the word displayed by French theatres when they are closed), symphonic drama SOCRATES, etc.

Satz (Ger., a setting), term of several different musical applications in German, including (1) a musical setting; so *Tonsatz* (note-setting), a com-

position; (2) a movement; so Schubert's isolated QUARTET MOVEMENT is called *Quartettsatz*; (3) a theme or subject – so *Hauptsatz*, main theme; *Nebensatz*, subsidiary theme.

saudades, Portuguese (plural) word of uncertain origin, but carrying the implication of wistful remembrance of things past; it has been used for two sets of piano pieces by Milhaud, *Saudades do Brasil* (... of Brazil), and for a set of songs by Warlock.

Sauguet, Henri (pen-name of Jean Pierre Poupard) (1901–89), French composer, pupil of Koechlin, disciple of Satie; also critic. Works, many in a light vein, include opera *Marianne's Caprices*; *The Strolling Players* (*Les Forains*) and other ballets; song cycle *The Fortune Teller* (*La Voyante*) with orchestra; three piano concertos, two string quartets.

Saul, oratorio by Handel, first performed in London, 1739. Text, based on the Bible, by C. Jennens. Contains a famous 'Dead March'.

Sauret, Émile (1852–1920), French violinist who taught in London (where he died), Chicago and elsewhere; composer of two violin concertos, etc.

sausage bassoon, an alternative and more informal name for the RACK-ET(T).

sautillé (Fr., springing), type of bowing on the violin, etc., in which the bow springs rebounding off the string.

Savile, Jeremy (17th century), English composer known only for a few songs (including 'Here's a Health unto His Majesty') and part-songs.

Sāvitri, one-act opera by G. Holst, produced in London, 1916. Libretto by composer, after an episode in the Hindu scriptures: Sāvitri is the devoted wife of a woodman.

Savoy Operas, name for the operettas (or light operas) composed by Sullivan with librettos by W. S. Gilbert. From IOLANTHE onwards, these were first heard at the Savoy Theatre, London, built specially for them. The name is also customarily held to cover COX AND BOX (libretto by F. C. Burnand, not by Gilbert) since this remained in the D'Oyly Carte company's repertory along with Gilbert's works.

saw, musical, a hand-saw used as a musical instrument for purposes of novel entertainment – very rare in serious composition (but see MAY-UZUMI): it is held by the knees and played with a violin bow, the left hand altering the tension (and thus the pitch of the note produced) by bending the saw. See also FLEXATONE.

Sawallisch, Wolfgang (b. 1923), German conductor, also well known as piano accompanist to leading singers. Since 1971, music director (later, general director) of the Bavarian State Opera, Munich; appointed conductor of Philadelphia Orchestra from 1992.

Sax, Adolphe (real first names Antoine Joseph) (1814–94), Belgian inventor of the SAXHORN and SAXOPHONE families of instruments.

saxhorn, type of brass instrument with valves invented by A. Sax in 1845. As to nomenclature, there is a great difference between authorities and between various countries (see also FLUGELHORN, a near relation). The instruments used in brass bands in Britain, which are TRANSPOSING IN-

STRUMENTS, are the *tenor saxhorn* in Eb and the *baritone saxhorn* in Bb, known simply as 'tenor horn' (or 'Eb horn') and 'baritone': the former is also used in military bands but neither is used in the orchestra. The series of instruments may be regarded as being continued downwards in pitch by the TUBA family, including EUPHONIUM.

saxophone, name of a family of wind instruments having a reed resembling a clarinet's – and therefore classified among the WOODWIND (not 'brass') despite a metal body. Invented by A. Sax about 1840. Made in various sizes, the lower-pitched ones in S-shape or with additional curves (the *alto saxophone* exists in both S-shaped and straight forms). The most common are the *alto* (TRANSPOSING INSTRUMENT in Eb) with compass from the Db below middle C upwards for about two and a half octaves, and the *tenor saxophone* in Bb a fifth lower. Both these are occasionally used in the symphony orchestra, and regularly in dance bands and military bands (not brass bands). Less frequently used are the *baritone* (below the tenor, in Eb) and *soprano* (above the alto, in Bb); still rarer are the *bass* (lower than the baritone, in Bb) and the *sopranino* (higher than the soprano, in Eb). The saxophones are thus alternately in Bb and Eb. Outside this series is the so-called C *melody saxophone* (pitched between alto and tenor), not transposing, and so easier to use for playing from song-copies with piano accompaniment, etc.

Scala, La, the common form of reference to the Teatro alla Scala in Milan, erected in 1788, and now ranking as Italy's main opera-house. It is so named because it was built on the former site of a church, Santa Maria alla Scala. Musical director since 1972, Claudio Abbado.

Scala di seta, La, see SILKEN LADDER.

scale, a progression of single notes upwards or downwards in 'steps'. (Cf. It. *scala*, stairway.) So *scalic* – e.g. 'a scalic figure', progressing upwards or downwards in steps. For the *major scale* and *minor scale*, see MAJOR. See also CHROMATIC, DIATONIC, PENTATONIC, WHOLE-TONE, MODE, TWELVE-NOTE.

Scaramouche, title of suite for two pianos by Milhaud: so called because the music is based on music by Milhaud for a play, *The Flying Doctor*, produced in Paris, 1937, at the Théâtre Scaramouche.

Scarlatti, Alessandro (1660–1725), Italian composer who worked chiefly in Naples; reckoned the founder of the type of Italian opera which conquered all Europe in the 18th century. Composed more than 100 operas, many now lost; 600 cantatas for solo voice and continuo; various other cantatas, oratorios, Masses, madrigals, etc.; also chamber music. Possibly a pupil of Carissimi in boyhood. Held various court and church posts. Father of Domenico Scarlatti.

Scarlatti, [Giuseppe] **Domenico** (1685–1757), Italian composer; at first wrote Italian opera, etc., on the model of his father (see preceding entry), and was known also as a harpsichord virtuoso; but went in 1720 to Portugal and later to Spain (dying in Madrid) and there wrote the greater number of his single-movement harpsichord sonatas. These, numbering over 550, and in their time also called 'exercises'

(It., *esercizi*), exploit with great variety the capabilities of the BINARY-form movement, and foreshadow later SONATA-FORM. (For a nicknamed one, see CAT'S FUGUE; for the numbering of the sonatas, see KIRKPATRICK.) Other works include a STABAT MATER and other church music.

scena (It., stage, scene), (1) a 'scene' (subdivision of an act); (2) in 19th-century operatic scores, a musical unit incorporating recitative, and leading to an aria, a duet, etc.: so *scena ed* [and] *aria*; (3) term sometimes meaning the double unit of recitative *plus* aria, etc.; (4) a concert item corresponding to this (third) dramatic form. Spohr gave the designation 'in the form of a song-scena' to his Violin Concerto no. 8.

Scenes from Goethe's 'Faust', see FAUST.

Scenes of Childhood (Ger., *Kinderscenen*), set of 13 short piano pieces by Schumann, 1838, with titles alluding to childhood life.

Sch-, German spelling for Russian names better spelt in English 'Sh-'; see, e.g., SHEBALIN.

Schaeffer, Pierre [Henri Marie] (b. 1910), French composer and author. Pioneer in 1948–9 of CONCRETE MUSIC, exemplified in his *Study with Objects* and (in collaboration with Pierre Henry) *Symphony for a Lonely Man*.

Schafer, R[aymond] **Murray** (b. 1933), Canadian composer; at Simon Fraser University, Vancouver, he promoted much musical activity and researched 'acoustic ecology'. Works include *Requiems for the Party Girl* for soprano and nine instruments; *From the*

Tibetan Book of the Dead (text in Tibetan) for soprano, instruments, chorus, tape.

Schäffer, Bogusław [Julian] (b. 1929), Polish composer, pioneer in Poland of specifically modern (12-note, etc.) style. Works include *Non-Stop* (eight hours of music for piano), *Little Symphony, Collage and Form* for eight jazz musicians with symphony orchestra.

Scharwenka, [Franz] **Xaver** (1850–1924), German pianist and celebrated teacher (in Berlin, and in 1891–8 in New York); composer of piano solos (including *Polish Dances*), four piano concertos, opera *Mataswintha*, etc. His brother Philipp Scharwenka (1847–1917) was also a composer.

Schat, Peter (b. 1935), Dutch composer, pupil of Seiber in London. Works include opera *Reconstruction* (jointly composed with Jan van Vlijmen, Louis Andriessen, Reinbert de Leeuw, Misha Mengelberg); *First Essay on Electrocution* for violin, guitar and metal percussion; *Improvisations and Symphonies* for wind quartet.

Schauspieldirektor, Der, see IMPRESARIO.

Scheherazade, see SHEHERAZADE.

Scheidemann, Heinrich (*c.* 1596–1663), German organist who held a church post in Hamburg, having studied with Sweelinck in Amsterdam. Composer of organ music, etc.

Scheidt, Samuel (1587–1654), German organist and composer, especially of organ works (including hymn-tune harmonizations); church music, dance music, etc. His *Tabulatura nova* (1624) advocated staff notation for organ, in place of TABLATURE.

Schein, Johann Hermann (1586–1630), German composer, church musician in Leipzig. Works include hymns (some to his own words), instrumental dances, madrigals; his music shows Italian influence.

Schelomo, see SHELOMO.

Schemelli Hymn-book, usual name for the *Musical Song-book* published in 1736 by Georg Christian Schemelli (*c.* 1678–1762); its musical editor was Bach, who afterwards wrote chorale preludes on some of its hymn-tunes.

Schenker, Heinrich (1868–1935), Austrian composer (pupil of Bruckner) who was mainly important as theorist: he claimed that a single type of basic music structure underlies all the masterpieces written in the period from Bach to Brahms.

scherzando, direction that an impression of light-heartedness is to be given. Cp. SCHERZO.

Scherzi, Gli, another name for Haydn's RUSSIAN QUARTETS. Alludes to the character of the 'minuet' movements: see SCHERZO. (The title means 'The Scherzos'.)

scherzo (It., joke), a type of lively movement which historically – chiefly through Haydn, and, especially, Beethoven – developed from the minuet as used in symphonies, string quartets, etc. Usually therefore it is in the characteristic minuet form, AABA; and the B section is called the TRIO (as in the minuet). Usually also it is in 3/4 time. The original implication of humour is by no means always maintained, but fast tempo is obligatory and sentimentality is avoided. Examples exist also of the scherzo not as a movement of a larger work, but as an independent work of its own – notably Chopin's four for piano. See preceding entries.

scherzoso = SCHERZANDO.

Schicksalslied, see SONG OF DESTINY.

Schiff, András (b. 1953), Hungarian pianist who made his London début in 1976; noted in Bach.

Schiff, Heinrich (b. 1951), Austrian cellist who made his London début in 1973; also conductor, musical director of Northern Sinfonia from 1990.

Schiller, Johann Christoph Friedrich von (1759–1805), German poet and dramatist. See CHORAL SYMPHONY, DON CARLOS, KLEBE, LUISA MILLER, MAID OF ORLEANS, TURANDOT, WILLIAM TELL.

Schipa, Tito (forenames originally Raffaele Attilio Amadeo) (1888–1965), Italian tenor with prominent operatic career in Chicago and New York; also well known for concert performances.

Schlaginstrument(e) (Ger.), percussion instrument(s).

schleppend (Ger.), dragging; *nicht schleppend*, direction that the pace is not to be allowed to drag.

Schlick, Arnolt (before 1460–after 1521), German composer (born blind); author of an influential treatise on the organ. Works include song-arrangements for organ or lute.

Schluss (Ger.), end; *Schluss-Satz*, final section (see SATZ).

Schlüssel (Ger.), clef. (Not 'key', though in German *Schlüssel* literally means 'key', as *clef* (or *clé*) does in French.)

Schmelzer, Johann Heinrich (*c.*1623–80), Austrian composer (also violinist) in service at the Austrian court. Composed trio-sonatas and other chamber works; also chamber music, a Nuptial Mass, etc.

Schmidt, Franz (1874–1939), Austrian composer of oratorio *The Book with Seven Seals* (after Revelation); four symphonies, etc., in traditional Austrian-symphonic style; also pianist, organist and cellist.

Schmidt-Isserstedt, Hans (1900–1973), German conductor; founder-conductor of the Hamburg Radio Symphony Orchestra, 1945–71; composer of opera and orchestral works.

Schmieder, Wolfgang (b. 1901), German musicologist. See BACH (J.S.).

Schmitt, Florent (1870–1958), French composer, pupil of Massenet, Fauré and others; also pianist and writer on music. Works include ballets *The Tragedy of Salome* and *Oriane and the Prince of Love*; choral setting of Psalm 46; Legend for saxophone and orchestra; various pieces of chamber music (including a quartet for three trombones and tuba); many piano solos.

Schnabel, Artur (1882–1951), Austrian pianist and noted teacher; driven from Germany by the Nazis, settled in USA, died in Geneva. Composer of three symphonies, etc.

Schnebel, Dieter (b. 1930), German composer (also Lutheran minister) whose works use non-musical and non-sound effects. Works include *Nostalgia* (*Visible Music II*) for conductor alone; *Ki-no*, night music for projectors and listeners, etc.

schnell (Ger.), fast; *schneller*, faster. See also following entry.

Schneller (Ger.), an ornament classified as a variety of MORDENT, the main note moving quickly to the note above (only once) and back again; often designated by a small wavy line above the written note.

Schnittke, Alfred [Garyevich] (b. 1934), Russian composer of part-German descent who spent boyhood years in Vienna. Works, many initially winning notice chiefly outside USSR, include four symphonies, four violin concertos, and *Minnesang* (old Ger., love-song) for 48 solo voices.

Schobert, Johann (c.1740–67), German harpsichordist and composer who lived in Paris from 1760 and died there (of eating toadstools mistaken for mushrooms). Wrote harpsichord solos and concertos, etc.; influenced Mozart, whose first four numbered keyboard concertos were arrangements of Schobert and other composers.

Schoek, Othmar (1886–1957), Swiss composer and conductor, pupil of Reger. Works include a violin concerto, horn concerto, operas and many songs – with accompaniments for piano, for chamber groups and for orchestra.

Schoenbach, Dieter, see SCHÖNBACH.

Schoenberg, Arnold (1874–1951), Austrian-born composer who worked in Germany and then (driven out by the Nazis as a Jew and a composer of 'decadent' music) from 1933 in USA, thereafter changing the spelling of his name from the original 'Schönberg'. Died in Los Angeles. At first composed in post-Romantic style (e.g. in TRANSFIGURED NIGHT, *Gurrelieder* – see SONGS OF GURRE); by 1908, however, he had developed a technique of ATONALITY (keylessness) shown e.g. in PIERROT LUNAIRE; afterwards he systematized this into TWELVE-NOTE technique (from about 1923) – later of great influence internationally. He himself varied in strictness of adherence to this technique, relaxing it (i.e. admitting the idea of key), e.g. in his late ODE TO NAPOLEON. Several works use SPEECH-SONG, invented by him (and also influential). Other works include opera MOSES AND AARON, monodrama EXPECTATION (*Erwartung*), cantata A SURVIVOR FROM WARSAW, a piano concerto, violin concerto, symphonic poem PELLÉAS AND MÉLISANDE, two CHAMBER SYMPHONIES, four string quartets, various songs and piano pieces. Also writer of textbooks on music, etc. See DONATONI, FLEXATONE.

Schönbach, Dieter (b. 1931), German-born composer, also conductor. Works include *Colours and Sounds* for orchestra, *Lyric Songs* for soprano and two prepared pianos.

Schönberg, Arnold, see SCHOENBERG.

Schöne Müllerin, Die, see FAIR MAID OF THE MILL.

School for Fathers, the title by which is known in England (in E. J. Dent's translation) Wolf-Ferrari's comic opera *I quatro rusteghi* (It. [Venetian dialect], The Four Boors), produced (in German) in Munich, 1906. Libretto (in Italian) by G. Pizzolato, after a play by Goldoni, dealing with the comic outwitting of four curmudgeons.

Schoolmaster, The, nickname for Haydn's Symphony no. 55 in E♭, 1774 (Hob. I: 55), perhaps from the grave character of its second movement.

Schöpfung, Schöpfungsmesse, see CREATION, CREATION MASS.

Schottische (Ger. pl., Scottish), type of ballroom dance similar to polka, popular in the 19th century. The origin of the name is unknown; the dance is not the same as the ÉCOSSAISE, despite the name.

Schrammel quartet, type of Austrian light-music combination of two violins, guitar and accordion (named after Joseph Schrammel, 1850–93, leader of such a quartet).

Schreier, Peter (b. 1935), German tenor, celebrated in Mozart at Salzburg Festival, etc.; former member of East Berlin State Opera. Also conductor.

Schreker, Franz (1878–1934), Austrian composer. He was also the director of the Berlin State Music High School, 1920–32. Works include *The Distant Sound* (*Der ferne Klang*) and eight other operas, ballet after Oscar Wilde's *The Birthday of the Infanta*, songs with orchestra; also CHAMBER SYMPHONY (1916, notable for cultivation of the chamber orchestra, in contrast to the 'outsize' orchestrations then in vogue).

Schubert, Franz [Peter] (1797–1828), Austrian composer who was born and died in Vienna, and hardly ever left it. At first a choirboy. Never held an official musical post, and gained little recognition in life. But matured early – wrote song 'Gretchen at the Spinning-wheel' (*Gretchen am Spinnrade*) at 17. Often worked very fast, once producing eight songs in a day. Composed more than 600 songs of great range and subtlety (see ERLKING); regarded as founding the type of 19th-century German song (*Lied*).

Showed high individuality also in piano pieces – including sonatas, dances, WANDERER FANTASY, IMPROMPTUS, MOMENTS MUSICAUX; wrote also works for piano duet (see MARCHE militaire). His admiration for Rossini is evident e.g. in his *Overture in the Italian Style*; for Beethoven, in his string quartets (15 including DEATH AND THE MAIDEN, and also a QUARTET MOVEMENT) and symphonies – of which he never heard a performance of no. 8 (UNFINISHED) or of no. 9 (and last) the GREAT C MAJOR (this is sometimes called no. 7, but the symphony properly so called is in E, left in skeleton form and completed e.g. by J. F. Barnett and by Weingartner. For another possible symphony see GASTEIN.) The TRAGIC Symphony is no. 4. Other works include ALFONSO AND ESTRELLA and other operas; music to the play ROSAMUNDE, PRINCESS OF CYPRUS; a piano quintet (TROUT) and other chamber music (see ARPEGGIONE); six Latin Masses, and other church music. Unmarried. Died of typhus. His works are indexed by 'D' numbers, after the thematic catalogue published by O. E. Deutsch in 1951.

Schulhoff, Erwin (1894–1942), Czech pianist and composer in a variety of styles – influenced by Schoenberg and also by jazz. Works include six symphonies (no. 6 *Symphony of Freedom*), Concerto for string quartet and wind orchestra, many piano solos. Died in a Nazi concentration camp.

Schuller, Gunther (b. 1925), American composer (formerly horn-player), also conductor; president of the New England Conservatory (Boston), 1967–77. Several of his works use jazz performers (e.g. *Variants* for jazz quartet; *Con-*

versations for jazz quartet and string quartet). Other works include opera *The Visitation*; *American Triptych* for orchestra; *Museum Piece* for Renaissance instruments and orchestra.

Schuman, William [Howard] (b. 1910), American composer, pupil of R. Harris and others; 1945–61, head of the Juilliard School of Music, New York. Works include 10 symphonies (no. 5 *Symphony for Strings*); *American Festival Overture*; *William Billings Overture* and *New England Triptych* (both with reference to themes by BILLINGS); *A Free Song* and other cantatas; opera *The Mighty Casey* (about baseball), ballet *Undertow* (and a suite drawn from it), a piano concerto, violin concerto, chamber music.

Schumann, Clara [Josephine] (born Wieck; 1819–96), German pianist and composer, chiefly for piano; daughter of the composer Friedrich Wieck (1788–1873) and wife of R. Schumann (below). Made many visits to Britain; internationally noted as a performer of her husband's and other works, and also as a teacher.

Schumann, Elisabeth (1888–1952), German-born soprano, admired in operas by Mozart and R. Strauss; naturalized American, 1944.

Schumann, Robert [Alexander] (1810–56), German composer, also pianist, conductor and noted as critic with wide sympathies. Married Clara Wieck (see SCHUMANN, C.), 1840. Developed mental instability, in 1854 throwing himself into the Rhine; afterwards was in a mental asylum, where he died. His work shows ROMANTIC outlook and literary associations – as in the fanciful titles (some given after composition, however) of various piano works, e.g. ABEGG VARIATIONS, CARNIVAL, CARNIVAL JEST FROM VIENNA, KREISLERIANA, PAPILLONS, SCENES OF CHILDHOOD (see also DAVIDSBÜNDLER). Other works include many songs (some in cycles, e.g. POET'S LOVE, WOMAN'S LOVE AND LIFE); three string quartets, a piano concerto, cello concerto, violin concerto (not heard till 1937, being suppressed by Clara Schumann and Joachim as unworthy); four symphonies (no. 1 SPRING SYMPHONY, no. 3 RHENISH; no. 4 originally written directly after no. 1, later re-scored); cantata PARADISE AND THE PERI, opera *Genoveva*, *Scenes from Goethe's Faust* (see FAUST), incidental music to Byron's MANFRED.

Schumann-Heink (née Rössler), **Ernestine** (1861–1936), Austrian-born contralto who became a favourite singer at the New York Metropolitan Opera and was naturalized American in 1908.

Schurmann, Gerard (b. 1928), Dutch composer, Indonesian-born, resident in England (pupil of Rawsthorne); also conductor. Works include *Variants* for orchestra, a piano concerto, violin concerto; *Chuench'i* (song-cycle based on English translations of Chinese texts) – optionally with piano or with orchestra.

Schütz, Heinrich (1585–1672), German composer; studied under G. Gabrieli in Venice and worked mainly as court composer in Dresden; influential in introducing Italian musical ideas (as to vocal declamation, concerted instrumental writing, etc.) to Germany. Worked also in Copenhagen. Works include the earliest German opera, *Daphne* (music now lost); Italian madrigals; *Sacred Symphonies*, etc., for voices and instruments; three PAS-SIONS (Matthew, Luke, John), 'Resurrection' and CHRISTMAS Oratorios.

Schwanda the Bagpiper, see ŠVANDA THE BAGPIPER.

Schwanengesang, see SWAN SONG.

Schwartzendorf, see MARTINI (G.P.).

Schwarz, Gerard (b. 1947), American trumpeter, active in modern music and since 1978 also well known as conductor.

Schwarzkopf, Elisabeth (b. 1915), German soprano active e.g. at the Vienna State Opera, at Covent Garden (from 1947), and in recital. Hon.D.Mus., Cambridge, 1976.

Schweitzer, Albert (1875–1965), French (Alsatian) theologian, medical missionary, and musician – organist, and writer on Bach. Awarded the Nobel Prize, 1952.

Schwertsik, Kurt (b. 1935), Austrian composer (also pianist and formerly orchestral horn player). Works include fairy-tale opera *Fanferlizzy Sunnyfeet* (authorized English translation!); Concerto for alphorn and chamber orchestra; *Moment musical* for clarinet and piano.

Sciutti, Graziella (b. 1927), Italian soprano, eminent in opera; sang at La Scala, Milan, from 1955, and has occasionally been an operatic stage director.

scoop, colloquial term for a fault in singing – to glide up to a note disagreeably from below instead of attacking it cleanly.

scordatura (It., mis-tuning), the tuning of a stringed instrument to notes other

than the normal, for special effects – much used in the 17th century and revived in modern times; e.g. in Mahler's Symphony no. 4, a solo violinist has to tune all his/her strings up a tone to represent the unearthly fiddling of a 'dance of death'. See CONTRASTS.

score, a music-copy combining in ordered form all the different PARTS allotted to various performers of a piece; so (e.g. in an orchestral library) *score and parts*, meaning both the combined music-copy (for the conductor) and the separate copies containing just the music for particular instruments. So also *full score*, a score displaying every different participating voice and instrument; *short score*, a compressed version of the preceding, such as a composer may write out at first, when the outlines of his instrumentation are decided on but not the details; *open score*, a score displaying every part on a separate line – particularly for study or academic exercise, in cases when normal reasons of economy and convenience would suggest compression on to fewer staves; *miniature score* or *pocket score* or *study score*, one which reproduces all the details of a full score but is of a size more suitable for study than for a conductor's desk; *vocal score* (or, US, *piano-vocal score*), one giving all the voice-parts of a work but having the orchestral parts reduced to a piano part; *piano score*, one in which not only the orchestral parts but also the vocal parts (if any) are all reduced to a piano part. So also *to score*, to arrange a work for a particular combination of voices and/or instruments (whether this is part of the process of original composition, or in itself a process of arrangement of an already existing work).

scorrevole (It.), scurrying, with rapid fluency.

Scots snap, name for a rhythmic figure consisting of a short note on the beat followed by a longer one held until the next beat, e.g. ♩♪ Found in Scottish folk-music, but also elsewhere, e.g. in Hungarian folk-music, and in Purcell (as in the setting of English words like 'ruin'd').

Scott, Cyril [Meir] (1879–1970), British composer who trained mainly in Germany and won considerable success there and in England up to about 1930 – particularly with songs and piano pieces; nicknamed 'the English Debussy'. Also composed three operas (only one produced, in Germany); a piano concerto and various other concertos; choral works; two string trios and other chamber music. Writer on music and also on occultism, food reform, etc.

Scott, Francis George (1880–1958), British composer (pupil of Roger-Ducasse in Paris) who composed mainly songs to Scottish verse, but also orchestral works, songs to French and German verse, etc.

Scott, [Sir] **Walter** (1771–1832), British novelist and poet. See BOÏELDIEU, FAIR MAID OF PERTH, IVANHOE, LUCIA DI LAMMERMOOR, MARSCHNER, PURITANS.

Scottish National Orchestra, orchestra founded in 1950, succeeding a previous Scottish Orchestra; conductor 1959–84, Alexander Gibson, then Neeme Järvi till 1988, succeeded by Bryden Thomson.

'Scottish' (in former use 'Scotch') **Symphony,** nickname for Mendelssohn's Symphony no. 3, completed in 1842, dedicated to Queen Victoria, and inspired originally by the composer's visit to Scotland, 1829. No detailed scheme of allusions, however, has been discovered to be behind the music.

Scotto, Renata (b. 1933), Italian soprano, eminent in opera; at La Scala, Milan, from 1953; has recorded over 30 operas.

Scriabin(e), Alexander, see SKRYABIN.

Sculthorpe, Peter [Joshua] (b. 1929), Australian composer, pupil of Rubbra and Wellesz at Oxford. Has written orchestral works (e.g. series entitled *Sun Music*); *Love 200* for two singers, pop group and orchestra; nine string quartets; film scores, etc.

Sea, The (Fr., *La Mer*), 'three symphonic sketches' by Debussy, first performed in 1905: (1) 'From Dawn to Midday on the Sea'; (2) 'Play of the Waves'; (3) 'Dialogue of the Wind and the Sea'. See also BRIDGE (F.).

Sea Pictures, cycle of five songs by Elgar for contralto and orchestra, 1899 – poems by various writers including (no. 2) Elgar's wife.

Searle, Humphrey (1915–82), British composer, pupil of Webern in Austria. Works include a trilogy using speakers and orchestra – *Gold Coast Customs* (text, Edith Sitwell), *The Riverrun* (James Joyce), *The Shadow of Cain* (Edith Sitwell); operas *The Diary of a Madman, The Photo of the Colonel* and HAMLET (respectively after Gogol, Ionesco, Shakespeare); five symphonies. CBE, 1968. Was also writer on music.

Seasons, The, (1) oratorio by Haydn (Ger., *Die Jahreszeiten*), first performed in Vienna, 1801 (Hob. XXI: 3), to a German text based on an English poem by James Thomson; (2) ballet with music by Glazunov, produced in 1900. See also FOUR SEASONS.

Sea Symphony, A, title of Vaughan Williams's Symphony no. 1 – which, however, was (in conformity with his practice) given no number by him. In four movements, it is a setting, for soprano, baritone, chorus, and orchestra, of verse by Whitman. First performed in 1910.

sec (Fr., dry), direction that a note or chord is to be struck and released sharply.

secco, see RECITATIVE.

Sechter, Simon (1788–1867), Austrian organist, composer, and noted theorist and teacher of counterpoint. Bruckner studied with him and Schubert intended to do so (dying before he could).

second (noun), an interval in melody or harmony, reckoned as taking two steps in the (major or minor) scale, counting the bottom and top notes: either a *minor second* (one semitone, e.g. C up to D♭), or *major second* (two semitones, e.g. C up to D), or *augmented second* (three semitones, e.g. C up to D♯). The last gives what is equivalent in practice to the minor third, e.g. C up to E♭, but the terms imply different harmonic contexts. See also following entries.

second (adjective), term implying the performance of a lower-pitched part (*second tenor, second trombone, second violins,* etc.) and usually – but not in

choirs – also implying an inferiority in rank to the 'first' of the kind. (For *second inversion,* see POSITION.)

secondary dominant, see DOMINANT.

secondo (It., second), the lower of the two parts in a piano duet.

Secret Marriage, The (It., *Il matrimonio segreto*), comic opera by Cimarosa, produced (in Italian) in Vienna, 1792. Libretto by G. Bertati, a comedy of intrigue based on the English play, *The Clandestine Marriage,* by Garrick and Colman.

Secret of Susanna, The, see SUSANNA'S SECRET.

Seefried, Irmgard (1919–88), German soprano resident in Austria, active 1943–77 at the Vienna State Opera, and internationally noted also as recitalist. Her husband was Wolfgang Schneiderhan (b. 1915), Austrian violinist: Henze's *Ariosi* (1963, on poems by Tasso) for soprano, violin and orchestra was written for them.

Seeger, Ruth Crawford, see CRAWFORD.

segno (It.), sign; *dal segno* (or *DS*), from the sign, i.e. repeat the preceding passage beginning at the appropriate sign (usually 𝄋).

Segovia, Andrés (1893–1987), Spanish guitarist, for whom many works (e.g. by Castelnuovo-Tedesco and Rodrigo) were specially written. His artistry was chiefly responsible for the 20th-century revival of the guitar as a 'classical' instrument.

segue (It., [it] follows), term used as a direction to the performer to proceed with the next section without a break.

seguidilla, type of quick Spanish dance

in triple time, often accompanied by castanets.

Seiber, Mátyás [György] (1905–60), Hungarian-born composer (formerly also cellist), pupil of Kodály, resident in England from 1935; was also conductor and noted teacher. Works include cantata ULYSSES, three string quartets, a violin concerto, clarinet concertino, two orchestral suites based on old lute music, folk-song arrangements, educational piano works, film and radio music.

Seixas, José (1704–42), Portuguese organist and composer of sonatas and dances, etc., for harpsichord; also choral works, etc.

Semele, work by Handel, first performed in 1744: it is of oratorio type, though not based on a biblical subject but on Semele's love for Jupiter. Text adapted from the libretto written by Congreve for John Eccles's opera *Semele*, intended for performance about 1705, but not then given.

semibreve, see WHOLE-NOTE.

semi-chorus, a section of a choral body – not necessarily exactly half of the full chorus.

semidemisemiquaver, an unusual equivalent of hemidemisemiquaver: see SIXTY-FOURTH-NOTE.

semi-opera, modern term for certain 17th- and 18th-century English stage works (particularly Purcell's, e.g. KING ARTHUR) in which music, although a principal element, is not so all-pervading as to justify the title of 'opera' as now understood. In Purcell's own time, however, the word 'opera' was freely used for these.

semiquaver, see SIXTEENTH-NOTE.

Semiramide, Semiramis, opera by Rossini, produced in Venice, 1823. Libretto by G. Rossi (after Voltaire) about the ancient queen of Nineveh. (Semiramis is the accepted historical form, Semiramide an Italianization of it.)

semitone, the smallest interval commonly used in European music – on the piano, the interval between any note and the next note, higher or lower (whether this next note happens to be white or black). Cp. TONE (3).

semplice (It.), simple, simply.

sempre (It.), always; *sempre più mosso*, always getting faster, i.e. getting faster and faster.

Senaillé [or Senallié], **Jean Baptiste** (1687–1730), French violinist and composer, pupil of Vitali in Italy; member of the orchestra at the French court. Wrote many sonatas for violin – from one of which comes an 'Allegro spiritoso' now heard in various arrangements.

Senesino (i.e. 'the man from Siena'), professional name of Francesco Bernardi (*c.* 1680–1759), Italian castrato who sang in 13 of Handel's operas, under the composer's direction.

Senfl, Ludwig (*c.* 1490–1543), Swiss-born composer who, after studying with Isaac, took service with the (Austrian) imperial court and then with the Bavarian court at Munich. Composed choral song-settings, more than 300 of which survive; also motets, Masses, etc.

senza (It.), without.

septet, (1) a performing group of seven instrumentalists or singers; (2) a com-

359

position for such: if instrumental, and actually entitled 'Septet', it will probably have the character of a SONATA for seven performers, in several movements.

septimole, septolet = SEPTUPLET.

septuplet, a group of seven notes (or notes and rests) of equal time-value, written where a group of three, four or some other number of notes is suggested by the time-signature, e.g. a seven-note group occupying a bar of 3/4 time, written

sequence, (1) the repetition of a phrase at a higher or lower pitch than the original: if the intervals within it are slightly altered in the repetition so as to avoid moving out of key, it is a *tonal sequence*, if they are unaltered, it is a *real sequence*; (2) hymn-like composition with non-biblical Latin text, sung during the Roman Catholic High Mass or Requiem Mass; some sequences have been set by various composers. See STABAT MATER; (3) term used by Berio (It., *sequenza*) as title of a series of works for different solo instruments, unaccompanied.

sequenza, see preceding.

Seraglio, The, workably short title for Mozart's comic opera. *The Abduction from the Seraglio* (Ger., *Die Entführung aus dem Serail*) (K384), produced in Vienna, 1782. Libretto by C. F. Bretzner and G. Stephanie, with a non-singing part for the benevolent Pasha who eventually releases his European captives. In 19th-century England this work was given in Italian, hence the style of title *Il seraglio*; but this has now no claim to general usage.

Serebrier, José (b. 1938), Uruguayan composer of orchestral *Variations on a Theme from Childhood* and other works; also conductor in USA, Europe, Australia; festival director in Miami. Resident in USA and Britain.

serenade, properly a piece of open-air evening music (cp. AUBADE), e.g. a lover's song outside his mistress's window, but now a term of the widest and vaguest significance. The classical (18th-century) use of the term indicates a piece for several instruments (often wind instruments only) written in several movements of which the first is in SONATA-FORM and one at least of the others is a minuet. A German equivalent is *Nachtmusik* (as in EINE KLEINE NACHTMUSIK), or, for the song-type, *Ständchen*. See also HASSAN and the following entries.

Serenade, title of a song-cycle by Britten for tenor with accompaniment of horn and string orchestra, first performed in 1943. The words, by various poets, have a general association with evening or night.

'Serenade' Quartet, nickname for a famous string quartet in F, long known as Haydn's op. 3 no. 5, but now thought to be by a contemporary of his, R. Hoffstetter: its slow movement (violin melody, plucked-string accompaniment) is reminiscent of a song sung as a serenade with guitar.

Serenade to Music, work by Vaughan Williams for 16 solo voices and orchestra, written in honour of Henry Wood's jubilee as a conductor and first performed in 1938. Words adapted from Shakespeare's *The Merchant of Venice*.

serenata (It.), (1) a serenade, e.g. the popular piece by Braga so entitled, or

Mozart's *Serenata notturna* (1776) for two orchestras (K239), or C. Nielsen's *Serenata in vano* (It., Serenade in Vain) for five instruments, 1914; (2) 18th-century English term for a type of cantata approaching operatic form, e.g. Handel's ACIS AND GALATEA.

seria, see OPERA SERIA.

serial technique, see SERIES.

series, a set of notes treated in composition not mainly as a recognizable theme, but as a kind of plastic material from which the composition is made. The order of the notes in the series is considered its main characteristic: though the series can be turned upside-down, backwards etc., a relationship to this order must be preserved. The 'note-row' in TWELVE-NOTE technique is the main example of such a series, but other serial techniques are possible. Hence *serialism*, usually referring to the practice of 12-note technique. The term *multi-serialism* or *total serialism* is applied to composition in which not only pitch is treated serially, but also other dimensions ('parameters') of music – e.g. time-values, volume, force of attack – these being similarly placed in a given mathematical order (e.g. certain works of Boulez, Berio, Nono in the 1950s).

Serious Songs, see FOUR SERIOUS SONGS.

Serkin, Peter (b. 1947), American pianist with public career from age 12. Founder of ensemble 'Tashi' (1973), devoted to modern music. Son of the following.

Serkin, Rudolf (b. 1903), Austrian pianist of Russian origin, naturalized American, 1939. Noted as soloist and as partner of Adolf Busch, violinist (1891–1952), whose daughter he married. Also composer. Father of preceding.

Sermisy, Claude (or Claudin) **de** (c. 1490–1562), French composer (and priest); wrote more than 200 chansons, also Masses, motets, etc. As a singer of the French Chapel Royal he attended François I at his meeting with Henry VIII at the Field of the Cloth of Gold, 1520. (See FAYRFAX.)

Serocki, Kazimierz (1922–81), Polish composer (also pianist), active in promoting modern music. Works include *Forte e piano* for two pianos and orchestra, *Niobe* for two narrators, chorus and orchestra; also song-cycles, some with orchestral accompaniment.

Serov, Alexander Nikolayevich (1820–71), Russian composer of operas (including *Judith* and *The Power of Evil*), orchestral works, a Stabat Mater, etc.

serpent, obsolete large S-shaped bass wind instrument (of a family related to the CORNETT) with finger-holes and sometimes keys; usually made of wood but sometimes of metal. It was used e.g. in military bands and in churches up to the mid 19th century. Modified versions were the so-called Russian bassoon and the (English) 'bass horn' from which developed the OPHICLEIDE which ousted the serpent from concert use.

serré (Fr., tightened), with increasing speed and tension (It., *stringendo*).

Serva padrona, La, see MAID AS MISTRESS.

service, term used for a musically unified setting of the Anglican canticles for morning or evening prayer, or for the Communion service; *short ser-vice* and *great service*, terms used in the 16th and early 17th centuries to distinguish between less and more elaborate settings. Note the antithesis between *service* (setting of prescribed liturgical text) and ANTHEM (to the composer's own choice of text).

sesquialtera, a type of MIXTURE stop on the organ. (From Latin, expressing the ratio of 3:2 between certain lengths of pipes.)

Sessions, Roger [Huntington] (1896–1985), American composer, pupil of Bloch and others; lived for several years in Europe; noted teacher. Works include eight symphonies, a violin concerto (with orchestra including five clarinets and no violins), operas *The Trial of Lucullus* and *Montezuma*, cantata *Turn O Libertad* (Whitman), three piano sonatas.

sestet, obsolete equivalent of SEXTET.

Seter, Mordecai (b. 1916), Russian-born Israeli composer who studied with Dukas and others in Paris. Works include *Ricercar* for strings, oratorio *Midnight Vigil*, symphony *Jerusalem* (with chorus).

Ševčík, Otakar (1852–1934), Czech violinist, famous as teacher in Prague, London and various US cities.

Seven Last Words of our Saviour on the Cross, The (Ger., *Die sieben Worte des Erlösers am Kreuz*), orchestral work by Haydn (Hob. XX: 2) in the form of seven slow movements for performance in Cadiz cathedral (1785) as 'incidental music' to a Lenten service when the 'Words' (actually sentences) were read and preached on. Haydn arranged the music later for string quartet and for piano, and later still

as a cantata, the text including the 'Words' themselves.

seventh, an interval in melody or harmony, reckoned as taking seven steps in the (major or minor) scale, counting bottom and top notes. The *major seventh* is the distance e.g. from A up to the next G♯; one semitone less gives the *minor seventh* (e.g. A up to G♮), and one further semitone less gives the *diminished seventh* (e.g. A up to G♭). This last is virtually equivalent in practice to the major sixth (e.g. A up to F♯), but is used in a different harmonic context, especially when the *diminished-seventh chord* (e.g. A, C, E♭, G♭), is sounded or implied – see DIMINISHED.

Sévérac, [Joseph Marie] **Déodat de** (1872–1921), French composer, pupil of Magnard and d'Indy. Works include three operas, orchestral and chamber works, songs (some in the old Provençal language), many piano pieces.

sextet, (1) a performing group of six instrumentalists or singers; (2) a piece for six performers; if instrumental, and actually entitled 'Sextet', it will probably have the character of a SONATA for six performers, in several movements.

sextolet = SEXTUPLET.

sextuplet, a group of six notes (or notes and rests) of equal time-value, written where a group of four, five or some other number of notes would be suggested by the time-signature, e.g. a group of six notes occupying a bar of

4/4, written 𝅘𝅥𝅘𝅥𝅘𝅥𝅘𝅥𝅘𝅥𝅘𝅥

sf., abbr. of SFORZANDO.

sfogato (It., evaporated), direction used

e.g. by Chopin to indicate an airy, delicate manner of performance.

sforzando, sforzato (It., reinforced), direction that a note or chord is to be played in a 'forced' manner, i.e. with special emphasis.

sfp., abbr. signifying that a SFORZANDO is to be followed by a (sudden) softness of tone.

sfz., abbr. of SFORZANDO.

Sgambati, Giovanni (1841–1914), Italian pianist (pupil of Liszt) and composer of two symphonies, various piano works, etc.

shake, see TRILL.

Shakespeare, William (1564–1616), English poet and dramatist. See BEATRICE AND BENEDICK, BENTOIU, BERLIOZ, CASTIGLIONI, CORIOLANUS, DITTERSDORF, EATON, ELGAR, ESPOSITO, FAIRY QUEEN, FALSTAFF, FIBICH, FINZI, FOERSTER, FOREST, GATTY, GERMAN (Edward), GIANNINI, GOETZ, GOLDMARK (Karl), GOUNOD, GREENSLEEVES, HAHN, HALÉVY, HAMLET, HARBISON, HOLST, HUMFREY, JOACHIM, JOHNSON (Robert, 2), JULIUS CAESAR, KABELÁČ, KETTING, KING LEAR, KNOT GARDEN, KREJČI, LOCKE, MACBETH, MACDOWELL, MACFARREN, MANCINELLI, MARTIN, MENDELSSOHN, MERRY WIVES OF WINDSOR, MIDSUMMER NIGHT'S DREAM, MIGNON, MINES OF SULPHUR, MORLEY, OBERON, ORFF, OTELLO, OTHELLO, PACINI, PERSICHETTI, PINSUTI, POMP AND CIRCUMSTANCE, PROKOFIEV, ROMEO AND JULIET, ROSSELLINI, SALIERI, SEARLE, SHEBALIN, SIBELIUS, STORACE, STRAUSS (Richard), SUTERMEISTER, SVIRIDOV, TALMA, TAMING OF THE SHREW, TCHAIKOVSKY, TEMPEST, VERACINI, WILSON, ZANDONAI, ZINGARELLI.

shakuhachi (or as two words, *shaku hachi*), type of Japanese endblown bamboo flute.

Shalyapin, Feodor Ivanovich (1873–1938), Russian bass singer noted in Russian opera – brought to London and Paris by Diaghilev, 1913 – and latterly in recital. After the 1917 Russian Revolution he was at first treated as a distinguished artist of the Soviet régime, but afterwards he settled abroad and died in Paris. (The form 'Chaliapin(e)' is a French spelling of his surname; the name has a stress on the 'ya'.)

shamisen, variant spelling of SAMISEN.

Shankar, Ravi (b. 1920), Indian sitarist, composer and lecturer. Works include a concerto for sitar and orchestra, music for *Pather Panchali* and other films. He was to a considerable degree responsible for the new vogue in the West for Indian music arising in the 1950s.

shanty, type of sailors' work-song, dating from the era of sail-power and unmechanized ships, suitable for aiding such rhythmical movements as pulling together on a rope. The spelling 'chanty' is a 'literary' form introduced to emphasize the probable derivation from the French imperative *chantez* (sing).

Shapero, Harold [Samuel] (b. 1920), American composer of a symphony, *Nine-minute Overture*, piano solos, cantata on Hebrew texts, etc.; also conductor and university teacher.

Shapey, Ralph (b. 1921), American

composer, also university teacher. Works include a symphony, chamber symphony, seven string quartets.

Shaporin, Yury [Alexandrovich] (1887–1966), Russian composer, pupil of Glazunov, N. Tcherepnin and others. Works include a symphony, patriotic cantatas, opera *The Decembrists* (alluding to a Russian political conspiracy of December 1825), piano sonatas, songs, etc.

sharp, term indicating a raising in pitch – either (1) indeterminately as when a singer is said to sing sharp, by mistake; or (2) precisely by a semitone, as represented by the sign ♯; so G♯ (G sharp), the note a semitone higher than G♮ (G natural); so also, e.g., *B*♯ – a notation which is sometimes required by the 'grammar' of music, though on e.g. the piano the note is identical with C♮ (C natural). So DOUBLE-SHARP; *sharp keys*, those having sharps in their key-signatures; *in four sharps*, in the key of E major or C♯ minor, the key-signature of which is four sharps (and similarly with other keys); *sharpened fourth* (US, *sharped . . .*), the raising of the fourth degree of the scale by a semitone.

Sharp, Cecil [James] (1859–1924), British musician who, after holding an organist's and other posts, concentrated on reviving English folk-songs and folk-dances – collecting, editing, performing and writing about them; regarded as the leader of the English folk-music revival in the late 19th century.

Shaw, George Bernard (1856–1950), Irish dramatist (also music critic). See CHOCOLATE SOLDIER, CONSTANT, CORNO.

Shaw, Martin [Fallas] (1875–1958), British composer (church music, songs, etc.), organist and editor of hymn-books, etc.

shawm, obsolete double-reed woodwind instrument, forerunner of the oboe; made in several sizes, the larger (lower-pitched) ones being called BOMBARD or 'pommer'. (Shawm and CHALUMEAU are cognate words.)

Shchedrin, Rodion [Konstantinovich] (b. 1932), Russian composer of ballet *The Little Hump-backed Horse*, opera *Not Only Love*, two piano concertos, songs, *Carmen Suite* (for ballet, transcribed from Bizet's CARMEN), etc. Is also pianist.

Shcherbachev, Vladimir [Vassilevich] (1889–1952), Russian composer (though born in Warsaw); pupil of Lyadov and others; noted teacher. Works include five symphonies, a piano suite on poems by Alexander Blok, opera, film music.

Shebalin, Vissarion [Yakovlevich] (1902–63), Russian composer, pupil of Myaskovsky. Works include five symphonies and a 'dramatic symphony' with singers entitled *Lenin*; opera THE TAMING OF THE SHREW; piano sonatas; music to plays and films. Made a completion of Musorgsky's SOROCHINTSY FAIR.

Sheherazade, (1) symphonic suite by Rimsky-Korsakov, 1888 – Sheherazade being a sultan's wife (in the *Arabian Nights*) who tells stories to stave off her execution (the ballet set to this music, 1910, is on a scenario quite distinct from Rimsky-Korsakov's); (2) a set of three songs with orchestra, 1903, by Ravel; the poems, by Tristan Klingsor, are on oriental subjects, but despite the title (in French 'Shéhér-azade') there is no direct allusion in the songs to the *Arabian Nights* charac-ter. (The form *Scheherazade*, common in references to Rimsky-Korsakov's work, represents the German spelling of the Russian title.)

Shelley, Percy, Bysshe (1792–1822), British poet. See GOLDSCHMIDT.

Shelomo (Heb., Solomon), rhapsody for cello and orchestra by Bloch, first per-formed in 1917; the reference is to Solomon as depicted in the Bible. The form *Schelomo*, more common, repre-sents a German spelling of the Hebrew name; *Shelomo* (accent on middle syll-able) represents an English translitera-tion.

Shepherd, Arthur (1880–1958), American composer of two sym-phonies (no. 1 originally called *Hori-zons* and incorporating some tradi-tional cowboy songs), string quartets, cantatas, etc. Also conductor and uni-versity teacher.

Shepherd, John, see SHEPPARD.

Sheppard, John (*c*.1515–*c*.1560), Eng-lish composer of Latin and English church music; organist of Magdalen College, Oxford, and a member of the Chapel Royal.

Sheridan, Richard Brinsley (1751–1816), Irish dramatist. See BARBER, DUENNA, GERHARD, GIORDANI (T.), LINLEY (both entries).

Sheriff, Noam (b. 1935), Israeli com-poser; born in Palestine, but studied with Blacher in Berlin. Works include *Metamorphoses on a Galliard* for orch-estra; electronic music for ballet *Cain*; a piano sonata.

Shield, William (1748–1829), British composer, also violinist and viola-player; pupil of Avison. Master of the King's Music, 1817, and composer to Covent Garden Theatre. Wrote operas and other stage pieces, often in-corporating (as was then customary in England) items by other composers; also songs, string quartets, etc. Excep-tionally for his period, composed some music in 5/4 time. Also writer of musi-cal textbooks.

Shifrin, Seymour (1926–79), Ameri-can composer, pupil of Milhaud (in Paris) and others; also university teacher. Works include *Satires of Cir-cumstance* for mezzo-soprano and six instruments; five string quartets; a chamber symphony.

Shirley, James (1596–1666), English dramatist. See CUPID AND DEATH.

Shirley-Quirk, John (b. 1931), British baritone, prominent in Britten's operas with the (former) English Opera Group; is also noted recitalist.

Shnitke, Alfred, see SCHNITTKE. (He prefers the ancestral German form of his Russian name.)

shofar (Heb.), wind instrument made of a ram's horn, stipulated in the Old Testament for religious ritual and still used on the most solemn occasions in the synagogue. Simulated, with refer-ence to this, in Elgar's oratorio THE APOSTLES.

Sholokhov, Mikhail Alexandrovich (b. 1905), Russian writer. See DZERZH-INSKY.

short score, see SCORE.

Shostakovich, Dmitry [Dmitrievich] (1906–75), Russian composer (pupil of Glazunov); also pianist. At 19, wrote very successful Symphony no. 1 (14 others followed, including no. 7, LENINGRAD Symphony; no. 13, BABI YAR; no. 14 for soprano and bass soloists with chamber orchestra). Denounced by Soviet officialdom for unmelodiousness, freakishness, etc. in 1936 (after his opera *Lady Macbeth of the Mtsensk District* – see KATERINA ISMAILOVA); again denounced, for FORMALISM and other 'faults', in 1948 (after such works as his orchestral *Poem of Fatherland*). In each case admitted his 'errors', and endeavoured to find a style reconciling his individuality and Soviet offical views on what music should be like. Also composed other operas; *The Golden Age* and other ballets; *Songs of the Forests* and other cantatas to patriotic Soviet texts; songs and piano pieces (including three sets of preludes and fugues); concerto for piano, trumpet, and orchestra; two violin concertos; 15 string quartets, a piano quintet; film music, etc. Re-orchestrated Musorgsky's BORIS GODUNOV and made a completion and orchestration of Musorgsky's THE KHOVANSKY AFFAIR. His son Maxim (b. 1938) is a pianist and conductor.

Shtcherbatchev, Vladimir Vassilevich, see SHCHERBACHEV.

si, the note B (in Latin countries and formerly elsewhere); cp. TE.

Sibelius, Jean (real first names Johan Julian Christian) (1865–1957), Finnish composer who studied in Berlin and Vienna. Was enabled by a Finnish government grant to give up teaching and concentrate on composing from 1897. Married a sister of Järnefelt. Much of his work has Finnish 'national' associations sometimes relating to the 'Kalevala' (Finnish national epic poem) – e.g. A SAGA, KARELIA (overture and suite), THE SWAN OF TUONELA, LEMMINKÄINEN'S HOMECOMING, FINLANDIA, TAPIOLA. In his last 30 years he published almost nothing. Of his seven symphonies, the last is in one movement only. Other works include a violin concerto; small orchestral pieces including *Valse triste* (see VALSE); an unpublished opera; many songs in Finnish and Swedish; incidental music to A. Paul's KING CHRISTIAN II, Maeterlinck's PELLÉAS AND MÉLISANDE, H. Procope's BELSHAZZAR'S FEAST, Shakespeare's THE TEMPEST, and other plays.

siciliana (It.), type of song or instrumental piece (also *siciliano* and in French *sicilienne*) derived presumably from some Sicilian dance: much cultivated in the 18th century, it is in slow 6/8 (or sometimes 12/8) time, usually in a minor key.

side-drum, see SNARE-DRUM.

Siege of Corinth, The (Fr., *Le Siège de Corinthe*), opera by Rossini, produced in Paris, 1826. It was a revised French version of Rossini's earlier Italian opera *Mahomet II* (It., *Maometto II*) produced in Naples, 1820, with libretto by C. della Valle. The plot concerns the love of an 18th-century Muslim conqueror for the daughter of the Christian Governor of Corinth.

Siege of Rhodes, The, opera produced in London (1656) and reckoned the first English opera. The music (now lost) was contributed by Locke, H. Lawes, H. Cooke, Coleman and Hudson. Libretto by W. Davenant, referring to the Turkish siege (1480–81) of the last Christian outpost then surviving in the Mediterranean.

Siegfried, see RING; also next entry.

Siegfried Idyll, work by Wagner, 1870, for small orchestra, celebrating the birth of his son Siegfried, and using themes from his opera of that name (not yet produced).

Siegmeister, Elie (b. 1909), American composer, also writer on music; pupil of Riegger and N. Boulanger. Works include eight symphonies; *The Plough and the Stars* (on O'Casey's play) and other operas; a sextet for brass and percussion.

Sienkiewicz, Henryk (1846–1916), Polish writer. See NOWOWIEJSKI.

Siepi, Cesare (b. 1923), Italian bass, eminent in opera, particularly at the New York Metropolitan for 23 seasons from 1950.

sight-reading, sight-singing, the playing or singing of music at first sight.

signature, see KEY-SIGNATURE, TIME-SIGNATURE; *signature-tune*, a piece (whether or not specially written) used by a radio or TV programme, etc., at each performance as a means of identification.

Silja, Anja (b. 1940), German soprano who made her operatic début at 16; celebrated particularly in Wagner (Bayreuth Festival from 1960); married Christoph von Dohnányi.

Silken Ladder, The (It., *La scala di seta*), comic opera by Rossini, produced in Venice, 1812. Libretto by G. Rossi; the ladder conveys a lover to his lady's room.

Sills, Beverly (real name Belle Miriam Silverman) (b. 1929), American soprano, celebrated chiefly in coloratura roles of Italian opera; at New York City Opera from 1955, at Metropolitan from 1975; Covent Garden, 1970. Director, New York City Opera, 1979–88.

Siloti, Alexander, see ZILOTI: the form 'Siloti', though common in Western references, assumes the German sound of 's' (= English 'z').

silver band, a BRASS BAND with instruments coated in what looks like silver.

similar motion, see MOTION.

simile (It., similar), term indicating that a phrase, etc., is to be performed in the same manner as a parallel phrase preceding it.

Simon Boccanegra, opera by Verdi, produced in Venice, 1857 (libretto by F. M. Piave); new version, with libretto altered by A. Boito, produced in Milan, 1881. Named after the historical 14th-century Doge of Venice, its hero.

simple interval, an interval of an eighth (octave) or less; see INTERVAL.

Simple Symphony, a symphony for string orchestra by Britten, 1934, 'entirely based on material from works which the composer wrote between the ages of nine and 12'. Used for a ballet, 1944.

simple time, a scheme of time-division in which the beat-unit is divisible by 2 – e.g. 4/4, in which the beat-time is the quarter-note (crotchet) divided into two eighth-notes (quavers). Cp. COMPOUND TIME.

Simpson (or Sympson), Christopher (c.1605–1669), English player of the (bass) viola da gamba, author of musical treatises, composer of various works for his instrument and for groups of strings. It is not certain whether he was related to Thomas Simpson (below).

Simpson, Robert [Wilfred Levick] (b. 1921), British composer (ten symphonies, 11 string quartets, piano solos, etc.), writer on music (book on C. Nielsen) and member of BBC music staff, 1951–80.

Simpson, Thomas (1582–after 1630), English viol-player and composer (dances, songs, etc.) who held various posts in Germany (by 1610 or earlier) and Denmark. It is not known whether he was related to Christopher Simpson (above).

Sinding, Christian (1856–1941), Norwegian composer (also pianist) who studied in Germany and in 1921–2 taught in USA. Besides RUSTLE OF SPRING and other piano pieces, wrote three symphonies, two concertos for violin and one for piano, etc., in Romantic style.

sinfonia (It.), symphony; *sinfonia concertante*, term applied to orchestral works of the Haydn–Mozart period with more than one solo instrument (see SYMPHONIE CONCERTANTE), and used by Walton and some other 20th-century composers for works with only one solo instrument (perhaps because it does not seem to emphasize, as 'concerto' does, the element of display). See also SYMPHONIA (the Greek form), SYMPHONY and the following entries. Also (mid-20th-century usage), a small symphony orchestra.

Sinfonia Antartica (It., Antarctic Symphony), title given by Vaughan Williams to his Symphony no. 7 (but, in conformity with his practice, not numbered by him), first performed in 1953. It is based on Vaughan Williams's music to the film *Scott of the Antarctic* (1949); each of the five movements is prefaced by a literary quotation, the last one from Scott's Journal.

Sinfonia da Requiem (It., Requiem Symphony), symphony by Britten, 1940, in three movements headed 'Lacrymosa', 'Dies Irae' and 'Requiem Aeternam' (titles of sections of the REQUIEM Mass).

sinfonietta (term formed as a diminutive from *sinfonia*, but not an authentic Italian word), a small (and probably rather light) symphony; also a performing name for a small orchestra.

Singakademie (Ger., singing-academy), title used by certain choirs in German-speaking countries.

singing saw, see SAW.

Singspiel (Ger., song-play), a type of opera. Although the term was more freely applied in the 18th century, modern usage confines it to the historical type of German opera popular in Germany and Austria in Mozart's time. Mozart's own THE SERAGLIO and THE MAGIC FLUTE are of this type – having spoken dialogue instead of recitative, and being in the vernacular tongue instead of Italian – but with music more central to the drama than with some earlier composers. Cp. HILLIER (J. A.).

Sinigaglia, Leone (1868–1944), Italian composer who, untypically, wrote no opera. Works include a string quartet and orchestral music – e.g. overture to Goldoni's comedy *The Row at Chioggia* (*Le baruffe chiozzotte*), and a suite of Piedmontese dances; pupil of Dvořák in Prague.

Sinopoli, Giuseppe (b. 1946), Italian conductor, also composer; conductor of the Philharmonia Orchestra since 1984. Appointed to Dresden post from 1992.

Sir John in Love, opera by Vaughan Williams, produced in London in 1929; libretto by composer, based on Shakespeare's *The Merry Wives of Windsor*; see also FALSTAFF and MERRY WIVES OF WINDSOR.

Sister Angelica (It., *Suor Angelica*), one-act opera by Puccini, produced in New York, 1918, along with two others – THE CLOAK preceding it and GIANNI SCHICCHI following, making a 'triptych' (It., *trittico*). Libretto by G. Forzano: Sister Angelica is a nun and the setting is a convent.

sistrum, ancient rattle-like percussion instrument with rings which jangled on a metal frame when the instrument was shaken.

sitar, an Indian long-necked lute with movable frets, and originally with three strings, now with 4–7, and sometimes sympathetic strings also. It is played with a plectrum worn on the right forefinger.

Sitkovetsky, Dmitry (b. 1945), Russian violinist who emigrated to the West in 1977; recorded the Mozart concertos as violinist-director.

Sitwell, Edith (1887–1964), British poet. See FAÇADE, SEARLE.

Sitwell, Osbert (1892–1969), British writer. See BELSHAZZAR'S FEAST.

Sitwell, Sacheverell (1897–1988), British poet. See RIO GRANDE.

Six, The (Fr., *Les Six*), name given to the French composers, Auric, Durey, Honegger, Milhaud, Poulenc and Tailleferre. It was invented in 1920 by the French critic Henri Collet (after these composers had together published an album of pieces) on the analogy of the Russian 'five' composers – see MIGHTY HANDFUL. Collet claimed that, inspired by Satie and Jean Cocteau, the 'Six' had brought a renaissance of French music. In fact the 'Six' did not remain a group, and only Honegger, Milhaud and Poulenc achieved wide fame.

sixteen-foot (as measurement of organ pipes, etc.), see FOOT.

sixteenth-note, the note ♬ considered as a time-value. This term is standard North American usage and, as mathematically corresponding to the element of time-signature represented by /16, should clearly be preferred to 'semiquaver', still surviving in British use. The corresponding rest is notated ♼

sixth, (1) an interval in melody or harmony, reckoned as taking six steps in the (major or minor) scale, counting the bottom and top notes. The *major sixth* is the distance e.g. from C up to A, *a minor sixth* (one semitone less) from C up to A♭, an *augmented sixth* (one semitone more) from C up to A♯. The last gives an interval which in practice is virtually the same as the 'diminished seventh' (C up to B♭) but the harmonic context implied is different. (2) term used in the phrase *Landino sixth* – see LANDINO. This refers to the sixth degree of the scale, not the interval of six notes as described above.

sixty-fourth-note, the note ♬ considered as a time-value. This term is standard North American usage and, as mathematically corresponding to the element of time-signature represented by

/64, should clearly be preferred to 'hemidemisemiquaver', still surviving in British use. The corresponding rest is notated ♪

Sjögren, [Johann Gustav] **Emil** (1853–1918), Swedish composer and organist who studied partly in Germany and wrote works for piano, organ, choir, etc., showing certain 'nationalist' characteristics.

Skalkottas, Nikos (1904–49), Greek composer (also violinist), pupil of Schoenberg; also made use of Greek folk-music. Works include suites for piano, *Greek Dances* for orchestra, three piano concertos, four string quartets – hardly any of this music being published in his lifetime.

Skelton, John (*c.*1460–1529), English poet. See CORNYSHE.

sketch, (1) a rough draft of a composition, or a musical jotting made by a composer as a 'germ' or reminder; so Beethoven's *Sketch-books*; (2) a short piece usually interpreting pictorial or other extra-musical ideas.

Skilton, Charles Sanford (1868–1941), American composer who studied American-Indian music and made use of it in many of his works – including operas and pieces for string quartet.

Skriabin, Alexander, see SKRYABIN.

Skrowaczewski, Stanisław (b. 1923), Polish conductor who worked in USA (naturalized in 1966) and was conductor of the Hallé Orchestra, 1984–91. Also composer.

Skryabin, Alexander [Nikolayevich] (1872–1915), Russian composer, pupil of Taneyev and others; also virtuoso pianist, touring greatly. Composer of early Chopin-like piano pieces, then of larger-scale works prompted by theoso-

phical beliefs and using a highly chromatic new type of harmonic style designed to express these beliefs. Invented the so-called 'mystic chord' of ascending fourths, C–F♯–B♭–E–A–D, as a replacement for ordinary major and minor chords. Works include orchestral DIVINE POEM, POEM OF ECSTASY, *Prometheus – The Poem of Fire* (see PROMETHEUS), 10 piano sonatas and many other piano works. Died of a tumour on the lip.

Slaatt(er), see the following entry.

Slått (Norw., pl. *Slåtter*), type of composition (originally a march, but afterwards more broadly treated) played by Norwegian folk-musicians on the Hardanger fiddle (see FIDDLE); Grieg transcribed several examples, and other Norwegian composers have also written works of this kind. (The spellings *slaatt* and *slaatter* were formerly current in Norwegian.)

Slavonic Dances, two sets each of eight dances by Dvořák – in folk-music vein but all 'original' – for piano duet, 1878 and 1886; also orchestrated by the composer.

Slavonic Rhapsodies, three orchestral works by Dvořák (1878) in the vein of Czech folk-music, but all 'original'.

Sleeping Beauty, The (Rus., *Spyashchaya krasavitsa*), ballet with music by Tchaikovsky, produced in St Petersburg, 1890. (*The Sleeping Princess* was the title adopted by Diaghilev for his London presentation of it, 1921, to avoid possible confusion with a Christmas pantomime.) It lasts a full evening; an extract from it is given as 'Aurora's Wedding'.

Sleeping Princess, The, see SLEEPING BEAUTY.

slentando (It.), becoming slower.

slide, a device on some brass instruments for altering the length of the tube (and thus the notes produced). The principal use today is on the TROMBONE. For the obsolete *slide-trumpet*, see TRUMPET.

Slonimsky, Sergey [Mikhailovich] (b. 1932), Russian composer of symphony; opera *Maria Stuart*; *Antiphones* for string quartet in which the performers walk about the platform and hall, etc. He is the nephew of the Russian-born American musicologist Nicolas Slonimsky (b. 1894).

slur, in musical notation, a curved line grouping notes together and indicating that in performance they are to be joined smoothly together – sung in one breath, played with one stroke of the bow, etc.

Smalley, Roger (b. 1943), British composer of *Beat Music* for 55 players; *Gloria tibi Trinitatis I* for orchestra; electronic works, etc. Resident in Australia as university teacher since 1976.

Smetana, Bedřich (1824–84), Czech composer, also conductor and pianist; encouraged by Liszt. Took part in the unsuccessful Czech revolt against Austria, 1848, and afterwards worked for some years in Sweden; but from 1861 settled again in Prague. Became totally deaf in 1874 but continued to compose – e.g. cycle of symphonic poems MY COUNTRY, two string quartets (no. 1 FROM MY LIFE), opera *The Kiss* and others. Previous works include operas THE BARTERED BRIDE and *Dalibor*, choral works, many piano pieces. Cultivated, and is regarded as founding, a Czech national style influenced by folk-music.

Smith, John Stafford (1750–1836), British organist, tenor singer, and composer of catches, glees, church music, etc.; see STAR-SPANGLED BANNER.

Smith, Ronald (b. 1929), British pianist (also composer) who has specialized in the works of Alkan and has written extensively on that composer.

Smyth, Ethel [Mary] (1858–1944), British composer who studied in Germany and had operas and other works performed there. Joined militant agitation for women's vote in Britain and was jailed, 1911; created Dame, 1922. Works, broadly conforming to traditional (German-influenced) idiom, include *The Wreckers*, *The Boatswain's Mate* and other operas; Mass; a concerto for violin, horn and orchestra; chamber music. In late years suffered from deafness and distorted hearing. Also writer of autobiographical and other books.

snare, see following entry.

snare-drum, small drum (slung slightly to one side when marching – hence alternative British [not US] name, 'side-drum'); used in the orchestra, military band, dance band, etc. It has a skin at either end of a shallow cylinder, the upper skin being struck with a pair of wooden sticks and the lower one being in contact with gut strings or wires (called snares). These snares add a rattling effect to the tone; they can be disengaged at will.

Snegurochka, see SNOW MAIDEN.

Snow Maiden, The (Rus., *Snegurochka*), opera by Rimsky-Korsakov, produced in St Petersburg, 1882.

Libretto by composer, after a play by Ostrovsky: the legendary Snow Maiden, daughter of Fairy Spring and King Frost, is wooed in vain by the Sun-God.

soap opera, not an opera but a radio or television serial of a sentimental type – in USA designed to sell the sponsor's product, e.g. soap.

soave (It.), sweet(ly), tender(ly).

Socrates (Fr., *Socrate*), work for voices and orchestra by Satie, first performed in 1920; called a 'symphonic drama' but not intended for the stage. Texts translated from Plato's dialogues.

Söderström, [Anna] **Elisabeth** (b. 1927), Swedish soprano, eminent in a wide range of operas; at Salzburg Festival from 1955, at Glyndebourne from 1957, etc.

soft pedal, see PIANO (2).

soh, in TONIC SOL-FA the spoken name for the fifth degree (dominant) of the scale, written s. Cp. SOL.

Sohal, Naresh (b. 1939), Indian composer, pupil in England of Goehr. Works with Indian or Sanskrit titles include *Asht Prahar* (Sanskrit: *asht* = eight, *prahar* is a division of the day) for orchestra. Other works include a harmonica concerto.

Soir (et la tempête), Le, title of one of a set of three symphonies by Haydn: see MORNING.

Soirées musicales (Fr., musical evenings), a collection of songs and duets by Rossini, published in 1835; an orchestral arrangement by Britten (1936) of five of its numbers bears the same title. Other arrangements include Respighi's in the ballet THE FANTASTIC TOYSHOP.

sol, the note G (in Latin countries, and formerly elsewhere); cp. SOH.

Soldiers, The (Ger., *Die Soldaten*), opera by Zimmermann, produced in Cologne, 1965, with libretto after J. Lenz's play; the heroine ends as a soldiers' prostitute.

Soldier's Tale, The (Fr., *L'Histoire du soldat*), stage work by Stravinsky, produced in Lausanne, 1918. Text by C. F. Ramuz, after a collection of Russian tales: it deals with a soldier, the Devil and a Princess. The work uses speech and dance but no singing, an 'orchestra' of seven, and an idiom indebted to jazz. See MULDOWNEY.

Soler, Antonio (1729–83), Spanish friar and composer of harpsichord sonatas, church music, incidental music to plays, etc.

sol-fa, see TONIC SOL-FA (and cp. SOL-FEGGIO, SOLMIZATION).

solfège, solfeggio, French and Italian terms for a method of ear-training and sight-reading by which the pupil names each note of a melody (*do* for C, *sol* for G, etc.) by singing it. The Italian is the original term; the French, derived from it, is also used in a broader sense to take in the whole system of rudimentary musical instruction in which the above is a prime element. The name *solfeggio* is also given to a vocal exercise written for the above method of study.

solmization, the designation of musical notes by a system of syllabic names – as applied to a nomenclature devised by Guido of Arezzo in the 11th century and now to a development of this. Such a development is represented by the current Italian *do, re, mi, fa, sol, la, si* (representing the notes from C up to B), paralleled in English TONIC SOL-FA by *doh, ray, me, fah, soh, lah, te* (though these are not fixed in pitch but relative, *doh* representing C in C major, D in D major, etc., the other notes ascending from it).

solo (It., alone), a piece or passage performed by one performer – either alone or with others in a subordinate, accompanying role. So *solo song* normally denotes a song for one singer with piano accompaniment. Plural in Italian, *soli*; in English, *solos*. The *solo organ* is a manual on some organs, having mainly stops suitable for the solo treatment of melodies. *Soloistic*, in musicologists' jargon, refers to the use of instruments in the orchestra not as contributing to massed effects but for their individual qualities.

Solomon, oratorio by Handel, produced in London, 1749. Text (based on the Bible) by someone now unknown.

Solomon (professional name used by Solomon Cutner) (1902–88), British pianist who appeared from age eight, and became internationally noted. CBE, 1946. Incapacitated after a stroke, 1956.

Solti, Georg (b. 1912), Hungarian-born conductor (also pianist); from 1939 resident in Switzerland and later in Germany; music director of the Frankfurt Opera, 1952; of Covent Garden Opera, 1961–71; of Chicago Symphony Orchestra, 1969–91; of London Philharmonic Orchestra, 1979–83. Naturalized British, 1972; his previous honorary KBE (1971) became a regular knighthood.

Sombrero de tres picos, El, see THREE-CORNERED HAT.

Somers, Harry [Stewart] (b. 1925), Canadian composer, pupil of Milhaud in Paris. Works include opera *Louis Riel*; five *Concepts* for orchestra; three string quartets; *Voiceplay* for singer-actor (any voice, any range).

Somervell, Arthur (1863–1937), British composer of choral works, songs, etc., and musical educationist. Knighted, 1929.

sommo, somma (It.), highest; *con somma passione*, with the utmost passion.

son (Fr.), sound; *musique de douze sons*, TWELVE-NOTE music; *sons bouchés*, 'stopped' notes on the horn (see STOP, verb, 2).

sonata (It., a piece sounded; as distinct from 'cantata', a piece sung), originally (in Italy, *c*.1600) any instrumental piece not in a prevailing form (e.g. CANZONA, RICERCAR or dance-form). Later, since the Haydn–Mozart era (regarded as the 'classic' era for this type of work), usually a work in three or four movements – or, following the example of Liszt's Piano Sonata (1852–3), in one movement deliberately conceived as equal to (and about as long as) several 'normal' movements combined. Only a work for one or two players is now normally called a sonata; a work of this type for three is called a trio, for four a quartet, etc., and for an orchestra a symphony. Such terms as *violin sonata, cello sonata* normally assume the participation also of a piano. Characteristic of the sonata is the use (normally in the first movement and often in others too) of what is called SONATA-FORM (below) or a modification of it. Among the notable forerunners of this now standard type are D. Scarlatti's short one-movement keyboard works, now usually also called sonatas; and in the immediate paving of the way for the Haydn–Mozart sonata, a chief part is ascribed to C. P. E. Bach. Earlier, the suite rather than the sonata was the prevailing type of instrumental piece in several movements; and indeed the 17th-century and early 18th-century *chamber sonata* (It., *sonata da camera*) represents virtually a suite (mainly in the form of dance-movements) for two or more stringed instruments with keyboard accompaniment, the restriction of the term to one or two players not having yet arisen. The *church sonata* (It., *sonata da chiesa*) was similar but of a 'graver' type, avoiding dance-movements. The pre-Haydn usage of *sonata* as applied to a work for orchestra or smaller ensemble has occasionally been revived since 1950: see, e.g., MATTHEWS (C.). See also SONATINA below.

sonata-form, term used to describe a certain type of musical construction normally used in the first movement of a SONATA (above) and of a symphony (which is in effect a sonata for orchestra) and similar works. An alternative name is 'first-movement form' – but the form is also found in movements other than first movements, just as it is also found in works not called sonatas. It may also be called 'compound binary form' (see BINARY). The essential of sonata-form is the division of a movement (sometimes after an introduction) into three parts – exposition, development, recapitulation. The exposition, having its first theme in the 'home' key of the movement, moves into another key normally presenting a fresh (second) subject in that key, and ends in that key; the next

section 'develops' or expands the material already presented; the last section is basically a varied repetition of the first, but ending in the home key, normally by bringing the second subject into that key. Afterwards may follow a further section, called coda ('finishing off' the movement). The key into which the first section moves is normally the dominant (if the piece is in the major key) or the relative major (if the piece is in the minor key). It will be gathered that sonata-form consists basically in the relationship of keys: if the term is applied to keyless (ATONAL) music, then it must be with an altered significance.

sonate (Fr., Ger.) = SONATA.

sonatina, sonatine (It., Fr.), a 'little sonata', usually shorter, lighter, or easier than most sonatas; *sonatina* is used in English.

Sondheim, Stephen [Joshua] (b. 1930), American composer of musicals, including *A Little Night Music*; also lyricist for his own works and for Bernstein's *West Side Story*, etc.

song, any short vocal composition, accompanied or not – usually for one performer, but cp. PART-SONG. The word has no precise meaning, but is effectively defined in various contexts by contrast with other terms – e.g. *songs and duets* (implying vocal solos and vocal duets). In opera the word 'aria' or 'air' is more usual. When, as normally, a song repeats the same tune for successive stanzas of a poem, it is said to be 'strophic'; if not, then the clumsy term 'through-composed' (from Ger., *durchkomponiert*) is sometimes applied to it – but see STROPHIC. A *song-cycle* is a set of songs grouped by the composer in a particular order (usually with reference to the sense of the words) and intended to be so performed. The term *song* is also applied in a generalized sense to certain large-scale works – see e.g. SONG OF THE EARTH, SONG OF DESTINY (below). The Song of the Three Holy Children is a book of the Apocrypha (also known in Anglican church use as the Benedicite) supposedly representing a prayer sung in the furnace by Daniel and his brothers: for Stockhausen's use of this source see GESANG. For *song-scena* see SCENA. See also the following titles.

song-form, name sometimes given to ordinary TERNARY form as used in an instrumental slow-movement. The term is better avoided ('ternary' itself being better) because not all songs are in this form – though it applies to the 'da capo' aria (see ARIA), and to most dance-tunes of the 1930s, etc.

Song of Destiny (Ger., *Schicksalslied*), work by Brahms for chorus and orchestra, 1871, to a poem by Hölderlin.

Song of the Earth (Ger., *Das Lied von der Erde*), work by Mahler for mezzo-soprano, tenor and orchestra, 1907–9 (first performed in 1911, after Mahler's death); called by him a symphony, and of symphonic dimensions, but not numbered among his symphonies. Text from German translations of Chinese poems.

Songs and Dances of Death (Rus., *Pesni i plyaski smerti*), cycle of four songs by Musorgsky, 1875–7, to poems by Golenishchev-Gutuzov evoking different aspects of death.

Songs for a Mad King, see EIGHT SONGS FOR A MAD KING.

Songs of a Wayfarer (Ger., *Lieder eines fahrenden Gesellen*), cycle of four songs by Mahler (1883–5); words by composer, expressing the sentiments of a young man scorned by his sweetheart.

Songs of Gurre (Ger., *Gurrelieder*), work by Schoenberg (1900–1911) for four solo singers, three male choruses, and one mixed chorus and huge orchestra (including eight flutes and a set of iron chains). Text is a German translation from the Danish of J. P. Jacobsen: Gurre is the castle where dwells Tove, beloved of Waldemar IV, a 14th-century Danish king.

Songs on the Death of Children (Ger., *Kindertotenlieder*), cycle of five songs (1901–4) by Mahler, to poems by F. Rückert. There are alternative accompaniments for orchestra and for piano.

Songs without Words (Ger., *Lieder ohne Worte*), 48 pieces for piano by Mendelssohn published at intervals (1832–45) in six books. They resemble song-melodies with accompaniment. Most of the titles (e.g. 'Spring Song' and 'The Bees' Wedding' for nos. 30 and 34) are not Mendelssohn's; but among those he did name are the three 'Venetian Gondola Songs' (nos. 6, 12, 29).

Sonnambula, La (It., The Sleepwalker), opera by Bellini, produced in Milan, 1831. Libretto by F. Romani, the heroine's sleepwalking habit leading her into a compromising situation.

sonore, direction often used by composers to mean 'sonorously', apparently under the impression that it is an Italian word. It could be, however, either the French for 'sonorous' or (if written *sonor^e*) an abbreviation for the correct Italian *sonoramente*.

sop., abbr. of SOPRANO.

Sophocles (495–406 BC), Greek dramatist. See ANTIGONE, ELEKTRA, HADLEY (P.), OEDIPUS REX, ORFF, PARTCH.

sopranino (It., little soprano), name for a size of instrument higher than the soprano size – e.g. *sopranino* RECORDER, *sopranino* SAXOPHONE.

soprano (It., upper), (1) the highest type of female voice, with approximate normal range from middle C upwards for two octaves; or a child's high voice (= TREBLE, 1); (2, *male soprano*) type of male adult voice of similar range, produced by castration, as used for some operatic and church singers, e.g. in the 17th and 18th centuries; (3, *soprano clef*) name of a clef (now obsolete) having middle C on the bottom

line of the staff: ⯑ (4) name given, in a 'family' of instruments (i.e. a group of different sizes), to the one with a range approximating to the soprano voice – and usually also carrying the implication of being higher than the 'normal'-sized instrument. E.g. *soprano* CORNET, *soprano* RECORDER, *soprano* SAXOPHONE; the small clarinet in E♭ is occasionally (though not commonly) called a *soprano clarinet* for the same reason.

Sor, Ferdinando (also called Fernando Sors) (1778–1839), Spanish guitarist; teacher of his instrument in Paris, London, and elsewhere; composer mainly for his instrument, but also of an Italian opera, produced when he was 19. Died in Paris.

Sorabji, Kaikhosru Shapurji (1892–1988), British composer (originally Leon Dudley Sorabji), son of a Parsi father and a Spanish-Sicilian mother; resident in Britain. Also pianist and writer on music. Works (for orchestra, piano, organ, etc.) including the two-hour *Opus clavicembalisticum* for piano. Until the mid-1970s he discouraged public performances of his works.

Sorcerer, The, operetta by Sullivan, produced in London, 1877. Libretto by W. S. Gilbert. A representative of a respectable firm of 'family sorcerers' administers a love-potion to an English village.

Sorcerer's Apprentice, The (Fr., *L'Apprenti sorcier*), symphonic poem by Dukas, also called a 'scherzo'; first performed 1897. It humorously illustrates Goethe's story (based on Lucian, second century AD) of the apprentice who finds he can start a spell but not stop it.

sord., abbr. of SORDINO.

sordina, an occasionally found alternative to SORDINO.

sordino (It., pl. *-i*), a mute; abbr. *sord.* So *con sordini*, with mutes, put on mutes; *senza sordini*, without mutes, take off mutes. As applied to the piano, *sordini* refers to the dampers which remain in operation unless the sustaining pedal (right-hand side) is depressed; *senza sordini*, i.e. without dampers, means that this pedal is to be brought into use.

Sorochintsy Fair (Rus., *Sorochintskaya yarmarka*), opera by Musorgsky; libretto by composer, after a rustic story (with faked supernatural happenings) by Gogol. Begun 1874, the opera was left unfinished at Musorgsky's death.

Various completions have been made – the most successful by N. Tcherepnin.

Sors, see SOR.

sostenuto (It.), sustained, i.e. in a smooth manner.

sotto voce (It., under the voice), whispered, barely audible – term used of instrumental as well as vocal music.

soubrette (Fr.), type of pert female character (often a servant) sung by a light soprano voice in opera or operetta – e.g. Despina in COSÌ FAN TUTTE (Mozart), Adèle in DIE FLEDERMAUS (Johann Strauss the younger).

sound-board, a wooden board on the piano and other keyboard instruments, located close to the strings, vibrating when they are struck, and serving to amplify the volume of their sound.

sound-hole, hole cut out of the upper surface of stringed instruments to assist resonance – the violin and related instruments having two holes shaped like an *f* and called *f*-holes, the lute and some guitars having one hole cut in an ornamented manner somewhat like a flower and called 'rose'.

sound-post, piece of wood connecting vertically the upper and lower surfaces of the body of a violin and other stringed instruments. It helps to support the pressure of the strings on the bridge (and hence on the upper surface) and serves to distribute the vibrations of the strings over the body of the instrument.

sourdine (Fr.), a mute (cp. SORDINO); *mettez, ôtez, les sourdines,* put on, take off, mutes.

Sousa, John Philip (1854–1932), American band-conductor and composer of marches ('The Washington Post', 'The Stars and Stripes Forever', etc.); also of *El capitán* and other operettas. The story that his name was a fabrication to include the letters USA is itself a fabrication. See also the following.

sousaphone, type of tuba (see TUBA, 1) made in a shape circling the player's body and ending in a big bell facing forward. It was associated with the band conducted by Sousa (above) and is still used in American bands; it was also used in some early manifestations of jazz.

Souster, Tim [Timothy Andrew James] (b. 1943), British composer, also writer on music, and formerly BBC producer; works include concerto for trumpet, live electronics and orchestra.

soutenu (Fr.), sustained, smoothly flowing (the French equivalent of SOSTENUTO).

Souzay, Gérard (real name Gérard Marcel Tisserand) (b. 1928), French baritone, with European and American reputation in performances of French and German songs; also opera singer (Metropolitan, New York, 1965).

Sowerby, Leo (1895–1968), American organist, and composer of works for organ alone, and for organ with orchestra; also of two piano concertos, chamber music, etc.

Spanisches Liederbuch, see SPANISH SONG-BOOK.

Spanish Caprice, orchestral work by Rimsky-Korsakov (first performed in

1887) on themes of Spanish 'folk-song' character. The usual form of the title, *Capriccio espagnol*, is bastard Italian-and-French.

Spanish Hour, The (Fr., *L'Heure espagnole*), opera by Ravel, produced in Paris, 1911. Libretto by Franc-Nohain, set in a Spanish clockmaker's shop.

Spanish Rhapsody (Fr., *Rapsodie espagnole*), orchestral work by Ravel, 1907, using themes of Spanish national character.

Spanish Song-book (Ger., *Spanisches Liederbuch*), Wolf's song-settings, 1890, of 44 Spanish poems in German translation.

Spanish Symphony (Fr., *Symphonie espagnole*), work by Lalo for violin and orchestra – really a violin concerto in five movements – first performed in 1875 and written for the Spanish violinist Sarasate. Has themes of Spanish national character.

species, name given to each of five types of academic 'strict counterpoint' (see COUNTERPOINT), progressively more complex (called *first species*, *second species*, etc.).

Spectre's Bride, The, usual English title for *Svatebni kosile* (Cz., the Wedding Shift), cantatas written to a text of K. J. Erben by – (1) Dvořák, first performed (in English) in Birmingham, 1885; (2) Novák, 1913 (called by composer 'A symphony of horror').

speech-song, type of vocal utterance midway between speech and song, originated by Schoenberg and used in the SONGS OF GURRE, PIERROT LUNAIRE and later works; the voice touches the note (usually notated in a special way, e.g. ♩) but does not sustain it. The German term is *Sprech-*

gesang, and a voice-part employing it is designated *Sprechstimme*.

Speer, Daniel (1636–1707), German musician, in municipal service at Göttingen as wind-player; composed songs (including collection of a whimsical nature), chamber music, etc.

Spelman, Timothy Mather (1891–1970), American composer who studied in Germany. Works include symphonic poem *Christ and the Blind Man*, a symphony, chamber music, piano works, many songs.

spianato (It.), smoothed out, smooth.

spiccato (It., separated), a certain method of playing rapid detached notes on the violin and related instruments, the bow rebounding off the strings.

Spider's Banquet, The (Fr., *Le Festin de l'araignée*), ballet with music by Roussel, first produced in Paris, 1913. (Prompted by Fabre's studies of insect life.)

Spies, Claudio (b. 1925), Chilean-born composer, who studied with Piston, Hindemith and others in USA and was naturalized there in 1966. Works include *Ensembles* for orchestra, *Times 2* for two horns, *Viopiacem* for viola with harpsichord/piano; also vocal settings from the Bible, from St Francis of Assisi, etc.

spinet, (1) wing-shaped keyboard instrument of harpsichord type, but smaller – current in 16th–18th centuries, revived in the 20th for old music; see VIRGINALS; (2) incorrect name for the 'square PIANO'.

spinetto, see VIRGINALS.

spinto (It.), pushed, urged on – especially in voice-classification; *lirico spinto*, a LYRIC voice (tenor or soprano) which has been 'pushed' into more forceful singing.

spirito, spiritoso (It.), spirit, spirited.

spiritual, name given to a type of religious folk-song of the American blacks, usually of solo-and-refrain design. Authorities also use the term *white spirituals* for similar songs among certain whites in the Southern States.

Spofforth, Reginald (1770–1827), British organist and composer, especially of glees – e.g. 'Hail, smiling morn'.

Spohr, Louis (1784–1859), German violinist, conductor and composer of 17 violin concertos (no. 8 'in the form of a song-scena'); also of operas (one on FAUST), oratorios, symphonies, much chamber music (including four 'double string quartets' and a nonet), etc., in mellifluous Romantic style. Was one of the first orchestral conductors to use a baton – but the story that he used one in London as early as 1820 (and thus introduced it there) is unsupported by any evidence outside his own unreliable autobiography.

Spontini, Gaspare [Luigi Pacifico] (1774–1851), Italian composer, in the main of operas of a heroic and historical kind – e.g. THE VESTAL (Fr., *La Vestale*), composed for Paris where he had settled in 1803. As musical director to the court in Berlin, 1820–41, continued to compose operas (e.g. *Agnes von Hohenstaufen*, in German) and made notable reputation as opera conductor. Became deaf, 1848; died at his birthplace, near Ancona.

Sprechgesang, Sprechstimme, see SPEECH-SONG.

springar (Norw.), Norwegian folk-

dance in 3/4 time, cultivated e.g. by Grieg and Svendsen.

springer, a musical ornament (used e.g. by Chopin) in which an extra note, notated in smaller type, robs the preceding note of part of its time-value. Thus: 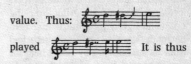 played It is thus the opposite of an APPOGGIATURA (1) in which the extra note robs the following (not the preceding) note of part of its time-value. The German term for *springer* is *Nachschlag* (literally 'afterstroke').

'Spring' Sonata, name (not the composer's) for Beethoven's notably cheerful Sonata in F for violin and piano, op. 24 (1801).

Spring Song, see SONGS WITHOUT WORDS.

'Spring' Symphony, (1) nickname, authorized by the composer, for Schumann's Symphony no. 1 in B♭, 1841; (2) title of a work by Britten, 1949, for three solo singers, mixed chorus, boys' chorus and orchestra (on poems on or near the subject of spring). The final section introduces the tune and words of SUMER IS ICUMEN IN.

square piano, see PIANO.

Staatsoper (Ger.), State Opera (house or company).

Stabat Mater, a devotional poem in medieval Latin about the vigil of Mary by the Cross; used as an authorized hymn (see SEQUENCE, 2) in the Roman Catholic Church since 1727, and even before then set by Josquin, Palestrina and other composers. There are also more recent settings (e.g. by Pergolesi and by Berkeley) – as well as a traditional plainsong melody.

stabile (It.), stable, firm; term used of an orchestra to denote 'permanent', 'regular', 'resident', etc.

staccato (It., detached), a method of performance denoted by a dot over the note, and signifying that the note is to be made short – and thus detached from its successor – by being held for less than its full length; so the superlative *staccatissimo*.

Stadler, Anton (1753–1812), Austrian clarinettist and basset-horn player, for whom Mozart wrote the Clarinet Quintet and Clarinet Concerto. He invented a specially extended clarinet capable of reaching lower notes. See BASSET CLARINET.

Städtische Oper (Ger.), Municipal Opera (house or company).

staff, the framework of lines and spaces on which music is ordinarily written; so *treble staff, bass staff*, the five-line framework respectively carrying the treble and bass clefs. So also *staff notation*, ordinary notation as distinct e.g. from TONIC SOL-FA notation; *Great Staff*, fictitious academic construction of 11 lines to include both the treble staff and bass staff with middle C in between. (An alternative name is *stave*, and the plural is always *staves*.)

Stainer, John (1840–1901), British organist, editor of old music, professor at Oxford, writer on music, and composer of oratorio THE CRUCIFIXION and of church music in mid-Victorian English idiom. Knighted, 1888.

Stamic, see STAMITZ.

Stamitz, German form of surname adopted by a Czech family of musicians (originally named Stamic), whose chief members were (1) Jan Václav Stamic (or Johann Wenzel Stamitz) (1717–57), violinist and composer of violin concertos, symphonies, harpsichord sonatas, etc., who became musical director at the court of Mannheim, 1745, and is regarded as the founder of the MANNHEIM SCHOOL; (2) his son Karel Stamic (or Karl Stamitz) (1745–1801), violinist and composer of symphonies, operas, etc.

Ständchen (Ger.), see SERENADE.

Stanford, Charles Villiers (1852–1924), Irish composer, also organist, conductor, professor at Cambridge, teacher at RCM. His pupils included Vaughan Williams, Howells, Bliss. Works include seven operas (including *Shamus O'Brien, The Critic, The Travelling Companion*); seven symphonies and five orchestral *Irish Rhapsodies; The Revenge* and other cantatas; church music; many songs (including Irish folk-song settings). Knighted, 1901.

Stanley, [Charles] **John** (1712–86), British composer, pupil of Greene. Was also noted organist, though blind from the age of two. Wrote organ music, concertos for strings, various vocal settings, etc.

Starer, Robert (b. 1924), Austrian composer, also pianist, who emigrated to Palestine and since 1949 has worked in USA. Compositions include several to Hebrew texts, e.g. Symphony no. 2 (with soprano, baritone, chorus) entitled *Kohelet* (Heb., Ecclesiastes); also a concerto for violin, cello and orchestra, etc.

stark (Ger.), loud, strong.

Starker, János (b. 1924), Hungarian

cellist who settled in USA (naturalized, 1954); he achieved high distinction.

Starokadomsky, Mikhail (1901–54), Russian composer, pupil of Myaskovsky and others; composed works inclining to NEOCLASSICISM, including Concerto for Orchestra – also an organ concerto (rare in Soviet music), string quartets, opera, etc.

Star-Spangled Banner, The, the national anthem of the USA, not officially adopted until 1931, although the words were written in 1814 to the tune at present in use. This tune had already been issued (in England) by John Stafford Smith, who in all probability was the composer.

stave, see STAFF.

steel band, ensemble of a type developed in the West Indies from the 1940s, the instruments made from the tops of oil drums, which are hammered into segments to sound at various pitches.

steel guitar (or Hawaiian guitar), instrument of guitar-like shape but held horizontally, the strings not 'stopped' with the fingers but with a small metal bar (called a 'steel') forming a movable NUT going right across all the strings. The particular intervals of the tuning can therefore be reproduced at any pitch by sliding the steel, making possible the sliding thirds characteristic of the instrument (e.g. in commercialized 'Hawaiian'-style dance music, popular before World War II). Modern examples are often electronic and placed on a stand, further reducing kinship to the traditional guitar.

Stefano, Giuseppe di (b. 1921), Italian tenor, prominent at La Scala, Milan (from 1947) and elsewhere; he partnered Callas on her final recital tour, 1973–4.

Steffani, Agostino (1654–1728), Italian composer, also priest and diplomat; became court musical director in Hanover (Handel afterwards succeeding him). Wrote notable vocal duets, some in his Italian operas; also church music, chamber music, etc. Died in Frankfurt on a diplomatic visit.

Steg (Ger.), bridge (of a stringed instrument); *am Steg*, on the bridge; see PONTICELLO.

Steibelt, Daniel (1765–1823), German pianist, composer (much piano music, also operas, etc.), and fashionable teacher in Paris and London. In 1808 he took a court musical post in Russia, where he died.

Steinberg, Maximilian [Osseyevich] (1883–1946), Russian composer, pupil and son-in-law of Rimsky-Korsakov; director of the Leningrad Conservatory. Works include five symphonies – no. 4 called *Turksib* (Turkestan–Siberia Railway). Wrote also ballets (including one on the same subject as R. Strauss's TILL EULENSPIEGEL), string quartets, etc.

Steinberg, William (originally Hans Wilhelm) (1899–1978), German-born conductor who after a period in Palestine settled in USA, becoming conductor of the Pittsburgh Symphony Orchestra; 1958–60, musical director of the London Philharmonic Orchestra; 1969–72, of Boston Symphony Orchestra.

Steinspiel, see STONE CHIMES.

Stenhammar, Vilhelm Eugen (1871–1927), Swedish pianist, conductor and composer – influenced by

Wagner, but also using Swedish folk-music. Wrote two operas, two symphonies, two piano concertos, etc.

Stern, Isaac (b. 1920), Russian-born American violinist, brought to USA in infancy; he toured widely (Russia, Australia, etc.), achieving the highest distinction.

stessa, stesso (It.), same.

Stevenson, Robert Louis (1850–94), British writer. See LIVIABELLA.

Stevenson, Ronald (b. 1928), British composer and pianist (of partly Scottish descent) whose work makes use of Scottish literary and musical sources; is also writer on music. Compositions include Prelude, Fugue and Fantasy for piano after Busoni's *Doctor Faust*; *Passacaglia on DSCH* (initials representing Shostakovich) for piano.

stile rappresentativo (It.), a 'style aimed at representation' – term used by early 17th-century Italian composers of opera and oratorio, alluding to the theatre and to their newly invented device of RECITATIVE, based on the natural spoken inflexions of the voice.

Still, William Grant (1895–1978), American composer, reputedly the first black musician to compose a symphony (1931) and to conduct a major symphony orchestra. Works include *Afro-American Symphony*, *Lenox Avenue* (for speaker, chorus and orchestra, later as ballet) alluding to Harlem; opera *Troubled Island*.

Stimme (Ger., pl. *-en*), voice, instrumental PART, stop (of an organ), etc. See next entries.

Stimmführung (Ger.) = PART-WRITING.

Stimmung (Ger.), (1) tuning; (2) atmosphere (in sense of 'prevailing mood'); (3) work by Stockhausen (1968), presumably drawing on both these senses, for six singers unaccompanied who vocalize without words.

stochastic (from Gk.), governed by the mathematical laws of probability – term applied by Xenakis to procedures whereby, having determined a total massive sound, a composer makes a mathematical calculation (worked out by himself or by computer) to decide the distribution of its component sounds over many MOMENTS and/or performers. This is Xenakis's own procedure in *Metastaseis* and other works for large numbers of individual players.

Stockhausen, Karlheinz (b. 1928), German composer, pupil of F. Martin and (in Paris) of Messiaen. Highly influential in trends of form, sound content, use of electronics: he was the first composer to have an electronic 'score' (or rather diagram) published, 1956. Later active in exploring spatial possibilities in music and a measure of free choice by performers – e.g. in *Groups* (Ger., *Gruppen*) for three orchestras (and three conductors); *Cycle* (*Zyklus*) for one percussion-player who may begin on any page (see CYCLE). Other works include *Stimmung* (Ger., atmosphere, tuning) for vocal ensemble; cycle of operas entitled *Light* (Ger., *Licht*), 'each part being named after a day', e.g. *Donnerstag* (Thursday). See also MOMENT.

Stokowski, Leopold (1882–1977), British-born conductor (*not* originally Stokes; father Polish), naturalized American, 1915. Conducted Philadelphia Orchestra, 1912–36, giving hundreds of first performances; appeared in Disney's *Fantasia* and other films; transcribed for orchestra Bach's organ Toccata and Fugue in D minor and other works. Latterly resident in Britain, where he died.

Stolz, Robert (1880–1975), Austrian composer and conductor who lived in USA, 1940–46; wrote over 50 operettas (including *Wild Violets*, *White Horse Inn*), etc.

stone chimes (Ger., *Steinspiel*, i.e. 'stone-play' on the analogy of *glockenspiel*), percussion instrument prescribed by (and specially made for) Orff's operas *Antigone* and *Oedipus the Tyrant*, etc.; it has a short, keyboard-like arrangement of different-sized stone bars, struck by beaters held in the hand.

Stone Guest, The (Rus., *Kamenny Gost*), opera by Dargomizhsky, begun in 1866, left not quite finished at his death; completed by Cui, orchestrated by Rimsky-Korsakov, and produced in St Petersburg, 1872. It is a setting of Pushkin's play, on the same story as Mozart's DON GIOVANNI.

stop (noun), (1) a row of pipes on an organ, all put in or out of operation by one lever; or the lever itself; (2) by analogy, the mechanism used in the harpsichord for similar purpose – e.g. *sixteen-foot stop* (see FOOT) for adding tone an octave lower, *harp stop* for simulating harp tone.

stop (verb), (1, *stringed instruments*) to place the finger on a string, thus determining the length of the portion of the string which is to vibrate; so *double-stopping*, *triple-stopping*, this action on 2–3 strings at once. The opposite of a *stopped string* is an 'open string', i.e. one vibrating its full length

without being shortened by the placing of a finger. Note that the phrase *double-stopping* is loosely used for 'playing on two strings', whether or not both strings are actually stopped or open (and *triple-stopping* similarly). (2, horn-playing) to insert the hand into the bell of the instrument, altering the pitch and tone-quality of the note. (3, acoustics, organ-building, etc.) to block the passage of air through one end of a pipe (thus creating a *stopped pipe* or *end-stopped pipe* as distinct from an 'open pipe'), producing a note an octave lower than would otherwise sound. See DIAPASON.

Storace, Stephen (1762–96), British composer whose training in Italy served him in Italian and English operas, including *The Comedy of Errors*, based on Shakespeare's play (It., *Gli equivoci*, The Errors) and *No Song, No Supper*. Also wrote chamber music, etc. Friend and presumed pupil of Mozart in Vienna.

Strad, colloquial name for an instrument made by the STRADIVARI family.

Stradella, Alessandro (1644–82), Italian composer of operas and cantatas with notable choral writing; also of church music, sinfonias for strings, etc. Of noble family. Was murdered. Legend says that he escaped from an earlier attempted assassination after an elopement, but evidence for this is lacking – though it forms the basis of an opera about him by Flotow, 1844.

Stradivari, Stradivarius, Italian and Latinized names of a family of Italian violin-makers at Cremona – principally Antonio Stradivari (1644–1737).

strascinando (It.), dragging – direction

referring not so much to tempo as to one note's 'dragging' the next behind it, e.g. in singing PORTAMENTO.

Stratas, Teresa (originally Anastasi Stratakis) (b. 1938), Canadian soprano of Greek descent; well known in opera, she sang the title-role in Berg's *Lulu* when it belatedly received its first full-length performance, 1979.

Straus, Oscar (not 'Strauss'; 1870–1954), Austrian composer, pupil of Bruch; wrote Viennese operettas including THE CHOCOLATE SOLDIER and A WALTZ DREAM – also music to film *La Ronde*, etc. Naturalized French, 1939.

Strauss, surname of a family of Austrian musicians – Johann the elder, Johann the younger, Joseph and Eduard (separately below); also of Richard Strauss (below), no relation.

Strauss, Eduard (1835–1916), Austrian composer of dance music, etc., and conductor; son of Johann Strauss the elder.

Strauss, Johann (the elder; 1804–49), Austrian violinist, conductor and composer who toured much – was in Britain in 1838 for celebrations of Victoria's coronation. Wrote waltzes, polkas, etc., but today chiefly famous for the RADETZKY MARCH. Father of Eduard Strauss (above) and Johann and Josef Strauss (below).

Strauss, Johann (the younger; 1825–99), Austrian violinist, conductor, and composer of enormously successful waltzes in noticeably artistic style – including THE BLUE DANUBE, ROSES FROM THE SOUTH, and TALES FROM THE VIENNA WOODS; called 'the Waltz King'. Wrote also polkas ('Tritsch-Tratsch', 'Thunder and Lightning',

etc.) and other dances; and 16 operettas including *The Bat* (see FLEDER-MAUS) and THE GIPSY BARON. Other operettas, e.g. VIENNA BLOOD, have been made by others from his music. Toured much (London, 1869; USA, 1872). Son of Johann Strauss (above). Collaborated in a few works with his brother Josef Strauss.

Strauss, Josef (1827–70), Austrian composer of 'Village Swallows from Austria', 'Music of the Spheres' and other waltzes; also other orchestral dance-music, piano pieces, etc. Collaborated with his brother Johann in a 'Pizzicato Polka' and two other works.

Strauss, Richard [Georg] (1864–1949), German composer, also conductor; no relation to the other Strausses. Born in Munich, later settling in Garmisch (also in Bavaria) where he died. Became the most celebrated German composer of his generation. After early leaning towards 'traditional' forms, took up and developed the SYMPHONIC POEM – composing e.g. MACBETH, DON JUAN, DEATH AND TRANSFIGURATION, TILL EULEN-SPIEGEL, THUS SPAKE ZARATHUSTRA (Ger., *Also sprach Zarathustra*), DON QUIXOTE, A HERO'S LIFE. Also of the character of symphonic poems are his SYMPHONIA DOMESTICA (see also PARERGON) and ALPINE SYMPHONY (1915), his last work of this illustrative type). His early operas (e.g. SALOME, ELEKTRA, DER ROSEN-KAVALIER) have a grandiloquent, Wagner-influenced style and a tendency to 'shocking' subjects; but from ARIADNE ON NAXOS (1912), there are signs of the more intimate manner that characterizes especially certain very late works – e.g. Horn Concerto no. 2, Symphony for wind (both in neo-Mozartian style). Wrote also incidental music to Molière's *Le Bourgeois gentilhomme* (see ARIADNE ON NAXOS); METAMORPHOSES for strings; many songs, several with his own orchestral accompaniments (see FOUR LAST SONGS); various further operas including ARABELLA, INTERMEZZO, CAPRICCIO; ballet *The Legend of Joseph*.

Stravinsky, Igor [Fedorovich] (1882–1971), Russian-born composer; also pianist, conductor, and author of autobiographical and other writings. Pupil of Rimsky-Korsakov; left Russia in 1914; lived mainly in Paris, naturalized French, 1934; settled in USA, 1939, naturalized there, 1945. Prodigiously successful and influential composer, initially winning fame with pre-1914 ballets THE FIREBIRD, PETRUSHKA and (using enormous orchestra and 'savage' dynamic elements) THE RITE OF SPRING. Later developed NEO-CLASSICAL tendency (compact forms, small forces, aversion from 'emotion', see SYMPHONY), though the austerity of this was modified from the 1930s. Showed interest in jazz (e.g. in THE SOLDIER'S TALE); based ballet PULCINELLA on music supposedly by Pergolesi; adopted a deliberate back-to-Mozart style in opera THE RAKE'S PROGRESS (1951). Other works include SYMPHONY OF PSALMS (with chorus), DUMBARTON OAKS CONCERTO, EBONY CONCERTO (for dance band); opera-oratorio OEDIPUS REX; PERSEPHONE; ballets APOLLO MUSAGETES, ORPHEUS, AGON; Mass. Notable rhythmic and harmonic innovator, but long adhered to tonality; however, from the choral-and-orchestral *Canticum sacrum* (Holy Canticle – in Latin, for St Mark's, Venice), 1955, he adopted a 12-note technique indebted to Webern's. Later works included ballet AGON; MOVEMENTS for piano and orchestra; THRENI; THE FLOOD; *Sacred Ballad* (in Hebrew, based on the biblical story of Abraham and Isaac) for baritone and small orchestra; *Elegy for J. F. Kennedy*. See also ODE and RAGTIME.

Strawinsky, German spelling of the Russian name STRAVINSKY.

street piano, type of instrument used by itinerant musicians, being basically a mechanical form of piano: a selection of tunes is available, played by the turning of a handle which operates a barrel-and-pin mechanism similar to that of a musical box. An alternative name (because the turning of the handle is similar to that of a BARREL-ORGAN) is 'piano-organ'.

Street Scene, opera by Weill, produced (as a musical, in continuous run) in New York, 1947; set in modern New York, it is an adaptation of a play by Elmer Rice, with lyrics by Langston Hughes.

stretta (It., drawn together; fem. form of following), term used in some Italian operatic scores for the section towards the end of a long ensemble when a quicker tempo succeeds a slower one.

stretto (It., drawn together), (1) direction that the pace is to become faster; (2) term used of the overlapping of entries in certain examples of FUGUE or similar composition, the subject beginning in one voice before the preceding voice has finished uttering it. A *stretto maestrale* (magisterial) occurs when the full length of the subject, and not just the first part of it, is subjected to overlapping. Cp. preceding.

strict counterpoint, see COUNTERPOINT.

Strindberg, August (1849–1912), Swedish writer. See RANGSTRÖM, REIMANN, ROREM, WEISGALL.

string(s), name given to the thin strands of wire or gut which are set in vibration e.g. on the piano (by hammers), violin (by the bow), harp and guitar (by plucking); hence the word *strings* is used for 'stringed instruments'. But in normal use *the strings* or *the string section* of an orchestra means only the violins (divided into first and second), violas, cellos and double-basses – not the harp and piano which, if used, are classified separately. Similarly a *string orchestra* normally implies violins (first and second), violas, cellos and double-bases only. The standard *string quartet* is two violins, viola, cello; *string trio*, violin, viola, cello.

stringendo (It., tightening), direction to a performer to increase the 'tension' of the music – in effect, to increase speed, often as preparation for a new section of basically faster tempo than the old one.

Stringfield, Lamar (1897–1959), American composer and conductor, also flautist; works include *From the Southern Mountains* and *The Legend of John Henry* for orchestra, and other works alluding to American life and legend.

stromento, see STRUMENTO.

strophic, term used of a song in which the same music is repeated (exactly or almost exactly) for each successive stanza of a poem. The opposite type, in which the music progresses continually, has usually been called in English a 'through-composed song' (from Ger., *durchkomponiert*); it would be less ugly and less awkward to say 'non-strophic' or 'non-repeating'.

strumento (It., pl. -i), instrument. The old form *stromento* is also encountered.

Stuart, Leslie (pen-name of Thomas A. Barrett) (1866–1928), British composer of *Florodora* and other musical comedies, song 'Lily of Laguna', etc.

study, an instrumental piece (usually solo) written to train or demonstrate the facility of the performer in certain points of technique – but sometimes having artistic value as well, e.g. the three sets (27 in all) by Chopin for piano. (The word translates the French *étude*, which is also, needlessly, used in English.) See also SYMPHONIC STUDY.

style, term used in different senses to differentiate the usages of a period, nationality or individual, in composition or performance. Thus *Monteverdi's style*, the *classical style* (often implying the Haydn–Mozart period), a *bravura style* (of performance). So also *style-modulation*, name applied to a composer's deliberate, temporary adoption of another composer's work or manner.

su (It.), on; *sul, sulla*, on the; *sul G*, on the G-string; *sul ponticello* (on, i.e. near, the bridge), *sul tasto* or *sulla tastiera* (on the fingerboard) – special methods of bowing the violin and related instruments.

subdominant, name for the fourth degree of the scale, e.g. F in key C (major or minor). It is so called because it dominates the scale to an extent subordinate to the DOMINANT or fifth degree.

subito (It.), immediately; *attacca subito*, go on (to the next section) without a break.

subject, term used in musical analysis to define a group of notes which appears to form a basic element in a composition and which is given prominence by its position, by being repeated or developed, etc. In SONATA-FORM the main musical ideas (usually two) announced in the 'exposition' and then developed are called subjects; in fugue the term is more narrowly restricted – see FUGUE.

submediant, the sixth degree of the scale, e.g. A in the key of C major, A♭ in the key of C minor. So called because it is halfway between the keynote and the subdominant (working downwards), whereas the MEDIANT (third degree of the scale) is halfway between the keynote and the dominant (working upwards).

Subotnick, Morton (b. 1933), American composer, active in electronic music (his *Silver Apples of the Moon*, 1967, is thought to be the first electronic work composed for issue as a recording). Has also written a series of works (for different performing groups) each called *Play!*; a *Ritual Game Room* with tape, lights, dancer, four game-players and no audience, etc.

Suchoň, Eugen (b. 1908), Czechoslovak composer of operas *The Whirlpool* and *Svätopluk*; cantata *Psalm of the Carpathian Land*; *Pictures of Slovakia* for piano, etc.

suite (Fr., a following), the most common name for an instrumental piece in several movements, usually (in older use) a sequence of dances. Its characteristic in the 17th and 18th centuries was the inclusion of the dance-forms 'allemande', 'courante', 'sarabande', and 'gigue' (these French names were widely used) with optional additions. The BINARY form characteristic of these dances was expanded in the mid 18th century into SONATA-FORM, and the suite was succeeded as the prevailing instrumental form by the sonata (and symphony, i.e. sonata for orchestra, etc.). Since then *suite* has lost a strict specification, and in the 19th and 20th centuries has often been used for a work rather lighter or more loosely connected than a work of sonata type: it may describe a set of movements assembled from an opera or ballet score, etc.

Suk, Josef (1874–1935), Czech composer – also violinist, for 40 years in the Bohemian String Quartet. Pupil and son-in-law of Dvořák; his music carries on Dvořák's ideas with some modernization. Works (nearly all instrumental) include symphony *Asrael*; *Prague* and other symphonic poems; cycle of piano pieces *Things Lived and Dreamed* (Cz., *Životem snem*) and other piano works.

Suk, Josef (b. 1929), Czech violinist, grandson of the preceding; trio-player with Katchen and Starker, 1967–9.

sul, sulla, see SU.

Sullivan, Arthur [Seymour] (1842–1900), British composer (also organist and conductor) who studied in Leipzig. Wrote much serious music – including symphony, *Overtura di ballo* (see BALLO), religious cantata *The Golden Legend*, opera *Ivanhoe* – but made his chief reputation in a long series of successful operettas, combining solid musical construction with apt reinforcement of verbal points. Those written with W. S. Gilbert as librettist are *Thespis* (lost, unpublished), TRIAL BY JURY, THE SORCERER, HMS PINAFORE, THE PIRATES OF PENZANCE, PATIENCE, IOLANTHE, PRINCESS IDA, THE MIKADO, RUDDIGORE, THE YEOMEN OF THE GUARD, THE GONDOLIERS and, finally and unsuccessfully, UTOPIA LIMITED and THE GRAND DUKE. Operettas without Gilbert include COX AND BOX and (unfinished) *The Emerald Isle*, completed by German. Knighted, 1883. See also PINEAPPLE POLL.

Sumer is icumen in, English mid-13th-century work, the oldest known canon and the oldest-known six-PART composition. It has alternative words in Latin for church use. Known also as the 'Reading Rota' (see ROTA) because its conjectural composer was John of Fornsete, monk of Reading Abbey. It is quoted in Britten's SPRING SYMPHONY.

summational tone, see RESULTANT TONE.

Suor Angelica, see SISTER ANGELICA.

supertonic, the second degree of the scale, e.g. the note D in the key C (major or minor) – lying immediately above the TONIC (first degree).

Suppé, Franz von (Germanized form of name used by Francesco Ermenegildo Ezechiele Suppé-Demelli) (1819–95), Austrian (Dalmatian-born) composer of Belgian descent. Wrote succession of popular operettas including *The Beautiful Galatea* and *Boccaccio*; overtures to plays including POET AND PEASANT; a Mass, etc.

sur (Fr.), on; *sur la touche, sur le cheva-*

let, on the fingerboard, on (i.e. near) the bridge – special methods of bowing a violin and related instruments.

Surinach, Carlos (b. 1915), Spanish-born composer, naturalized American, 1959; also concert and operatic conductor. Works include three symphonies and Symphonic Variations for orchestra; *Songs of the Soul* for chorus, *Flamenco Meditations* for voice and piano; ballet scores; etc.

'Surprise' Symphony, nickname for Haydn's Symphony no. 94 in G (Hob. I:94), composed in 1791 – so called because of the sudden loud chord in the slow movement.

Survivor from Warsaw, A, work by Schoenberg (first performed in 1948) for speaker, men's chorus and orchestra; text by the composer (in English, apart from German interpolations and a Hebrew prayer) alluding to the Nazis' murder of Jews.

Susanna, oratorio by Handel, first performed in 1749; text after the Apocrypha by author now unknown.

Susanna's Secret (It., *Il segreto di Susanna*), one-act comic opera by Wolf-Ferrari, produced (in German) in Munich, 1909. Libretto by E. Golisciani: Susanna's terrible secret is that she smokes.

Susato, Tielman (?–c.1561), German music publisher and composer; from 1529 town trumpeter in Antwerp, where he died. Composed songs, dances, etc.

suspension, a device in harmony by which a note in a chord is kept sounding when that chord has been succeeded by another in which the prolonged note forms a discord. This discord is then normally resolved when the prolonged note falls to a note forming part of the new chord. If it rises instead of falling, then the process is in some textbooks called 'retardation', presumably on the linguistically pedantic ground that a thing 'suspended' must fall. The reverse process to both of these, when the note precedes the chord of which it forms a part, is called ANTICIPATION.

Süssmayr, Franz Xaver (1766–1803), Austrian composer of operas, church music, etc., and conductor. A pupil of Mozart, he completed the Requiem which Mozart left unfinished at his death.

sustaining pedal, see PIANO (2).

Sutermeister, Heinrich [Paul] (b. 1910), Swiss composer of operas, including *Romeo and Juliet*, *The Magic Island* after Shakespeare's *The Tempest* and *Raskolnikov* (after Dostoyevsky's *Crime and Punishment*); also three piano concertos, a two-piano concerto, etc. Pupil of Orff.

Sutherland, Joan (b. 1926), Australian soprano; joined Covent Garden Opera Company, 1952; attained international celebrity in Donizetti's LUCIA DI LAMMERMOOR (Covent Garden, 1959) and continued to enjoy operatic prominence into her mid-60s. Created Dame, 1979; retired in 1990. Married to Richard BONYNGE.

Suzuki, Shin'ichi (b. 1898), Japanese violinist who evolved a technique of teaching very young children the violin (and other instruments) which won world-wide success from the 1950s.

Švanda the Bagpiper (Cz., *Švanda dudák*), opera by Weinberger, pro-

duced in Prague, 1927. Libretto by M. Kares, on a Czech folk-tale of which Švanda is the hero. (The spelling 'Schwanda' is inappropriate in English, being only the German representation of the sound of the Czech name.)

Svendsen, Johan [Severin] (1840–1911), Norwegian composer, also conductor and pianist; studied in Leipzig, was associated with Liszt and Wagner and wrote two symphonies and other music showing German influence. But also wrote four *Norwegian Rhapsodies* and other works of Norwegian associations; *Carnival in Paris* for orchestra; chamber music; etc.

Sviridov, Georgy [Vasilyevich] (b. 1915), Russian composer of many songs (some translated into Russian from Shakespeare and Burns), *Miniature Triptych* for orchestra, *Pathetic Oratorio*, etc. Is also pianist.

swanee whistle, crude woodwind instrument, mainly used as a toy; at one end is a recorder-type mouthpiece, at the other a slide which is worked backwards and forwards to vary the length of the tube and so produce different notes. Continued accuracy of pitch is almost impossible and a sliding effect is characteristic; but it has been very occasionally used in the orchestra – e.g. in Ravel's opera THE CHILD AND THE SPELLS and in G. Gordon's ballet THE RAKE'S PROGRESS to simulate a shaky singing voice.

Swan Lake (Rus., *Lebedino ozero*), ballet with music by Tchaikovsky, produced in St Petersburg, 1895. The swans are maidens transformed by a wicked magician.

Swan of Tuonela, The, 'symphonic legend' by Sibelius, 1893 – originally

Swan Song

written as a prelude to an opera, but published as one of four pieces on Finnish legendary subjects; see LEMMINKÄINEN'S HOMECOMING. Tuonela is the land of death surrounded by waters on which the swan floats, singing.

Swan Song (Ger., *Schwanengesang*), name given – by the publisher, not by Schubert – to a collection of 14 songs by Schubert, published in 1828 (after his death). They were not grouped by Schubert and do not form a unity like his genuine song-cycles.

Swedish Rhapsody, see ALFVÉN.

Sweelinck, Jan Pieterszoon (1562–1621), Dutch composer – also organist and harpsichordist. Wrote organ works, notable for their development of the fugue, and for their pioneering of an independent part for the pedals; taught many German organist-composers. Wrote also various vocal works, some for the church.

swell, a device for increasing and diminishing the volume of sound on an organ, or on certain 18th-century harpsichords. See next entry.

swell organ (or simply *swell*), name given to a section of the organ in which the pipes are set in an enclosed space; the player can consequently regulate the volume of sound through a pedal (*swell pedal*) which opens and closes a shutter. The manual controlling this (placed directly above the GREAT) is called the *swell manual*. But note that the *swell effect* (of being able to increase and decrease volume) can usually be obtained also on the 'Choir' and 'Solo' manuals of the modern organ.

Swift, Jonathan (1667–1745), English writer. See KELLEY.

Swinburne, Algernon Charles (1837–1909), English poet. See BANTOCK, CHORAL SYMPHONY.

Sylphides, Les, ballet with music arranged from piano works by Chopin; produced in Paris, 1909. Various orchestrations are used. (Title is merely French for 'The Sylphs'.)

Sylvia, ballet with music by Delibes, produced in Paris, 1876; the heroine is a mythical huntress.

sympathetic, term used in allusion to the capacity of strings and other bodies to vibrate (and thus give a note) when this note is sounded near them by some other agent. So *sympathetic strings*, e.g. on the viola d'amore, not touched by the bow but vibrating by their proximity to the bowed strings lying above them.

symphonia, Greek word taken into Latin and used in certain modern contexts as equivalent to 'symphony' – e.g. in R. Strauss's *Symphonia Domestica* (i.e. Domestic Symphony), 1904, describing with semi-realistic touches the composer's home life.

symphonic band = CONCERT BAND.

symphonic poem, term introduced by Liszt for an orchestral work which is approximately of the size and seriousness customarily associated with a symphony, but which is meant as an interpretation of something non-musical, e.g. a work of literature. A not quite satisfactory synonym is TONE POEM; see next entry.

symphonic study, term not in standard use, but used by Elgar (more or less as an equivalent for SYMPHONIC POEM) for his FALSTAFF. Schumann's *Symphonic Studies* (1836, revised 1852) are a set of variations for piano solo. See STUDY.

symphonie (Fr.), symphony; *Symphonie concertante*, see following entry; *Symphonie espagnole*, see SPANISH SYMPHONY. *Symphonie fantastique*, see FANTASTIC SYMPHONY.

symphonie concertante, the French equivalent (and the original form) of what is now more often called the *sinfonia concertante* (Ital.), i.e. a concerto-type work featuring more than one solo instrument, such as Mozart's Sinfonia Concertante for violin and viola.

symphony, term literally meaning 'a sounding-together', formerly indicating (1) an overture, e.g. to an opera; (2) the instrumental section introducing, or between the verses of, a vocal work. Occasionally such archaic meanings are revived, e.g. in Stravinsky's work entitled *Symphonies for Wind Instruments* (1920). But, in general, since the mid 18th century, the word has ordinarily indicated an orchestral work of a serious nature and a substantial size, in the shape of a SONATA for orchestra. Most such works are in four movements; some are in three; some are in one ('telescoping' a larger number of movements together) or five; other numbers are very rare. Symphonies may have a name (e.g. Beethoven's PASTORAL SYMPHONY), or may include vocal parts (since Beethoven's CHORAL SYMPHONY); but such remain the minority. A *symphony orchestra* (or, in USA, just 'a symphony') is an orchestra large enough to play symphonies and having a repertory of 'serious' music (see ORCHESTRA); a *symphony concert* is one including a symphony or other work of similar type. See also SINFONIA and following entries.

Symphony of a Thousand, nickname for Mahler's Symphony no. 8, first performed in 1910 – because of the huge forces employed (large orchestra, an extra brass group, seven vocal soloists, boys' choir, two mixed choirs).

Symphony of Psalms, work for chorus and orchestra by Stravinsky, 1930, 'composed to the glory of God, dedicated to the Boston Symphony Orchestra'. In three movements; text from Psalms, in Latin.

Symphony on a French Mountaineer's Song (Fr., *Symphonie sur un chant montagnard français*), work for piano and orchestra by d'Indy, first performed in 1887.

syncopation, a displacement of accent on to a beat that is normally unaccented.

Synge, John Millington (1871–1909), Irish poet and dramatist. See RABAUD, RIDERS TO THE SEA.

synthesizer, general word for an electronic apparatus by which any one of a number of musical sounds can be put together from its physical components (harmonic constituents, characteristics of attack and decay, etc.) at such a speed and with such convenience as to make possible the performance of a piece from a musical score; generally (e.g. MOOG synthesizer) with a piano-like keyboard.

system, a grouping of staves in a score (with a vertical left-hand line joining the staves) to show a group of instruments and/or voices performing together; thus, where four voices each on a separate line are notated on a page of 12 staves, they are joined in four-stave systems, with three systems to the page.

391

Szabó, Ferenc (1902–69), Hungarian composer, resident in USSR, 1931–45; works include Concerto for Orchestra, cantatas, piano pieces.

Szeligowski, Tadeusz (1896–1963), Polish composer of opera *The Revolt of the Schoolboys*, ballet *The Peacock and the Girl*, and orchestral *Epitaph for Szymanowski*, choral works, etc.

Szell, Georg (originally György Széll) (1897–1970), Hungarian-born conductor who grew up in Vienna, naturalized American in 1946; won particular fame as conductor of the Cleveland Orchestra, 1946–70. See FROM MY LIFE.

Szervánszky, Endre (1911–77), Hungarian composer, also critic and academic teacher. Works include a symphony, a clarinet concerto, flute concerto, pieces for two violins, Hungarian folk-song arrangements.

Szeryng, Henrik (1918–88), Polish-born violinist who settled in Mexico (naturalized, 1946); eminent in concertos, etc.; touring internationally from the mid-1950s.

Szigeti, Joseph (originally József) (1892–1973), Hungarian-born violinist, naturalized American in 1951; made London début in 1907 and pioneered many new works.

Szokolay, Sándor (b. 1931), Hungarian composer of opera *Blood Wedding* (based on Lorca's play); *Déploration* (Fr., Lament), in memory of Poulenc, for chorus and orchestra; a trumpet concerto, etc.

Szymanowski, Karol (1882–1937), Polish composer (also pianist) born in the Russian Ukraine. After study in Berlin was influenced by R. Strauss and Debussy, but later took to a simpler harmonic style with some debt to Polish folk-music. Works include operas *Hagith* and KING ROGER; two violin concertos; three *Myths* for violin and piano (no. 1, 'The Fountain of Arethusa'); four symphonies; a Stabat Mater; song-settings of James Joyce, Tagore and other poets. Died in a Swiss sanatorium.

T

t, symbol in TONIC SOL-FA for the seventh degree (leading-note) of the scale, pronounced *te*. Cp. SI.

Tabachnik, Michel (b. 1942), Swiss conductor (also composer) of Russian extraction, an associate of Boulez and a specialist in interpreting complex modern works.

Tabarro, Il, see CLOAK.

tabla, a type of Indian small-size drum with a single head (membrane) but a double body of two truncated cones; played with the fingers.

tablature, a system of writing down music by symbols which represent not the pitch (as in ordinary modern notation) but the position of the performer's fingers. Such a system was formerly used for the lute, and another one for keyboard (see SCHEIDT). The diagrammatic notation used in popular music for guitar is a tablature.

Tábor, see MY COUNTRY.

tabor, small drum used e.g. to accompany folk-dancing – the player beating the drum with one hand (not with sticks) while the other hand fingers a three-holed pipe.

tacet (Lat., is silent), indication that a particular performer or instrument has no part for considerable time, e.g. for a whole movement.

Taddei, Giuseppe (b. 1916), Italian baritone, a noted performer with the Vienna State Opera from 1949; sang more than 135 roles.

Tafelmusik (Ger., table-music), music suited to convivial gatherings, e.g. for performance at or after dinner. (See TELEMANN.)

Tagore, [Sir] Rabindranath (1861–1941), Indian poet. See HAGEMAN, ROTA (N.), SZYMANOWSKI.

Tailleferre, Germaine (1892–1983), French composer (also pianist), member of the former group THE SIX; she wrote a piano concerto, a harp concertino, songs, etc.

Takemitsu, Toru (b. 1930), Japanese composer, mainly self-taught. Works include several on tape, and also *November Steps No. 1* for shakuhachi, biwa (Japanese instruments) and orchestra; *Requiem* for strings, *Coral Island* for soprano and orchestra.

Tal (originally Gruenthal), **Josef** (b. 1910), Polish-born Israeli composer who studied in Germany. Works on Hebrew texts include operas *Ashmedai* and *The Temptation*, cantata *Call of the Fallen Soldiers*; has also written ten six piano concertos (no. 4 with tape).

Talbot, Howard (pen-name of Richard

Lansdale Munkittrick) (1865–1928), American composer who settled in England and wrote music for *The Arcadians* (see also MONCKTON) and other musical comedies.

Tales from the Vienna Woods (Ger., *Geschichten aus dem Wienerwald*), waltz by Johann Strauss the younger, 1868.

Tales of Hoffmann, The (Fr., *Les Contes d'Hoffmann*), opera by Offenbach, produced in Paris, 1881, after the composer's death. Guiraud completed the scoring and supplied the recitatives which in most productions replace the original spoken dialogue. Libretto by J. Barbier and M. Carré. The hero represents the German Romantic writer E. T. A. HOFFMANN, and the succession of amorous adventures is drawn from his works.

Talich, Václav (1883–1961), Czechoslovak conductor, one of his country's most prominent musicians; a leading orchestral and operatic conductor in Prague.

Tallis, Thomas (*c.*1505–85), English composer and organist; from 1572 joint organist with Byrd at the Chapel Royal, and from 1575 joint holder with Byrd of a State monopoly of music-printing in England. Cultivated a solemn style of great contrapuntal ingenuity, as seen e.g. in his Latin motet 'Spem in alium' in 40 parts, i.e. for eight choirs each of five voices. Wrote mainly church music, in Latin (see CANTIONES SACRAE) and then in English; also some pieces for keyboard, viols, etc. The so-called 'Tallis's Canon' is an adaptation from one of a set of psalm-tunes, 1567; Vaughan Williams's *Fantasia on a Theme of Tallis* (first performed in 1910) is based on another of the same set.

talon (Fr.), heel (of the bow of a stringed instrument), i.e. the end of the bow which is held by the player.

Talvela, Martti (1935–89), Finnish bass, prominent in opera – Bayreuth Festival, 1962; La Scala, Milan, from 1964.

Tamagno, Francesco (1850–1905), Italian tenor, noted in opera; chosen by Verdi to sing the title-role of OTELLO at its première.

Tamberlik, Enrico (1820–89), Italian tenor for whom Verdi wrote the principal tenor role in THE FORCE OF DESTINY; prominent performer in Paris and London.

tambour (Fr.), drum; *tambour de Basque* = TAMBOURINE; tambour militaire = SNARE-DRUM.

tambourin (Fr., originally diminutive of *tambour*, drum), a type of drum, especially the long, narrow drum from Provence; hence a dance-movement, e.g. in the works of Rameau, simulating a rustic drum-beat.

tambourine, type of small drum struck with the fingers and rattled with the hand; it has little jingles inserted into its wooden frame. It is of Arab origin but was known in Europe before 1300; brought into the modern orchestra by Weber, Berlioz and later composers mainly to evoke revelry, gipsies, exotic scenes, etc.

tambura (also *tanbura*, *tanpura*), a long-necked Indian lute having four wire strings and no frets; plucked with the fingers, it is used only to provide a drone.

tamburo (It.), drum; *tamburo piccolo* (literally, little drum) = SNARE-DRUM.

Taming of the Shrew, The, title of operas (after Shakespeare's play) by several composers – notably by Goetz (produced at Mannheim, 1874, as *Der widerspänstigen Zähmung*, with libretto by J. V. Widmann), and by Shebalin (Moscow, 1955).

tam-tam, see GONG. (Not the same as TOM-TOM.)

Tancred, name of operas by various composers – from poem by Tasso, concerning a fabled hero of the Crusades and his love for a woman on the enemy side – notably (1) Campra (*Tancrède*), produced in Paris, 1702, with a libretto by A. Danchet; (2) Rossini (*Tancredi*) produced in Venice, 1813, with a libretto by R. Rossi. Monteverdi's *Combat of Tancred and Clorinda* (*Il combattimento di Tancredi e Clorinda*, 1624) is a non-operatic cantata, though in modern times it has been staged.

Taneyev, surname of two distantly related Russian composers (separately, below). The surname without qualification indicates the second.

Taneyev, Alexander Sergeyevich (1850–1918), Russian composer of operas, orchestral works, etc.; pupil of Rimsky-Korsakov.

Taneyev, Sergey Ivanovich (1856–1915), Russian pianist and composer of four symphonies, songs and choral works, etc.; pupil and friend of Tchaikovsky. Noted teacher. See preceding entries.

tangent, the metal 'tongue' which, on the clavichord, touches a string when a key is struck and so sounds that string. It remains in contact with the string for as long as the note sounds, unlike the hammers of the piano. (From Lat. *tangere*, touch.)

tango, Argentinian dance supposed to have been imported by African slaves into the American continent; taken into general use in ballroom dancing about the time of World War I. Its characteristic rhythm is ♩.♪♩♩

Tannhäuser and the Singing Contest at the Wartburg (Ger., ... *und der Sängerkrieg auf der Wartburg*), opera by Wagner, produced in Dresden, 1845. (What is called the 'Paris version' refers to the revision made by Wagner for the Paris production of 1861.) Libretto by composer: Tannhäuser is a medieval minstrel torn between 'sacred' and 'profane' love.

Tansman, Alexandre (1897–1986), Polish-born composer, naturalized French; settled in Paris, 1919. Works, in an individual but not 'revolutionary' style, include eight symphonies, eight string quartets, operas, ballets, pieces for one and two pianos. Was also pianist and conductor.

tanto (It.), so much; *allegro ma non tanto*, fast but not too fast.

Tantum ergo, name for part of a Latin hymn by St Thomas Aquinas, which is used in Roman Catholic services; it has its own plainsong melodies and has also been set afresh by various composers.

Tanz (Ger.), dance.

tape, term which in musical references stands for electronic-recording tape, particularly in reference to music which the composer has assembled from electronic components directly on to tape. The play-back of this tape then constitutes the performance or is combined with 'live' elements: as in music 'for piano and tape', etc. See ELECTRONIC MUSIC.

Tapiola, symphonic poem by Sibelius, 1926 – named after Tapio, the forest god of Finnish mythology.

tarantella, fast Italian dance in 6/8 time with alternating major-key and minor-key sections. named from the South Italian town of Taranto, habitat of the tarantula: superstition declared the tarantula poisonous, and the dance was said to be the result of (or sometimes the cure for) this poison.

tarentelle, French form of TARANTELLA.

tárogató, Hungarian single-reed woodwind instrument, related to the clarinet and saxophone; it has sometimes been used to perform part of the shepherd's piping in Act III of Wagner's TRISTAN AND ISOLDE.

Tárrega, Francisco (1852–1909), Spanish guitarist, and composer and arranger of many works for his instrument.

Tartini, Giuseppe (1692–1770), Italian violinist and composer, founder of a famous school for violin-playing. Travelled much in Italy, and for three years worked in Prague. Wrote concertos and sonatas (including the DEVIL'S TRILL) for violin; also trio sonatas, church music, etc. Improved the violin-bow. Also author of theoretical writings on music, and discoverer of what modern acoustics calls RESULTANT TONES.

Tasso, Torquato (1544–95), Italian poet. See ARMIDA, RINALDO, SEEFRIED, TANCRED.

tasto (It.), (1) the fingerboard of a keyboard instrument; *sul tasto*, on the fingerboard; (2) the finger-key of a keyboard instrument: *tasto solo*, finger-key only – i.e. (in music which has a CONTINUO part) instruction to play only the single bass-note written and not the supporting chords which a continuo-player would normally add.

Tate, Jeffrey (b. 1943), British conductor who trained first as a doctor; active in opera (Covent Garden from 1982). He suffers from curvature of the spine and conducts seated.

Tate, Nahum (1652–1715), English poet. See DIDO AND AENEAS.

Tate, Phyllis [Margaret Duncan] (1911–87), British composer; works include opera *The Lodger*, songs, a saxophone concerto, *A Secular Requiem* for voices, organ and orchestra.

Tauber (originally Denemy), **Richard** (1892–1948), Austrian tenor, naturalized British. Well known in opera, recital and (especially) Lehár's operettas. Also composer and conductor.

Tausig, Carl (1841–71), Polish pianist who settled in Germany, becoming pupil of Liszt; made arrangements for the piano of some organ works of Bach, orchestral pieces by various composers, etc. Also composer. Died of typhoid.

Tavener, John [Kenneth] (b. 1944), British composer, also pianist and organist; pupil of Berkeley. Works on religious subjects (both before and after his conversion to Russian Orthodoxy) include cantata *Ultimos ritos* (Sp., Last Rites), and *The Protecting Veil* for cello and orchestra; has also written operas *Thérèse* and *A Gentle Spirit* (after Dostoyevsky).

Taverner, opera by Peter Maxwell Davies, produced in London, 1972; libretto by composer, about the 16th-century musician – see following.

Taverner, John (*c*.1490–1545), English composer and organist: wrote chiefly church music in Latin, including eight Masses – one based on the then popular song, 'The Western Wind'. His mass *Gloria tibi Trinitas* was the starting-point of the 'In nomines' for strings (see IN NOMINE) and a few other works. The oft-retailed story that in later life he became an active agent in the political suppression of the monasteries is now held to be a fiction.

Taylor, [Joseph] Deems (1885–1966), American composer of operas (including *The King's Henchman* and *Peter Ibbetson*), orchestral works (including suite *Through the Looking-Glass*, after Lewis Carroll, originally for chamber-music group), etc.; also writer and radio commentator on music.

Taylor, Samuel Coleridge-, see COLERIDGE-TAYLOR.

Tchaikovsky, Boris [Alexandrovich] (b. 1925), Russian pianist and composer, pupil of Shostakovich and others; works include opera *The Star*, two symphonies, four string quartets.

Tchaikovsky, Pyotr Ilyich (1840–93), Russian composer, aloof from the overt nationalism of THE MIGHTY HANDFUL group, but nevertheless writing in a distinctively Russian style. A homosexual, left his wife a few weeks after marriage (1877); 1876–90, carried on an extensive correspondence with Nadezhda von Meck, a wealthy widow who made him a monetary allowance – but they hardly met. Visited USA, 1892; England, 1893 (D.Mus., Cambridge). Developed cholera after drinking unboiled water (perhaps deliberately?) in St Petersburg, and died there a few days after

the first performance of his last symphony, the PATHETIC. His Second Symphony is nicknamed UKRAINIAN (or 'Little Russian'), and his Third Symphony POLISH; his MANFRED Symphony is unnumbered. Other works – notable for vivid, forceful scoring and for an often-expressed melancholy – include three piano concertos (no. 1 the popular one, no. 3 unfinished), a violin concerto; orchestral works (see, e.g., MOZARTIANA, THE TEMPEST, ROMEO AND JULIET, HAMLET, FRANCESCA DA RIMINI, EIGHTEEN-TWELVE); YEVGENY ONEGIN, THE QUEEN OF SPADES, YOLANDE, MAZEPPA and seven other operas; ballets SWAN LAKE, THE SLEEPING BEAUTY, THE NUTCRACKER; chamber works, songs.

Tcherepnin, Alexander Nikolayevich (1899–1977), Russian-born composer and pianist, settled in Paris, 1921; university teacher in Chicago, 1949; married a Chinese singer. Works include operas, six piano concertos; various piano solos. Son of Nikolay Tcherepnin (below).

Tcherepnin, Nikolay Nikolayevich (1873–1945), Russian composer of ballets, symphonic poems, a piano concerto, etc.; also pianist and conductor. Made a completion of Musorgsky's unfinished opera, SOROCHINTSY FAIR. Settled in Paris, 1921, with his son (above).

te, in TONIC SOL-FA, the spoken name for the seventh degree (leading-note) of the scale, written t. Cp.SI – the initial letter *t* was adopted in tonic sol-fa because *s* might be confused with *soh* (fifth degree).

Tear, Robert (b. 1939), British tenor, prominent in British opera (Britten, Tippett, Crosse) and noted in varied concert repertory including Russian and Polish songs. Also occasional conductor.

Tebaldi, Renata (b. 1922), Italian soprano, active in opera – at La Scala, Milan, from 1946; first sang in Britain (with La Scala company at Covent Garden), 1950.

tedesco (It., fem. -a), German; alla tedesca, in German fashion – usually meaning 'in the manner of a GERMAN DANCE', but Vaughan Williams's 'Rondo alla tedesca' in his Tuba Concerto (1954) apparently indicates merely a rondo as in a symphonic work by German composers, e.g. by Beethoven.

Te Deum, a Latin hymn of thanksgiving to God, used in the Roman Catholic Church and as 'We praise thee, O God' in the Anglican Church, etc. There is a traditional plainsong melody for it, and other settings for liturgical use; also settings by Handel and other later composers for concert or ceremonial use. Walton wrote one for the coronation of Queen Elizabeth II.

Teil (Ger.), part, section (not in the sense of a voice-part, etc. – see PART, 1 and 2).

Te Kanawa, Kiri (b. 1944), New Zealand soprano, of mixed Maori and European origin, resident in Britain since 1966; internationally celebrated in opera (Covent Garden from 1970). Created Dame, 1982.

Telemann, Georg Philipp (1681– 1767), German composer of 40 operas, many oratorios, church cantatas, concertos and other vocal and instrumental works. His chamber music includes instrumental suites

classified as Musique de table – see TAFELMUSIK. Friend of Bach. Held a leading church music post in Hamburg from 1721 until his death.

Telephone, The, one-act comic opera by Menotti, produced in New York, 1947. Libretto by composer. For two characters only (lovers) – plus the distracting telephone.

tema (It.), theme.

Temirkanov, Yuri (b. 1938), Russian conductor; conducted the Kirov Opera in Leningrad, then from 1988 appointed principal conductor of the Leningrad Philharmonic Orchestra.

temper(ed), see TEMPERAMENT.

temperament, the 'tempering' (i.e. slight lessening or enlarging) of musical intervals away from the 'natural' scale (that deducible by physical laws), in order to fit them for practicable performance. In particular the piano, the modern organ, and other fixed-pitch modern instruments are tuned to equal temperament, meaning that each semitone is made an equal interval. In this way the notes D♯ and E♭ are made identical, and other pairs similarly (though by physical laws they differ slightly); it is therefore equally easy to play in any key or, having started in one key, to modulate to any other. (Bach's 48 Preludes and Fugues, called THE WELL-TEMPERED CLAVIER, were among the first works to require some such system as this, being set in all the major and minor keys.) An earlier system was mean-tone temperament, which gave a nearer approximation to 'natural' tuning than does equal temperament for C major and keys nearly related to it; but it was so far out for keys remote from C major that playing in them was virtually impossible, unless such devices as separate notes for D♯ and E♭ were adopted (as they were on some old organs). It is to be noted that instruments where the notes are not 'preset' (e.g. the violin family) can have no 'system' of temperament, since the player alone determines the pitch of the note and checks it by ear: and he or she may, indeed, get nearer to 'natural' intonation than a keyboard's fixed notes allow.

Tempest, The, play by Shakespeare, to which Sibelius wrote incidental music (1926), and on which Tchaikovsky based his orchestral fantasy, *The Tempest* (1873); it is the source also of Frank Martin's opera of the same name (Ger., *Der Sturm*), an almost literal setting of the text, produced in Vienna, 1956. See also SUTERMEISTER, WELDON.

temple block (or Korean temple block), type of hollowed-out wooden vessel, approximately in the shape of a human head; it is struck with a stick as a percussion instrument, particularly in dance-bands etc. (and occasionally in the symphony orchestra, e.g. in Gould's 'Philharmonic Waltzes'). There are several sizes, giving different pitches though not tuned to any one clear note.

tempo (It., time), pace (pl. *tempi* or, as naturalized Eng, word, *tempos*). So *tempo primo* or *a tempo*, direction to return to the original pace; *tempo di* . . ., at the pace of (a specified dance-movement, for instance); *tempo giusto*, strict time (but see GIUSTO).

ten., abbr. of (1) tenor; (2) *tenuto*.

tenero (It.), tender; *teneramente, tenerezza*, tenderly, tenderness.

Tennyson, Alfred [Lord] (1809–92), British poet. See LISZT, PRINCESS IDA.

tenor, (1) the highest normal male voice, apart from the ALTO (which uses falsetto) – so named because, when polyphonic music emerged in the late Middle Ages, its function was to hold (Lat., *tenere*) the plainsong or other 'given' tune while the other voices proceeded in counterpoint to it; (2) name given, in 'families' of instruments, to that instrument considered to have a position parallel to that which the tenor voice has among voices – so *tenor* SAXOPHONE, *tenor* TROMBONE, etc.; the word *tenor* by itself means in a dance band the tenor saxophone, in a brass band the tenor SAXHORN, and in obsolete English usage meant the viola; (3, *tenor clef*) type of clef (now little used, but sometimes encountered for cello, bassoon, tenor trombone) written ![tenor clef] , in which the note middle C is indicated on the top line but one of the staff. See also following entries.

tenor cor, see MELLOPHONE.

tenor drum, percussion instrument of similar type to snare-drum (and capable of similar rolls, etc.) but deeper in pitch, bigger and without snares. Occasionally used in the orchestra, from the 19th century; also in the military band.

tenor tuba, see TUBA.

tenuto (It., held), direction that a note is to be fully sustained, up to (and sometimes even over) its full written time value.

Termen, Lev Sergeyevich, see THEREMIN.

ternary, in three sections; *ternary form*, classification used of a movement in three sections of which the third is a repetition (exact or near) of the first – i.e. a movement which may be represented as ABA or ABA'. Note that the term is also used even if the first section is initially stated twice (AABA or AABA') as in the conventional 'minuet and trio', in which the 'minuet' section is given twice on its first statement but only once on its return. Cp. BINARY.

Tertis, Lionel (1876–1975), British viola-player who raised his instrument to a new importance, many (chiefly British) composers writing new works specially for him; he himself introduced new technical specifications for the making of the instrument.

tessitura (It., texture), the compass of notes to which a particular singer's voice naturally inclines ('he has a high *tessitura*') though exceptional notes may be produced outside it; similarly, the general compass (not counting exceptional notes) of a vocal part.

tetrachord, an obsolete scale-pattern (ancient Greek, also medieval) grouping four adjacent notes a whole-tone or semitone apart. (Originally from *tetrachordon*, Greek four-stringed instrument.)

Tetrazzini, Luisa (originally Luigia) (1871–1940), Italian soprano who made London début in 1907 and was one of the earliest singers to become a household name mainly on the basis of recordings.

texture, the relative density of sound as perceived in a composition or orchestration; hence 'Brahms's orchestral texture is thicker than

Bizet's', etc. (The literal Italian equivalent, TESSITURA, has a quite different meaning.)

Teyte, Maggie (originally Margaret Tate) (1888–1976), British soprano who became famous on the French opera stage (studying the role of Mélisande with Debussy) and in recitals, especially in French song. Created Dame, 1958.

Thaïs, opera by Massenet, produced in Paris, 1894. Libretto by L. Gallet. Named after its heroine, a fourth-century courtesan who becomes a nun. The well-known orchestral *Meditation* is an intermezzo between the second and last acts.

Thalben-Ball, George [Thomas] (1896–1987), Australian-born organist (also composer) resident in Britain; well-known recitalist, from 1923 to 1981 organist of the Temple Church in London, and from 1949 to 1982 Birmingham City Organist. Knighted, 1982.

Thalberg, Sigismond (1812–71), Austrian (Swiss-born) virtuoso pianist (pupil of Hummel) and composer of a piano concerto and many solos exploiting piano technique; contributor to the HEXAMERON. Wrote also operas, songs, etc.

theatre organ (also called *cinema organ*), type of instrument in vogue particularly 1925–50 for use in intermissions at cinema performances, etc.; it was usually a 'unit organ' (see ORGAN) with some 'freak' stops, e.g. piano, motor-horn.

theme, a group of notes constituting (by repetition, recurrence, development, etc.) an important element in the construction of a piece. In some types of musical analysis it is broadly equated with SUBJECT; but it is sometimes also applied to separately recognizable elements within a subject. In the phrase *theme and variations* it refers to the whole musical statement on which the variations are based (i.e. something much longer than *theme* in most other senses). *Metamorphosis of themes*, the process by which a theme can be altered in character (e.g. by changing its rhythm, say, to suit the dramatic progress of a SYMPHONIC POEM) while retaining its essence – e.g. in Liszt's symphonic poems; *representative theme*, a theme which carries some extra-musical indication (e.g. a person or object or emotion) for dramatic or narrative purpose – e.g. the Wagnerian LEADING-MOTIVE. In the term *theme-song* (recurring in a musical play, etc., in association with a particular character) the word *theme* is used in a general and not a technical musical sense.

theme-song, see preceding.

Theodora, oratorio by Handel, first performed in London, 1750. Libretto by T. Morell: the heroine is a Christian martyr.

theorbo, type of archlute (bass lute) with long, off-the-fingerboard extra strings and an extra (S-shaped) neck; used in 16th–18th centuries to accompany singing and generally as a continuo instrument. The alternative term *theorbo-lute* (more rarely *theorboed lute*) is also found in English 17th- and 18th-century use.

theremin (or *thereminovox*), type of ELECTRONIC instrument having an upright sensitive 'pole' which produces sound from the motion of the hand in space round it; invented in Russia,

1920, by Lev Sergeyevich Termen (b. 1896) who adopted 'Theremin' as the Western form of his name and patented an improved version of the instrument in USA, 1928. Composers using it in ensemble have included Varèse (*Equatorial*, 1934) and Martinů (*Phantasy* with string quartet, oboe, piano, 1945). It has a range of five octaves and a diversity of tone-colour.

Thibaud, Jacques (1880–1953), French violinist, noted as a soloist and as a duo-partner with Marguerite LONG; he never retired, performing when over 70, and was killed in an air crash.

Thieving Magpie, The (It., *La gazza ladra*), opera by Rossini, produced in Milan, 1817. Libretto by G. Gherardini: the magpie is the real perpetrator of the theft for which a maidservant is condemned to death.

Thill, Georges (1897–1984), French tenor with a long and distinguished opera career in Paris (1924–53) embracing about 50 major roles.

third (noun), an interval in melody or harmony, reckoned as taking three steps in the (major or minor) scale, counting the bottom and top notes: either a *major third* (four semitones, e.g. C up to E) or *minor third* (three semitones, e.g. C up to E♭) or *diminished third* (two semitones, e.g. C♯ up to E♭). The last of these is of little practical application, the interval being for practical performing purposes considered as a major second, e.g. D♭ to E♭. See also following entries.

third inversion, see POSITION.

third sound, Tartini's name (It., *terzo suono*) for the acoustical phenomenon he discovered, now known as a RE-SULTANT TONE.

third stream, hopeful term originated about 1957 by Gunther Schuller for music which should be neither jazz nor classical but should absorb both traditions.

thirty-second-note, the note ♪ considered as a time-value. This term is standard North American usage and, as mathematically corresponding to the element of time-signature represented by /32, should clearly be preferred to 'demisemiquaver', still surviving in British use. The corresponding rest is notated ♭

Thomas, [Charles Louis] Ambroise (1811–96), French composer – also pianist, and director of the Paris Conservatory. Wrote MIGNON, HAMLET, RAYMOND and other operas in a light, melodious style (see also CARNIVAL OF VENICE), and ballets, church music, instrumental pieces, etc.

Thomas, Arthur Goring (1850–92), British composer, pupil of Sullivan and Bruch. Works include operas *Esmeralda* and *Nadeshda*, cantata *The Sun Worshippers*, songs. Became insane, 1891.

Thomas, Dylan (1914–53), British poet. See JONES (D.).

Thomas, Michael Tilson (b. 1944), American conductor and pianist, also noted as television presenter; principal conductor of the London Symphony Orchestra since 1988.

Thomas, Theodore [Christian Friedrich] (1835–1905), German-born American conductor, a major activator of orchestral life in New York and Chicago; founder of the Chicago Symphony Orchestra (1891).

Thomé, Francis (real first names Joseph François Luc) (1850–1909), French (Mauritius-born) composer of *Simple Aveu* (Simple Avowal), piano piece later subject to multitudinous arrangements; also of operas, operettas, etc.

Thompson, Randall (1899–1984), American composer, pupil of Bloch and others; also noted teacher. Wrote three symphonies, *The Peaceable Kingdom* and other choral works, opera *Solomon and Balkis*, etc.

Thomson, James (1700–1748), Scottish poet. See ALFRED, SEASONS.

Thomson, Virgil (1896–1989), American composer, pupil of N. Boulanger in Paris; also organist and noted critic. Works include operas FOUR SAINTS IN THREE ACTS, *The Mother of Us All* (both to librettos of Gertrude Stein), and *Lord Byron*; *Symphony on a Hymn-tune*, a cello concerto, *Portraits* of various named people (some for orchestra, some for piano, some for unaccompanied violin), songs in English and French, stage and film music.

thorough-bass, see CONTINUO.

Three-Cornered Hat, The (Sp., *El sombrero de tres picos*), ballet with music by Falla, first produced in London, 1919.

Threepenny Opera, The (Ger., *Die Dreigroschenoper*), opera by Weill, produced in Berlin, 1928, with libretto by Brecht – a modernization (using jazz) of the idea of THE BEGGAR'S OPERA.

threni, term from Greek, used as equivalent of LAMENTATIONS and hence employed by Stravinsky as title of his (Latin) setting of part of this ecclesiastical text, 1958.

through-composed, see STROPHIC.

thunder-machine, a piece of theatre machinery imitating thunder and brought into a few orchestral scores, e.g. R. Strauss's ALPINE SYMPHONY.

Thus Spake Zarathustra (Ger., *Also sprach Zarathustra*), symphonic poem by R. Strauss, first performed in 1896; after a literary text by Nietzsche, who used a variant name for the ancient Persian prophet Zoroaster.

tie, a line in musical notation joining two adjacent notes of the same pitch indicating that the sound of the first is to be prolonged continuously into the second, instead of the latter's being struck afresh. So also *to tie, tied note,* etc.

tief (Ger.), deep, low-pitched.

tierce de Picardie, see PICARDY THIRD.

Till Eulenspiegel, usual abbreviated title for *Till Eulenspiegel's Merry Tricks* (Ger., *Till Eulenspiegels lustige Streiche*), symphonic poem by R. Strauss, first performed in 1895. The hero is a traditional rogue of German folklore, dating at least from the 15th century; other composers have also written works based on his exploits (e.g. Alpaerts, a symphonic poem; Reznicek, an opera; M. Steinberg, a ballet). He is sometimes referred to in English as Tyll Owlglass (literal translation of his surname).

timbale (Fr.) = KETTLEDRUM.

timbre (Fr.) = TONE COLOUR.

timbrel, old English name for TAMBOURINE; it is also a word in biblical translation for a Hebrew instrument thought to be of this type.

time, term used in music to classify

basic rhythmical patterns: thus a movement is said to be in *six-eight time* (6/8 time), having six eighth-notes (quavers) to the bar. (See next entry.) So also, e.g., *common time* (4/4); *waltz time* (3/4, with a characteristic lilt); *march time* (usually 4/4 or 6/8); in *free time,* without any regular accent. (The term is also used more loosely for 'speed'; e.g. *in quick time.*) See also DUPLE, TRIPLE time.

time-signature, sign at the beginning of a composition or movement (and thereafter only when a change has to be indicated) conveying by means of figures the kind of beats in the bar and (above it) the number of such beats, E.g. $\frac{3}{2}$ indicates three half-notes (minims) to the bar, $\frac{3}{8}$ indicates three eighth-notes (quavers). See also DUPLE, TRIPLE TIME.

timpani (It., not *tympani*) = KETTLEDRUMS. (The singular *timpano* is not generally used in English, though it is standard Italian.)

tin-whistle, rudimentary, six-holed, keyless wind instrument of RECORDER type but made of metal. Also called *penny-whistle.*

Tippett, [Sir] **Michael** [Kemp] (b. 1905), British composer, pupil of C. Wood and R. O. Morris – and of Boult and Sargent for conducting; musical director at Morley College, London, 1940–51. He continued to compose into his 80s, with the opera *New Year* (1989), succeeding THE MIDSUMMER MARRIAGE (the choral-and-orchestral 'Ritual Dances' come from this), KING PRIAM, THE KNOT GARDEN, and *The Ice Break,* all with his own librettos; four symphonies, a concerto for double string orchestra and Concerto for Orchestra, *Fantasia Concertante on a Theme of*

Corelli, piano concerto and four piano sonatas, four string quartets, song-cycles *Boyhood's End* and *The Heart's Assurance*; oratorio A CHILD OF OUR TIME, cantatas *The Vision of St Augustine* and *The Mask of Time* (see MASK). Knighted, 1966.

Titan, name given by Mahler to his Symphony no. 1 when he conducted its second performance (1893); the label was later discarded by him but is sometimes retained as a nickname.

toccata (It.), an instrumental piece, usually for one performer and usually consisting of a single rapid movement exhibiting the player's touch (It., *toccare*, to touch); but there are specimens, e.g. by Bach for harpsichord, which are in several movements, and here the term is of imprecise significance. The celebrated Toccata by Widor comes from the fifth of his 'symphonies' for organ alone (*c.*1880).

Toch, Ernst (1887–1964), Austrian-born composer (also pianist) naturalized in USA, 1940, and a prominent teacher and composer of film music there. Also wrote *The Princess and the Pea* and three other operas, seven symphonies, orchestral fantasy *Big Ben* (on the Westminster chimes), chamber music, piano solos, etc.

Toeschi, Carlo Giuseppe (1731–88), see MANNHEIM SCHOOL.

Togni, Camillo (b. 1922), Italian composer, pupil of Casella and others; also pianist. Has written flute sonata, piano works, choral settings of T. S. Eliot, a Missa Brevis, etc.

Tokyo Quartet, string quartet founded in 1969 by Japanese players (led by Koichiro Harada) at the Juilliard School, New York.

Tolstoy, Leo Nikolayevich [Count] (1828–1910), Russian writer. See CIKKER, HAMILTON, LOURIÉ, WAR AND PEACE.

Tomaschek, Wenzel Johann, a Germanized form of the following name.

Tomášek, Václav Jan (1774–1850), Bohemian composer of operas, church music, etc., and especially of piano works and songs. Was himself also pianist and organist.

Tomasi, Henri (1901–71), French composer of operas including *Sampiero Corso* and *The Silence of the Sea*; also of concertos for 13 different instruments, choral works, etc. Was also conductor.

tombeau (Fr., tomb, tombstone), term used by French 17th-century composers for memorial works – a usage revived by Ravel in *The Grave of Couperin* (*Le Tombeau de Couperin*), for piano, 1917, four of the six movements being later orchestrated.

Tom Jones, stage works based on Fielding's novel – (1) opera by Philidor, produced in Paris, 1765 (libretto by A. A. H. Poinsinet); (2) operetta by German, produced in Manchester, 1907 (libretto by A. M. Thompson, R. Courtneidge and C. H. Taylor); (3) opera by Oliver, produced in Aldeburgh, 1976 (libretto by composer).

Tomkins, name of an English family of musicians of whom the most important was Thomas Tomkins (1572–1656), pupil of Byrd, organist of the Chapel Royal, composer of much church music, also of madrigals and music for keyboard and for viols.

Tommasini, Vincenzo (1878–1950), Italian composer; arranged D. Scarlatti's music for the ballet *The Good-humoured Ladies*, and wrote operas, orchestral works, chamber and choral music, etc. Also writer on musical aesthetics.

Tomowa-Sintow, Anna (b. 1941), Bulgarian soprano; began her operatic career in East Germany, was 'discovered' by Karajan and rose to international prominence in Mozart, R. Strauss, etc.

tom-tom, type of high-pitched drum (imitation of African drum) used in Western dance-bands since the 1920s, and occasionally from the 1950s in the orchestra – often in sets of two or more, either tuned to definite notes or otherwise. (Not the same as TAM-TAM.)

ton (Fr.), term which as used in various contexts may mean 'note', 'tone' (interval of two semitones), or 'key'. See next entry.

Ton (Ger., pl. *Töne*), note, sound (not the interval of a 'tone', i.e. two semitones). So *Tonreihe*, note-row (see TWELVE-NOTE); *Tondichtung*, symphonic poem (this German word in fact providing the origin of the unsatisfactory English term TONE POEM); *Tonkunst*, music (literally, 'sound-art'); *Tonkünstler*, musician(s). See preceding entry.

tonada (Sp.), tune, air. (Used e.g. as title of some works by Allende.) Cp. next entry.

tonadilla (Sp.), type of Spanish stage entertainment employing a few singers.

tonal, (1) of notes (so *tonal structure* of a piece); (2) of tonality, as distinct from e.g. ATONALITY (so *a tonal com-

position*; (3) opposite to 'real' in certain technical contexts – see ANSWER, SEQUENCE (1).

tonality = key – especially in the effect made on the listener by the observance of a single key, as opposed (in the 20th century) to POLYTONALITY (simultaneous use of several keys) or ATONALITY (absence of key).

Tondichtung, see TON (Ger.).

tone, (1) quality of musical sound ('he plays with a pleasing tone'); (2) a musical sound consisting of a 'pure' note, as in acoustical analysis ('a note on the violin may be analysed as containing several different tones'); (3) the interval consisting of two semitones, e.g. from C up to D – see WHOLE-TONE; (4) one of the plainsong melodies (see GREGORIAN TONE) used for the singing of psalms in the Roman Catholic Church; (5, US) a note (in such usages as 'a chord consisting of four tones'). It is because of this last use, derived from German (see TON) and needlessly confusing, that there have arisen such American compounds as *tone-row* and *twelve-tone* (Eng., note-row, twelve-note). See also following entries.

tone-cluster, see CLUSTER.

tone-colour, the quality which distinguishes a note as performed on one instrument from the same note as performed on other instruments (or voices). The French word *timbre* is also used in English in this sense. On analysis the differences between tone-colours of instruments are found to correspond with differences in the harmonics represented in the sound (see HARMONIC SERIES).

tone poem = SYMPHONIC POEM. (The

term is a 'translation' of Ger., *Tondichtung*, but is somewhat misleading – 'sound poem' would be better. See TON and TONE.

tongue, to articulate a note on a wind instrument with a certain use of the tongue; so *single-*, *double-* and *triple-tonguing*, making for progressively faster articulation; *flutter-tonguing*, the articulation of sound as if trilling an *r* (e.g. on the flute, where the resulting tone sounds pigeon-like, and on the trumpet).

tonic, the first degree, or keynote, of the scale, e.g. F in the keys of F major and F minor. See also TONIC SOL-FA.

tonic sol-fa, English system of notation and sight-reading introduced in the 1840s by J. S. Curwen (1816–80), though partly anticipated by others. According to this the notes of the major scale are named (ascending) *doh*, *ray*, *me*, *fah*, *soh*, *lah*, *te* – where *doh* is the keynote (tonic), the other notes being thus related to the keynote of the moment, not fixed in pitch as in ordinary (STAFF) notation. Time-values are indicated by bar-lines and dots, and there is other symbolization. The chief use of the written system has been in amateur choral music. See SOLMIZATION.

Tonkunst, Tonkünstler, see TON (Ger.).

tonus (Lat.), (1) Gregorian tone – see TONE, 4; (2) MODE. See also next entry.

tonus peregrinus (Lat., foreign tone), (1) medieval term for what is now called the minor scale, not 'recognized' in the modal system then prevalent; (2) the plainsong sung in the Roman Catholic Church to Psalm 114, being in the above scale. See GREGORIAN TONE.

Torelli, **Giuseppe** (1658–1709), Italian violinist and composer who worked largely in Bologna; was one of the pioneer practitioners of the CONCERTO GROSSO, and also wrote other music for stringed instruments. See CHRISTMAS CONCERTO.

Toronto Symphony Orchestra, Canadian orchestra which took that name in 1926; principal conductor from 1990, Günther Herbig.

Torroba (actually Moreno-Torroba), **Federico** (1891–1982), Spanish composer of music for guitar (including a concerto) and of zarzuelas (Spanish operettas), etc.

Tortelier, **Paul** (1914–90), French cellist, also conductor and composer of three violin concertos, Concerto for two cellos and orchestra, *Israel Symphony*. Lived in Israel 1955–6. His wife, Maud Martin Tortelier (b. 1926), is a cellist, his daughter, Maria de la Pau (b. 1950), a pianist, and his son, Yan Pascal Tortelier (b. 1947), a violinist and conductor.

Tosca, opera by Puccini, produced in Rome, 1900. Libretto by G. Giacosa and L. Illica, after Sardou's French play *La Tosca*. The title-role is that of an operatic prima donna.

Toscanini, **Arturo** (1867–1957), Italian conductor (formerly cellist), eminent in concert and opera; his many important 'first performances' included that of Puccini's TURANDOT. Refused to perform under German or Italian fascism and settled in New York, where the National Broadcasting Company's orchestra was specially created for him (1937). Conducted always from memory, being too short-sighted to read a score from the rostrum. His daughter Wanda married Vladimir HOROWITZ.

Toselli, Enrico (1883–1920), Italian composer of songs, including a famous 'Serenata', and also of operettas, chamber music, etc.

Tosti, [Francesco] Paolo (1846–1916), Italian composer and singing-master who settled in London, taught the British royal family, and was knighted (1908). Wrote 'Good-bye' and other songs in English, also songs in French and Italian.

Tost Quartets, name given to 12 string quartets by Haydn, 1789–90, Hob. III: 57–68 (op. 54 nos. 1–3, op. 55 nos. 1–3, op. 64 nos. 1–6), dedicated to a violinist named Johann Tost.

total serialism, see SERIES.

touche (Fr.), fingerboard (of stringed instruments); *sur la touche,* direction to play 'on the fingerboard' (a special method of bowing).

toujours (Fr.), always, still.

Tournemire, Charles Arnould (1870–1939), French organist and composer of many organ works (also of operas, chamber music, etc.); noted recitalist. Pupil of d'Indy.

Tourte bow, see BOW.

Tovey, Donald Francis (1875–1940), British pianist, composer (opera *The Bride of Dionysus,* a cello concerto, etc.), conductor, professor at Edinburgh University; celebrated for his programme-notes, collected as *Essays in Musical Analysis,* and other writings on music. Made, with great technical skill, a conjectural completion of the final unfinished fugue in Bach's THE ART OF FUGUE. Knighted, 1935.

toy(e), old English term sometimes used for a light piece for the keyboard or lute.

toy symphony, a symphony of a simple kind in which toy instruments are employed. The best-known example, formerly ascribed to Joseph Haydn, is now considered to be the work of Leopold Mozart. Another example was written by Malcolm Arnold (1957).

tr., abbr. of (1) TRILL; (2) TRUMPET.

tracker action, see ACTION.

Traetta, Tommaso [Michele Francesco Saverio] (1727–79), Italian composer of more than 40 operas including *Iphigenia in Tauris* and *Antigone;* also of church music, etc. Pupil of Durante. Worked for a time in St Petersburg and London.

tragédie lyrique (Fr., 'sung' tragedy), the usual term for French serious opera in the period of Lully and Rameau (17th–18th centuries).

Tragic Overture (Ger., *Tragische Ouvertüre*), concert-overture by Brahms, first performed in 1881; it does not refer to any particular tragedy.

'Tragic' Symphony, name given (by the composer) to Schubert's Symphony no. 4 in C minor, 1816 (D417).

Traherne, Thomas (*c.*1636–74), English poet. See BUTTERLEY, DIES NATALIS.

transcribe, (1) to arrange a piece of music for a performing medium other than the original – or for the same medium but in a more elaborate style. The term usually implies a freer treatment than the simple verb 'to arrange' by itself; (2) to convert a piece from one system of notation to another, e.g. from medieval notation to the modern. So also *transcription*.

Transfigured Night (Ger., *Verklärte Nacht*), work by Schoenberg (op. 4, composed in 1899) for string sextet – in effect a 'symphonic poem' for this combination, after a poem by R. Dehmel about a moonlit walk by a man and a woman. The composer's arrangement for string orchestra appeared in 1917.

transition, (1, in analysis) a passage serving mainly to join two passages more important than itself; (2) a change of key, particularly one of a sudden kind, not going through the regularly ordered process called 'modulation' (see MODULATE).

transpose, to write down or perform music at a pitch other than the original. So certain instruments on which the player produces a note different from the written note are called TRANSPOSING INSTRUMENTS; e.g. an English horn, playing a perfect fifth below the written note, is said to *transpose down a fifth*. A song is often *transposed* to a higher or lower key to suit a singer's convenience. So also a piece written in one of the old MODES may be said to be in, e.g., the *Dorian mode transposed*, meaning with the same intervals as the Dorian mode but ending elsewhere than D on which the Dorian ends. So also *transposing keyboard*, one on which the performer can transpose by mechanical aid – he strikes the keys as usual, but the sideways shifting of the keyboard causes strings higher or lower than normal to be struck. See also the following.

transposing instrument (see preceding entry), an instrument on which the player produces a sound at a fixed interval above or below the note written. The chief reason for this is the convenience of a player changing between different sizes of instrument. A player of e.g. the clarinet knows that when seeing the note middle C in the printed music, he or she always puts down the same fingers in the same way. On the 'clarinet in C' the note sounded is the note written, i.e. middle C; other clarinets' names indicate the note each produces instead of C. E.g. on the 'clarinet in B♭', the note written C sounds as B♭ – the instrument transposing the C (and all other notes) one tone lower; the 'clarinet in A' transposes one and a half tones below the written note; the 'clarinet in E♭', one and a half tones higher; the 'bass clarinet in B♭' an octave and one tone lower. The horn and trumpet usually work as transposing instruments (e.g. 'horn in F', 'trumpet in B♭'); but when a brass instrument is described as being 'in' a key this does not necessarily mean that it transposes but merely that it is built to a certain basic pitch – e.g. the normal orchestral tuba is 'in' F or E♭. See IN.

transposition, the process of transferring music to a pitch other than the original. See TRANSPOSE.

transverse flute, name for the ordinary flute, to distinguish it (as held crosswise) from the recorder (of the same basic instrumental type, but held downwards).

trascinando (It.), dragging.

Traubel, Helen (1899–1972), American soprano, noted in Wagner at the New York Metropolitan Opera – which she left when Rudolf Bing, its director, objected to her also performing in night-clubs.

Trauer (Ger.), mourning. So *Trauermarsch*, funeral march. So also Haydn's so-called *Trauersymphonie* (see MOURNING SYMPHONY); Mozart's *Maurerische Trauermusik* (Masonic Funeral Music); Hindemith's *Trauermusik* (Mourning Music) for viola and strings.

Trautonium, trade name for a type of ELECTRONIC instrument invented in Germany in 1930; it produced only one note at a time. It could be fixed to a piano, one hand playing each instrument. R. Strauss and Hindemith wrote for it.

traversa, name occasionally found instead of TRAVERSO.

traverso, name sometimes used in old scores as abbreviation of *flauto traverso* (It.), i.e. the transverse flute – to distinguish this instrument (the ordinary flute, held cross-wise) from the recorder, held downwards.

Traviata, La (It. The Woman Gone Astray), opera by Verdi, produced in Venice, 1853. Libretto by F. M. Piave, after the younger Dumas's *The Lady of the Camellias* – the heroine being a self-sacrificing courtesan who eventually dies.

Travis, Roy [Elihu] (b. 1922), American composer, pupil of Milhaud in Paris. Works include opera *The Passion of Oedipus*, a concerto for flute, pre-recorded African instruments and synthesizer.

treble, (1) type of high voice – the term usually being kept today to children's voices, the adult female equivalent being 'soprano'; (2) the upper part of a composition, or the upper regions of pitch generally – especially in antithesis to BASS; (3) name given to high-pitched members of certain 'families' of instruments: e.g. *treble* RECORDER, *treble* VIOL; (4, *treble clef*) clef written ⨪ indicating the G above middle C as the next-to-bottom line of the staff. It is normally used for high-pitched instruments and for women's and children's voices; also for right-hand piano parts. It is moreover used for the tenor voice, by a convention according to which the notes are sounded an octave lower than written: occasionally, to indicate this, a figure 8 is written below the clef-sign.

Tremblay, Gilles (b. 1932), Canadian composer, pupil in Paris of Messiaen and others; also university teacher in Montreal. Works include *Sonorization* – electronic sounds on 24 tape-channels; *Kekoba* for three voices with martenot and percussion; *Canticle of Durations* (Fr., *Cantique des durées*) for orchestra; piano solos.

tremolando (It., trembling), having the effect of a TREMOLO.

tremolo (It., a shaking, a trembling), (1, in string-playing) the rapid reiteration of a single note by back-and-forth strokes of the bow; (2, in string-playing, and on other instruments) the alternation between two notes as rapidly as possible; (3) term used (misleadingly) by some singing-teachers for the effect in the voice that should rightly be called VIBRATO. Note that *tremolo*, as in (1) above, is strictly the rapid regular fluctuation of intensity, i.e. of volume; 'vibrato' is a fluctuation of pitch, i.e. of the frequency of vibrations.

tremulant, device on the organ imparting a wobbling effect to the note through variation of the wind-pressure: an element both of TREMOLO and VIBRATO is involved.

trepak, lively Russian dance in 2/4 time.

Tretyakov, Viktor (b. 1946), Russian violinist who won the Moscow Tchaikovsky competition (1966) and became known as violinist-director of orchestral performances; conductor of the USSR State Chamber Orchestra.

triad, a three-note chord consisting of a particular note plus its third and fifth above – e.g. C-E-G, which is called the 'common chord' of C major, no matter whether C remains the bass-note or is replaced by one of the other notes. Similarly C-E♭-G is the 'common chord' of C minor. So also *augmented triad*, containing the augmented fifth (e.g. C, E, G♯); *diminished triad*, containing the diminished fifth (e.g. C, E♭, G♭).

Trial by Jury, operetta (but styled a 'dramatic cantata') by Sullivan produced in London, 1875. Libretto by W. S. Gilbert, burlesquing an action for breach of promise. (It is the only Gilbert-and-Sullivan stage piece that is sung throughout, with no spoken dialogue.)

triangle, three-cornered metal-framed percussion instrument, struck with a metal stick; its tinkling sound is without definite pitch.

trill, a musical ornament (usually designated by *tr* ⌁ over the note) also called 'shake', consisting of the rapid alternation of the written note and the note above. Whether this note is a whole-tone or a semitone above depends on which of these notes occurs in the scale in use at the moment – unless the composer directs otherwise. See also TURN. See also following entry.

trillo (It.), (1) trill; *Trillo del Diavolo*, see DEVIL'S TRILL; (2) a 17th-century vocal ornament in which a single note was repeated, the repetitions getting ever faster.

trio, (1) a combination of three performers; *string trio*, violin, viola, cello; *piano trio*, piano, violin, cello; (2) a work for three performers – if instrumental and actually called a 'trio', it will probably have the character of a SONATA for three performers, in several movements; (3) the centre section of a MINUET, so called because formerly it was conventionally written in three-part harmony only, as for a 'trio' in the normal sense; so also when a scherzo or a march is constructed in minuet form (AABA), the 'B' section may be called a trio; (4) name given also to certain works by Bach for organ (or for harpsichord with two manuals and pedals) having three melodic PARTS but played by one performer; these are more reasonably called TRIO-SONATAS or sonatas.

trio-sonata, type of composition favoured in the late 17th and early 18th centuries, usually for two violins and a cello (or bass viol), with a keyboard instrument also playing the bass-line and supporting it with harmonies worked out by the player – see CONTINUO. See also preceding entry.

triple concerto, concerto with three soloists, e.g. Beethoven's (piano, violin, cello), 1805, or Tippett's (see IMAI).

triple counterpoint, see COUNTERPOINT.

triplet, a group of three notes (or notes and rests) of equal time-value, written where a group of two, four or some other number of notes is suggested by the time-signatures. E.g. a three-note group occupying a bar of 2/4 time,

written $\overset{3}{}$ ♪♪♪

triple time, time in which the primary division is into three beats, as distinct particularly from DUPLE TIME (primary division into two). Triple time is normally indicated by the figure 3 or 9 as the upper digit of a TIME-SIGNATURE: e.g. $\frac{3}{4}$ indicates three quarter-notes (crotchets) to the bar, $\frac{9}{8}$ indicates nine eighth-notes (quavers), split into three groups of three. It is to be remarked that the upper digits 6 and 12 do not denote triple time: $\frac{6}{4}$ indicates two pulses each of three quarter-notes, $\frac{12}{8}$ four pulses of three eighth-notes, etc.

Triptych, see TRITTICO.

Tristan and Isolde (Ger., *Tristan und Isolde*), opera by Wagner, produced in Munich, 1865. Libretto by composer, after the Arthurian legend. The two lovers (also known in English as Tristram and Yseult) drink a love-potion in mistake for poison, but eventually die just the same. See also KING'S HENCHMAN, MARTIN (F.).

tritone, the interval of three whole-tones (see TONE, 3), e.g. from F up or down to B. This is a relatively awkward interval to sing, and its use in composition was formerly (in medieval and later practice) hedged round with various prohibitions. Hence the jingle, 'Mi contra fa diabolus est in musica' (Mi against fa [the old names for these notes according to the system of HEXACHORDS] is the devil in music).

Trittico (It., Triptych), Puccini's name for the three contrasted one-act operas produced in a single evening in New York in 1918. See CLOAK, SISTER ANGELICA, GIANNI SCHICCHI.

Triumphs of Oriana, The, English collection of madrigals by various composers, edited by Morley and published in 1601; in the form (modelled on an Italian collection) of tributes, each poem ending 'Long live fair Oriana'. It is generally recognized that 'Oriana' was Elizabeth I. Among the 23 English composers represented in the first edition were J. Bennet, Hilton (the elder), Kirbye, Milton, Morley, J. Mundy, Norcombe, Tomkins, Weelkes, Wilbye; an Italian madrigal (translated into English) by Croce was also included. Works by Bateson and Pilkington were added in later editions.

Troilus and Cressida, opera by Walton, produced in London, 1954. Libretto by C. Hassall, principally after Chaucer's (not Shakespeare's) version of the story.

Trojans, The (Fr., *Les Troyens*), opera by Berlioz, with libretto by composer, after Virgil's *Aeneid*. In two parts – (1) 'The Taking of Troy' (*La Prise de Troie*), produced (in German) in Karlsruhe, 1890, after Berlioz's death; (2) 'The Trojans at Carthage' (*Les Troyens à Carthage*), produced in Paris, 1863.

tromba (It.), trumpet (also with special significance – see under TRUMPET); *tromba da tirarsi*, slide-TRUMPET; *tromba marina*, TRUMPET MARINE.

Tromboncino, Bartolomeo (*c.*1470-after 1534), Italian composer, singer, and lutenist. Works include madrigals, canzonets, church music.

trombone (from It., literally 'large

trumpet'), type of brass instrument, generally possessing a slide which serves to vary the effective length of the tube. (But see *valve-trombone*, below.) In any one position of the slide, the notes of the HARMONIC SERIES can be produced; and there are seven recognized positions of the slide, producing harmonic series a semitone apart. A combination of moving the slide (i.e. picking a particular series) and controlling the breath (i.e. picking a note within a series) yields a chromatic range – *tenor trombone*, from E below the bass stave upwards for about two and a half octaves; *bass trombone*, from the B lower. (Below this, a few isolated 'pedal notes' can be produced: they are actually the first tones of the harmonic series in various positions, and are not usually called for.) Two tenor and one bass trombones are regarded as the standard within the orchestra, but the (generally obsolete) *alto trombone* has been revived, e.g. by Britten (*The Burning Fiery Furnace*), and the lower *double-bass trombone* (or *contrabass trombone*) was occasionally used by Wagner and a few others. The *tenor-bass trombone* is basically a tenor with a mechanism permitting access to an extra length of tubing for conversion to bass. (The *valve-trombone*, with valves instead of slide, is rarely met with but exists in both tenor and bass sizes: see CIMBASSO.) The trombones, previously confined largely to church music, entered the opera orchestra in the late 18th century and the symphony orchestra shortly afterwards; now standard also in military, brass and dance bands, etc. Solo and chamber music using them is rare.

Trommel (Ger.), drum; *grosse Trommel*, bass drum.

tronco, tronca (It.), broken off short (of a note, especially in vocal music).

trope, (1) type of musical interpolation into traditional liturgical plainsong, from about the ninth to the 15th century – the ecclesiastical SEQUENCE being a survival of this; hence *Troper*, a medieval book containing tropes; (2) term used, in quite a different sense from the above, of the form of 12-note technique invented and practised by HAUER.

troppo (It.), too much; *allegro non troppo*, or *allegro ma non troppo*, fast but not too fast.

troubadour, type of itinerant poet-musician of southern France flourishing in the 11th–13th centuries, writing and singing songs in the Provençal language. Cp. TROUVÈRE, TROVATORE.

Trouble in Tahiti, see QUIET PLACE.

'Trout' Quintet, name for Schubert's Quintet (D667), 1819, for piano, violin, viola, cello and double-bass; the fourth of its five movements comprises variations on Schubert's song 'The Trout' (Ger., *Die Forelle*).

trouvère, the northern French counterpart of the TROUBADOUR, writing and singing his songs in Old French, not in Provençal.

Trovatore, Il (It., The Troubadour), opera by Verdi, produced in Rome, 1853. Libretto by S. Cammarano: the hero, though eventually revealed as a nobleman's son, has been brought up by a gipsy and has become a troubadour.

Troyanos, Tatiana (b. 1938), American mezzo-soprano with a varied international operatic career including works by Britten and Penderecki.

trumpet, metal wind instrument, cylindrically bored, used for signalling, etc., from ancient times, and regularly appearing in the orchestra from the 17th century. The standard modern form (from mid 19th century) has three valves. The trumpet in most common use is either a TRANSPOSING INSTRUMENT in B♭ with compass from E below middle C upwards for nearly three octaves, or a non-transposing instrument in C (one tone higher). Trumpets in D and in E♭ (higher, smaller) are in increasing use. The trumpet is found in dance bands and other popular formations as well as in the orchestra; in the brass band and some military bands it is replaced by the cornet. The *bass trumpet* (rare) is similar, but in C an octave lower. The so-called *piccolo trumpet* is pitched an octave higher than the standard instrument (and sometimes has four valves). The so-called *Bach trumpet* is a late-19th-century type of high-pitched trumpet (sometimes made in long, straight form), suitable for playing high-pitched trumpet parts as written by Bach – but having valves, so not being a historical reconstruction. *Fanfare trumpets* are a set in various sizes for ceremonial purposes, made in long, straight form on which banners can be hung. Before the modern valve trumpet the normal instrument was a 'natural' (valveless, keyless) trumpet producing one HARMONIC SERIES only, like a bugle; but the use of different instruments and of changeable CROOKS (altering the instrument's total length of tube) went some way to allow a choice of different harmonic series as the music required it. In Bach's time, trumpeters specialized in high (*clarino*) or low (*principale*) parts, the name *tromba* sometimes being

used for middle parts. Attempts before the valve-trumpet to enlarge the number of notes available led to the invention of various types of *slide-trumpet* (having a slide like a trombone's) and of the *keyed trumpet* for which Haydn wrote his concerto.

trumpet marine, obsolete bowed instrument (sometimes 6 feet long), one end of which rested on the floor. By the pressing of a finger at correct points on its single string, notes of the HARMONIC SERIES could be obtained. This reliance on harmonics perhaps explains the name 'trumpet', though 'marine' remains baffling. The Italian name *tromba marina* is also sometimes found in English references.

trumpet tune, trumpet voluntary, pieces not composed for a trumpet, but imitating one – e.g. as solo for a trumpet-like stop on the organ. *Trumpet Voluntary* was the name Henry Wood gave to a keyboard piece which he arranged for a combination of organ, brass and kettledrums and which he followed another editor in mistakenly attributing to Purcell. Its original title was *The Prince of Denmark's March*, and it is now known to be by J. CLARKE.

Tsar and Carpenter, or The Two Peters (Ger., *Zar und Zimmermann, oder Die Zwei Peter*), opera by Lortzing, produced in Leipzig, 1837. Libretto after a French play by A. H. J. Mélesville, J. T. Merle and E. Cantiran de Boirie; concerns Peter the Great.

Tschaikowski, -sky, German spellings of the name TCHAIKOVSKY.

tuba, (1) type of bass brass valved instrument made in several sizes and shapes – when circular, called 'helicon', of which the SOUSAPHONE is a variety. The standard orchestral tuba (or *bass tuba*) is in F, with compass from the F an octave below the bass clef, upwards for about three octaves, or in E♭, a tone lower; since its invention (1835) it has become the normal lowest brass instrument of the orchestra. (Very rarely used as soloist, though Vaughan Williams has composed a concerto for it.) *Double-bass tuba* signifies a lower and much rarer instrument, used e.g. by Wagner in THE RING in conjunction with the WAGNER TUBAS, of which it is not one. *Tenor tuba* signifies an instrument higher than the bass tuba – in Britain equated with the euphonium. The lowest and therefore largest instruments of the brass and military band are tubas (often called just 'basses'): they are the E♭ (same as standard tuba) and the B♭ (same as double-bass tuba) – the latter often in band usage called BB♭ bass (spoken as 'double B flat'); (2) trumpet-like organ stop; (3) ancient Roman straight trumpet.

Tubin, Eduard (1905–82), Soviet-Estonian composer who settled in Sweden; works include 10 symphonies (plus another unfinished), a balalaika concerto, two operas.

tubular bell, SEE BELL.

Tucker, Richard (originally Reuben Ticker) (1913–75), American tenor, famous chiefly for his performances (more than 600) at the New York Metropolitan Opera.

tucket, obsolete English word (found in Shakespeare) for a fanfare.

Tuckwell, Barry [Emmanuel] (b. 1931), Australian horn-player active in Britain since 1951; internationally eminent soloist, leader of his own wind quintet. OBE, 1965.

Tudor, David (b. 1926), American pianist who gave first performances of works by Cage, Stockhausen, etc., and is also composer, mainly of pieces using theatrical and lighting effects – *4 Pepsi Pieces* for sound-and-light resources of Pepsi-Cola Pavilion at Expo '70, Osaka (Japan), etc. Collaborated with Cage in joint compositions.

Tudway, Thomas (*c.*1650–1726), English composer of church music, organist, professor at Cambridge, and compiler of a collection of English cathedral music.

Tunder, Franz (1614–67), German organist, composer of organ works, choral cantatas, etc. Buxtehude was his son-in-law and successor in church post in Lübeck.

tune, (1) melody, especially the upper part of a simple composition; (2) term (noun and verb) referring to correct intonation – so *in tune, out of tune, to tune a piano*, etc. ('Dancers dancing in tune' is a phenomenon observed only by Tennyson.) See also next entry.

tuning-fork, a two-pronged metal object set in vibration to produce a sound which serves to check the pitch of instruments and to give the pitch to voices. Its note is virtually a 'pure' tone – lacking the upper harmonics (see HARMONIC SERIES) which enter into the tone of normal instruments.

Turandot, (1) opera by Puccini, produced in Milan, 1926; completed by Alfano, Puccini having died; libretto by G. Adami and P. Simone; (2) opera by Busoni, produced in Zurich, 1917; libretto (in German) by composer; (3) play by Schiller for which

Weber wrote incidental music, 1809. The source of all these is an Italian play by Gozzi: Turandot is a cruel Chinese princess eventually conquered by love.

Turangalîla, title of a symphony by Messiaen, with a solo piano part, 1948. It is influenced (especially as to rhythm) by Indian music, to which the title refers, and 'the whole work is a love-song' (Messiaen).

turca, alla (It.), in the Turkish style – in effect having, or simulating, the percussion instruments brought to Austria (and so introduced to Western Europe) by Turkish military bands in the 18th century. (Cp. JANISSARY MUSIC.) So the *Rondo alla turca* forming the last movement of Mozart's Piano Sonata in A (K331), 1778 – arranged by others for various combinations.

Turchi, Guido (b. 1916), Italian composer of opera *The Good Soldier Schweik*; *Concerto breve* (in memory of Bartók) for string quartet or string orchestra; *Invective* for choir and two pianos; etc. Also critic.

Turina [y Pérez], **Joaquín** (1882–1949), Spanish composer, pupil of d'Indy in Paris. Works include symphonic poem *The Procession of the Virgin of the Dew* (Sp., *La procesión del rocío*); piano concerto; *The Bull-Fighter's Prayer* (*La oración del toreto*) for string quartet; piano solos and songs.

turn, musical ornament normally indicated by a special mark, as follows:

 played

Turnage, Mark-Anthony (b. 1960),

British composer of opera *Greek* (after Berkoff's play), *Night Dances* for orchestra, *Lament for a Hanging Man* (text from the Bible and Sylvia Plath).

Turner, Eva (1892–1990), British soprano who sang at La Scala, Milan, from 1924; noted as Turandot (Puccini). Later taught in USA and London. Created Dame, 1962.

Turn of the Screw, The, opera by Britten, produced in Venice, 1954. Libretto by M. Piper, after Henry James's story about the ghostly possession of children.

tutti, see TUTTO.

tutto (It., fem., *-a*, pl. *tutti, tutte*), all. So, in piano works, *tutte le corde*, all the strings, i.e. not with soft pedal (see CORDA). The word *tutti*, meaning 'all the performers', is loosely used e.g. in a concerto as signifying a passage for the orchestra without the soloist – whether or not every member of the orchestra is actually playing. In choral works *tutti* can mean chorus as opposed to soloists, or full chorus as opposed to semi-chorus.

Tveitt, Geirr (1908–81), Norwegian composer; also pianist and writer on music. Studied in Germany, Austria and France. Works include six piano concertos, a concerto for Hardanger fiddle (see FIDDLE) and orchestra, operas, choral works, chamber music.

Twain, Mark (real name Samuel Langhorne Clemens) (1835–1910), American writer. See FOSS, KERN.

twelfth, on the organ, a MUTATION STOP sounding a 12th (i.e. an octave plus a fifth) above the note depressed.

twelve-note, term used to describe a technique of composition in which all

12 notes within the octave (i.e. the seven white and five black notes of the piano) are treated as 'equal' – i.e. are subjected to an ordered relationship which (unlike that of the major-minor key system) establishes no 'hierarchy' of notes (but see below). One such technique was invented by J. M. HAUER; but the term is now virtually confined to the technique invented by Schoenberg, described by him as a 'method of composing with 12 notes which are related only to one another'. This method works through the 'note-row' (or SERIES), in which all the 12 notes are placed in a particular order as the basis of a work. No note is repeated within a row, which accordingly consists of 12 different notes and no others. The note-row does not necessarily form a theme or part of one, but it is used as the 'tonal reservoir' from which the piece is drawn; it may be used as it stands, or transformed (see INVERT and RE-TROGRADE) or transposed. The total structure of the work, not merely the shape of the particular melody, must conform to the observance of the note-row. Originally 12-note technique developed as a standardization of ATONAL music; but certain composers (e.g. Dallapiccola, F. Martin), while using 12-note methods of construction, allowed the resultant music to present a definitely implied relation to the major-minor key system; and many composers who do not follow 12-note technique in Schoenberg's rigorous sense have nevertheless deployed complete series of all the 12 notes without repetition of any one note – e.g. Walton, violin sonata; Britten, THE TURN OF THE SCREW.

Twilight of the Gods, The, usual translation of Wagner's *Götterdämmerung* – see RING.

Tye, Christopher (*c*.1505–?1572), English composer who became a clergyman in the newly reformed Church of England. Wrote notable church music in Latin and English, including settings of the Acts of the Apostles in his own metrical rhymed English translation. Also wrote IN NOMINES. See also WHITE (R.).

tzigane (Fr.), gipsy (both sexes), equivalent to Ger. *Zigeuner*, etc.; used by Ravel as title of an extended, virtuoso piece for solo violin with piano or orchestral accompaniment (1924).

U

Uccelli, Gli, see BIRDS.

Uchida, Mitsuko (b. 1948), Japanese pianist who trained in Vienna; well known in Mozart, she often directs the piano concertos from the keyboard.

Uhr, Die, German nickname (The Clock) for Haydn's CLOCK Symphony.

Uillean pipes, see BAGPIPES.

'Ukrainian' Symphony, nickname for Tchaikovsky's Symphony no. 2 in C minor, first performed in 1873; so called from the use of folk-tunes in the first and fourth movements. More often called 'Little Russian' Symphony (meaning the same); but 'Ukrainian', as the more intelligible term nowadays, is preferable.

ukulele (sometimes spelt *ukelele*), small guitar-like four-stringed instrument from the South Pacific islands (but of Portuguese origin); having some vogue since the 1920s in the USA and Europe, being cheap and easily learnt. A special notation is used – see TABLATURE.

Ullmann, Viktor (1898–?1944), Austrian composer who, as a Jew, died at Auschwitz concentration camp. His works include the unfinished opera *The Emperor of Atlantis*; it was first performed, in a version completed by the British conductor Kerry Woodward, in Holland, 1975.

Ulysses, (1) cantata by Seiber, first performed in 1949; text (philosophically speculative) from James Joyce's novel; (2) opera (It., *Ulisse*) by Dallapiccola, produced in Berlin, 1968; libretto by the composer, after Homer. See also RETURN OF ULYSSES.

un, una, uno (It.), a. (For entries beginning thus, see under second word.)

un, une (Fr.) a. (For entries beginning thus, see under second word.)

unaccompanied, see ACCOMPANY.

und (Ger.), and.

unda maris (Lat., wave of the sea), organ stop similar to 'voix céleste' (see VOIX).

'Unfinished' Symphony, name given to Schubert's Symphony no. 8 in B minor, 1822 (D759). It has only two completed movements, though sketches exist for a third (Scherzo). Schubert presumably either (1) intended to complete the work later; or (2) forgot about it; or (3) actually did complete it, the two final movements having been lost. Not performed until 1865. Various completions have been made, some re-using other Schubert material.

Union pipes, see BAGPIPES.

unison, a united sounding of the same

417

note: thus *unison song*, a song for several people all singing the same tune (not harmonizing). Expressions such as *singing in unison* are generally (but loosely) also applied to the singing of the same tune by men and women an octave apart – where 'singing in octaves' would be more strictly accurate.

unit organ (also called *extension organ*), type of organ which saves space by having various stops 'borrow' pipes from each other. Thus an eight-FOOT stop and a four-foot stop will share pipes for the part of their range that overlaps, instead of having completely separate sets of pipes as on a 'normal' organ. The THEATRE ORGAN is usually of this type.

unprepared (discord), see PREPARATION.

Unquenchable, The (Dan., *Det Uudslukkelige*), title of Symphony no. 4 by C. Nielsen, 1916. The title – more usually and more awkwardly translated as 'The Inextinguishable' – comes from the composer's dictum, 'Music is life, and as such is unquenchable'.

up-beat, the upward motion of the conductor's stick or hand, especially as indicating the beat preceding the barline, i.e. the beat preceding the main accent; term therefore also used for the beat preceding such an accent, whether or not the piece is being 'conducted'. Cp. DOWN-BEAT.

up-bow, the motion of the bow of a stringed instrument when pushed by the player – the opposite (pulling) motion being a DOWN-BOW.

upper partial, see HARMONIC SERIES.

upright piano, see PIANO.

Ursuleac, Viorica (1894–1985), Romanian soprano who settled in Vienna, gave more than 500 performances of roles in R. Strauss's operas, and was married to Clemens Krauss.

Urtext (Ger., original text), an edition purporting to present a composition exactly as written down by the composer, without changes, additions or aids (such as tempo directions) supplied by an editor.

Ussachevsky, Vladimir [Alexis] (b. 1911), Manchurian-born composer of Russian parents, resident in the US since 1930; innovator and instructor in electronic music. Works include *Creation-Prologue* for four choruses and electronic sounds; *We* (computer-synthesized tape score for radio-dramatic production).

ut, French name for the note C in SOLMIZATION.

utility music, English equivalent for the original German form *Gebrauchsmusik*, utilized by Hindemith, Weill and others in Germany in the 1920s to indicate music directed to a social or educational purpose and not merely constituting art for art's sake. Hindemith disowned the term in his book *A Composer's World* (1951) as a misleading and useless label.

Utopia Limited, or The Flowers of Progress, operetta by Sullivan, produced in London, 1893. Libretto by W. S. Gilbert, postulating a Utopia run on the lines of a British limited-liability company.

va., abbr. of VIOLA.

Valen, Fartein [Olav] (1887–1952), Norwegian composer who spent his early years in Madagascar and then studied in Berlin, coming (uniquely among Scandinavian composers of his generation) under the influence of Schoenberg. Works include five symphonies (no. 5 unfinished), a violin concerto, two string quartets.

Valkyrie, The, see RING.

valse (Fr.) = WALTZ. So *La Valse*, 'choreographic poem' by Ravel for orchestra, 1920; *Valses nobles et sentimentales*, a set by Ravel for piano, 1911, afterwards orchestrated (Ravel intended homage to Schubert, who composed for piano some 'Valses nobles' and some 'Valses sentimentales'). So also *Valse triste* ('sad'), by Sibelius – originally for strings and occurring in the incidental music to the play *Death* by Arvid Järnefelt, afterwards scored for full orchestra and in this version first performed in 1904.

valve, mechanism on brass instruments whereby, at the pressure of the player's finger, the current of air is diverted round an additional length of tubing. Thus the vibrating air-column becomes longer, giving a different HARMONIC SERIES from that of the unlengthened tube. By means of three valves, each giving a different additional length of tubing, and usable singly or in combination, the modern trumpet (and other instruments) can produce a complete chromatic scale; whereas the valveless triumpet of e.g. Bach's day, like a modern bugle, could produce only one harmonic series leaving large gaps in the scale. All the brass instruments now normally used in the orchestra, military band, brass band and dance band have valves varying the length of tube for this purpose – except the (normal) trombones, which have slides. (For the exceptional *valve-trombone*, see TROMBONE.) A valve is also used (e.g. on a horn in F/B♭ or a cornet in B♭/A) to convert the instrument's basic length to another, thus saving the player the necessity of changing between two instruments.

Valverde, Joaquín (1846–1910), Spanish composer of songs including 'Clavelitos' (Sp., Carnations), etc.

vamp, to improvise an instrumental accompaniment or introduction, e.g. to a song.

van, van den, van der, prefixes to names – see next word of the name.

Vaňhal, Vanhall, see WANHAL.

Varèse, Edgard (1883–1965), French-born composer (pupil of d'Indy and

Roussel) who settled in USA, 1915, and cultivated music involving extremes of dissonance, unusual instrumentation, and (often) 'scientific' titles – e.g. *Ionization* (percussion instruments only), *Density 21.5* (flute solo, referring to specific gravity of platinum), *Octandre* (Fr. form of Lat. *octandria*, plant with eight stamens). Was also an influential pioneer in the use of taped and electronic music: see ELECTRONIC POEM; THEREMIN.

variation, a passage of music intended as a varied version of some 'given' passage. So *Variations on . . .* a tune (whether or not the tune has been specially composed by the composer of the variations), the tune being called the 'theme' of the variations. Such variations may diverge only slightly from the theme, mainly by melodic ornamentation (as in Mozart), but usage since the mid 19th century has tended to a looser type allowing a much freer form of composition, e.g. Elgar's ENIGMA VARIATIONS. The terms CHACONNE, GROUND BASS and PASSACAGLIA also imply variations, of a specific type, and the term RHAPSODY may do so. See also following entries.

Variations and Fugue on a Theme of Purcell (Britten), see YOUNG PERSON'S GUIDE.

Variations on a Theme of Haydn, see 'ST ANTHONY' VARIATIONS.

Varnay, Astrid [Ibolyka Maria] (b. 1918), Swedish-born American soprano of Hungarian parentage; distinguished in Wagner at the New York Metropolitan Opera (from 1941) and elsewhere.

Varviso, Silvio (b. 1924), Swiss conductor, eminent in opera; first appeared at the Metropolitan Opera, New York, 1961, at Covent Garden and Glyndebourne, 1962. Became musical director of the Paris Opera, 1980, but resigned in 1981.

Vásáry, Tamás (b. 1933), Hungarian pianist who gave a full evening's recital at age nine; left Hungary in 1956 and later settled in London. Also conductor – see BOURNEMOUTH SINFONIETTA.

vaudeville, French theatrical term of varying meanings, among them that of a song with verses sung by different characters in turn, each verse followed by the same refrain – as in the final number of Mozart's THE SERAGLIO.

Vaughan Williams, Ralph (1872–1958), British composer, pupil of Stanford, Bruch (in Berlin) and Ravel (in Paris). Close associate of Holst; much influenced by English folk-music, some of which he collected and arranged (see GREENSLEEVES). Based his SINFONIA ANTARTICA (Symphony no. 7) on his score for film *Scott of the Antarctic*, and brought out his last symphony (no. 9) at the age of 85. He numbered only the last, identifying the others by key or by name (see SEA SYMPHONY, LONDON SYMPHONY, PASTORAL SYMPHONY). Other works include operas HUGH THE DROVER, RIDERS TO THE SEA, THE PILGRIM'S PROGRESS, SIR JOHN IN LOVE; ballet JOB; many choral works (see MAGNIFICAT); SERENADE TO MUSIC, originally for 16 solo voices and orchestra; orchestral works with solo instruments including THE LARK ASCENDING, ROMANCE (harmonica solo), a tuba concerto (see TEDESCA); *Fan-*

tasia on a Theme of Tallis (see TALLIS) for strings; Latin Mass; two string quartets; songs, including 'Linden Lea' and cycle *On Wenlock Edge*. Also conductor, especially choral, and hymnbook editor. OM, 1935.

Vautor, Thomas (c.1580–c.1620?), English composer of 'Sweet Suffolk Owl' and other distinctive madrigals in a collection published in 1619. (He was one of the last of the English madrigal school.)

Vecchi, Orazio (1550–1605), Italian composer, also priest; holder of church and court musical posts. Works include madrigals, church music, and THE AMPHIPARNASSUS (It., *L'Anfiparnaso*), a work of dramatic form made up of madrigals.

Végh Quartet, string quartet led by Sándor Végh (b. 1905), active 1940–80, first in Hungary and then after World War II in Switzerland.

Vejvanovský, Pavel [Josef] (1633/9–1693), Moravian composer (also trumpeter), who served for 30 years at the court of the prince-bishops at Kroměříž, latterly as musical director. Works include Masses, other church music, chamber music.

veloce (It.), quickly – normally a direction to give an impression of uninterrupted swiftness, rather than to increase actual speed.

vent (Fr.), wind; *instruments à vent*, wind instruments.

Ventadorn, Bernart de (?–1195), French troubadour, some of whose surviving poems and melodies have been transcribed variously for modern use.

Venus and Adonis, masque with music by Blow, produced in London about 1684; librettist unknown.

Veracini, Francesco Maria (1690–1768), Italian violinist, composer of 44 violin sonatas, etc. Thrice visited London as performer, and his other works include opera *Rosalinda* (after Shakespeare's *As You Like It*).

Verbunkos (Hung., from Ger. *Werbung,* recruiting), a lively Hungarian dance associated with the recruitment of Hungarian soldiers for the Austrian army before 1850, the music being provided by gipsy bands. It is related to the CSÁRDÁS.

Verdelot, Philippe (?-before 1552), Flemish composer who held church musical posts in Italy. Was one of the first madrigal-composers (see MADRIGAL, 1) and wrote also Masses, motets, etc.

Verdi, Giuseppe [Fortunino Francesco] (1813–1901), Italian composer, born in Busseto of a poor family; became organist and composer in boyhood, but rejected by Milan Conservatory as over-age and insufficiently gifted. First opera, *Oberto,* 1839. Later operas – grafting an individual mastery (vocal, orchestral and dramatic) on to traditional Italian models – include NABUCCO, MACBETH, RIGOLETTO, IL TROVATORE, LA TRAVIATA, SIMON BOCCANEGRA, A MASKED BALL, THE FORCE OF DESTINY, DON CARLOS, LUISA MILLER, AIDA, OTELLO and FALSTAFF. The last two are products of his 70s, and rely less on the appeal of successive 'set' numbers. Wrote also REQUIEM and a few other works to religious texts, though not himself a churchman; also a string quartet – little else. In his earlier operas he became the symbol of resurgent Italian nationalism, and frequently clashed with censorships suspecting revolutionary implications: in 1860–65, he himself sat as deputy in that part of Italy already unified. But later lived in seclusion. Founded a home for aged musicians in Milan. After early death of his first wife he lived with and then married the singer Giuseppina Strepponi. Died in Milan. See also KING LEAR.

Veress, Sándor (b. 1907), Hungarian composer (also pianist), resident mainly in Switzerland since 1950. He was associated with Bartók in collecting and editing Hungarian folk-music. Works include a concerto for two trombones and orchestra; *Homage to Paul Klee* (one movement for each of seven pictures) for two pianos and strings; *Sinfonia Minneapolitana* (for what is now the Minnesota Orchestra), *Songs of the Seasons* and other works for chorus.

verismo (It.), realism – term applied particularly to Italian opera of about 1900 (e.g. Mascagni, Puccini) with reference to its 'contemporary' and often violent plots, sometimes amid sordid surroundings – e.g. Puccini's THE CLOAK, aboard a canal barge.

Verklärte Nacht, see TRANSFIGURED NIGHT.

Verrett, Shirley (b. 1931), American soprano who performed with the New York City Opera from 1958, then internationally; she sang Dido in Berlioz's *The Trojans* at the opening of the Bastille Opera in Paris, 1990.

Verschiebung (Ger., a displacing), use of the soft pedal of the piano.

verse, (1) term used in Gregorian chant in the sense of a biblical verse, i.e. a sentence from the Psalms or other text; (2) term indicating, in Anglican church music, the use of solo voice as contrasted with full choir;

verse anthem, one using such a contrast; (3, as equivalent to Fr., VERSET) a short organ piece replacing a 'verse' in the first sense.

verset (Fr.), a short organ piece, originally as an instrumental replacement for the verse of a psalm in Catholic church usage.

Vestal, The (i.e. The Vestal Virgin: Fr., *La Vestale*), opera by Spontini, produced in Paris, 1807. Libretto by V. J. E. de Jouy. The heroine's religious vows conflict with human love.

via (It.), away with; *via sordini*, take off mutes.

Via Crucis (Lat., The Way of the Cross), work by Liszt for solo singers, chorus and organ, completed in 1879; text, partly biblical, on the Stations of the Cross. Not performed until 40 years after Liszt's death.

Viardot-Garcia, [Michelle Ferdinande] **Pauline** (1821–1910), French mezzo-soprano, daughter of Manuel Garcia the elder, and sister of Maria Malibran. Outstanding in opera, she was much admired by composers: sang the title-role of Gluck's *Orpheus* more than 150 times in the edition which Berlioz made for her.

vibraharp (US) = VIBRAPHONE.

vibraphone, percussion instrument on which tuned metal bars (laid out on the pattern of a piano keyboard) are struck with small padded beaters held in both hands; beneath the bars are resonators which, constantly opened and closed electronically, impart a vibrating sound to the tone. Compass most commonly from F below middle C, upwards for three octaves. Used by modern composers occasionally in symphonic and operatic music (e.g. by Berg in LULU) and also in jazz, etc.

vibration, the side-to-side motion of a string, a struck surface, or air-column, by which musical sounds are produced. See FREQUENCY.

vibrato (It., vibrated), a rapid regular fluctuation in pitch – whether tasteful (e.g. as imparted by the oscillatory motion of a violinist's left hand) or exaggerated to a fault, as in a singer's 'wobble'. (Note the difference from TREMOLO, which is a fluctuation of intensity, i.e. loudness, not of pitch.) See also TREMULANT.

Vickers, Jon (originally Jonathan) [Stewart] (b. 1926), Canadian tenor, eminent in such 'heavy' operatic roles as Verdi's Otello and Wagner's Tristan – at Covent Garden from 1957, Bayreuth Festival from 1958, Metropolitan Opera (New York) from 1960.

Victoria, Tomás Luis de (1548–1611), Spanish composer (also poet) who worked in Rome for nearly 20 years (hence 'Vittoria', the sometimes encountered Italian form of his name). Then took up a church choirmaster's post in Madrid and died there. Composed only church music, including settings of all the hymns of the Roman Catholic liturgical year; 19 Masses, among them a Requiem Mass for the Spanish Dowager Empress; motets. Associated in Rome with Palestrina, to whose style his own is related.

Victory, Gerard (form of name used by Alan Loraine) (b. 1921), Irish conductor and composer, music director of Irish Radio and Television, 1967–82. Works include operas (in Gaelic and in English); *Short Symphony*; *Homage to Petrarch* for strings.

vide (Lat., 'See!'), instruction to make a cut in performance, usually indicated by putting the letters 'vi–' at the point of cut and '–de' at the point of resumption.

vielle (Fr.), term normally meaning a HURDY-GURDY, but also used for the medieval fiddle (see FIDDLE, 2).

Vienna Blood (Ger., *Wiener Blut*), operetta compiled from the music of J. Strauss the younger, with the composer's consent, by A. Müller; produced in Vienna, 1899. Libretto by V. Leon and L. Stein. Concerns romantic intrigue in Vienna, 1815, and is named from a Strauss waltz (1871) incorporated in it.

Vienna Boys' Choir, usual English appellation for the Wiener Sängerknaben (Ger., Viennese Singing Boys), descending from the chapel establishment of the former Austrian imperial court, and performing on their own or with adult males.

Vienna Philharmonic Orchestra, an orchestra tracing its history to the Philharmonic Concerts begun in Vienna by Otto Nicolai in 1842. The orchestra also plays for the Vienna State Opera. It is self-governing. Conductors associated with it since World War II have included KARAJAN, SOLTI, BÖHM, BERNSTEIN, ABBADO.

Vier ernste Gesänge, see FOUR SERIOUS SONGS.

Vierne, Louis (1870–1937), French organist and composer, pupil of Franck and Widor; blind from birth. Organist of Notre Dame, Paris; died while playing there. Noted travelling recitalist. Composer of six 'symphonies' and other solo pieces for organ; also of a Mass, string quartet, etc.

Viertel (Ger., quarter) = QUARTER-NOTE, crotchet.

Vieuxtemps, Henri [Joseph François] (1820–81), Belgian violinist (touring from age seven) and composer of seven violin concertos and other works for his instrument. For a time taught in Russia. Died while visiting Algeria.

vif (Fr.), lively.

vihuela, old Spanish musical instrument, shaped like the guitar but strung like the lute; plucked either with the hand (*vihuela da mano*) or with a plectrum. It fell into disuse in the 17th century, being superseded by the guitar.

Village Romeo and Juliet, A, opera by Delius, produced in Berlin, 1907. Libretto (after a story by G. Keller) by composer, in German (*Romeo und Julia aus dem Dorfe*), though no librettist's name is given in the printed score. The two lovers are the children of quarrelling landowners, and eventually commit suicide together.

Villa-Lobos, Heitor (1887–1959), Brazilian composer, the first South American composer to become world-famous; was also pianist and teacher. Prolific output, including operas, ballets, 12 symphonies, 17 string quartets, songs, etc., in varied styles but frequently with pronounced 'national' flavour. Composed 14 works characterized as 'chôros' (see CHÔRO) for various combinations (some including Brazilian native instruments), explaining the title as synthesizing 'the different modalities of Brazilian, South-American Indian and popular music, and having for principal elements rhythm and typical melody of popular

character'. His BACHIANAS BRAS-ILEIRAS are supposed evocations of Bach in a Brazilian spirit. Wrote also *New York Skyline Melody* (on melodic 'shape' suggested by skyline) for piano or orchestra; works for piano solo, for guitar, etc.

villancico, (1) a Spanish poetical and musical song-form usually to amorous or devotional words, current in the 16th century; (2) a Spanish 17th-century term for an extended cantata with orchestra.

villanella, villanelle (It., Fr.), a countrified or rustic song (or an instrumental piece suggestive of such); especially a type of 16th-century Italian part-song of less complexity than the madrigal.

Vinay, Ramón (b. 1912), Chilean tenor famous in 'heavy' operatic roles such as Verdi's Otello and Wagner's Tristan; previously sang baritone and reverted to baritone in later career, when he also directed operas.

Vinci, Leonardo (*c.*1690–1730), Italian composer and church musician; wrote operas, some in Neapolitan dialect. No relation of da Vinci the artist.

Viñes, Ricardo (1875–1943), Spanish pianist who settled in Paris, giving early performances of Debussy, Ravel and Falla.

viol, type of bowed stringed instrument of various sizes, current up to about 1700 and thereafter superseded by instruments of the VIOLIN type; resuscitated in the 20th century, however, for old music. The viols differ from the violin family in shape, in having frets, and in the kind of bow and style of bowing used. The three principal sizes (often encountered in ensemble) were the *treble viol, tenor viol* and *bass viol.* All, being rested on or between the legs, are properly called *viola da gamba* (... for the leg) though that term most commonly indicates the bass viol (approximately cello size). *Viola da braccio* (... for the arm) indicates not a viol but a violin or viola. The *division viol* was a small bass viol suitable for solos (such as the playing of DIVISIONS, i.e. variations); the *violone* was a larger (double-bass) viol. Note that the *bass viol* may occasionally (in non-specialist usage, chiefly US) indicate modern double-bass.

viola, (1) bowed stringed instrument, a lower-pitched relative of the violin, invariably present in the orchestra and the string quartet (and used also as a solo instrument); its compass is from the C below middle C, upwards for more than three octaves. See FELDMAN. The *viola pomposa* was a rare 18th-century viola with an extra (fifth) higher string. (2) Italian for VIOL; hence the following entries.

viola da braccio, see VIOL.

viola d'amore (It., love-viol), bowed stringed instrument related primarily not to the modern viola but to the VIOL family – but, unlike them, having no frets, and played under the chin. It has (usually) seven strings touched by the bow, and seven SYMPATHETIC strings beneath them (hence the instrument's name) whose vibration is induced by the sounding of the upper set. The instrument is occasionally encountered in music of the 17th–18th centuries and there are some later exceptional uses (e.g. in Meyerbeer's THE HUGUENOTS).

violin, bowed four-stringed instrument, the principal (and highest) member of the family of instruments (called 'the violin family') which superseded the VIOLS from about 1700. The other members are the viola, cello and double-bass, which has a superficial resemblance to the corresponding member (violone) of the viol family. The violin is prominently used in the orchestra (where the players normally divide into first and second violinists, a division usually corresponding to higher- and lower-pitched parts) and in solo and chamber music. Its compass is from the G below middle C, upwards for three and a half octaves and more.

violino (It.), violin; *violino piccolo*, small-sized, higher-pitched violin occasionally used in 16th–18th centuries, e.g. in Bach's Brandenburg Concerto no. 1.

violoncello, see CELLO.

violone, see VIOL.

Viotti, Giovanni Battista (1755–1824), Italian violinist and composer (pupil of Pugnani) who came to London in 1792, and afterwards had varied career including the directorship of the Italian Opera in Paris. Died, impoverished, in London. Wrote 29 violin concertos and other violin works; also 10 piano concertos, songs, etc.

Viozzi, Giulio (b. 1912) (he used German form of surname, Weutz, until 1931), Italian composer of operas including *Allamistakeo* (after Poe; title based on English words); ballet *Stage Rehearsals*; orchestral *Concerto on a 12-note Theme from Mozart's 'Don Giovanni'*, two string quartets, etc. Also critic.

virelai, type of medieval French song.

Virgil [Publius Vergilius Maro] (70–19 BC), Roman poet. See COLGRASS, DIDO AND AENEAS, ECLOGUE, IDOMENEUS, LOEFFLER, TROJANS.

virginal(s), (1) term in English 16th-century sources for all types of keyboard instruments, including *virginal* proper (see (2) below), harpsichord, and even organ. (2) 16th- and 17th-century keyboard instrument of harpsichord type (i.e. the strings being plucked), but smaller and of different shape – oblong, and with its one keyboard along the longer side of the soundboard (not at the end). Revived for old music in the 20th century. Its name may be derived from Lat. *virga* (rod or jack) or *virgo* (maiden or virgin), possibly because it used to be played by maidens (or because some analogous instrument had been so played), but certainly not because of the Virgin Queen, as the instrument was known before her time. The Italian term *spinetto* is used both for this and for the wing-shaped but otherwise similar instrument; but the best English practice is to confine the term SPINET to the latter type. Hence *virginalist*, a player on or composer for the virginals.

virtuoso (It.), a performer of exceptional skill, especially in the technical aspects of performance.

Vishnevskaya, Galina [Pavlovna] (b. 1926), Russian soprano who sang at the Bolshoi Theatre, Moscow from 1953 and became internationally eminent. Married to Rostropovich, she went into forced emigration with him.

Visit of the Old Lady, The (Ger., *Der Besuch der alten Dame*), opera by von Einem, produced in Vienna, 1971; based on the play by Dürrenmatt about a long-delayed revenge.

Vitali, Giovanni Battista (1632–92), Italian violinist and composer who held church and court posts; wrote dance music, sonatas for two and more instruments, psalm-settings, etc. Father of Tommaso Antonio Vitali (below).

Vitali, Tommaso Antonio (1663–1745), Italian violinist and composer of famous Chaconne for violin with keyboard accompaniment, also of other works for strings; edited a volume of music by his father, Giovanni Battista Vitali (above).

Vito, Gioconda de, see DE VITO.

Vitry, Philippe de (1291–1361), French composer – also poet, priest and French court official. Much esteemed in his day, but only a few of his motets survive. Exponent of ARS NOVA and author of a treatise on it; thought to have originated the ISO-RHYTHMIC motet.

Vittoria, see VICTORIA.

vivace (It.), lively.

Vivaldi, Antonio (1678–1741), Italian violinist and composer; also priest, nicknamed 'the red priest' (*il prete rosso*) from the colour of his hair. Pupil of Legrenzi. Long in charge of music at an orphanage-conservatory in Venice, but died in obscure circumstances in Vienna. Wrote more than 450 concertos (broadly conforming to the CONCERTO GROSSO type) with various solo instruments, many with illustrative titles, e.g. THE FOUR SEASONS; also operas, church music, oratorios, including *Juditha triumphans* (see

JUDITH). Bach admired him and transcribed many of his works (e.g. Bach's Concerto for four harpsichords and strings is a transcription of Vivaldi's Concerto for four violins and strings); and there has been a notable revival of interest in his works in the mid 20th century. The currently accepted numbering of his works (superseding various others) follows the thematic catalogue made by Peter Ryom: numbers are prefaced RV = *Ryom-Verzeichnis* (Ger., . . . index).

vivo (It.), lively.

Vlad, Roman (b. 1919), Romanian-born Italian composer and writer on music; also pianist. Works include ballet *The Lady of the Camellias* (after Dumas); *Sonnet to Orpheus* for harp and orchestra, *Variations on a 12-note Theme from Mozart's 'Don Giovanni'* for piano and orchestra; stage and film music.

Vladigerov, Pancho (1899–1978), Bulgarian composer (also pianist) who studied in Berlin; works include opera *Tsar Kaloyan*, a violin concerto, and five piano concertos.

Vltava, see MY COUNTRY.

vocal cords (not 'chords'), see VOICE (1).

vocalise (Fr., noun), a wordless composition for solo voice, whether for training purposes or for concert performance. Rakhmaninov's work of this name, though most commonly heard in the purely orchestral version, was originally for voice and piano (1912, revised in 1915).

vocal score, see SCORE.

voce (It.), voice; *colla voce*, direction to play 'with the voice' (i.e the accompaniment accommodating the singer on matters of tempo; *sotto voce*, 'under the voice', i.e. in a subdued tone; *voce di petto*, CHEST VOICE; *voce di testa*, HEAD VOICE.

Vogel, Vladimir [Rudolfovich] (1896–1984), Russo-German composer; born in Moscow, studied in Berlin under Busoni and settled in Switzerland, 1939. Works include memorial works to Busoni (for orchestra) and to Berg (for piano); secular oratorios *The Fall of Wagadu* and *Thyl Claes* (the latter nearly four hours long, about the 16th-century revolt of the Netherlands).

Vogelweide, Walther von der (*c.*1170–*c.*1230), German singer and composer (of the MINNESINGER variety), mentioned by Wagner in THE MASTERSINGERS.

Vogler, Abt, see next entry.

Vogler, Georg Joseph (1749–1814), German pianist, organist and composer who travelled much and taught many, including Meyerbeer and Liszt; was also priest, and known as the Abbé Vogler ('Abt Vogler' in Robert Browning's poem).

voice, (1) the human (and animal) means of sound-production using the two vibrating agents called the vocal cords (not 'chords'); hence (2) a separate 'strand' of music in harmony or counterpoint, whether intended to be sung or played. Thus a fugue is said to be in, say, four voices (for four PARTS), whether its four 'strands' are sung by individual voices, sung by several voices each, played by instruments, or all played on one instrument (e.g. piano). (3, verb) to adjust a wind instrument or organ-pipe in the process of construction so that it exactly fits the required standards of pitch, tone-colour, etc.

voice-leading, see PART-WRITING.

voix (Fr.) = VOICE (1 and 2); *voix céleste* (Fr. heavenly voice), a type of organ stop with two pipes to each note, tuned slightly apart and producing a wavering effect.

Volkmann, [Friedrich] Robert (1815–83), German composer of symphonies, songs, etc.; encouraged by Schumann; taught much in Vienna and in Budapest, where he died.

Volkonsky, Andrey [Mikhailovich] (b. 1933), Russian (Swiss-born) composer, also pianist; pupil of N. Boulanger in Paris. In Moscow, directed an early-music ensemble. Works include cantata *Dead Souls* (after Gogol); *Serenade to an Insect* for chamber orchestra; a piano quintet, string quartet. Left USSR in 1973.

Volkslied, see FOLK-SONG (the two terms not being quite identical).

Volles Werk (Ger., full apparatus) = FULL ORGAN.

volta (It.), time (in the sense of *prima, seconda volta*: (first, second time). See also LAVOLTA.

Voltaire, François Marie Arouet de (1694–1778), French writer. See BERNSTEIN, KNIPPER.

volti (It.), turn (imperative); *volti subito* (abbr. VS), turn over the page immediately – direction used especially in old music to prevent a performer's ending or making a break in the music at the bottom of a page, or to warn,

after 'rests' at the bottom of a page, that notes begin immediately overleaf.

voluntary, an organ piece of the kind used chiefly at the beginning and end of a church service. (For *trumpet voluntary* see TRUMPET TUNE.)

von, von der, prefixes to names – see under next word of the name.

Voříšek, Jan [Hugo] (1791–1825), Czech composer (also organist and pianist); works include symphonies, IMPROMPTUS and other works for piano solo, a piano concerto.

Vorspiel (Ger.), prelude. (Term used also e.g. by Wagner in the sense of overture, e.g. that to THE MASTERSINGERS.)

vox (Lat.), voice; *vox humana*, a reed-stop on the organ supposedly reminiscent of the human voice.

Vranický, Antonín (1761–1820), Czech (Moravian) violinist and composer of 15 violin concertos, chamber music, etc., who worked from 1783 in Vienna and died there. Brother of the following.

Vranický, Pavel (1756–1808), Czech (Moravian) violinist and composer of *Oberon* and other operas, 51 symphonies, etc. He worked in Vienna from 1785 and died there. Brother of the preceding.

VS, (1) abbr. for 'vocal score' (see SCORE); (2) see VOLTI.

vuoto, vuota (It.), empty – applied e.g. to a bar of music in which all performers' parts have a 'rest' (i.e. a GENERAL PAUSE); *corda vuota*, open string.

Vyšehrad, see MY COUNTRY.

W, abbr. for *Werk(e)*, i.e. work(s) (Ger.); equivalent to OPUS.

Waart, Edo [abbreviation of Eduard] **de** (b. 1941), Dutch conductor, formerly orchestral oboist; musical director of the Rotterdam Philharmonic, 1973–9, of the San Francisco Symphony Orchestra, 1977–85, and currently of the Minnesota Orchestra.

Wagenaar, Bernard (1894–1971), Dutch-born composer who settled in USA, 1921, as orchestral violinist and then college teacher. Composed opera *Pieces of Eight*, Triple Concerto (flute, cello, harp), four symphonies, songs, etc. Pupil of his father, Johan Wagenaar (1862–1941).

Wagenseil, Georg Christoph (1715–77), Austrian composer, pupil of Fux; also harpsichordist and organist. Composed at least 30 symphonies (of 'pre-classical') type and 10 operas, also church music, keyboard works, etc.

Wagner, [Wilhelm] Richard (1813–83), German composer – also writer (of his own librettos, and of essays on musical and philosophical topics); also noted conductor, in which function he earned a living and visited London in 1855 and 1877. Born in Leipzig, travelled greatly, met much opposition. From RIENZI (1842) went on to write successful operas THE FLYING DUTCH-MAN, TANNHÄUSER and LOHENGRIN; then, exemplifying his new theories of the proper relation of music and drama, composed TRISTAN AND ISOLDE, THE RING (cycle of four operas), and PARSIFAL. These show a 'symphonic' conception of opera, proceeding by LEADING-MOTIVES (i.e. themes), not through the contrast of set 'numbers'. Wagner aimed at the *Gesamtkunstwerk*, the work of art uniting all the arts; the Festival Theatre at Bayreuth (opened 1876) was built to his own revolutionary design with this in mind. His only mature comic opera is THE MASTERSINGERS OF NUREMBERG. Other compositions include A FAUST OVERTURE, SIEGFRIED IDYLL, and five song-settings (with piano) of poems by Mathilde Wesendonk, at that time his mistress. Afterwards he took as mistress Cosima, wife of Bülow and daughter of Liszt, and married her when his first wife died. He died in Venice. Influenced the course of music as much as any composer – as to operatic structure, harmony and orchestration. Introduced the WAGNER TUBA.

Wagner-Régeny, Rudolf (1903–69), German composer, especially of operas, including *The Favourite* and *The Mine at Falun*.

Wagner tuba, type of instrument (more like a modified orchestral HORN than the usual tuba; see TUBA), made in two sizes (tenor and bass), designed to Wagner's specification and used by him (two of each) in THE RING. The compass of the tenor is from the B♭ in the bass stave upwards for about two and a half octaves; the bass has a compass an octave lower. The instruments have been used also by Bruckner, R. Strauss, and a few others. (Note that the 'double-bass tuba', which Wagner uses with these instruments in *The Ring*, is not of this family: it is a 'real' TUBA.)

wait, (1) a salaried musician acting as town watchman, or as a member of a court band, etc., in medieval England (the outdoor functions of the waits being alluded to in the modern application of the title to street-singers at Christmas-time); (2) old English name for SHAWM, an instrument much used by the medieval waits.

Walcha, [Arthur Emil] **Helmut** (b. 1907), German organist, noted in recitals, almost exclusively of Bach (Royal Festival Hall, London, from 1955); became blind at age 16.

Wald flute, Waldflöte (Ger., forest flute), organ stop of flute-like tone.

Waldhorn (Ger., forest horn), hunting-horn, i.e. a 'natural' horn having no valves. See HORN.

'Waldstein' Sonata, nickname for Beethoven's Piano Sonato in C, op. 53 (1804), dedicated to Count Waldstein, a musical amateur who was one of Beethoven's patrons.

Waldteufel, Emil (1837–1915), French (Alsatian) pianist and composer of waltzes (including the well-known 'Skaters' Waltz') and other dance-music. Was pianist to the Empress Eugénie of France.

Walker, Sarah (b. 1943), British mezzo-soprano, active in opera (noted in Handel), also soloist in the ritual Last Night of the Proms, etc.

Walküre, Die, see RING.

Wallace, William (1860–1940), British composer of *The Passing of Beatrice* (1892), thought to be the first symphonic poem by a British composer; also of other symphonic poems, songs, etc. Was also writer on music, and ophthalmologist. No relation of William Vincent Wallace.

Wallace, William Vincent (1812–65), Irish composer of a once very popular opera MARITANA and also of other operas, a violin concerto, piano solos, etc. Originally violinist. Visited Australia and New Zealand as a young man, and North and South America later. Died in France.

Wallfisch, Raphael (b. 1953), British cellist, prominent in concertos and as recitalist, often with his father, the pianist Peter Wallfisch (b. 1924).

Wally (name of heroine; original Italian title *La Wally*), opera by Catalani, produced in Milan, 1892, with libretto by L. Illica: an Alpine drama in which the heroine and her lover are finally engulfed in an avalanche.

Walmisley, Thomas Attwood (1814–56), British organist, professor of music at Cambridge, and composer chiefly of church and organ music.

Walond, William (*c*.1725–*c*.1770), British composer of keyboard pieces, an *Ode on St Cecilia's Day* to Pope's words, etc.; also organist. Another composer of the same name (?–1836) was probably his son.

Walter, Bruno (originally Bruno

Walter Schlesinger) (1876–1962), German-born conductor, also pianist; settled in Austria, then (penalized as a Jew under the Nazis) took French (1938) and later US (1946) nationality. Disciple and advocate of Mahler; noted also in opera.

Walther, Johann (1496–1570), German composer and publisher, adviser to Luther; he issued in 1524 the first Protestant hymn-collection. Composed also secular songs and instrumental music.

Walton, William [Turner] (1902–83), British composer, largely self-taught. Showed early influence of jazz and Stravinsky, e.g. in FAÇADE (reciter and instruments; later arranged for ballet). Other works include two symphonies, concertos for viola (see HINDEMITH), violin and cello; *Improvisations on an Impromptu by Benjamin Britten* for orchestra (see IMPROMPTU); march CROWN IMPERIAL; BELSHAZZAR'S FEAST and smaller choral works (see TE DEUM); operas TROILUS AND CRESSIDA and THE BEAR; film music (including *Henry V*); two string quartets, a violin sonata (see TWELVE-NOTE). Knighted, 1951. OM, 1968. Lived in Ischia (Italy).

waltz, dance in triple time becoming universally known in the 19th century; characteristically harmonized with only one chord to each bar. (See also VALSE, and the following entries.)

Waltz Dream, A (Ger., *Ein Walzertraum*), operetta by Oscar Straus, produced in Vienna, 1907. Libretto by F. Dörmann and L. Jacobson; a waltz is treated as the symbol of a nostalgic longing for Vienna.

Walzer (Ger.) = waltz(es).

Wand, Günter (b. 1912), German conductor, principal conductor of North German Radio since 1982; has toured widely, making London début, 1951, with London Symphony Orchestra.

'Wanderer' Fantasy, nickname given to Schubert's Fantasy for piano in C, 1822 (D760), because it makes use of material found also in his song 'The Wanderer' (1816). Best known as arranged by Liszt for piano and orchestra.

Wanhal(l), Johann Baptist (German form of Jan Křtitel Vaňhal) (1739–1813), Bohemian composer; his name was sometimes (e.g. on English editions) spelt 'Vanhall', and he has thus been erroneously said to be of Dutch descent. Visited Italy but worked mainly in Vienna, where he died. Friend of Haydn and Mozart: composed about 100 symphonies, 100 string quartets, much church music, etc.

War and Peace (Rus., *Voyna i mir*), opera by Prokofiev; libretto, after Tolstoy's novel, by the composer and M. Mendelson-Prokofiev. First performance of first version (the work was later extended), Moscow, 1944 (in concert form).

Ward, John (1571–1638), English composer; published a set of madrigals – the type of work for which he is noted – in 1613; wrote also music for viols, and for keyboard, church music, etc.

Ward, Robert [Eugene] (b. 1917), American composer of operas *He Who Gets Slapped* and *The Crucible* (after Arthur Miller); also of six symphonies, choral works, etc.

Warlock, Peter pseudonym used (as composer) by Philip Heseltine, (1894–1930), who also wrote about music (e.g. a book on Delius) under his own name. Works include song-cycle THE CURLEW and many other songs; also suite CAPRIOL, choral works, orchestral serenade for Delius's 60th birthday, etc. Also transcribed old English music, e.g. by Dowland. His sudden death is often presumed to have been a suicide.

War Requiem, A, work by Britten for soprano, tenor, baritone, chorus and orchestra, first performed in Coventry, 1962; text – from Roman Catholic Requiem (in Latin) and Wilfred Owen's poems – carries an anti-war message.

Water Music, name commonly used to designate a set of orchestral pieces by Handel, composed for a royal procession on the Thames (1715, 1717?) – the exact circumstances being uncertain. Published later as set of 20 pieces, of which six were arranged by Harty in a celebrated suite using modern orchestration, published in 1922.

water-organ, see HYDRAULIS.

Watkins, Michael Blake (b. 1948), British composer (also guitarist), pupil of Lutyens and Richard Rodney Bennett. Works include Double Concerto (oboe, guitar, orchestra), a horn concerto and a quartet (four guitars).

Watts, André (b. 1946), American pianist of Hungarian and black American parentage; made London concerto début and gave first New York solo recital in 1966.

Wat Tyler, opera by A. Bush, produced in Leipzig, 1953. Libretto by Nancy Bush (the composer's wife) about the leader of the Peasants' Revolt in England, 1381.

Wayenberg, Daniel [Ernest Joseph Carel] (b. 1929), French-born pianist of Dutch family, resident in France. Also composer of a symphony, concerto for three pianos and orchestra, etc.

Webbe, Samuel (1740–1816), British organist, composer of vocal music from Roman Catholic Masses and motets to glees and catches; father of Samuel Webbe (below).

Webbe, Samuel (c.1770–1843), pianist, organist, composer of vocal music, etc.; also writer of textbooks. Son of the above.

Webber, Andrew Lloyd and **Julian Lloyd,** see LLOYD WEBBER.

Weber, surname of two unrelated composers (separately below): the surname alone indicates reference to C. M. von Weber.

Weber, Ben (1916–79), American composer, largely self-taught; works include a piano concerto, a 'symphony' for baritone and chamber orchestra on poems by Blake, piano solos, ballet *Pool of Darkness*.

Weber, Carl Maria [Friedrich Ernst] **von** (1786–1826), German composer, pupil of M. Haydn and Vogler; also conductor and pianist. Exponent of German ROMANTIC opera, particularly in DER FREISCHÜTZ, a lasting international success. Other operas include ABU HASSAN, EURYANTHE and OBERON – the last written in English for England; Weber died in London after superintending the first production. (He had poor health, and was financially driven to over-work.) Also wrote incidental music to plays, including PRECIOSA and TURANDOT; two concertos and *Concert Piece* for piano and orchestra; two concertos and a concertino for clarinet and orchestra; a bassoon concerto; INVITATION TO THE DANCE and other piano solos; church music, songs, etc. Also writer on music; wrote an unfinished novel *A Composer's Life*, criticism, poems.

Webern, Anton von (1883–1945), Austrian composer, pupil of Schoenberg, whose TWELVE-NOTE technique he adapted with a special concern for the relationship between a particular tone-quality and a particular note. His works, mainly vocal or in the nature of chamber music, are few and tend to extreme brevity: no. 4 of his *Five Pieces for Orchestra* (1913), scored for nine instruments including mandolin, takes six and one-third bars and lasts 19 seconds. Other works include a symphony; Variations for orchestra; cantatas; five works for string quartet. He was accidentally shot dead in the Allied occupation of Austria. His posthumous influence on younger composers (and older, e.g. Stravinsky) was conspicuous.

Wechseldominante, see DOMINANT.

Weckerlin, Jean-Baptiste Théodore (1821–1910), French composer of operas, chamber music, etc., and editor of much old French music.

We Come to the River, opera by Henze, produced in London, 1976; libretto by Edward Bond, castigating war and social injustice.

Wedding, The (Rus., *Svadebka*), ballet with music by Stravinsky (for chorus, four pianos and percussion) produced in Paris, 1923. (The work having Russian words, there is no reason, outside

French-speaking countries, to use the name *Les Noces*.)

'Wedge' Fugue, nickname given to the longer of Bach's two Organ Fugues in E minor, composed between 1727 and 1736; the opening subject proceeds in gradually widening intervals.

Weelkes, Thomas (*c.*1575–1623), English composer of many strongly individual madrigals – including 'As Vesta was from Latmos hill descending' in THE TRIUMPHS OF ORIANA; also of BALLETTS and other secular vocal music, and of church music and pieces for viols including IN NOMINES. Also organist. Friend of Morley, in whose memory he wrote a three-part song.

Weidinger, Anton (1767–1852), Austrian trumpeter; he played the newly evolved keyed trumpet, and for him and his instrument Haydn wrote his Trumpet Concerto, 1796.

Weigl, Joseph (1766–1846), Austrian composer of operas (chiefly comic) in German and Italian; also of church music, etc. Worked and died in Vienna, where he became musical director of the Opera. Godson of Haydn.

Weigl, Karl (1881–1949), Austrian-born, American-naturalized composer of six symphonies, eight string quartets (no. 2 has a viola d'amore), etc. Also teacher and (1904–6) assistant coach at the Vienna Court Opera under Mahler.

Weihnachtsoratorium (Ger.) = CHRISTMAS ORATORIO.

Weihnachtssymphonie (Ger., Christmas Symphony), another nickname for Haydn's LAMENTATION symphony.

Weill, Kurt [Julian] (1900–1950), German-born composer, pupil of Humperdinck and Busoni. Using some jazz-based idioms, he had early success with THE THREEPENNY OPERA (Ger., *Die Dreigroschenoper*), and with RISE AND FALL OF THE CITY OF MAHAGONNY – both to texts by Brecht with satirical criticism of capitalist society. Penalized by the Nazis as a Jew and a composer of 'decadent' music, he settled in USA, 1935. His American works include operas STREET SCENE and *Down in the Valley*, music to various Broadway musical plays including *Lost in the Stars*. Other works include cantata *Lindbergh's Flight* (1929), two symphonies.

Weinberger, Jaromir (1896–1967), Czech composer who studied with Reger in Berlin, lived in USA, 1922–6, and settled in USA, 1939. Works include opera ŠVANDA THE BAGPIPER, formerly much performed; also orchestral Variations and Fugue based on 'Under the Spreading Chestnut Tree', etc.

Weiner, Leó (1885–1960), Hungarian composer, also teacher and writer on music. Works include five Divertimentos for orchestra, two violin concertos, three string quartets.

Weingartner, [Paul] **Felix,** Count von Münzberg (1863–1942), German conductor (also composer) of unsurpassed reputation (London début 1908), making famous Beethoven recordings in the 1930s.

Weinzweig, John Jacob (b. 1913), Canadian composer, also conductor and teacher. Works include a symphony and *Symphonic Ode* for orchestra; a harp concerto; *Around the stage in 25 minutes during which a variety of instruments are struck* for percussionist.

Weir, Gillian [Constance] (b. 1941), New Zealand organist (also harpsichordist) who trained in London and has been prominent as organ soloist in Britain and elsewhere since 1965; noted interpreter of Messiaen.

Weisgall, Hugo [David] (b. 1912), American composer (born in Czechoslovakia); works include operas *Six Characters in Search of an Author* (after Pirandello), *The Stronger* (after Strindberg) and other operas; also *Graven Images* (chamber music).

Weiss, Sylvius Leopold (1686–1750), German lutenist and composer for his instrument, working at various courts.

Weissenberg, Alexis (b. 1929), Bulgarian-born pianist who made his début in Israel at 14, then trained at Juilliard School, New York; naturalized French, 1956. Celebrated soloist, e.g. on records with Karajan and the Berlin Philharmonic.

Weldon, John (1676–1736), English organist and composer of church and stage music. His music to a Restoration version of Shakespeare's *The Tempest* was formerly attributed to Purcell, his teacher.

Welitsch (originally Velichova), **Ljuba** (b. 1913), Bulgarian-born Austrian soprano who began a notable operatic career in Sofia, extending to Vienna, London, etc.; famous as Salome in R. Strauss's opera.

Wellesz, Egon (1885–1974), Austrian-born composer (pupil of Schoenberg) who settled in England, 1939, as Oxford University lecturer. Works include *Alkestis*, *Incognita* (in English) and other operas; *The Leaden Echo and the Golden Echo* (Gerard Manley

Hopkins) for soprano and four instruments; Roman Catholic church music; a violin concerto, songs.

Wellington's Victory, or The Battle of Vitoria (Ger., *Wellingtons Sieg, oder Die Schlacht bei Vitoria*), orchestral work by Beethoven, 1813. (He wrote 'Vittoria' by mistake.) Also known as the 'Battle Symphony', it is illustrative of a British and allied victory over Napoleonic forces at Vitoria, Spain, and quotes various national airs.

Wells, H. G. [Herbert George] (1866–1946), British writer. See BRINDLE.

Well-tempered Clavier, The (Ger., *Das wohltemperierte Clavier*), title given by Bach to his 24 Preludes and Fugues, 1772, in all the major and minor keys, and applied also to a further similar 24 (1744); the title is thus now applied to the two sets together, which are also known as 'the 48'. The use of all the major and minor keys demonstrated the facilities offered by the system of 'equal TEMPERAMENT'. The word 'clavier', meaning any keyboard instrument, is correct here – not clavichord, Bach not intending the work exclusively for that instrument.

Wenzinger, August (b. 1905), Swiss cellist, viol-player and conductor; influential in establishing 'authentic' baroque orchestral performances, particularly with the (Swiss) Schola Cantorum Basiliensis.

Werle, Lars Johan (b. 1926), Swedish composer of operas *Dreaming about Thérèse*, designed with special instrumentation to be performed 'in the round' (orchestra encircling audience encircling singers) and *The Journey*; *Sinfonia da camera*; ballet *Zodiac*; etc.

Werner, Gregor [Joseph] (1693–1766), Austrian composer of 40 Masses, fugues for string quartet, etc.; in service to the Esterházy family, succeeded after his death by Haydn.

Wert, Giaches de (or Jaches de) (1535–96), Flemish composer who went to Italy as a boy chorister and settled there, dying in Mantua. Wrote madrigals, motets, etc., and held court and church musical posts.

Werther, opera by Massenet, produced (in German) in Vienna, 1892; libretto, in French, by E. Blau, P. Milliet and G. Hartmann – after Goethe's *The Sorrows of Werther*, the hero being driven by sentimental love to suicide.

Wesley, Charles (1757–1834), British organist, harpsichordist and composer (concertos, anthems, etc.); a youthful prodigy who did not fulfil his early promise. Pupil of Boyce. Nephew of John Wesley, the founder of Methodism, and brother of Samuel Wesley.

Wesley, Samuel (1766–1837), British organist and composer; despite his family background (see preceding entry) became Roman Catholic, and wrote mainly Roman Catholic (but some Anglican) church music; also symphonies, organ concertos, etc. A head injury in youth caused his later mental instability. Was among the first British enthusiasts for Bach; hence, doubtless, the middle name of his son (below).

Wesley, Samuel Sebastian (1810–76), British composer, illegitimate son of the preceding; also organist, finally at Gloucester Cathedral, and a fighter against the slackness in Anglican cathedral music at that time. Wrote much church music; also choral 'Ode to Labour' and some piano pieces.

whip, percussion instrument imitative of the crack of a whip and consisting of two pieces of wood joined in a V-shape: the player snaps the 'arms' loudly together.

whistle, (1, verb) to produce a vocal sound through a small aperture in the lips, the pitch being governed by the shaping of the mouth as a resonating chamber. A few professional whistlers have occasionally penetrated to the concert-platform. (2, noun) general name for various wind instruments, usually of primitive construction (and sometimes played with the nose) giving a sound similar to human whistling – a Western mouth-blown example being the TIN-WHISTLE.

White, Maude Valérie (1855–1937), British composer, born in France; wrote mainly songs, in French, English and German; also a few piano pieces, etc.

White, Patrick (1912–90), Australian writer. See MEALE.

White, Robert (or Whyte) (c.1538–74), English composer who died of the plague; wrote church music (chiefly but not entirely to Latin texts), and also music for viols, etc. Married Ellen Tye, probably a daughter of the composer Tye.

White, Willard (b. 1946), Jamaican bass, resident in Britain; celebrated as Porgy in Gershwin's *Porgy and Bess* (Glyndebourne, 1986).

White Peacock, The, work for piano by Griffes (1915), later orchestrated; after a poem by 'Fiona Macleod' (William Sharp), and originally forming one of four *Roman Sketches*.

Whithorne (originally Whittern),

Emerson (1884–1958), American composer – also pianist, pupil of Leschetizky in Vienna; lived for a time in England and China. Works include *New York Days and Nights* and other piano pieces; symphonic poems, chamber music, etc.

Whithorne, Thomas, see WHYTHORNE.

Whitlock, Percy [William] (1903–46), British organist, and composer chiefly of organ and church music.

Whitman, Walt (1819–92), American poet. See REQUIEM.

whole-note, the note ○ considered as a time-value. This term is standard North American usage and, as mathematically corresponding to the element of time-signature represented by /1, should clearly be preferred to 'semibreve', still surviving in British use. The corresponding rest is notated ▬

whole-tone, the interval of two semitones, e.g. from C up to the adjacent D – divisible into the two semitones C–C♯ and C♯–D. So *whole-tone scale*, a scale progressing entirely in wholetones, instead of partly in whole-tones and partly in semitones like the major and minor scales and the old MODES. Only two such whole-tone scales are possible – one 'beginning' on C, one on C♯, though in fact each scale can equally well begin on any of its notes, since (owing to the equal intervals) there is no note which presents itself as a point of rest equivalent to a key-note. Debussy and other composers have used the whole-tone scale pronouncedly for chords and short passages, but not for an entire piece consistently.

Whyte, Robert, see WHITE (R.).

Whythorne, Thomas (1528–96), English composer who travelled in Italy and elsewhere, and wrote music for voices, for viols, etc., including some duos expressly with option for voices or for instruments. His autobiography, written in phonetic script, was rediscovered in 1955.

Widor, Charles-Marie [-Jean-Albert] (1844–1937). French organist, composer and noted teacher, holder of a church appointment at St Sulpice, Paris, for 64 years. Works include many solos for organ including 10 'symphonies' (see TOCCATA), as well as orchestral symphonies, two piano concertos, operas.

Wiegenlied (Ger.), cradle-song; the one sometimes attributed to Mozart ('Schlafe, mein Prinzchen' – Sleep, my little prince) is really by J. Bernhard Flies, an amateur composer born about 1770.

Wiener Blut, see VIENNA BLOOD.

Wiener Sängerknaben, see VIENNA BOYS' CHOIR.

Wieniawski, Henryk (1835–80), Polish violinist, composer of two concertos (no. 2 is the well-known one) and other music for his instrument. Toured much (in USA with Anton Rubinstein), taught many years at the Brussels Conservatory, and died in Moscow.

Wilbye, John (1574–1638), English composer, particularly of madrigals (including 'Flora gave me fairest flowers'). His other works, which are very few, include a little church music (in Latin and English), and some pieces for viols. Contributor to THE TRIUMPHS OF ORIANA. In service to noble English families.

Wild, Earl (b. 1915), American pianist, celebrated in Liszt and other virtuoso-style music, who made his London début in 1973.

Wilde, David [Clark] (b. 1935), British pianist, pupil of Reizenstein and (in Paris) of N. Boulanger; first prize in a Liszt-Bartók competition, Budapest, 1961. Teaches in Hanover; is also television presenter, writer and occasional conductor.

Wilde, Oscar (1854–1900), Irish writer. See IBERT, LUTYENS, SALOME, ZEMLINSKY.

Wilder, Thornton (1897–1975), American novelist and dramatist. See REUTTER.

Wilhelmj, August [Emil Daniel Ferdinand] (1845–1908), German violinist who in 1893 settled in London as teacher, and died there. Wrote cadenzas for celebrated violin concertos, arrangements for violin, etc. – e.g. the so-called *Air on the G String* (see AIR).

Wilkinson, Marc (b. 1929), Australian (French-born) composer, pupil of Messiaen in Paris and of Varèse in New York; music director to the Old Vic (theatre company), 1964–7. Works include cantata *Voices* based on Beckett's play *Waiting for Godot*.

Willaert, Adriaan (c.1490–1562), Flemish composer who worked chiefly in Venice as church musician, achieving high influence and dying there. Was one of the first to compose madrigals, to write independent instrumental pieces (of the type of the RICERCAR, etc.) and to employ double choirs antiphonally. Composed Masses, motets, a Magnificat and various vocal pieces to secular words.

Willan, Healey (1880–1968), British-born organist and composer who settled in Canada (Toronto University post, 1914). Composed symphony, cantatas, church and organ music, etc.

Willcocks, David [Valentine] (b. 1919), British organist, conductor, and music editor. Music director of the Bach Choir (London) since 1960; director, Royal College of Music, 1974–85. Knighted, 1977.

Williams, Grace (1906–77), British composer, pupil of Vaughan Williams (no relation) in London and of Wellesz in Vienna. Works include PENILLION for orchestra, symphonic variations *Owen Glendower*, and other works with Welsh associations; also opera *The Parlour*, a trumpet concerto, etc.

Williams, John [Christopher] (b. 1941), Australian guitarist (resident in Britain), for whom works have been written by Stephen Dodgson (two concertos) and others; eminent soloist and guitar-duettist with Julian Bream, formerly leader of his own ensemble embracing jazz and pop as well as classical traditions. OBE, 1980.

Williams, John [Tower] (b. 1932), American conductor and composer; he wrote the music to *Star Wars* and many other films. Conductor of the Boston Pops Orchestra since 1980.

Williams, Ralph Vaughan, see VAUGHAN WILLIAMS.

Williams, Tennessee (1912–83), American dramatist. See BANFIELD.

Williamson, Malcolm [Benjamin Graham Christopher] (b. 1931), Australian composer resident in Britain since 1953; also organist and pianist.

Works include OUR MAN IN HAVANA, *The Violins of St Jacques* and other operas; also three piano concertos, five symphonies, and Roman Catholic church music in popular-song style. Master of the Queen's Music, 1975. CBE, 1976.

William Tell (Fr., *Guillaume Tell*), Rossini's last opera, produced in Paris, 1829, Libretto by V. J. E. de Jouy and H. L. F. Bis – after Schiller's drama about the Swiss national hero.

Wilson, John (1595–1674), English lutenist, singer, viol-player, and composer of songs (some to words by Shakespeare), catches, psalms, etc. Is thought to be identical with the 'Jack Wilson' who acted in Shakespeare's company in *Much Ado About Nothing*. Later, court musician to Charles I and Charles II.

Wimberger, Gerhard (b. 1923), Austrian composer of *Dame Hobgoblin* (Ger., *Dame Kobold*, after Calderón's *La dama duende*) and other operas; piano concerto *Resonances* (It., *Risonanze*) for three orchestral groups; cantatas, etc.

wind band, term used to describe a band of mixed wind instruments (usually with percussion also); MILITARY BAND is, however, the traditional British term (a BRASS BAND being of brass alone, not mixed with woodwind). Haydn's so-called *Wind Band Mass* (in B♭, 1802, Hob. XXII: 14; Ger., *Harmoniemesse*), however, got its nickname only because wind instruments are used in it prominently, not exclusively.

Windgassen, Wolfgang (1914–74), German tenor, a leading Wagner singer (Covent Garden, Bayreuth, etc.) of the 1950s and beyond.

wind instrument, generic name for musical instruments in which the sound is produced through the vibrations of a column of air which is set in motion by the player's breath – such instruments being commonly divided into WOODWIND and BRASS (convenient labels to classify differing types of mechanism, though the implication that all the former are made of wood and the latter of brass is misleading). Instruments in which the effect of the breath is mechanically simulated, e.g. organ and accordion, are not normally understood by the term *wind instruments,* though all may be classified as AEROPHONES.

wind-machine, theatrical 'effects' machine simulating wind (usually by means of the rotation of a fabric-covered barrel) used in a few musical works – e.g. R. Strauss, DON QUIXOTE.

Winter Journey, The, song-cycle by Schubert, 1827 (Ger., *Die Winterreise*), on 24 poems by W. Müller about an unrequited love.

Winterreise, Die, see WINTER JOURNEY.

'Winter Wind' Study, nickname for Chopin's Study in A minor, op. 25, no. 11, 1834.

wire brush, type of drumstick with a head of several stiff wires, used to give a 'brushing' sound to a side-drum – an effect chiefly used in dance bands.

Wirén, Dag [Ivar] (1905–86), Swedish composer (also formerly music critic) who studied in Paris and became influenced by Honegger. Works include Serenade (for strings), five symphonies, a violin concerto, piano concerto, cello concerto, stage and film music, five string quartets.

Wise, Michael (*c.* 1647–87), English singer, organist and composer of anthems, catches, etc.; killed in a street brawl.

Witches' Minuet, see FIFTHS QUARTET.

Witt, Jeremias Friedrich (1771–1837), Austrian composer of Masses, orchestral works, etc.; see JENA.

Wittgenstein, Paul (1887–1961), Austrian pianist (naturalized American, 1946) who lost his right arm in World War I and for whom R. Strauss, Ravel, Britten and others wrote piano works for left hand alone (with orchestra).

Wohltemperierte Clavier, Das, see WELL-TEMPERED CLAVIER.

wolf, (1) a jarring sound sometimes occurring through unintentional vibrations on stringed instruments; (2) an out-of-tune effect occurring in certain keys on old organs tuned in 'mean-tone temperament' – not in 'equal temperament' by which all keys are equally 'in tune'. (See TEMPERAMENT.)

Wolf, Hugo [Filipp Jakob] (1860–1903), Austrian composer chiefly of songs, usually grouped by their literary sources – e.g. ITALIAN SONG-BOOK and SPANISH SONG-BOOK (German translations of Italian, Spanish poems), MÖRIKE SONGS (57) and songs to texts by Goethe (51). These are reckoned to constitute a peak within the general German Romantic type of song; as in Schumann's, the piano parts are very important. A few of the songs also have orchestral (as well as piano) versions of the accompaniments. Wolf wrote also opera *The Corregidor*; ITALIAN SERENADE; and a few other works. Lived largely in poverty; proved himself unfitted to conducting; was an aggressive music critic (extolling Wagner, decrying Brahms); became insane in 1897 and was confined from 1898 till death.

Wolff, Christian (b. 1934), French-born American composer who studied with Cage; university teacher of classics and music. Has written music using tapes, music for prepared piano and for non-fixed ensembles ('for one, two or three people' on any instruments), etc., and has evolved his own notation.

Wolf-Ferrari, Ermanno (1876–1948), Italian-born composer, son of a German father and Italian mother; pupil of Rheinberger. Works are principally operas (in Italian, though some were first given in German). They include SCHOOL FOR FATHERS (*I quatro rusteghi*), SUSANNA'S SECRET, THE JEWELS OF THE MADONNA and CINDERELLA. Wrote also cantatas, chamber music, etc.

Wolpe, Stefan (1902–72), German-born composer who emigrated to Austria, to Palestine, then (1938) to USA, teaching there. Works include song-settings to Hebrew texts, piano pieces, chamber music, *Solo Piece for Trumpet*, a symphony.

Wolstenholme, William (1865–1931), British organist and composer, blind from birth; composed chiefly for the organ. Also violinist (taught by Elgar) and pianist.

Woman of Arles, The (Fr., *L'Arlésienne*), play by Alphonse Daudet, 1872, for which Bizet wrote incidental music; the second of the two suites drawn from this is an arrangement made by Guiraud after Bizet's death. See FARANDOLE.

Woman's Love and Life (Ger., *Frau-*enliebe und -leben), song-cycle by Schumann, 1840, to eight poems by Chamisso – male poet proclaiming woman's adoring submission.

WoO, abbr. for German *Werk ohne Opuszahl* (work without opus number), referring particularly to those works by Beethoven to which the composer did not give a number but which were listed in the thematic catalogue by G. Kinsky.

Wood, Charles (1866–1926), Irish organist, composer, professor of music at Cambridge. Composed cantatas, church music, songs, etc.

Wood, Haydn (1882–1959), British composer chiefly famous for 'Roses of Picardy' and similar popular sentimental songs; also wrote a piano concerto, Fantasy Quartet for strings, etc.

Wood, Henry [Joseph] (1869–1944), British conductor who in 1895 began a famous series of Promenade Concerts in London ('the Proms') and continued to conduct them until his death. Also arranger e.g. of the so-called *Trumpet Voluntary* (misattributed to Purcell, see CLARKE) for organ, brass and kettledrums, and, under the name 'Paul Klenovsky', of Bach's Organ Toccata and Fugue in D minor for orchestra. Knighted, 1911.

Wood, Hugh (b. 1932), British composer, pupil of Hamilton and Seiber. Works include a cello concerto, four string quartets and *Scenes from 'Comus'* (Milton) for soprano, tenor and orchestra.

Wood, Thomas (1892–1950), British composer (pupil of Stanford), and author. Travelled to Australia and popularized the song 'Waltzing Matilda' outside Australia. Works include cantatas *Chanticleer* (after Chaucer; unaccompanied) and *The Rainbow* (male voices and brass band).

wood block (or *Chinese block*), a rectangular block of wood, hollowed out for resonance, and used as a percussion instrument in certain 20th-century works, e.g. Lambert's THE RIO GRANDE. A related type is the TEMPLE BLOCK.

Woodward, Roger (b. 1942), Australian pianist who studied in London and Warsaw and won the Warsaw International Chopin Competition in 1970. Notable also in performing modern works. OBE, 1980.

woodwind, collective name for those types of wind instrument historically and generally made of wood – either blown directly (e.g. flute, recorder), or blown by means of a reed (e.g. clarinet, oboe), and in either case consisting basically of a tube with holes which, closed or opened by the player's fingers, shorten or lengthen the vibrating air-column and thus vary the pitch of the note emitted. The term *woodwind* is also used of instruments conforming to this but made of metal (e.g. saxophones, and some models of flute and clarinet). The distinction between *woodwind* and BRASS, apart from material, is that in the latter the player blows not by the methods described above but by pressing his lips against a cup-shaped or funnel-shaped mouthpiece. In the symphony orchestra, *double woodwind* indicates two players of each 'standard type' (flute, oboe, clarinet, bassoon), as usually specified e.g. by Beethoven; *triple woodwind* indicates three of each, one player normally also taking an 'extra' related to the four 'standard'

instruments above – respectively, piccolo, English horn, bass clarinet, double-bassoon.

Wordsworth, William [Brocklesby] (1908–88), British composer; a descendant of Christopher Wordsworth, brother of the poet. Works include six symphonies, six string quartets, songs.

working-out, synonym for DEVELOPMENT, e.g. in SONATA-FORM.

World of the Moon, The (It., *Il Mondo della luna*), comic opera by Haydn (Hob. XXVIII: 7), produced in Eszterháza, 1777. Libretto by Goldoni, about an astronomer so absorbed in his study of the moon that he allows his daughters to accept 'unsuitable' suitors.

Wotquenne, Alfred (1867–1939), Belgian musicologist. See BACH (C. P. E.).

Wozzeck, opera by A. Berg, completed in 1922, produced in Berlin, 1925. Libretto by composer; Wozzeck is a simple, persecuted, feeble-minded private soldier. The play on which the opera is based is by Georg Büchner, 1836; another opera on it, by M. Gurlitt, appeared in 1926.

Wq., abbr. for 'Wotquenne' (in numbering the works of C. P. E. BACH).

Wranitzky, German spelling of VRANICKÝ.

Wührer, Friedrich (1900–75), Austrian pianist and teacher; his recital tours in Europe and USA gave prominence to modern works.

Wunderlich, Fritz (1930–66), German tenor with a distinguished career in concert and opera (Covent Garden from 1965) which was cut short by his early death.

Wuorinen, Charles (b. 1938), American composer of an octet and much other chamber music; various concertos including one for tuba, 12 wind instruments and 12 drums; *Making Ends Meet* for piano duet; electronic music. Is also pianist and conductor.

Wurlitzer, American firm of organ-builders (founded in 1858) which became famous for theatre-organs (originally pipe-organs) in the period 1919–39.

Wyner, Yehudi (b. 1929), Canadian-born American composer of Jewish liturgical music, a piano sonata, *On This Most Voluptuous Night* for soprano and seven instruments, etc.; is also pianist, conductor and teacher.

X

Xenakis, Iannis (b. 1922), Romanian-born composer of Greek parentage; uses complex mathematical formulas – and sometimes a computer, as in part of *Eonta* (Gk., Beings) for piano and five brass instruments. His *Metastaseis* (After-standstill) is for 61 individual instrumentalists; *Polytope* (Many-placed) is for four orchestras of 17 players each, distributed among the audience. Some works, e.g. *Duel* (for two orchestras), have the form of a game with rules (and unpredicted result). See also STOCHASTIC.

Xerxes (It., *Serse*), opera by Handel, produced in London, 1738. Libretto by N. Minato about a Persian king. Contains the famous aria 'Ombra mai fu' (In Praise of a Tree's Shade) known as 'Handel's Largo' – arbitrarily, since Handel actually headed it 'Larghetto'.

xylophone, percussion instrument consisting of tuned wooden bars (hence the name, from Greek for 'wood' and 'sound'), arranged in order as on a piano keyboard and struck with small hard-headed sticks. Compass from middle C upwards for three octaves. Introduced from Eastern Europe; used in the orchestra in Saint-Saëns' DANSE MACABRE, 1874, and afterwards gaining general currency for special effects. See also MARIMBA.

xylorimba, percussion instrument (name combining xylophone and marimba), combining the compass of xylophone and marimba, about five octaves.

Y

Yamash'ta, Stomu (originally Tsutomu Yamashita) (b. 1947), Japanese percussionist (active as soloist in modern music) and composer (*Prisms* for solo percussion, etc.); directed his own *Red Buddha Ensemble*, etc.

Yansons, Arvid (1914–84), Soviet-Latvian conductor, prominently associated with the Hallé Orchestra (Manchester) from 1964. His son Mariss Yansons (b. 1943) is also a conductor.

Years of Pilgrimage (Fr., *Années de Pèlerinage*), title of four sets of piano pieces by Liszt, expressing his experiences of Italy and Switzerland – arranged in three 'years', plus a supplementary set, published 1855–83. See DANTE SONATA.

Yeats, William Butler (1865–1939), Irish poet and dramatist. See CURLEW, EGK, PARTCH.

Yeomen of the Guard, The, or The Merryman and his Maid, operetta by Sullivan, produced in London, 1888. Libretto by W. S. Gilbert, the title referring to the Warders of the Tower of London; the action is set in the 16th century.

Yepes, Narciso (b. 1927), Spanish guitarist who has toured internationally since 1948; has also composed film music. Plays a 10-string guitar.

Yevgeny Onegin, opera by Tchaikovsky, produced in Moscow, 1879. Libretto by composer and K. S. Shilovsky, after Pushkin. The hero lives to regret his blasé rejection of a young woman's love. (The title is often given in English-speaking contexts as *Eugene Onegin.*)

Yevtushenko, Yevgeni (b. 1933), Russian poet. See BABI YAR.

yodel (Ger., *Jodel*), type of singing for men alternating between natural voice and falsetto, practised particularly in the Swiss and Austrian Alpine region. It is used for simple dance-like tunes.

Yolande, opera by Tchaikovsky, produced in St Petersburg, 1892. Libretto (after Henrik Hertz) by M. I. Tchaikovsky, the composer's brother: the name part is that of a blind medieval princess. The Russian form of the title is *Yolanta,* sometimes spelt *Iolanta.*

Yonge, Nicolas (?–1619), English singer; see MUSICA TRANSALPINA.

Young, La Monte (b. 1935), American composer who studied with Stockhausen. His works often incorporate nonmusical elements – as in *Poem for Chairs* [*Tables, Benches,* etc.] – or may consist of non-musical instructions, e.g. 'Draw a straight line and follow it'; earlier works include a string trio, etc.

Young, William (?–1672), English flautist, violinist and composer who worked abroad and published (at Innsbruck, 1653) the earliest English sonatas for two or more violins with bass viol and continuo – i.e. the type of TRIO-SONATA later used by Purcell. Afterwards returned to England and became a member of the court band.

Young Lord, The (Ger., *Der junge Lord*), opera by Henze, produced in Berlin, 1965; in Ingeborg Bachmann's libretto, the 'English nobleman' is really a dressed-up ape.

Young Person's Guide to the Orchestra, The, variations and fugue by Britten (1945) on a theme of Purcell (from the play *Abdelazer*, 1695).

Youth's Magic Horn, The (Ger., *Des Knaben Wunderhorn*), an anthology of German poetry supposedly of folk origin; Mahler set 13 of these poems to orchestral accompaniment, 1900.

Yradier, Sebastián (1809–65), Spanish composer of 'La paloma' (Sp., The Dove) and other popular songs. The 'Habanera' in Bizet's CARMEN is an adaptation of one of Yradier's songs.

Ysaÿe, Eugène (1858–1931), Belgian violinist, pupil of Wieniawski and Vieuxtemps; toured much, played many new works (including Franck's Violin Sonata) and led his own celebrated string quartet. Was also conductor and composer – mainly of six concertos and other works for violin, but also of an opera in Walloon (a Belgian dialect of French).

Yun, Isang (b. 1917), Korean-born composer who trained in Paris and Berlin (pupil of Blacher) and now lives and teaches in Berlin; works include operas *The Dream of Liu-Tung* and *The Butterfly's Widow*; *Fluctuations* for orchestra; *Images* for flute, oboe, violin and cello; etc.

Z

Z, abbr. for Zimmerman in numbering the works of Henry PURCELL.

Zabaleta, Nicanor (b. 1907), Spanish harpist who studied in Madrid and Paris and became internationally known; works were specially written for him by Milhaud, Krenek and other composers.

Zachau, Friedrich Wilhelm (1663–1712), German composer, chiefly of church and organ music; teacher of Handel.

Zacher, Gerd (b. 1929), German composer, also organist, giving first performances of works by Kagel, Ligeti, etc. His own works include *The Prayers of Jonah in the Fish's Belly* for soprano and organ, *Transformations* for piano; choral music.

Zadok the Priest, no.1 of four anthems by Handel for the coronation of George II, 1727; performed at every English coronation since.

Zagrosek, Lothar (b. 1942), Austrian conductor, noted in London and other capitals as a specialist in modern music; conductor of the Austrian Radio Symphony Orchestra since 1984.

Zampa, or The Marble Betrothed (Fr., ... *ou la Fiancée de marbre*), opera by Hérold, produced in Paris, 1831. Lib-

retto by A. H. J. Mélesville; Zampa, a 16th-century pirate, is dragged down to death by a marble statue. (The statue is female, but cp. DON GIOVANNI.)

Zandonai, Riccardo (1883–1944), Italian composer of operas in the conventional Italian style of his period – including *Giulietta e Romeo* (on Shakespeare's *Romeo and Juliet*) and *Francesca da Rimini* (after D'Annunzio's play). Also composed orchestral works, songs, etc.

zapateado (Sp.), vigorous Spanish dance for a single performer, in which the heels tap out rhythmic patterns.

Zar und Zimmermann, see TSAR AND CARPENTER.

zarzuela (Sp.), type of traditional Spanish musical stage entertainment, with spoken dialogue, often satirical.

Zauberflöte, Die, see MAGIC FLUTE.

Zelenka, Jan Dismas (1679–1745), Czech composer (also double-bass player) active in Germany; in 1735 became court musical director at Dresden, where he died. Wrote overture *Hypochondria*, 21 Masses, many motets, etc.

Zelter, Carl Friedrich (1785–1832), German composer, chiefly of vocal music, including song-settings of Goethe which won Goethe's approval; teacher of Mendelssohn.

Zemlinsky, Alexander von (1872–1942), Austrian composer of operas, including *A Florentine Tragedy* and *The Dwarf* (or *The Birthday of the Infanta*), both after Wilde, also of two symphonies, etc. Conductor in Vienna and Berlin, mentor (and brother-in-law) of Schoenberg.

Ziehharmonika (Ger.) = ACCORDION.

Zigeuner (Ger.), gipsy; so *Zigeunerbaron* – see GIPSY BARON; *Zigeunerweisen* (Gipsy Airs), work in gipsy style for violin and piano (or orchestra) by Sarasate, published in 1878.

Ziloti, Alexander [Ilyich] (1863–1945), Russian pianist and conductor; his piano pupils included his cousin Rakhmaninov. Conducted his own orchestra in St Petersburg, then settled in USA, 1922.

Zimbalist, Efrem [Alexandrovich] (1889–1985), Russian-born American violinist, noted as soloist and as teacher at the Curtis Institute in Philadelphia – he was its director, 1941–68.

Zimerman, Krystian (b. 1956), Polish pianist who won the Warsaw International Chopin Competition, 1975, and later gave the first performance of Lutosławski's Piano Concerto.

Zimmerman, Franklin Bershir (b. 1923), American musicologist. see PURCELL (H.).

Zimmermann, Bernd Alois (1918–70), German composer, pupil of Jarnach, Fortner and Leibowitz; works include two symphonies, a violin concerto, cello concerto; *Requiem for a Young Poet* for speaking and singing choruses, solo singers, jazz group, organ, orchestra and electronics; cantata *In Praise of Stupidity* (on texts by Goethe); opera THE SOLDIERS.

Zingarelli, Niccolò Antonio (1752–1837), Italian composer of many operas (one on *Romeo and Juliet*), also of church music, etc.; holder of church music posts. Teacher of Bellini.

Zipoli, Domenico (1688–1726), Italian composer and Jesuit priest who went as church organist to Argentina, where he died; wrote toccatas and other pieces for harpsichord or organ, also Italian oratorios, etc.

zither, type of flat-backed stringed instrument laid on the knees or table, and plucked; usually, some strings can be 'stopped' (as on a violin), and others are fixed in pitch and used for accompaniment. In its best-known form it is a folk-instrument native to Central Europe and widely adopted elsewhere.

Zola, Émile (1840–1902), French novelist. See BRUNEAU.

zoppa (It.), a limp; *alla zoppa*, term used of music having a prominent SCOTCH SNAP or a pronounced regular syncopation.

Zukerman, Pinchas (b. 1948), Israeli violinist who trained in USA, 1962–7; winner of Leventritt Prize (jointly with Kyung-Wha Chung), New York, 1967. Prominent soloist since then, often conducting his own accompaniment in concertos. Is also viola-player and, since 1974, an occasional conductor.

Zwölf (Ger.), 12; *Zwölftonmusik*, TWELVE-NOTE music.

FOR THE BEST IN PAPERBACKS, LOOK FOR THE

In every corner of the world, on every subject under the sun, Penguin represents quality and variety – the very best in publishing today.

For complete information about books available from Penguin – including Puffins, Penguin Classics and Arkana – and how to order them, write to us at the appropriate address below. Please note that for copyright reasons the selection of books varies from country to country.

In the United Kingdom: Please write to *Dept E.P., Penguin Books Ltd, Harmondsworth, Middlesex, UB7 0DA.*

If you have any difficulty in obtaining a title, please send your order with the correct money, plus ten per cent for postage and packaging, to *PO Box No 11, West Drayton, Middlesex*

In the United States: Please write to *Dept BA, Penguin, 299 Murray Hill Parkway, East Rutherford, New Jersey 07073*

In Canada: Please write to *Penguin Books Canada Ltd, 2801 John Street, Markham, Ontario L3R 1B4*

In Australia: Please write to the *Marketing Department, Penguin Books Australia Ltd, P.O. Box 257, Ringwood, Victoria 3134*

In New Zealand: Please write to the *Marketing Department, Penguin Books (NZ) Ltd, Private Bag, Takapuna, Auckland 9*

In India: Please write to *Penguin Overseas Ltd, 706 Eros Apartments, 56 Nehru Place, New Delhi, 110019*

In the Netherlands: Please write to *Penguin Books Netherlands B.V., Postbus 195, NL–1380AD Weesp*

In West Germany: Please write to *Penguin Books Ltd, Friedrichstrasse 10–12, D–6000 Frankfurt/Main 1*

In Spain: Please write to *Alhambra Longman S.A., Fernandez de la Hoz 9, E–28010 Madrid*

In Italy: Please write to *Penguin Italia s.r.l., Via Como 4, I-20096 Pioltello (Milano)*

In France: Please write to *Penguin Books Ltd, 39 Rue de Montmorency, F-75003 Paris*

In Japan: Please write to *Longman Penguin Japan Co Ltd, Yamaguchi Building, 2–12–9 Kanda Jimbocho, Chiyoda-Ku, Tokyo 101*

A Lover's Discourse Roland Barthes

'*A Lover's Discourse* … may be the most detailed, painstaking anatomy of desire we are ever likely to see or need again … The book is an ecstatic celebration of love and language and … readers interested in either or both … will enjoy savouring its rich and dark delights' – *Washington Post Book World*

The New Pelican Guide to English Literature Boris Ford (ed.)

The indispensable critical guide to English and American literature in nine volumes, erudite yet accessible. From the ages of Chaucer and Shakespeare, via Georgian satirists and Victorian social critics, to the leading writers of the 1980s, all literary life is here.

The Theatre of the Absurd Martin Esslin

This classic study of the dramatists of the Absurd examines the origins, nature and future of a movement whose significance has transcended the bounds of the stage and influenced the whole intellectual climate of our time.

The Theory of the Modern Stage Eric Bentley (ed.)

In this anthology Artaud, Brecht, Stanislavski and other great theatrical theorists reveal the ideas underlying their productions and point to the possibilities of the modern theatre.

Introducing Shakespeare G. B. Harrison

An excellent popular introduction to Shakespeare – the legend, the (tantalizingly ill-recorded) life and the work – in the context of his times: theatrical rivalry, literary piracy, the famous performance of *Richard II* in support of Essex, and the fire which finally destroyed the Globe.

Aspects of the Novel E. M. Forster

'I say that I have never met this kind of perspicacity in literary criticism before. I could quote scores of examples of startling excellence' – Arnold Bennett. Originating in a course of lectures given at Cambridge, *Aspects of the Novel* is full of E. M. Forster's habitual wit, wisdom and freshness of approach.

The English Novel   Walter Allen

In this 'refreshingly alert' (*The Times Literary Supplement*) landmark panorama of English fiction, the development of the novel is traced from *Pilgrim's Progress* to Joyce and Lawrence.

Film as Film   V. F. Perkins

Acknowledging the unique qualities of cinema as essentially a bastard medium – neither purely a visual nor a dramatic art – this pioneering text remains 'one of the most sophisticated and commendable works of film criticism' – *Tribune*

The Anatomy of Criticism   Northrop Frye

'Here is a book fundamental enough to be entitled *Principia Critica*,' wrote one critic. Northrop Frye's seminal masterpiece was the first work to argue for the status of literary criticism as a science: a true discipline whose techniques and approaches could systematically – and beneficially – be evaluated, quantified and categorized.

The Modern World   Ten Great Writers   Malcolm Bradbury

From Conrad to Kafka, from Proust to Pirandello, Professor Bradbury provides a fresh introduction to ten influential writers of the modern age and the Modernist movement. Each, in their individual way, followed Ezra Pound's famous dictum – 'Make it new'.

Art and Literature   Sigmund Freud

Volume 14 of the *Penguin Freud Library* contains Freud's major essays on Leonardo, Dostoyevsky and Michelangelo, plus shorter pieces on Shakespeare, the nature of creativity and much more.

The Literature of the United States   Marcus Cunliffe

'Still the best short history [of American literature] ... written with notable critical tact' – Warner Berthoff. 'Cunliffe retains the happy faculty (which he shares with Edmund Wilson) of reading familiar books with fresh eyes and of writing in an engaging style' – Howard Mumford Jones

FOR THE BEST IN PAPERBACKS, LOOK FOR THE

PENGUIN REFERENCE BOOKS

The New Penguin English Dictionary

Over 1,000 pages long and with over 68,000 definitions, this cheap, compact and totally up-to-date book is ideal for today's needs. It includes many technical and colloquial terms, guides to pronunciation and common abbreviations.

The Penguin Spelling Dictionary

What are the plurals of *octopus* and *rhinoceros*? What is the difference between *stationary* and *stationery*? And how about *annex* and *annexe*, *agape* and *Agape*? This comprehensive new book, the fullest spelling dictionary now available, provides the answers.

Roget's Thesaurus of English Words and Phrases   Betty Kirkpatrick (ed.)

This new edition of Roget's classic work, now brought up to date for the nineties, will increase anyone's command of the English language. Fully cross-referenced, it includes synonyms of every kind (formal or colloquial, idiomatic and figurative) for almost 900 headings. It is a must for writers and utterly fascinating for any English speaker.

The Penguin Dictionary of Quotations

A treasure-trove of over 12,000 new gems and old favourites, from Aesop and Matthew Arnold to Xenophon and Zola.

The Penguin Wordmaster Dictionary
Martin H. Manser and Nigel D. Turton

This dictionary puts the pleasure back into word-seeking. Every time you look at a page you get a bonus – a panel telling you everything about a particular word or expression. It is, therefore, a dictionary to be read as well as used for its concise and up-to-date definitions.

FOR THE BEST IN PAPERBACKS, LOOK FOR THE

PENGUIN REFERENCE BOOKS

The Penguin Guide to the Law

This acclaimed reference book is designed for everyday use and forms the most comprehensive handbook ever published on the law as it affects the individual.

The Penguin Medical Encyclopedia

Covers the body and mind in sickness and in health, including drugs, surgery, medical history, medical vocabulary and many other aspects. 'Highly commendable' – *Journal of the Institute of Health Education*

The Slang Thesaurus

Do you make the public bar sound like a gentleman's club? Do you need help in understanding *Minder*? The miraculous *Slang Thesaurus* will liven up your language in no time. You won't Adam and Eve it! A mine of funny, witty, acid and vulgar synonyms for the words you use every day.

The Penguin Dictionary of Troublesome Words   Bill Bryson

Why should you avoid discussing the *weather conditions*? Can a married woman be *celibate*? Why is it eccentric to talk about the *aroma* of a cowshed? A straightforward guide to the pitfalls and hotly disputed issues in standard written English.

The Penguin Spanish Dictionary   James R. Jump

Detailed, comprehensive and, above all, modern, *The Penguin Spanish Dictionary* offers a complete picture of the language of ordinary Spaniards – the words used at home and at work, in bars and discos, at cafés and in the street, including full and unsqueamish coverage of common slang and colloquialisms.

The New Penguin Dictionary of Geography

From *aa* and *ablation* to *zinc* and *zonal soils*, this succinct dictionary is unique in covering in one volume the main terms now in use in the diverse areas – physical and human geography, geology and climatology, ecology and economics – that make up geography today.

FOR THE BEST IN PAPERBACKS, LOOK FOR THE

PENGUIN DICTIONARIES

Abbreviations
Archaeology
Architecture
Art and Artists
Biology
Botany
Building
Business
Chemistry
Civil Engineering
Computers
Curious and Interesting
  Words
Curious and Interesting
  Numbers
Design and Designers
Economics
Electronics
English and European
  History
English Idioms
French
Geography
German

Historical Slang
Human Geography
Literary Terms
Mathematics
Modern History 1789–1945
Modern Quotations
Music
Physical Geography
Physics
Politics
Proverbs
Psychology
Quotations
Religions
Rhyming Dictionary
Saints
Science
Sociology
Spanish
Surnames
Telecommunications
Troublesome Words
Twentieth-Century History